Commercial Bank Management

Commercial Bank Management

Frank P. Johnson
Colorado State University

Richard D. Johnson
Colorado State University

The Dryden Press
Chicago   New York   Philadelphia
San Francisco   Montreal   Toronto
London   Sydney   Tokyo   Mexico City
Rio de Janeiro   Madrid

Acquisitions Editor: Elizabeth Widdicombe
Developmental Editor: Judy Sarwark
Project Editor: Nancy Shanahan
Managing Editor: Jane Perkins
Design Director: Alan Wendt
Production Manager: Mary Jarvis

Text and Cover Designer: Quarto
Copy Editor: Mary Englehart
Compositor: The Clarinda Company
Text Type: 10/12 Trump Medieval

Library of Congress Cataloging in Publication Data

Johnson, Frank P., 1940–
  Commercial bank management.

  Includes bibliographies and index.
  1. Bank management. I. Johnson, Richard D., 1947–
II. Title.
HG1615.J59 1984   332.1′2′068   84-6013
ISBN 0-03-063582-9

Printed in the United States of America
567-016-987654321

Address orders:
383 Madison Avenue
New York, NY 10017

Address editorial correspondence:
One Salt Creek Lane
Hinsdale, IL 60521

CBS College Publishing
The Dryden Press
Holt, Rinehart and Winston
Saunders College Publishing

The Dryden Press Series in Finance

Reilly
Investments

Weston and Brigham
Essentials of Managerial Finance, Seventh Edition

Tallman and Neal
Financial Analysis and Planning Package

Weston and Copeland
Managerial Finance, Eighth Edition

PREFACE

This text is a departure from the traditional bank management text. There are several reasons for this departure. First, we, the authors, have been trained in unit bank and branch bank management programs in addition to our academic training. Our "real world" banking exposure has given us broad and diverse experience, which we have attempted to bring to the organization and development of this text.

Second, our teaching of commercial bank management has confirmed our view that other texts are written from an outsider's view of banking. This outside view has separated academics and professional bankers, particularly with respect to how readily graduates are accepted in the job market. As a remedy, this text includes many flowcharts, giving an insider's view of the bank operations that support all bank functions (for example, see Chapters 6 through 10). Also, the order of chapters incorporates the integration of bank functions as they would be incorporated in a comprehensive bank management training program.

Third, many areas of banking are presently becoming deregulated, and banks are no longer clearly distinguishable as a distinct line of commerce. Banks now participate in a broader industry known as the *financial services industry*. The first three sections of the book emphasize and develop current management philosophies, strategies, and techniques of banking. In describing the management of banking functions, we have attempted to describe the elements of change implied by the broader concept of the financial services industry. The fourth section develops the opportunities for expansion that banks can employ to become effective competitors in the financial services industry.

Fourth, changes in regulation and the operating environment of banks have made it more difficult to maintain profits. While the primary goal in managing a bank has been to maximize the return to the owners, the profit maximization goal assumes greater importance in a deregulated environment. The profit subsidy associated with regulated deposit interest rates has disappeared. To remain profitable, banks have been forced to change the pricing on existing products and offer innovative products. We emphasize the profit maximization goal throughout the text and integrate new pricing and product strategies.

Finally, in our initial planning we asked ourselves how we could best prepare our banking students for acceptance by future employers. Whereas other texts emphasize regulatory issues and deal with management and policy issues in a less direct fashion, we chose to develop management strategies that are used by senior-level management and also to attempt to provide a greater understanding of how a bank operates at lower management levels. This integration of senior- and lower-level management strategies is intended to provide students with a more useful background for entry into the banking industry. It is our hope that students entering the industry will thus have a more thorough understanding of the industry, one that will allow faster progression from training assignments to middle management positions.

Although we have endeavored to make this book as up to date as possible, we also recognize that changes occur daily. The *Instructor's Manual* incorporates those significant changes that occurred between the typesetting of the text and the completion of the *Instructor's Manual*. Because so many changes have occurred in the last two years, our updating has been a continual process. The text includes current materials on contemporaneous reserve accounting, regulatory changes, modifications in financial statement reporting, and changes in banking structure and laws.

ORGANIZATION

The text is divided into four parts, with a total of twenty-four chapters. Part One, Introduction to Banking, concentrates on (1) the role of the commercial bank in the financial services industry; (2) organizational structure of banks, with emphasis on the delivery of financial products; (3) risks and returns in banking; and (4) bank financial statements.

Part Two, Bank Functions, develops asset and liability management as a foundation for discussing the deposit, lending, investment, short-term funds management, and capital functions. Specific topics include gap and spread management, loan administration processes and management systems, management of potential loan losses, investment securities strategies, contemporaneous reserve accounting, capital funds management, and capital adequacy.

Part Three, Analysis of Performance and Planning, covers the analysis of bank performance, management of interest margin, bank cost accounting, pricing of bank services, and planning. The planning chapter pulls together all of the previous chapters in a planning framework.

Part Four, Bank Expansion and the Future of Banking, has an institutional framework encompassing bank structure in unit, branch, and bank holding company environments, mergers and acquisitions, activities related to banking, trust, international banking, and possible future scenarios for the banking industry. The placement of the institutional framework in the last part of this text reflects our belief that a sound foundation in banking enables the student to grasp the significance of changes within the banking industry and of the bank's role in the financial services industry.

SPECIAL FEATURES

A building-block approach has been used in the organization of this text. Part One provides the student with a foundation for understanding bank organization, financial management theory as it relates to banking, and bank financial statements. Chapter 5 develops the intricate interrelationships of asset and liability management. This chapter provides sufficient knowledge of banking so that the instructor can begin employing computer simulation models early in the course. The remainder of Part Two concentrates on the basic functions of banks and the management activities related to those functions.

The building-block approach continues with Part Three, which provides analytical techniques for judging performance in relation to peer banks and for setting prices for services. Given the background of Part Two and the analysis of bank operations, the planning chapter brings together all of the previous chapters in a planning framework. Finally, expansion into banking or related markets completes the structure. In summary, the building-block approach provides general background (Chapters 1–4), basic functional foundation (Chapters 5–14), analysis and planning (Chapters 15–19), and future expansion opportunities (Chapters 20–24).

Several other special features are included. Boxed items provide related topical material from real world events or situations that enhance the basic textual materials. Flowcharts of specific processes such as deposit processing and types of loan processes help the student to visualize what goes on inside a bank. Each chapter is summarized and includes questions that serve as review points on the major areas covered in the text. Teaching footnotes are included to expand concepts or to offer alternative points of view. Diagrams, which assist in explaining key materials, and exhibits are presented to highlight and condense key information.

Part Five consists of the following case problems which illustrate key points in certain chapters:

- Chapter 8: Johnco Manufacturing Company (*increase in revolving line of credit*)
- Chapter 9: Ramco Inc. (*problem loan*)
- Chapter 10: Rocky Ford National Bank (*scoring charge card applications*)
- Chapter 15: Laramie County Bank (*analysis of bank performance*);
  Laramie County Bank (*projection of bank performance*)
- Chapter 16: Eighth National Bank (*interest margin planning*)
- Chapter 18: Computer Software, Inc. (*customer profitability analysis*)

An appendix at the end of the book (1) contains sample accounting entries for bank transactions and indicates their impact on financial statements; (2) provides additional reference material not found in other books in the field; and (3) presents the tax treatment of the allowance for loan losses as well as the SEC disclosure requirements for banks and bank holding companies.

A comprehensive *Instructor's Manual* has been prepared for the professor. The manual includes suggested course content and alternative outlines. In addition, materials have been included that update changes in the industry. For each chapter the manual includes:

- —chapter objectives
- —chapter key points
- —answers to end-of-chapter questions and problems
- —solutions to cases
- —true–false, multiple-choice, and essay questions for use in quizzes and examinations.

The material in this book was class tested at Colorado State University, with students identifying areas in which clarification was required. An attempt was made to incorporate their suggestions in the textual changes.[1]

POSSIBLE COURSE OUTLINES

The material in the text offers wide flexibility for use in a course in bank management. At Colorado State University the text is used in conjunction with a bank simulation in a 15-week semester course. The outline used in the course is presented below.

It is difficult to cover all of the text material in detail in a semester course if any outside material is used. Less lecture time should be devoted to the material in Part Four, with the students being relied upon to gain the necessary background from their reading. If cases are used, lecture coverage in some chapters will have to be eliminated. In a one-quarter course it is impossible to cover all of the material in detail. It is suggested that Chapters 1–15 be covered in sequence, with coverage on additional chapters limited according to the emphasis the instructor wishes to employ. For a more detailed management approach, the remaining chapters in Part Three could be covered. For a more descriptive approach, the chapters on expansion in Part Four could be used.

---

[1] In this text where we used the masculine gender, we did so for the sake of simplicity. There was no intent to overlook either the contributions made by women in banking or the opportunities available for women in the industry.

Week No.	Lecture Material	Chapters
1	Introduction	1
	Bank organization	2
2	Risk and return concepts	3
	Financial statements	4
3	Asset and liability management	5
4	Deposit functions	6
5	Loan management	7
6	Commercial loans	8
7	Commercial loans	8
	Problem loan management	9
8	Consumer loans	10
	Mortgage loans	11
9	Investments	12
	Short-term funds management	13
10	Capital	14
	Analysis of bank performance	15
11	Interest margin management	16
12	Cost and pricing of bank services: Part 1	17
	Cost and pricing of bank services: Part 2	18
13	Planning	19
	Expansion—banking activities	20
14	Expansion—activities related to banking	21
	Trust	22
15	International banking	23
	Future of banking	24

ACKNOWLEDGMENTS

We are indebted to many friends, colleagues, and students for criticism and encouragement during the preparation of this book. The manuscript was extensively reviewed at various stages by Larry Frieder of Florida Agriculture and Mechanical University, Jack Hayden of the University of Nevada at Las Vegas, James Hugon of Portland State University, James Kehr of Miami University of Ohio, Paul Leonard of the State University of New York at Albany, John Lewis of Stephen F. Austin State University, Robert Rogowski of Washington State University, James Tipton of Baylor University, and William Wilbur of Northern Illinois University.

We also appreciate the technical assistance of George Cooke of Deposit Guaranty National Bank (Jackson, Mississippi), William Kesler of

Bank of the Southwest (Houston), David Pringle and Debra Levine of Central Bank of Denver, Richard Pede of Security Pacific National Bank, Michael Travis of First Interstate Bank of Denver, and Karen Tinley and Gary Mulder of the American Bankers Association. A special note of appreciation goes to John Olienyk of Colorado State University, good friend and colleague, who provided direction and assistance in capturing the essence of international banking.

Drafts of the manuscript were skillfully typed by Kathy Corcelius, Harriet Sykes, and Caryn Becker. Kathy also assisted in completing the index and *Instructor's Manual.*

The staff of The Dryden Press was helpful in providing direction and encouragement. Doris Milligan, Deborah Ruck, Judy Sarwark, Nancy Shanahan, and Elizabeth Widdicombe deserve special mention for guiding the manuscript through various stages of development and production to the final bound book.

We thank Professor Emeritus Eugene T. Halaas of the University of Denver, Professor George A. Racette of the University of Oregon, and Marvin F. Owens, Jr., formerly of the Central Bank of Denver, all of whom influenced our careers in finance and banking.

Finally, we are grateful to Jennifer, Lisa, and Jan for their patience with us while we worked to meet deadlines. In particular, we appreciate their understanding and generosity in giving of their time to allow us to complete this project.

Frank P. Johnson
Richard D. Johnson

Fort Collins, Colorado
September 1984

ABOUT THE AUTHORS

Frank P. Johnson, Ph.D. (Colorado State University), CPA, is Assistant to the Director, Experiment Station, and Associate Professor of Finance and Real Estate, College of Business, Colorado State University. He previously served on the faculty of the University of Denver. Professor Johnson holds memberships in the American Institute of Certified Public Accountants, the AICPA banking committee, and Beta Alpha Psi, national accounting fraternity. He was the recipient of the College of Business Everitt Grant for Professional Development. A consultant to various banks and bank holding companies, his banking experience also includes the positions of credit officer (Central Bank of Denver), chief financial officer (First Wyoming Bancorporation and American Stock Exchange listed multibank holding company), and organizer and director (Foothills National Bank, Fort Collins, Colorado). Professor Johnson has contributed articles to *Management Accounting* and *Colorado Agribusiness Review*. He is the author of *Accounting and Reporting Systems for Banks* (AICPA, 1981) and co-author of *Bank Management* (American Bankers Association, 1983). He has presented seminars for Bank Administration Institute and the Colorado Society of CPAs and has been an instructor for the American Institute of Banking. Professor Johnson has taught undergraduate and graduate courses in commercial banking, corporate finance, financial and managerial accounting, and taxation.

Richard D. Johnson, Ph.D. (University of Oregon) is Director of the Office of Special Programs and an Associate Professor in the Department of Finance and Real Estate in the College of Business at Colorado State University. He previously served on the faculty of California Polytechnic State University at San Luis Obispo. Professor Johnson holds memberships in the American Finance Association, the Western Finance Association, the Financial Management Association, and Beta Gamma Sigma, the National Business Administration Honorary Fraternity. His banking experience was with Security Pacific National Bank–Los Angeles, where he was an assistant to a division vice president in the Installment Loan Division. He has extensive commercial and consumer lending and business development experience. An administrator of BankSim for the American Bankers Association, he has presented seminars and programs in commercial and consumer lending and asset and liability management for the professional community. He is co-author of *Bank Management* (American Bankers Association, 1983) and has contributed to articles in *Taxes, Les Nouvilles,* and *Journal of Licensing Executives Society.* He has presented papers and served as discussant for the Financial Management Association and national and regional American Institute of Decision Sciences. Professor Johnson has taught graduate and undergraduate courses in commercial banking, financial institutions management, corporate finance, and investments.

CONTENTS

Commercial Bank Management

PART ONE

◆

Introduction to Banking

CHAPTER 1

Introduction

Before spending hours reading and examining principles involved in the management of a commercial bank, we ought to be familiar with the definition of a bank. Ten years ago the definition of a commercial bank was clear and precise. There were neatly defined distinctions between a commercial bank and nonbank financial institutions. Commercial banks offered a product that was not offered by nonbank institutions. The unique product distinction has become increasingly blurred and the task of defining a bank today is a much more difficult task.

Traditionally a bank was distinguished from a nonbank in terms of two activities: accepting demand deposits and engaging in commercial lending activity.[1] Commercial banks were the only financial institutions authorized to offer checking accounts that allowed customers access to deposit funds by writing checks or drafts. The distinction of not being engaged in commercial lending was applied to other deposit institutions. Banks were the only deposit institutions that could make commercial loans. Traditionally, then, a commercial bank was an institution that offered demand deposit accounts and was engaged in commercial lending.

While that traditional definition still works well to describe most commercial banks, today it also describes many other financial institutions. Commercial banks no longer uniquely offer those products. The two-activities criterion currently describes mutual savings banks and savings and loan institutions. It also describes Sears and Merrill Lynch. Sears has put together a financial services network that includes savings and loan institutions, stock brokerage, real estate brokerage, and insurance services. Merrill Lynch, through its Cash Management Account, offers its customers the ability to transfer funds by issuing third-party drafts or checks and it has opened a commercial lending subsidiary. Nar-

---

[1]The two-activities criterion for defining a commercial bank is the definition used in the Bank Holding Company Act. For excellent discussion see J. J. DiClemente, "The Meeting of Passion and Intellect: A History of the Term Bank in the Bank Holding Company Act," *Occasional Paper 83–1, Federal Reserve Bank of Chicago*: 1–41.

rowly interpreted, the definition also includes money market mutual funds which offer investment accounts that customers can access through drafts. In an indirect sense money market mutual funds also make commercial loans by purchasing commercial paper issued by corporations.

The separation of commercial banks from nonbank financial institutions is no longer clear if we look at the distinction on the basis of product line. We are seeing the development of the financial services industry in which banks and nonbanks offer services that include lending and transaction deposit services to customers in a targeted market segment. About the only difference between banks and nonbanks on a product line basis is the extent to which the institutions are involved in lending and deposit services. For commercial banks, their primary business is characterized by securing funds from depositors and using those funds to make commercial and consumer loans. For some institutions such as brokerage firms, such services are not the primary services offered. For other institutions such as thrift institutions, regulatory limits apply to the percentage of loans that can be made in the consumer and commercial classification.

The changes in the competitive environment in which banks operate have made banking more risky and difficult than it was in the past. The main business of banking still involves the two activities of providing transaction deposit services and commercial lending, but commercial banks no longer enjoy the insulation from competition that they once enjoyed.

If a commercial bank is no longer uniquely described in terms of being a financial intermediary offering demand deposit and commercial lending services, what then is a commercial bank? A commercial bank is a financial intermediary that provides a financial services product in an evolving industry. The industry is characterized by changing competition, regulation, and technology. The central activity of banking remains the securing of deposit funds and the making of consumer and commercial loans. Those two activities will likely remain as the major activities of commercial banks. Changes in competition, regulation, and technology will have an impact on how those two activities are delivered as a product to consumers and commercial enterprises.

If the current trend in deregulation persists, the product offered by commercial banks will be broadened. The bank of the future may offer investment management and brokerage, real estate brokerage, and insurance services in addition to traditional loan and deposit services. In addition to the new services being offered, traditional services will be offered in different packages. Developments in technology will lead to greater automation in deposit and lending services. Commercial banks are making more extensive use of electronic funds transfer systems in delivering transaction services. That trend will continue and is likely to be expanded to loan services as well.

REGULATION OF COMMERCIAL BANKS

Commercial banking is a highly regulated industry. While the extent of regulation and the type of regulation imposed on banks have historically varied significantly, the importance of banking to the performance of the economy mandates regulation to protect participants in the economy.

The goals of bank regulation include:

- *Protection of monetary stability.* The stability of the banking system is necessary to allow the monetary authorities to control the volume of money circulating in the economy. A stable payment system is necessary to promote economic development and to avoid financial panics associated with periods of economic recession.
- *Protection of depositors.* Our fractional reserve system is complicated and it is inefficient and impractical for depositors to investigate the safety of banks. To gain transaction services consumers must maintain deposits, which makes them creditors of the bank. If banks are regulated, depositors are not required to investigate banks as extensively.
- *Protection of consumers.* Related to depositor protection, banking regulation also has as its purpose to protect all consumers. Specific goals in this area include protection against unfair lending practices, fair disclosure of charges for loans, and assurance of equal opportunity for credit services.
- *Development of an efficient and competitive financial system.* A goal of regulation is to develop a regulatory framework which encourages the development of a competitive system in which consumers are able to secure efficient banking services at reasonable costs.[2]

OVERVIEW OF U.S. BANK REGULATION

The early development of banks in the United States brought about a number of unsafe practices. Bad loans and the simultaneous withdrawal of depositor funds resulted in many bank failures. A bank failure has four major effects: (1) it induces fears about the solvency of other banks; (2) it reduces the money supply in the community, thereby dampening spending, and it induces declines in employment and income production; (3) it reduces time deposits, which next to money supply form the

---

[2]G. G. Kaufman, *Money, the Financial System, and the Economy* (Boston: Houghton Mifflin, 1981), 118.

most liquid part of the financial wealth, further reducing spending, employment, production, and income; and (4) it breaks ongoing credit relationships, leaving bank borrowers without sufficient financing to conduct their operations.[3]

During the Great Depression approximately 40 percent of all banks closed, primarily due to bank failure. As a result important banking legislation was adopted in the early 1930s. A primary impact of the legislation was to limit entry into banking. Until that time banks had not been required to demonstrate a need and capacity for delivering bank services. Commercial and investment banking activities were separated (Glass-Steagall Act). Prior to this separation banks had been self-dealing in securities to the detriment of investors.

Significantly, the Federal Deposit Insurance Corporation was established, making a major advance in the restoration of depositor confidence. Also, interest rate ceilings were established on deposits. In the past, banks had increased their risk by bidding up interest on deposits to meet or beat the competition. To compensate, greater lending risks were taken in order to increase yields. Competition for deposits through spiraling interest rates contributed to bank failures.

The U.S. banking system is based upon the concept of dual banking—the existence of state and nationally chartered banks. Exhibit 1.1 illustrates the major banking authorities governing bank chartering and examinations. National banks are chartered and examined by the Comptroller of the Currency, are required to be members of the Federal Reserve System, and are required to obtain FDIC insurance. State-chartered banks are not required to be members of the Federal Reserve System nor to obtain FDIC insurance. However, most state banks do obtain FDIC insurance. State nonmember banks were not required to maintain reserve requirements on deposits with the Federal Reserve System until 1980.

State laws govern a bank's expansion through branch offices. Certain states allow limited branching in geographic or political subdivisions while others allow statewide branching. In states with limited or no branching (unit banks), bank holding companies have formed to acquire banks to create a larger banking corporation, but these banks may have a common identity such as First Interstate Bank of Denver and First Interstate Bank of Los Angeles. Unless permitted by state law, a bank holding company is not allowed to expand beyond the state boundary of the parent corporation. Nevertheless, certain bank holding companies had expanded across state lines prior to the enactment of the

---

[3]For an excellent discussion on the purposes of bank regulation and an overview of banking regulation in the United States, see K. Sprong, *Banking Regulation: Its Purposes, Implementation, and Effects* (Kansas City: Federal Reserve Bank of Kansas City, 1983). This overview draws heavily on Chapter 1.

EXHIBIT 1.1   Major Banking Authorities

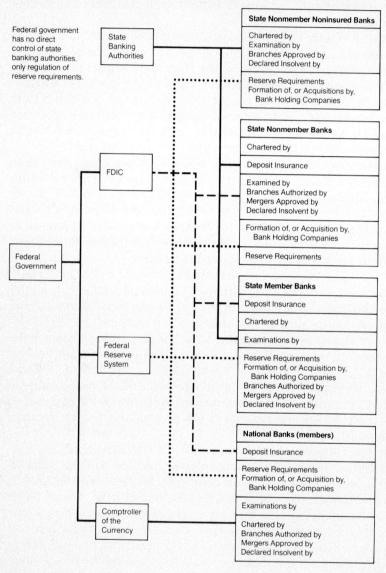

Source: D. S. Kidwell and R. L. Peterson, *Financial Institutions, Markets, and Money*, (Hinsdale, IL: The Dryden Press, 1981), 21.

Bank Holding Company Act of 1956 and were allowed to retain out-of-state banks.[4]

CHANGES IN THE REGULATORY ENVIRONMENT

The basic structure of bank regulation that grew out of the depression of the 1930s remained effective until the late 1960s. The inflation experienced in that period caused significant problems for banks because market interest rates rose far above the ceiling rates allowed by regulation. When that occurred, banks lost deposit funds as depositors withdrew savings and invested directly in the market to secure higher rates.

Regulations continued to become outdated in the 1970s. Inflation and the high market interest rates that accompanied inflation made it increasingly difficult for banks to retain deposit funds. Banks offered innovative types of deposit accounts designed to skirt the regulatory ceilings that applied to traditional types of deposit accounts. Nonbank financial institutions began to offer products that competed with traditional banking products, thereby putting pressure on regulators and Congress to change legislation to allow banks to compete with less-regulated financial institutions. In March 1980 Congress enacted the Depository Institutions Deregulation and Monetary Control Act of 1980, hereafter DIDMCA. This landmark legislation authorized the eventual elimination of interest rate ceilings on deposit accounts and allowed nonbank deposit institutions to offer interest-bearing checking accounts. The DIDMCA also called for a broadening of the powers of thrift institutions. The Garn-St. Germain Act, which was passed in 1982, granted thrift institutions limited authorization to offer commercial and consumer loans as mandated by the DIDMCA.[5]

The changes in regulation and the competitive environment of the last decade have created additional regulatory issues that must be addressed. In a matter of just a few years the participants offering banking services have changed and the product offered by banks has changed. Major regulatory questions remaining to be addressed include:

- Who should be allowed to own a bank? Specifically, should investment institutions such as Merrill Lynch be allowed to own banks? Should nonfinancial firms such as Sears be allowed to own banks?

---

[4]For in-depth discussion of regulatory issues related to bank expansion, see the following in the *Journal of Bank Research* (Summer 1980): H. C. Nathan, "Nonbank Organizations and the McFadden Act," 80–99; A. S. McCall, "The Impact of Bank Structure on Bank Service to Local Communities," 101–109; D. T. Savage and E. H. Solomon, "Branch Banking: The Competitive Issues," 110–121; and A. S. McCall and D. T. Savage, "Branching Policy: The Options," 122–126.

[5]P. S. Nadler, "Garn-St. Germain in Perspective," *Bankers Monthly Magazine*, Nov. 15, 1982, 12–22.

- Should banks be allowed to operate banking facilities on an interstate basis? If so, should that operation be on a national or regional basis?
- Should banks be allowed greater freedom in offering investment-type services? If so, what activities should be allowed? Should banks be able to offer more extensive underwriting services? Should banks be able to offer personal investment management?
- Should the Federal Deposit Insurance Corporation program be modified to reflect the change in the product offered by banks today? If so, how should that modification be accomplished? Should banks be charged variable-rate insurance premiums? If so, how will those premiums be assigned?
- Should the regulatory framework be reorganized to avoid the duplication present in our current system? If so, how should that reorganization be accomplished?

The regulatory issues outlined must be addressed, and the decisions made on these issues will further shape the environment in which banks will operate. At this time the exact operating environment for the future is uncertain. Until these issues are resolved, managers of banks are forced to maintain flexibility in business plans and strategies.

MODERN BANK MANAGEMENT

The transformation of banking from an environment in which banks were isolated from direct competition from other financial institutions to an environment in which banks are in direct competition with many financial institutions and the recent volatile economic environment have made banking increasingly risky. As new entrants to the banking market price products competitively to gain market share, to remain competitive banks have also lowered prices. This leads to lower margins on services. Recent examples of this pricing practice include the pricing on NOW accounts and on the newly authorized Money Market Deposit Accounts (MMDAs). Some banks and thrift institutions offered MMDAs at yields of 25 percent for short time periods to gain market share.

The recent volatility of the economy has caused serious disruptions in the banking industry. Since 1978 we have seen very large swings in interest rates in short cycles. Banks operating under old strategies that were more suitable for stable economic environments experienced difficulties. The recession that began in the late 1970s caused loan losses to soar to new highs. Most notable loss areas included energy loans and international loans. Poor performance on loans combined with mismanagement by banks have led to bank failures reaching levels not seen since the depression of the 1930s. Forty-eight banks failed in

1983, breaking the post depression record of forty-three failures in 1940.[6]

The changes in a bank's operating environment make it necessary for management to develop new strategies, develop carefully considered business plans, and develop control systems that allow performance to be tracked. The business of banking in the mid-1980s is not the same business that existed in the previous two decades.

To be successful in the 1980s, banks must decide which elements of banking they want to be involved in, since all banks will not offer the same products. A basic decision that must be made by each bank is what business to be in. Services offered by banks in a modern environment include:

+ Originating credit contracts—involves locating loan customers, performing credit analyses, and structuring loans
+ Inventorying credit contracts—involves holding and servicing loans for the bank's portfolio
+ Financing the bank's assets—involves securing deposit and other borrowed funds that support the bank's asset portfolio
+ Originating and processing noncredit transactions—involves marketing efforts for developing additional deposit customers and developing electronic funds transfer systems and automated processing systems noncredit transactions
+ Selling financial advisory and management services—involves developing and delivering management services for both consumer and commercial customers[7]

Although originating and inventorying credit transactions and financing the bank's assets must be performed to some extent by all banks, an individual bank can specialize in certain aspects of these areas and de-emphasize others. In other words, not all banks will be alike. The future is likely to be characterized by banks that specialize in certain business lines, and the successful banks will be those that deliver their specialized services most efficiently.

ORGANIZATION OF THIS BOOK

From our viewpoint, a bank is a set of portfolios varying in volume, rate, and mix. Assets as well as liabilities must be managed. Although it is important to describe the functions in which a bank engages, it is equally or more important to provide a systematic framework within

---

[6]"48 Banks Fail in '83; S&Ls Fare Better," *Rocky Mountain News*, Jan. 4, 1983, 60.

[7]For an in-depth discussion on separate business activities, see E. V. Bowden, *Revolution in Banking* (Richmond, VA: Robert F. Dame, 1980).

Why So Many Banks Go Belly up: Misconduct, Mismanagement Lead to a Near Record Failure Rate

A financial thunderbolt struck the tiny farm community of Danvers (pop. 920) in west-central Illinois one Friday this month. The First National Bank of Danvers, the only bank in town, with 2,560 accounts and about $11 million in deposits, was declared insolvent by federal authorities and shut down until new owners could reopen it under another name. That same day 2,000 miles away, the Oregon Mutual Savings Bank in Portland also closed its doors before being taken over by an Idaho holding company. The bank had seen its net worth fall nearly 20% in just six months. Said President Jack Goetze: "Without a capital infusion, our net worth would have been seriously impaired in another ten months."

Bank failures used to come in isolated outbreaks. During the 1960s and '70s, they averaged fewer than ten a year. But despite the stronger-than-expected economic recovery, they are now occurring at a worrisome rate. Across the U.S., more than one bank a week is failing. By year's end, the number of failures, now 35, should easily beat the post-Depression record of 43 set in 1940. (Runner-up: 1982 with 42 failures.)

In Texas, anxious depositors withdrew $447 million during the first half of the year from the First National Bank of Midland (assets: $1.5 billion), whose loans to oil and gas producers turned sour. Earlier this month, the bank reported a second-quarter loss of $109.3 million. Many banks are now teetering on the brink of collapse. At the end of July, the Federal Deposit Insurance Corporation listed 540 "problem" banks, ranging from small state-chartered ones with too many weak agricultural loans to nationally chartered banks with bad business loans. Among the 540, the FDIC secretly lists dozens as likely to fail unless they are soon merged with healthier financial institutions. Says John Downey, chief national bank examiner for the Comptroller of the Currency: "The number is the highest I've ever seen it."

No longer does a bank failure result in angry customers milling outside locked doors, or widows and orphans being stripped of their life savings. Closings have become so routine that agencies like the FDIC perform them with robot-like precision. Typically, authorities move in after business hours on Friday and freeze accounts. By the following Monday, they have either paid off the depositors or allowed another bank to assume control. But such transitions are not without cost. The FDIC spent $870 million last year, mostly to compensate private financial institutions for taking over bad loans. Moreover, bank shareholders can see their investments vanish when the financial institution goes under.

Part of the blame for the rising number of failures belongs to the recession and its complement of bankruptcies and defaulted loans. But increasingly, the problems are due to poor bank management. Says an FDIC attorney: "We find examples of actionable negligence on the part of bank officers and directors in virtually every case of a closed bank."

Some examples involve sheer stupidity or the failure to make a move at the right time. Two weeks before First National Bank of Danvers failed, its officers filed a suit against former President Terry Winterland, claiming he made loans without adequate collateral. Replies Winterland, 41: "I can't comment without getting my nose crossways, but I'm not the culprit they say I am."

Other cases may involve outright criminal misconduct, such as intentional fraud or dishonesty, by bank officials. In California, scene of a rash of failures, Consultant Gerry Findley says there has been "a pattern of insider abuses that included sweetheart loans and deals to organizations that officers are involved in." After the collapse of Jake Butcher's United American Bank of Knoxville, Tenn., in February brought down another bank formerly controlled by him and five other financial institutions directed by his younger brother C.H., the FDIC identified bad loans totaling hundreds of millions of dollars. Many of them had been made to friends, relatives and business associates.

Bank failures are one effect of the growing deregulation of financial institutions. Since interest rate ceilings on savings deposits were lifted last year, banks have been cut off from easy sources of cheap money and have had to increase sharply the rate of return they pay on deposits. In addition, deregulation has made banking more competitive. In California, the number of banks has surged from 242 four years ago to 387. They must now also compete with such firms as Shearson/American Express, Merrill Lynch and Prudential-Bache, which offer accounts that operate much like the savings and checking accounts once offered only by banks. With everyone striving for more business, risks grow and profit margins shrink.

A banker's job has not been made any easier by the rapid and unpredictable changes in the economy over the past 18 months. Banks that gambled on interest rates going down when they actually went up find themselves paying out more for deposits than they were charging for loans. Real estate investments turned sour after mortgage rates hit 17.5%; oil and gas deals fell apart when energy prices dropped. Other loans that looked profitable when the rate of inflation was expected to be running at 15% became disasters when the rate dropped below 5% and stayed there.

Despite the hard times and high risks, the number of new commercial banks being started still outnumbers failures 10 to 1. A bank is still a good place to make money, and the outlook will improve even more as the recovery gathers force.   —by Alexander L. Taylor III.
Reported by Ross H. Munro/Washington, with other bureaus.

which bank funds may be managed. That framework is developed around the financial statements. Each portfolio decision results in financial statement impact. Each bank function is examined from a descriptive viewpoint together with the management tools required to maximize earnings within the regulatory constraint. These tools are quantitative in nature, yet we stress the quality factors in managing a bank.

The structure of this text is designed to build upon prior material and to culminate in the tools of analysis and planning of bank financial objectives. Part I develops a basic foundation of the financial environment in which banks operate. Included in Part I are chapters that describe the bank's financial statements, basic organizational concepts, and banking risks and returns, with an overview of asset and liability management. Part One is designed to set the stage for detailed analyses of the individual bank functions.

Part Two begins with the development of current bank management theory and includes the integration of various operational theories of bank management. A discussion of the flow of bank operations, beginning with deposit acquisitions and followed by lending practices and an in-depth examination of lending services, sets the stage for developing investment security requirements. A key chapter deals with balancing the bank, i.e., providing bank liquidity, and the short-term management of bank assets and liabilities for profit maximization. Finally, capital adequacy and policies complete Part Two.

In Part Three we examine the analytical tools employed by bankers and analysts in evaluating performance. Profit strategies and hedging are also discussed. Cost accounting and planning are examined as they apply specifically to banking.

In Part Four bank expansion and regulatory constraints complete the treatment of commercial bank management. The international aspects of modern commercial banking are a separate area and are viewed as an expansionary role for banks.

A manager who has an understanding of the underlying operational systems of a bank is one who can use the resulting daily financial data to improve or maintain profitability. Without a knowledge of sound financial principles and accounting data, a manager is in the position of running a ship without a rudder.

Our purpose in this text extends beyond a description of the various banking functions. While we believe that a student of banking must be aware of the various functions, our purpose is to go beyond that description of functions to identify how a bank actually manages each of the functions. We tie each of the decisions that a bank makes to the financial statements and, in an appendix, we assess the impact of such decisions on the financial statements.

Our emphasis is on how a bank operates, how it generates financial data, how it reports to various vested interests for the purpose of evaluating performance, making projections, and reacting to internal and external changes. We believe a banker should know the costs of doing business and should be in a position to control performance. This knowledge of costs in setting service prices allows the banker the luxury of beating or ignoring competition.

References

Bowden, E. V. *Revolution in Banking.* Richmond, VA: Robert F. Dame, 1980, 1–203.

DiClemente, J. J. "The Meeting of Passion and Intellect: A History of the Term Bank in the Bank Holding Company Act." *Occasional Paper 83–1, Federal Reserve Bank of Chicago:* 1–41.

"48 Banks Fail in '83; S&Ls Fare Better." *Rocky Mountain News,* Jan. 4, 1983, 60.

Kaufman, G. G. *Money, the Financial System, and the Economy.* Boston: Houghton Mifflin, 1981, 117–144.

Kaufman, G. G., L. R. Mote, and H. Rosenbloom. "The Future of Commercial Banks in the Financial Services Industry." *Occasional Paper 83–5, Federal Reserve Bank of Chicago:* 1–60.

Kidwell, D. S., and R. L. Peterson. *Financial Institutions, Markets, and Money.* Hinsdale, IL: The Dryden Press, 1981, 81–98.

Nadler, P. S. "Garn-St. Germain in Perspective." *Bankers Monthly Magazine,* Nov. 15, 1982, 12–22.

Rosenblum, H., and D. Siegel. "Competition in Financial Services: The Impact of Nonbank Entry." *Staff Study 83–1, Federal Reserve Bank of Chicago:* 1–43.

Sprong, K. *"Banking Regulation: Its Purposes, Implementation, and Effects.* Kansas City: Federal Reserve Bank of Kansas City, 1983, 1–145.

Taylor, A. L., III. "Why So Many Banks Go Belly Up." *Time,* Aug. 29, 1983, 47.

West, R. C. "The Depository Institutions Deregulation Act of 1980: A Historical Perspective." *Economic Review, Federal Reserve Bank of Kansas City,* February 1982: 3–13.

CHAPTER 2

Bank Organization

Organizational structure depends on bank size, services offered, personnel expertise, and permitted legal structure. Money-center and regional banks exhibit portfolio characteristics that serve the larger corporate customer and also offer services that extend beyond traditional banking services. Their organizational structures reflect the diversity of their operations. The structure of a very small bank is typically oriented toward two functions—lending and operations. As the bank grows, its lending and operational functions become departmentalized, eventually leading to separate divisions.

There is no prototype for an organizational structure that serves all operating situations. Banks organize their functions to serve customers or to tap the specific talents of existing or new personnel. Many states permit branching whereas others permit bank holding companies that acquire banks to expand their market share without the benefit of branching laws. In a branching or holding company environment, organizational structures and authority accorded to managers will vary from those of a single bank organization. Therefore each organizational structure represents its management's view of the most effective way to operate the bank.

TRADITIONAL APPROACH TO BANK ORGANIZATION

The traditional approach to bank organization is through an integration of functions. A *function* is a natural division of operation according to a major activity. Typically, functions are defined on the basis of balance sheet activities such as loans, investments, cash, and deposits. In a bank with these traditional services, the organizational structure separates into three basic functions—loans, investments, and operations. Operations include deposit acquisition, "back-room" processing of deposit transactions, cash management, and the accounting department. The head of the operations division usually holds the title of cashier.

As a bank expands, it may departmentalize certain activities. For example, loans may be divided into commercial, installment, and mortgage loans, and operations may be divided into tellers, proof, bookkeeping, and accounting. In a small bank the president usually manages the investment portfolio, and the cashier assumes cash management respon-

14

sibilities because they are related to maintaining reserve requirements on deposits. In larger banks the investment portfolio and cash management activities may be combined to centralize the primary (cash) and secondary (investment) reserve activities. If cash balances are not sufficient to meet withdrawals or loan demand, investments may be sold to provide the necessary funds. Integration of cash and investment portfolio management reflects a larger organization's need to react to more volatile deposit and loan demands than a smaller bank experiences.

TRENDS TOWARD ORGANIZING INTO BANK PRODUCT DIVISIONS

Banks have become more aware of customers' demands for services along product lines. A consumer typically uses checking, savings and time deposits, and installment and mortgage loans. Some banks have "packaged" these services so that the consumer has a single point of contact with the bank. Other bank functions may be similarly packaged.

Bank Markets

Product Markets.   Banking has diversified its product mix in recent years to take advantage of interest and fee income opportunities. The four basic product types are credit services (lending), operations (deposit-related services and nondeposit functions such as safekeeping and data processing), operations-credit (checking accounts with overdraft loan privileges), and investments (money market certificates and trust functions). These products are evolving as nonbanking competitors create product lines, including packages of interrelated financial services, to tap investor funds.

Customer Markets.   A recent trend in bank organization is the concept of relationship banking. Relationship banking is concerned with tying services used by a particular type of customer into an organizational structure that best delivers the package of services. There are three basic customer groups—retail, wholesale, and trust. Retail banking defines a customer market consisting of consumers. Wholesale banking includes corporate, institutional (correspondent banking), and governmental customers. Large banks may act as another, usually smaller, bank's bank. Just as consumers and corporations require banking services, banks also require banking services. The smaller bank is usually referred to as the respondent bank and the larger bank as the correspondent. Trust represents a special case because a trust function is an adjunct to normal banking operations and represents a different customer market. Exhibit 2.1. identifies the integration of customer and product markets and the key services offered to each group. It is important to note that all product types may not be demanded by a specific customer market.

EXHIBIT 2.1   Organization of Product Types and Key Services for Customer Markets

Customer Market	Product Type	Key Services	
Retail	Credit	Consumer financing Installment loans Mortgage loans	Credit cards Credit loan insurance Check guarantee cards
	Operations	Checking accounts Safe deposit NOW accounts Traveler's checks Debit cards Budget planning	Bill paying Automated teller machines Collections Foreign exchange Account reconciliation
	Operations-credit	Overdraft banking	
	Investment	Savings accounts Time certificates of deposit Money market certificates	IRAs Keogh plans Personal trusts Investment advice Repurchase agreements
Corporate	Credit	Commercial loans Commercial mortgage loans Commitments	Discounting Leases Factoring
	Operations	Cash management Electronic data processing Wire transfers Lockboxes Stock transfers Corporate custodianship Freight payments	Collections Foreign currency exchange Treasury tax and loan deposits Demand deposits Automatic payments Bill paying Account reconciliation
	Operations-credit	Credit reports Acceptances	
	Investment	Corporate trusts Pension funds Profit sharing Investment advice	Private placements Purchase and sales of debt securities Time deposits—open accounts

		Corporate savings accounts Merger/acquisition services	Time certificates of deposit
Institutional **(correspondent banking)**	Credit	Bank stock loans Loan participation	Direct loans
	Operations	Demand deposits Check clearing Electronic data processing	Safekeeping of securities Consulting
	Operations-credit	None	None
	Investment	Federal funds purchases and sales	Securities purchases and sales Cash management
Governmental	Credit	Private placement—municipal securities	Project financing
	Operations	Cash management Lockboxes Electronic data processing	Safekeeping of securities Demand deposits
	Operations-credit	None	None
	Investment	Securities purchases and sales	Fiduciary services Time deposits
Trust	Credit	None	Registrar
	Operations	Stock transfers Property management Corporate trust administration Employee stock ownership plans Business advisory services Paying agency for bond issues	Personal trust administration Pension and profit sharing Money purchase pension and thrift accounts
	Operations-credit	None	
	Investment	Trust investments	Pooled investments

Geographic Markets. In addition to product and customer markets, a market may be defined by location. The location may be local or metropolitan, branch, regional, national, or international. Banks are limited by banking laws in the extent to which they may expand geographically. However, certain types of banking activities are allowed outside geographic boundaries.

Depending on state laws, a bank may be operated as a unit or as a branch bank. In many states only unit banks are permissible. States permitting branching may allow limited branching, such as countywide, contiguous-county, or statewide branching. In states that do not allow branching, many banking organizations have formed multibank holding companies to acquire unit banks and to "act" as branching organizations. Some states permit only one bank holding company. To accomplish the equivalent of a multibank holding company, another holding company may be formed to own the one bank holding company, thereby linking the banks in the complex legal structure.

The unit bank is typically limited to a single location. However, certain states allow detached facilities offering limited services. In Colorado, for instance, such facilities are allowed within 3000 feet of the main bank. They provide drive-in service and service for depository activities; they do not provide loan services. Colorado also permits loan production offices. These offices cannot accept depository transactions but can process loan applications.

Branching allows banks to extend their market areas. Branch banks may confine their activities to the retail or wholesale market or they may serve both markets. The types of services offered at the branches depend on the kinds of customers in the market areas. Some branches provide deposits in excess of loan demand, whereas others have greater loan demand than deposits. Many branch organizations establish branch locations that tap only lending markets and other locations that tap only deposit markets. The overall objective is to match as closely as possible all fund-using locations with fund-providing locations.

Establishment of a branch with full or limited services depends on the market area. Geographic location of branch offices is a way of delivering customer services and of stretching the organization beyond the main office to tap specific markets. Branch offices may be small or large, depending on the type of customer and product market to be accessed. In metropolitan areas the branch usually is not accessible by automobile and relies mainly on foot traffic. In suburban areas, where the automobile is a primary means of access to a bank, branches are more likely to have drive-in facilities.

With regard to subsidiaries, holding company operational structures vary. Some organizations operate each bank as an independent unit. Others operate the banks like a branch system. No one structure is followed by all institutions.

Alternative Organizational Structures

The simplest organizational structure is the unit bank. Exhibit 2.2 portrays a unit bank divided into traditional functions and an alternative design incorporating retail and wholesale concepts. In the small bank many staff functions are assigned to the operations functions, such as personnel and accounting. In the retail-wholesale structure operations functions may be separated. In the retail division customer services operations, such as new accounts, may be included with consumer-lending functions in a personal banker concept. The personal banker concept allows the customer to contact a single person who can handle all facets of the customer relationship. The customer accounting support responsibilities may be assigned to data processing in a staff service relationship and may be administered by a separate administrative division head.

Centralization versus Decentralization

Branch and multibank holding company organizations may centralize certain line and staff functions and decentralize other functions. These structures permit different degrees of autonomy to branch managers or bank presidents. There are advantages and disadvantages to different degrees of centralization. Phillip Searle summarizes the pros and cons associated with the various degrees of centralization in *The Bankers' Handbook.*

A. Little authority and decision making at the branch or subsidiary bank level (this is the situation when most of the authority is retained and exercised at the head office or at the holding company headquarters).

Pros

Functional Expertise. Obviously, it is less costly overall to have a few experts in the head office or the holding company headquarters for functions such as loans, operations, and marketing than to have such expertise in every branch or subsidiary bank.

Minimum Training of Personnel. The less expertise required at the branch or subsidiary bank level, the less training of such personnel will be necessary.

Maximum Control. Since most decisions are made centrally, there is little difficulty in controlling the decision makers.

Little or No Reporting, Reviewing, and Discussions. Conversely, to the extent that decisions are made in the branches or the subsidiary banks, maintenance of some control over application of policy is necessary.

EXHIBIT 2.2   Unit Bank Organization

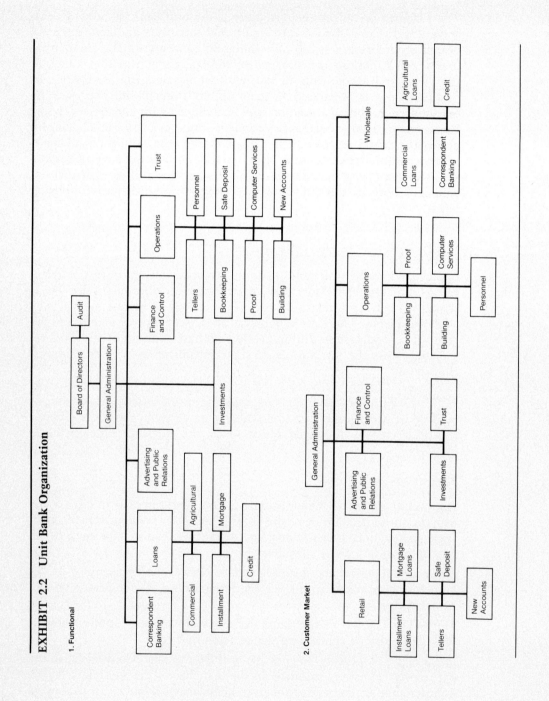

1. Functional

2. Customer Market

This can result in time-consuming preparation, review of reports, and ensuing discussions or correspondence.

Centralized Processing. There is a natural tendency towards centralization of processing when decisions are made in the head office or in the headquarters of the multibank holding company.

Cons

Fewer Services in Branches or Banking Subsidiaries and Perhaps in the Banking Organization as a Whole. Many services cannot be rendered, at least acceptably, unless those in the branches or subsidiary banks having contact with the customer are able to perform them. Some services have a time factor or a person-to-person relationship that will not permit referral to headquarters for decision or action.

Slower Service. Akin to the foregoing are the services that can be performed by referral to the head office or the holding company headquarters but that are delayed because of the time of communication, the multiple handling, or the reference to off-premise records.

Impersonal Service and Customer Dissatisfaction. Lack of opportunity for the customers to state their cases face to face with the decision maker can be disturbing and frustrating for them. Coupled with this is the decision maker's lack of personal knowledge of, and to some degree interest in, customers and their problems.

Less Interest in Local Welfare and Local Activities. Unless the decision makers participate actively in local affairs, it is difficult for the banking organization, whatever its structure, to demonstrate its good citizenship. In competition with unit bankers or branch managers and subsidiary bank CEOs, who possess a relatively high degree of autonomy, it is unlikely that a branch manager with little authority can become "the local banker."

Imbalance of Functional Effects. When each head office or headquarters of a multibank holding company exercises substantial functional authority over the branch manager or the subsidiary bank manager, it is inescapable that there will be "pushing and pulling." The effect of the activities of various functional heads in the home office can hardly be a balanced mix that represents top management's intentions. The head office or headquarters operation function may strive for efficiency and economy at the same time that the business development function is pressing for promotion, good public relations, and the ultimate in customer service and satisfaction. While these are not necessarily incompatible, the degree of emphasis that each branch manager or subsidiary bank CEO will give to the respective functions is likely to be influenced by the effect of the representative of each function, rather than by the best overall interests of the bank. This violates one of the cardinal principles of organization—i.e., no person should have more than one "boss."

B. Maximum authority in decision making at the branch or the subsidiary bank level (this is in contrast to the foregoing centralization in the organizational structure that occurs when the head office or the headquarters of the multibank holding company functions only in advising, assisting, observing, and reporting).

Pros

Widest Variety of Services Conveniently Rendered. When possessed with sufficient expertise and authority, branch or subsidiary bank personnel can render almost any service without reference to administrative specialists. This is to the advantage of the customer in obtaining desired services conveniently and promptly. It is to the advantage of the bank because it can sell services it could not otherwise sell.

Most Personal Service. Not only can the services be rendered more conveniently and promptly but also the likelihood of personal interest is greater on the part of the staff member. Also, the staff member can adapt the service to the needs and preferences of the customer.

Greatest Knowledge of, and Interest in, Local Conditions. This is the basis for good corporate citizenship. Active participation in community affairs by the bank staff not only discharges a civic obligation but also reflects credit on the institution.

Maximum Job Satisfaction. This is an advantage particularly applicable to branch managers and subsidiary bank CEOs. Instead of being the proverbial "cog in a wheel," the manager or subsidiary CEO is the "wheel." Managers have the challenge of the authority, responsibility, and accountability for a full-service banking operation and are measured and rewarded on the basis of the growth, soundness, and profitability of the banking unit. Their contribution to the welfare of the overall banking organization can be measured not only by their superiors but also by themselves. Furthermore, there exists the prestige of being the local banker, not merely the paid functionary of a distant head office or multibank holding company headquarters.

Maximum Motivation to Develop Branch or Subsidiary Bank. When a person is operating on his or her own, pride and self-interest stimulate the individual to greater ingenuity and effort.

Minimum Problems of Communication. When the authority to make most decisions is vested in the branch or subsidiary bank, the necessity for communication with the head office or holding company headquarters is lessened substantially.

Broadest Development of Personnel. It is incumbent on the local banking unit to work with its staff to develop the competencies necessary to make the right decisions and otherwise to discharge responsibilities of a nearly autonomous banking entity. This development is in the best interests of each employee, the local banking entity, and the community. It provides opportunities for advancement to the individual and a needed pool of talent for the banking organization overall.

Cons

Problem of Achieving Uniformity. A high degree of decentralized decision making may result in undesirable differences in the interpretation and implementation of institutional policies. Effective communication of top management's desires is more difficult.

Problems of Control. Not only must policies be communicated but also there must be adequate means of detecting noncompliance or misinterpretation without in effect removing the authority of the branch manager or subsidiary CEO. It is therefore essential that there exist within the organization methods of measurement and control by which the superior can measure achievement, performance, and status.

Problems of Training and Development. The more numerous the technical services rendered in the branches or the subsidiary banks and the wider the dispersion of such banking facilities, the greater the problem of providing training and assistance in self-development. Carefully tailored programs for training and development, capably executed, are an absolute necessity.[1]

Each organization must decide on the degree of centralization by weighing the advantages and disadvantages in concert with meeting its corporate goals and objectives. Centralized bank functions, such as investments, result in greater efficiency than could be achieved through decentralization. The centralize-decentralize decision is not so clear-cut for many other bank functions.

A Branch Structure.   Let us examine a more complex organizational structure. Security Pacific Bank, based in Los Angeles, is a branching organization. Exhibit 2.3 is Security Pacific's organization chart. The key features include the retail functions dispersed through its branches in the California Banking Group. Wholesale banking functions, such as international, corporate, and fiduciary services, are offered through the main office. Support services, such as the financial group, are assigned to the vice-chairman and chief financial officer.

The branches are supported by such staff functions as consumer service centers and product management. This support, coordinated through the vice-chairman for the California Banking Group, serves the various geographic structures, including divisions, regions, and branch

---

[1]P. F. Searle, "Alternative Organizational Structures," in *The Bankers' Handbook*, 2d ed., ed. W. H. Baughn and C. E. Walker (Homewood, Ill: Dow Jones-Irwin, 1978), 32–35.

EXHIBIT 2.3   Security Pacific Bank

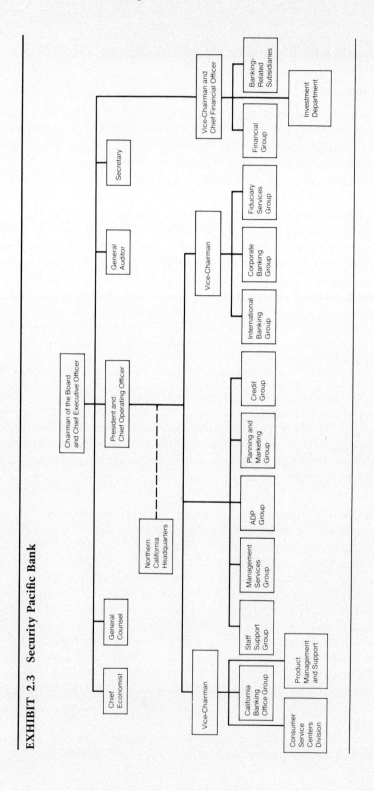

banks. The various subdivisions are also assigned specific support staff (see Exhibit 2.4). The consumer service centers process loan applications taken by automobile dealers, for example, and they may also handle specialized transactions such as leasing. The branches conduct mainline retail activities and refer specialized banking relationships to the service centers. Deposit and check-clearing processing occurs in central locations (off-premise from the branches). Wholesale activities may also be conducted at certain branches but are usually limited to smaller businesses. Large corporate banking relationships are conducted through the Corporate Banking Group.

Innovative Structure in a Holding Company Environment. An example of an innovative organization is the First Bank Holding Company based in Colorado. This holding company owns 21 banks and has several *de novo* charter applications pending. Although branching is not permitted in Colorado, First Bank has structured its banks operationally and physically as a branching system. The key features of its organization are:

1. The members of the holding company's board of directors are also directors of each unit bank. Board meetings are held on the same day at a single location, with each bank president attending his respective meeting.

2. Holding company expansion is through *de novo* banks (banks formed through new charters).

3. All new banks are housed in prototype buildings, which are extremely efficient and austere, yet comfortable.

4. Backroom operations, such as proof, bookkeeping, and data processing, are centrally located in the Denver area.

5. The bank premises consist of areas for lending and customer depository contact as well as drive-in facilities. The banks look and act like branch operations.

6. The organization hires and trains new personnel in all phases of the operations. Employees are young; it is not unusual for a bank president to be 28 years old.

7. The holding company performs investment and audit functions for all units.

8. A significant but less-than-majority ownership of the holding company is held by an Employee Stock Ownership Plan (ESOP).

9. The corporation employs a bonus plan that allocates bonus

EXHIBIT 2.4   Security Pacific Bank: Banking Office System

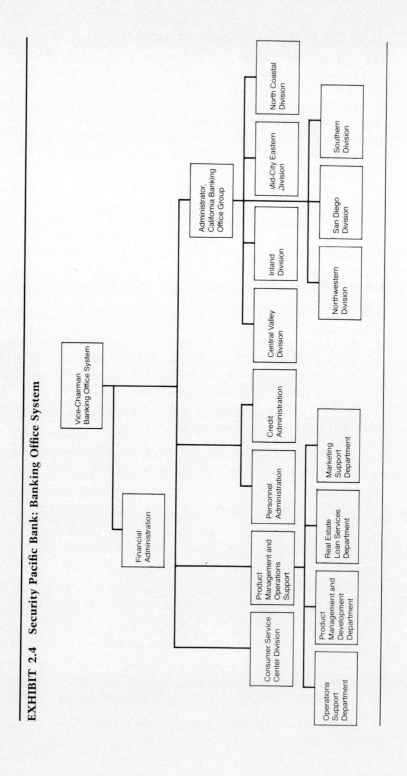

monies based on individual bank performance and distributed by the bank president to key employees.

10. Each bank is identified as First Bank of *(location)* for common corporate identity.[2]

The above examples illustrate several organizational styles. These styles are obviously not the only possibilities. Each organization will adapt its own services to a particular organizational style. The important consideration is whether the structure enhances accomplishment of corporate goals through distribution of authority and responsibility and through defined communication at all levels, and whether it increases productivity.

PERSONNEL STRUCTURE

A bank's organizational structure involves several levels of authority and responsibility. A bank must have a board of directors and a management. Banks also form several committees, some at the board level and others interlaced among various management levels. These committees provide concentrations of expertise, control, and communication of bank policies and procedures.

Lines of Authority

Board of Directors.   The board of directors represents the highest echelon of authority. Under national banking laws a board must consist of at least 5 but no more than 25 directors elected annually by the shareholders. In the smaller bank it is appropriate to have a small board. As the bank grows, it may become appropriate to add directors. Normally a board will include both inside and outside directors. Inside directors include the bank's president and may include other senior bank officers. Outside directors should be selected from a cross section of the community served by the bank. As a practical consideration, although a bank directorship is an honor to the individual, it also carries significant responsibilities and liabilities.

Inside directors, who represent management, are familiar with the business of banking. But outside directors, though knowledgeable about their own businesses, are usually unfamiliar with banking operations. They are therefore at a disadvantage when discussing technical issues affecting policy. In recognition of this disadvantage, several banking associations, including the American Bankers Association and the Bank

---

[2]Interview with W. P. Johnson, Chairman, First Bank Holding Company, Denver, CO, January 1982.

Ineffective Board Action Leads Regional Administrator to Intercede

Several years ago, a community bank in Wyoming that was owned by a bank holding company found itself in significant trouble. The bank president was the former owner of the bank. His board represented a cross section of the community but lacked any knowledge or expertise in banking. At that time the holding company had no representatives on the bank board. The Regional Administrator of National Banks in Denver was concerned about the bank's practice of borrowing substantial amounts of short-term funds and its longer-run effect on the bank's soundness. The holding company's internal audit staff and management made several recommendations to the holding company board, which were largely ignored.

The Regional Administrator called a meeting of the bank board in his office and in no uncertain terms indicated to the board the gravity of the situation. He indicated that he would remove the directors from office if they did not become more aware of and more active in bank policy and if they did not direct the bank president to take corrective action. The task was more easily assigned than accomplished. None of the outside directors had enough financial training to fully comprehend the bank's operations, and all continued to rely on the bank president as their sole source of information.

Sadly, approximately one year later, the bank experienced unprecedented losses on loans made by the president. It was also determined that the president had indirect interest in the companies to which the loans were made. The effect on the community was traumatic, as the bank lost approximately one quarter of its deposit base, and the holding company experienced a significant depression in earnings per share as a result of the losses. The holding company replaced management and certain board members. This experience has had a dramatic effect on the holding company's policies to improve the caliber of its banks' managements and directors.

Administration Institute, have designed seminars to increase directors' knowledge of banking. Management should encourage director participation in these seminars, for directors can be valuable in establishing policy, goals, and objectives. Management that controls policy, goals, and objectives because of lack of director participation is self-serving and may act to the detriment of the bank.

The outside director contributes his knowledge of the community and can effectively promote the bank's services within his sphere of influence. An active director can bring new customers to the bank, often more easily than bank personnel can. At board meetings a well-prepared director may ask probing and challenging questions, in effect serving as the "devil's advocate." As a result, policies, goals, and objectives may take broader perspective.

Bank directorships differ from nonbank directorships. Bank directorships are governed by numerous laws and regulations, whereas nonbank directorships are not. The primary differences are:

1. Bank directors take an oath of office; nonbank directors do not.

2. Bank directors have residence and citizenship requirements; nonbank directors do not.

3. Certain occupations involving successful and honorable men are barred from bank boards. There is no parallel in other businesses.

4. A bank director must own some stock. Again, the parallel condition does not exist in nonbanking firms.

5. A bank director's conduct of his affairs may result in his being subject to a cease-and-desist order or, quite possibly, even being separated from his office by public authority.[3]

Banking laws prohibit individuals from serving as directors if they are engaged in investment banking. The law also prohibits a director serving concurrently on the board of another bank, savings and loan association, mutual savings bank, or other financial institution within the same Standard Metropolitan Statistical Area (SMSA) unless that institution is also owned by the owners of the bank.

A director must avoid conflict of interest. His personal interests must be subordinated to the bank's interest when he is conducting business. When he is privy to information concerning bank customers, he should not use that information to the customers' detriment nor to further his own interests. What he learns in the boardroom should stay there. With regard to his own interests, the director should not make a request of the bank that will give him favored treatment. Indeed, banking law to some degree controls such situations. However, a director may be able to obtain certain loans or services on terms more favorable than if he were not a director.

In addition to directors who lack sufficient knowledge of banking or who do not carry out their responsibilities, there are occasions when

---

[3]G. T. Dunne, "Legal Responsibilities of Bank Directors," in *The Bank Director,* ed. R. B. Johnson (Dallas: SMU Press, 1974), 54.

directors step across the line and interfere with management. The directors establish policies that management is expected to execute. When an individual director "suggests" that an officer or employee perform some action, he steps out of the role of director and into that of management. Unfortunately, such an action may result in a poor decision, with the director conveniently stepping back into his director role and disclaiming responsibility for the consequences. If directors act as a team in setting policy and leave execution to management, the board can clearly evaluate results and suggest alternatives to management. If management personnel cannot carry out policies or are ineffective, then they may be replaced. A clear delineation of the director's role is certainly necessary to establish the line between directors and management.

National bank regulations require that certain committees be established by the board. These are the loan and discount, investment, examination, and trust committees. Other committees may be established, including the executive and salary committees. Typically, the examination and salary committee members are outside directors. The examination committee is charged with conducting an annual examination of the bank. National bank regulations prescribe the minimum tests that must be performed in a directors' examination. The directors may conduct the examination themselves or engage an outside firm.

In small banks the loan and discount and investment committee functions may be conducted by an executive committee. The loan committee is responsible for reviewing loan activity, particularly larger credits that exceed officer lending limits. The investment committee is charged with the responsibility of establishing investment policy and ensuring that purchases and sales of investment-grade securities conform to established policy.

Directors may become personally liable for losses sustained by the bank because of actions in which the director participated, assented, or was negligent. Certain actions by directors in violation of antitrust and securities laws subject the directors to liabilities and penalties prescribed by law. Criminal acts include (1) falsifying entries, reports, or certification of checks; (2) theft, embezzlement, or misapplication by a bank officer, director, or employee; (3) false representation of federal deposit insurance coverage; (4) making loans to bank examiners; (5) lending trust funds to directors or directors receiving fees for procuring loans; and (6) frauds and swindles. Principal violations of banking law may include granting loans in excess of legal lending limits, falsifying reports, issuing improper dividends, exceeding statutory limits on the payment of interest on deposits, and exceeding limits on loans to officers.

The duties and responsibilities may be summarized in a statement by George S. Sloan, director, Division of Examinations, Federal Reserve Board:

If I were to find myself elected a director of a bank, I would consider it my first duty to know my bank and not just by name, location, size, and magnificence of quarters, capital, surplus and total deposits. I would want to know the character and needs of its customers, the economic conditions under which it must exist and both generally and particularly applicable to it; the stability of its deposits and how much weight this factor had in the determination of loan and investment policies; and the prospects for its development or, to say the same thing, the improvement of its services to the community. I would feel that I should satisfy myself that the officers of the bank were able, efficient and completely trustworthy. I would insist on sound loan, investment and operating policies and I would supervise operations to see that the procedures and practices conformed with such policies.[4]

Management. Banking has long been a people-oriented business. In dealing with customers' money, concern for depositor safety and confidence has required an interpersonal contact with the customer. Although there has been an increase in the use of electronic devices, such as automated teller machines, and proposals for telephone and in-home banking, customers still want contact from time to time with bank management and personnel. It has been said that a bank takes on the personality of its officers and employees, and it is with that personality that the customer identifies his banking relationship.

Bank management is concerned with managing the resources of the bank, including capital, time, and people. Much has been said about managing the financial aspects of the balance sheet, but time and people management are equally important. Time is an important factor in all banking functions. We all have heard the expression "time is money," but in banking an investment not made today will be income lost forever. In daily operations the processing of checks is generally governed by the Uniform Commercial Code, wherein checks must be processed within certain time limits or the legal right to collection is lost. Losses can occur if these limits are not met.

Management groups bank activities into an organizational structure that emphasizes general and specialized services, discrete markets, regional needs, and internal support functions. In the small organization services and functions will be grouped around individuals having the specific training to guide the specific services and functions. The larger organization defines the organization and selects the appropriate personnel to manage the various functions. The smaller organization tends to employ more generalists, whereas the larger organization tends to be

---

[4]American Bankers Association, *A Bank Director's Job* (Washington, DC: American Bankers Association, 1979), 24.

Organizational Transition: A Troubled Bank Merges

When IntraWest Bank, formerly The First National Bank of Denver, experienced exuberant expense growth and deteriorating loan quality and found itself earning only about two thirds of the return on assets of its peers, the board of directors went outside to hire the chief executive officer (CEO) and chief operating officer (COO). The new executives developed a plan to cut expenses and improve customer service. When they took over, they observed six layers of personnel between the customer and the CEO and began a concerted effort to reduce the number of layers to four. The reductions were accomplished by eliminating personnel between department and divisional heads. The result is better accountability for decisions.

The bank has also reduced its head count of full-time-equivalent employees from 1680 in June 1983 to 1380 in July 1983 and expect it to fall to 1250 by mid-1985. The old rule of thumb in banking was to have one person per million dollars of assets. The bank believes it can reduce its ratio to one-half person per million dollars of assets.

The desire to shore up its capital position led the new management to seek out a merger with First Interstate Bank of Denver. Not only is the "old" bank faced with consolidating its operations and personnel levels but also it will be interesting to watch the process required to merge two of Denver's largest banks into a single operation.

more specialized. Historically, lending personnel have had the best opportunities to reach the presidency of a bank. Recently, with greater emphasis on financial and administrative skills, operational and financial managers are gaining increased access to the president's chair.

Personnel.   A personnel structure may include the president, executive vice-presidents, senior vice-presidents, and other officers, supervisors, and employees. The size of the bank and the number of functions and offices determine the number and mix of officers and employees. Lending functions differ from operations functions in the mix of officers and employees. Loan officers manage portfolios, while the concentration of personnel management is in operational support activities.

Officers are selected by the board and granted specific authority to carry out bank functions. In the lending area, officers manage loan portfolios. Operationally, officers and supervisors carry out backroom operations, which are people intensive. Exposure to public contact also plays a role in determining need for combining officer status with job responsibility. An officer title implies ability and authority within certain limits to conduct bank transactions with the public. The authority of an officer is defined by the corporate bylaws and further refined by board policy.

Most banks operate with a committee structure. The executive or management committee consists of the senior officers in charge of the major bank divisions. Executive or management committees evaluate progress toward meeting overall goals and objectives and the problems experienced in meeting these goals. Such committees also provide a forum for senior management to become informed about internal and external matters affecting the bank. Additional formal or informal committees may operate within each division. These committees include the division head and department managers. For example, the loan committee reviews and discusses lending limits and lines of credit. For large lines of credit the loan committee approves or disapproves recommendations to the board of directors. In large banks each major lending division may have separate loan committees.

Personnel hiring and training are two important operations at every level of management. Some organizations hire, train, and promote from within. Others hire trained personnel and place them in key positions as expertise in specific tasks is required. Whatever the philosophy, a bank must continually examine its organization and evaluate its personnel skills as new markets are attacked. Additionally, because changes in banking technology occur rapidly and frequently, a bank must continually plan to afford personnel the opportunity to engage in formal and informal training to increase skills and awareness of banking trends.

SUMMARY

A variety of organizational structures is observed in banking. The issue of efficient organization is an important one in the current environment characterized by increased competition. Efficient organization is critical to delivery of services at the lowest possible cost.

Traditionally banks were organized around the major functions of lending and operations. This structure is still the most commonly observed for small banks. Larger banks also organize around functions, although in recent years the trend has been to set up the organizational structure around product or customer markets rather than on a straight functional basis. The advantage of organizing around customer markets is that all services offered by the bank are delivered through one organizational unit.

A management decision that is related to the basic organizational structure is the decision to centralize or decentralize key functions. Key factors that must be considered in the decision include the costs of per-

sonnel training, control aspects, and the ability to deliver services in a
timely fashion.

Questions and Problems

1. Identify the regulatory differences between bank and nonbank
directorships.

2. Describe the difference between an organizational structure based
on function and one based on customer markets.

3. Describe the various legal structures that apply to banking
organizations.

4. Differentiate between a centralized and a decentralized philosophy
in structuring a multioffice banking organization.

5. Identify the major advantages and disadvantages of different degrees
of centralization employed in branching or multibank holding
companies.

6. What criminal acts subject directors to liabilities and penalties
prescribed by law?

7. What is the purpose of the directors' audit committee? Investment
committee?

8. Describe the committees typically used in the day-to-day
management of banks.

References

American Bankers Association. *A Bank Director's Job*. Washington, DC: American Bankers Association, 1970, 24.

Buckwalter, N. "Bankers Trust Goes Wholesale." *United States Banker*, August 1981: 38–39.

Comptroller of the Currency. *Duties and Liabilities of Directors of National Banks*. Washington, DC: U.S. Government Printing Office, 1978, 3–14.

Dunne, G. T. "Legal Responsibilities of Bank Directors." In *The Bank Director*, ed. R. B Johnson, Dallas: Southern Methodist University Press, 1974.

Ellison, D. E. "Fiduciary Services by Business Line." In *The Bankers' Handbook*, 2d ed., ed. W. H. Baughn and C. E. Walker, 929–935. Homewood, IL.: Dow Jones-Irwin, 1978.

Hazeltin, S. "The Bank's Board of Directors—Functions and Responsibilities." In *The Bankers' Handbook*, 2d ed., ed. W. H. Baughn and C. E. Walker, 15–25. Homewood, IL.: Dow Jones-Irwin, 1978.

Oliver, A. G. "The Function of Retail Banking." In *The Bankers' Handbook*, 2d ed., ed. W. H. Baughn and C. E. Walker, 837–847. Homewood, IL.: Dow Jones-Irwin, 1978.

Rideout, T. P., and S. Seidler. "Fed's Changes Will Help Correspondents, They Say in Survey." *ABA Banking Journal*, November 1981: 67–70.

Robertson, R. R. "Developing Corporate Services." In *The Bankers' Handbook*, 2d ed., ed. W. H. Baughn and C. E. Walker, 961–972. Homewood, IL.: Dow Jones-Irwin, 1978.

Searle, P. F. "Alternative Organizational Structures." In *The Bankers' Handbook*, 2d ed., ed. W. H. Baughn and C. E. Walker, 32–35. Homewood, IL.: Dow Jones-Irwin, 1978.

Stous, T. I., M. J. Shapiro, and M. J. Frieder. "An Orderly Transition to Interstate Banking." *Bankers Magazine*, March-April 1981: 47–53.

Thompson, T. W., L. L. Berry, and P. H. Davidson. *Banking Tomorrow*. New York: Van Nostrand Reinhold, 1978, 185–186.

CHAPTER 3

Banking
Return and Risk

The management of a bank is concerned with implementing short-term and long-term goals and objectives, with the ultimate goal being the maximization of return to the bank's owners. Each decision made by management will have some effect on achieving the ultimate goal. The success of management depends on its ability to recognize what effect a particular decision will have on potential return and how it will affect the riskiness of the bank.

The goal of maximizing shareholder wealth is implemented on a short-term basis by managing a pool of funds that changes daily. Management must coordinate the inflow to and outflow from that pool of funds in a manner that meets the long-term goal of maximizing the owners' wealth. In this chapter we survey the basic process of managing the pool of funds and examine the elements of return and risk present in the banking industry.

SOURCES AND USES OF FUNDS

In a dynamic sense a bank is a pool of funds that is constantly changing as new funds flow in and out of the bank. As the bank receives new deposits or existing depositors increase the holdings in their accounts, management employs these funds in assets that will contribute earnings to the bank. Conversely, if the bank's depositors reduce their deposits, management must secure funds to cover these withdrawals. If the bank holds surplus cash, it may be able to cover the withdrawals without further adjustments. If no surplus cash is held, the bank will have to secure the funds by either liquidating some of its earning assets or by borrowing the funds from other sources.

The process of funds management entails managing an ever-changing pool of funds with a goal of maximizing profit and minimizing risk exposure to the bank shareholders. Sufficient flexibility must be maintained in the management process to meet unexpected inflows and outflows.

Funds-Providing Functions

Banks secure funds from these major sources: deposits, other borrowed funds, and capital. These sources of funds, or funds-providing functions, can be differentiated according to their maturity and cost to the bank.

Deposits.   The largest and most important funds-providing function for banks is deposits. Deposits account for approximately 80 to 90 percent of a bank's sources of funds, with larger money center banks at the lower end of the range and smaller banks at the higher end of the range. Deposits are classified into three groups: demand, savings, and time.

Demand deposits are payable on demand and, at least in a legal sense, have the shortest maturity. Savings deposits as a matter of practice are also payable on demand, although legally a bank can require a depositor to give 30 days notice prior to withdrawal. Time deposits have specific maturity dates that may extend for several years. Because of the specified maturities, these deposits, in a legal sense, are the most permanent deposits.

It is useful to distinguish between the concepts of legal maturity and practical maturity. Although in a legal sense demand and savings deposits have very short maturities, not all of these accounts are viewed as being short-term deposits. The bank will have a certain level of deposits that are permanent and a remaining portion that will fluctuate. From a planning standpoint, a portion of demand and savings deposits can be viewed as permanent and are typically referred to as "core" deposits.

In general, demand deposits are considered the lowest-cost source of funds and one of the most stable. Traditionally banks were prohibited from paying *explicit* interest on demand deposits, but they have paid *implicit* interest on such deposits by offering checking services at prices less than the banks' costs. Under current regulation banks can offer interest on certain types of checking accounts.[1] The maximum rate of interest that can be offered on savings and most time deposits is set by Regulation Q, and in recent periods banks have offered the maximum allowable rate on such deposits. The cost of such funds is viewed as being fixed or as not being interest sensitive. Regulation Q is being phased out pursuant to the passage of the Depository Institutions Deregulation and Monetary Control Act of 1980. Interest rate ceilings will be removed and banks will compete for deposits at market rates. Large negotiable certificates of deposit are interest sensitive because they are excluded from Regulation Q ceilings. Rates paid for such deposits vary with general money market conditions.

---

[1]Under the Depository Institutions Deregulation and Monetary Control Act of 1980, banks now can offer checking with interest. The Act also calls for the eventual elimination of Regulation Q, which sets the limit on interest banks can offer on small nonnegotiable deposits.

Borrowed Funds. Banks also secure funds by borrowing on either a short-term or a long-term basis. Long-term debt is more permanent and may be considered bank capital if it meets certain regulatory criteria.

The major instruments used by banks in securing short-term borrowed funds include: federal funds purchased, securities sold under repurchase agreements, acceptances outstanding, borrowings from the Federal Reserve Bank, and Eurodollar borrowings. All of these instruments are secured loans payable that have very short maturities, in many cases overnight.

Rates of interest paid on borrowed funds are quite volatile, particularly on those instruments that are extensively used in the daily cash management process. Since rates are determined through the interaction of supply and demand in the market and the maturities are so short, it is not uncommon to observe large swings in rates on these instruments in a matter of days.

In recent years banks have made extensive use of borrowed funds, with many banks using them on a permanent ongoing basis. When a bank uses short-term funds to support long-term assets, rate variability can affect interest spreads. When a bank uses short-term funds to support short-term assets, the effect on margins is not so significant. Large money center and regional banks tend to be net borrowers of these funds, with smaller banks being net suppliers.

Capital. The third major funds-providing function is capital. Banks secure additional funds through the issuance of long-term debt and through increases in equity securities. Funds secured through increases in capital accounts are differentiated from other funds-providing functions by the permanence of the funds.

The main source of bank capital is common stock. A bank secures funds initially when the owners commit their funds to the bank through stock purchase. Following the initial injection of funds, additional funds are provided through either profit retention or sales of additional shares of stock.

In an ongoing sense, funds are provided to banks from profits that are retained and not distributed as dividends to the owners. This source of funds depends on both the profitability of the bank and its dividend-paying practices. The more profitable the bank and the larger the percentage of earnings it retains, the larger will be the source of funds. A typical bank dividend payout ratio is 30 percent of current-period profits.

A bank may secure additional funds by selling additional shares of stock. This source of funding is more accessible to large banks whose common stock trades in active secondary markets than to small banks whose stock is closely held and usually not traded.

In recent years banks have issued long-term debt. Regulators monitor the relationships between total outstanding liabilities to capital and total assets to capital. By considering long-term debt as capital, a bank may expand other liabilities and assets. Regulations require that such debt be subordinated to depositor claims. To be classified as capital debt, its maturity must equal or exceed 7 years.[2] Maturities on these subordinated debentures may be as long as 20 to 25 years. The long-term permanent nature of these funds distinguishes them from other liabilities of the bank. A bank that issues subordinated debt obtains funds having a fixed cost and has use of these funds until the bonds mature.[3]

Funds-Using Functions

Banks invest in a variety of assets the funds secured through deposits, short-term borrowings, and capital. The majority of these funds are employed in interest-bearing assets such as loans and investments. Some funds are also employed in nonearning assets such as cash and facilities. Investment in nonearning cash assets is necessary to provide liquidity to accommodate outflows of funds and to meet reserve requirements. Banks must also have facilities to support their investment and funds-providing functions. Funds-using functions are classified into four major groups: loans, investments, cash assets, and facilities.

Loans.   The single most important funds-using function for commercial banks is the lending function. For a typical bank, loans account for approximately 55 percent to 60 percent of total assets. Banks earn the highest gross yield on loans.

Commercial and industrial loans account for approximately 40 percent of total loans for all banks. The next two largest categories of loans are real estate and loans to individuals, which account for approximately 30 percent and 20 percent, respectively, of total loans. For all banks these three classes account for approximately 90 percent of total loans. Other types of loans made by commercial banks include agricultural loans, loans to other financial institutions, and lease financing.

Larger money-center banks are most active in commercial and industrial loans. Larger banks also are very active in lending to other financial institutions, with as much as 10 percent of their loans being made to other financial institutions. Smaller regional banks tend to have heavier concentrations in real estate and agricultural loans.

It is important to differentiate loans on the basis of maturity and pricing characteristics. A bank is primarily a short- to intermediate-term

---

[2]R. D. Watson, "Banking on Debt for Capital Needs," *Business Review, Federal Reserve Bank of Philadelphia*, December 1974: 17–28.

[3]The subordinated notes may have a sinking fund provision that effectively shortens the maturity of the source of funding. Subordinated notes are discussed in greater detail in Chapter 14.

lender, although certain loans may have maturities as long as 30 years. Loans may also vary with respect to the interest rate negotiated by the lending bank. Loans may be made on either a fixed-rate or variable-rate basis. The maturity and pricing characteristics of assets are important since they can be different from the maturity and pricing characteristics of a bank's source of funds.

The average maturity of the major types of loans varies. Most commercial and industrial loans have maturities of one year or less. In contrast, the maturities on consumer loans and on many of the real estate loans in a bank's portfolio extend for several years. The average maturity of the loan portfolio will therefore depend to some extent on the concentration of lending activity. A bank that concentrates its lending in the commercial and industrial category will have a shorter average maturity on its loan portfolio than will a bank that concentrates in consumer and real estate loans. The average maturity of the loan portfolio is also dependent on whether loans are installment or single payment loans. Installment loans, which are characterized by systematic repayment of principal and interest over the term of the loan, have an average life that is less than the stated maturity. The bank will recover a portion of the principal as the loan is systematically retired. On a single payment loan all of the principal is repaid at maturity. Although installment loans have average lives that exceed single payment loans, their average lives are less than the stated maturity.

Loan portfolios can also be differentiated according to the pricing characteristics of the loans that make up the portfolios. A fixed-rate loan is negotiated with an interest rate that is fixed over the term of the loan. A variable-rate loan is negotiated with an interest rate that fluctuates over the term of the loan. The rate on such loans fluctuates with money market conditions.

The combined effect of both the maturity and pricing characteristics is important to the concept of asset and liability management. Loans with very short maturities and longer-term loans with variable interest rates are classified as interest-sensitive loans. Interest earned on these loans is sensitive to movements in the general level of interest rates. Long-term fixed-rate loans are characterized by rates that will not vary with money market rates; such loans are therefore classified as nonsensitive to changes in interest rates. The loan portfolio must be managed with respect to a bank's sources of funds since sources of funds also vary with respect to interest rate sensitivity.

Investments.   The second major funds-using function of banks is investment in debt securities. The major investments include obligations of the U.S. Treasury, agencies of the federal government, and state and local governments or political subdivisions thereof. Banks may also purchase obligations of other financial institutions and debt issued by foreign and domestic corporations.

Investments in obligations of the federal, state, and local government units are differentiated with respect to risk of default, maturity, marketability, and tax treatment. Obligations of the federal government are essentially free of risk of default. Obligations of state and local governments vary with respect to risk of default. Risk of default is dependent on whether the security is a general obligation bond or a revenue bond on which the source of repayment is tied to particular sources of revenue, and it is also dependent on the financial strength of the issuer. Municipal securities are generally classified as low-risk securities but are riskier than investments in federal securities.

Maturities on obligations of the U.S. Treasury range from 13 weeks on Treasury bills to more than 20 years on some Treasury bonds. Agency securities and municipal securities tend to be longer-term bonds and notes whose maturities can extend upwards of 30 years.

Various government obligations possess different degrees of marketability. Obligations of the U.S. Treasury trade in active secondary markets, enabling a bank to sell such securities quickly if the bank needs funds.[4] U.S agency securities also trade in active secondary markets but are usually considered to be slightly less marketable than Treasury obligations. Most municipal securities are less marketable than either agency or Treasury obligations, as less active secondary markets exist for many municipal securities.

Another significant difference in a bank's investments in municipal obligations is the tax treatment of interest income. Because interest income on municipal securities is not subject to federal income taxes, the interest rates are lower than the interest rates on taxable federal government securities. The yield that a bank earns on its investment portfolio is influenced by the tax treatment, risk of default, maturity, and marketability of the securities.

Cash Assets. The third major funds-using function of banks is investment in cash assets. Cash assets include vault cash, reserves held at the Federal Reserve Bank, balances due from other banks, and cash items in the process of collection. This use of funds can be differentiated from loans and investments in that a bank does not earn an explicit rate of interest on cash assets. Investment in cash assets is necessary to support the deposit function of the bank and in some cases to obtain correspondent services related to loans and investments.

Vault cash consists of currency and coin that a bank holds in its vault. The bank must accommodate depositors who wish to withdraw funds from their accounts in the form of cash, although a bank will

---

[4]Marketability refers to the ability to sell a reasonable quantity of securities at a price close to the equilibrium price within a short period of time. A liquid security is highly marketable and has a stable equilibrium price.

attempt to limit investment in cash since it is costly to hold cash on its premises.

The remainder of cash assets is held in the form of accounts with the Federal Reserve Bank, balances due from other banks (hereafter referred to as *due from banks*), and items in the process of collection. Banks are required to maintain deposit reserve accounts directly with the Federal Reserve Bank or through correspondent banks in accounts identified as pass-through accounts. These required reserves are determined by the amount and types of deposits. Banks use the reserve and correspondent accounts to process checks drawn on other banks.

Banks will also hold cash on deposit with other banks. Banks maintain such balances as compensation for services obtained from these correspondent banks, such as check clearing, transaction services related to investments, and participation in lending arrangements. Balances due from correspondent banks can be used to meet reserve requirements for banks that are not members of the Federal Reserve System. Cash items in the process of collection represent checks or drafts presented for payment on which the bank has not yet received credit. These items are in the process of clearing through either the Federal Reserve System or correspondent banks.

Facilities.   The final funds-using function is a bank's investment in facilities. As with cash assets, a bank does not earn an explicit return on its investments in facilities, but investment in facilities is necessary to support physically the funds-using and funds-providing functions of the bank.

Investment in facilities includes buildings constructed on property that is owned or leased by the bank, leasehold improvements that are made in leased buildings, and all owned equipment used by the bank in providing its services.

MANAGEMENT OF THE POOL OF FUNDS

In a static sense, the bank's statement of financial position represents two portfolios that the bank has constructed: a portfolio of assets and a portfolio of liabilities. These portfolios indicate the current state of past management decisions by the bank. The portfolio of assets is a summary of how the bank has used its funds. Composition of the loan and investment portfolio represents management's decision on employment of funds in interest-bearing assets. The liability portfolio is a summarization of how the bank secured its funds.

In a dynamic sense, characteristics of the portfolios of assets and liabilities represent a starting point for future funds management decisions. The coordination of inflows and outflows of funds to maximize

EXHIBIT 3.1   Funds Flow Diagram

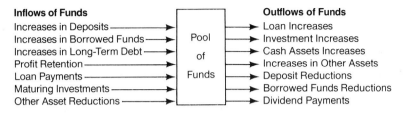

rate of return and at the same time control or limit portfolio risk is the daily operational goal of the bank's management.

Exhibit 3.1 displays the process of funds flow. The pool of funds that the bank manages changes continually. Funds flow into the pool as deposits increase or the bank increases its borrowing. Funds flow out of the pool as loans are made or securities are purchased. The bank must manage the flow of funds in and out of the pool on both a short-term basis and a long-term basis. On a short-term basis, the bank must manage the flow to assure that reserve requirements are met and substitute sources of funds are acquired to offset outflows. On a long-term basis, the funds flow must be coordinated so that the bank has funds or access to funds that can be used to meet expected or unexpected outflows. The bank can always assure that adequate funds are available to meet outflows by holding the funds in nonearning cash. When the bank employs funds in interest-bearing assets, the maturities of these assets must be coordinated with the maturities or potential maturities of the liabilities used to fund these investments.

In an ongoing sense, then, management of the bank's funds requires that the portfolios of assets and liabilities be constructed to assure that this process of funds flow produces the desired interest margin and limits the interest-rate risk exposure.

BANK RETURNS

The level of profits (net income) generated by a bank is affected by controllable and uncontrollable factors. Controllable factors, which management can influence, include business mix (wholesale/retail orientation), income production (net interest margin, service fee income, and trading profits), loan quality, and expense control. Uncontrollable, or external, factors that influence bank performance include level of interest rates, general economic conditions, and the competitive environment in which the bank operates. Banks cannot control these external factors, but they can build flexibility into their operating plans to react to changes in these factors.

Two ratio measures are commonly used in comparing bank performance—return on assets and return on equity. Return on assets (ROA) is defined as net income divided by average assets. Return on equity (ROE) is defined as net income divided by average equity (owners' investment), which is referred to as capital. From the owners' standpoint, return on equity is the most important measure, since it relates return to their ownership interest.

Generation of return to the owners of the bank results from both profitability on assets and the degree of leverage used. The relationship between return on assets and leverage is illustrated below:

$$\text{Return on assets} \times \text{Leverage multiplier} = \text{Return on equity}$$

$$\frac{\text{Net income}}{\text{Average assets}} \times \frac{\text{Average assets}}{\text{Capital}} = \text{ROE}$$

$$1.0\% \times 15 = 15\%$$

If the bank can generate a 1 percent net income as a percent of assets, the owners' ROE is 15 percent. This result is obtained because of the high degree of financial leverage employed by banks.

Students of finance will note the large difference in the return-generating mechanisms of a bank compared with those of a nonfinancial enterprise. A more common relationship between ROA, financial leverage, and ROE for nonfinancial enterprises would be as follows:

$$\text{ROA} \times \text{Leverage multiplier} = \text{ROE}$$

$$10\% \times 1.5 = 15\%$$

While returns to the owners of the bank and the nonfinancial enterprise are both equal to 15 percent, the leverage factors are significantly different. A leverage factor of 1.5 for the nonfinancial firm represents a capital structure that is one-third debt, or borrowed funds, and two-thirds equity. For the commercial bank the leverage factor of 15 represents borrowed funds as approximately 93 percent of funds and capital (owners' investment of 7 percent). The nature of a financial intermediary differs in that most of the funds are supplied by creditors, and banks are able to generate larger returns for the owners with small margins on assets.

Small vs. Large Banks

Systematic differences are observed in the return-generating process for large and small banks. While ROE may be similar for large and small banks, differences in ROA and leverage are usually present. Large banks usually experience ROAs of less than 1 percent, whereas small banks often experience ROAs in excess of 1 percent, with some experiencing ROAs in excess of 1.5 percent.

Small banks tend to have higher ratios of capital to assets, while large banks tend to have lower ratios of capital to assets. This circumstance is not accidental. Although large banks make larger loans, these loans, usually to large corporations, tend to be of high quality. Although small banks do not make loans to the very largest corporations, their customers require sizable financing with potentially greater risks, necessitating more capital to absorb losses. Therefore, to protect their depositors, small banks need a capital base proportionally higher than that of the larger banks.

The systematic difference in ROA and leverage results in differences in the return-generating process. Differences in small and large banks' returns are displayed below. In the example both the small and large bank generate a ROE of 15 percent, but the return to the owners is generated by different sources. Within limits, a bank can generate greater return to its owners by operating with a smaller capital base. Regulatory authorities limit the extent to which leverage can be used by imposing capital constraints. A bank that increases ROE through greater leverage increases its risk in that a smaller capital base is available to absorb losses.

$$\frac{\text{Net income}}{\text{Average assets}} \times \frac{\text{Average assets}}{\text{Average capital}} = \text{Return on equity}$$

Case 1 (small bank):

$$1.5\% \times 10 = 15\% \text{ ROE}$$

Case 2 (large bank):

$$1.0\% \times 15 = 15\% \text{ ROE}$$

Although bank managers strive to generate the highest possible level of earnings, they must simultaneously be concerned with the stability of earnings over time, i.e., with the quality of earnings. Quality refers to the predictability and degree of reliance that can be placed on earnings to maintain normal relationships.

The variability of returns to the bank's owners can be attributed to variation in ROA and the degree of leverage. The greater the use of financial leverage, the greater will be the variability in returns to owners. The multiplier effect translates small changes in ROA to large changes in ROE. Variation in ROA is a function of both controllable and uncontrollable factors. Specific sources of risk that cause variability in returns include liquidity, interest rate, credit, and capital risk. Some elements of these sources of risk are controllable and can be limited through managerial action, whereas other elements remain uncontrollable.

Liquidity Risk

Banks must meet demand for liquidity when customers withdraw deposits or when customers demand loanable funds. To meet potential demands for liquidity, banks must maintain liquidity in assets or must rely on creating liquidity by borrowing funds. Liquidity risk refers to the variability in earnings that results from satisfying a demand for liquidity.

The U.S. banking system operates with a fractional reserve system, where for each dollar deposited the bank is required to hold a portion of deposits in cash or balances with the Federal Reserve. State nonmember banks are required to maintain reserve balances and may use Fed-member correspondent banks as depositories. In addition to reserve balances, banks maintain balances with correspondent banks to process checks for collection.

Cash and balances with banks are primary reserves. Short-term investment securities are secondary reserves held to meet unexpected withdrawals or loan demands. The securities are important because, although they are not required, they earn revenues. When liquidated to meet depositor withdrawals, however, future revenue is lost. In addition, if interest rates have risen, the securities may be liquidated at a lower price, resulting in a trading loss. When securities are sold to meet loan demand, higher yields are substituted for lower investment yields.

A bank can create deposits by crediting loan proceeds to a depositor's account. If the reserves required on such deposits are not available in existing cash and balances with correspondent banks, then the bank has two alternatives to cure the revenue deficiency. It may borrow short-term funds at market rates of interest, or it may liquidate securities if the deficiency is a long-run problem normally related to the repayment cycle of the loan.

Measuring liquidity risk is complex. Banks have two basic sources of liquidity—assets and liabilities. If a bank holds assets such as securities, which can be sold to meet a need for funds, it may lower its liquidity risk. At the same time, holding securities limits return, since the bank can earn higher yields on loans. The bank can also borrow to meet a need for funds. Larger banks rely heavily on liabilities as a source of liquidity, which allows them to invest larger percentages of funds in higher-earning loans.

The key factor is that banks are unable to maximize revenue because of the liquidity constraint. Therefore a bank must be concerned with the appropriate amount of liquidity. Too much liquidity sacrifices earnings; too little imposes borrowing requirements in an unknown interest rate environment, which in turn increases costs and reduces earnings.

Interest Rate Risk

Interest rate risk is the risk of making a loan today that is financed at a known rate but that during the loan life may be required to be refinanced at a higher interest rate. If the loan rate is fixed and funding rate rises, the net yield to the bank is reduced. The timing of loan decisions does not ordinarily correspond one to one with the deposit acquisition opportunities. A bank is therefore subject to certain degrees of earnings variability as interest rates fluctuate.

The degree of interest rate risk that a bank is subject to can be controlled to some extent by management. A bank can control interest rate risk by matching assets and liabilities, that is, by employing interest-sensitive funds in assets that are also interest sensitive. A bank can also attempt to secure larger profits by adjusting its assets and liabilities portfolios over cyclical moves in interest rates. If interest rates fall, a fixed-rate loan funded with interest-sensitive liabilities will result in larger profits than a matched transaction with a fixed-interest spread.

A proxy of interest rate risk is interest-sensitive assets divided by interest-sensitive liabilities. By definition, interest sensitivity refers to the degree that the rate on an asset or liability moves in the same direction as the general movement in market interest rates. By examining assets and liabilities at a specific point in time, one can determine the degree of imbalance in matching rate-sensitive assets with liabilities. It is not enough simply to know the ratio value, but one must also consider the point in the interest cycle and the projected direction of rates. Again, interest rate risk is complex. In subsequent chapters, therefore, considerable attention is given to managing portfolios in order to minimize the effect of interest rate changes.

Credit Risk

Credit risk refers to the variability in earnings that could result from loan losses and security defaults. Banks can control credit risk through conservative lending practices, although they may pass up potentially profitable loans by restrictive credit policies.

Credit risk is difficult to assess without thoroughly examining the loan portfolio. Key factors that affect credit risk are diversification of loan types, diversification of commercial loans among different industries, the collateral margin on loans, and, most importantly, the credit standards that are employed.

Because loans are made in a competitive environment, higher yields on loans are generally achieved by assuming greater risk. A bank can increase its expected return by making loans to riskier customers at

**Bank Frauds and Embezzlement Schemes Lead to
Dramatic Headlines and Interesting Reading**

We have described the basic elements of risk involved in banking.
These elements are far more important determinants of earnings variability for the banking system than are cases of fraud and embezzlement, but a bank's exposure to potential losses from such white-collar
crime can be significant. Although portions of these losses are insurable, a bank can experience sizable losses if controls are not adequate.
The degree of sophistication found in control systems must be expanded if a potential increase in computer-based crimes is to be
avoided.

Two recent examples point to the need for sophisticated control
systems to protect against fraud and embezzlement. Both cases occurred at large West Coast banks. One case involving a loan officer at
a Wells Fargo branch concerned an embezzlement scheme that extended over two years and resulted in a $21.3 million loss ($20 million
was insured). The other case, in which an outsider successfully transferred over $10 million in a faudulent wire transfer, netted Security
Pacific a $4 million loss. Both examples point to the importance of
controls.

In the first case, L. Ben Lewis embezzled funds for over two years
by means of a branch settlement account used to transfer money
among branches. Lewis, who had formerly worked in the bank's regional computer center, knew that items entered into the branch settlement account must be cleared within five days or a tracer would be
issued by the computer to the branch involved. He also knew that

higher rates. To mitigate potential losses, a bank can require collateral
to serve as an alternative means of payment in the event a borrower is
unable to make the promised payments.

Diversification of loan types, commercial loans, and geographic locations of borrowers serves to limit risk since it protects earnings from
loan losses due to concentration. If a bank concentrates its lending to a
particular industry, disruption unique to that industry will have a significant effect on the bank's earnings. The recent performance of banks
that concentrate their loans in the energy industry demonstrates the
effect of lack of diversification.

Capital Risk

The fourth element of risk related to banking is capital risk, which reflects the degree of leverage employed by the bank. Capital, the owner's
equity, serves to protect creditors (depositors) against losses a bank may

items of $1 million or more triggered an inquiry from the computer. Although the scheme started with smaller amounts, toward the end Lewis was being forced to create 25 different credit entries averaging $900 thousand every five business days to stay under the computer flag limit. In January 1981 Lewis filled out the wrong side of a ticket and sent it through the system, revealing the embezzlement scheme.

The other case involved a fraudulent wire transfer, which had elements that would have made it a potential script for "Mission Impossible." In October 1978 Stanley Mark Rifkin entered the wire transfer room posing as a consultant from the Federal Reserve in Washington. In the past he had worked as a computer consultant at the bank while he was employed by another consulting firm, and no one in the wire transfer room questioned his authority to be there.

Having secured information from employees in the wire transfer room during the day, Rifkin left the banking office and made a phone call from a phone booth in the lobby of the bank. He successfully transferred over $10 million to an account at the Wozchod Bank in Zurich. He had made prior arrangements with a diamond dealer and immediately purchased $8 million in diamonds. The bank did not discover the loss until Rifkin's lawyer informed the bank of the caper. It took the bank an additional eight days to confirm the loss. The bank eventually recovered most of the diamonds, but after expenses it still suffered a $4 million loss.

incur. The amount of capital required to protect creditors is related to the quality, or riskiness of a bank's assets.

A bank's assets can be classified as riskless and risk assets. Risk assets generally include but are not limited to securities issued by municipalities and loans not guaranteed by the federal government. Riskless assets include but are not limited to federal government and federal government agency securities and loans, which are federally guaranteed.

In assessing capital risk, the level of capital must be related to the quality of assets. Banks that employ a large percentage of their funds in risky assets may be required to have large capital cushions to fall back on if the assets do not perform. The level of capital necessary is also a function of liquidity and interest rate risk.

In addition to the major sources of risk associated with banking described above, banks also face risks in terms of employee fraud, such as embezzlement, losses from bank robberies, and computer fraud.

Although many of these risks are at least partially insurable, managements must establish controls to guard against losses from these elements. Events such as computer fraud and bank robberies may capture the public's attention; nevertheless they are not the primary elements of risk to a banking enterprise.

BANK PERFORMANCE

To analyze the performance of a bank, the returns and risks must be simultaneously considered. Exhibit 3.2 graphically displays the process involved. Quality performance essentially entails increasing returns while at the same time minimizing risks.

At any given time a bank may experience very large ROA and ROE measures, but these returns must be balanced against the level of risk the bank has assumed. For example, a bank may be able to generate large ROA and ROE measures through operational efficiencies by controlling expenses without affecting the quality of earnings. A bank may also increase ROA and ROE in a given period by increasing credit, interest rate, and liquidity risk. The future earnings may be more variable and the owners of the bank may experience losses in the future. To analyze performance, risk and return must be balanced. Why did the

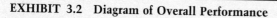

EXHIBIT 3.2   Diagram of Overall Performance

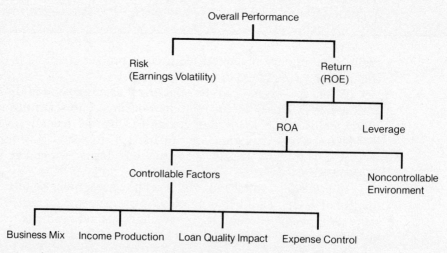

Source: H. N. Gillis, R. W. Lumbry III, and T. J. Oswald, "A New Approach to Analyzing Bank Performance," in *Funds Management Under Deregulation*, ed G. H. Hempel (Washington, DC: American Bankers Association, 1981), 155.

bank experience higher returns in this period? Were they achieved by making riskier loans and increasing credit risk? Were they achieved by funding fixed-rate loans with interest-sensitive sources of funds? Were they achieved by reducing the liquidity of the assets portfolio? Questions such as these must be answered to assess future earnings variability.

Goals in Managing a Bank

A variety of goals exist for the managers of commercial banks. One goal, which is related to the granting of a charter, is to service the needs of the community in which the bank is located. Management may also set goals related to asset growth and loan growth or to becoming the dominant institution in the bank's service area. The ultimate goal of bank management is or should be to maximize the wealth or long-term return to owners of the bank. Bank owners make an investment of capital, and the goal of bank managers should be to maximize the long-term return on that investment.

The goal of the financial manager in any enterprise is usually stated in terms of maximizing the wealth of its owners. For large publicly held firms, that goal is usually translated into an operational goal of maximizing share price.[5] Through managerial actions that maximize the share price, the managers of a firm can best satisfy the diverse needs or desires of its large group of shareholders.

For closely held firms whose stock does not trade in public markets and in which the managers are the owners of the firm, it is possible for the managers to maximize the utility obtained from ownership without strict adherence to the shareholder wealth criterion. For example, the managers of a firm might recommend dividend policies directly related to their personal consumption desires without worrying about the selection of an optimal policy that would maximize the price of the stock.[6]

The goal of the shareholder wealth maximization via share price maximization also applies to the management of commercial banks, but the structure of the commercial banking industry limits that goal in terms of being universally applicable. There are approximately 15,000 commercial banks, and the vast majority of these institutions do not have actively trading markets for their common stock. Many banks are closely held and controlled by families. In addition, many individual

---

[5]For example, see E. F. Brigham, *Financial Management: Theory and Practice*, 3rd ed. (Hinsdale, IL: Dryden Press, 1982), chap. 1.

[6]The owner-manager has greater flexibility in a variety of managerial decisions that range from satisfying nonpecuniary wants, such as overplush carpets and luxurious facilities, to paying management larger salaries than efficiency suggests. There are limits to deviation from efficient operation, but owner management has greater flexibility than management of publicly traded firms. For discussion, see Brigham, op. cit., chap. 1.

banks are solely owned or effectively controlled by multibank holding companies. For these banks maximizing share price is not a meaningful operational goal.

Share price maximization is appropriate mainly for large national and regional banks whose stock trades in active national or regional markets. For a bank whose stock trades in an active market, the managers can best satisfy the owners by maximizing the value of their ownership claims.

Assuming that the goal of share price maximization is appropriate, making such a goal operational requires extension to the underlying factors that influence share value. Management must specify some model or models that identify factors which influence value so that appropriate action can be taken to maximize share price.

The most commonly applied valuation model employed in financial management is the approach of current value of future cash flow. As indicated in Equation 3.1, the general dividend model asserts that the price of the stock is the current value of future dividends, which accrue to the owners of the stock.

$$P = \sum_{t=1}^{N} \frac{D_t}{(1 + k)^t} \qquad\qquad (3.1)$$

where D_t = dividends to the owners of the firm for period t

k = required rate of return for investors in the stock

The factors that influence value, then, are the dividends, which in turn are dependent on the firm's earnings, and the return required by shareholders, which is influenced by the riskiness or variability of the earnings stream. The cash flow model balances the risk and return associated with cash flows and also explicitly accounts for the timing of cash flow receipts through the discounting process.[7]

The shareholder wealth maximization criterion is more inclusive than an alternative goal of maximizing earnings in that explicit considerations of risk and timing are included. Management can increase expected future earnings by making investments or altering the financing mix of the firm, but that action may not be in the best interest of the owners if it substantially increases the variability of future cash flows.

---

[7]The influence of dividend policy on the value of stock is another factor considered in the shareholder wealth criterion. The influence of dividend policy per se on the value of common stock is a widely debated and unresolved issue in finance theory. Dividend policy is an important issue for management of commercial banks because of its direct influence on capital. We discuss this issue in greater detail in Chapter 14. For a general discussion of the issues, see Brigham, op. cit., chap. 8.

Operationally, managers of publicly traded banks that are attempting to maximize the firm's share price must undertake managerial actions that positively influence expected earnings and simultaneously limit the risk exposure. To best serve the interests of the owners of the bank, the risk must be balanced with increases in expected earnings. Increases in earnings accomplished through making riskier loans may cause the value of the stock to decline if the market perceives the increased credit risk to more than offset the rise in earnings. The possible variability in expected future earnings could cause an increase in the required rates of return by investors, causing a downward adjustment in share price.

Research on determinants of returns on bank common stock is limited. In theory, we would expect that investors would demand higher rates of return for the common stock of those banks that assume higher levels of the elements of risk described in the previous section.

Much of the research on equity valuation and required rates of return has focused on the capital asset pricing model, or security market line, approach.[8] Research specifically related to the banking industry indicates that bank equity returns are more sensitive to returns on debt instruments than are nonfinancial firm equity returns. Limited evidence indicates greater explanatory power is attained when indexes of short- and long-term debt returns are included along with the returns on equity indexes.[9] Researchers hypothesize that such findings are consistent with the notion of the importance of interest rate risk to financial intermediaries.

In related research Jahankhani and Lynge investigated the effect of financial statement measures of risk on the beta coefficient of commercial bank stocks.[10] Using financial statement measures of variability in earnings and deposits, financial leverage, liquidity, and payout ratio, the authors employed regression analysis to assess the effect of such measures on market-determined measures of risk. They found market measures of risk to be significantly influenced by financial statement measures of risk.

The effect of dividend policy on the valuation of bank stock is complicated by regulatory constraints relating to capital adequacy. The ability of a bank to support asset growth is constrained by appropriate levels of capital. Dividends paid out to investors reduce capital and con-

---

[8]Brigham, op. cit., chap. 5.

[9]W. P. Lloyd and R. A. Shick, "A Test of Stone's Two-Index Model of Returns," *Journal of Financial and Quantitative Analysis*, September 1977: 363–376; and M. Lynge, Jr., and J. K. Zumwalt, "An Empirical Study of Interest Sensitivity of Commercial Bank Returns: A Multi-Index Approach," *Journal of Financial and Quantitative Analysis*, September 1980: 731–742.

[10]A. Jahankhani and M. Lynge, Jr., "Commercial Bank Financial Policies and Their Impact on Market Determined Measures of Risk," *Journal of Bank Research*, Autumn 1980: 169–175.

strain growth unless new equity capital is secured through the sale of new common stock.[11]

For smaller banks, whose access to equity markets is limited, dividends are constrained. Limited evidence from research indicates that large banks tend to pay out larger percentages of earnings in dividends than small banks. Large banks that trade in public markets appear to meet investor demand for return by paying out more in dividends.[12]

For management of a closely held nontraded bank, the key factors remain the balance between earnings growth and risk. The quality of earnings must be maintained to assure success of the bank. The difference of managerial objectives between a closely held and a publicly traded bank is really not all that significant. The level of earnings and the stability or quality of earnings are still key factors. One meaningful difference is the ability of the managers of closely held banks to adopt more flexible dividend policies.

SUMMARY

The management of a bank can be viewed as the management of a pool of funds that constantly experiences inflows and outflows. Successful management requires coordination of these flows in a manner that maximizes profit and at the same time limits risk.

Returns to the owners of a bank arise from return on assets and leverage. A typical bank earns far less on assets than does a nonbanking firm but it generates returns for its owners because of leverage. A small change in the return on assets results in a large change in return to the owners because of the high degree of leverage.

Risk to the bank as measured by variability in earnings arises from four elements: credit risk, liquidity risk, interest rate risk, and capital risk. Some elements of these risks are controllable, whereas others arise from the business of banking and are not controllable.

The objective in managing a bank is to maximize the wealth of the owners of the bank. Shareholder wealth maximization requires that management balance expected return with risk.

---

[11]The effect of dividend policy on equity valuation is a highly complex issue that is not resolved. Potentially, dividend policy could affect share value through informational or clientele effects. For a discussion of these issues, see Brigham, op. cit., chap. 18.

[12]L. S. Mayne, "Bank Dividend Policy and Holding Company Affiliation," *Journal of Financial and Quantitative Analysis,* June 1980: 469–482; and T. K. Mukheyee and L. M. Austin, "An Empirical Examination of Small Bank Stock Valuation and Dividend Policy," *Financial Management,* Spring 1980: 27–31.

Questions

1. What are the major funds-providing and funds-using functions?

2. Describe return generation for commercial banks using the return-on-assets and return-on-equity ratios.

3. Describe the major elements of risk present in commercial banking.

4. Describe potential goals that the management of the bank should pursue.

References

Brigham, E. F. *Financial Management: Theory and Practice,* 3rd ed. Hinsdale, IL: Dryden Press, 1982.

Gillis, H. N., R. W. Lumry III, and T. J. Oswald. "A New Approach to Analyzing Bank Performance." In *Funds Management Under Deregulation,* ed. G. H. Hempel, 152–161. Washington, DC: American Bankers Association, 1981.

Hempel, G. H. "The Interrelationships Between Banking Risks and Returns." In *Funds Management Under Deregulation,* ed. G. H. Hempel, 162–173. Washington, DC: American Bankers Association, 1981.

Jahankhani, A., and M. Lynge, Jr. "Commercial Bank Financial Policies and Their Impact on Market Determined Measures of Risk." *Journal of Bank Research*, Autumn 1980: 169–175.

Lloyd, W. P., and R. A. Shick. "A Test of Stone's Two-Index Model of Returns." *Journal of Financial and Quantitative Analysis,* September 1977: 363–376.

Lynge, M., Jr., and J. K. Zumwalt. "An Empirical Study of Interest Sensitivity of Commercial Bank Returns: A Multi-Index Approach." *Journal of Financial and Quantitative Analysis,* September 1980: 731–742.

Mayne, L. S. "Bank Dividend Policy and Holding Company Affiliation." *Journal of Financial and Quantitative Analysis,* June 1980: 469–482.

Mayne, L. S. "Bank Holding Company Characteristics and the Upstreaming of Bank Funds." *Journal of Money, Credit and Banking,* May 1980: 209–214.

Meeker, L. G., and J. O'Maurice. "Price Premiums for Controlling Shares of Closely Held Stock." *Journal of Business,* July 1980: 297–314.

Mukheyee, T. K., and L. M. Austin. "An Empirical Examination of Small Bank Stock Valuation and Dividend Policy." *Financial Management,* Spring 1980: 27–31.

Peltway, R. H. "The Effects of Large Banks' Failures Upon Investors' Risk Cognizance in the Commercial Banking Industry." *Journal of Financial and Quantitative Analysis,* September 1976: 465–477.

Watson, R. D. "Banking on Debt for Capital Needs." *Business Review, Federal Reserve Bank of Philadelphia,* December 1974: 17–28.

CHAPTER 4

Introduction to
Bank Financial Statements

Even though each bank is organized differently, certain transactions are basic to all banks. Exhibit 4.1 is a simplified visual description of the types of transactions that flow to the general ledger from operating departments. The exhibit is based on the assumption that the bank has three functional divisions: (1) loans, (2) deposits, services, and support, and (3) investments and federal funds. Transactions are created by the functions and are accumulated in the proof department. The proof departments sorts and balances the transactions on a daily basis. The daily transactions include checks, deposits, and tickets for entries to the general ledger system. Checks and deposits are sorted for keeping customer accounting records, and the tickets are used to make entries to the general ledger. The entries are added to the previous day's balances for a preparation of an updated balance sheet and income statement for management.

A background in the details of operations and an understanding of bank financial statement construction are necessary before one can analyze or implement changes in the portfolios of assets and liabilities to improve profits. Appendix A, at the end of this text, contains the primary accounting and financial statement impact of deposits, loans, investment securities, short-term funding, and capital transactions. In addition, this appendix presents formats for regulatory and director reports and a discussion of bank taxation.

The financial statements summarize activity in each of the functional areas, the balance sheet represents a summary of past management decisions in the functional areas, and the income statement measures the profitability of management decisions over a specific period of time.

The financial results of operations vary among banks, depending on the size, location, and type of business in which each bank engages. Certain banks may show the same rate of return on assets and return on equity as other banks but may differ significantly from other banks in terms of asset, liability, and capital structure and in terms of mix of earnings from interest and noninterest income. Accounting policies may also vary significantly among banks, resulting in different financial statement presentations for essentially the same types of transactions.

EXHIBIT 4.1   Flow of Data to General Ledger

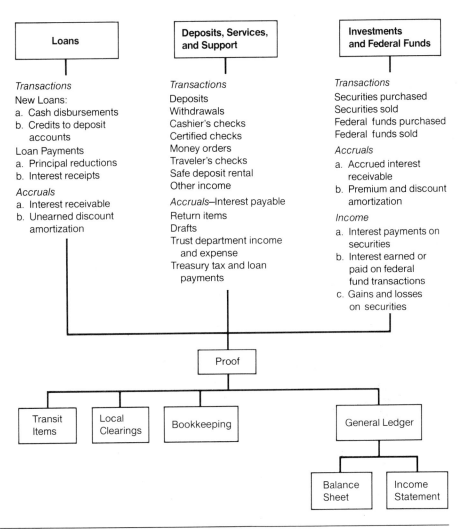

FINANCIAL REPORTING CONSIDERATIONS

The general accounting system is usually structured in the call report format. The call report is the basic financial statement prepared by a commercial bank and is the statement submitted to the appropriate regulatory agency. The general ledger system is important for preparing the basic balance sheet and income statement information; however, it provides limited information for the detailed disclosures required for auditing financial statements and for the preparation of securities offerings regulated by the Comptroller of the Currency or the Securities and Exchange Commission.

Subsidiary accounting records provide the information for internal analysis and external reporting requirements. For example, information regarding maturities and interest rates of the various loans and securities and the amounts of deposits, interest rates, and maturities can be obtained only from subsidiary records. Therefore it is extremely important that a bank give sufficient consideration to the structure of subsidiary systems for the preparation of external reports. For the purpose of compiling information for the call report and other financial reporting requirements, considerable attention is given below to the structure of the information contained in the commercial-loan, consumer-loan, mortgage-loan, investments, and deposits subsidiary systems. In addition to the analytical work performed for determining bank profitability, certain information is important in managing the various portfolios of loans and deposits.

Regulatory authorities view subsidiary records as an important source of information for management purposes. A certain degree of time and effort should therefore be taken to construct these records.

The Call Report

The balance sheet of the standard call report is fairly simple and requires only basic information found in the general ledger system. A bank prepares a quarterly "call report" for regulatory agencies. This report contains a balance sheet, an income statement, and other schedules (see Appendix A). The term *call* was derived from the earlier regulatory practice of telephoning banks to provide financial statements on a specified date near the end of a calendar quarter. All banks are required by regulation to have a calendar fiscal year. Each quarter every bank is required to publish its balance sheet in a local newspaper. Although income statements and other schedules are considered confidential, they are available from regulatory authorities on request.

National banks report to the Comptroller of the Currency, who makes the reports available to the Federal Reserve and the Federal Deposit Insurance Corporation. State-chartered banks report to the state banking authority and to the Federal Deposit Insurance Corporation if insured and to the Federal Reserve if a member.

The balance sheet is ordered in a format progressing from the most liquid to the least liquid assets. Correspondingly, the liabilities are also in liquidity format, beginning with deposits, followed by the longer-term debt of the bank and finally by equity capital.

The income statement format is presented with operating income followed by operating expenses. The income after income taxes is separated from extraordinary items.

In addition to the basic information required for the income statement and balance sheet and the balance sheet memoranda, there are various schedules required with the standard call report. Schedule A, Loans, reports the classifications of real estate loans, loans to financial institutions, loans for purchasing or carrying securities, loans to farmers, commercial and industrial loans, and loans to individuals for household, family, and other personal expenditures. Most of the data required in the preparation of Schedule A must be obtained from a loan subsidiary ledger or from an analysis of the loan portfolio.

Schedule B, Securities, covers the distribution by maturity for each category of securities, including one year or less, over one year through 5 years, over 5 and through 10 years, and over 10 years. In Chapter 15 we will cover the basic formats for the information required for Schedule B and indicate that the securities information 's generally contained in a subsidiary ledger. The categorization is important to an analyst for determining liquidity and investment policies.

Schedule C details the amounts of interest-bearing balances for cash and due from depository institutions. Schedule I provides other data for deposit insurance assessments, including the amounts of unposted debits and credits split into amounts due to demand and time and savings deposits. It also includes investment trust funds and deposits of consolidated subsidiaries that are not included in the total liabilities.

Schedule K requires average total assets for the quarter end, liabilities for borrowed money maturing in more than 12 months, and total public time deposits of $100,000 or more. Additionally, the changes in equity capital and possible loan loss information is required as part of Schedule K.

The Director Report

Monthly financial statements are prepared for internal management review and for informing directors, who generally are unfamiliar with bank financial statements, of how well bank goals and objectives are being met.

Appendix A includes a set of director reports, which are useful in reporting operating results. These reports include:

1. *Balance Sheet:* Comparative statements in amount and percent of total assets for the prior year to date, the current year to date, and the plan or budget for the current year.

2. *Income Statement:* Comparative statements in amount for the prior year to date, the current year to date, the plan, and the variance of the current year to date from the plan.

3. *Analysis of Net Interest Income:* Prior year to date, current year to date, the plan, and the variance to plan, including the average balance sheet amount and the yield or rate.

4. *Statement of Stockholders' Equity:* Three prior years and the current year to date.

5. *Statement of Changes in Financial Position:* Prior year and the current year to date.

6. *Schedule of Investment Securities:* Fully tax-equivalent basis for several maturity periods, including amount and yield by period and the total.

7. *Loan Maturities and Sensitivity to Changes in Interest Rates:* Amounts over several maturity periods and in total and rate structure in amounts of loans due after one year.

8. *Nonperformance Loans:* Past due, renegotiated, and total loans and interest for original period and actually recorded.

9. *Summary of Loan Loss Experience:* For five prior years and current year to date.

10. *Average Deposits:* For each period indicated.

11. *Significant Ratios.*

12. *Delinquency Lists.*

Management should be prepared to answer several basic questions regarding the director reports. An effective way to inform the directors about bank operations is to conduct a seminar in which many of the following questions may be addressed:

1. What is the normal relationship of the account balance to the overall financial statement?

2. What are the kinds of account relationships that are important to bank examiners?

3. How do we balance profitability and sound banking in the account makeup?

4. What are the bank's goals?

5. Does the bank have a profit plan?

6. How do written policies for investment securities and loans contribute to bank profitability and soundness?

Director reports should be confidential. Some banks distribute reports to the directors at the directors' meeting, and others mail the reports so the directors may have an opportunity to review the data and formulate questions. The directors should have an opportunity to review the data before their meeting, and the preferred procedure is to mail the reports even at the risk of the reports falling into nondirector's hands.

The Shareholder Report

Many banks take great care in reporting annual information. A typical annual report of a large bank is prepared in booklet form and includes a letter to the shareholders from the chairman or president regarding current operations and future plans. The report may contain a variety of information and data on performance, often presented by means of graphs, charts, and color photographs. The annual report serves as a promotional tool, incorporating marketing plans and the bank's goals and objectives for the following year.

Audits of Banks That Failed

The investing public relies on financial statements audited by CPA firms. In two recent cases unqualified opinions were issued shortly before the banks collapsed. In the Penn Square Bank example, its auditor, Peat Marwick Mitchell & Company, was sued by a money broker, who maintained that the CPA firm was negligent in rendering its opinion. In the United American Bank collapse, although Ernst & Whinney rendered an unqualified opinion, the bank failed. At the same time that Ernst & Whinney was in the bank, the FDIC was conducting its examination. Ironically, Ernst & Whinney did not confer with the FDIC examiners, who declared the bank insolvent three weeks after Ernst & Whinney rendered its opinion.

One should ask how an auditor can miss the signs of insolvency. The answer lies partly in the approach used to determine the adequacy of the allowance for loan losses. Auditors tend to take an aggregate view, whereas bank examiners take a detailed approach toward determining collectible loans. It is important, however, that auditors and examiners understand how a bank operates and what policies are apparent from the makeup of the bank's financial statement.

So it is with management, which must understand where it has been, where it is, and where it is going. The financial statements provide the information for the past and present and form the basis for projections of the future. An inadequate understanding of financial statements leads to poor decisions, which affect bank solvency.

The content of the annual report varies among banks. Small banks and some medium-sized banks present only the basic call report balance sheet and income statement data. Banks that are audited by certified public accounting firms present complete financial statements, including balance sheet, income statement, statement of changes in stockholders' equity, statement of changes in financial position, and explanatory footnotes. Since banks desire access to money markets for borrowed funds, sophisticated depositors rely on audited financial statements before placing funds on deposit. In the following pages are examples of annual financial statements prepared by CPAs.

BALANCE SHEET

Assets

In Exhibit 4.2 the assets are presented in liquidity order from highest to lowest. Cash and due from banks includes operating cash and accounts with correspondent banks and the Federal Reserve Bank. Just as consumers have checking accounts with banks to facilitate the acquisition of goods and services, banks use and keep accounts with other banks to facilitate their transactions. Accounts must be maintained with the Fed-

---

EXHIBIT 4.2   Balance Sheets for a Sample Bank

Sample Bank
Balance Sheets
December 31, 19X2 and 19X1

Assets	19X2	19X1
Cash and due from banks	$ 5,498,000	$ 5,425,000
Interest-bearing deposits in banks	1,000,000	1,000,000
Investment securities (approximate market value of $32,886,000 and $41,567,000 respectively) (Note 2)	37,695,000	43,528,000
Trading securities	4,640,000	5,915,000
Federal funds sold and securities purchased under reverse repurchase agreements	2,100,000	—
Loans, less allowance for loan losses of $830,000 and $823,000, respectively (Note 3)	48,586,000	43,772,000
Investment in leveraged leases, net (Note 4)	1,897,000	1,113,000
Office buildings, equipment, and leasehold improvements, net (Note 5)	2,144,000	1,878,000
Customers' acceptance liability	237,000	379,000
Other assets	1,408,000	794.000
	$105,205,000	$103,804,000

(continued)

EXHIBIT 4.2 *(continued)*

Sample Bank
Balance Sheets
December 31, 19X2 and 19X1

Liabilities and Stockholders' Equity

Deposits

Demand	$ 19,427,000	$ 24,061,000
NOW accounts	7,107,000	——
Savings	30,135,000	33,449,000
Time, $100,000 and over	15,500,000	12,200,000
Other time	17,574,000	19,181,000
	89,743,000	88,891,000
Federal funds purchased and securities sold under repurchase agreements	2,279,000	2,558,000
Acceptances outstanding	237,000	379,000
Accrued interest and other liabilities (Note 6)	1,918,000	2,062,000
Subordinated debentures (Note 7)	1,000,000	1,000,000
Total liabilities	95,177,000	94,890,000
Commitments and contingent liabilities (Note 9)		
Stockholders' equity		
Common stock, par value $10; 150,000 shares authorized and outstanding	1,500,000	1,500,000
Surplus	4,500,000	4,500,000
Retained earnings (Note 11)	4,028,000	2,914,000
Total stockholders' equity	10,028,000	8,914,000
	$105,205,000	$103,804,000

The accompanying notes are an integral part of these financial statements.[a]

[a]The notes are presented in Appendix 4.1 at the end of this chapter.

---

eral Reserve Bank as required by the Depository Institutions Deregulation and Monetary Control Act of 1980. Interest-bearing deposits are accounts with other banks that bear interest and may be converted to cash in the near future.

Investment-account securities are short-, intermediate- and long-term investments in securities. Short-term securities provide liquidity to meet depositor withdrawals or loan demand. Intermediate- and long-term securities produce a base of income for banks, and obligations of states and political subdivisions produce income exempt from federal income taxes. Other securities include Federal Reserve Bank stock and corporate debt securities. Banks are not allowed to invest in corporate common or preferred stocks except for investments in certain bank-related activities.

In addition to maintaining investment security portfolios for their own accounts, certain larger banks act as market makers for some federal government and state and political subdivision securities. In that capacity the banks act as either brokers or dealers in these securities by buying and selling investment-grade debt securities for customers. Trading-account securities repesent the value of the inventory position banks are holding for this market-making activity. Banks buy and sell securities and generate income for the banks on the "spread," or difference, between purchase and sales price.

Federal funds sold are one-day transactions wherein a bank having cash and due from banks in excess of operating cash needs and reserve requirements lends funds to other banks by transferring deposits from its correspondent banks through the Federal Reserve System to a bank needing reserves. On the following business day the transaction is reversed, with the borrowing bank transferring the loaned amount and one day's interest for the use of the funds.

An alternative for a borrowing bank is to sell certain of its investment securities to a liquid bank. The purchasing bank agrees to sell the securities back to the borrowing bank within a specified period (securities sold under repurchase agreements). At termination of the agreement, the same securities are returned in exchange for cash including interest.

Loans include commercial, installment, mortgage, and agricultural loans. Certain installment loans include interest in the face amount of the note. The actual loan amount is calculated by deducting unearned interest. The balance sheet reflects the remaining amount to be collected and the remaining unearned discount to be amortized to income.

Most loans are subject to some degree of default risk. Estimates of potential losses are computed at financial reporting dates. The aggregate of the estimated losses is the allowance for loan losses. The allowance for loan losses and the unearned discount are deducted from gross loans in presenting estimated net collectible loans.

Leveraged leases are special loans. The bank purchases assets for customers and leases the assets back to the customers. Interest is the return on the leased assets. Any unearned interest is deducted from gross leases in the financial statements.

Office buildings, equipment, and leasehold improvements are presented net of accumulated depreciation. Customers' acceptance liability represents liability on drafts that the customer will use in future transactions to pay for goods or services and that the bank will pay when presented. Drafts are presented for payment by other banks. When the bank accepts liability for the issuance of the drafts, it creates a liability account recognizing payments to be made to presenting banks. Other assets include real estate owned by the bank as a result of a foreclosure on a bank loan and normal accruals such as accrued interest.

Liabilities

Liability presentation begins with deposits followed by other liabilities. Deposits include demand, savings, and time deposits. Demand deposits are checking accounts of individuals, partnerships, corporations, states, municipalities, the U.S. government, and other banks. Savings deposits are passbook accounts and are subject to interest rate ceilings. Time deposits include money market certificates and certificates of deposit.

Federal funds purchased and securities sold under repurchase agreements are the opposite of the assets transactions. When a bank requires funds to meet liquidity needs, it may purchase federal funds or sell specific securities to be returned at a later date.

Acceptances outstanding are liabilities to other banks that will present customer drafts for payment. Accrued interest and other liabilities represent normal accruals of expense. Subordinated debentures are long-term debt instruments that are issued by banks to secure longer-term or more permanent funds. This debt is subordinated to deposits and other liabilities in the case of liquidation.

Stockholders' Equity

The stockholders' equity section includes three accounts—capital stock, surplus, and retained earnings. Surplus is equivalent to paid-in capital in a nonbanking corporation; it is not available for cash dividends and is periodically increased by transfers from retained earnings for the purpose of increasing loan limits. Capital stock and surplus are considered permanent capital for the computation of a bank's legal lending limit, i.e., maximum loan to a single borrower.

INCOME STATEMENT

The income statement, which is displayed in Exhibit 4.3, is presented in an interest margin concept. Interest expense accounts are deducted from interest income accounts to derive net interest income (interest margin). Provision for loan losses (equivalent to bad debt expense) is deducted from net interest income. Net interest income after provision for loan losses represents net income from interest-earning assets less cost of interest-bearing liabilities and associated risks of lending money. Net interest income after provision for loan losses is available to meet all other banking costs.

EXHIBIT 4.3 Income Statements for a Sample Bank

Sample Bank
Statements of Income
Years Ended December 31, 19X2 and 19X1

	19X2	19X1
Interest income		
Interest and fees on loans (Note 4)	$6,859,000	$5,527,000
Interest on investment securities		
U.S. Treasury securities	741,000	836,000
Obligations of other U.S. government agencies and corporations	186,000	268,000
Obligations of states and political subdivisions	1,248,000	1,256,000
Other securities	58,000	42,000
Interest on trading securities	221,000	241,000
Interest on federal funds sold and securities purchased under reverse repurchase agreements	332,000	105,000
Interest on deposits in banks	86,000	72,000
	9,731,000	8,347,000
Interest expense		
Interest on deposits	6,446,000	5,340,000
Interest on federal funds purchased and securities sold under repurchase agreements	253,000	78,000
Interest on subordinated debentures (Note 7)	80,000	80,000
	6,779,000	5,498,000
Net interest income	2,952,000	2,849,000
Provision for loan losses (Note 3)	60,000	68,000
Net interest income after provision for loan losses	2,892,000	2,781,000
Other income		
Trust department income	187,000	166,000
Service fees	106,000	103,000
Trading profits and commissions	174,000	67,000
Securities gains (losses)	131,000	(30,000)
Other	74,000	77,000
	672,000	383,000
Other expense		
Salaries	727,000	718,000
Pensions and other employee benefits (Note 8)	153,000	130,000
Occupancy expenses, net	356,000	304,000
Other operating expenses	747,000	648,000
	1,983,000	1,800,000
Income before income taxes	1,581,000	1,364,000
Applicable income taxes (Note 6)	146,000	33,000
Net income	$1,435,000	$1,331,000
Per share of common stock		
Net income	$ 9.57	$ 8.87

The accompanying notes are an integral part of these financial statements.[a]

[a]The notes are presented in Appendix 4.1 at the end of this chapter.

The next two sections of the income statement measure income and expenses from other activities in which the bank may engage. The largest noninterest expenses that banks incur are salaries and occupancy expenses. Other operating expenses include legal and accounting services, FDIC insurance, blanket bond insurance, regulatory fees for examinations, directors' fees, and advertising.

STATEMENTS OF CHANGES IN STOCKHOLDERS' EQUITY AND FINANCIAL POSITION

These two statements are part of the basic financial statements presented by certified public accountants. The statement of changes in stockholders' equity details the transactions in the stockholders' equity section between reporting periods. The statement of changes in financial position begins with the funds provided by operations and adds back noncash expenses. Financing activities are separated from changes in earning assets (see Exhibits 4.4 and 4.5).

EXHIBIT 4.4   Statements of Changes in Stockholders' Equity for a Sample Bank

Sample Bank
Statements of Changes in Stockholders' Equity
Years Ended December 31, 19X2 and 19X1

	Common Stock			Retained	
	Shares	Par Value	Surplus	Earnings	Total
Balance, December 31, 19X0	150,000	$1,500,000	$4,500,000	$1,904,000	$ 7,904,000
Net income				1,331,000	1,331,000
Cash dividends declared, $2.14 per share				(321,000)	(321,000)
Balance, December 31, 19X1	150,000	1,500,000	4,500,000	2,914,000	8,914,000
Net income				1,435,000	1,435,000
Cash dividends declared, $2.14 per share				(321,000)	(321,000)
Balance, December 31, 19X2	150,000	$1,500,000	$4,500,000	$4,028,000	$10,028,000

EXHIBIT 4.5 **Statement of Changes in Financial Position for a Sample Bank**

Sample Bank
Statement of Changes in Financial Position
Years Ended December 31, 19X2 and 19X1

	19X2 ($000)	19X1 ($000)
Financial resources were provided by (applied to):		
Operations:		
Net income	$1,435	$1,331
Noncash charges (credits): Provision for interest on savings accounts, depreciation, loan losses, deferred income taxes	1,923	2,043
Financial resources provided by operations	3,358	3,374
Cash dividends declared	(321)	(321)
	3,037	3,053
Deposits and other financing activities:		
Deposits:		
Demand	(4,634)	(2,521)
NOW	7,107	
Savings	(4,914)	(2,910)
Time	1,693	2,087
	(748)	(3,344)
Short-term borrowings	(279)	1,721
Subordinated debentures		1,000
Common stock issued	500	500
	(527)	(123)
Other activities—(increase) decrease in nonearning assets:		
Cash and due from banks	(73)	(129)
Premises and equipment, net	(473)	(315)
Other, net	(1,367)	959
	(1,913)	515
Increase in financial resources invested in earning assets	$ 597	$3,455
Increase (decrease) in earning assets:		
Interest-bearing deposits in banks		$ 500
Federal funds sold and securities purchased under reverse repurchase agreements	$2,100	
Trading account securities	(1,275)	2,850
Investment securities	(5,833)	(3,248)
Loans	4,821	2,983
Lease financing	784	360
	$ 597	$3,445

NOTES TO FINANCIAL STATEMENTS

Required by generally accepted auditing standards, notes are essential to the meaningful and fair presentation of financial statements. The notes describe the major accounting policies of the bank and provide additional detail regarding certain balance sheet and income statement accounts. By reading the notes, one may obtain a more complete understanding of a bank's transactions (see Appendix 4.1)

Let us examine some of the more important aspects of the notes. Significant accounting policies outline the particular accounting methods applicable to the banking industry. In certain notes the valuation of certain asset accounts leads to an income statement impact in terms of collectibility or return of principal funds invested. For example, normally an investment security is carried at cost and not at market value, even if market value is lower. However, if permanent decline in value is anticipated, the loss is recognized immediately in the income statement. Banks may be holding securities that have had significant decline in market value due to rising interest rates, but in the long run they are likely to be redeemed at prices approximating par value. Meanwhile, interest income will reflect the lower yields.

If a security is purchased at a discount, the amount of discount is accreted, i.e., coupon interest income is increased to yield the market rate at date of purchase. Correspondingly, the amount of discount is decreased, resulting in a higher carrying value of the security. When the market rate at date of purchase is lower than the coupon rate at the date of purchase, bonds will be acquired at a premium. Premium amortization is deducted from coupon interest received on a security to bring interest yield to that at the date of purchase.

National banks with assets over $10 million are required by regulation to use the accrual method of accounting. However, as a matter of regulatory practice, all new banks are required to use the accrual method. As a practical managerial consideration, a bank should adopt the accrual method because it best represents matching of income and expense.

Accounting for loan losses includes balance sheet and income statement impact (allowance for loan losses and provision for loan losses, respectively). Interest income on installment loans is recognized by reductions of unearned discount and increases to income. Nonperforming loans are loans on which the borrower is not making principal and/or interest payments. Interest is not accrued on these loans because income would be overstated and ultimately would have to be removed. Prudent accounting calls for immediately stopping accrual of interest income when the loan is determined to be nonperforming.

The provision for income taxes is based upon net income reduced by tax-exempt income and statutory tax expenses exceeding expenses reported in the income statement. Many banks use tax accounting methods that create deferrals of tax liability to future periods. Whereas the income statement presents the tax expense on reported net income, the corresponding liability accounts separate current taxes due and deferred taxes.

The remaining notes provide further detail of asset and liability accounts and include disclosure of the market values of the respective securities accounts, portfolio mix, amounts of interest forgone on non-accrual loans, the allowance for loan losses, and fixed assets by major asset classification. Composition of the income tax liability and the major tax accounting methods that produce tax deferrals are disclosed. Leases, accounted under generally accepted accounting principles, are categorized as either capitalized leases or operating leases. Operating leases (noncapitalized leases) are not presented in the balance sheet; however, prudent disclosure indicates the impact such leases will have upon future reporting periods.

The degree of financial disclosure in notes required by generally accepted auditing standards assumes significant prior knowledge. We have presented the financial statements and notes to illustrate the scope of banking activity and the implications of the complexity of certain financial transactions.

IMPORTANCE OF UNDERSTANDING BANK FINANCIAL STATEMENTS

Today's banker cannot simply rely upon balance sheets and income statements as reporting vehicles. The banker must understand bank accounting methods and operational procedures. It is one thing to know what a loan is by definition. It is another to understand the composition of the portfolio, its valuation, and the accounting for income and related expense. The latter approach is mandated to attain the levels of high-performance banks. Financial statements reflect the results of policy and operational decisions.

Franklin National Bank of New York, one of the largest banks in the United States, failed in part because its management systems, including financial statements, were not fully understood by all levels of management. Management failed to understand the basic difference between marginal interest rates and average interest rates. While it was securing deposit funds at higher interest rates, it failed to make loans at interest rates that would ensure its interest margin. Eventually, the margin contracted and the bank was unable to meet its operating costs.

Interest rates in recent years have become extremely volatile, with levels reaching their all-time highs. To manage a bank profitably in such an environment requires a thorough and complete understanding of the bank's financial statements. These statements not only represent a summary of information for use by shareholders and regulators, but also represent the central source of information for management. In today's environment a bank cannot be managed with basic statements; it is essential that statements be broken down into component systems for in-depth analysis.

The aim of this text is to extend beyond the basic financial statements and descriptive aspects of banking to the framework for analytical planning. Because the financial statements are the central source of information in the construction of this analytical framework, an understanding of the basic statements is imperative.

SUMMARY

Banks are subject to several financial reporting requirements. Reports to regulatory agencies meet a basic compliance requirement and also are included in reports that contain national and state financial statistics. Director reports allow directors to meet their statutory responsibilities and to define policies and operating objectives. Shareholders' interest is met through annual statements that present the summary of transactions for the period. These financial statements present an aggregate framework for the study of the various transactions in which a bank engages.

Questions and Problems

1. Discuss the primary uses of financial statements for banks.

2. Describe the presentation of the balance sheet and the accompanying notes for loans. What information is covered by notes to the financial statements that is not included in the balance sheet or income statement?

3. Describe the order of presentation of liabilities on the balance sheet.

4. Why are financial statements important in managing a bank?

5. First National Bank maintains the following accounts. Prepare a balance sheet and income statement in proper format for the year ending 19X1. Include appropriate headings and other descriptive terminology as necessary.

Loans, net of unearned discount
   and allowance for loan losses
Retained earnings
Demand deposits

Federal funds purchased
Surplus
Interest-bearing deposits in banks
Capital stock

Interest of deposits
Interest on federal funds sold
Cash and due from banks
Office buildings, equipment, and leasehold improvements, net
Savings deposits
Interest and fees on loans
Securities gains, net of related taxes
Other time deposits
Accrued interest and other liabilities
Income taxes
Interest on deposits in banks
Other operating expenses
Investment account securities

Salaries and wages
Interest on investment account securites:
  U.S. Treasury securities
  Obligations of states and political subdivisions
Occupancy expenses, net of revenue
Federal funds sold and securities purchased under reverse repurchase agreements
Interest on federal funds purchased
Furniture and equipment expenses
Pensions and other employee benefits
Provision for loan losses

References

American Institute of Certified Public Accountants. *Audits of Banks*, December 4, 1980.

Johnson, F. P. *Accounting and Reporting Systems for Banks.* New York: American Institute of Certified Public Accountants, 1981.

APPENDIX 4.1

Notes to the Financial Statements for a Sample Bank

**Sample Bank
Notes to Financial Statements
Years Ended December 31, 19X2 and 19X1**

1. Summary of Significant Accounting Policies

Investment Securities. Investment securities are stated at cost adjusted for amortization of premiums and accretion of discounts, which are recognized as adjustments to interest income. Gains or losses on disposition are based on the net proceeds and the adjusted carrying amount of the securities sold, using the specific identification method.

Trading Securities. Trading securities are carried at market value. Gains and losses on sales and changes in market values are included in other income.

Loans and Allowance for Loan Losses. Loans are stated at the amount of unpaid principal, reduced by unearned discount and an allowance for loan losses. Unearned discount on installment loans is recognized as income over the terms of the loans by the interest method. Interest on other loans is calculated by using the simple interest method on daily balances of the principal amount outstanding. The allowance for loan losses is established through a provision for loan losses charged to expenses. Loans are charged against the allowance for loan losses when management believes that the collectibility of the principal is unlikely. The allowance is an amount that management believes will be adequate to absorb possible losses on existing loans that may become uncollectible, based on evaluations of the collectibility of loans and prior loan loss experience. The evaluations take into consideration such factors as changes in the nature and volume of the loan portfolio, overall portfolio quality, review of specific problem loans, and current economic conditions that may affect the borrowers' ability to pay. Accrual of interest is discontinued on a loan when management believes, after considering economic and business conditions and collection efforts, that the borrowers' financial condition is such that collection of interest is doubtful.

73

Leveraged Leases.   Income on leveraged leases is recognized by a method that yields a level rate of return on the lease investment.

Depreciation.   Office equipment and buildings are stated at cost less accumulated depreciation computed principally on the straight-line method over the estimated useful lives of the assets. Leasehold improvements are amortized on the declining-balance method over the shorter of the estimated useful lives of the improvements or the terms of the related leases.

Pension Plan.   The bank has a noncontributory pension plan covering substantially all employees. The bank's policy is to fund accrued pension costs. Prior service costs are being amortized over 30 years.

Income Taxes.   Deferred income taxes are reported for timing differences between items of income or expense reported in the financial statements and those reported for income tax purposes. The differences relate principally to depreciation of office buildings and equipment, accretion of discounts on investment securities, provision for loan losses, and differences in method of recognizing income from leases. Investment tax credits resulting from purchases of equipment for the bank's use are accounted for under the flow-through method as a reduction of income tax expense in the period the assets are placed in service. Investment tax credits on equipment leased to others are recognized over a period related to the recovery of the lease investment that gives rise to the credits.

Earnings Per Share.   Earnings per share are calculated on the basis of the weighted average number of shares outstanding.

2. Investment Securities

Carrying amounts and approximate market values of investment securities are summarized as follows:

	December 31, 19X2	
	Carrying Amount	Approximate Market Value
U.S. Treasury securities	$11,023,000	$ 9,801,000
Obligations of other U.S. government agencies and corporations	2,493,000	2,192,000
Obligations of states and political subdivisions	23,279,000	20,056,000
Other securities	900,000	837,000
	$37,695,000	$32,886,000

	December 31, 19X1	
	Carrying Amount	**Approximate Market Value**
U.S. Treasury securities	$14,674,000	$13,858,000
Obligations of other U.S. government agencies and corporations	4,690,000	4,540,000
Obligations of states and political subdivisions	23,364,000	22,442,000
Other securities	800,000	727,000
	$43,528,000	$41,567,000

Investment securities with a carrying amount of $6,892,000 and $13,524,000 at December 31, 19X2 and 19X1, respectively, were pledged to secure public deposits and securities sold under agreements to repurchase and for other purposes required or permitted by law.

3. Loans

Major classifications of loans are as follows:

	December 31	
	19X2	**19X1**
Commercial	$14,634,000	$11,823,000
Construction	4,200,000	4,223,000
Mortgage	10,346,000	10,482,000
Installment	22,222,000	19,889,000
	51,402,000	46,417,000
Unearned discount	(1,986,000)	(1,822,000)
	49,416,000	44,595,000
Allowance for loan losses	(830,000)	(823,000)
Loans, net	$48,586,000	$43,772,000

Loans on which the accrual of interest has been discontinued or reduced amounted to $373,000 and $596,000 at December 31,19X2 and 19X1, respectively. If interest on those loans had been accrued, such income would have approximated $37,100 and $59,600 for 19X2 and 19X1, respectively. Interest income on those loans, which is recorded only when received, amounted to $9,300 and $18,700 for 19X2 and 19X1, respectively.

Changes in the allowance for loan losses were as follows:

| | Year Ended December 31 | |
	19X2	19X1
Balance, beginning of year	$823,000	$819,000
Provision charged to operations	60,000	68,000
Loans charged off	(80,000)	(103,000)
Recoveries	27,000	39,000
Balance, end of year	$830,000	$823,000

4. Investment in Leveraged Leases

Leveraged leases of equipment to customers comprise the following:

| | December 31, | |
	19X2	19X1
Gross rents receivable	$4,248,000	$2,760,000
Nonrecourse debt	(1,219,000)	(785,000)
Net rentals receivable	3,029,000	1,975,000
Estimated residual value	222,000	115,000
Unearned income	(1,354,000)	(977,000)
Investment in leveraged leases	$1,897,000	$1,113,000

Income on leveraged leases of $223,000 for 19X2 and $122,000 for 19X1 is included in interest and fees on loans.

5. Office Buildings, Equipment, and Leasehold Improvements

Major classifications of these assets are summarized as follows:

| | December 31 | |
	19X2	19X1
Land	$ 535,000	$ 526,000
Buildings	1,417,000	1,144,000
Equipment	691,000	596,000
Leasehold improvements	112,000	125,000
	2,755,000	2,391,000
Accumulated depreciation and amortization	(611,000)	(513,000)
	$2,144,000	$1,878,000

Depreciation and amortization expense amounted to $173,000 in 19X2 and $162,000 in 19X1.

6. Income Taxes

The total income taxes in the statements of income are as follows:

	Year Ended December 31	
	19X2	**19X1**
Currently payable		
Federal	$ 20,000	$(105,000)
State	36,000	25,000
Deferred		
Federal	85,000	100,000
State	5,000	13,000
	$146,000	$ 33,000

Accumulated deferred income taxes of $1,102,000 and $1,012,000 at December 31, 19X2 and 19X1, respectively, are included in accrued interest and other liabilities.

Deferred income taxes according to the timing differences that caused them were as follows:

	Year Ended December 31	
	19X2	**19X1**
Income on leases recognized under the finance method for financial statement purposes but recognized under the operating method for income tax purposes (Note 4)	$73,000	$ 22,000
Excess of provision for loan losses over deduction for federal income tax purposes	(3,000)	(2,000)
Accretion of discount on investment securities	6,000	78,000
Accelerated depreciation	10,000	10,000
Other	4,000	5,000
	$90,000	$113,000

Interest income on loans and securities totaling $1,258,000 and $1,266,000 for 19X2 and 19X1, respectively, is exempt from federal income taxes; accordingly, the tax provision is less than that obtained by using the statutory federal corporate income tax rate.

7. Subordinated Debentures

Subordinated debentures consist of 8 percent notes due June 1, 19X5. The notes are subordinated to all other indebtedness of the bank, and they may be prepaid, in whole or in part, at a premium of 1.833 percent to May 1, 19X3, and at reducing premiums thereafter. The terms also restrict incurrence of debt, mergers, and payment of cash dividends. As of December 31, 19X2, none of the restrictions effectively limit the bank's operations.

8. Pension Plan

The bank has a noncontributory pension plan covering substantially all of its employees. The total pension expense of 19X2 and 19X1 was $39,000 and $27,000, respectively, which includes amortization of prior service cost over 30 years. The bank contributed annually to the plan amounts equal to the accrual for pension expense. A comparison of accumulated plan benefits and plan net assets for the bank's defined benefit plan is presented below:

| | January 1 | |
	19X2	19X1
Actuarial present value of accumulated plan benefits		
Vested	$1,500,000	$1,350,000
Nonvested	2,800,000	2,650,000
	$4,300,000	$4,000,000
Net assets available for benefits	$2,050,000	$1,900,000

The weighted average assumed rate of return used in determining the actuarial present value of accumulated plan benefits was 8 percent for both 19X2 and 19X1.

9. Commitments, Contingent Liabilities, and Rental Expense

The bank leases three branch offices under noncancellable agreements, which expire between December 31, 19X6, and November 30, 19X9, and require various minimum annual rentals. One of the leases requires payment of the property taxes and insurance on the property.

The total minimum rental commitment at December 31, 19X2, under the leases is $498,000, which is due as follows:

Due in the year ending December 31	19X3	$ 85,000
	19X4	85,000
	19X5	85,000
	19X6	85,000
	19X7	60,000
Due in the remaining terms of the leases		98,000
		$498,000

The total rental expense was $85,000 and $55,000 in 19X2 and 19X1, respectively.

In the normal course of business, the bank makes various commitments and incurs certain contingent liabilities that are not presented in the accompanying financial statements. The commitments and contingent liabilities include various guarantees, commitments to extend credit, and standby letters of credit. At December 31, 19X2, commitments under standby letters of credit and guarantees aggregated $150,000. The bank does not anticipate any material losses as a result of the commitments and contingent liabilities.

The bank is a defendant in legal actions arising from normal business activities. Management believes that those actions are without merit or that the ultimate liability, if any, resulting from them will not materially affect the bank's financial position.

10. Related-Party Transactions

At December 31, 19X2, certain officers and directors, and companies in which they have 10 percent or more beneficial ownership, were indebted to the bank in the aggregate amount of $600,000.

11. Retained Earnings

Banking regulations limit the amount of dividends that may be paid without prior approval of the bank's regulatory agency. Retained earnings against which dividends may be charged were $2,000,000 at December 31, 19X2.

PART TWO

◆

Bank Functions

CHAPTER 5

Overview of Asset / Liability Management Strategies

Asset/liability management strategies entail coordinating return and risk characteristics of the bank's portfolio of assets and liabilities. Every investment decision a bank makes requires a simultaneous decision on how to fund the investment. The risk to the bank depends not only on the characteristics of the assets but also on the characteristics of the liabilities used to fund the assets.

Modern management strategies involve control of both the asset portfolio and the liability portfolio. Traditionally banks emphasized management of the asset portfolio, using deposit funds to build a portfolio of assets that was appropriate for the liability portfolio. Beginning in the 1960s, banks became more aggressive and expanded their use of short-term borrowing to support assets. The extended use of liability management led to the development of interest margin management strategies, which allow banks to profit from movements in interest rates. Broader use of liability management techniques while increasing profit potential has also increased the risk and complexity in managing banks.

THE SIMULTANEOUS NATURE OF INVESTMENT DECISIONS

We recall from our discussion in Chapter 3 that management can exhibit some degree of control over the elements of risk in banking. Of special concern to us in this chapter are the concepts of interest rate and liquidity risk. Banks can earn higher returns if they assume higher levels of interest rate and liquidity risk. Historically a portion of bank returns has been attributed to the bank's assuming interest rate and liquidity risk because banks fund loans with sources of funds that do not match the maturity of loans. As a matter of practice, most banks adjust their funding strategies over expected interest rate cycles to earn higher returns.

When individual decisions are examined, it is important to recognize the simultaneous nature of asset and liability decisions. Every fund-using or asset employment decision requires a simultaneous funding decision. For example, the decision to employ funds in consumer loans requires some decision regarding the funding of those loans. The risk in the decision must consider both the risk of the assets and the risk in funding the loans.

To see how the funding decision affects risk, consider two banks that have decided to increase their consumer loans. Consumer loans are generally longer-term loans of small amounts. Assuming that the two banks making the loans apply similar credit standards, the loans will entail similar levels of credit risk. The risk to the bank making the loans will depend not only on the asset risk but also on how the loans are funded.

Bank A decides to fund the loans with core deposits. It plans to use the funds it anticipates from maturing assets and predicted growth in deposits. Core deposits in this example are assumed to be a stable source of funding with a predictable cost. Bank B decides to fund the loans by issuing short-term certificates of deposits.

The risk in making the loans is greater for Bank B than for Bank A. Bank B will increase both its interest rate and its liquidity risk. The net yield from making the consumer loans will be affected by changes in market interest rates. If rates rise, the net return on the loans will fall. Of course, if rates decline, the net yield will rise. Since Bank B has funded the longer-term loans with short-term liabilities, it will also incur greater liquidity risk than Bank A. It will have refinanced the loans by rolling over the CDs as they mature. So, even though the banks have made asset decisions involving similar risk, the risk to the individual banks is not the same because of the selection of different sources of funding.

The risks in asset and liability decisions are interdependent. The funding of assets will affect the risk to the bank. The characteristics of assets must be considered in terms of their funding. The simultaneous nature of investment decisions is therefore an important aspect of risk evaluation.

FUNDING DECISIONS AND LIQUIDITY RISK

Over the last three decades we have seen a major restructuring in the asset and liability portfolios of commercial banks. This restructuring has resulted in increased opportunities for profits, but it has also increased the amount of risk in banks' portfolios of assets and liabilities. Restructuring of asset and liability portfolios arose because of changes in liquidity management strategies, inflationary pressures on sources of funds, and generally more aggressive management by commercial banks. In the 1960s and 1970s inflation pushed market rates above rates that banks were able to offer on deposits. As traditional deposit sources of funds became more inaccessible, banks turned to the money markets to secure funds. Once operating in the money markets, many banks continued to expand loans, funding them with borrowed funds instead of with deposits.

Traditionally banks incorporated liquidity into asset portfolios. Asset portfolios were constructed so that outflows of funds could be satisfied by liquidating assets. In the 1960s and 1970s managements shifted liquidity emphasis to the liability portfolios. Rather than liquidating assets, banks borrowed funds in the money market.

Asset Management

Asset management, as it pertains to liquidity, entails construction of assets so that outflows of funds can be accommodated without making adjustments in liabilities. Investment in assets is constrained by the ability to transform the asset into usable funds.

Liquidity of an asset comes from one of two sources: the asset's self-contained liquidity or its marketability. Self-contained liquidity reflects the maturity of the asset. For example, federal funds sold would be more liquid than an investment in Treasury bonds since federal funds sold will mature or convert into cash in most cases on an overnight basis, whereas the maturity of the bond issue may extend upwards of 20 years. The second source of liquidity arises from the marketability of the asset: the ability to exchange the asset for money through its sale to another investor in the secondary market. In this sense a Treasury bond could be viewed as being more liquid than a 90-day loan because even though the maturity of the bond is much longer than the loan, the bank can, at its option, sell the bond in the secondary market. Asset liquidity depends on the ease with which the asset can be converted into cash to meet a funds need.[1]

Assets are ranked in terms of their liquidity characteristics (see Exhibit 5.1). Cash assets are viewed as the most liquid and loans as the least liquid. (Recall from our discussion in Chapter 4 that financial statements are constructed in terms of liquidity characteristics.)

From a liquidity planning standpoint, it is important to recognize that not all assets in the various categories are liquid in the sense that the bank can, at its discretion, use these assets to meet a funds outflow. For example, balances held at correspondent banks, while appearing to be liquid, may not be at all liquid. The bank may be holding at correspondent banks the minimum amounts necessary to compensate those banks for services rendered. The only elements of these balances that represent liquid assets are the amounts of excess or surplus correspondent balances over and above the minimum necessary to obtain the services of the correspondent banks.

---

[1] J. L. Pierce, "Commercial Bank Liquidity," *Federal Reserve Bulletin,* August 1966: 1093–1101.

EXHIBIT 5.1   Banking of Assets by Liquidity Characteristics

Liquidity	Asset Category
Most Liquid	**Cash Assets**
	Investments
	Federal funds sold
	Repurchase agreements
	Treasury securities
	Agency securities
	Municipal securities
	Loans
	Short-term
Least Liquid	Long-term

The process of securing liquidity through asset construction is not without its costs. Traditionally loans yield the highest return but are the least liquid of interest-bearing assets. Greater degrees of liquidity in asset portfolios are available only if lower-yielding assets, such as Treasury securities, are included in the portfolios. To assure liquidity, banks are forced to trade off profitability.

Liability Management

The decades of the 1960s and 1970s witnessed a change in liquidity planning away from primary emphasis on asset management to emphasis on both asset and liability management. Bankers realized that another potential source of liquidity could be used—funds could be borrowed through increasing liabilities as well as liquidating assets. Some of the change in emphasis was also caused by changes in the economic environment. Increases in inflation and interest rates coupled with limits on the rates that could be paid on deposits resulted in periods in which banks witnessed significant deposit outflows. Faced with severe liquidity problems and regulatory constraints, banks were forced to innovate to accommodate the outflow of funds.

This change in emphasis from sole reliance on asset liquidity to a combination of asset and liability liquidity has greatly changed the structure of asset and liability portfolios. As shown in Exhibit 5.2, the composition of asset portfolios changed dramatically from 1950 to 1980. Banks have lowered the percentage of liquid assets (cash and securities) and have increased the percentage of assets in higher-yielding loans. Banks have been able to reduce liquidity in their asset portfolios because of the ability to obtain liquidity from their liability portfolios. They

EXHIBIT 5.2   Balance Sheet Ratios—All Commercial Banks

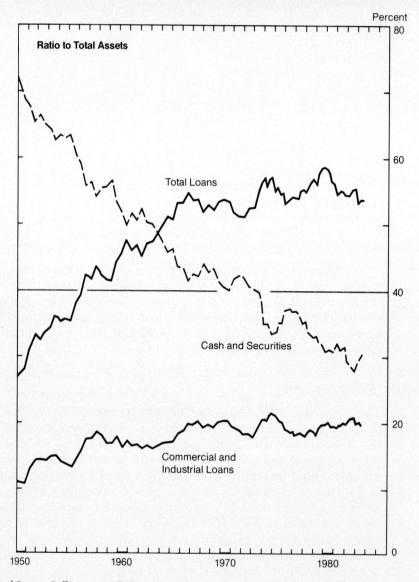

Source: *Federal Reserve Bulletin, Annual Chart Book, 1981.*

have relied more heavily on borrowed funds to meet liquidity needs, thereby allowing a higher-yielding composition of assets.

As we indicated in our discussion of asset management, banks must trade off profitability to obtain greater liquidity in their asset portfolios. There are also costs to assuring liquidity through liability portfolios. Reliance on borrowed funds to meet the liquidity needs of banks means that banks will most likely pay a higher rate of interest on borrowed funds (compared to demand and savings deposits) and will also experience greater variability in costs of its funds.

To appreciate the impact of liability management on a bank's profitability, the difference between the increased rate earned on the asset portfolio and the increased cost of the funds borrowed in the open market must be analyzed. Increased return on the asset portfolio is produced because of the increased concentration in higher-yielding loans. The increased cost in securing liquidity through borrowed funds is the market rate of interest that must be paid on these funds. The spread between the increased return on assets over liabilities measures the change in interest margin.

A bank that secures funds by borrowing must pay the market rate of interest. The cost of these funds is more volatile than traditional deposit sources, which can potentially result in increased variability in bank profits. How the use of liability management will affect the profits of the bank depends on the characteristics of the assets that are funded by the borrowed funds. If the bank uses the borrowed funds to support or fund long-term loans with fixed rates of interest, profits will vary as market interest rates vary. If the bank uses the borrowed funds to fund assets with returns that also fluctuate with market rates, profits would not be impacted, or at least not to the same extent.

Increased reliance on liability management has reduced liquidity pressures and has allowed banks to use larger percentages of their funds in higher-yielding assets. At the same time the increased use of borrowed funds has complicated the process of managing banks' portfolios. To assure profitability and minimize risk, banks must simultaneously manage the maturity, rate, and volume characteristics in their portfolios of assets and liabilities. This has led to the development of interest margin management strategies, which are designed to coordinate the maturity, rate, and volume characteristics of the asset and liability portfolios.

MARGIN MANAGEMENT TECHNIQUES

To achieve the long-range goal of maximizing the wealth of the owners of the bank, management strives to control interest margins. It is through management of interest margin that banks establish profit goals and attempt to translate the goals into realities.

To analyze the strategies of managing interest margin, it is necessary to be familiar with a few key definitions. *Interest margin,* expressed in terms of dollars, is the difference between the interest revenue on earning assets and the interest expense on liabilities. Interest margin is also expressed as a percentage of earning assets to give a mea-

sure of net yield on the portfolio of earning assets. *Spread* is the difference between the percentage rate earned on assets and the percentage
interest rate paid on liabilities. The concept of spread can be used for
the overall portfolios of assets or liabilities or used to evaluate the profitability of individual assets compared with the funds supporting those
assets. The concept of spread is used extensively in loan pricing.

The concepts of interest margin and spread are income statement
measures. On an *ex post* basis, the measures are derived directly from
the income statement. The concepts are also used on a planning, or *ex
ante*, basis. On a planning basis the expected spread is estimated by
predicting the return on assets and the expected cost of funds. Variance
in expected spread can arise if funding mismatch exists. (This topic is
analyzed in Chapter 16.)

Another key concept used in interest margin analysis is *gap*,
which is a balance sheet concept. The gap measures the imbalance of
variable- and fixed-rate assets and liabilities. Gap management is used
to increase interest margin over interest rate cycles. For any period the
gap is measured by the dollar amount that variable-rate (or interest-sensitive) assets exceed variable-rate liabilities. When a bank has a positive
gap, it is funding some variable-rate assets with fixed-rate liabilities.

To increase the spread, the bank must alter the composition of its
portfolios of assets and liabilities in accordance with predicted cycles of
interest rate moves. In short, the bank must assume greater risks to
achieve higher levels of returns. If the portfolios are adjusted to maximize returns in a given interest rate environment and the bank incorrectly assesses that rate environment, the bank is likely to experience
decreased spreads and could very well experience negative spreads and
losses. Margin management techniques require that managers carefully
assess the risk–return trade-offs involved with the adjustment in portfolios. The more aggressive management is in trying to capture returns
from movements in interest rates, the greater the risk.

Three characteristics of the asset and liability portfolios must be
managed simultaneously for successful margin or spread management.
These characteristics are the maturity composition, the rate structure,
and the default risk. Simultaneous management of these characteristics
requires a delicate balancing act in which management tries to coordinate the flows of funds into and out of the bank's pool of funds.

The maturity composition of assets and liabilities can be matched
or unmatched. When the rate earned on a bank's investment and loan
portfolio exceeds the rate paid for borrowed funds and deposits, a
locked-in spread results when maturities are matched. If maturities are
mismatched, the bank will be unable to lock in a spread. For example,
if the maturity of its liabilities exceeds the maturity of its assets, the
bank will have to reinvest funds at an uncertain future rate. If the opposite is true, i.e., the maturity of its assets is greater than the maturity
of its liabilities, the bank will be forced to secure additional funds, at an

uncertain future rate, to support the longer-maturity assets. In either of the above cases, the realized spread will be unknown at the time of investment.

Of course, if the bank can accurately predict the future rates that it could earn on its assets or that it would have to pay for its funds, a larger interest spread could be earned. For example, if rates on short-maturity borrowed funds are expected to decline, the bank could make longer-term investments and secure funds in the future to support the longer-term investments and earn a larger spread.

A simple example of how this could be accomplished is shown in Exhibit 5.3. If a bank makes a 180-day loan and secures funds for the full period of the loan, a 3 percent spread can be locked in. If rates behave as predicted, a bank could earn a larger spread average of 4.25 percent by lending longer than the maturity of its borrowed funds. The risk to the bank in such a strategy is that rates could behave differently than predicted. If the rate on shorter-maturity funds rose, the spread earned by the bank would be less.

In addition to maturity composition, effective margin management requires that rate structures be coordinated. The rate structure refers to the interest sensitivity of assets and liabilities. The rate structure and maturity composition actually interact to determine the critical aspects of returns to a bank.

Interest sensitivity depends on whether interest earned on an asset or paid on a liability changes with market rates of interest and on the speed of adjustment to these changes in market rates. Variable-rate assets and liabilities are interest sensitive since the rate paid or earned will fluctuate with changes in market rates. Examples include prime-

---

EXHIBIT 5.3   Comparative Spread on Matched and Mismatched Assets and Liabilities

	Maturity	Borrowed Funds[a]	Loans[a]	Spread[a]
Current observed rates	90 days	16 %	19 %	3%
	180 days	16.5	19.5	3
Next period's expected rates	90 days	14	17	3

Alternative Strategies

1. Loan for 180 days—secure funds for 180 days.
   Spread—3% for 180 days (19.5% − 16.5%).
2. Loan for 180 days—secure funds for 90 days today; in 90 days secure additional funds:

Spread:	1st 90 days	3%	(19.5% − 16.5%)
	2nd 90 days	5.5%	(19.5% − 14%)
Average spread for 180 days		4.25%	

[a]The borrowed-funds rate, loan rate, and spread are expressed in annual rates for the example.

rate loans and short-term borrowed funds such as federal funds purchased. Fixed-rate assets and liabilities are not sensitive to changes in market rates of interest. Examples include installment loans and subordinated debentures issued by the bank. The rate earned or paid on the fixed-rate components of the asset and liability portfolios are fixed to the bank for the maturity of the instrument.

The rate structure and maturity structure together determine the degree of interest sensitivity. Term loans that have variable rates even though the maturities may extend for several years are, in fact, interest sensitive. Even though the maturities are longer, the pricing characteristics effectively create short-term assets as far as the interest spreads are concerned.

The final characteristic of the asset and liability portfolios that must be considered for effective margin management is default risk. The risk of default to the bank on its asset portfolio exceeds the default risk to depositors for its liabilities. A portion of the spread the bank makes is compensation for risk pooling and credit evaluation. Depositors are willing to accept lower rates on the funds they lend to the bank because they cannot evaluate the creditworthiness of the ultimate borrower of the funds in a cost-effective manner.

The bank can adjust the spread through management of default risk in the loan and investment portfolio. A larger expected spread can be achieved by making higher-risk loans and investing in lower-grade debt securities. The management of the bank must make a prudent assessment of the risk/return trade-offs in undertaking such a strategy. Increasing the spread through assuming greater default risk can cause problems, especially in periods of economic turndown.

Gap Management

Gap management is a strategy employed to maximize interest margin over the interest rate cycle. This strategy basically involves adjusting the variable- and fixed-rate components in line with the phase of the interest rate cycle to achieve maximum profitability.

To understand the elements of gap management, we begin by classifying assets and liabilities (funds) into three categories: matched, variable, and fixed.[2] Matched assets and liabilities are specific sources that have matched maturities with predetermined spreads. An example of a matched transaction would be an acceptance transaction. Variable assets and liabilities are characterized by interest rates that fluctuate with money market conditions, such as negotiable CDs, short-term business loans, and short-term investments. Fixed-rate assets and liabilities are characterized by fixed rates for relatively long periods of time. Examples include installment loans and core demand and fixed-rate time deposits.

---

[2]This section draws heavily on J. T. Clifford, "A Perspective on Asset-Liability Management, Parts I and II," *The Magazine of Bank Administration*, March 1975: 16–21; April 1975: 32–36.

The gap is defined by the dollar amount by which variable-rate assets exceed variable-rate liabilities.[3] The gap is positive when that dollar amount is positive and negative when that amount is negative. When the gap is positive, the bank is supporting variable-rate assets with fixed-rate liabilities. When the gap is negative, the bank is supporting fixed-rate assets with variable-rate liabilities.

The basic strategy used in gap management is to change the gap size in accordance with predicted movements in interest rates. A large positive gap is ideal when rates are rising. With a positive gap the bank will earn higher rates on its assets while supporting those assets with fixed-rate funds. When rates are predicted to decline, the bank will want to lock in the high rates on assets and use more variable-rate funding. As rates fall, the bank's cost of funds will decline and the spread will increase, since the bank has acquired fixed-rate assets.

For illustration, assume that fixed rates earned on assets and fixed rates paid on liabilities do not vary over the cycle and that the spread earned on matched variable-rate transactions remains constant. As rates on matched variable-rate transactions rise and fall over the cycle, the bank will earn a constant spread. Let us see what will happen to a bank's spread when it successfully gaps.

Suppose that a bank starts out with a gap of $200 million as shown in Exhibit 5.4. The spreads on the various categories of assets

EXHIBIT 5.4   Illustration of Gap Management and Interest Margin Determination (Narrow Gap at Low Interest Rates)

Assets[a]	Funds	Spread	$Margins (millions)
Matched assets $50 million @ 14%	Matched liabilities $50 million @ 13.5%	.5%	0.25
Variable-rate assets $200 million @ 15%	Variable-rate liabilities $200 million @ 13%	2%	4.00
$200 million @ 15% (total $400 million)	Fixed-rate liabilities $200 million @ 12%	3%	6.00 GAP
Fixed-rate assets $900 million @ 15%	Fixed-rate liabilities $900 million @ 12% (total $1,100 million)	3%	27.00
Totals $1,350 million	$1,350 million	2.76%	$37.25

[a]This form for analyzing the gap is used in J. T. Clifford, "A Perspective on Asset-Liability Management, Part I," *The Magazine of Bank Administration*, March 1975; 16–21.

[3]The term *gap* can also be defined as the dollar amount by which fixed-rate liabilities exceed fixed-rate assets. Authors also use a number of other terms for various classifications. Two commonly used terms are *interest-sensitive* and *floating-rate*.

and liabilities are shown, and the bank's overall spread is 2.76 percent with a total interest margin of $37.25 million.

If the bank could increase the amount of variable-rate assets funded with fixed-rate funds as rates rose, the bank's profit margin could be improved. This is shown in Exhibit 5.5. Rates on short-term assets increased from 15 percent to 21 percent, and the bank funded an additional $100 million in the short-term assets with fixed-rate funds whose average cost remained at 12 percent. The strategy resulted in additional interest margin of $6 million over what the bank would have earned with a $200 million gap.

Strategies to manage the gap over the interest rate cycle will result in larger spreads and interest margins. A conservative strategy is to maintain a positive gap at all times but to narrow the gap as rates move from cyclical highs to cyclical lows, with the gap reaching its lowest level when rates reach their low point.

An aggressive strategy is to move to a negative gap position when rates are predicted to decline. With a negative gap the bank will be supporting fixed-rate assets with variable-rate liabilities. The bank will lock in the high rates on assets and the cost of funds supporting those assets will decline.

We should at least mention a few of the difficulties and problems associated with "gapping." First, although it is true that margins can be improved if interest rate movements are correctly predicted, "gapping" does increase variability in the spread. In our example the bank in-

EXHIBIT 5.5 Illustration of Gap Management and Interest Margin Determination (Wide Gap at High Interest Rates)

Assets	Funds	Spread	$ Margin (millions)
Matched assets $50 million @ 20%	Matched liabilities $50 million @ 19.5%	0.5%	0.25
Variable-rate assets $200 million @ 21%	Variable-rate liabilities $200 million @ 19%	2.0%	4.00
Variable-rate assets $300 million @ 21% (total $500 million)	Fixed-rate liabilities $300 million @ 12%	9.0%	27.00 GAP
Fixed-rate assets $800 million @ 15%	Fixed-rate liabilities $800 million @ 12% (total $1,100 million)	3.0%	24.00
Totals $1,350 million	$1,350 million	4.09%	$55.25

creased the gap correctly for the movement in interest rates. If the bank had predicted rates incorrectly, increasing the gap would have reduced margin. Second, there is a problem with respect to the timing of the change in the size of the gap. It may take a considerable amount of time to change the size of the gap significantly. Interest rate cycles must be of sufficient duration to accomplish the changes. Finally, "gapping" implicitly assumes that the bank can effectively alter the gap. Banks operate in very competitive environments, and the ability of banks to make significant changes in the structure of assets and liabilities is often affected or limited by competition.

ASSET AND LIABILITY MANAGEMENT IN THE CURRENT ENVIRONMENT

Aggressive management of asset and liability portfolios depends on the degree of certainty about inflows and outflows and about rates earned on assets and paid on liabilities. To apply gap management as it is traditionally defined, banks must be able to predict flows and rates. Banks must accurately predict levels of fixed-rate funds that will be available. To maximize interest margin, banks must also be able to time movements in interest rates.

A second requirement for aggressive management of assets and liabilities is the assurance that the duration of the interest rate cycle will be sufficiently long to accomplish the required changes. Banks cannot instantaneously change the composition of their asset and liability portfolios. Significant changes in the size of the gap may take months or years to accomplish. If the duration of the interest rate cycle is not long enough for a bank to change its asset and liability structure and therefore gap size (which may be positive or negative), the bank could experience a disruption in adjustments to obtain a planned gap and declining interest margin.

The competitive environment in which a bank operates also limits the ability of a bank to be successful in aggressive management of its assets and liabilities. In our discussions of gap management, we assumed that the bank would move to increase and decrease the gap in line with its prediction on rates. Competition will limit the ability of the bank to achieve these goals in many cases. If most banks share the same expectations and all are attempting to pursue the same strategy, prices and rates will reflect the anticipated changes very quickly.

Recent Developments

Stating that the economic environment in which banks must operate has become more volatile is the ultimate exaggeration. To compare today's environment with the environment 15 years ago is to compare day and night. Two major factors have contributed to the change—interest rate volatility and changes in the competitive environment. Mounting interest rate volatility and increased competition have made the process of asset and liability management more difficult and demanding.

Interest Rate Volatility

Rate volatility and duration of interest rate cycles have changed dramatically in the last two decades. This coupled with the fact that banks have relied more on borrowed funds as a source of funds has caused the banks' cost of funds to shift more dramatically and to change more quickly than in any period since the 1930s. The changes were particularly perceptible in the 1970s.

The period following the Great Depression until the mid-1960s was characterized by infrequent and small changes in the prime rate. The typical change in the prime rate was ¼ to ½ percent and the prime rate changed on average less than once a year. In the late 1960s the prime rate changed more frequently but the changes were still relatively small. In the 1970s changes in the prime rate were made much more frequently, with the average incremental change in the prime rate being larger.

In each of the decades of the 1950s and 1960s there were 16 changes made in the prime rate, but from 1970 to 1979 there were 139 changes made.[4] The changes in the prime rate were nearly 10 times as volatile in the 1970s as they were in the 1950s and 1960s.

Recent periods have been even more volatile. From October 1979 through December 1980 there were approximately 50 changes in the prime rate. Even more significant than the number of prime rate changes was the magnitude of the change in rates. During the short period from August 1979 to January 1981, rates rose from the 11 percent level to 20 percent, back down to slightly under 12 percent, then upward again to over 20 percent.

For a bank to profit from movements in interest rates when the duration of the cycles is so short is nearly impossible. Even if the bank were to accurately predict the rate movements, with the short duration in interest rate cycles there would be insufficient time for the bank to make significant changes in the composition of its assets and liabilities. To profit from gapping, the interest rate cycle must be long enough for the bank to change the composition of its assets and liabilities. If rates move too quickly, the bank could end up implementing a strategy that results in lower profits because of its inability to adjust in a timely fashion.

---

[4]R. L. Olson et al., "Margin Management in the 1980's, Part I," in *Funds Management Under Deregulation*, ed. G. H. Hempel (Washington, DC: American Bankers Association, 1981), 89–95.

In the past banks have profited through the prediction of interest rate levels. If the rate volatility displayed in recent periods continues, it will become increasingly difficult for banks to continue to profit from rate cycles. If banks are unable to profit from rate cycles, their profit margins will be reduced.[5] At a minimum, accurate estimations of flows and greater flexibility in asset and liability construction are necessary to react to this increasingly volatile market.

Changes in the Competitive Environment

The problems faced by banks in asset and liability management have also increased because of changes in the environment in which the banks operate. These changes have resulted from increased competition from nonbank financial institutions and from changes in regulation.

In the last decade many nonbank institutions have begun to offer services that compete either directly or indirectly with services traditionally offered by commercial banks. High rates of inflation and high money market rates have enhanced the development of money market funds. Most of these funds offer check-writing privileges and rates that exceed the rates that banks can offer on deposits with similar characteristics. The investment industry has offered competitive services in both the wholesale and retail industry. The characteristics of services offered by the investment industry have been very competitive since such institutions are not subject to regulations that are as restrictive as those imposed on commercial banks.[6] The Sears Financial Network demonstrates just how competitive the market is becoming. The idea of department store financial service has arrived.

The Depository Institutions Deregulation and Monetary Control Act of 1980 will eventually change the operating environment for commercial banks. The major provisions, which include expanded powers for thrift institutions, eventual elimination of Regulation Q, and explicit changes in the services offered by the Federal Reserve banks, will increase the competition faced by banks and alter the cost structure of many of the banks' sources of funds. Also, serious discussions by legislators concerning possible changes in the banking laws to allow interstate banking and expanded underwriting powers are taking place. If interstate branching is allowed, banks in a given region will face greater competition not only from nonbank institutions but also from other banks.

---

[5]For an interesting discussion of the impact on profit margins when banks are unable to profit from interest rate movements, see S. Rose, "Dark Days Ahead for Banks," in *Funds Management Under Deregulation*, ed G. H. Hempel (Washington, DC: American Bankers Association, 1981), 81–88.

[6]M. Mayer, "Merrill Lynch Quacks Like a Bank," *Fortune*, Oct. 20, 1980, 134–144.

Changes in the regulatory environment bring both a blessing and a curse. The blessing is that elimination of rate ceilings will allow banks to compete more effectively for funds currently being attracted to non-bank institutions. The curse is that banks will experience increased cost of funds from some of their traditional sources.

These changes in a bank's operating environment from both competition and interest rate volatility complicate the process of asset and liability management. To manage their portfolios of assets and liabilities effectively in the current environment, banks must be able to assess their costs of funds and expected returns very accurately. Planning is critical in today's environment because of the pressure on interest margins and the extreme volatility of the market. The balancing act that management must perform in trading off risk and return and in coordinating flows of funds is essential for consistent profits.

Asset/Liability Management Committee

If management is committed to asset/liability management, it has taken the first important step—recognition and support of the function. The organization of the function in a small bank might include the president and key officers active in decisions about loans, investments, and the money market. In larger banks an asset/liability management committee would include the managers of the key portions of the balance sheet—the chairman and/or president, the chief financial and accounting officers, heads of lending divisions, the investment manager, heads of deposit and liability acquisition functions, economists, and the supervisor of credit policy.

> The responsibilities of the asset/liability management committee usually include directing the overall acquisition and allocation of funds to maximize earnings and ensure demand and funding sources, so that the committee can assess liability and loan pricing strategies; establishing funds acquisition practices and options for the allocation of loans; monitoring earnings spread, asset/liability distributions, and maturities; determining how to deal with reserve requirements for money market activities; reviewing budget variances; and, most important, developing action plans based on the causes of these variances.[7]

Management in each bank has made decisions that affect interest margin, including concentration in nonsensitive assets while taking on rate-

---

[7]B. F. Binder, "Asset/Liability Management, Part I," *The Magazine of Bank Administration,* November 1981: 46.

sensitive liabilities. Periodic financial analysis is an important technique for identifying the causes of past fluctuations in interest rates as well as assisting in predicting the future direction of key variables. Attention to economic trends, particularly forecasts of interest rates, also assists in predicting key variables.

The asset/liability management committee should develop financial planning tools, including spread management, gap management, and interest-sensitivity analysis. These tools emphasize quantitative measures that indicate conditions of the bank's portfolios in the past and present as well as what future decisions might be made and their potential effect on the balance sheet and income statement.

SUMMARY

In this chapter we have examined the simultaneous nature of the asset and liability decisions that a bank makes. Every decision to employ funds in assets requires another decision on how to fund the assets. The risk in making investments or loans depends not only on the characteristics of the assets but also on the characteristics of the liabilities used to support those assets.

Banks use strategies to maximize interest margins or the spread over interest rate cycles. A strategy used to increase interest margins is gap management, which adjusts the balance between fixed- and variable-rate assets and liabilities. The gap, defined as the dollar amount by which variable-rate assets exceed variable-rate liabilities, is adjusted to predicted interest rate cycles. To maximize interest margins, a bank should increase the gap when rates are expected to rise and narrow the gap when rates are expected to decline. Although aggressive margin management increases the expected returns to the bank, it also increases risk.

We have found that banking's current operating environment is characterized by increased interest rate variability, increased uncertainty, and greater competition. The changes in operating environment present modern-day bankers with a challenge. In today's environment the process of asset and liability management has been shown to be a complex process requiring accurate information and careful planning.

Questions and Problems

1. Why is it important to consider both the asset and liability components of an investment decision?

2. Describe the effect of aggressive liability management on the structure of a bank's asset portfolio.

3. Exhibit 5.1 ranks assets according to liquidity characteristics. Describe some potential problems in assessing liquidity according to that ranking.

4. Discuss the trend in liability management techniques from 1950 through 1980. What significance does that trend have on banking risks and returns?

5. Define the following terms: *Net interest margin (dollars), spread,* and *gap.*

6. Describe the appropriate gap management strategies when (a) interest rates are expected to rise, and (b) interest rates are expected to fall.

7. Discuss the problems involved with gap management in the current economic and competitive environment.

References

Beebe, J. "A Perspective on Liability Management and Bank Risk." *Economic Review, Federal Reserve Bank of San Francisco,* Winter 1977: 12–24.

Binder, B. F. "Asset/Liability Management, Part I." *The Magazine of Bank Administration,* November 1981: 42–48.

Clifford, J. T. "A Perspective on Asset-Liability Management, Parts I and II." *The Magazine of Bank Administration,* March 1975: 16–21; April 1975: 32–36.

Goodfriend, M. "Eurodollars." In *Instruments of the Money Market,* ed. T. Q. Cook and B. J. Summers. Richmond, VA: Federal Reserve Bank of Richmond, 1981: 123–132.

Hervey, J. L. "Bankers Acceptance." *Business Conditions, Federal Reserve Bank of Chicago,* May 1976: 3–11.

Howard, D. S., and G. M. Hoffman. *Evolving Concepts of Bank Capital Management.* New York: Citicorp, 1980.

Kaufman, D. J., Jr., and D. R. Lee. "Planning Liquidity: A Practical Approach." *The Magazine of Bank Administration,* March 1977: 55–63.

Lucas, C. M., M. T. Jones, and J. Thurston. "Federal Funds and Repurchase Agreements." *Quarterly Review, Federal Reserve Bank of New York,* Summer 1977: 33–48.

Luckett, D. G. "Approaches to Bank Liquidity Management." *Economic Review, Federal Reserve Bank of Kansas City,* March 1981: 11–27.

Mayer, M. "Merrill Lynch Quacks Like a Bank." *Fortune,* October 20, 1980, 134–144.

Olson, R. L., et al. "Margin Management in the 1980's, Parts I–IV." In *Funds Management Under Deregulation,* ed. G. H. Hempel, 89–95, 562–599. Washington, DC: American Bankers Association, 1981.

Olson, R. L., and H. M. Sollenberger. "Interest Margin Variance Analysis: A Tool for Current Times." *The Magazine of Bank Administration,* May 1978: 45–51.

Parthemos, B. J., and W. Varvel. "The Discount Window." In *Instruments of the Money Market,* ed. T. Q. Cook and B. J. Summers. Richmond, VA: Federal Reserve Bank of Richmond, 1981: 59–71.

Pierce, J. L. "Commercial Bank Liquidity." *Federal Reserve Bulletin,* August 1966: 1093–1101.

Ratti, R. A. "Pledging Requirements and Bank Asset Portfolios." *Economic Review, Federal Reserve Bank of Kansas City,* September-October 1973: 13–23.

Rose, S. "Dark Days Ahead for Banks." In *Funds Management Under Deregulation,* ed. G. H. Hempel, 81–88. Washington, DC: American Bankers Association, 1981.

Summers, B. J. "Negotiable Certificates of Deposit." *Economic Review, Federal Reserve Bank of Richmond,* July-August 1980: 8–19.

Watson, R. D. "Bank Board Management: The Maturity Dilemma." *Business Review, Federal Reserve Bank of Philadelphia,* March 1972: 20–23.

Watson, R. D. "Banking on Debt for Capital Needs." *Business Review, Federal Reserve Bank of Philadelphia,* December 1974: 17–28.

CHAPTER 6

Deposit Functions

Deposit structures of commercial banks are changing so rapidly that traditional discussions of deposit types and their structure have very little meaning in today's environment. Market demands for explicit interest payments and changes in regulation have transformed the structure of deposits. Demand deposit accounts have been declining and interest-bearing time deposits and transaction accounts have been increasing.

Following passage of the Depository Institutions Deregulation and Monetary Control Act of 1980 (DIDMCA), the regulatory agencies have been eliminating interest rate regulations imposed on banks and other depository institutions. Effective October 1, 1983, the only deposit accounts subject to Regulation Q interest rate restrictions are savings accounts, small-balance interest-bearing NOW (negotiable order of withdrawal) accounts, and small-balance time deposits with maturities of less than 31 days.

The result of the provisions of the DIDMCA will be much greater interest sensitivity in banks' sources of funds. The increased volatility in the rates banks pay for their funds will necessitate important changes in management practices and is likely to result in significant changes in how banks market their deposit services. Cost control and innovation in the management of deposit services will become even more critical in the coming years. The ability of banks to survive will depend on their ability to coordinate asset and liability management to protect growth.

LIABILITY MANAGEMENT

In a broad sense liability management refers to the overall process of controlling and coordinating a bank's sources of funds. These sources of funds include traditional deposits, such as demand and time accounts, and other funds a bank borrows in the money markets either temporarily or permanently. Banks can borrow funds to provide needed liquidity in the event of an unexpected outflow of funds or to secure additional funds to invest. The process of overall liability management refers not only to these short-term borrowed funds but also to a bank's deposits.[1]

---

[1]Many authors use the term *liability management* to refer to the use of short-term borrowed funds to meet an unexpected liquidity need. We refer to the term in a broader sense to include all of the bank's sources of funds.

Types of Deposits

For commercial banks deposits are divided into three major categories—demand deposits, savings deposits, and time deposits. Demand deposits, which comprise slightly over 20 percent of total deposits for all banks as of October 1983, are payable on demand to depositors. Savings deposits are ordinary passbook accounts, which can be withdrawn on very short notice. Time deposits are characterized by a fixed maturity that can range from 7 days to 8 years or longer.

As elements of the DIDMCA have been phased in, some deposits can be offered with no interest ceilings and others are still subject to fixed ceilings. Exhibit 6.1 displays the current requirements that apply on deposits.

As indicated in Exhibit 6.1, very few restrictions currently apply to deposits. The only public deposits still subject to interest rate regulations are savings accounts, NOW accounts that have an average balance of less than $2500, and time deposits with an average balance of less than $2500 and maturities that range from 7 to 31 days. Also, deposits of governmental units that are less than $2500 remain subject to an 8 percent interest ceiling. Unless extended by legislation, no restrictions will apply to bank deposits by 1986.

The transition from a highly regulated deposit structure has been swift. Following the passage of the DIDMCA in June 1980, several transitional changes were incorporated. Prior to the change in October 1983, the largest change was made in December 1982. That change allowed banks to pay market rates on money market deposit accounts. These accounts were very popular and accounted for much of the deposit growth in 1983. Following the change in 1983, very few restrictions remain.

Other Liabilities

Banks secure funds to satisfy liquidity needs or to increase assets by borrowing in the money markets or by making specialized lending arrangements through the Federal Reserve System. These borrowed funds have become an increasingly important source of funds for banks in recent years. The major instruments banks use to borrow funds include federal funds purchased, securities sold under repurchase agreements, Eurodollar deposits, and bankers' acceptances. Maturities on these instruments are short; some borrowings are made overnight. In general, rates are market determined and are not subject to rate ceilings. The instruments differ with respect to whether or not they are secured. Some instruments, such as repurchase agreements, are collateralized, whereas other instruments are unsecured. Banks also secure funds by borrowing from the Federal Reserve Bank through the discount window.

A key factor affecting the cost of borrowing funds through these various instruments is the reserve requirement. If a bank is required to

EXHIBIT 6.1 Maximum Interest Rates Payable on Time and Savings Deposits at Federally Insured Institutions (Percent per Annum)[a]

Type of Deposit	Commercial Banks (In Effect Oct. 30, 1983)		Savings and Loan Associations and Mutual Savings Banks (Thrift Institutions)[a] (In Effect Oct. 30, 1983)	
	Percent	Effective Date	Percent	Effective Date
Savings	5½	7/1/79	5½	7/1/79
Negotiable order of withdrawal accounts	5¼	12/31/80	5¼	12/31/80
Negotiable order of withdrawal accounts of $2500 or more	—[b]	1/5/83	—[b]	1/5/83
Money market deposit accounts	[b]	12/14/82	[b]	12/14/82
Time Accounts by Maturity				
7–31 days of less than $2500[c]	5½	9/1/82	5½	9/1/82
7–31 days of $2500 or more	—	1/5/83	—	1/5/83
More than 31 days	—	10/1/83	—	10/1/83

[a]Effective Oct. 1, 1983, restrictions on the maximum rates of interest payable by commercial banks and thrift institutions on various categories of deposits were removed. For information regarding previous interest rate ceilings on all categories of accounts, see earlier issues of the *Federal Reserve Bulletin*, the *Federal Home Loan Bank Board Journal*, and the *Annual Report of the Federal Deposit Insurance Corporation* before November 1983.
[b]Effective Dec. 14, 1982, depository institutions are authorized to offer a new account with a required initial balance of $2500 and an average maintenance balance of $2500 not subject to interest rate restrictions. No minimum maturity period is required for this account, but depository institutions must reserve the right to require seven days notice before withdrawals. When the average balance is less than $2500, the account is subject to the maximum ceiling rate of interest for NOW accounts; compliance with the average balance requirement may be determined over a period of one month. Depository institutions may not guarantee a rate of interest for this account for a period longer than one month or condition the payment of a rate on a requirement that the funds remain on deposit for longer than one month.
[c]Deposits of less than $2500 issued to governmental units continue to be subject to an interest rate ceiling of 8 percent.

Source: *Federal Reserve Bulletin*, November 1983.

hold reserves against borrowed funds, the cost of borrowing such funds is increased. The Federal Reserve authorities have at various times put marginal reserve requirements in place on borrowed funds.[2]

To see how reserve requirements increase the cost of deposit funds, let us consider an example of a negotiable CD. Suppose that a 15 percent reserve requirement applies to such CDs and that the market rate is 12 percent. The effective cost to the bank is equal to

$$\frac{\text{Market rate}}{1 - \text{Reserve requirement percentage}}$$

The cost of funds therefore equals

$$14.12\% = \frac{12\%}{1 - 15\%}$$

Since the bank has use of only 85 percent of the funds borrowed (15 percent must be held in nonearning reserves), we see that the effective cost of funds increases when reserves must be held.[3]

Mix, Volatility, and the Cost of Funds

The process of liability management must be coordinated with the management of a bank's assets to ensure the level and stability of profits. Key factors that affect a bank's cost of funds include the mix of deposit funds and other borrowed funds, the volatility of deposit funds, and the services provided to depositors.

The mix of deposit funds refers to the breakdown of demand, savings, and time deposits. A bank can reduce its interest costs by attracting lower-cost types of deposits, such as demand and savings deposits. Although no interest is paid on traditional demand deposits, the processing costs on such accounts are higher, thereby increasing the cost of such funds.

The volatility of the level of deposit funds and of the rates paid on deposits also affects the cost of funds. Fluctuations in the level of deposit funds must be coordinated with a bank's investments. If loans are funded with deposits and the bank experiences significant outflows of funds before those loans mature, the bank must seek additional funds

---

[2]For example, the Federal Reserve imposed a marginal reserve requirement of 8 percent on managed liabilities in October 1979. The marginal requirement applied to managed liabilities above the base of managed liabilities a bank had outstanding. Managed liabilities include large time deposits, Eurodollar borrowings, repurchase agreements against Treasury and federal agency securities, and federal funds borrowed from nonmember institutions. The percentages were altered and eventually eliminated in July 1980.

[3]The above analysis considers only the reserve requirement. The same methodology may be employed for any additional changes that apply to deposits. For example, the effect of FDIC insurance premiums is often used when comparing costs of traditional and Eurodollar deposits. The FDIC premium is expressed as a percentage incorporated in the denominator in the same fashion as the reserve requirement percentage.

to support the loans. The net return will be lower on those loans if the new funds are more costly. As we indicated in the previous chapter, volatility in interest rates on deposits may also affect profits. If fixed-rate assets are financed with variable-rate deposits or borrowed funds, profits will be squeezed in rising-rate markets.

As displayed in Exhibit 6.2, the mix of deposit funds of commercial banks changed drastically between 1950 and 1980. In 1950 demand deposits accounted for approximately 70 percent of the banks' total sources of funds, whereas in 1980 they accounted for approximately 20 percent of total liabilities and capital. In 1950 time and savings deposits accounted for approximately 20 percent of total liabilities and capital, whereas in 1980 they accounted for nearly 50 percent of the total. During the same period the equity capital accounts for commercial banks, expressed as a percentage of total liabilities and capital, declined slightly while borrowed funds increased as a percentage of the total.

The change in the mix of deposit funds has transformed the cost structure of commercial banks into a structure in which interest expense on deposits has become increasingly important. In short, the entire structure of a bank's sources of funds has become more interest sensitive. Exhibit 6.3 graphically illustrates the effect of the changing structure on operating expenses. Interest expense has steadily increased as a percentage of total operating expenses.

The change from noninterest- to interest-bearing deposits represents only part of the change in banks' liabilities portfolios. The liability portfolio has become progressively interest sensitive as well. The composition of savings and time deposits has shifted from fixed-rate to variable-rate deposits. Increased percentages of funds that are sensitive to market interest rates and increased volatility in market rates have combined to have a dual effect on the cost of funds—increasing both the cost of funds and the variability of the cost of funds.

The types of deposits experiencing the largest growth at commercial banks in recent years have been a function of changing regulations. In the early 1970s most of the growth in deposits occurred in the large negotiable CDs. In 1978 financial institutions were able to offer 6-month money market CDs whose rates were tied to the 26-week Treasury bill rate. Banks experienced large growth in these deposits following their introduction. From 1978 to December 1982 banks offered various innovative types of accounts designed to compete with accounts offered by less-regulated financial institutions. From their introduction in the late 1970s, the assets of money market mutual funds had grown to $75.8 billion by December 1980. From December 1980 to December 1981, their assets had grown to $184.5 billion, a growth rate of 143 percent for the period. During the same period deposits at commercial banks grew at a rate of 9.9 percent.[4]

---

[4]"Financial Developments in 1981," *Financial Letter, Federal Reserve Bank of Kansas City,* Jan. 28, 1982.

EXHIBIT 6.2.   Deposit Structure

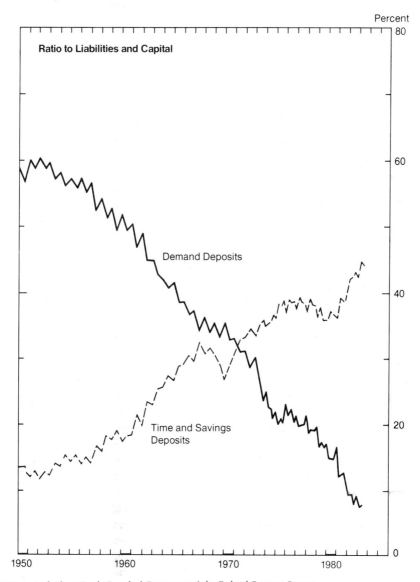

Source: *1981 Historical Chart Book,* Board of Governors of the Federal Reserve System.

     To compete with the less-regulated money market funds, banks offered many different accounts designed to skirt regulations. With the passage of the DIDMCA and the phase-in of the deregulation of deposit restrictions, many of the innovations have disappeared. The major changes following the DIDMCA that have influenced deposit structure

EXHIBIT 6.3   Operating Expenses of Commercial Banks

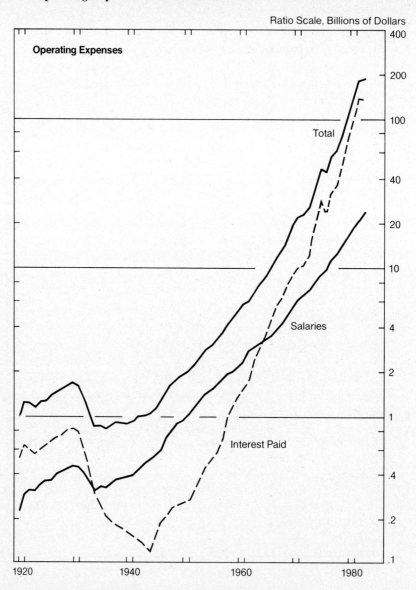

Ratio Scale, Billions of Dollars

Operating Expenses

Total

Salaries

Interest Paid

Source: *1981 Historical Chart Book,* Board of Governors of the Federal Reserve System.

include the nationwide introduction of NOW accounts in December 1980 and the introduction of the money market deposit and Super NOW accounts in December 1982.

From a base of $28.1 billion in December 1980, NOW and other checkable deposits at financial institutions had grown to $77.8 billion by the end of 1981.[5] Most of the funds transferred to NOWs have come from demand deposits, although some transfers have also been made from low-yielding savings accounts. Transfers from traditional demand deposit accounts have influenced the cost of funds because of the explicit interest expense. Transfers from savings accounts increase the cost of funds because of increased processing costs, even though the interest rate is the same for savings and NOW accounts.[6]

In December 1982 banks were authorized to offer money market deposit accounts. From their introduction in December 1982 to mid-April 1983, these accounts grew to $340 billion.[7] The rate of growth was phenomenal. In four months the money market deposit accounts grew to a level that the money market certificate had taken two years to achieve. Characteristics of the money market accounts are described in the following section.

The change that has taken place in deposits for commercial banks can be summarized in terms of trends toward explicit interest payment and increased volatility in the rates paid. The structure has changed and has become increasingly interest sensitive.

RETAIL DEPOSITS: CHARACTERISTICS

Deposit funds secured from retail customers include traditional demand deposits, savings deposits, and various types of certificates of deposit. As provisions of the DIDMCA are put into place, banks have offered a variety of deposit accounts characterized by variable rates that are not subject to ceilings.

Given the competitive nature of the market for deposit funds, most banks have developed or are developing integrated packages of services to attract consumer funds, rather than offering services such as lending and deposits as discrete services. Competition has been particularly acute in the market for large-scale or up-scale consumer accounts.

Exhibit 6.4 describes the different types of deposit services offered to consumers. Banks typically offer a variety of transaction accounts, ranging from traditional checking account services to a package of bundled services, which may include checking account services tied to other services typically desired by consumers. Passage of the DIDMCA authorized the development of NOW accounts nationwide. In January 1983 banks were authorized to offer Super NOW accounts. Banks can offer these accounts, which are not subject to any rate ceilings, as long

---

[5]Ibid.

[6]Robert O. Metzger, "Coping With the Cost of NOW's," *Bankers Magazine*, January-February 1981: 55–58.

[7]F. F. Furlong, "New Deposit Instruments," *Federal Reserve Bulletin*, May 1983: 320.

EXHIBIT 6.4 Retail Accounts—Overview of Basic Accounts and Services

Type of Account	Characteristics	Services Provided	Revenues	Expenses
Transaction Accounts				
Regular checking accounts	Transferable on demand, small or no minimum balance	Traditional transaction services, monthly statements	Service charges typically tied to minimum or average balances, charges for returned items and special requests such as stop payments, etc.	All costs associated with processing checks and deposits, preparation and mailing of statements
Special checking accounts	Transferable on demand, small balance	Limited transaction services and periodic statements	Service charges typically at a charge per item with some minimum charges for special items	All costs associated with processing checks and deposits, preparation and mailing of statements
Bundled-services accounts	Same as regular checking except wider variety of services provided	Transaction services and all other services in the bundle, for example, safe deposit, traveler's checks, overdrafts, and credit cards	Service charges, typically a flat fee per month, which may be varied with balance	All processing costs and costs of providing to customers the related services in the bundles
NOWs	Interest-bearing transaction account with rate ceiling by Regulation Q	Traditional transaction services, monthly statements	Service charge typically tied to minimum or average balances, charges for special items	All costs associated with processing checks and deposits, preparation and mailing of statements, interest paid on average or minimum balance

Super NOWs	Minimum balance of $2500, no rate ceilings apply	Traditional transaction services, monthly statements	Service charges typically based on average balances	All costs associated with processing checks and deposits, preparation and mailing of statements, and paying interest on average balances
Money market deposit accounts	$2500 minimum initial deposit and minimum monthly average, no minimum maturity, limited third-party or automatic transfers	Limited transaction services and monthly statement processing	Possible charges for transactions	All processing costs associated with transfers and variable interest expense
Savings Accounts	Immediately withdrawable, maximum rate set by Regulation Q	Traditional passbook services	Charges for excess withdrawal	Processing costs and interest expense
Time Deposit Accounts				
Maturity of from 7 to 31 days	$2500 minimum balance, no rate ceilings; if balance is less than $2500, subject to Regulation Q	Time deposit	Penalty yield charges for early withdrawal	Processing costs and interest expense
Maturity of 31 days or longer	No Rate ceilings	Time deposit	Penalty yield charges for early withdrawal	Processing costs and interest expense

as the account maintains an average balance of $2500 per month. Currently banks are limited in the interest rate they can offer on NOW accounts whose average balance is less than $2500.

Banks have marketed bundled-service accounts, which offer a package of services in addition to transaction services, since the early 1970s. The types of services frequently included in the package are unlimited checking, free checks, free traveler's and cashier's checks, safe deposit boxes, credit card services, overdraft protection, check guarantee cards, and reduced rates on certain types of consumer loans. The purpose of such accounts is to offer services that are attractive to a large number of consumers, thereby increasing a bank's deposits as well as its lending services. Banks have also marketed services to particular segments of the market such as senior citizens or young consumers.[8]

Deposit accounts that offer retail customers explicit interest payments include transaction accounts (NOWs, Super NOWs, and money market deposit accounts), traditional savings accounts, and time deposits. Although traditional savings accounts are still offered, high rates of inflation and regulatory changes have rendered these accounts a minor source of funding for today's banks.

Time deposits can be classified into three groups. Banks can offer market rates on all time deposits that have a maturity of more than 31 days regardless of balance. On accounts with maturities of from 7 to 31 days, market rates can be offered on deposits of $2500 or more. Time deposits with maturities of from 7 to 31 days with balances of less than $2500 are subject to a maximum rate of 5½ percent.

The above classification is much simplified from the previous classification that included fixed-rate, variable-rate, and unregulated-rate categories. Previous regulations created an elaborate structure based on minimum balance, maturity, and purpose of the account.[9]

Under current regulation banks are able to offer market rates with very few restrictions. Specialized types of accounts that have an attractive market potential are the IRA agreement and Keogh (H.R. 10) plans. These individual retirement accounts offer the retail customer the advantage of shielding income from current taxes. Changes in tax regulations have extended this privilege to virtually all individuals whether or not they are covered by other retirement plans. Banks are able to compete at market rates for these deposits.

From 1977 until the most recent regulatory changes, banks found themselves at a competitive disadvantage. The growth of money market mutual funds and specialized accounts, such as Merrill Lynch's Cash

---

[8]For specific examples of such accounts see T. W. Thompson et al., *Banking Tomorrow: Managing Markets Through Planning* (New York: Van Nostrand Reinhold, 1978).

[9]An example of a special purpose account was the All-Savers Certificate, which was offered until December 1982. Banks were able to offer this special account at a variable rate set in accordance with the Treasury bill rate. Interest on the account was not subject to federal taxes for the depositor.

Management Account, drained deposit funds, and regulations did not allow banks to compete for funds through traditional deposit sources.

Several innovative accounts appeared during this period that were designed to skirt regulations. Most of these accounts, which were designed to avoid interest rate ceilings, have become unnecessary with the recent money market deposit account authorization. Examples included the retail repurchase agreement, check-access certificate of deposit, and an automatic transfer account, which was proposed by Master Charge International.[10] The need for these innovative accounts has disappeared with regulatory changes.

The competition for deposits has changed the structure of retail deposits. Retail customers have minimized transaction balances and have become more aware of interest rates in selecting deposit services. Banks competing for deposit funds in the market must design accounts that will meet the needs of their customers and at the same time be cost effective.

Revenue

Revenue from retail deposits can be classified as explicit and implicit. Explicit revenue arises from service charges or fees collected by a bank for services rendered. The most significant component of explicit revenue arises from transaction accounts, although charges for excessive withdrawals on savings accounts are commonly imposed. Implicit revenue arises from earnings on the balances a bank can invest. The balances that can be invested depend on the average balances maintained in the account and the reserve requirements that apply to the funds.

Service charges for transaction accounts involve a pricing decision between monthly maintenance fees and charges for each check processed. The pricing decision has an effect on the behavior of the individual account. A service charge that assesses a monthly maintenance fee with no charge for individual items encourages account holders to write larger numbers of checks. A service charge that charges per item encourages account holders to minimize the number of checks written.[11]

Most banks use a conditional pricing arrangement for transaction accounts. Conditional pricing involves charges for transaction services

---

[10]The list of innovative accounts is not meant to be complete. During the period many different types of automatic transfer or sweep accounts were designed to skirt regulation. With the change in regulations, most accounts of this type have disappeared.

[11]For an analysis of how pricing affects the type of customers a bank attracts, see Constance Dunham, "Unraveling the Complexity of NOW Account Pricing," *New England Economic Review, Federal Reserve Bank of Boston*, May-June 1983: 30–45. The article uses examples to illustrate trends in NOW account pricing and considers issues a bank must consider in developing pricing schemes for transaction accounts. We investigate the topic of pricing in greater detail in Chapter 18.

that are based on an average or a minimum balance maintained in the account over the statement period. A common example is no charge for checking services if the average balance exceeds $X; if the average balance is less than $X, a maintenance fee and a per-item charge are assessed.

The service charges are based on an analysis of the earnings credit on the average balances. An earnings credit is calculated by multiplying the average balance on an account that the bank can invest by the average spread on the bank's loans and investments. The revenue from investment of the funds plus the service charges collected on the account represents the total revenue from the account. Expenses for maintenance and processing transactions on the account are subtracted from the total revenue to determine net income. The service charges depend on the average balance of the account, and banks typically price the services in relation to the average or the minimum balance over the statement period.

Commercial banks also offer special checking accounts for retail customers who do not have large numbers of monthly transactions. Service charges on such accounts are for each item, such as $.15 to $.25 per check. Banks commonly also set some minimum charge per month to recover at least a portion of the expenses associated with this type of account.

Since the early 1970s banks have offered bundled-service accounts. Revenue on such accounts is usually based on a flat fee per month. Maintenance fees on such accounts typically range from $3 to $5 per month. As in regular checking account services, banks can also use a combination minimum- or average-balance and maintenance-fee arrangement. When a bank employs such a pricing scheme, the minimum balance for no-charge checking typically exceeds the minimum balance in a similar arrangement for a regular account, as the bank must cover the expenses associated with the additional service. That is, the revenue from the earnings credit and service charges must be large enough to cover the additional expenses of the services provided.

By packaging services, a bank might lose some revenue it would have received for services like safe deposit boxes that customers would otherwise purchase; but at the same time the package might include certain services that customers might not have purchased. Depending on the pricing, such an arrangement can increase revenue to the bank. The question of indirect revenue associated with the lending revenues included in the package of services further complicates the ability to determine the profitability on bundled accounts.

Service charges for interest-bearing transaction accounts involve the same basic trade-offs as noninterest-bearing accounts. The most common arrangements include some minimum- or average-balance and maintenance-fee or per-item charge. The minimum balance necessary to obtain no-charge checking is typically larger for interest-bearing NOW accounts, as the earnings credit is reduced by the interest paid on the account. To offset the costs of providing additional services, the minimum balance is also higher for no-charge checking on interest-bearing accounts that include bundled services.

Expenses

Expenses on all retail accounts include all costs associated with processing the accounts and interest paid on the funds deposited by retail customers. Processing costs include all of the costs associated with clearing checks and preparing and mailing monthly statements as well as the direct costs of services provided with the retail accounts. Interest expense for the various consumer accounts varies with the size and maturity of each deposit.

Measuring the operating expenses of providing transaction services is neither easy nor straightforward. Operating costs associated with delivering the services include the salaries of employees who spend a portion of their time delivering transaction services but who also perform other tasks not directly related to deposits. The Functional Cost Analysis (FCA), a computerized cost analysis program available to subscribing banks, is a system that allocates costs to the various functions a bank performs and develops measures of profitability for those functions.

Anderson has reported on the profitability of various functions for banks participating in the FCA program.[12] Results of his investigation indicate that the cost of processing each check is $0.30. Based on the average of 15 checks per month, the processing costs for an average account are $4.50, while the average service charge collected is $1.23. Thus, before consideration of revenue earned on funds the bank can invest in loans and securities, the cost not recovered with service fees is nearly $40 per year.[13]

Examination of the 1981 data from the FCA program also shows a similar pattern of expenses exceeding service charges. For personal transaction accounts, explicit revenue was less than expenses; losses ranged from $4 to $6 per month. When the earnings credit on average balances was considered, the accounts were profitable. Recent FCA

---

[12]Paul Anderson, "Cost and Profitability of Bank Functions," *New England Economic Review, Federal Reserve Bank of Boston,* March-April 1979: 43–61. The estimate of $.30 is based on both direct costs and indirect costs.

[13]This is based on an average of 15 checks per month and an average balance of $921. When revenue on the balances is considered, the accounts are still profitable but not as profitable as commercial demand-deposit accounts. See Anderson, ibid.

results confirm Anderson's findings that personal transaction accounts are less profitable than commercial accounts.[14]

As movement toward explicit interest on transaction accounts continues, banks will have to increase revenue or decrease expenses to maintain the same degree of profitability on transaction accounts. The increase in interest expense must be offset. Options to increase revenue include increasing service charges or increasing the balances that the bank can invest. Evidence from recent FCA figures indicates that a larger earnings credit for average accounts, which indicates a larger minimum balance, is being required for no-charge transaction services.[15]

Several options are available to banks to reduce expenses incurred in offering transaction services. These options include use of electronic funds transfer (EFT), check truncation, and automated clearing. EFT involves the transfer of funds via electronic wire rather than by paper entry. Operating expenses can be reduced if transfer expenses via EFT are less costly than processing paper transactions. Examples of EFT types of processing include automated clearing services, check truncation, point-of-sale systems, and automated teller machines.

Check truncation involves abbreviating the flow of paper checks through the payment-processing system. Various levels of truncation are possible. The most sophisticated truncation system stops the flow at the point of entry to the payment system, with the remaining transfer of funds being done electronically. The bank in which the check was first deposited microfilms the check and stores the actual check for a limited period. Less sophisticated systems truncate the flow of paper at the bank on which the check is drawn. This process eliminates returning the check to the customer by mail. The depositor's bank retains the actual check for a limited period and provides customers with photocopies of their checks if they are requested. Check truncation, if offered to satisfy customers, can appreciably lower the costs of providing services. For example, mailing costs in recent years have increased at a rate twice that of the consumer price index. The savings realized by reducing the number of items mailed can be considerable.

A Colorado bank holding company provides an example of the reduction in operating expenses available from a partial check-truncation

[14]A warning must be made concerning interpretation of FCA figures. The sample of participating banks is not representative of the population of commercial banks. The figures are dominated by smaller commercial banks, as only 65 of the 614 participating banks had deposits in excess of $200 million. The basic results of Anderson's study are confirmed by the most recent figures, indicating that banks' service charges are less than the expenses of providing services. The accounts are still profitable when earnings credits are considered.

[15]The larger earnings credit can arise from two factors: larger average balances and higher yields on earnings assets. Given the high levels of rates in 1981, some of the higher earnings credits are attributed to higher yields.

system.[16] The holding company has been able to increase its earnings $100,000 a year by reducing the number of checks it returns to customers. The holding company estimates that it costs $.02 per check to return checks to customers by mail. With 30 percent of its regular accounts converted to the truncated service, the holding company has eliminated the mailing of 5 million items per year.

Automated clearing systems have been in existence since the early 1970s. Under automated clearing, instructions for deposits to or payments from a depositor's accounts are transmitted by electronic tape rather than by individual deposits or checks. A common example of automated clearing is the direct-deposit system used by the federal government to make Social Security payments.[17] Rather than mailing individual checks to recipients, the government deposits payments directly in the recipient's bank account. Instructions for the payments are processed through the clearinghouse on magnetic tape, eliminating the handling of individual deposits and reducing processing costs.

Debit processing of payments from consumer accounts is an area of potential growth that could reduce processing costs. Although automation has been used extensively for payments of a fixed amount, such as mortgage loans and insurance payments, future uses of debit processing for payments of uneven amounts could further cut processing costs by reducing the handling of individual checks. Giro systems (bill-paying systems), in which depositors authorize automated payments, are beginning to be used more extensively.[18] Phone bill-paying systems and some electronic home computer bill-paying systems are currently operating.

As technology develops, extensive use of electronic funds transfer systems and automated clearing systems offers potential reductions in service costs. If operating expenses are not reduced, banks will have to charge more for services. The evidence from the introduction of NOW accounts indicates that banks have increased charges to consumers for transaction services. The primary means of increasing pricing has been to raise the minimum balance necessary to obtain no-cost checking, with service charges imposed as a penalty.[19] Analysis of NOW accounts indicates that, for banks to break even, larger balances are necessary as the interest rate paid on such accounts increases.[20]

---

[16]Roger Reisher and Dennis Barrett, "$100,000 Savings from Check Truncation System," *ABA Banking Journal*, November 1981: 142–145.

[17]C. M. Gambs, "Automated Clearinghouse: Current Status and Prospects," *Economic Review, Federal Reserve Board of Kansas City*, May 1978: 3–16.

[18]Ibid.

[19]D. G. Simonson and P. C. Marks, "Breakeven Analysis on NOW Accounts: Perils in Pricing," in *Funds Management Under Deregulation*, ed G. H. Hempel (Washington DC: American Bankers Association, 1981), 201–209.

[20]Ibid.

Future Retail Accounts

As the changes mandated by the DIDMCA are put into effect and as banks compete with other financial institutions for retail deposits, the services offered and the costs of those services will change drastically. If a bank pays money market rates for its deposit funds, the costs of providing such services will have to be recovered. To be competitive, transaction services will have to be provided efficiently. Increased use of automated transfer of funds and check truncation is likely to become commonplace.

Rather than offering the bundled-service accounts that grew out of regulation, banks will find that the retail accounts of the future might be constructed much more like commercial accounts. Services might be provided cafeteria style.[21] Consumers will pay only for services they actually choose to use. The future account might be constructed with earnings credits on collected balances and charges for services used by the retail customer.

It is clear that transaction services and the basic character of retail deposits will change greatly in the coming years. The more innovative and efficient a bank is in providing desirable services, the greater will be its ability to effectively compete for retail deposits.

WHOLESALE DEPOSITS: CHARACTERISTICS

Wholesale deposits can be classified into three major groups: commercial and industrial, governmental units, and other financial institutions. Like retail deposits, wholesale deposits consist of both traditional deposits and interest-bearing time deposits. As displayed in Exhibit 6.5, (see pages 118–119), more varied services are provided for wholesale depositors. In general, the overall account relationship of both lending and deposit services is more closely integrated in wholesale deposits than in retail deposits. The level of deposits carried by a commercial customer might be determined by lending arrangements. Consequently, the calculation of expenses and revenues from wholesale accounts is much more complicated than for retail accounts because of this broader account relationship. Overall expenses and revenues from deposits and loans are combined to analyze profitability on wholesale accounts.

---

[21]For a discussion on the influence of prohibition of payment of interest on demand deposits, see F. E. Morris, "The Costs of Price Controls in Banking," *New England Economic Review, Federal Reserve Bank of Boston,* May-June 1979: 49–54. Often inefficiencies such as overbranching were also influenced by regulation. With elimination of price controls, we will also probably see significant reductions in branches or in the services offered at branches.

Commercial and Industrial Deposits

Demand deposits for nonfinancial businesses have averaged slightly over 50 percent of commercial banks' demand deposits in recent years. This compares with approximately 33 percent for consumer demand deposits. Commercial demand deposits are therefore the most significant source of demand deposits.

Services provided in connection with commercial demand deposits include traditional transaction services, collection and disbursement, electronic funds transfers, payroll services, investment services, and foreign exchange services. Much of the compensation commercial firms pay for these services is in the form of compensating balances. A recent study of large corporate customers indicated that approximately 85 percent of the compensation for services was in the form of compensating balances.[22] The services used most often included electronic funds transfers, short-term-investment services, and collection services.[23]

Because much of the compensation for services rendered by banks in connection with deposit services is in the form of compensating balances, the average balance for commercial and industrial accounts is much larger, with the average ledger balance for commercial accounts approximately $9000. Additionally, such accounts are much more profitable than retail demand deposits.[24] Because of the importance of the overall relationship of both deposit and lending services, determination of profitability on demand deposit accounts is really a part of the overall customer profitability analysis.

The other major source of deposit funds from commercial and industrial firms is large negotiable CDs. Large corporations use CDs in cash management. Given that firms are usually continually investing surplus balances, an active secondary market is desirable. CDs issued by money center banks offer the greatest marketability. Large CDs therefore are more important for large money center banks.

Governmental Unit Deposits

Banks also obtain deposit funds from federal, state, and local governmental units. Services provided to state and local governments are more extensive than those provided for federal government accounts. State and local government accounts are similar to commercial accounts in terms of customer relationships. Deposits in excess of the insured amounts must be protected by pledged securities in most states, although the requirements vary widely from state to state.

---

[22]L. J. Gitman, E. A. Moses, and I. T. White, "An Assessment of Corporate Cash Management Practices," *Financial Management*, Spring 1979: 32–41.

[23]Ibid.

[24]Anderson, op. cit.

EXHIBIT 6.5 Characteristics of Wholesale Accounts

	Characteristics	Services Provided	Revenues	Expenses
Commercial and Industrial Deposits				
Demand deposits	Traditional transaction services, typical for minimum-balance requirement that is related to service	Transaction services, collection and dispursement services, electronic funds transfer, cash management, zero-balance accounts, investment management, foreign exchange services, etc.	Compensating minimum balance and for-fee-based pricing on services; compensating balance typically tied to lending arrangements	Processing and servicing costs for all services provided
Certificates of deposit	Large negotiable CDs at money market rates with varying maturities	Traditional certificate of deposit		Interest determined by money market rates, processing costs
Governmental Unit Deposits State and local governments				
Demand deposits	Traditional transaction services, typical for minimum balance requirement	Transaction services, collection and dispursement services, electronic funds transfer, cash management, investment management, etc.	Compensating balance and/or for-fee-based pricing on services	Processing and servicing costs of all services provided; pledging requirements possibly requiring greater holdings of investment securities

Interest-bearing deposits Time deposits	Interest-bearing deposits currently subject to Regulation Q requirements	Traditional time deposits		Processing costs and interest costs. Pledging requirements possibly requiring greater holdings of investment securities
Treasury deposits Treasury tax and loan accounts	Deposits that Treasury transfers on demand	Collection of tax receipts and proceeds of sales of certain Treasury securities	Service fees paid on schedule by Treasury	Processing costs and interest fees if note option is elected
Deposits of Other Financial Institutions				
Demand deposits of correspondent banks	Balances required for services provided	Check clearing, loan participation, investment services, general management services	Compensating balance and/or fee income for services provided	Processing and servicing costs for all services provided
Balances of foreign banks and central banks of foreign countries	Balances required for services provided	Transaction services related to international banking	Fees on compensating balance	Processing costs for all services provided

U.S. Treasury Deposits.   Treasury tax and loan (TTL) accounts serve as depositories for taxes collected on behalf of the U.S. Treasury, including withheld income taxes, corporate taxes, Social Security taxes, and federal unemployment taxes. Proceeds of sales of U.S. Treasury securities, particularly savings bonds, are also collected in these accounts.

Until 1978 banks could use these funds until the Treasury withdrew the funds from the banks and placed them in accounts at Federal Reserve banks. The deposits served as compensation for services provided to the Treasury for collecting its payments. A study by the Treasury in 1974 indicated that banks were being overcompensated for services because of increasing market rates, resulting in the legislation passed in 1977.[25] Under the new legislation the Treasury earns interest on funds left at banks.

Two options exist for handling TTL accounts: a remittance option and a note option. Under the remittance option a bank must forward, after one business day, all receipts in the TTL account to the Treasury's account at the appropriate Federal Reserve bank. During the day those funds are held at the bank, they are subject to reserve requirements at the bank's rate for demand deposits. Under the note option the bank agrees to transfer the previous day's receipts to an interest-paying note account, which is payable on demand of the Treasury. The rate paid on the note is 25 basis points below the prevailing weekly average federal fund rate. The Treasury compensates the bank directly by paying fees for services provided under either option.[26]

Deposits from State and Local Governmental Units.   Banks also secure deposits from state and local governmental units. Deposits can be in the form of demand deposits or interest-bearing time deposits. As with commercial deposits, the level of state and local deposits is a function of the services provided to the governmental units.

Deposits of state and local units typically require that the bank collateralize deposits in excess of the amount insured by the FDIC. Requirements vary from state to state as to what securities are eligible to be pledged against the deposits and what percentage of the excess amount must be backed by collateral.[27] In making a decision to secure such deposits, management must consider the profitability of the deposits compared with the pledging requirements, which could restrict either the bank's investment policy or its liquidity position. If a bank uses

---

[25]R. W. Lang, "TTL Note Accounts and the Money Supply Process," *Review, Federal Reserve Bank of St. Louis,* October 1979: 3–14.

[26]Ibid.

[27]For a thorough discussion of the various pledging requirements and their effect on bank liquidity and lending policies, see R. Ratti, "Pledging Requirements and Bank Asset Portfolios," *Economic Review, Federal Reserve Bank of Kansas City,* September-October 1979: 13–23.

securities it currently holds to meet pledging requirements, then the bank's liquidity is reduced. If the bank purchases additional securities to meet the requirements, profitability could be affected in that funds might be diverted away from loans that offer higher rates of return.[28]

The rates offered on state and local governmental time deposits are subject to little regulation. Currently only deposits of less than $2500 are subject to Regulation Q. On these deposits a ceiling of 8 percent applies.

Deposits of Other Financial Institutions

Banks also hold deposits of other financial institutions, which include correspondent banks and foreign central banks. The most significant and important category of these deposits is that of the correspondent bank balances. Correspondent bank balances arise from the market for interbank services and transactions. Just as nonfinancial corporations hold balances at banks to compensate for services rendered, banks hold balances at other banks to compensate for services rendered. Banks typically establish several correspondent relationships and may use different correspondent banks for different services.

The services offered by correspondent banks range from traditional check clearing to management consulting related to the management of the respondent bank. Among the services reported as most important are loan participation, check clearing, securities safekeeping, and federal funds transactions. Larger banks can offer smaller banks services they cannot efficiently provide for themselves. Larger banks also benefit by loan participation and by borrowing excess funds from smaller banks through the federal funds market.

Many of the services provided through the correspondent bank system are also offered through the Federal Reserve System. Traditionally services such as check clearing and cash services were offered to Federal Reserve System members at no charge. Since passage of the DIDMCA in 1980, the Fed charges for its services, which are available to both members and nonmembers. Services that must be priced include currency and coin services, check clearing and collection services, electronic transfer services, automated clearinghouse services, settlement services, securities safekeeping, Federal Reserve float, and any new service the Fed offers.[29] The DIDMCA called for the Fed to publish a list of prices it intended to charge within 6 months of the act's introduction and to begin charging for services September 30, 1981.

---

[28]Ratti, op. cit., provides some evidence that pledging requirements do have a negative effect on bank liquidity and do divert some funds away from loans.

[29]Federal Reserve Bank of Chicago, *Depository Institutions Deregulation and Monetary Control Act of 1980: A Summary* (Washington, DC: Federal Reserve Board, March 1980).

Under the traditional system, member banks could obtain services at no charge from the Fed or through correspondents. To obtain services through the correspondent system required that correspondents be compensated. Several studies have analyzed the practices of member banks and found that many member banks do not extensively use the Fed. This is particularly true for larger banks.[30] Services were offered more efficiently through the correspondent system. How effective a competitor the Federal Reserve System will be under explicit pricing remains to be seen, but several authors predict that it will attempt to maintain its market share in the payments-clearing system.[31]

Analysis of revenues and expenses associated with correspondent balances is very similar to profitability analysis of commercial accounts. (Chapter 18 contains a detailed explanation of that analysis.) To assess revenues from these deposits, management estimates the yield on collected funds after making allowance for reserves that must be held against the deposits.[32] Expenses include expenses for services rendered to secure the deposits. Normally an earnings credit is estimated and charges are made against that credit for services rendered. Because the services provided for correspondent balances are significant, the expenses associated with those deposits are also significant.[33]

Primary compensation for correspondent services takes the form of compensating balances. A recent study of correspondent banking practices indicates that more than 80 percent of the compensation for services is in the form of correspondent balances held; the remainder is in the form of fees.[34]

With changes in the competitive environment and changes in regulations, future types of correspondent bank services and the costs of such services could be significantly different. Some banks are competing very effectively for correspondent services, and many are considering offering expanded types of services in the future. For example, Continental Illinois Bank has 2800 respondent banks and clears as many checks as the Federal Reserve Bank of Cleveland.[35] A greater concentration in correspondent bank services is possible as new technology is

---

[30]B. J. Summers, "Correspondent Services, Federal Reserve Services and Bank Cash Management Policy," *Economic Review, Federal Reserve Bank of Richmond,* November-December 1978: 29–38.

[31]For examples, see P. Merrill, "Big Change Foreseen in Correspondent's Share of the Market," *ABA Banking Journal,* January 1981: 97–103; and B. Streeter, "The Fed Faces a Tough Competitor in Continental," *ABA Banking Journal,* November 1981: 75–82.

[32]R. E. Knight, "Account Analysis in Correspondent Banking," *Monthly Review, Federal Reserve Bank of Kansas City,* March 1976: 11–20.

[33]For an analysis of costs, see C. Dunham, "Commercial Bank Cost and Correspondent Banking," *New England Economic Review, Federal Reserve Bank of Boston,* September-October 1981: 22–36.

[34]Ibid.

[35]Streeter, op. cit.

introduced and correspondents compete with the Fed for check-clearing services.

Management of the Deposit Function

The principal responsibilities in managing the deposit function are the coordination of deposit activities related to meeting bank objectives and the planning and execution of strategies for obtaining and retaining funds; the latter includes setting interest rates, managing and controlling transaction-processing systems, and developing product lines and setting them into operation. As a member of the asset/liability management committee, the manager must be sensitive to the types of customer markets served and the pricing of products according to estimated demand. The manager must also be concerned with structuring customer-contact areas that are both convenient and cost effective. Training employees to deliver services and process transactions is an ongoing management function. If the manager can accomplish the responsibilities outlined above, the deposit function can provide sources of funds at reasonable processing and interest rate costs.

OVERVIEW OF OPERATION: DEPOSIT SUMMARY

Deposit processing involves opening new accounts and processing checks, deposits, and withdrawals on customers' accounts. The overall process involves recording the individual transactions of all accounts and processing them so that the transactions are reflected in the individual accounts and summarized in the bank's books to indicate totals in the various types of deposit accounts.

Exhibit 6.6 displays an overview of deposit processing from the opening of new accounts to the bank's general bookkeeping system, indicating the interrelationships of the various functions or departments. New accounts and teller operations are areas of customer contact, whereas the remaining areas are back-room operations that require no direct customer contact. These operations process individual transactions, record the transactions on individual customers' accounts, and generate overall statements for the bank.

The structure of each department or function displayed in Exhibit 6.6 depends on the volume of transactions, the number of separate banking facilities, and the geographic dispersion of the facilities. Significant differences between large and small banks are found in regard to the structure of functions and degree of automation employed in the processing of deposit transactions. Generally, large banks with large volumes of transactions can profitably employ highly automated processing equipment, whereas smaller banks with smaller volumes of transactions

EXHIBIT 6.6   Overview of Deposit Processing

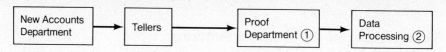

New Accounts Department	Tellers	Proof Department ①	Data Processing ②
Open New Accounts	Accept deposits, withdrawals, bond coupons	Encode dollar values on checks and deposits	**Set up New Accounts**
Checking: Inform customers about types of and charges for accounts	Cash checks	Balance deposit transactions	Demand deposit accounts (DDA): Check on-us and sort deposits
Assist customers in selecting account type	Issue traveler's checks, cashier's checks, money orders, advances on credit cards	Sort checks, drafts, etc., into on-us, local clearings, Federal Reserve, and transit	Update customers' DDA records
Send check order to vendor	Process mail-in deposits, night depository bags, armored car deliveries, change orders, bulk payroll deposits	Batch on-us and transit Federal Reserve checks for computer sorting ②	Create DDA trial balance
Complete signature cards			Transmit checks, deposit slips, and trial balance to bookkeeping ⑥
Obtain resolutions for authorized signatures if corporation, partnership, or trust	Transmit deposit items (checks, deposit slips, cash-in and -out tickets, etc.) to proof department ①	Transmit drafts and other noncheck items to cash items ⑤	Savings and time deposits: Process savings and time transactions
		Receive and encode general ledger tickets	Update trial balance
Savings and time deposits: Inform customer of account types and regulations		Balance bank's debit and credit transactions by department and general ledger categories daily	Transmit items and trial balance to savings and time deposit department
Provide savings register or certificate of deposit		Prepare proof recap of daily transactions and transmit to accounting ④ with general ledger tickets	Prepare interest statements periodically
Complete signature cards			Prepare year-end interest statements
Obtain resolutions for authorized signatures		Receive in-clearings from local banks and correspondent banks	Transit items for Federal Reserve: Sort checks for clearing on transit routing symbol to obtain immediate or deferred credit
All deposits: Code new account entries and transmit to data processing ②			Transmit sort and listing to transit ③
Deposit customer funds with teller			
Handle Customers' Inquiries			
Solve problems on request (balancing, stop payments, etc.)			
Perform Cross-Selling Services			
Inform customer of other bank services			

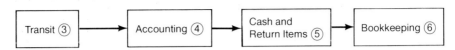

Transit ③ → **Accounting ④** → **Cash and Return Items ⑤** → **Bookkeeping ⑥**

Prepare cash letters for transmittals to Federal Reserve Bank, local banks, and correspondent banks

Microfilm cash letters and items

Transmit cash letter

Prepare daily statements for management

File and control bank expense checks

File and control cashier's checks and money orders

File general ledger tickets

Cash Items:

For drafts, coupons, bonds, and other transactions not acceptable to normal check collection process; prepare and send transmittal letters to collection sources

Returned Items:

For customer overdrafts, send checks to account officer for approval/ disapproval for payment

If disapproved, return to presenting banks and charge fee to customers' accounts

If approved, reprocess against customers' accounts to override insufficient-fund edit ①

Process Other Irregularities:

Missing endorsements, accounts closed, stop payments drawn on uncollected funds, etc.

Prepare appropriate general ledger and customer account entries

Reconcile proof recap totals with DDA trial balance

Transmit unprocessed checks to cash and return items ⑤ including uncollected funds and insufficient funds

Trace reasons for and correct missorts; send to proof department ①

Send adjusting entries to accounting ④ for account reclassification

Match customers' statements, deposit slips, and checks; mail to customers

do not have sufficient volume to employ fully automated processing equipment. The geographic dispersion of the banks also has a significant effect on the structure of functions and the automation in processing equipment. A large, statewide, branching bank will employ structures different from those of a large unit bank with essentially one physical facility.

The new accounts department or function is responsible for opening accounts, informing customers about different types of accounts, and securing the necessary documentation and agreements to open the accounts. The process includes obtaining signature cards, ordering checks, and processing the initial deposits. The new accounts personnel are also responsible for cross-selling other services the bank has available for customers.

The degree of specialization in the function depends on bank size. In a very small bank one individual may be responsible for processing both consumer and commercial new accounts. In larger banks with larger volumes of transactions, consumer and commercial new accounts are handled separately. This specialization allows greater efficiency in informing customers of the various services available and in the cross-selling of services available on consumer and commercial accounts. Servicing of commercial accounts may be physically separated from retail service by housing the commercial new accounts function on a separate floor or, in branching operations, servicing commercial accounts in a limited number of the larger branches. Again, the degree of specialization depends on volume of business.

Tellers are responsible for accepting deposits and withdrawals, cashing checks, issuing traveler's checks, and processing items such as mail-in deposits and change orders. Tellers transmit deposits, checks, cash-in and cash-out tickets, and the like to the proof department for processing.

Organization of tellers' functions also varies with the size of the banking operation. Functions can be specialized to handle special types of transactions to increase efficiency and provide greater convenience for customers. Examples of specialization in the tellers' functions include specialized commercial tellers, who handle only commercial transactions; express tellers, who handle routine deposits and withdrawals but not lengthy transactions such as issuing traveler's checks and certified checks; and drive-up-window tellers, who handle routine transactions.

With the advances in EFT systems, routine transactions can also be handled through automated teller machines (ATMs) at the banking facility. Delivery of service to customers is designed to improve convenience by allowing customers to transact their business in the least amount of time. Increased use of ATMs allows the extension of banking service hours for customers with routine transactions. In states that allow off-site ATMs (typically states with restrictive branching laws), it is possible to deliver teller services electronically at various distances from the actual banking facility.

The first step in back-room processing of deposits takes place in the proof department, where dollar values are encoded on checks, withdrawals, and deposits. In the proof department, checks are roughly sorted into basic categories for the data-processing department, which typically does the fine sorting of items. The proof operation sorts such items as on-us checks, local clearings, Federal Reserve and other transit items, and nonroutine items such as drafts and coupon bonds not acceptable to normal check collection.

Routine items like checks drawn on the bank, on-us checks, and deposits are sorted in data processing. Customer deposit records are updated in savings and demand-deposit accounts, and checks drawn on customers' accounts are recorded with the customer statement information prepared and sent to the bookkeeping department. Checks not drawn on the bank are sorted by routing symbols to obtain immediate or deferred credit. These sorted items are then sent to the transit department.

The transit department then prepares cash letters[36] for transmittal to Federal Reserve banks, local banks, and correspondent banks. Through this process checks drawn on outside banks are actually cleared. Checks and cash letters are microfilmed and actual cash letters are transmitted.

Cash items[37] and returned items require special processing. Cash items such as drafts must be prepared and sent for collection. Returned items include checks that exceed customers' deposit amounts, overdrafts, and checks deposited by the bank's customers that have been returned unpaid by outside banks. Customer overdrafts must be approved for payment and the information recorded in the customers' accounts and appropriate charges made to the customers' accounts. Appropriate adjustments are made for items returned by outside banks.

SUMMARY

Managing a bank's portfolio of borrowed funds is referred to as liability management. Borrowed funds include deposits and other short-term borrowings that banks secure in the money markets. Deposits, which include demand, savings, and time deposits, are the largest source of funding for banks. The mix of deposits and other borrowed funds affects the

---

[36]Cash letters are, in effect, deposit documents that accompany checks to be collected from other banks.

[37]Cash items are transactions that are similar to checks but require special handling and cannot be processed through normal check-clearing channels. Cash items include drafts, bond coupons, and foreign exchange.

volatility of a bank's cost of funds. In recent years bank deposits have become more interest sensitive, which complicates overall management.

Banks secure deposit funds from two major groups of customers: retail customers and wholesale customers. Deposits of retail customers include traditional demand deposits and interest-bearing savings and time deposits. Retail deposits have become increasingly interest sensitive, and the characteristics of retail deposits have changed significantly in recent years. Wholesale deposits include demand and time deposits secured from commercial firms, governmental units, and other banks. In general, banks provide broader services for wholesale customers, and the level of demand deposits for these customers is determined by the level of services provided to them. Wholesale customers are sources of time deposits primarily in the form of negotiable certificates of deposit.

Changes in regulations and market conditions have drastically altered the deposit structure of banks in the last three decades. When the changes mandated by the DIDMCA are fully in place, deposit characteristics will be unregulated. Banks face formidable challenges in redesigning deposit specifications to meet the demands of the marketplace. When explicit interest is paid on most deposits, banks will be required to charge higher rates for services, curtail services, or reduce the cost of delivering services to maintain profitability. Product redesign in retail deposits is the most pressing area in the immediate future.

Questions and Problems

1. Define *bundled-service account.*

2. As banks move to a market in which interest rates are not restricted by Regulation Q, what potential changes are likely in deposit services?

3. Describe the options available for a bank in handling Treasury tax and loan deposits.

4. Describe the trend in deposit mix and operating-interest expense from 1950 to the present.

5. Define *check truncation* and *automated clearinghouse.*

6. Identify the basic steps involved in processing a check drawn on another bank and deposited by a customer of our bank. How would that process be simplified if both parties were depositors of our bank?

References

American Bankers Association. "CHIPS Clears Same Day, at $200 Billion on a Day." *ABA Banking Journal,* November 1981: 84–86.

Anderson, P. S. "Cost and Profitability of Bank Functions." *New England Economic Review, Federal Reserve Bank of Boston,* March-April 1979: 43–61.

Bank Administration Institute. *Bank Administration Manual.* Vols. I & II. Park Ridge, IL: Bank Administration Institute, 1974.

Baughn, W. H., and C. E. Walker, eds. The *Bankers' Handbook.* 2d ed. Homewood, IL: Dow Jones-Irwin, 1978.

Bowsher, N. N. "Repurchase Agreements." *Review, Federal Reserve Bank of St. Louis,* September 1979: 17–22.

Dince, R. R., and J. A. Verbrugge. "The Rush to Retail Repos." In *The Bankers' Handbook,* 2d ed., ed. W. H. Baughn and C. E. Walker, 77–82. Homewood, IL: Dow Jones-Irwin, 1978.

Dunham, C. "Commercial Bank Costs and Correspondent Banking." *New England Economic Review, Federal Reserve Bank of Boston,* September-October 1981: 22–36.

Dunham, C. "Unraveling the Complexity of NOW Account Pricing." *New England Economic Review, Federal Reserve Bank of Boston,* May-June 1983: 30–45.

Federal Reserve Bank of Chicago. *Depository Institutions Deregulation and Monetary Control Act of 1980: A Summary.* Washington, DC: Federal Reserve Board, March 1980.

Federal Reserve Bank of Kansas City. "Financial Developments in 1981." *Financial Letter of Federal Reserve Bank of Kansas City,* (no. 1, Jan. 28, 1982).

Federal Reserve Bank of New York. *Annual Report: 1981, Federal Reserve Bank of New York,* Dec. 31, 1981: 1–36.

Feinstein, M. "Advice From the Northeast: You Can Live With NOW's Profitably." *ABA Banking Journal,* August 1980: 40–45.

Furash, E. E. "The Not-So-Obvious Impact of Inflation." *ABA Banking Journal,* July 1980: 87–89.

Furlong, F. T. "New Deposit Instruments." *Federal Reserve Bulletin,* May 1983: 319–326.

Gambs, C. M. "Automated Clearinghouses—Current Status and Prospects." *Economic Review, Federal Reserve Bank of Kansas City,* May 1978: 3–16.

Gilbert, R. A. "Effects of Interest Rates on Demand Deposits—Implications of Compensating Balances." *Review, Federal Reserve Bank of St. Louis,* November 1977: 8–15.

Gitman, L. J., E. A. Moses, and I. T. White. "An Assessment of Corporate Cash Management Practices." *Financial Management,* Spring 1979: 32–41.

Goodfriend, M. "Eurodollars." In *Instruments of the Money Market,* ed. T. Q. Cook and B. J. Summers. Richmond, VA: Federal Reserve Bank of Richmond, 1981.

Gushee, J. W. H. "Correspondent Bank Services." In *The Bankers' Handbook,* 2d ed., ed. W. E. Baughn and C. E. Walker, 973–989. Homewood, IL: Dow Jones-Irwin, 1978.

Hayes, D. A. "Retail Banking in an Interest Sensitive World." *Bankers Magazine,* July-August 1980. Reprinted in *Funds Management Under Deregulation,* ed. G. H. Hempel, 368–375. Washington, DC: American Bankers Association, 1981.

Hervey, J. L. "Bankers Acceptance." *Business Conditions, Federal Reserve Bank of Chicago,* May 1976: 3–11.

Knight, R. E. "Account Analysis in Correspondent Banking." *Monthly Review, Federal Reserve Bank of Kansas City,* March 1976: 11–20.

Knight, R. E. "Customer Profitability Analysis." *Monthly Review, Federal Reserve Bank of Kansas City,* April 1975: 11–20.

Lang, R. W. "TTL Note Accounts and the Money Supply Process." *Review, Federal Reserve Bank of St. Louis,* October 1979: 3–14.

Lucas, C. M., M. T. Jones, and J. Thurston. "Federal Funds and Repurchase Agreements." *Quarterly Review, Federal Reserve Bank of New York,* Summer 1977: 33–48.

Mayer, M. "Merrill Lynch Quacks Like a Bank." *Fortune,* Oct. 20, 1980, 134–144.

Melton, W. C., and J. M. Mahr. "Banker's Acceptances." *Quarterly Review, Federal Reserve Bank of New York,* Summer 1981: 39–55.

Merrill, P. "Big Change Foreseen in Correspondent's Share of the Market." *ABA Banking Journal,* January 1981: 97–103.

Metzger, R. O. "Coping With the Cost of NOW's." *Bankers Magazine,* January-February 1981: 55–58.

Morris, F. E. "The Costs of Price Control in Banking." *New England Economic Review, Federal Reserve Bank of Boston,* May-June 1979: 49–54.

Motley, L. "Four Strategies for Pricing NOW's." In *Funds Management Under Deregulation,* ed. G. H. Hempel, 190–200. Washington, DC: American Bankers Association, 1981.

Ratti, R. A. "Pledging Requirements and Bank Asset Portfolios." *Economic Review, Federal Reserve Bank of Kansas City,* September-October 1979: 13–23.

Reisher, R. L., and D. E. Barrett. "$100,000 Savings from Check Truncation System." *ABA Banking Journal,* November 1981: 142–145.

Schaadt, P. "How to Compare Prices Between Correspondents." *ABA Banking Journal,* October 1981: 88–92.

Simonson, D. G., and P. C. Marks. "Breakeven Balances on NOW Accounts: Perils in Pricing." In *Funds Management Under Deregulation,* ed. G. H. Hempel, 201–209. Washington, DC: American Bankers Association, 1981.

Streeter, B. "The Fed Faces a Tough Competitor in Continental." *ABA Banking Journal,* November 1981: 75–82.

Summers, B. J. "Correspondent Services, Federal Reserve Services and Bank Cash Management Policy." *Economic Review, Federal Reserve Bank of Richmond,* November-December 1978: 29–38.

Summers, B. J. "Demand Deposits: A Comparison of Household and Business Balances." *Economic Review, Federal Reserve Bank of Richmond,* July-August 1979: 214.

Summers, B. J. "Negotiable Certificates of Deposit." *Economic Review, Federal Reserve Bank of Richmond,* July-August 1980: 8–19.

Thompson, T. W., L. L. Berry, and P. H. Davidson. *Banking Tomorrow: Managing Markets Through Planning.* New York: Van Nostrand Reinhold, 1978.

Weber, A. J. "New Concepts in Correspondent Banking." *Bankers Magazine,* January-February 1981: 74–76.

CHAPTER 7

Loan Administration and the Process of Lending

Loan administration involves the creation and management of risk assets. The process of lending takes into consideration the people and systems required for the evaluation and approval of loan requests, negotiation of terms, documentation, disbursement, administration of outstanding loans, and workouts. Knowledge of the process and awareness of its strengths and weaknesses are important in setting objectives and goals for lending activities and for allocating available funds to various lending functions such as commercial, installment, and mortgage portfolios.

The senior loan manager must be concerned with managing the process, including such mundane activities as documentation, maintaining credit files and records, and credit officer follow-through, to minimize the operational risks associated with lending.

Internal risks with which the manager must also be concerned include portfolio diversification, loan size, and number of loans. Undue concentration by industry, geography, or customer type submits the portfolio to nonperforming risks in the event, for example, that the particular industry experiences a downturn in economic activity. Loan repayment may be slowed, which results in the stagnation of future lending until the situation is worked out. Profits will also suffer since unforeseen losses usually will occur concurrent with the slowing of the industry's activity. If the lending terms do not provide for an orderly liquidation of outstanding loans, the bank may be faced with cash flow problems as well.

Loan size is governed by regulation for maximum loans to one borrower. The maximum loan to one borrower under national banking laws is 15 percent of capital. Bank policies may set lower limits on size and may require that oversized loans be partitioned. The "excess" loan portion may be sold to a correspondent bank under a participation agreement. The loan manager must monitor each large credit to ensure that the loan officer conforms each large request to bank policies.

The loan manager must also monitor the number of loans assigned to each loan officer. This ensures that the officer can effectively administer and monitor the loans under his supervision. If the number of loans is substantial, risk is increased because the officer may not be able to monitor all of the loans efficiently enough to exact performance.

In addition to monitoring the number of loans, the complexity and size of loans must be considered as well. If the loans are complex and require significant individual follow-up, fewer loans can be effectively handled by a single loan officer. Importantly, the object of controlling loan categories and limiting concentration is to prevent a single occurrence of loan default from having a significant adverse effect on the bank's profits and liquidity.

The lending process differs among commercial, consumer, and mortgage loans. The skill and expertise for lending in each type of portfolio differs. Accordingly, the risks, costs, profits, and effects of economic trends also differ and must be considered in portfolio allocation. This chapter is concerned with the different processes and, more specifically, with the support systems and policies that ensure overall effective loan administration, particularly with regard to commercial lending. Chapter 8 concentrates on the trends, policies, and practices for commercial lending. Chapter 9 is concerned with the systems and problems related to identifying and administering possible loan losses. The techniques discussed apply also to consumer and mortgage loan portfolios but concentrate on commercial loan portfolios. The lending chapters are completed with the examination of trends, policies, and practices for consumer loans (Chapter 10) and for mortgage loans (Chapter 11).

ELEMENTS OF LOAN ADMINISTRATION

The administration of loan portfolios may be divided into the general management objectives of planning, organizing, and controlling lending activities. Planning involves the consideration of the risks and returns of loans that meet profit objectives and the allocation of loan assets among commercial, installment, and mortgage loan portfolios. Organizing is putting planned objectives and goals into action through definition of policies and processes, including the establishment of support functions and the dissemination of services through the organizational structure. Controlling is the ongoing process of making and monitoring loans in a manner that maintains performance and attains profit objectives and goals.

Risks and Returns

Lending involves risk taking and includes assessment of default risk and interest rate risk. The assessment of default risk is performed by analyzing the creditworthiness of the borrower. Assessment of interest rate risk considers (1) changes in the level of interest rates over the expected life of the loan and (2) funding risk—the risk relating to the availability of fund sources to continue the funding of new and existing loans at interest rates that will ensure the continued profitability of the loan.

Loan pricing must be flexible to ensure adequate returns. The pricing must take into consideration the cost of funds, the default risks, and the costs associated with making and processing the loan. Commercial lending involves many more variables with regard to risk and costs of administering individual loans. Whereas consumer and mortgage loans are generally more standardized and incur approximately the same costs for each loan, with commercial loans all of the variables must be considered in each loan request.

Portfolio risk is the risk that overconcentration in a particular portfolio will lead to potential default problems in the event that a certain segment of the economy or a specific geographic location experiences economic difficulties. The minimization of portfolio risk leads to an orderly liquidation of loans with the proceeds shifted to new or better-quality loans. In this regard, theoretically, the bank can fund more profitable and less risky loans from loan runoff without seeking additional and more costly funds in a no-growth or recessionary scenario.

Limiting portfolio risk may include some of the following alternatives:

- Establish loan-size limits by type of borrower.
- Restrict credit to certain industries or types of borrowers to avoid undue concentration.
- Restrict credit in specific geographic areas where default risk may be greater due to locational or borrower difficulties.
- Use loan participations to reduce size and concentration of bank's borrower's requirements.
- Purchase participations to induce industry and borrower diversification.

Portfolio Allocation

Decisions regarding allocation of funds to specific portfolios take into consideration the capacity to handle specific types of loan requests and to conduct loan operations activities in support of loan requests, accounting for loans, and collecting loans. The loan portfolio administrator must consider the specific loan processes and their differences for commercial, consumer, and mortgage loans.

Other decisions include identifying the market for specific loans, the loan purposes that will be acceptable risks, personnel capabilities, pricing, funding sources, portfolio liquidation rates, and general and specific profit objectives. These factors will become part of a plan for current and future years and should be incorporated in a formal loan policy.

Numerous factors impact portfolio allocation. For example, a "large" bank in a small community must consider the balance of demand for commercial, consumer, and mortgage loans. The small bank in a small community may set different strategies, concentrating primarily on consumer loans and secondarily on commercial loans and ignoring mortgage lending. The large bank may set geographic, industry, and customer objectives that are totally different from those of a small to medium-size bank in a large city. The allocations and strategies depend on available funds, lending expertise, and support systems.

Some basic economic factors must be considered by senior loan administrators in allocating loan assets. An understanding of the national, regional, and local economic environment is important. For example, large corporations that produce consumer goods in a period of high product demand may expand their workforces or extend their working hours. Employees enjoy the additional income and are more likely to spend for consumer and housing products. Home building may also benefit. However, if the credit markets are constrained by high interest rates, consumers may defer spending for large-dollar products and/or housing. Understanding the linkage between the stage of the business cycle and its impact on consumer-oriented markets plays an important role in determining what emphasis should be placed on contraction or expansion of specific portfolios.

In expansionary periods of our economy we may find equal demand for commercial, consumer, and mortgage loans. The duration of the stage of the business cycle has varied significantly in recent years. This produces lagged-demand effects between businesses and consumers. For example, as interest rates remain high, businesses reduce production to decrease inventories and carrying costs. The consumer may absorb some inventories, but they may also defer spending and borrowing until interest rates turn lower. As business activity increases, businesses increase production, employment and income may increase, and with lower interest rates consumers are more willing to borrow and spend. However, these activities may occur over different periods of time.

If we concentrate on the interrelationships of the credit and business cycle, particularly with regard to commercial loans, we may better understand the lending strategies that may be adopted by bankers and consequently the effects of these strategies on overall portfolio allocation.

Linkage between the Credit and Business Cycle.   Some of the questions that might be asked in determining the risks associated with lending at various stages of the credit and business cycle are:

1. At which stage of the business cycle are we? How does the borrower relate to it?

2. Does the borrower's business track the business cycle, or does its inherent volatility cause it to move independently? Does it lead or lag the business cycle?

3. What is the life of the borrower's industry cycle, and at what stage is it now? Is there serious overcapacity? Is industry activity tapering off?

4. Is the borrower in a new product business that is subject to booms and busts?

5. What is the borrower's main business, and how does it relate to the industry cycle?

6. Is the industry function performed by the borrower one that will endure, or is the borrower's role losing ground?

7. Are industry consolidations taking place or likely to occur?

8. What are the distinct risk characteristics of each of the borrower's business segments? What must the borrower do well to succeed?

9. At what stage of the business cycle is the borrower most strongly affected? How is his performance affected by those cyclical pressures?

10. What is the borrower's historic ability to weather recession?[1]

Grasping a "feel" for the trend and timing of economic events is important in determining where the borrower and lender are in terms of the cycle. Exhibit 7.1 is an overview of the regular patterns in the behavior of borrowers and lenders throughout the cycle.

Determining the Borrower's Requirements.   Portfolio allocation also involves an assessment of the purposes for which loans are demanded. The aim is to determine how the purposes of the loans fit overall bank objectives and what implications may be present in terms of the maturity of the loans. Correspondingly, funding must be provided for the short- and longer-term loans.

Theoretically, short-, medium-, and long-term loans should be funded with short-, medium-, and long-term liabilities or capital, respectively. As we discovered in Chapter 5, there generally is a funding gap between assets and liabilities in terms of interest rates and maturities. For this reason a bank may determine that loans of a certain purpose may cause funding requirements of longer terms than the bank is willing to risk. Consumer and mortgage loans normally have terms longer than one year. Prediction of future interest rates and the amount of future core (dependable-base) deposits may be difficult, yet it is necessary in allocating the loan portfolio to consumer and mortgage loans.

---

[1]P. H. Mueller, "What Every Lending Officer Should Know About Economics," in *Classics in Commercial Bank Lending,* ed. W. W. Sihler (Philadelphia: Robert Morris Associates, 1981), 51.

EXHIBIT 7.1 How Borrowers and Lenders Behave over the Cycle

Stage of Business Cycle	Behavior of Borrower	Behavior of Lender
Recession—unemployment and idle capacity	Liquidation in the case of marginal borrowers. Faced with melting backlogs and order cancellations, repairs balance sheet liquidity; pares inventory and cuts production; receivables run off; cost-cutting programs undertaken; fixed costs are hard to trim quickly. Reduces bank borrowing. Defers nonessential capital.	Repairs liquidity. Excess liquidity, which erodes pricing; push for market share; irrational tendency to accept "caps" and fixed-rate deals. Cautious on credit quality; security-conscious.
Recovery and expansion, commencing with pickup in consumer spending	Continues to repair balance sheet liquidity. Inventory and receivables build. Increases productivity and earnings. Updates plant and equipment and contemplates future capital needs. More liberal on wage settlements. Overtime payments grow. Introduces new products, and new ventures appear. Large borrowers make extensive use of the commercial paper market.	Loan volume shows signs of pickup in the face of excess bank liquidity. Intense competition tends to push bankers into unsound deals. Rates rise and business borrowers turn to banks rather than to bond market.
Boom—acceleration of inflation beyond economy's potential growth rate	Optimism mounts. Orders and prices soar above historic norms, often at unsustainable levels. Raises wages sharply. Reluctant to turn to long-term financing, increases short and intermediate credit substantially. Supply of internally generated business funds increasingly constrained by low rates of increase in productivity and slow rates of increase in physical output, which narrow profit margins.	Optimism mounts. Increasing amounts loaned against increasing cash flow; overgenerosity on the part of lenders. In some instances the liquidity supplied by the bank is all that's keeping the borrower afloat. Susceptibility to euphoria and loss of perspective of what constitutes a good credit. Mania for growth, going down market to get it.

(continued)

EXHIBIT 7.1 (continued)

Stage of Business Cycle	Behavior of Borrower	Behavior of Lender
	Probes limits of physical capacity. Uses less productive facilities and workers; productivity declines.	High dependence on cash flow for collectibility.
	Backlogs increase as cycle ages. Builds inventory.	Demand for short-term funds increasingly strengthens.
	Finds cost of replacing depreciated capital equipment rising. Acquisitions and tender offers more attractive.	Lending for capital spending grows and heats up toward the end of a maturing "up" cycle.
	Finds cost of replacing stocks of raw materials and components high.	Acquisition loans increase.
	Working capital needs rise to accommodate rising unit costs and inefficiencies.	Banks tend to become proxies for the equity and long-term debt markets.
	Overall profit performance swells because of inventory profits.	Wise lenders exercise caution—stress avoidance of exposure to weakening borrowers.
	Profitable lines obscure weak performance of other lines.	
	Fears credit controls. Anticipatory buying of supplies and raw materials. Increases prices wherever possible. Wages increased in anticipation of a freeze.	
	Liquidity declines; leverage sometimes excessive.	
	Large borrowers that have relied heavily on the commercial paper market return to banks for at least part of their short-term cash needs. In anticipation of a credit squeeze, borrowers negotiate revolving and other forms of committed credit.	
	Marginal borrowers find it difficult to hold on.	
Crunch—restrictive monetary policy, with restraint on the growth of bank reserves. Credit conditions and general frustration with inflation	Cuts production as backlog orders decrease.	Cautious and selective in extending new credit.
	To the extent possible, limits borrowing as credit restraint takes hold, although inflation	Allocates funds formally, or informally; basic needs of established business customers for

(continued)

EXHIBIT 7.1   (continued)

Stage of Business Cycle	Behavior of Borrower	Behavior of Lender
spawn proposals for credit allocation	usually accentuates demand for credit. Pressure on working capital affects debt servicing ability. Tries to improve collection of receivables as payments slow. Takes large write-downs in recognition that assets are inflated. This could precipitate further problems, depending upon how the marketplace interprets the action.	normal operations met to assure production and distribution of goods and services. Discourages loans for: 1. Purely financial activities—acquisitions or purchase of own shares. 2. Speculation. 3. Use outside domestic economy, funded from domestic sources. 4. Discretionary spending that might be deferred. Displays less flexibility on moratorium or grace periods but more flexibility on repayments. Raises interest rates and hardens fee structure.

Source: P. H. Mueller, "What Every Lending Officer Should Know About Economics," in *Classics in Commercial Bank Lending*, ed. W. W. Sihler (Philadelphia: Robert Morris Associates, 1981), 52–54.

Determining the maturity and funding implications for commercial loans represents a special problem. Commercial loans are classified into two basic types. Short-term working capital loans are normally over the operating cycle or one-year. Term loans have maturities that extend beyond one year. Term loans are made for longer-term support of working capital needs, equipment financing, and financing of the expansion of commercial enterprises. Larger banks also provide lease financing to commercial and agricultural enterprises, which serves as an alternative to term loans. Traditionally banks concentrated their lending to enterprises in short-term working capital loans, but in the last two decades they have become active in term loans as well.

Portfolio Funding.   Although there are many aspects of the administration of the loan portfolio, from a funds management standpoint the critical issue is the planning of the coordination of fund sources with demand for loans. The portfolio generates funds inflow from payment of interest and repayment of principal, which can be reemployed in loans or other earning assets. The characteristics of the overall portfolio determine the funds that will flow back to the bank in any given period. Generally, larger percentages of short-term loans will generate larger inflows that can be reemployed. Consumer and residential mortgage loans produce monthly inflows from customer payments.

Management must also plan for funding demands for new loans that arise from new requests and reduction on commitments. A commitment is an approved loan that the customer expects to use in the future. The reduction of the committed amounts is termed a *takedown.* Management must forecast the percentage of committed lines that will be taken down in a given period and must have funding available for these requests. Basic questions that management must ask include: What percentage of commitments will be taken down? How will these loans be funded? What will be the impact on interest margin and profits? Management may also use simulation analysis to determine the impact of alternative percentages of takedown so that the impact on interest margin and profits under various conditions can be assessed.

Demand for loans and takedowns of commitments often follow a cyclical pattern. In general, at the end of expansionary periods, demand increases for short-term borrowing by businesses to finance inventories. Banks may experience a larger percentage of takedowns at this point in the cycle. To meet these commitments, the bank may be forced to obtain new high-rate funds. If all banks are in a similar position, increased demand for these funds will result in higher rates. Increases in prime rates tend to lag increases in costs of funds when rates are rising, and these factors could result in lower interest margin.

Importantly, short-term commercial loans should be funded from similar-maturity sources, and consumer and mortgage loans should be funded from long-term sources in periods of relatively stable interest rates. In periods of volatile rates, however, greater caution needs to be taken in locking-in high-rate fund sources for extended maturities.

Setting Objectives and Goals.   The primary considerations in setting annual objectives and goals include target values for each loan portfolio, specific loan types to be promoted, and pricing objectives and profit goals. Objectives and goals should be communicated through a formal written plan and through implementation policies.

Loan Policies

The purposes of a written loan policy are (1) to assure compliance by lending personnel with the bank's policies and objectives regarding the portfolio of loans and (2) to provide personnel with a framework of standards within which they can operate.

Arguments can be made that *all* banks should have a written loan policy that is complete in the sense that it clearly defines the acceptable types of loans, servicing arrangements, pricing policies, loan authority, and responsibility of lending personnel to adhere to the written policy. The advantage of a complete written policy is that it forces management to clearly identify and formulate policies concerning lending. A complete written loan policy is essential for larger banks. Without such a policy, lending personnel must spend time getting verbal clearance on loans and confirmation of policies from upper managers to assure compliance. The more specific and exact the written policy is, the better the chances of compliance and the more efficient the lending operation will be.

Loan policy should be written by senior loan administrators with contributions from associates and subordinates. After the policy is established, it should be carefully discussed with the board of directors and their approval obtained.

Major elements of a written loan policy should include the following sections:

Statement of Policy Objectives

Included under this section should be statements concerning the purpose of the bank's lending policy and the importance of adherence with the policy.

Organization of the Lending Function

This section should identify departments responsible for the administration of the various types of loans, and identify reporting responsibilities of the various personnel in the department. The loan committee specification for the bank is also developed in this section and loan officer's authority is delineated.

Loan Standards

In this section of the written policy, exact standards for the various types of loans are described. General standards which apply to all types of loans made by the bank are first developed, followed by specifications of specific types of loans. General standards include factors such as deposit relationship required with loans, policy concerning commitments made on loans, and maximum loans made to any one customer. Specific standards include specific types of loans.

Other elements developed in the loan standard section include acceptable personal conduct of loan officers, loan servicing instructions, and instructions on compliance with regulation. The detail in this section is important since it provides the basic information on the characteristics of loans in various departments.

Handling of Problem Loans

Procedures for handling of problem loans are contained in this section. Included are basic elements of the bank's collection policy, procedure for referring accounts to special collection departments, and charge-off procedures.

Loan Review and Rating Process

Exact specifications for loan review and responsibilities for the loan review function are detailed here as well as specifications of any rating system employed by the bank in rating loan customers. The purpose of a rating system is to provide information on both individual loan quality (1 being the highest rating and 5 being a marginal customer) and characteristics of the loan portfolio in various departments in geographic areas.

Appendix

Information concerning the definition of terms used in the loan policy, such as ratings on marketable securities, etc., should be provided. Also included would be examples of all forms used in the lending process along with instructions for completion of the forms.[2]

The following areas should be incorporated in a comprehensive statement of loan policy, although there may be variations among banking organizations:

1. *Legal considerations:* The bank's legal lending limit and other legal constraints should be set forth to avoid inadvertent violation of banking regulations.

2. *Delegation of authority:* Each individual authorized to extend credit should know precisely how much and under what conditions he may commit the bank's funds. These authorities should be approved, at least annually, by written resolution of the board of directors and kept current at all times.

3. *Types of credit extension:* One of the most substantive parts of a loan policy is a delineation of which types of loans are acceptable and which are not.

4. *Pricing:* In any profit-motivated endeavor, the price to be charged for the goods or services rendered is of paramount importance. Relative uniformity within the same market is necessary. Without it, individuals have few guidelines for quoting rates or fees, and the variations resulting from human nature will be a source of customer dissatisfaction.

5. *Market area:* Each bank should establish its proper market area, based upon, among other things, the size and

---

[2]See L. E. Davids, *The Bank Board and Loan Policy* (Washington, DC: Director Publications, 1972); H. F. McHugh, "Credit and Loan Administration," in *The Bankers' Handbook,* ed. W. H. Baughn and C. E. Walker (Homewood, IL: Dow Jones-Irwin, 1978), 556–567; and H. C. Mott, "Establishing Criteria and Concepts for a Written Loan Policy," in *Classics in Commercial Bank Lending,* ed. W. W. Sihler (Philadelphia: Robert Morris Associates, 1981), 415–429.

sophistication of its organization, its ability to service its customers, and its ability to absorb risks. From the bank's capital standpoint, defining one's market area is probably more important in the lending function than in any other aspect of banking.

6. *Credit-granting procedures:* This subject may be covered in a separate manual, and usually is in larger banks. At any rate, it should not be overlooked because proper procedures are essential in establishing sound policy and standards. Without proper procedures that are meticulously carried out, the best-conceived loan policy will not function and, inevitably, problems will develop.[3]

In setting provisions for loan approval, the following might be stated:

1. A definition as to what constitutes "secured and unsecured" lending for loan approval purposes.

2. A definition of "borrower's total liability" to protect the bank against maximum extensions of credit to various affiliates, subsidiaries, principals, and related entities all dependent on one basic enterprise. Such a credit extension could be undertaken by an officer or combination of officers lacking the expertise to handle a credit of that magnitude. This is known as the "one ball of wax" principle, and it continues to be a sound one.

3. The establishment of officers' loan committee(s), naming the members, the chairman and secretary, quorum and voting procedures, and the maximum amount of each type of loan the committee may approve. Possible variations may include separate commercial, mortgage, installment, and international loan committees, senior and junior committees, and regional loan committees in the case of extensive branch operations.

4. Establishment of combination authorities, whereby certain individuals, with one or more others, may approve loans up to certain dollar amounts.

5. Listing of individual authorities by name and amount, secured and unsecured, and by type, where appropriate (mortgage officers limited to mortgage loans, for example). The maximum authority would range from very modest amounts for inexperienced individuals and those in junior positions to very

---

[3]Mott, op. cit., 417.

large amounts for senior lending officers and executive officers.[4]

A statement regarding acceptable as well as unacceptable loans is important. It is important also to distinguish which loan types are illegal and which types are speculative and therefore unacceptable. Examples of acceptable loans might include:

1. Short-term working capital loans that are self-liquidating in nature.
2. Loans to experienced farmers where the source of repayment is clear, such as crop loans.
3. Loans to finance the carrying of commodities where the collateral is negotiable warehouse receipts.
4. Nonspeculative construction loans with firm take-out commitments from reliable long-term lenders.
5. Floor plan lending (if it appeals to you).
6. Various kinds of consumer loans.
7. Construction loans on housing.
8. Term and revolving credits.[5]

Depending on a bank's expertise, the types of loans that may be unacceptable include term loans of more than a certain maturity, nonresidential long-term real estate loans, revolving credits, and loans to other finance organizations. Although some banks may make some of the following types of loans, other unacceptable loans may include:

1. Loans to finance change in business ownership.
2. Construction loans without a firm take-out.
3. Loans secured by second mortgages on real estate.
4. Construction loans on condominiums unless they are presold.
5. Loans to a new business without a track record, unless it is well-collateralized.
6. So-called "bullet" loans or nonamortizing term loans.
7. Unsecured loans for real estate purposes.

---

[4]Ibid., 421.
[5]Ibid., 420.

8. Loans where the source of payment is solely public or private financing, not firmly committed.

9. Loans based on unmarketable securities.[6]

The basic lending process is displayed in Exhibit 7.2. This process includes obtaining the loan request and application, performing credit analysis, structuring the loan terms, preparing loan documents, servicing the loan, monitoring progress, and resolving problem loans.

Each of the basic lending functions has a different organizational structure. One of the reasons for the variation in structure is the difference in control exercised by lending officers. Commercial loan officers usually have complete control of a loan. The particular aspects of commercial lending that differentiate it from other lending activities include the origination, administration, and operations related to credit and

---

EXHIBIT 7.2 Lending Process

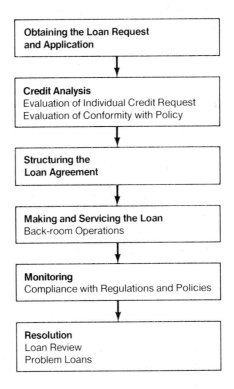

---

[6]Ibid.

other back-room functions. The commercial loan officer not only administers the loan portfolio but is also held accountable for the ultimate collection of the loan. He is responsible for the complete customer relationship, including the deposit acquisition function.

The commercial loan officer interviews the customer and obtains information and financial statements. He makes the basic credit decision to grant, reject, or qualify a loan. Qualifying a loan request involves determination of specific terms, collateral requirements, and noncollateral considerations such as guarantees of corporate debt by principal officers of the firm. In the event of collection difficulties, the officer contacts the customer and arranges terms that will bring the loan current. If the loan is deemed to be uncollectable, the officer will liquidate the collateral. If the collateral is insufficient to pay principal and interest, legal action may result.

The officer is supported by credit and loan operations personnel. The credit department supports commercial loan officers through analysis of the financial statements and maintenance of credit files that include complete histories of customer relationships. Loan operations includes preparation of collateral documents, safekeeping functions, periodic valuation of collateral, and collection of principal and interest payments. Loan operations personnel include any support such as secretarial and teller personnel.

Consumer lending is differentiated from commercial lending in that the installment loan officer who originates the loan may not necessarily be the one who collects the loan. Consumer lending is much more specialized, with activities separated into such specialized departments or divisions as origination, credit investigation, loan servicing, and collection functions. In addition, consumer lending normally involves direct and indirect lending. A direct loan is made to a customer on a face-to-face basis with the lending officer. An indirect loan is generated by an automobile dealer or another business that processes the loan application and sends it to the bank, usually by telephone communication. At that point the application is reviewed by an officer. Indirect lending demands considerable skill in the analysis of applications and requires integrity between the dealer and the lending officer.

Mortgage lending also involves divided responsibility. A mortgage loan officer will take the application and administer the support activities necessary to close the loan. The support activities include obtaining appraisals, procuring credit reports, and preparing mortgage instruments and closing statements. In large banks the loan may be closed by personnel other than the loan officer. Servicing and collection normally is conducted by specialists.

In larger banks another important department or function of the lending process is the loan review. Loan reviews are periodically conducted to review the specific portfolios of commercial, consumer, and mortgage loans. A loan review may include:

1. An analysis of the lending techniques employed by individual officers.

2. Grading loan quality according to risk.

3. An examination of portfolio concentration by industry or type of customer.

Commercial Loans.   As outlined in Exhibit 7.3, the commercial loan process involves eight principal steps. These are:

1. Application
2. Credit analysis
3. Decision
4. Document preparation
5. Closing
6. Recording
7. Servicing and administration
8. Collection

The application process is conducted by the loan officer and includes the initial interview and screening of the loan request. Initially the loan officer obtains as much information as possible about the borrower, including previous credit history, current outstanding loans, and current financial statements. The loan officer obtains information about the company, its legal status, and the principal officers and directors of the company. He obtains market information, including chief products or services sold, production techniques employed, and important competitors.

The next step is the credit analysis conducted by the credit department. The credit analyst receives the information gathered by the loan officer and spreads the financial statements. This process involves a comparative analysis from year to year or period to period of the company's balance sheet and income statement. The analyst also obtains verification of deposit and loan balances and the customer's borrowing history. After completing the financial statement analysis and obtaining additional information, the credit analyst prepares his report and makes recommendations to the loan officers. The report outlines suggestions for the type and amount of borrowing and whether the loan should be granted, rejected, or qualified.

The loan officer reviews the credit analyst's report and the financial statements and concludes whether the report accurately portrays the borrowing capacity and character of the borrower. The loan officer

EXHIBIT 7.3 An Overview of the Commercial Loan Process

Application → Credit Analysis → Decision → Document Preparation → Closing → Recording → Servicing and Administration → Collection

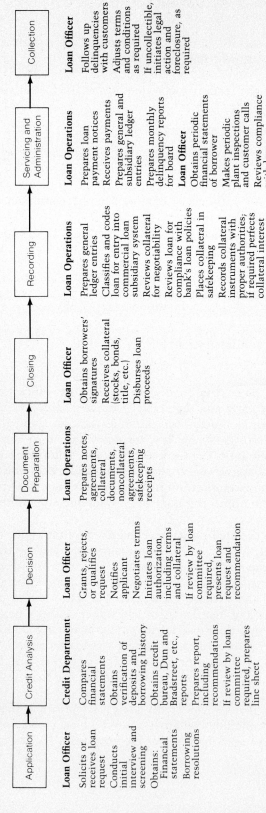

Application

Loan Officer

Solicits or receives loan request

Conducts initial interview and screening

Obtains:
Financial statements
Borrowing resolutions

Credit Analysis

Credit Department

Compares financial statements

Obtains verification of deposits and borrowing history

Obtains credit bureau, Dun and Bradstreet, etc., reports

Prepares report, including recommendations

If review by loan committee required, prepares line sheet

Decision

Loan Officer

Grants, rejects, or qualifies request

Notifies applicant

Negotiates terms

Initiates loan authorization, including terms and collateral

If review by loan committee required, presents loan request and recommendation

Document Preparation

Loan Operations

Prepares notes, agreements, collateral documents, noncollateral agreements, safekeeping receipts

Closing

Loan Officer

Obtains borrowers' signatures

Receives collateral (stocks, bonds, title, etc.)

Disburses loan proceeds

Recording

Loan Operations

Prepares general ledger entries

Classifies and codes loan for entry into commercial loan subsidiary system

Reviews collateral for negotiability

Reviews loan for compliance with bank's loan policies

Places collateral in safekeeping

Records collateral instruments with proper authorities; if required perfects collateral interest

Files notes

Files receipts of recording collateral instruments

Credit Department

Files loan authorization in credit file

Servicing and Administration

Loan Operations

Prepares loan payment notices

Receives payments

Prepares general and subsidiary ledger entries

Prepares monthly delinquency reports for board

Loan Officer

Obtains periodic financial statements of borrower

Makes periodic plant inspections and customer calls

Reviews compliance with loan agreements

Credit Department

Reviews periodic financial statements

Tests compliance with loan agreement

Loan Review

Grades loan risk; reviews loans for compliance with bank's loan policy, credit standards, officer's lending skills, and trends

Collection

Loan Officer

Follows up delinquencies with customers

Adjusts terms and conditions as required

If uncollectible, initiates legal action and foreclosure, as required

basically has three choices in the lending process: (1) to reject the loan outrightly; (2) to grant the loan without any consideration of collateral or other documents necessary to secure the loan; or (3) to grant the loan with some qualification, that is, to obtain guarantees of the borrower's principal officers or certain stockholders of the company, to obtain collateral, or to obtain pledges or collateral from the corporate officers and stockholders.

Upon making a decision, the lending officer notifies the applicant and proceeds to negotiate terms if the loan is to be granted. Assuming the borrower and loan officer are in agreement, the loan officer then initiates a loan authorization. The loan authorization is the primary document that indicates to loan operations personnel the term, rates, and conditions of the borrowing. If collateral is required, the amounts of collateral and types of additional documentation are indicated.

Consumer Loan Process.   Consumer loans are typically divided into two main operations—direct and indirect lending. Exhibit 7.4 illustrates the basic process of consumer lending. The consumer loan process is similar to the commercial loan process, the primary difference being that the loan officer is involved only through the decision stage. Subsequent processes are performed by specialized groups, notably the collection phase or, as commonly called, adjustments.

Adjustments involves telephone collectors who contact customers to determine the reasons for delinquency. Typically, consumer lending involves more personalized contact in the collection process. Consumers are affected by many external factors, such as loss of employment or family crises, which lead to delinquency. With proper understanding and care, a nonperforming loan can be brought current by delaying payments or otherwise adjusting the terms of the loan.

Unlike the commercial loan process, in which credit analysts are the primary source of new loan officers, the adjustment department is considered the initial training ground for consumer lending officers. The adjuster becomes familiar with consumers' attitudes toward debt obligations and with the factors affecting borrowers' employment, professions, incomes, assets, and liabilities. He also becomes familiar with such consumer traits as character and stability.

Mortgage Loan Process.   The residential and commercial mortgage loan process is illustrated in Exhibit 7.5. The primary differences between mortgage and other types of lending relate to the collateral. The residential and commercial mortgage loan processes include appraisals of the property by inside or outside appraisers. The commercial appraisal will include values based upon income flows to the property. Residential owner-occupied loans may also require approvals from the Veterans Administration (VA) or Federal Home Administration (FHA).

EXHIBIT 7.4 An Overview of the Consumer Loan Process

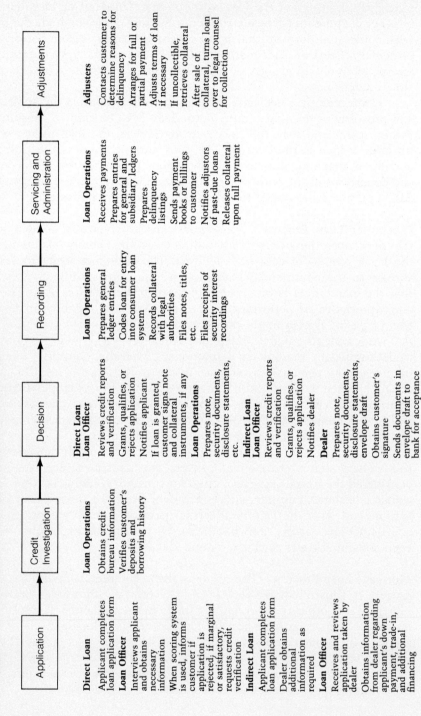

| Application | Credit Investigation | Decision | Recording | Servicing and Administration | Adjustments |

Direct Loan

Applicant completes loan application form

Loan Officer

Interviews applicant and obtains necessary information

When scoring system is used, informs customer if application is rejected, if marginal or satisfactory, requests credit verification

Indirect Loan

Applicant completes loan application form

Dealer obtains additional information as required

Loan Officer

Receives and reviews application taken by dealer

Obtains information from dealer regarding applicant's down payment, trade-in, and additional financing

Loan Operations

Obtains credit bureau information

Verifies customer's deposits and borrowing history

Direct Loan
Loan Officer

Reviews credit reports and verification

Grants, qualifies, or rejects application

Notifies applicant

If loan is granted, customer signs note and collateral instruments, if any

Loan Operations

Prepares note, security documents, disclosure statements, etc.

Indirect Loan
Loan Officer

Reviews credit reports and verification

Grants, qualifies, or rejects application

Notifies dealer

Dealer

Prepares note, security documents, disclosure statements, envelope draft

Obtains customer's signature

Sends documents in envelope draft to bank for acceptance

Loan Operations

Prepares general ledger entries

Codes loan for entry into consumer loan system

Records collateral with legal authorities

Files notes, titles, etc.

Files receipts of security interest recordings

Loan Operations

Receives payments

Prepares entries for general and subsidiary ledgers

Prepares delinquency listings

Sends payment books or billings to customer

Notifies adjustors of past-due loans

Releases collateral upon full payment

Adjusters

Contacts customer to determine reasons for delinquency

Arranges for full or partial payment

Adjusts terms of loan if necessary

If uncollectible, retrieves collateral

After sale of collateral, turns loan over to legal counsel for collection

EXHIBIT 7.5 An Overview of the Mortgage Loan Process

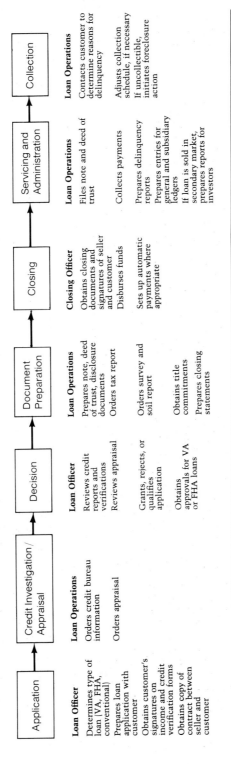

Application	Credit Investigation / Appraisal	Decision	Document Preparation	Closing	Servicing and Administration	Collection

Application

Loan Officer

Determines type of loan (VA, FHA, conventional)

Prepares loan application with customer

Obtains customer's signatures on income and credit verification forms

Obtains copy of contract between seller and customer

Credit Investigation / Appraisal

Loan Operations

Orders credit bureau information

Orders appraisal

Decision

Loan Officer

Reviews credit reports and verifications

Reviews appraisal

Grants, rejects, or qualifies application

Obtains approvals for VA or FHA loans

Document Preparation

Loan Operations

Prepares note, deed of trust, disclosure documents

Orders tax report

Orders survey and soil report

Obtains title commitments

Prepares closing statements

Closing

Closing Officer

Obtains closing documents and signatures of seller and customer

Disburses funds

Sets up automatic payments where appropriate

Servicing and Administration

Loan Operations

Files note and deed of trust

Collects payments

Prepares delinquency reports

Prepares entries for general and subsidiary ledgers

If loan is sold in secondary market, prepares reports for investors

Collection

Loan Operations

Contacts customer to determine reasons for delinquency

Adjusts collection schedule, if necessary

If uncollectible, initiates foreclosure action

As in the consumer loan process, the loan officer has complete responsibility through the decision stage. Depending on bank size and loan volume, the closing may be conducted by the loan officer or delegated to personnel specializing in loan closing.

A special type of lending is the construction loan. Here the lending process is basically the same but with specific exceptions. The loan is handled similarly to a commercial loan in that a complete credit analysis of the contractor is required. The mortgage loan officer may prepare the analysis or delegate the responsibility to the credit department. In addition to an analysis of the borrower, the loan officer evaluates the construction project, including its plans and specifications.

Once the loan is approved, a schedule is established with the contractor for increases to the outstanding loan as construction progresses. Importantly, the project is physically inspected to determine that the payments made to subcontractors reflect actual stages of construction. As final payments to subcontractors are made, contractor liens must be released simultaneously so that the title to the property will be unencumbered. Inspections may be made by the loan officer or assigned to other department personnel.

Credit Department Operations. The commercial credit department is a valuable support function of the bank. In larger banks analysts support general commercial lending and consumer and mortgage lending for dealer floor plan and contractor credit lines, respectively.

The credit department activities include:

- Gathering financial information about persons and business enterprises.
- Organizing and summarizing information to facilitate analysis and use when required.
- Analyzing stored information upon request.
- Making recommendations about credit accommodations based upon the analysis.
- Answering credit inquiries received from banks or other legitimate sources.[7]

The credit files are an important source of information for the lending officer. Most credit files include sections for customer histories, credit memorandums, financial spread sheets, and credit investigations. The history section contains information the loan officer needs to understand the bank's relationship with the borrower. The information normally is a summarization of the deposit accounts, specific loan requests, and past loans that have been granted and collected. For a new

---

[7]Bank Administration Institute, *Bank Administration Handbook* (Park Ridge, Ill: Bank Administration Institute, 1974), 215.

customer the loan officer will conduct an interview to obtain basic information on the customer's prior banking experience with the officer's bank and with other banks. He will collect other information helpful in establishing the credit relationship, including the high and low borrowings, history and amount of payments, the borrower's accounting firm, suppliers to and customers of the borrower, and any other necessary information.

The credit memorandum section contains information relating to every contact that the loan officer makes with the customer. This is typically accomplished with short memorandums. The memorandums include the amounts of loans and terms for repayment or renewal. Typically they include the source of the repayment funds, the borrower's planned use of the money, and any other supporting information that the loan officer determines is important for inclusion in the history of the lending relationship. Many times the memorandums become very important in clarifying understanding between the loan officer and the customer.

The financial statement section of a credit file includes spread sheets of the financial information provided by the customer. Financial statements obtained from the customer's accountants are typically segregated from the spread sheet. The statement spread is the analytical portion prepared by the credit analyst. The loan analyst will portray in several columns the customer's financial history from period to period, and in addition he will develop pertinent ratios that describe the customer's financial performance. Any other written analysis prepared by the analyst will also be included in this section.

Another section of the credit file includes all responses to credit inquiries received by the bank. Applicable credit agency or bureau reports will be updated periodically to obtain the most current information. In addition, the loan officer and the analyst may determine that inquiries of the borrower's creditors and suppliers will be performed to ensure that the loan proceeds are applied in a manner that will maintain normal credit relationships. For example, if the proceeds are used to take advantage of trade supplier discounts, the loan officer and analyst will want to ensure that the proceeds are being applied in accordance with the purpose intended.

The terms of borrowing may include a loan agreement. The loan agreement is a written statement of the performance terms required of the customer in the granting of the credit and will be included in the credit file. In certain cases the loan may also be guaranteed by such agencies as the Small Business Administration. The loan agreement will specify certain terms that the agency requires of the lender in order to monitor loan performance. A review for compliance to those terms is certainly warranted and is performed on a periodic basis by the credit analyst. Many banks establish a tickler system to review the loan periodically and to obtain current financial statements. This activity is not necessarily done during the time at which a loan is due for renewal or repayment nor is it necessarily used to determine whether repayment will be made on the loan.

Credit files for consumer and mortgage loans are normally maintained in the consumer and mortgage loan departments, respectively. The files contain the loan application, credit verifications, and any other supporting documentation. The files are less extensive but more standardized than commercial credit files.

Loan Operations. Loan operations, including secretarial and clerical support, prepares notes, agreements, collateral documents, and safekeeping receipts for collateral received. An important part of the documentation process is perfecting legal interests in collateral. Loan operations personnel record the loan on bank records by preparing entries for both the subsidiary ledger and the general ledger. These personnel bill customers for principal and interest payments and prepare delinquency reports for the use of lending officers in contacting customers for payments.

If collateral such as marketable securities have been received to secure a loan, they are held in safekeeping. Importantly, any collateral received must be in negotiable form so that the bank can liquidate collateral in the event the customer defaults. On a periodic basis the value of marketable securities taken as collateral is verified to ensure that loans are adequately collateralized. If the valuation process shows decreased value, the loan officer may contact the customer to obtain either a loan reduction or additional collateral to maintain the collateral value-to-loan relationship desired.

When the loan documents are received by loan operations, they are reviewed to ensure that they are properly signed and conform to the loan authorization criteria. Collateral or security interests may require recording to perfect a legal claim, and the assignments of interests signed by the customer must be sent to the proper governmental agencies. Liens on tangible collateral are perfected by one of the following means:

1. Vehicle liens are perfected by a filing with the Motor Vehicle Department in the state in which the vehicle is registered. The lender's lien will be entered on the certificate of title issued.

2. Liens on nontitled property are perfected by a Uniform Commercial Code filing in the county of residence and, in the case of a multilocated business, dual filing with the secretary of state's office may be required.

3. Nonfiling insurance may be substituted to insure lender's investment in loans secured by personal property where the balances do not exceed the dollar limit provided by the policy.

4. Aircraft liens filing is provided by the Federal Aviation Authority with a centralized service in Oklahoma City.

5. Security interest in real property is perfected by deed of trust recorded in the county in which the property is located.[8]

Loan operations personnel must have thorough knowledge of the loan policy of the bank and the various levels of loan authority and approval systems. They must understand the various documents required for each type of loan and how each form is to be completed. The loan operations supervisor must bring any deficiency or deviation from policy to the attention of the loan officer. Accordingly, the supervisor must be given the responsibility and authority for such action.

Loan operations functions for commercial loans require significant personnel expertise since a wide variety of loans are made and serviced. The operations function for consumer and mortgage loans also requires skill, although the loan documentation and legal requirements for perfecting security interests are very standardized. This standardization is due to the types of collateral and loan purposes, which are also very standardized and repetitive.

SUMMARY

Lending processes vary among commercial, consumer, and mortgage loan functions. Portfolio allocation is dependent on a complete understanding of the characteristics of each portfolio, funding sources, and customer demand. Written loan policies are important in defining lending objectives and goals and ensuring that lending standards are consistent. The end results should be minimization of loan losses, portfolio diversification, and profits.

Questions and Problems

1. Describe the returns and risks in lending and the steps that may be taken to limit portfolio risk.

2. Describe the commercial loan process.

3. Describe the consumer loan process.

4. Describe the mortgage loan process.

5. Why must security interests in collateral be perfected?

---

[8]W. B. McNeil, "Primary Areas of Consumer Credit," in *The Bankers' Handbook*, ed. W. H. Baughn and C. E. Walker (Homewood, IL: Dow Jones-Irwin, 1978), 758.

6. What factors should be considered in allocating assets among commercial, consumer, and mortgage loans?

7. Briefly describe the economic cycle faced by lenders, and the corresponding actions taken by lenders in each stage of the economic cycle.

8. Why is it important to understand the working capital cycle in determining loan purposes?

9. Outline a written policy statement for secured working capital loans.

References

Bank Administration Institute. *Bank Administration Manual.* Park Ridge, IL: Bank Administration Institute, 1974, 167–173.

Davids, L. E. *The Bank Board and Loan Policy.* Washington, DC: Director Publications, 1972, 1–96.

Gallaudet, J. R. "Constructing Mortgage and Real Estate Warehousing Loans." In *The Bankers' Handbook,* ed. W. H. Baughn and C. E. Walker, 703–715. Homewood, IL: Dow Jones-Irwin, 1978.

McHugh, H. F. "Credit and Loan Administration." In *The Bankers' Handbook,* ed. W. H. Baughn and C. E. Walker, 556–567. Homewood, IL: Dow Jones-Irwin, 1978.

McNeil, W. B. "Primary Areas of Consumer Credit." In *The Bankers' Handbook,* ed. W. H. Baughn and C. E. Walker, 750–753, 758. Homewood, IL: Dow Jones-Irwin, 1978.

Mott, H. C. "Establishing Criteria and Concepts for a Written Loan Policy." In *Classics in Commercial Bank Lending,* ed. W. W. Sihler, 415–429. Philadelphia: Robert Morris Associates, 1981.

Mueller, P. H. "What Every Lending Officer Should Know About Economics." In *Classics in Commercial Bank Lending,* ed. W. W. Sihler, 51–54. Philadelphia: Robert Morris Associates, 1981.

Pearson, J. H., and F. Watson. "The Bank Credit Department." In *Bank Credit,* ed. H. V. Prochnow, 72–77. New York: Harper & Row, 1981.

Shanahan, R. B. "The Organization and Operation of a Consumer Loan Department." In *The Bankers' Handbook,* ed. W. H. Baughn and C. E. Walker, 862–878. Homewood, IL: Dow Jones-Irwin, 1978.

Summerfield, H. G., Jr. "Commercial Bank Real Estate Lending." In *Bank Credit,* ed. H. V. Prochnow, 173–185. New York: Harper & Row, 1981.

CHAPTER 8

Commercial Loans

Commercial lending is the area of banking that receives the greatest publicity and greatest managerial emphasis. It is with good reason, since commercial loans constitute the largest category of loans for the industry. Although the importance of commercial loans varies with bank size, commercial loans typically amount to about 25 percent of total loans. For large banks commercial loans often account for over 50 percent of total loans.

Commercial loans tend to be large and complex, requiring careful credit analysis and loan structuring. Commercial loans are also less uniform than consumer or real estate loans and require greater loan officer involvement in the administration and collection of loans.

Management of the commercial loan function requires a set of coordinated systems and policies. The loan policy sets forth basic guidelines on types of acceptable loans, return requirements, and systems that are to be followed in the documentation, monitoring, and collection of loans made to commercial enterprises. The key factor in managing the function is setting up a system in which personnel implement the policy that governs the delivery of commercial loan services.

This chapter discusses the major elements involved in structuring the commercial loan department and administering individual commercial loans. Our emphasis is on the identification of the key elements involved in qualifying and structuring individual commercial loans. In Chapter 9 we shall discuss the systems employed in managing problem loans.

TREND AND COMPOSITION OF COMMERCIAL LOANS

Exhibit 8.1 presents a breakdown of loan classes as a percentage of assets for all commercial banks and for banks segmented by size. For all banks commercial and industrial loans comprised 22.8 percent of average assets in 1982, representing 40.6 percent of total loans. The data indicate a slight trend toward commercial and industrial loans being a larger component of earning assets and total loans for all banks.

Examination of Exhibit 8.1 demonstrates the difference in relative importance of commercial and industrial loans for large and small

EXHIBIT 8.1 Loans as a Percentage of Assets for Banks, by Size of Bank

	Balance-Sheet Items as Percent of Average Consolidated Assets			
	1979	1980	1981	1982
All Banks				
Loans	56.3	55.4	55.2	56.1
Commercial and industrial	20.6	20.8	21.5	22.8
Real estate	14.6	14.6	14.4	14.2
Personal	11.4	10.6	9.6	9.2
Banks with Less than $100 Million in Assets				
Loans	58.5	55.9	53.6	52.5
Commercial and industrial	12.1	11.9	12.3	12.9
Real estate	21.6	20.8	19.6	18.4
Personal	17.2	15.5	14.0	12.9
Banks with $100 Million to $1 Billion in Assets				
Loans	56.8	55.4	54.1	53.4
Commercial and industrial	16.1	15.9	16.3	16.9
Real estate	20.6	20.5	20.0	19.4
Personal	16.4	15.4	14.0	13.2
Thirteen Money-Center Banks				
Loans	54.8	55.4	57.5	61.0
Commercial and industrial	29.7	29.9	31.2	33.6
Real estate	6.2	6.9	7.5	8.1
Personal	4.2	4.3	4.2	4.3
Large Banks Other than Money-Center Banks				
Loans	56.1	55.0	54.4	55.1
Commercial and industrial	19.9	20.8	20.7	21.8
Real estate	14.4	14.7	14.6	14.6
Personal	11.5	10.9	9.7	9.3

Adapted from B. N. Opper, "Profitability of Insured Commercial Banks in 1982," *Federal Reserve Bulletin,* July 1983: 502–506.

banks. Commercial and industrial loans are a larger component of assets and total loans for large banks. For the largest banks in the United States (the 13 money-center banks) in 1982 commercial and industrial loans comprised 33.6 percent of assets, while such loans comprised 12.9 percent of assets for banks with assets of less than $100 million for the same period. For the largest banks commercial and industrial loans were 55.1 percent of total loans, while such loans were 24.6 percent of assets for small banks. Smaller banks tend to concentrate more in real estate and personal loans than do larger banks, but the data indicate commercial and industrial loans have become a larger component of total loans for smaller banks since 1979.

Greater concentration in commercial lending by large banks develops for two reasons. First, the credit demands of many corporations are large, and only large banks can service large loan requests. Second, large firms are in the large metropolitan areas where large banks are also located.

The Market for Commercial Loans

In this chapter our discussion will be limited to analysis of loan arrangements. We shall discuss credit analysis, pricing of loans, and methods for controlling risk. Because commercial lending includes more than lending services and the market includes other services provided by banks, we shall be considering relationship banking.

Since commercial loans are only part of the package offered to corporate customers, the overall package must be considered in pricing and estimating profitability for a particular customer. The bank must consider not only interest and service fees from the loan but also returns for other services provided to the corporate customer. Revenues and expenses from related services, together with revenues and expenses from the lending arrangements, are considered as a package in establishing profitability and in pricing loan arrangements.

What services are included in corporate banking relationships? Beyond corporate lending services, other key services provided to corporate customers by commercial banks include planning and money management services, consulting and analysis services, and bookkeeping and accounting services. Although loans remain the cornerstone of the corporate relationship, these related services are also very important. Therefore, while our major attention in this chapter is directed to an analysis of loans, it is important to recognize that this is just a component of the overall services offered to commercial customers.

Competition for commercial loans is clearly increasing. Commercial banks have been and continue to be the dominant financial institutions in commercial lending, but they are facing ever-expanding competition from a variety of institutions. Banks face increased competition for commercial loans from thrift institutions, which were granted extended lending powers with the passage of the DIDMC Act of 1980. Banks also face competition for commercial loans from commercial and sales finance companies.

Investment institutions that typically offer underwriting services to commercial enterprises have expanded their product lines as well. We are beginning to see lending services offered by investment institutions. In a *Fortune* article, the development of Merrill Lynch's new subsidiary,

Capital Resources, was discussed. The author labeled Capital Resources "a grand and vague name that really means loan window."[1] In the future we can expect to see greater development of the lending services provided by investment institutions as well as by depository institutions.

Banks are also facing increased competition from direct lending in the commercial paper market. Many large firms with high credit ratings have chosen to secure funds directly through the issuance of commercial paper. This direct borrowing has eliminated some high-quality loan customers from commercial bank portfolios, resulting in a loss of interest income.

As more and more competitors enter the commercial loan market, profit margins will be squeezed. To remain profitable, banks must deliver services to corporate customers with greater efficiency than at any time in history. Efficient organization of marketing for corporate services is essential to the maintenance of profitability in commercial loans.

OVERVIEW OF TYPES OF LOANS AND PRICING CHARACTERISTICS

A variety of loan types are used in financing commercial enterprises. The type of lending arrangement used depends on the purpose and needs of the customer and is determined following credit investigation. To set the stage for our discussion of qualifying loan requests, we begin with a discussion of the various types of loans and key concepts.

Loan Types: Maturity

Commercial loans are classified into two groups according to maturity. Short-term loans have maturities of one year or less. Longer-term loans, referred to simply as "term loans" in the industry, have maturities that exceed one year. Short-term commercial loans are made primarily to support working capital needs. Term loans are made to support equipment purchases and more permanent funding needs. Traditionally, short-term loans were emphasized, but in recent years term loans have become an important component of the bank's loan portfolio. In many cases term loans comprise more than 50 percent of a bank's commercial loan portfolio.

To understand working capital loans, it is necessary to understand the funds-flow process for a nonfinancial firm. Exhibit 8.2 displays this

---

[1]L. Smith, "Merrill Lynch's Latest Bombshell for Bankers," *Fortune,* April 19, 1982, 67. The author indicates that Merrill Lynch hired three dozen seasoned commercial lenders from major banks to staff its new subsidiary.

EXHIBIT 8.2   Working Capital Cycle

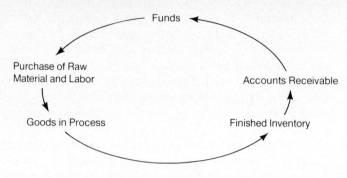

flow process for a manufacturing firm. Funds flow out of the firm when raw materials and labor are purchased to produce goods, as material and labor inputs are combined. When the production process is completed, finished inventory results. When the product is sold, an account receivable is created, and funds return to the firm when the purchaser pays off the account receivable.

Working capital refers to the level of capital that the producer must commit to support this production process. The firm may obtain some spontaneous financing for the funds required via accounts payable, but the remainder of funds must be supported through debt or equity by the producing firm. Working capital loans are loans made to support this production process. A natural process develops wherein funds are generated to repay a working capital loan; as funds move through the cycle, funds will be generated to repay the loan.

Working capital can be viewed as either temporary or permanent. Exhibit 8.3 displays the asset needs of a firm with growing sales over time. To support sales over time, firms will need fixed assets and some threshold level of current assets on a permanent basis. These asset needs will grow over time as sales increase. In addition, most firms experience some fluctuation or variation in sales over time, which creates temporary or fluctuating asset needs. Some firms experience pronounced seasonal sales patterns that require predictable levels of working capital over the year.

Temporary fluctuations should be viewed as occurring within one operating cycle or one year, whichever is shorter. Permanent working capital financing should be viewed as requiring longer-term funding as a firm grows. This distinction becomes important both in determining the customer's need and in planning portfolio allocation over periods exceeding one year.

Exhibit 8.4 displays the various lending arrangements used in short-term and term loans. In addition to the breakdown by maturity,

EXHIBIT 8.3   Permanent and Fluctuating Asset Needs

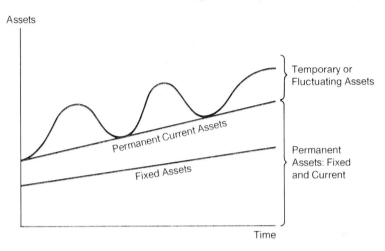

EXHIBIT 8.4   Loan Types: Maturity

Maturity Designation	Characteristics
Short-Term Loans	Maturity of up to one year.
Fixed	Loan for a set amount, with maturity of one year or less.
Revolving credit line	Approval to borrow up to a designated amount for a period up to one year. The borrower can borrow, repay, and reborrow up to the approved amount over the approved period.
Standby credit line	Standby credit lines are often employed in conjunction with a firm issuing commercial paper. Purchasers of commercial paper require a backup source of repayment and the bank guarantees that it will make funds available to the issuing firm, if necessary, so that commercial paper can be redeemed.
Term Loans	Maturity that extends beyond one year.
Fixed	A set amount of funds is borrowed, with periodic interest payments and principal repayment on maturity.
Serial	A set amount of funds is borrowed, with periodic repayment of both principal and interest. Functions similar to an installment loan.
Revolving credit line	Approval of borrowing up to a designated limit, with ability to borrow, repay, and reborrow. Maturity extends beyond one year.
Nonrevolving credit line	Approval to borrow up to a designated amount with a maturity that exceeds one year. The borrower does not have the option to repay and reborrow as with a revolving line. This type of loan may be used with project loans and real estate construction loans, with funds disbursed at stages of completion.

loans are also distinguished by whether they are fixed-amount loans or credit lines. With a fixed-amount loan the entire loan proceeds are borrowed at one time. Under a credit line relationship, the borrower can borrow up to the lending limit. Credit lines are also distinguished by whether they are revolving or nonrevolving. With a revolving line the borrower can borrow, repay, and reborrow over the period for which the credit line is approved. A nonrevolving credit line does not allow the borrower to repay and reborrow.

Loan Types: Security Position

Exhibit 8.5 displays a breakdown of loan types based on the bank's security position. Loans can be either secured or unsecured. With a secured loan the bank perfects a lien on specific, identifiable assets of the borrower. In case of default the bank can take possession of the assets and use the proceeds of liquidation to reduce or pay off the outstanding loan balance. With an unsecured loan the bank is a general creditor. No specific assets are used as collateral to back the loan.

The decision to make the loan secured or unsecured depends on the financial strength of the borrower, the size of the loan, the type of collateral available, and the costs of using assets as security. In general, the lender would always have the preferred position in a secured loan, but the additional protection offered by the security must be weighed against the costs of securing the loan. Administrative and monitoring costs may limit the benefit of the security.

EXHIBIT 8.5 Major Types of Loans

Loan Type	Characteristics
Unsecured	The loan is made with no particular collateral backing the loan. The lender is a general creditor of the corporation.
Secured	The loan is secured by specific, identified assets of the borrower. Any asset in which the lender can perfect a lien may serve as collateral. The collateral serves as an alternative means of loan repayment.
Asset-based	The loan is secured by specific assets of the borrowing enterprise, where the basis of the loan is related to an underlying security. The lender looks to the underlying security in a dynamic sense to generate cash flow to repay the loan. Most inventory and accounts-receivable loans are asset-based.
Lease	A true lease differs from a loan in that the bank actually owns the asset and is renting it to the lessee. Leasing is an alternative to term lending and is used extensively as a means of financing equipment.

Asset-based financing differs from a secured loan in the degree of reliance on the particular security as a means of liquidation of the loan. With a secured loan the collateral is used as additional protection to the lender in case of default. The lender looks primarily to cash flow to repay the loan. In case the borrower's cash flow is inadequate to repay the loan, the lender can rely on the liquidation of the security as an alternative means of repayment.

With an asset-based loan the asset used to secure the loan assumes paramount importance in creation of cash flow to repay the loan. As the name implies, the asset itself is the basis for the loan. An inventory floor plan loan is an example of an asset-based loan. The lender looks to inventory in a dynamic sense as repayment basis for the loan. The natural process of the retail enterprise's sale of inventory generates cash flow for repayment of the loan. The major types of asset-based loans are accounts-receivable and inventory loans.

Since the 1950s lease financing has grown to be a very significant component of financing arrangements for equipment. Banks provide lease financing either directly or indirectly. In direct-lease financing, banks actually lease assets to corporate borrowers or are participants in specialized leverage leases. Banks also participate in lease financing indirectly through loans made to leasing companies, which, in turn, act as lessors.

Firms have found that leasing rather than purchasing equipment is advantageous, and banks are facing competition with leasing companies for term loans. Banks, particularly large banks, have found lease financing to be profitable. In terms of overall importance, lease-financing receivables account for less than 3 percent of total loans, but they do offer some profitable opportunities for employing funds. The return offered through leasing is higher than the interest that could be earned on loans made to a purchaser, but leasing is also riskier.

In a true lease the bank acts as a lessor and owner of the property and assumes the risk of ownership. The bank, as the owner of the property, receives the lease payments from the lessee and retains the tax benefits associated with ownership.[2] In a leveraged lease, which is a three-party lease, the bank provides financing for purchase of the asset to be leased and receives a predetermined rate of return. Other parties to the lease are the lessor and lessee. The lessor makes an equity investment that ranges between 20 percent and 40 percent, and the remainder of the funds are borrowed from the bank.[3]

---

[2]For specific requirements on lease provisions allowable for commercial banks, see W. G. Brannen, "Equipment Leasing," in *Bank Credit*, ed H. V. Prochnow (New York: Harper & Row, 1981), 254–256.

[3]For a thorough treatment of leases, see Brannen, ibid., and M. M. Harris, "Equipment Leasing," in *The Bankers' Handbook*, 2d ed., ed. W. H. Baughn and C. E. Walker (Homewood, IL: Dow Jones-Irwin, 1978), 673–690.

Pricing Characteristics

A description of the terms used in the pricing of commercial loans is given in Exhibit 8.6. The yield on commercial and agricultural loans depends not only on the interest rate charged for borrowed funds but also on the charges a bank makes for commitments and compensating-balance requirements that may apply to the loan. On certain types of lending, service fee income is also a component of total return.

The interest rate charged on commercial and industrial loans can be either fixed or variable. Most banks offer these large loans on variable-rate or floating-rate terms to protect against a rise in the general level of interest rates, which in turn increases the bank's cost of funds. Such loans can be offered on fixed-rate terms if the bank expects that rates will not increase (or perhaps that they will decline) and if customers are willing to accept fixed rates. Most commercial loans, particularly large ones, are made on variable-rate terms in today's environment.

EXHIBIT 8.6   Key Pricing Terms for Commercial Loans

Term	Definition
Fixed Rate	The loan is written at a fixed interest rate, which is negotiated at origination. The rate is fixed until maturity.
Variable Rate (balloon)	The loan is written with a variable rate. Interest will vary depending on the base rate.
Prime base	Prime rate offered to highest-grade commercial customers.
Prime-plus	Prime rate plus a fixed percentage. Rate will fluctuate at a fixed percentage rate over prime.
Prime-times	Prime rate times a fixed multiple. With prime-times pricing the rate will increase (decrease) by the multiple. When rates rise, the interest rate will rise by a larger percentage than the prime-plus.
Other base rate	Similar to prime rate except that the base is different. Examples include a regional index or other market interest rate, such as the CD rate.
Caps and floors	For loans extended at variable rates, limits are placed on the extent to which the rate may vary. A cap is the upper limit, and a floor is the lower limit.
Commitment Fees	Charges on the used and unused portion of a credit line. These charges are compensation to the bank for agreeing to make the funds available.
Compensating Balances	Deposit balances that a lender may require to be maintained for the period of the loan. Balances are typically required to be maintained on average rather than at a strict minimum.

Interest rates are typically tied to prime rates, using a prime-plus or a prime-times percentage. For example, a loan with a prime-plus-3-percent rate will fluctuate with prime, being 3 percentage points higher than prime. With the use of the prime-times method, prime times 1.2 results in the rate on the loan remaining 20 percent higher than prime. In periods of rising rates a prime-times rate will increase by more than a prime-plus rate. Banks also employ combinations of prime-times and prime-plus in pricing loans.[4]

It is common for both cap rates and floor rates to apply to the loan arrangements as well. Cap and floor rates establish a maximum and minimum rate on the loan. These maximum and minimum rates can be accomplished by exact rate limits or by an average rate on the loan. From the bank's point of view, this limits both the upside and downside potential. From the borrower's point of view, the cap serves to protect against a large increase in rate on the loan.

Banks often require commercial borrowers to maintain deposit balances in relation to outstanding loans and/or unused portions of lines of credit the bank has committed to the borrower. These compensating balances increase the yield to the bank. Common examples of compensating-balance requirements include 15 percent on outstanding loan balance or 10 percent on average outstanding loan balance and 10 percent on the amount of the committed line of credit. The structure of the compensating-balance requirement relative to the amount of committed funds borrowed affects the yield on the loan.

The final element that affects the yield on loans is the commitment, or facility, fee. Banks usually charge commercial borrowers a percentage rate based either on the commitment amount or on the amount of funds not borrowed on the committed line. Commitment fees increase the revenue to the bank and provide additional compensation for the bank making funds available on demand to the borrower. With a formal commitment the bank must maintain additional liquidity to assure availability of funds in the event the customer draws down the line.

Yields on commercial loans depend on the rate of interest charged, compensating-balance requirements, and commitment fees. All of these factors must be considered together to estimate yield. Banks may be able to structure loans with a lower stated interest rate (or a variable rate based on the prime) by favorably structuring the compensating-balance and commitment-fee provisions.[5]

Pricing commercial loans is a complex process that requires estimating the return the bank should earn on a particular loan and then

---

[4]R. C. Merris, "Business Loans at Large Commercial Banks: Policies and Practices," *Economic Perspectives, Federal Reserve Bank of Chicago,* November-December 1979: 61–69.

[5]For a detailed discussion of how alternative structuring can affect yields, see G. R. Severson, "Determining Pricing Alternatives," *Journal of Commercial Bank Lending,* November 1974: 2–8.

constructing a loan agreement that will generate the desired return. The actual return generated on a loan is a function of interest income, fee income, and return earned on compensating balances.

An overview of the process of pricing is displayed in Exhibit 8.7. Return generated on a loan must be sufficient to cover all costs (including capital costs) associated with providing the lending service. In addition, return must be sufficient for the risk level of the loan.

The first factor influencing required return is the marginal cost of the funds that support the loan. Funds that support loans include not only deposits and other borrowed funds but also the owners' capital. Loans are supported by permanent capital, and suppliers of that capital demand a return for supplying funds for loans. Failure to consider the owners' required return will underestimate the return that must be earned on a loan.

For example, consider a bank that is funding a loan by issuing negotiable CDs. The interest margin on the loan must cover not only the cost of the negotiable CDs but also the return to the investors who supply capital to support the loan. If equity capital is 5 percent of total liabilities and equity (or assets) and the owners of the bank require a 20 percent return on investment, the interest income must exceed the cost of the negotiable CDs by an amount large enough to provide a 20 percent return on the portion of the loan supported by equity capital.

In measuring the cost of funds, the marginal, not average, cost of funds is relevant. In making the loan, the bank will have to secure additional funds, and the cost of the new funds is relevant to the pricing

EXHIBIT 8.7   Overview of Return Requirements and Return Generation on Commercial Loans

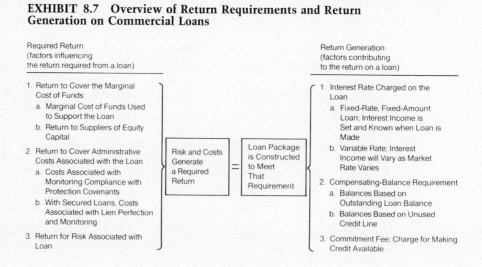

decision. When rates are rising, use of an average cost of funds will underestimate the return that must be earned on the loan. The opposite would be true when rates are falling.[6]

The return on the loan must be sufficient to cover additional administrative costs incurred in providing the loan service. Some loans, such as secured-inventory and accounts-receivable loans, require considerable administrative costs. For example, a floor loan requires that the inventory be inspected to assure that the borrower is performing according to the terms of the trust agreement. Administrative costs are incurred as new inventory is added to, and sold inventory is deleted from, the loan collateral. Finally, the return should be adequate for the risk of the loan as determined or estimated by the credit investigation. The spread earned on a risky loan must be higher to provide additional compensation for the higher risk.

Once the desired rate of return is estimated, the pricing characteristics of the loan can be constructed to achieve that return. The return depends not only on the rate but also on the compensating-balance requirements and commitment fees. A variety of combinations can be employed to obtain the desired yield.

On credit lines, the contribution of compensating balances and commitment fees to overall loan yield depends on use. For example, if a 10 percent compensating-balance requirement applies to both the unused commitment and the amount of the credit line borrowed, the yield on the loan will be affected by the amount of the line used. With this pricing arrangement, lower utilization will increase the yield from compensating balances on the loan. The contribution of commitment fees to loan yield will also increase with lower utilization.

Given the importance of utilization in determining loan yield, the loan officer must estimate utilization in pricing the loan to obtain the desired yield. If utilization is incorrectly assessed, the realized yield on the loan will differ from the expected yield. If high utilization of the credit line is expected, the yield on the loan can be increased by increasing the compensating-balance requirement on oustanding loan balances and reducing the compensating-balance requirement on the committed but unused portion of the line. If low utilization is expected, the opposite strategy will increase yield.[7]

Additional detail on pricing is provided in Chapter 18.

---

[6]One of the factors contributing to the failure of Franklin National Bank in the mid-1970s has been identified as failure to correctly assess the marginal cost of funds. Reportedly, Franklin National was pricing loans on an average-cost basis. For a complete discussion on alternative measures of cost of funds, see B. M. Johnson, "An Analysis of Modern Concepts of Loan Yields," *The Magazine of Bank Administration*, August 1977: 31–36.

[7]For detailed examples of the effect of utilization on loan yields, see Johnson, ibid.

ORGANIZATION OF THE COMMERCIAL
LOAN DEPARTMENT

Administration of the commercial lending function involves structuring
the department to deliver its services in the most efficient fashion. As
we indicated in Chapter 7, administration of this function is more decentralized than other lending areas. Individual loan officers are responsible for all functions related to delivering the loan service, from securing the initial application to routine collection.

Although the servicing of individual loans is decentralized, the organization or grouping of loans into service areas can result in managerial efficiencies. As banks have increased services offered to commercial
enterprises, many banking firms have integrated commercial loan and
other services into a centralized department where major borrowers are
serviced by specialized personnel. Given the specialized nature of borrowing by different types of industries, most banks also employ some
organizational structure by industry classification. This allows the bank
to employ personnel who are knowledgeable in the various types of industries in which they will be applying their analytical skills.

The degree of centralization and/or specialization of commercial
lending is a function of the volume of lending and whether the bank is
a unit or branching bank. Larger volume allows greater specialization in both unit and branching banks. Large branching organizations
have the additional consideration of the location of personnel in the
branch system. The basic decision is whether commercial loan services
are to be offered at all locations or whether such activity is to be region-
alized in key branch locations or, in some cases, separate regional locations.

Exhibit 8.8 displays possible organizational structures for a unit
banking organization. Assuming adequate volume to warrant some specialization, the first type of breakdown involves the separation of lending into commercial, agricultural, real estate, and consumer lending. In
the agricultural and commercial area, individual lending officers are assigned particular loans and are responsible for customer relationships.
Depending on volume and expertise, responsibility could be divided according to type of industry or size of the customer.

Sections II and III of Exhibit 8.8 display finer organizational break-
downs that can be used. With sufficient volume a bank may structure
its lending operation with separate functional units according to basic
industry types. Organized in this fashion, all commercial loans in a
given industry are serviced under a particular unit. Alternatively, a bank
may structure its operation according to the size of its customers. The
distinction according to size allows specialization in servicing large-,
medium-, and small-sized accounts. Very large major corporate accounts
involve larger loans, wider geographic dispersion, and greater use of

EXHIBIT 8.8   Organizational Structure for Unit Banks

Option 1.

Option 2.

Option 3.

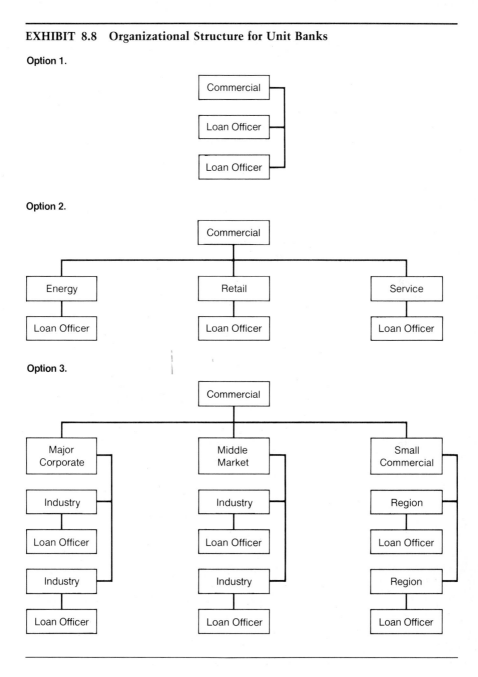

complicated participations and specialized related services than do medium- or small-sized firms. The bank can effectively service the needs of these firms through a centralized department. Many banks have found they are able to better deliver and compete for loan and related services if they have a separate organizational function to service medium- and small-sized firms.

Exhibit 8.9 displays alternative organizational structures for a branching organization. The degree of centralization depends on volume, but with a branching organization an additional consideration is involved. Management must decide whether to deliver corporate lending services through its individual branches or through specialized service centers. Specialized centers could operate as separate units or they could be centralized in large branches in key service locations.

Option I of Exhibit 8.9 displays a geographic breakdown by regions in the bank's service area. With this type of organization, loans are housed and serviced in individual branches within the system. Options II and III display separation of organizational structure according to account size. Alternative specialization could include either separation of major corporate accounts from all other loans or a finer breakdown into major and middle-market loans with routine smaller commercial loans being serviced in the branch system.

Many banks have found that concentration results in increased efficiency, better service, and greater control of lending activity. In very large banking organizations with 500 to 1000 branches, control and efficient utilization of resources are very important issues. Through centralization or regionalization of larger commercial loan services, banks are able to better maintain and service larger numbers of customers with fewer personnel.

ADMINISTRATION OF INDIVIDUAL LOANS

The administration of individual loans includes credit analysis, loan agreement structuring (which includes pricing and construction of the loan agreement with covenants to protect the bank's interest), monitoring of existing loans, and resolution of problem loans. Credit evaluation and loan structuring are critical elements in the process. Monitoring is also important in that it provides timely identification of potential problem loans and allows management to take action to limit losses.

Credit evaluation results in an assessment of the riskiness of the loan and provides information on factors of special concern that are useful in structuring the loan to limit risk. This section presents an overview of credit analysis and loan structuring.

EXHIBIT 8.9   Organizational Structures for Branch Banks

Option 1:

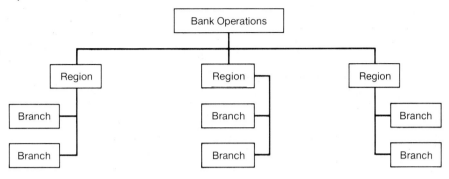

Option 2:

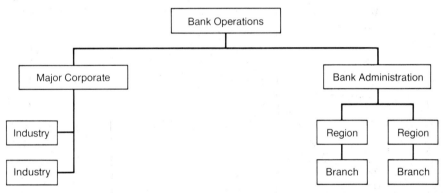

Option 3:

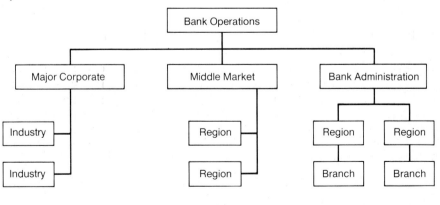

Credit Analysis

Analyzing a credit request includes analysis of the character, capacity, and capital position of the potential borrower and an evaluation of those characteristics in terms of the current economy and the economic conditions predicted over the loan period.

The basic questions the loan officer attempts to answer in the credit analysis include:

- What is the character and managerial ability of the borrower?
- What is the borrower's capacity to repay the loan as requested?
- What is the capital position of the borrower in case the borrower experiences difficulties?
- How will current and predicted economic conditions affect the ability of the borrower to repay the loan?
- Do any special elements of risk exist that could affect the borrower's cash flow and thus repayment?

The answers to these questions allow the loan officer to assess the probability that the borrower will be able to repay the loan under the terms requested, and they provide information that can be used to structure the loan to minimize the risk of default. Thorough credit analysis often results in determination that the loan as requested cannot be serviced or does not meet the needs of the borrower. Information generated from the analysis can be used to redesign the loan so that it meets the credit needs of the borrower and, at the same time, meets the risk/return characteristics desired by the bank.

An overview of the process of forming and updating credit judgments and the use of the information in structuring loans is displayed in Exhibit 8.10. The process of credit analysis is divided into the following eight categories or steps:

1. Acquiring basic information about the borrowers.

2. Acquiring basic information about loans.

3. Making a preliminary review of risk, including identification of need for more information or clarification.

4. Acquiring more complete information.

5. Verifying the critical information.

6. Making a refined analysis of the risk.

7. Making an overall decision.

8. Structuring the loan.[8]

---

[8]B. C. Eisenreich, "Credit Analysis: Tying It All Together, Part I," *Journal of Commercial Bank Lending*, December 1981: 4–6.

EXHIBIT 8.10   Steps in the Credit Analysis

Formulating Credit Judgments for Prospects	Updating Credit Judgments for Existing Customers

1. Acquire Basic Information About Borrower

A. Historical and current financial statements	A. Current financial statements
B. Background information	B. Broad explanation of current performance

2. Acquire Basic Information About Loans

A. Size and purpose of proposed needs	A. Size and purpose of new loans
B. Sources of repayment	B. Status and use of existing loans
	C. Sources of repayment
	D. Condition and value of collateral if any

3. Perform Preliminary Review of Risk, Including Identification of Need for More Information or Clarification

A. Assess commitment, experience, and track record of human variables	A. Evaluate change or inconsistencies in human variables
B. Assess broad political and economic risks	B. Reevaluate changing political or economic risks
C. Identify operating strengths and weaknesses apparent in track record	C. Evaluate current operating performance against expectations
D. Evaluate strength and stability of cash flow in relation to historical demands	D. Evaluate recent cash flow and investment decisions in relation to plans and financial consequences
E. Anticipate future operating performance and investment needs considering proposed loan and capacity to service debt	E. Anticipate future operating performance and investment needs considering proposed loan and capacity to service debt
F. Evaluate balance sheet strengths and weaknesses and consequences of loan	F. Evaluate balance sheet strengths and weaknesses and consequences of loan
G. Determine superficial risk rating to guide rest of process	G. Evaluate loan covenants and supplementary information
	H. Determine any likely change in existing risk rating

4. Acquire More Complete Information

A. Details of proposed deal	A. Details of proposed deal
B. Details of important human considerations	B. Explanation of changes in human variables
C. Details of important operating considerations	C. Explanations of significant operating issues or problems
D. General financial objectives and plans	D. Expectations of significant investments or problems requiring financing
E. Supplemental financial information such as projections	E. Supplemental financial information such as projections

5. Verify Critical Information

A. On-site visits	A. On-site visits
B. Routine bank, trade, and possibly customer checks	B. Specific investigation
C. Routine trade information	C. Routine trade information
D. Broad industry checks (public sources or direct investigation)	D. Industry problems and outlook
E. Audited statements	E. Audit collateral

(continued)

Exhibit 8.10 (continued)

Formulating Credit Judgments for Prospects	Updating Credit Judgments for Existing Customers

6. Perform Refined Analysis of Risk

A. Establish commitment of owners and labor	A. Reassess commitment
B. Assess management's success and determination to pay loans	B. Assess recent decision making
C. Judge political and economic risk for future	C. Interpret changes in political and economic risks
D. Identify and weigh operating strengths and weaknesses	D. Identify and weigh operating strengths and weaknesses
E. Evaluate expectations for operating performance considering proposed loan	E. Evaluate expectations for operating performance considering proposed loan
F. Evaluate project and estimate strength of cash flow in relation to all demands, including proposed debt service	F. Evaluate project and estimate strength of cash flow in relation to all demands, including proposed debt service
G. Estimate current or potential pressures on working capital	G. Estimate current or potential pressures on working capital
H. Evaluate secondary protection of balance sheet, collateral, or guarantees	H. Evaluate secondary protection of balance sheet, collateral, or guarantees

7. Make Overall Decision

A. Assign an overall risk rating (formally or informally)	A. Keep or change existing risk rating
B. If rating is unacceptable, the process ends	B. If rating becomes unacceptable, collection must be assessed and a plan proposed

8. Structure Loan

A. Determine appropriate type, maturity, and pricing to fit needs and risk	A. For new loans, determine appropriate type, maturity, and pricing to fit needs and risk
B. If terms required are unacceptable, the process ends	B. If terms are unacceptable, project may need to be reconsidered
C. Seek appropriate approvals	C. Seek appropriate approvals
D. Negotiate acceptable terms	D. Negotiate acceptable terms
E. Document and close loan	E. Restructure deal to meet changing needs for existing loans
	F. Review problem loans with appropriate collection area
	G. Document and close new loans

Source: B. C. Elsenreich, "Credit Analysis: Tying It All Together, Part I." *Journal of Commercial Bank Lending,* December 1981: 4–6.

The key to credit analysis is to use the information gained in the initial analysis to refine and revise the evaluation of elements of risk of the loan. The steps listed in Exhibit 8.10 show the coordination in the process that leads to the decision to grant or deny the credit request. On credit requests that are approved, information gained in the credit analysis is used to construct the loan agreement and the protective covenants. The protective covenants protect against any special elements of risk identified in the credit analysis.

Ratio analysis is employed in the initial stages of the credit analysis. The goal of ratio analysis is to reduce the large number of individual items on the financial statement to a small number of meaningful ratios that assist the lending officer in analyzing the current position of the borrower. Ratio analysis is used to identify critical areas for further and more detailed analysis.

Exhibit 8.11 displays a list of ratios commonly used in financial statement analysis. The basic types of ratios include liquidity, management efficiency, debt or leverage, and profitability. The ratios displayed in Exhibit 8.11 are not meant to be a universal set meaningful to the analysis of all types of statements. For example, inventory turnover is meaningless in an analysis of service firms but is very important in an analysis of a retail or manufacturing firm.

Ratio analysis includes both comparative and trend analysis. Comparative analysis compares a firm's ratios to the ratios of similar firms in the same industry. Trend analysis compares the firm's ratios over time.

Several credit service firms, among them Dun & Bradstreet and Robert Morris and Associates, publish ratio information for different industries. Large banks may construct their own data, which combine individual financial statements on present customers, to obtain industry averages. For large publicly traded firms, computerized data bases are available that provide financial statement information for various industries.

It is important to note that although ratio analysis is used to gain a quick insight into the financial position of a firm, it is subject to some limitations. Since financial ratios are constructed from balance sheet and income statement data, the analyst must be aware of various reporting practices that have an effect on statement data. For example, inventory valuation methods and exclusion of liability items must be considered when evaluating financial ratios.[9] Further, to properly evaluate ratios, the analyst must be familiar with the accounting practices in particular industries.

---

[9]E. E. Comiskey and C. A. Tritschler, "On or Off the Balance Sheet—Some Guidance for Credit Analysts," in *Classics in Commercial Bank Lending*, ed. W. W. Sihler (Philadelphia: Robert Morris Associates, 1981), 57–70.

EXHIBIT 8.11   Financial Ratios Used in Credit Analysis

Liquidity: Measures the ability of the firm to generate cash to meet short-term obligations.	Current ratio	$\dfrac{\text{Current assets}}{\text{Current liabilities}}$
	Acid-test ratio	$\dfrac{\text{Currents assets} - \text{inventory}}{\text{Current liabilities}}$
Management efficiency: Measures the efficiency with which management utilizes assets in the generation of sales and profits.	Average collection period	$\dfrac{\text{Average accounts receivable}}{\text{Sales per day}}$
	Inventory turnover	$\dfrac{\text{Sales}}{\text{Average inventory}}$
	Fixed asset turnover	$\dfrac{\text{Sales}}{\text{Net fixed assets}}$
	Total asset turnover	$\dfrac{\text{Sales}}{\text{Total assets}}$
Leverage: Measures the amount of debt or financial leverage employed by the firm and the coverage of interest payments on debt.	Debt to assets	$\dfrac{\text{Total debt}}{\text{Total assets}}$
	Debt to equity	$\dfrac{\text{Long-term debt}}{\text{Total equity (net worth)}}$
	Times interest earned	$\dfrac{\text{Earnings before interest \& taxes}}{\text{Annual interest expense}}$
	Acounts payable turnover	$\dfrac{\text{Average accounts payable}}{\text{Average purchases per day}}$
Profitability: Measures the profitability of the firm relative to its assets or sales.	Return on sales	$\dfrac{\text{Net income}}{\text{Sales}}$
	Return on assets	$\dfrac{\text{Net income}}{\text{Total assets}}$
	Return on equity	$\dfrac{\text{Net income}}{\text{Total equity (net worth)}}$

Following the initial analysis of the financial statements, the next steps is to analyze the cash flow of the borrower to determine whether it is adequate to service the loan as requested. Historical analysis of financial statements gives information on the past operation of a firm, but it is the future that is important in evaluating the ability of a borrower to service a loan. The goal in this stage is to project the borrower's expected cash flow from operations and determine if it is adequate. The evaluation of cash flow also provides information on whether the amount requested is adequate. Potential borrowers often underestimate the amount of funds they need to support projected operations.

Analysis of cash flows includes assessing the sales forecasts, estimating the net cash flows that will result if the sales forecast is accurate, and assessing the variance from expected sales and net cash flows. The analyst also must anticipate what factors or events could cause expected sales and net cash flows to vary.

Cash flows are typically defined as net income plus such noncash expenses as depreciation, but that definition is really oversimplified.[10] It is oversimplified because of accrual income measurement and because depreciation inflow can be only a temporary inflow, since eventually depreciated equipment must be replaced. The analyst must forecast actual net-cash-flow generation, taking into consideration leakages that may occur.

In analyzing cash flows, the analyst must evaluate projected sales and cash needs for realism. Of particular concern is whether the forecast sales are realistic and whether the asset levels projected to support the sales are realistic. Increasing sales requires increasing assets to support the sales. The increased asset levels must be financed with equity and debt. Some of the required assets are supported by profits retained by the firm. The remainder of the asset needs must be supported by some form of debt. The analyst must assess whether the requested loan is sufficient to meet the projected sales.[11]

Assessing the quality of projected cash flows is also an important element. The sensitivity of cash flows to changing economic conditions will affect the risk of default. If the flows are very sensitive to general economic conditions, any downturn in the economy could affect performance.[12] Analysis of any special risk factors associated with cash flows should also be included. For example, in the case of an agricultural loan, the sensitivity of cash flows to changes in the prices of commodities must be analyzed. The elements of risk may be hedged through the use of future contracts. Awareness of special risk elements may allow a loan agreement to be constructed so as to reduce risk to the bank. The key is to *anticipate* potential problems, which allows the risk to be assessed

---

[10]For detailed analysis see D. R. Denison, "The Banker's Shell Game—Lending Against Cash Flow," 105–114; and P. J. Tischler, "Evaluating a Firm's Liquidity and the Bank Credit Risk," 115–137, both in *Classics in Commercial Bank Lending*, ed. W. W. Sihler (Philadelphia: Robert Morris Associates, 1981). This collection of readings contains several good sources that discuss credit analysis in greater detail. The two articles cited are specifically directed at analysis of cash flow.

[11]For an overview of determining the level of growth a firm can sustain, see R. C. Higgins, "Sustainable Growth: New Tool in Bank Lending," in *Classics in Commercial Bank Lending*, ed. W. W. Sihler (Philadelphia: Robert Morris Associates, 1981), 79–89.

[12]G. G. Anderson, "The Role of Economic Information in Commercial Lending Analysis," in *Classics in Commercial Bank Lending*, ed. W. W. Sihler (Philadelphia: Robert Morris Associates, 1981), 138–154.

and a loan agreement (if the loan is approved) to be structured in a way that protects against any special elements of risk.

The horizon over which cash flows must be forecast is related to the maturity of the loan. For term loans, which may have maturities extending up to five years or longer, the analyst must project long-run profitability. Most term loans have greater risk because of greater uncertainty. Over the long run, changes in economic or industry conditions are possible, and the analyst must be able to anticipate how these possible changes will affect loan performance. The character and ability of the borrower's management are critical concerns in long-term lending, since the management's reaction to changing conditions will determine the firm's profitability.

The ability of any borrower to repay a loan depends on cash flow, but the critical aspects of cash flow analysis will vary with different types of loans. The analysis of cash flows for an asset-based loan will focus on cash flow from the conversion of the asset that is the basis for the loan. In an unsecured credit line, general cash flow from operations is the determining factor. Cash flow analysis is the decisive element in credit analysis, since cash flow is the basis for all loan repayment.

Structuring the Loan

The final stage in qualifying the loan is constructing the loan. The credit investigation identifies the elements of risk, the amount of funds needed by the applicant, and the likely timing of the borrowing. This information is used by the lending officer in putting together a loan proposal or package. From this information the type of loan to meet the borrower's needs and the bank's requirements must be decided on. The terms of repayment must be constructed. Furthermore, the loan officer must determine the special conditions or covenants needed to protect the bank against risk of default. All of these factors are put together in a comprehensive loan agreement that identifies all of the terms and conditions of lending, what constitutes default, and what remedies are available to the bank in case of default.

Structuring the loan is not separate from credit analysis—it is the final stage of the overall analysis. The loan officer uses the information gained in the credit analysis to construct the loan to make it a bankable credit.

The decision whether to make the loan on a secured or an unsecured basis may depend on information gained from the credit analysis. For some loans, such as asset-based loans, the loan officer is not concerned with the security decision since the collateral is the underlying basis for the loan. For special-purpose loans, such as term loans for purchase of capital assets and lease financing, the decision to make the loan on a secured basis is automatic. On other loans the loan officer may decide whether to make the loan secured or unsecured.

For most secured commercial loans, the purpose of collateral is to provide a backup source of repayment in case of default and to limit the borrower's capacity to borrow from other sources. The key to qualifying a loan is cash flow, and the existence of available security does not make a loan bankable. Perfecting a security interest in the assets of the borrowing firm will improve the bank's position in case of default, since the bank has the right to take possession of the assets and sell them in case of default. The added protection must be balanced against the costs associated with lien perfection and monitoring/controlling the assets.

Phases in a secured credit transaction include valuation of the proposed collateral and determination of proper lending margin, determination of how the bank can control and evaluate the collateral throughout the life of the loan, actual perfection of a security interest in the collateral, and implementation of regular monitoring and control of the loan.[13]

If the borrower is unable to repay the loan through the generation of cash flow from operations, the bank can take possession of the collateral that is used as security. Except for receivables (which are generally nonmarketable), the lender must sell the asset(s) to generate cash to satisfy the loan. The key factor in determining the protection offered by collateral is to estimate the market value of the asset(s). When receivables are used as security, the lender looks for cash flow from repayment of the receivables. Therefore the quality of receivables is more important than the estimated market value of the assets in most cases.

If the decision is made to secure the loan, the bank must perfect a security interest in the asset used as collateral. The particular form or instrument used to perfect the lien depends on the type of collateral. The most common type of lien is a consensual lien filed under the Uniform Commercial Code. The lender must make certain that no prior liens on the collateral exist.[14]

For certain types of inventory, trust receipts are used. A trust receipt is an instrument that acknowledges that the borrower holds the goods in trust for the lender and that when the inventory is sold the borrower is expected to immediately pay off the loan against the particular goods in the trust receipt. Trust receipts are issued for specific goods, and the goods must be identifiable to use this form of financing agreement. Examples of assets that can be controlled under a trust receipt arrangement are automobiles and equipment, which are identifiable by serial number. Trust receipts are typically used in inventory loans to retail dealers.

---

[13]K. L. Lott and R. G. Meyers, "Secured Lending," in *The Bankers' Handbook*, 2d ed., ed. W. H. Baughn and C. E. Walker (Homewood, IL: Dow Jones-Irwin, 1978), 622–649.

[14]G. D. Quill, J. C. Cresci, and B. D. Shuter, "Some Considerations About Secured Lending," in *Classics in Commercial Bank Lending*, ed. W. W. Sihler (Philadelphia: Robert Morris Associates, 1981), 197–212.

Loan Agreement and Protective Covenants. Once the decision has
been made on whether the loan is to be secured or unsecured, the next
step is the construction of a loan agreement. A written loan agreement
details all of the expectations of the bank concerning performance on
the loan.[15]

Loan agreements comprise the following major elements:

- *Description of the loan:* The loan is described by size of
  commitment, type, interest rate, repayment schedule, and
  security if the loan is secured.
- *Representations and warranties by the borrower:* The bank
  looks to the borrower to attest to the truthfulness of
  statements made in securing the loan. For example, the
  borrower may warrant that the financial statements are correct
  and that no material changes have taken place since the
  statements were drawn up.
- *Protective covenants:* The bank sets forth in a set of covenants
  certain conditions that will be met by the borrower. The
  covenants are designed to protect the bank's interest once the
  loan is made.
- *Conditions of lending:* Before actual disbursement of funds, the
  bank protects itself by assuring that the loan agreement is
  approved by both the bank and the borrower and gains
  assurance that the borrower is in compliance with all terms
  and conditions specified in the covenants.
- *Events of default:* In this section the bank specifies what
  events will be considered default. Beyond delinquent payments,
  other events that may be considered default include change of
  ownership, insolvency proceedings, and any violation of the
  covenants in the loan agreement.
- *Remedies:* This section spells out what action the bank may
  take in case of default. Remedies always include the bank's
  right to accelerate payments and effectively call the loan. The
  timing of the acceleration is also detailed—the borrower may
  be given a grace period to correct the conditions that constitute
  default.

Protective covenants are the central factors in the loan agreement.
In construction of the covenant package, the loan officer sets forth conditions to protect the bank against potential losses. Investigation of previous credit and cash-flow projections results in identification of the

---

[15]For large and complex loans, loan agreements are essential. For a small commercial loan
which does not involve collateral, a loan agreement may not be required. This section draws heavily
on C. S. Zimmerman, "An Approach to Writing Loan Agreement Covenants," in *Classics in Commercial Bank Lending,* ed. W. W. Sihler (Philadelphia: Robert Morris Associates, 1981), 213–228.

special elements of risk in the loan, and the covenant package is designed to protect against those elements of risk.

Covenants protect against material changes in conditions subsequent to the making of the loan. They serve a variety of functional objectives, including maintenance of asset quality, liquidity, cash flow to service the loan and net worth, timely disclosure of ongoing operations, limits on the growth of the borrowing firm, and assurance that the borrowing firm exists in essentially the same condition as when the loan was granted.

Exhibit 8.12 displays examples of the types of covenants used to protect the bank's interest. The list of covenants is not meant to be universal but rather representative of the types of covenants that can be used.[16]

Care must be taken in constructing the covenant package. First, the covenants must be realistic. For example, maintenance of certain financial ratios at target levels must be consistent with the borrower's projections of sales and cash flows. To set up unrealistic levels will cause unnecessary additional negotiations. Second, the lending officer must not only construct the covenant package but also monitor compliance with the covenants. Since most covenants are related to the financial statements, forms accompanying the periodic statements to certify levels of covenant ratios can be required. This enables the reviewing officer to verify compliance efficiently. Finally, the package should be designed to meet the elements of risk of the loan. The purpose of the covenant and the effect of the covenant should be related to a significant concern for the loan.

Loan Participation.   Participation loans are an integral part of the commercial banking system. A participation involves two or more banks jointly providing credit to a single borrower. The bank that originates the loan is responsible for servicing the loan and preparing the loan documents. Several methods of accomplishing the participation are possible, but the essence of the participation is that the loan is jointly made by the participating banks.[17]

Loan participations are classified as upstream or downstream. In a downstream participation a large bank originates the loan and the small bank(s) provide(s) funds for a portion of the loan. In an upstream participation a small bank originates the loan and sells a portion of the loan to the large bank(s). Both upstream and downstream participations are common.

---

[16]Zimmerman, op. cit., provides an extensive list of typical covenants with different functional objectives.

[17]For a discussion of the different documents used in loan participation, see F. W. Vandiver, Jr., "Loan Participations—Upstream/Downstream," in *Classics in Commercial Bank Lending*, ed. W. W. Sihler (Philadelphia: Robert Morris Associates, 1981), 229–235.

EXHIBIT 8.12   Sample Protective Loan Covenants

Purpose	Covenant
Timely disclosure on operations	Within 30 days of the reporting quarter, the borrower will provide financial statements.
	The borrower will immediately inform the bank of any changes in accounts or changes in accounting procedures that will materially affect the financial statements.
Maintenance of liquidity and loan coverage and limits on the use of debt.	The following financial ratios will be maintained at the following levels during the period of the loan:
	Current ratio $\geq x$ times Acid-test ratio $\geq x$ times Fixed charge coverage $\geq x$ times Inventory turnover $\geq x$ times Debt/assets $\leq x\%$
	Sales of assets shall not exceed $X for any given year.
	Net working capital shall never be less than $X.
	Net worth shall never be less than $X.
	Long-term debt shall not exceed $X, and total debt shall not exceed $X.
	Loans made to any officers of the corporation shall not exceed $X.
Maintenance of cash flow and limitations on growth and scope of business	The borrower shall not engage in any business other than the business currently engaged in.
	Capital expenditures are limited to $X for each year.
	Dividends shall not be paid except out of net accrued earnings after the date of this agreement and are further limited to $x\%$ of net earnings.
	Officers' salaries combined shall not exceed $X.
Maintenance of management and the basic business entity	The corporate existence must be maintained.
	The borrower shall not enter into any merger or consolidation or acquire the assets of an existing enterprise.
	No changes in management or ownership that change ownership philosophy are to be undertaken during the term of the loan.
	Key-man insurance on Mr. X in the amount of $X is to be maintained during the term of the loan, naming the bank as beneficiary.

Participation is made for a variety of reasons, but the major reason is to spread the risk. Through participation a bank is able to meet a customer's request that it may not be able to meet by itself because the amount of the loan may exceed its legal lending limit. Other reasons for loan participation include industrial and geographic diversification and greater employment of funds in loans. A bank can make loans to firms outside its service area through participation. If demand for loans in a bank's service area is depressed, funds can be employed in profitable areas through participation.

The decision to make commercial loans through participation imposes all the elements of risk involved in making loans directly but with one additional element—performance of the originating, or lead, bank. The participating bank must rely on the lead bank for loan documentation and monitoring. Participating in loans requires analysis of the underlying loan and analysis of the originating bank.[18]

Although loan participation provides an opportunity to lend funds profitably and reduce risk through diversification, it presents special management problems as well. Careful analysis of the lead bank is necessary to limit risks. The Penn Square Bank affair is a vivid example of special risks. Several major banks have experienced or apparently will experience large losses on energy loan participation originated by Penn Square Bank.[19] These losses point to the need for careful evaluation of participation loans.

SUMMARY

Commercial loans are a very significant component of a bank's portfolio of earning assets. For the banking system commercial loans are the largest single category of loans, although the concentration of commercial loans varies with the size of the bank. For large banks commercial loans are the largest and most important category of earning assets.

The administration of commercial loans requires carefully formulated policies, control systems, and personnel to complement the policies and systems. Efficient administration requires an organizational structure to deliver loan services. The degree of specialization of the department depends on the volume of loans. Alternative organization of commercial loan departments includes structuring by type of industry or by size of borrower. Both types of organizational structures are ob-

---

[18]The lead bank's lending philosophy, lending record, and overall performance must be evaluated to determine the risk of participation.

[19]Several major banks reported large losses, with Continental Illinois apparently experiencing the largest loss. Continental Illinois had purchased $1 billion in Penn Square loans and estimates its loss at $220 million on these participations. "Continental Illinois Posts a $61 Million Loss," *The Wall Street Journal*, July 22, 1982, 2.

served in modern banking organization. Specialization allows the efficient delivery of loan services.

The administration of individual loans involves credit analysis, loan structuring, monitoring compliance with loan agreements, and collection activity. In this chapter we have presented a discussion of the major elements involved in credit analysis, loan structuring, and monitoring compliance with loan agreements. The key factor in the administration of overall loans is coordination of all areas. The information gained in the credit analysis is used to structure the loan and to formulate protective covenants to protect the bank's position. The final area involved in the administration of commercial loans is the collection and resolution of problem loans, which is the subject of the following chapter.

Questions and Problems

1. Describe the following terms related to commercial loans: *revolving credit line, standby credit line, asset-based loan, serial term loan, commitment fee,* and *compensating balances.*

2. Differentiate prime-plus versus prime-times pricing as each relates to variable-rate loans. Which type of loan-pricing arrangement is more sensitive to changes in market interest rates? Explain.

3. List the major elements employed to determine the return or yield on a commercial loan.

4. Describe the effect credit line usage has on the return on a commercial loan if a commitment fee is employed.

5. Describe the relationship between credit analysis and loan structuring.

6. What are the major elements included in a loan agreement?

7. Describe any special elements of risk involved in making participation loans.

Suggested Case

Case 1, Johnco Manufacturing Company. This case illustrates an increase in revolving line of credit.

References

Anderson, G. G. "The Role of Economic Information in Commercial Lending Analysis." In *Classics in Commercial Bank Lending,* ed. W. W. Sihler, 138–154. Philadelphia: Robert Morris Associates, 1981.

Booker, C. H., and C. W. Henry. "Longer Term Lending to Business." In *The Bankers' Handbook,* 2d ed., ed. W. H. Baughn and C. E. Walker, 665–672. Homewood, IL: Dow Jones-Irwin, 1978.

Brannen, W. G. "Equipment Leasing." In *Bank Credit*, ed. H. V. Prochnow 248–260. New York: Harper & Row, 1981.

Castle, G. R. "Project Financing—Guidelines for the Commercial Banker." In *Classics in Commercial Bank Lending*, ed. W. W. Sihler, 242–258. Philadelphia: Robert Morris Associates, 1981.

Comiskey, E. E., and C. A. Tritschler. "On or Off the Balance Sheet—Some Guidance for Credit Analysts." In *Classics in Commercial Bank Lending*, ed. W. W. Sihler, 57–70. Philadelphia: Robert Morris Associates, 1981.

"Continental Illinois Posts a $61 Million Loss." *The Wall Street Journal*, July 22, 1982, 2.

Cunningham, J. S. "Term Loans." In *Bank Credit*, ed. H. V. Prochnow, 236–247. New York: Harper & Row, 1981.

Denison, D. R. "The Banker's Shell Game—Lending Against Cash Flow." In *Classics in Commercial Bank Lending*, ed. W. W. Sihler, 105–114. Philadelphia: Robert Morris Associates, 1981.

Diamond, S. C. "Asset-Based Lending in a Changing Environment." *Journal of Commercial Bank Lending*, May 1981: 43–48.

Duncan, M., and A. L. Adair. "Farm Structure: A Policy Issue for the 1980's." *Economic Review, Federal Reserve Bank of Kansas City*, November 1980: 15–27.

Eisenreich, B. C. "Credit Analysis: Tying It All Together, Part I." *Journal of Commercial Bank Lending*, December 1981: 4–6.

Harris, M. M. "Equipment Leasing." In *The Bankers' Handbook*, 2d ed., ed. W. H. Baughn and C. E. Walker, 673–690. Homewood, IL: Dow Jones-Irwin, 1978.

Higgins, R. C. "Sustainable Growth: New Tool in Bank Lending." In *Classics in Commercial Bank Lending*, ed. W. W. Sihler, 79–89. Philadelphia: Robert Morris Associates, 1981.

Johnson, B. M. "An Analysis of Modern Concepts of Loan Yields." *The Magazine of Bank Administration*, August 1977: 31–36.

Lott, K. L., and R. G. Meyers. "Secured Lending." In *The Bankers' Handbook*, 2d ed., ed. W. H. Baughn and C. E. Walker, 622–649. Homewood, IL: Dow Jones-Irwin, 1978.

Mansfield, C. F., Jr. "The Function of Credit Analysis in a U.S. Commercial Bank." *Journal of Commercial Bank Lending*, September 1979: 21–34.

Merris, R. C. "Business Loans at Large Commercial Banks: Policies and Practices." In *Bank Management: Concepts and Issues*, ed. J. R. Brick, 61–69. Richmond, VA: Robert F. Dame, 1980.

Merris, R. C. "Loan Commitments and Facility Fees." In *Bank Management: Concepts and Issues*, ed. J. R. Brick, 49–60. Richmond, VA: Robert F. Dame, 1980.

Mueller, H. P. "Lending Officers & Lending." In *Bank Credit*, ed. H. V. Prochnow, 92–103. New York: Harper & Row, 1981.

Opper, B. N. "Profitability of Insured Commercial Banks in 1982." *Federal Reserve Bulletin*, July 1983: 489–507.

Quill, G. D., J. C. Cresci, and B. D. Shuter. "Some Considerations About Secured Lending." In *Classics in Commercial Bank Lending*, ed. W. W. Sihler, 197–212. Philadelphia: Robert Morris Associates, 1981.

Redding, H. T. "Sources of Credit Information for Bank Credit Departments." In *Bank Credit*, ed. H. V. Prochnow, 48–71. New York: Harper & Row, 1981.

Robertson, R. R. "Developing Corporate Services." In *The Bankers' Handbook*, 2d ed., ed. W. H. Baughn and C. E. Walker, 961–972. Homewood, IL: Dow Jones-Irwin, 1978.

Sayre, W. H. "Seasonal and Revolving Credit Arrangements." In *Bank Credit*, ed. H. V. Prochnow and C. E. Walker, 613–621. Homewood, IL: Dow Jones-Irwin, 1978.

Severson, G. R. "Determining Pricing Alternatives." In *Bank Management: Concepts and Issues*, ed. J. R. Brick, 71–76. Richmond, VA: Robert F. Dame, 1980.

Smith, L. "Merrill Lynch's Latest Bombshell for Bankers." *Fortune*, Apr. 19, 1982, 67–70.

Stephens, D. B., and L. J. Silence. "Coping with 'Risky Shift' in the Loan Committee." *Journal of Commercial Bank Lending*, September 1981: 50–57.

Tischler, P. J. "Evaluating a Firm's Liquidity and the Bank Credit Risk." In *Classics in Commercial Bank Lending*, ed. W. W. Sihler, 115–137. Philadelphia: Robert Morris Associates, 1981.

Vandiver, F. W., Jr. "Loan Participations—Upstream/Downstream." In *Classics in Commercial Bank Lending*, ed. W. W. Sihler, 229–235. Philadelphia: Robert Morris Associates, 1981.

Zimmerman, C. S. "An Approach to Writing Loan Agreement Covenants." In *Classics in Commercial Bank Lending*, ed. W. W. Sihler, 213–228. Philadelphia: Robert Morris Associates, 1981.

CHAPTER 9

Management and Control of Potential Loan Losses

The control of loan losses is an important facet of bank operations. A poorly administered loan portfolio can have significant negative impact on earnings and capital. Larger than normal or expected loan losses require greater provisions for loan losses in the income statement, with consequent lower profits and possible losses that produce less than expected increases or decreases, respectively, to the capital base.

A sound systematic approach for administering loans requires management to:

1. Develop and implement a sound written loan policy.

2. Develop a strong departmental organization with clear-cut lines of responsibility.

3. Develop a strong loan review program to facilitate control over quality of the loan portfolio, and to identify weak loans as soon as possible.

4. Set up comprehensive credit files on each borrower containing general history and background information, complete financial information, a repayment agreement, and a record of all loan transactions with the borrower.

5. Develop the necessary techniques and procedures for identifying a problem loan as early as possible.

6. Develop the special skills and techniques required in the supervision of problem loans.

7. Recognize that each collection case is highly individualistic.

8. Institute an effective program of follow-up on charged-off loans to maximize recoveries.

9. Examine the loan loss experience periodically in relation to past experience and in relation to national averages and accordingly revise loan policy and lending procedures.[1]

---

[1]H. Albergo, "Building Better Controls in the Commercial Lending Function," *Management Accounting*, February 1980: 17.

In previous chapters we discussed the development of policy, loan organization, and the development of the borrower's credit history. In this chapter we shall examine the important tools for administering the loan portfolio on an ongoing basis and the control of problem loans. We shall concentrate on the commercial loan portfolio and large consumer and mortgage credits. While losses may be taken in the consumer portfolio, the smaller size and collateral assigned to the loan usually keep such losses small. Similarly, residential mortgage loans are collateralized and have smaller impact on bank financial statements.

MANAGEMENT INFORMATION SYSTEM
FOR COMMERCIAL BANKS

Access to information regarding attributes of loans is an important tool for effective administration. The commercial loan accounting system is particularly important for obtaining rate, dollar volume, and maturity information. In addition, loans are usually coded by collateral class, loan officer, and industry classification. Standard operating procedures usually provide for monthly or more frequent reporting. The monthly reports are constructed to identify loans that are delinquent and require immediate attention.

The loan accounting system usually creates statements for maturing loans and prepares copies or summaries for each loan officer. Summaries of all maturing and past-due loans are available to senior loan management for monitoring each loan officer's progress in collection efforts. If adverse trends appear to be developing in an individual loan officer's lending or collection efforts, the officer may be counseled by more experienced officers. This counseling serves two purposes: it puts pressure on the loan officer to correct his lending and collection techniques and provides guidance to the officer in enhancing his career development.

A bank may improve its access to information by developing a management information system for loans. The benefit of a data base for loans is to access information regarding performance by collateral class, geographic location, and industry classification. Also, dollar aggregates by these same attributes can be compared to assess concentration of the portfolio and to plan adjustments in portfolio allocation if necessary. The data base can also be used to measure compliance with banking regulations and with bank goals and objectives. An important byproduct of the system is a maturity analysis of outstanding loans for managing gap.

The data base is important in linking deposits with loans and other related accounts for profitability analyses and determining marketing strategy. Exhibit 9.1 illustrates a minimum of attributes and data that

Exhibit 9.1   Data Base Elements

Static Data for Each Customer
1. Customer's name
2. Customer's account number
3. Name of any affiliated companies being grouped with the customer for analysis
4. Geographic location
5. Primary SIC
6. Bank officer responsible for the credit relationship
7. Information on present borrowing arrangements
   a. Type of arrangements
   b. Explicit and implicit compensation for borrowing arrangements
   c. Dates established
   d. Dates of maturity
   e. Dates that revolving or advance provisions end
   f. Basis on which rates are determined
   g. Rates
   h. Second rates (for term portion of revolving loans)
   i. Commitment fees
   j. Other arrangements

Dynamic Data for Each Customer
1. Date
2. Demand deposit balances
3. Demand deposit activity
4. Savings deposit balances
5. Savings deposit activity
6. Profit or loss on demand deposit accounts
7. Escrow balances
8. Balances maintained by other banks as compensation for a participation we have taken
9. Commitment fee income
10. Other fees
11. Other expenses
12. Average loan (this may be classified by type, secured, unsecured, etc.)
13. Interest on loan
14. Nominal interest rate
15. Method of accrual
16. Amount of total commitment
17. Amount of unsecured commitment

should be collected to assist loan officers and management in making timely and accurate decisions regarding loans.

A data base management system differs from the loan accounting system. The loan accounting system is used primarily for such control purposes as providing entries to the general ledger system and producing customer accounting for new loans and repayments of principal and interest and delinquency data. The data base concept extends beyond the accounting system in that it gathers attribute data that can be retrieved by specifying criteria. For example, dollar attributes by industry, geographic region, and delinquency status could be selected. The primary advantage of data base retrieval is that the information needed can be reduced to a manageable report rather than obtained from a complete listing of the loan system, which requires manual effort to relate the pertinent attributes. Although data base management is expensive to design and operate, the advantages to management are the speed of retrieval and the ability to select key attributes for monitoring or planning purposes.

LOAN REVIEW

Loan reviews are conducted by regulatory agencies whose function is to perform periodic supervisory examinations. The purpose of the regulatory examination for loan review is to appraise the value of loans. After studying the supporting documents for the loan, including collateral and credit file information regarding the customer's financial statements, the examiner evaluates the quality and liquidity of each loan. Based upon the review, the examiner grades loans as substandard, doubtful, loss, or other specially mentioned loans.

Loans classified as substandard convey the existence of positive weaknesses that will jeopardize the liquidity of the loans. Doubtful ratings are assigned where there are high probabilities of losses but where other factors strengthen the loans such as personal guarantees provided by the borrowers. Loss-rated loans are considered uncollectible and must be immediately charged off. Other specially mentioned loans are normally those that have collateral deficiencies or lack proper documentation to perfect a collateral interest. If such problem loans do not perform, the collateral would probably be of little value.

The scope of the examiner's review depends on the statistical techniques used to select loans to be examined and the degree to which the bank reviews and grades the loan portfolios. The degree of reliance on the internal review depends on their quality and frequency.

Internal Loan Reviews

Organizational size determines the degree of difficulty in monitoring loan portfolios. In the small organization it is possible for senior loan administrators to have intimate knowledge of the overall quality of loans. In the larger organization it is unlikely for senior loan administrators to be completely informed regarding loan quality. Several factors contribute to lack of management involvement in loan administration, including multibranch operations, highly sophisticated and ever-changing methods of business financing, and the diverse nature of such specialized financing as accounts receivable, agricultural, international, and lease financing.

At some point in the growth of a bank, it becomes necessary to establish an independent function to examine loan quality. The ongoing procedures developed to determine loan quality become the province of the loan review function. Loan review may encompass three separate procedures: the preloan review, the postloan review, and the exception loan review.

Preloan Review. The purpose of the preloan review is to assist loan officers in structuring a loan before it is made. The involvement of the loan review function depends on management's perception of the need for assistance. The preloan review should not be viewed as a requirement before the loan is approved nor should the loan review officer necessarily approve the loan request. The review might be required, for example, on all new and restructured loans over a specified amount. Also, any credits that are required to be presented to the loan committee might also require review.

The type of assistance the loan officer receives from the loan review function varies but can include:

1. Analyzing the related financials.

2. Evaluating the appropriateness of the loan proceeds and of the proposed source and method of repayment.

3. Comparing the proposed credit to the bank's lending policy.

4. Assisting with the structuring and documentation of credit.

5. Posing credit-oriented questions to the lending officer that might be applicable to the situation.[2]

Postloan Review. Loan officers have been saying for years that "I have never made a bad loan, but, of course, several have gone bad after I initially approved them."[3] The need for monitoring loans after they have been made is the joint responsibility of the loan officer and the loan

---

[2]R. E. Davis, "Don't Miss Those Natural Loan Review Opportunities," in *Classics in Commercial Bank Lending*, ed. W. W. Sihler (Philadelphia: Robert Morris Associates, 1981), 455.

[3]Ibid., 454.

review function. The loan officer maintains the primary customer relationship. As the loan officer faces considerable pressure in making new loans and in monitoring existing loans, the postloan review function provides invaluable service in bringing possible loan problems to the loan officer's attention.

The postloan review serves to detect, as early as possible, credit weaknesses, documentation discrepancies, and violations of lending regulations and policies, and to initiate prompt corrective action. The postloan review process involves classifying or grading loans according to quality. The grading process is an ongoing activity over the life of the loan. Changing conditions force continual review.

The postloan review may be conducted on a priority basis. For example, tiers of review may establish the frequency of review. One bank holding company follows this practice:

1. First tier—constant review. All loans exceeding 2½% of capital.

2. Second tier—review every nine months. All loans over ½ of 1% of bank's capital but less than 2½%.

3. Third tier—random 10% review. Nine-month reviews. Random sampling of all loans under ½ of 1% of bank's capital.[4]

As a result of focusing on these loans, certain loans are placed on a "watch loan" list. The list may include loans so classified by regulatory examiners or internal examiners, loans that have been placed on non-accruing status, loans whose principal and interest payments are past due 15 days or more, and loans that deserve special attention because of other possible weaknesses.

Exception Loan Review.   The exception loan review is a specific loan review specially initiated because the bank senses that certain loans may experience difficulty in repayment. This difficulty may result from general or specific economic conditions affecting certain loan customers or certain industries.

Loan Review Organization

The independence of the loan review function is essential in that it provides a clear separation between line functions and review. The principal purpose of the review function is to advise management of potential problems. In turn, management can bring forth corrective action with

---

[4]A. C. Sinclair, "Monitoring Your Loan Portfolio," *The Journal of Commercial Bank Lending,* October 1981: 9.

line officers. Independence is important to the objectivity necessary in rendering appropriate loan reviews.

The questions of independence and objectivity are important in defining how loan review is accomplished in the organizational structure of a bank. There are at least four possible alternatives for placing the function in the organizational structure. These alternatives include (1) the audit department reporting to the board of directors, (2) loan review reporting to the board of directors, (3) loan review reporting to the senior loan management, or (4) loan review reporting to the chief executive. The strengths and weaknesses of each alternative are listed in Exhibit 9.2.

Loan-Rating System

A loan-rating or loan-grading system is a means of classifying loans for monitoring. Loans falling into certain classes require continual monitoring and follow-up, whereas others require only minimal monitoring. A subsequent review of each loan may necessitate a change in the loan's rating, either upward or downward. The rating system is therefore dynamic rather than static. Depending on the type of review—postloan or exception—a loan may be selected for review because changing conditions in the economy or in the industry have caused a change in the loan's rating.

EXHIBIT 9.2   Loan Review Organization

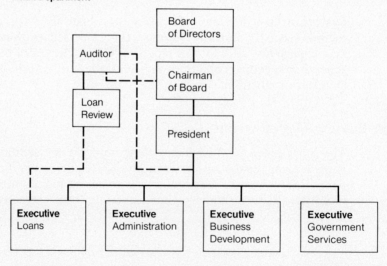

EXHIBIT 9.2 (continued)

Strengths
1. Existing independence
2. Established lines of communication to management and the board of directors
3. Authorized access to all records and information
4. Availability of a pool of staff auditors when needed
5. Formalized system of reporting, replies, and follow-up

Weaknesses
1. Lack of expertise in, and understanding of, the lending function
2. Rigid structure—lack of informal communication links to senior lending management
3. Suppression of information by line personnel (not an acute problem, but nevertheless possible)

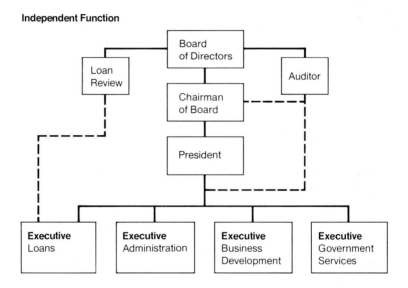

Strengths
1. Independence from lending management—increased objectivity
2. Less rigid structure than in the audit department
3. Relative ease in working with lending management
4. Staffed by personnel trained in the lending function
5. Elimination of audit's being too critical

Weaknesses
1. Lack of lines of communication
2. Increases the number of groups reporting to the directors
3. Decreasing scope of review

(continued)

EXHIBIT 9.2 (continued)

Function Reporting to Loan Executive

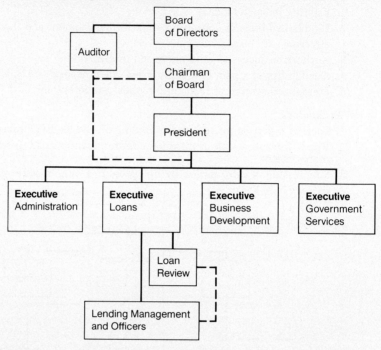

Strengths
1. Complete and immediate accessibility to all information on loans
2. Personnel trained in the lending function
3. Concentration of responsibility in one center
4. Good communication between loan review and loan officers

Weaknesses
1. Possible lack of objectivity and independence in evaluation of loan portfolios
2. Possibility of too much reliance on loan reviews to resolve problems

(continued)

Two types of rating systems have evolved. The *objective* type quantifies certain financial statement statistics, collateral, documentation, and financial statement quality. Financial statement quality refers to the bank's confidence in the level of the statements provided by the customer, such as certified financial statements with unqualified or

EXHIBIT 9.2 (continued)

Function Reporting to Chief Executive Officer

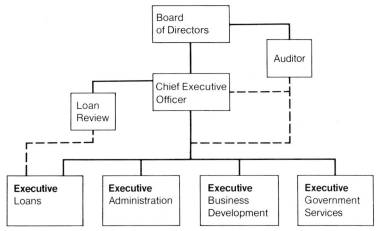

Strengths

1. Effective communication up to board of directors and down to senior lending management
2. Good probability of independent evaluation
3. Support from both board of directors and senior lending management
4. Demonstration of the importance of loan review
5. More time allocated to total picture rather than to specific problems

Weaknesses

1. Increased number of people reporting to chief executive
2. Necessitates hiring a separate loan review staff
3. Decreased scope of review

Source: C. Ellis, "Loan Review: An Organizational Dilemma" in *Classics in Commercial Bank Lending*, ed. W. W. Sihler (Philadelphia: Robert Morris Associates, 1981), 434, 437, 440, and 442.

qualified opinions. Depending on the numerical values of each category, a composite numerical rating is derived for classifying each loan.[5]

The *subjective* type of rating system relies on the judgment of the loan reviewer to place a loan in one of several defined classes without assigning numerical values to specific data such as financial statement ratios. The classifications within a subjective rating system may distin-

---

[5]S. F. Sherrod, "An Objective Risk Rating System for Commercial Banks," *The Journal of Commercial Bank Lending*, November 1981: 12–32; and D. K. Ashford, "Risk Assessment—Calculating the Odds in a Small or Medium-Sized Bank," *The Journal of Commercial Bank Lending*, March 1979: 2–13.

guish between examiner-classified loans and loans classified on the basis of internal loan-review evaluations. The internal-review evaluations may include classes for loans that correspond to examiner classes. The difference is that the internal-review classes are assigned to loans that probably will be classified by the examiners at the time of their next review.

Exhibit 9.3 illustrates a subjective rating system. We should note that the same classes may be used for an objective system by assigning numerical values corresponding to loan liquidity, etc., and placing the composite numerical rating in one of the classes in the exhibit.

Each loan grade should be entered into the loan accounting system or the management information system as a discrete data element. Periodically reports should be produced on at least two levels. One level identifies all loans in a classification with additional data such as customer name, loan amount, terms, industry code, geographic location, and loan officer. The second level includes the same information but the primary emphasis is on all loans by a particular loan officer. This serves to pinpoint responsibility for follow-up and also may be indicative of the officer's skills in making and administering loans.

Identifying Problem Loans

Early detection of a problem loan increases the possibility that the loan will be repaid. The longer a loan goes undetected, the more difficult it becomes to resolve. Certain early warning signs should indicate to the loan officer that problems exist or are about to develop. These warning signs include the following:

1. Delayed financial statements. If the customer fails to provide current financial statements as agreed or requested, it may indicate the customer is experiencing financial difficulty.
2. Delinquency.
3. Loss of borrower rapport. An uncooperative borrower or a change in attitude toward the lending officer may indicate financial difficulties.
4. A recessionary economy.
5. Miscellaneous:
   a. Illness or death of a principal.
   b. Marital problems of a principal and, especially, divorce. The division of properties and pecuniary judgments associated with divorce may seriously damage a proprietorship and cause dissolution of a business partnership.
   c. Irresponsible behavior of a principal, including excessive drinking, gambling, or absence from his business.

EXHIBIT 9.3 A Flexible Loan-Grading System

Class A: Prime loans based on liquid collateral with adequate margin or supported by strong financial statement of recent date. Character and ability of individuals or company principals are excellent and unquestioned. Position of company in its industry and in its community is excellent. High liquidity, minimum risk, good ratios, low handling cost.

Class B: Desirable loans of somewhat less stature than Class A but with strong financial statements or secured by other marketable securities (where there is no significant concentration or impairment to liquidation). Probability of serious financial deterioration is unlikely. Possessing a sound repayment source (and backup) that definitely will allow repayment in a reasonable (to purpose) period of time. Individual loans backed by sound assets and personal integrity. (Some potential Class A borrowers who don't provide a valuable relationship for your bank might fall here.)

Class C: Satisfactory loans of average or mediocre strength having some deficiency of vulnerability to changing economic or industry conditions but currently collectible. Secured loans lacking in margin or liquidity. Loans to individuals perhaps supported in dollars of net worth but with supporting assets that are illiquid. Sometimes a temporary classification for untested borrowers or where information is not entirely complete or acceptable.

Class C−: First classification that has relevance to a bank examiner class—i.e., Other Assets Especially Mentioned (OAEM). A warning classification that portrays one or more deficiencies that cannot be tolerated even in the short run. Pertinent ratios have deteriorated that deserve immediate attention and correction. Sometimes represents an interim or temporary classification of credits, new or on probation, moving to C or D.

Class D: Substandard because of steadiness on your books or other deficient nature (also related to bank examiner grade). Company or individual loans with no evident future, which are unfavorably affecting the loan-to-deposit ratio or cost of funds. Heavy leverage accounts, with no immediate relief in sight or compensating features. Accounts requiring excessive attention of the loan officer because of lack of borrower cooperation. Credits unable to adjust to unfavorable industry or general economic conditions. Individual loans where character or ability has become suspect. Credits going to the brink of potential charge-off for whatever reason, particularly loss operations.

Class E: Loans relating to bank examiner Doubtful and Loss classifications where an element of probable loss exists; at least a portion would be charged off if liquidated at present. Critical credits requiring immediate and drastic action. Secured loans with insufficient collateral or other sources to see the bank fully paid. Nonperforming assets where day-to-day circumstances leave the loans in question. Loans believed not to be tolerated as live assets by the examiners at their next visit or review.

Class O: Bank examiner OAEM class.

Class S: Bank examiner Substandard class.

Class Q: Bank examiner Doubtful class.

Source: K. A. Kehlbeck, "An Effective Loan Review Program: Some Options and Some Musts," *The Journal of Commercial Bank Lending*, October 1980: 8.

    d. Unexpected loan renewals, advances against a line during an off season, or unanticipated request for a new loan.

    e. Overdrafts.

    f. Excessive trade payables, especially when substantial discounts are being passed up.

    g. Unusually rapid or slow inventory turnover.

h. Strikes or hostile adversary relations with labor.

i. Natural disasters, such as flood or fire. Disasters wrought by man, including excessive accidents, burglaries, embezzlements, and arson may reflect poor management controls; in the extreme, either type of disaster may destroy the business.

j. Cancellation of insurance policies. This may suggest a severe cash shortage and can also create a serious deficiency in insurance coverage for bank collateral.

k. Unusual Internal Revenue Service inquiries. These may foretell a major unanticipated tax judgment in the near future.[6]

HANDLING PROBLEM LOANS

Once a problem loan is identified, the lending officer must decide upon a course of action. The initial step involves identifying the cause of the customer's difficulty. If the customer is cooperative, the officer may take a wait-and-see attitude and closely monitor progress. If progress is not forthcoming, the officer must take more aggressive action. This action may involve calling the loan, which may lead to a rehabilitation of the company or to the liquidation of the company.

Rehabilitation

Theoretically a rehabilitation is the transformation of a weak company into a stronger company, with loan performance the end product. Rehabilitation involves significant time and effort. The decision to rehabilitate must take into consideration how involved the bank will be and the costs and benefits. Another consideration is that the bank may not have sufficiently qualified personnel to assign to a rehabilitation effort.

An alternative is to bring in a management consultant to assist. If the bank's objective is to have a sound customer after the rehabilitation, the consultant should be hired by the customer. If, however, the bank's objective is to get out of the loan as cleanly and quickly as possible, the bank should hire the consultant.

The rehabilitation plan may involve all or some of these actions:

1. Eliminate or reduce every expense possible.

2. Reduce inventory and analyze accounts receivable regarding collection.

---

[6]E. E. Pace and D. G. Simonson, "Solving Problem Loans (A Training Feature)," *The Journal of Commercial Bank Lending,* July 1977: 27.

3. Dispose of idle or nonessential equipment or plant.

4. Analyze debt structure and plan cash flow to service debt. This may involve postponing payments and gaining the cooperation of other creditors.

5. Seek additional equity capital.

6. Prune unprofitable operating divisions.

7. Find a merger or purchase candidate.

The bank may also seek to improve or replace the existing management. Early in the rehabilitation planning, the lender needs to get the cooperation of the company's board of directors. If cooperation is not given, the lender is faced with dealing more forcefully with the company while avoiding any action that would place the bank in the position of management. If the bank takes the place of management, it loses status as a creditor and is also subject to legal liability for mismanagement.

Rehabilitation may also involve modification of the terms of the loan or a debt restructuring. A company is a candidate for restructuring or modification of terms if two positive factors exist:

1. There must be a market for the customer's product or service.

2. There must be a sufficient amount or number of viable assets to work with in liquidating the borrower's various liabilities.[7]

If the lender has confidence in the borrower's integrity and long-run viability, a restructuring or modification can be acceptable. A moratorium in principal and interest payments may assist the borrower in overcoming a short-term cash flow problem. A more definitive arrangement may include the lengthening of the repayment schedule, converting from a full amortization loan to one with a substantial balloon payment at the end of the original term, obtaining guarantors, taking a lien or additional collateral, or converting from a nonrecourse to a recourse obligation. The important consideration is that the lender maintains the continuity of security interest and liens granted and perfected before the date of the modification. Another alternative is to consider consolidating the borrower's debt to concentrate cash flows to the overall reduction of debt.

---

[7]D. J. McDonald, "Problem Loans: Their Prevention, Handling and Cures," in *Classics in Commercial Bank Lending*, ed W. W. Sihler (Philadelphia: Robert Morris Associates, 1981), 368.

Liquidation

The bank may conclude that the possibility of the borrower's long-range survival is minimal and decide to bring about a liquidation in order to satisfy creditors. This is usually a course of action that most borrowers resist. Once the decision to liquidate is accepted, a plan of action should be adopted that includes the method of liquidation and the settlement of debt obligations.

Several liquidation methods may be used. One is to sell the company as a going concern. If this is not possible, either a bulk sale of certain assets or a piecemeal liquidation may follow. The liquidation process is lengthy. The important consideration in a liquidation is that the bank gains control of the assets to ensure that the sale proceeds will be used to liquidate debt.

Use of a Workout Team

Many larger banks employ specialists who conduct rehabilitations or liquidations. These specialists usually have significant lending experience. The usual procedure for initiating the use of the workout team is for the loan officer to step aside and allow the workout team to address the grim facts of the situation. In this manner a clear separation of the bank's and customer's interests is made.

The task of the workout team differs depending on the assignment—rehabilitation or liquidation. Whatever the assignment, the workout specialist is the bank's consultant.

Legal Remedies

If a bank calls a loan, it has several rights that it may exercise. The right of setoff allows the bank to use any of the borrower's deposits to satisfy a loan obligation. To the extent that security instruments are perfected, accounts receivable of the borrower may be directed to the bank rather than to the borrower. The account debtors must be notified. Sometimes, the debtor requires written authorization from the borrower before turning over payments directly to the bank.

Inventory, plant, and equipment may be seized under the provisions of the Uniform Commercial Code. Importantly, the decision to seize these assets should be made when the company is shut down or the lender is prepared to liquidate the company.

The lender may force an involuntary bankruptcy if certain other creditors also agree to the action. The legal aspects of bankruptcy are very technical. A lender in a workout situation should be aware that certain provisions in the bankruptcy code may set aside an action taken by the bank to seek satisfaction of a borrower's obligation. Additionally, a lender may confront securities laws in a rehabilitation. Regardless of the nature of the problem loan, any action contemplated should be reviewed with the bank's legal counsel.

PENN SQUARE—A PROBLEM LOAN BANK

History may record the collapse of Penn Square Bank, an Oklahoma-based bank, as one of the banking system's greatest failures. The impact of the failure was especially significant because so many other banks and financial institutions were involved. Most of the bank's trouble resulted from poor lending and management practices and possibly fraud.

As facts evolve, it appears that Penn Square, which was chartered in 1960 as a consumer bank in a shopping center, began developing an energy-based loan portfolio in 1975. When the bank collapsed in July 1982, it had assets of approximately $525 million with $325 million in loans. Yet since 1975 Penn Square had generated in excess of $2.5 billion in energy-related loans and had sold over $2 billion to participating banks including Continental Illinois, Seafirst Corporation, Michigan National, and Chase Manhattan Bank. Penn Square's loan portfolio was 80 percent concentrated in energy loans.

To finance its growth, Penn Square solicited deposit funds from other banks, thrift institutions, and credit unions. Uninsured deposits resulting from the collapse are estimated at $250 million.

Exhibit 9.4 illustrates the events that led to Penn Square's closing. A number of practices and conditions contributed to its collapse:

+ Inadequate control of lending officers' activities.
+ Overconcentration of loans in a single industry.
+ Loans to related parties exceeding the bank's legal limit.
+ Loans to insiders (directors) exceeding prudent loan practices.
+ Making interest payments for customers to participants.
+ Loans made without adequate credit analysis.
+ Loans made without sufficient documentation or collateral.
+ Absence of a loan review system.
+ Noncompliance with agreements made with regulatory examiners to correct deficiencies.

One can ask, How did large banks allow themselves to forgo good credit standards? The answer may lie in greed. The oil industry had appeared to be a gold mine of activity with increasing demand for oil and increasing oil prices. One theory is that large-bank lending officers got too friendly with Penn Square officials and did not take adequate precautions in accepting more loans. Several other questions that might be asked are:

+ Why weren't Penn Square's examiner reports, which would have identified Penn Square's condition, made available to participants?

EXHIBIT 9.4   The Collapse of Penn Square Bank

April, 1980 An examination by the Office of the Comptroller of the Currency reveals problems due to rapid and uncontrolled growth and assigns to the bank a rating of "3" on a scale in which "5" identifies a bank on the verge of collapse.

September, 1980 The bank's board of directors signs an agreement to correct deficiencies and to sell $3.3 million of stock to increase bank capital. A limited review is performed and a "3" rating is assigned.

February, 1981 A general examination reveals continued deterioration, and an overall rating of "3" is assigned.

July, 1981 The board of directors and management review problems with the Regional Administrator and promise to correct them.

October, 1981 The bank shows some improvement but continues to be rated "3."

June, 1982 After conducting a general examination, the Regional Administrator notifies the Washington office and the FDIC about the problems in the bank and assigns to the bank a "5" rating. A notice of charges and a Temporary Order to Cease and Desist is issued.

July, 1982 The FDIC is requested to assess the prospects of an FDIC-assisted transaction. The Federal Reserve Bank of Kansas City is notified of the bank's condition. The Federal Reserve Bank says it will make no further loans to the bank. The bank is declared insolvent and the FDIC is appointed receiver.

Source: C. T. Conover, "Statement on Penn Square Bank," presented to the Subcommittee on Commerce, Consumer, and Monetary Affairs of the Committee on Government Operations, U.S. House of Representatives, July 16, 1982, and R. Rescigno, "Why Penn Square Failed," *Barrons*, Aug. 23, 1982, 7.

- Why didn't participants request the reports and the bank's financial statements?
- It is reported that loan reviews on energy loans were not performed at Continental Illinois, and at Chase Manhattan, although they were performed, they were handled by inadequately trained and inexperienced review officers. Why were these practices initiated, much less allowed to continue?

Congress is examining the conditions that were allowed to exist and has challenged regulatory officials to answer these questions:

- Why did it take the Comptroller's office so long to act?
- What additional disclosures should be required in bank financial statements to alert depositors and loan participants of bank problems?
- Why weren't the examiners in the large bank districts bringing Penn Square's problems to the attention of the participant banks?
- Why didn't Penn Square's audited financial statements alert investors, depositors, and loan participants to its financial condition?

It will take a long time for all the facts to surface and the loan problems to be worked out. Importantly, bankers can profit from the valuable lessons this event has brought. It reinforces the need for proper evaluation of credit applications, portfolio allocation, documentation, loan review, and control.

EVALUATING THE ADEQUACY OF THE ALLOWANCE FOR LOAN LOSSES

Several factors affect risk of the loan portfolio. A change in the concentration of loans outstanding with regard to a group of borrowers or a group of related industries increases the risk. If the concentration is removed, risk goes down. An increase in loans in relation to deposits also increases the risk of loss. Also, the more loans outstanding, the greater the odds that some will be bad unless staffing to handle loans is increased to maintain adequate controls.

A loan portfolio containing many loans that approach the bank's lending limit increases risk; a portfolio containing many small loans is less risky. Loans that have a tendency to be renewed rather than paid off also pose greater risk.

Numerous methods have been devised to assess the adequacy of the loan loss allowance. They range from management's best estimate to those methods implying a degree of precision through statistical calculations. The allowance should provide for normal loss expectancy plus additional amounts for loans that carry greater than normal risk.

Using information from the loan review system and the examiner classification of loans, we can arrive at an estimate of an adequate allowance through the following calculations:

Total Outstanding Loans	Nonclassified Loans	Specially Mentioned Loans	Substandard Loans	Doubtful Loans
$1,000,000,000	$98,600,000	$1,000,000	$300,000	$100,000
Average charge-off ratio	0.009%	0.009%	0.009%	—
Risk factor	$\times$ 1	$\times$ 2.5	$\times$ 10	100%
Weighted ratio	0.009%	2.25%	9%	

Expected loss:	Nonclassified	$ 867,400
	Specially mentioned	225,000
	Substandard	27,000
	Doubtful	100,000
	Allowance	$1,219,400

Ratio of allowance to outstanding loans: 1.22%

The risk factor is a weighting of the average charge-off ratio. For non-classified risks the risk is a normal risk. The risk factor for specially mentioned loans assumes 2.5 times the normal risk and 10 times the normal risk for substandard loans. The weights are subjective and may result from examining the charge-off history by classified loan categories. A comparison of the results of the examination to the average charge-off ratio determines the multiplier of normal risk. The above example considers all loans in the aggregate. The same methodology can be applied to the individual loan categories (commercial, installment, etc.) and summed to arrive at the aggregate loan allowance.

The purpose of providing for an adequate allowance is to insulate earnings from actual loan losses during the year. The practice of making adequate adjustments to the allowance matches revenue and expense for the period and makes earnings more meaningful to readers of the financial statements.

If a bank is an aggressive lender, the portfolio risk increases as well as interest income. Without recognition of the additional risk, earnings will appear to increase. When losses actually occur, the allowance will be inadequate to provide for normal risk, and additional bad debt expense will have to be recognized in the income statement to restore the allowance to an adequate level. The recognition of additional expense will depress earnings for the year. Readers of the financial statements will certainly question the reliability of the bank's reported income.[8]

SUMMARY

The management and control of potential loan losses is one of the most important aspects of banking practice. Important features of the control system are sufficient and easily retrieved information regarding loans and a loan review system. The adequacy of the allowance for loan losses protects bank earnings from fluctuations due to poor banking practices. Since loans are the largest class of assets and at the same time are the most risky class of assets, inadequate management and control can lead to bank insolvency.

Questions and Problems

1. Describe important data elements used to control and monitor loan portfolios.

2. Why is a data base important for controlling and monitoring loan portfolios?

---

[8]See Appendix A for accounting and taxation consequences of loan loss transactions.

3. What are the loan-rating classifications used by regulators? What does each classification describe?

4. Contrast preloan and postloan reviews.

5. Compare alternative loan review organizations.

6. Differentiate objective from subjective loan-rating systems.

7. Identify possible early warning signs for detecting problem loans.

8. What are key elements of a rehabilitation plan?

9. How may loan portfolios be evaluated with regard to risk for determining the adequacy of the allowance for loan losses?

10. Obtain information regarding the events that have occurred since the fall of Penn Square. Evaluate those events in terms of violations of good loan practices and policies.

Suggested Case

Case 2, Ramco, Inc. This case involves a problem loan.

References

Albergo, H. "Building Better Controls in the Commercial Lending Function." *Management Accounting*, February 1980: 13–17.

Alexander, W. "Handling Problem Loans." In *The Bankers' Handbook*, 2d ed., ed. W. H. Baughn and C. E. Walker, 602–610. Homewood, IL: Dow Jones-Irwin, 1978.

Antley, H. S., B. Hodge, and C. G. Wood, Jr. "Costs, Benefits, and Uses of a Management Information System for the Commercial Loan Function." *The Journal of Commercial Bank Lending*, May 1978: 29–37.

Ashford, D. K. "Risk Assessment—Calculating the Odds in a Small or Medium-Sized Bank." *The Journal of Commercial Bank Lending*, March 1979: 2–13.

Carpenter, D. A. "Analysis of Alternative Courses of Action for a Debtor's Troubled Business." *The Journal of Commercial Bank Lending*, September 1981: 38–49.

Cotton, N. D. "Legal Implications of Actions Taken by Lenders Against Troubled Borrowers." *The Journal of Commercial Bank Lending*, August 1981: 35–49.

Davis, R. E. "Don't Miss Those Natural Loan Review Opportunities." In *Classics in Commercial Bank Lending*, ed. W. W. Sihler, 453–463. Philadelphia: Robert Morris Associates, 1981.

Gigot, P. A. "Banks Hurt by Penn Square Collapse Were Victims of Oil Slump, Greed." *The Wall Street Journal*, July 19, 1982, 19, 31.

Hill, G. C., and J. Salsman. "Crumbling Credits, Many Banks Are Hurt by Bad Loans, but Few Are Likely to Collapse." *The Wall Street Journal*, July 30, 1982, 1, 8.

Kehlback, K. A. "An Effective Loan Review Program: Some Options and Some Musts." *The Journal of Commercial Bank Lending*, October 1980: 2–9.

McDonald, D. J. "Problem Loans: Their Prevention, Handling and Cures." In *Classics in Commercial Bank Lending*, ed. W. W. Sihler, 368. Philadelphia: Robert Morris Associates, 1981.

McHugh, H. F. "Credit and Loan Administration." In *The Bankers' Handbook*, 2d ed., ed. W. H. Baughn and C. E. Walker, 556–567. Homewood, IL: Dow Jones-Irwin, 1978.

Metz, T., and G. C. Hill. "Wildcat Banking, Penn Square Blowout Ended a Lending Spree as Risky as Oil Drilling." *The Wall Street Journal*, July 27, 1982, 1, 10.

Pace, E. E., and D. G. Simonson. "Solving Problem Loans (A Training Feature)." *The Journal of Commercial Bank Lending*, July 1977: 24–31.

Rescigno, R. "Why Penn Square Failed." *Barrons*, Aug. 23, 1982, 6–7, 33, 36.

Sherrod, S. F. "An Objective Risk Rating System for Commercial Banks." *The Journal of Commercial Bank Lending*, November 1981: 12–32.

Sinclair, A. C. "Monitoring Your Loan Portfolio." *The Journal of Commercial Bank Lending*, October 1981: 2–13.

Soderberg, R. K. "Assistance to Financially Troubled Companies." In *Classics in Commercial Bank Lending*, ed. W. W. Sihler, 386–397. Philadelphia: Robert Morris Associates, 1981.

Ziegler, H. G., Jr. "A Binary System of Loan Control." *The Journal of Commercial Bank Lending*, September 1980: 37–44.

CHAPTER 10

Consumer Loans

TREND AND IMPORTANCE

In today's environment consumer loans are a very important component of most banks' total loan portfolios, but this has not always been the case. Originally consumer loans were thought to be an undesirable or unproductive use of funds, and banks therefore limited loans to commerce to assist in the production of goods and services.

Commercial banks first entered consumer lending in the 1920s. Since then loans to consumers have grown to become a major portion of the total loan portfolio. The growth in consumer loans was particularly rapid in the 1960s and 1970s. By the end of the 1970s consumer loans represented 22 percent of total outstanding loans for all insured commercial banks. As indicated in Exhibit 10.1, the percentage of consumer loans has declined slightly since then, but such loans are still a very significant component of the banking system's loan portfolio.

The relative importance of consumer loans varies for commercial banks of different sizes located in different geographic regions (see Exhibit 10.2). In general, consumer loans comprise a larger percentage of total loans for most small- and medium-sized banks than for large banks with deposits of over $500 million. For example, in the New England area consumer loans range from 28 percent to 33 percent of total loans for banks with deposits of under $500 million, whereas such loans comprise only 9 percent of total loans for banks with deposits of $500 million or more.

Differences in importance of consumer loans exist in various geographic regions. Consumer loans are a much larger percentage—21 percent—of total loans for large banks in the Mountain region, compared to 9 percent in the New England area. Differences in customer base and emphasis on commercial loans are apparent from examination of Exhibit 10.2. Large Western banks have a greater retail orientation than do their counterparts on the East Coast.

Although consumer loans vary in importance among individual commercial banks, the importance of the commercial banking industry to consumer credit should not be underemphasized. Commercial banks

EXHIBIT 10.1   Percentage Breakdown for Different Types of Loans for All Insured Commercial Banks

Type of Loan	1980	1981	1982	1983
Commercial and industrial loans	36%	37%	38%	37%
Real estate loans	29	29	29	30
Loans to individuals	20	19	18	19
Security loans	2	2	2	2
Loans to NB financial institutions	3	3	3	3
Agricultural loans	3	3	3	3
Lease financing receivables	1	1	1	1
All others	6	5	5	5

Source: "Loans and Securities of All Commercial Banks," *Federal Reserve Bulletin.*

EXHIBIT 10.2   Banks' Ratios of Consumer Loans to Total Loans at Year-End 1982

Census Region	Deposit Size Categories (in Millons of Dollars)				
	Under 25	25–50	50–100	100–500	500 and over
New England	30%	28%	28%	33%	9%
Middle Atlantic	28	21	48	26	6
South Atlantic	23	42	33	32	22
East North Central	25	26	21	22	13
East South Central	21	32	24	29	16
West North Central	23	21	19	19	11
West South Central	36	39	30	23	6
Mountain	45	24	27	30	21
Pacific	45	18	34	27	15

Source: American Bankers Association, *1983 Retail Bank Credit Report* (Washington, DC: American Bankers Association, 1983), 15.

are the dominant institutions in all areas of consumer credit (see Exhibit 10.3). Based on percentages of outstanding credit, commercial banks hold 50 percent or more of all revolving and mobile home credit and 45 percent of automobile credit. Consumer loans are a very important and significant use of bank funds. For some banks, particularly small- and medium-sized banks, their consumer loan portfolios are as large or larger than their commercial loan portfolios.

EXHIBIT 10.3 Installment Credit Outstanding as Percentage of Total by Type and Holder

Type and Holder	1980	1981	1982
Automobile Credit			
Banks	53%	46%	45%
Credit unions	18	18	17
Finance companies	29	36	38
Revolving Credit			
Banks	51	52	55
Retailers	41	41	39
Gasoline companies	8	7	6
Mobile Home Credit			
Banks	60	55	51
Finance companies	21	25	26
Savings & loans	16	17	20
Credit unions	3	3	3
Other Credit			
Banks	37	37	36
Finance companies	32	32	32
Credit unions	19	19	19
Retailers	4	3	3
Savings & loans	6	7	8
Mutual savings banks	2	2	2

Source: Based on figures from American Bankers Association, *1983 Retail Bank Credit Report* (Washington, DC: American Bankers Association, 1983), 15.

CONSUMER LOANS AS A PRODUCT MARKET

Banks entered the consumer market when they recognized the potential profit of lending directly to consumers rather than to finance companies that in turn lent their funds to consumers. The market is large and has steadily increased in size. The demand for consumer loans is less sensitive to business cycles than demand for commercial loans. The stability of the market ensures greater employment of resources in the consumer area. All of these factors make the market attractive to commercial banks.

By lending to consumers banks have opportunities to sell related services, thus building a solid base of clients and contributing to long-term profitability. For example, a bank could sell related credit life and disability insurance as part of the loan package, increasing the total return on the loan. Banks can also obtain related commercial loan business through consumer lending activity. Some banks are active in indirect lending (discussed in the following section), which involves loans originated by retail dealers. Through these lending arrangements a bank is able to attract additional commercial loan business. Regulatory requirements mandate that a bank meet the credit needs of the community it services, and consumer loans contribute to satisfying this requirement.

The risk and return characteristics of consumer loans differ significantly from those of commercial loans. The dollar amount of each individual loan is small, which results in a lower dollar profit and less exposure to loss. The potential profit from an individual loan is small, but the potential for overall return from the portfolio of consumer loans can be large if the loan services are delivered at low cost.

The key element in management of the consumer loan portfolio is efficiency in delivery of service. Although administrative organizational structures are important to all functions of banking, an efficient structure is critical to consumer lending. Profitable management requires delivery of service with the lowest possible administrative and personnel costs. Consumer loan management also entails greater use of the computer than do other areas of lending. The computer is typically used in credit analysis, preparation of loan documents, and routine collection.

CHARACTERISTICS OF CONSUMER LOANS

Consumer loans differ from commercial loans in several important ways. First, consumer loans tend to be much more uniform than commercial loans, which allows for the greater specialization and centralization of services associated with consumer loans. Second, most consumer loans are longer-term installment loans at fixed rates, which increases the interest rate risk for these assets. The interest spread, or margin, on these fixed-rate loans will therefore likely vary with changes in interest rates. Third, consumer protection legislation passed since the mid-1960s has complicated the administration of consumer loans. Compliance with consumer protection legislation places a significant burden on the consumer loan department not imposed on the commercial loan department.

The standardization associated with consumer loans allows specialization in the organization of the consumer loan department. For example, the primary responsibility for collection of commercial loans lies with the lending officer. Collection of consumer loans is often centralized, with specialists handling delinquent loans. In most organizational structures, consumer revolving-credit lines are administered entirely in a centralized department. The uniform and centralized nature of the consumer lending process thus makes it possible to reduce operational costs, ensure compliance with the bank's loan policy, and maintain control more efficiently.

Given the smaller size of each installment credit compared to a typical commercial credit, one of the primary objectives of managing the consumer loan portfolio is to control the costs associated with the entire process of credit administration. The fewer the employees required to administer the consumer loan portfolio, the greater will be the net return on the portfolio. For example, centralizing collections might significantly increase the average number of accounts each employee can handle, in turn increasing the net return on the entire loan portfolio.

BASIC LOAN CLASSIFICATION

Consumer loans can be classified into three major categories: installment loans, single payment loans, and revolving lines of credit. The largest category on the basis of loans outstanding is installment loans. Single payment loans are offered by most banks to consumers, but they are not a major component of the overall consumer loan portfolio. This type of loan is much more like a commercial loan and many banks process them through the commercial loan department. Revolving lines of credit, which include credit cards and check overdraft lines, have been growing in importance and compose a significant portion of the consumer loan portfolio.

Installment Loans

Installment loans are characterized by periodic repayment of principal and interest over the maturity of the loan. The consumer borrows an amount of funds and repays both principal and interest in fixed monthly installments over the maturity of the loan. Typically, installment loans are entered on the books with interest added to the cash advanced to the customer. Some banks are converting to simple-interest loans from "add-on" interest loans to reduce the complexity involved in accounting. Maturities can extend to five years or longer, and installment loans can be made on a secured or an unsecured basis. With a secured loan, the bank records a security interest on an asset that can be used as an alternative source of repayment in case of default. With an unsecured loan the bank does not have claim to any particular asset as a source of repayment.

The vast majority of installment loans are made at a fixed rate, with the interest rate remaining constant over the life of the loan. However, recent market conditions characterized by high levels of and extreme variability in interest and by declining availability of fixed deposit rates have caused bank managers to reconsider, and in some cases they are making installment loans at a variable rate with simple interest.

Some banks with extensive consumer loan portfolios have experienced significant declines and, in some cases, negative interest margins on installment loans as rates have increased over the maturities of the loans.

A recent survey of commercial banks indicates that many banks are planning to offer installment loans on a variable-rate basis. Large banks responding to the survey indicated that 17.8 percent of the banks currently offer variable-rate installment loans and 63.2 percent of these respondents are planning to offer variable-rate installment loans.[1] Small- and medium-sized banks are not as active in variable-rate loans to consumers, but the trend is toward more variable-rate offerings.

Unsecured Installment Loans.   Unsecured personal loans typically involve smaller loan amounts and shorter maturities than do secured loans. In 1982 the average unsecured personal loan was under $2400, and the most common maximum maturity was 24 months.[2] Such loans are also a small component of the total installment portfolio. Personal consumer loans compose less than 11 percent of the total dollar amount of outstanding loans and their importance has been declining in recent years.[3]

Two major factors have contributed to the decline of unsecured personal installment loans. First, profit from small loans is limited. Many of the costs associated with the administration of installment loans are fixed, and interest revenue on such loans is not sufficient in many cases to cover the administrative costs. Second, with the advent of charge cards and revolving lines of credit, management has recognized that it is more efficient to handle small loans of a personal nature through a revolving-line relationship. A revolving line of credit allows the customer to draw all or part of the loan limit, repay, and redraw at will, subject to the loan limit. Except for larger requests, personal loan requests can thus be handled more efficiently on a revolving-line basis.

Secured Installment Loans.   Secured loans are made on either a direct or an indirect basis. A direct secured loan involves a two-party transaction wherein the loan is negotiated directly between the borrower and the bank. An indirect secured loan involves a three-party transaction wherein the loan application is generated by a dealer (third party) and the loan is made to the borrower through the bank. The dealer is the merchant who sells such consumer goods as automobiles and mobile homes. The bank approves the loan, and the dealer closes the loan with the customer.

---

[1]American Bankers Association, *1983 Retail Bank Credit Report* (Washington, DC: American Bankers Association, 1983), 58–62.

[2]Ibid., 22, 55.

[3]Ibid., 22.

Direct Secured Loans. Direct secured loans are collateralized loans in which the bank takes security interest in property to secure the loan. The largest single category of such loans are loans made to purchase automobiles. Other types of collateral used to secure loans include mobile homes, recreational vehicles, boats, large appliances, securities, passbooks, and cash values of life insurance policies. In the event that the consumer defaults on a loan, the bank will have the right to the collateral that secures the loan. The potential loss to the bank is clearly less on secured loans as long as the collateral is easily marketable and the loan-to-value ratio provides significant protection.

The maturity on secured installment loans typically exceeds that of unsecured loans (see Exhibit 10.4). Most banks offer automobile loans that can have maturities of four years. Maturities offered on mobile home loans range from five to ten years. Maturities of five to seven years are commonly offered on aircraft and recreational vehicle loans.

Indirect Secured Loans. Indirect secured loans are generated by dealers who sell merchandise to consumers and arrange for financing of the purchases through a bank or other lending institution. The majority of indirect secured loans are automobile loans. Other types of purchases for which indirect financing arrangements are common include mobile homes, construction and farm equipment, recreational vehicles, and aircraft.

Indirect financing arrangements made through dealers typically include a package of services and are not limited to just the installment loans to retail customers. It is common for a bank also to provide financing for the dealer's inventory (referred to as floor plan loans), and often the bank provides a variety of services and loans in addition to the floor plan—related real estate loans, working capital lines of credit, equipment leasing, or term loans. Indirect lending is therefore usually only one component of the overall package of services to dealers.

The dealer takes the credit application for an indirect loan and forwards it to the bank for processing. Once the credit has been approved, the dealer is notified and he prepares the loan documents, closes the loan, and forwards the documents to the bank. The bank books the loan and deposits the proceeds in the dealer's account. If the dealer has financed the inventory through the bank, the dealer must pay off the amount financed for the automobile (or other item) on the flooring loan.

The dealer can write the loan to the customer at any rate acceptable to both dealer and purchaser. The bank in turn provides the financing to the dealer on the basis of a predetermined rate structure. The particular rate depends on the maturity of the loan and whether the loan is being made to finance the purchase of new or used assets. The dealer usually writes the loan at a higher rate than the rate he is charged by the bank. This type of indirect lending is referred to as "discounting."

EXHIBIT 10.4   Most Common Maximum Maturity for Various Loans in Number of Months

Type of Loan	Deposit Size Categories (in million of dollars)				
	Under 25	25–50	50–100	100–500	500 and over
Personal—direct and indirect	24	24	24	24	36
Automobile, used and new —direct	36	48	48	48	48
Automobile, used and new —indirect	36	48	48	48	48
Home improvement, own plan—direct	60	60	60	60	60
Home improvement, own plan—indirect	60	60	60	60	60
Mobile homes, new and used—direct	60	60	60	60	120
Mobile homes, new and used—indirect	84	120	120	120	120+ [a]
Farm equipment—direct	24	60	60	36	60
Farm equipment—indirect	24	36	60	48	60
Recreational vehicle, used and new—direct	36	36	48	60	84
Recreational vehicle, used and new—indirect	24	48	48	60	84
Installment, small business —direct and indirect	36	36	60	60	60
Aircraft—direct	60	60	60	60	60
Aircraft—indirect	36	—	—	60	60
Second mortgages—direct and indirect	60	60	60	120	120

[a]Over 120 months.
Source: American Bankers Association, *1983 Retail Bank Credit Report* (Washington, DC: American Bankers Association, 1983), 55.

The dealer takes advantage of the difference between the bank's rate and the note's rate as an origination fee.

It is common for the bank to reserve a portion of the dealer's interest-differential income. The bank books the loan and credits the dealer's reserve with interest that will eventually be earned by the dealer when the loan is repaid in monthly installments. The bank holds the interest income in reserve until it builds up to a certain percentage of outstanding loans and then releases the excess interest to the dealer.

The percentage held in dealer reserve varies according to the dealer's recourse agreement (see below) and the bank's experience with the dealer. If the dealer makes some guarantee concerning repayment on the loan, a larger percentage is reserved. If the bank has had extensive credit experience with the dealer, it may be willing to hold a smaller percentage in reserve. Reserve percentages of 3 percent to 5 percent of outstanding loans are common.

It is customary for the dealer to make some guarantee arrangements concerning repayment of the loan. The dealer is able to arrange the loan through the bank at the discounted rate because of the guarantee. The types of dealer guarantees vary from full recourse (unconditional guarantee) to limited recourse. For a full-recourse guarantee, the dealer is responsible for the loan balance plus any collection costs incurred by the bank. At the other extreme, under a nonrecourse purchase the bank approves the loan and has no guarantees against default from the dealer. The loan is similar to a direct loan. Between these extremes are limited-recourse agreements in which the dealer who initiates the loan guarantees the loan if certain conditions are met.[4]

Credit Cards and Revolving Lines of Credit

Banks are increasingly using charge cards and revolving lines of credit to make unsecured consumer loans. The cost to a bank in making loans to consumers by using revolving credit lines is lower because operating and processing costs are reduced.

Standardization allows the bank to process revolving credits in a centralized department, thus reducing administrative cost. Cost advantages also arise from continued borrowing arrangements. Once the credit line is established, the customer can borrow and repay according to his needs, and the bank can provide the funds to the customer at lower cost. It costs nearly $50 to process a loan request.[5] Instead of having to process later loan requests individually, once the line is in place no further processing is required. This type of lending entails somewhat greater risks in that each loan request is not approved, although the bank can control its exposure through the line limit.

The two most common revolving-credit agreements are charge cards and credit lines tied to demand deposit accounts. Often the credit card and overdraft lines are combined as to terms. Banks have also begun to offer larger revolving-credit lines to "upscale consumers."

Credit Cards.   Banks have offered credit card services since the 1960s. The most successful and widely used cards currently are MasterCard

---

[4]An example is a 90-day limited-recourse agreement. If the bank returns the repossessed collateral within 90 days of default, the dealer is responsible for paying off the account balance. Dealers may limit their risk to a specific dollar amount, thereby sharing risk with the bank.

[5]Paul S. Anderson, "Costs and Profitability of Bank Functions," *New England Economic Review, Federal Reserve Bank of Boston*, March-April 1979: 43–61.

(formerly Master Charge), offered by the Interbank Card Association, and Visa (formerly BankAmericard). Although some banks have offered individual cards from time to time, MasterCard and Visa remain dominant.[6]

Size advantages exist with the operation of charge cards. Charge card operations are usually highly centralized with credit-granting, payment-processing, and collection activity being handled in a central location. This centralization allows greater operating efficiencies and therefore increased returns.

To become members of Visa and/or the Interbank Card Association, banks must pay an initiation fee plus an annual fee based upon the number of active accounts in their portfolios. In addition, member banks reimburse each other for the costs of processing interchange transactions.

Banks earn revenues on charge cards from merchants who accept the cards and from their cardholders. Revenue from merchants takes the form of discounts on drafts presented to the banks for payment. Discounts on drafts range from 2 percent to 5 percent. Revenue from cardholders includes interest on unpaid balances and fees charged to cardholders. Interest income is the largest component of income from charge card operations, but in the recent high-interest period banks have also begun to charge monthly or yearly fees to cover the higher cost of funds.

Special risks are inherent in credit card operations. Control aspects are very important because a bank can incur significant losses for fraudulent use of cards from customers using cards over their limits. Although most banks reported very large profits from bank card operations in the late 1960s to mid-1970s, profit margins were severely squeezed in the late 1970s and early 1980s. Over one half of the large banks in a recent survey indicated that they experienced financial losses on their charge card operations in 1980. In 1982 between 80 percent and 90 percent of surveyed banks reported that their charge card operations were either profitable or broke even.[7]

Automatic Overdraft Lines.   Most banks offer unsecured revolving-credit loans that a customer can use simply by writing a check for more than the amount in his checking account. Banks typically use descriptive titles for these accounts such as "Balance Plus," "Ready Assets," and "Ready Reserve." These lines operate as revolving-credit lines that may be separate from or tied into customers' charge card accounts.

---

[6]For a historical development of bank charge cards, see D. Dale Browning, "Bank Cards," in *The Bankers' Handbook*, 2d ed., ed. W. H. Baughn and C. E. Walker (Homewood, IL: Dow Jones-Irwin, 1978), 879–894.

[7]American Bankers Association, op. cit., *1981* and *1983 Retail Bank Credit Report* (Washington, DC: American Bankers Association, 1981, 1983), 63–64, 78.

The advantages of making unsecured loans in this way are similar to those for charge cards. The bank can achieve operational efficiencies and thus increase profits.

Larger Credit Lines. The competition for the upscale consumer has been extreme in recent periods. In an attempt to acquire both deposit balances and the loan business of customers who have large amounts of liquid assets, banks have begun to offer large revolving-credit lines. Larger revolving-credit lines may be secured or unsecured, and most are offered on a variable-rate basis with many tied to prime. Some innovative proposals have been made to offer large credit lines secured by a second deed of trust with variable rates. More innovative credit lines will probably be offered as competition for the upscale consumer intensifies.

Single-Payment Loans

Occasionally retail customers need to borrow larger amounts of funds for a short term than can be repaid in a single payment. These special-purpose loan requests do not have the same characteristics as the typical retail loan and thus require special handling. Many banks process single-payment requests through the commercial loan department because this form of loan is common in the commercial area.

The distinguishing characteristics of a single-payment loan are that the funds are needed for a short period of time and a source of funds will become available to retire the loan. A common example is a loan made against a certificate of deposit. When the certificate matures, funds will be available to retire the loan.

Single-payment loans are usually not a major component of a bank's consumer loan portfolio. They are made to accommodate the special needs of a retail customer. When making a single-payment loan, management must take special care to be certain that funds will be available to retire the loan.

FUNCTIONAL ORGANIZATION AND POLICY CONSIDERATIONS

Consumer loan services are delivered through banks or indirectly through subsidiaries of banks or bank holding companies. Several advantages occur from the formation of consumer finance subsidiaries. These subsidiaries can service markets outside of the geographic constraints to full-service banking activities. This allows banking organizations to compete in higher-growth markets and also provides geographic diversification. Banking organizations with managements that are highly trained and specialized in consumer lending can increase their market potential through subsidiaries.

Large banking organizations have used consumer finance subsidiaries to position for interstate banking as well. Examples include BankAmerica's Finance America and Citicorp's Person to Person Finance. Through operation of subsidiaries, retail lending personnel can be in place and the capabilities of delivering retail banking services when interstate banking is approved are greatly enhanced.

The organizational structure of the consumer loan function depends on the size of the individual bank and whether the bank is a unit or a branch bank. Exhibit 10.5 displays possible organizational structures for a small unit bank, a large unit bank, and a large branch system. The key organizational factor for large banks is the typical separation of operations for direct, indirect, and charge card loans.

In a small unit bank, lending and operations are separated. A loan officer is usually in charge of all loans for the bank. The smaller volume of loans does not make a finer organizational structure feasible. Additionally, most small banks do not have sufficient volume in charge card activity to offer those services directly to their customers. Charge card services are available through a correspondent bank arrangement in which the smaller bank acts as agent.[8] In a larger unit bank, consumer and commercial loan functions are usually separated. Further subdivision into direct, indirect, and charge card loans is warranted if volume is sufficient.

Indirect consumer loans are often centralized because of the specialized nature of the service. Indirect consumer loans involve installment, inventory, and other commercial loans, and the total package is usually centrally administered. Indirect consumer loans require specialized personnel, and efficient operation necessitates a separate organizational structure.[9]

Indirect consumer lending requires a large staff to properly administer the portfolio. To be profitable, the volume of indirect lending must be sufficient to cover the administrative costs. For this reason the majority of indirect loans are made by medium- and large-sized banks. In 1982, 26 percent of banks with deposits of $25 million or less offered indirect loans, whereas 96.3 percent of banks with deposits in excess of $500 million offered them.[10]

The functional breakdown in Exhibit 10.5 indicates separate organizational units for direct, indirect, and charge card operations for large

---

[8]A smaller bank can offer credit card services as an agency of a correspondent bank. This enables the small bank to offer services it could not provide itself because of limited volume.

[9]For an excellent discussion of the considerations involved in indirect lending, see William B. McNeill, "Primary Areas of Consumer Credit," in *The Bankers' Handbook,* 2d ed., ed. W. H. Baughn and C. E. Walker (Homewood, IL: Dow Jones-Irwin, 1978), 759–766. The author points out the special risks of indirect lending and the importance of a specialized staff.

[10]American Bankers Association, op. cit., 23. Greater detail on various aspects of the indirect lending arrangements of survey banks is also available in this report.

EXHIBIT 10.5   Organizational Structure of the Consumer Loan Function

1. Small Unit Bank

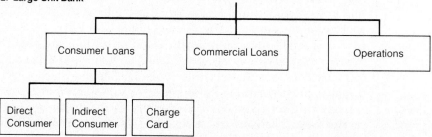

2. Large Unit Bank

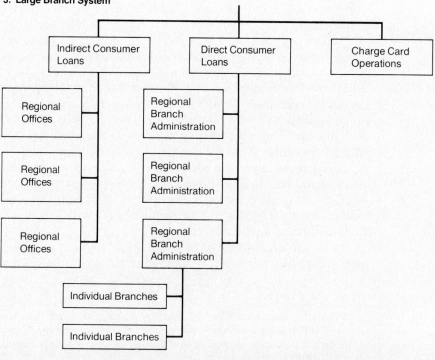

3. Large Branch System

unit banks. The administration of all loans involved with indirect lending typically falls under that unit. To concentrate expertise in similar operations, the charge card operation and revolving-credit lines are administered from the direct installment loan operation. Depending on volume, each of these functional areas may be responsible for such procedures as credit analysis and booking. If volume does not warrant separate functional areas, centralized credit-checking and administrative functions may be shared.

For a large branch system the organizational structure is also separated into direct, indirect, and charge card operations. The difference in administration of the loan areas necessitates separate physical locations for the operations. The charge card operation for the entire branch system is usually centralized, with credit approval, line size determination, and most collection activity being done centrally. The indirect loan function is administered in specialized centers that may be housed in locations separate from the branches. Operational efficiencies are realized through this organizational structure since personnel can administer all dealer loans in a given area through the regional center. This reduces the need for specialized personnel in the various branches in the system. Direct loans are under line authority for the central administration of the branches.

Policy Considerations

Some special considerations for policies on consumer loans include:

- *Lending terms:* Because most consumer installment loans are more standardized than commercial loans, the written loan policy can be more exact for consumer loans. The written policy can be constructed to specify maximum maturities and rates for the various maturities for the different types of loans. Acceptable collateral and steps that are taken to perfect the lien on collateral can be specified in the written loan policy.
- *Compliance:* The extensive consumer protection legislation enacted since the mid-1960s requires that the written loan policy carefully and thoroughly describes steps that must be met for compliance. This compliance involves various stages associated with consumer lending—from credit analysis, notification of approval or disapproval, and closing of loans to collection procedures. The written policy must contain precise and clear instructions to ensure that all legislative requirements are met.
- *Operations:* The written loan policy must also identify procedures to meet bank policy with respect to collections, loan servicing, and reporting. The policy should identify steps to be taken in administering collection of the loans. Specific

instructions should be contained for follow-up for insurance on collateral (e.g., collision insurance on automobile loans) to protect the bank's interest in case of default.[11]

ADMINISTRATION OF CONSUMER LOANS

Administration of consumer loans involves the entire process from credit application to final resolution of loans. It involves approving credit, managing collections, establishing policy for interest income and accrual, and complying with legislation and regulations.

Credit Approval

The purpose of credit analysis is to assess (if the credit request is approved) the likelihood that the customer will repay the loan in accordance with the stipulated terms. In determining whether or not to grant the credit, the loan officer must evaluate the loan request in line with the customer's ability and desire to repay the loan.

The time-honored "C's of credit"—character, capacity, capital, collateral, and conditions—are used as a basis for approving credit (see Exhibit 10.6). Each characteristic is important in evaluating the risk involved with a particular credit.

In assessing the likelihood that the loan will be repaid according to the terms offered, two of the most important characteristics that must be examined are the customer's character and capacity. Assessing character involves determining the customer's willingness to repay, and assessing capacity involves determining his ability to repay. Both factors are critical if the credit is to be repaid according to the terms offered.

The primary information used to assess character is the customer's credit history. If the credit request is from a current customer, the bank may have extensive experience on which it can rely. If the request is from a potential customer, the credit history data will be obtained from credit bureaus and supplied references.

Capacity involves an analysis of the level and stability of the income that can be used to meet the required loan payment. In establishing capacity, income available after living expenses and other loan payments are met is used to gauge the ability to repay. The larger the income after payments, the greater the capacity.

The analyst is also concerned with the stability of the income used to make the loan payments. For salaried individuals, the analyst is con-

---

[11]For additional discussion of policy considerations, see Robert B. Shanahan, "The Organization and Operation of a Consumer Loan Department," in *The Bankers' Handbook*, 2d ed., ed. W. H. Baughn and C. E. Walker (Homewood, IL: Dow Jones-Irwin, 1978), 866–871.

EXHIBIT 10.6   Overall Credit Evaluation—C's of Credit

C's	Attribute	How Measured
Character	Will the customer repay the loan according to terms offered?	Previous credit experience Other credit references Accuracy of application
Capacity	Does the customer have the ability to repay the loan according to terms offered?	Monthly income in excess of monthly outflows Stability of income source Stability of the customer Liquidity of the customer
Capital	Does the customer have alternative sources of capital to repay the loan in the event of adverse circumstances?	Customer's net worth Equity in home and other assets
Collateral	Is the loan backed by collateral that could provide for repayment if the customer is unable to repay the loan?	Loan-to-value ratio relative to terms of the loan Marketability of the collateral
Conditions	Do current economic conditions indicate any potential problems in the customer's ability to repay the loan?	General economic conditions that are forecast over the life of the loan Stability of the customer's income source relative to those conditions

cerned with job stability. For self-employed individuals and persons whose income is based on commissions, the analyst must evaluate stability very carefully.

In assessing capital and collateral, the loan officer is looking at alternative sources of repayment in the event of adverse circumstances. The level of capital, which involves an analysis of the customer's net worth, is important in establishing the customer's ability to repay the loan by falling back on other assets that could be used to generate cash to repay the loan. If the value of the customer's assets substantially exceeds liabilities, the credit is less risky.

If the loan is secured by collateral and the customer fails to repay the loan as promised, the bank has the right to the assets used to secure the loan. To provide an alternative source of repayment, the collateral must be marketable and the value of the collateral must exceed the balance of the loan at the time of default. Collateral should serve only as an alternative source of repayment and in most cases should not be a major consideration in granting credit. It serves to limit loss if the bank is forced to resolve the loan through repossession. Figures for losses in repossession involved with automobile loans in 1982 indicated average losses in excess of $1000 per loan in cases where the bank repossessed the collateral.[12]

The final "C," conditions, is related to general economic conditions and the impact that such conditions will have on capacity and to a lesser extent on the remaining characteristics. Consideration of the potential impact that general economic conditions may have on the ability of the customer to repay the loan is particularly important during recessionary times.

General economic conditions may impact the customer's ability to repay credit through income reduction due to a general economic slowdown or in some cases loss of income source through layoff.[13] In evaluating capacity, the credit analyst must not only look at current capacity, but must also evaluate likely capacity to service the loan over its term.

Implementation of Credit Analysis.   A bank has a choice on the implementation process of credit evaluation. The bank can employ a judgmental process or a credit-scoring process in which a mathematical evaluation of creditworthiness is constructed that relies on historical experience with consumer loans. A judgmental process, as the name implies, requires judgment by loan officers in making the decision to approve or decline a loan request. The loan officer, following the credit policy of the bank, evaluates the credit in terms of meeting that policy.

When a credit-scoring process is employed, the request for credit is evaluated through the use of a point system, in which requests are assigned points for such factors as years at one residence, years on the job, and level of income. Points for these items are based upon analysis of past performance of loans. The credit scoring does not replace judgment for all credit requests; it merely streamlines the process. Most institutions that use credit scoring use a process by which loan requests with scores below a certain number are rejected, loan requests with scores above a certain number are accepted, and loan requests with scores between those two numbers are referred to a loan officer for further analysis.[14]

---

[12]American Bankers Association, *1983 Retail Bank Credit Report,* op. cit., 35.

[13]A recent study indicated that delinquency rates on consumer and real estate loans were related to general economic conditions. From 1951 to 1974 delinquency rates on short- to intermediate-term consumer loans were strongly related to the average manufacturing work week. See Richard L. Peterson and Charles A. Luckett, "Determinants of Delinquency Rates, 1951–74," *Journal of Consumer Credit Management,* Fall 1978: 44–57.

[14]John Day, "Credit Scoring: The Seattle First System for Bank Card Applications," *The Credit World,* April 1978: 13–14; O. D. Nelson, "Credit Scoring Outlook for the 80's," *The Credit World,* April-May 1979: 34–37; and Yair E. Orgler, *Analytical Methods in Loan Evaluation* (Lexington, MA: Lexington Books, 1975), 50–51.

Advantages of Credit Scoring.   There are a number of advantages in the use of a credit-scoring tool:

- *Lower processing costs:* Consumer loans tend to be more uniform than commercial loans, and the key to profitability in consumer lending is operational efficiency. Larger numbers of applications can be screened by fewer employees when a scoring device is used. When the two-score procedure is utilized (low score reject, high score accept), the loan officer's time can be focused on marginally acceptable credits. Most adopters of credit scoring indicate very positive savings in personnel and operating costs.
- *Improved control:* Because evaluation is formalized, the bank potentially gains increased control in quality of the loan portfolio and better adherence to loan policy. This may be very important in a large branch system with thousands of lending officers involved in the process.
- *Reduction in bias or discrimination:* A sound credit-scoring system based upon empirical experience will less likely be as subject to discrimination violations as a judgmental system. The use of a scoring system may be easier to defend against claims of discrimination violations than a judgmental system.[15]
- *Greater flexibility:* Changes in the credit-scoring process can be made to adjust for changes in economic or other conditions with greater ease than may be possible through a judgmental system. The bank may be able to tighten credit standards on certain types of loans more efficiently through adjustment in the minimum score.
- *Improved response time:* The bank may be able to reduce the processing time required to approve a loan and therefore improve customer attitude. Individual branches or lending officers may also get better and quicker responses concerning the status of individual requests.[16]

Developing a Credit-Scoring System.   To develop a credit-scoring system, a bank must obtain a sufficiently large number of good and bad loans with a large quantity of characteristics or variables that are different for good and bad loans.[17] Since the purpose of developing the model

---

[15]Nelson, op. cit., and David C. Hsia, "Credit Scoring and The Equal Credit Opportunity Act," *Hastings Law Journal,* no. 2, 1978: 371–448.

[16]Day, op. cit. Seattle First reported significant gains in this area. With on-line capabilities the status on each credit could be found immediately.

[17]The development of scoring systems presented here is not technical. Readers interested in the technical aspects of a scoring system should see Gilbert A. Churchill, J. R. Nevin, and R. R. Watson, "Credit Scoring: How Many Systems Do We Need?" *The Credit World,* November 1977: 6–11; Bernie J. Grablowsky, "Credit Scoring: New Discriminant Methodology," *Journal of Consumer Credit Management,* Winter 1979: 86–92; Orgler, op. cit.; and Robert A. Eisenbeis, "Pitfalls in the Application of Discriminant Analysis in Business, Finance and Economics," *Journal of Finance,* June 1977: 875–900.

is to identify high- and low-risk loans on the basis of application data, the variables selected should be from applications taken on both good and bad loans. Bad loans are usually defined as charged-off loans and good loans are defined as paid-off loans.[18]

Once a large sample of good and bad loans has been identified and the appropriate data from the applications has been collected, this information is analyzed by using discriminant analysis or multivariate regression analysis. Results of this analysis are an identification of variables that discriminate between good and bad loans and a weighting and scoring system that allows a specific loan to be classified as being a good or a bad loan. From this analysis a manual or automated scoring device can be developed for analysis of future applications.

Given the computer technology available in today's market, the scoring can be done most efficiently through the computer. The data from the application can be entered into the scoring model and the score on the application can be obtained immediately. One bank using a scoring system reported that they automated the system to the point of ordering credit bureau reports on all applications in the marginal area (scores between the automatic accept and reject scores).[19] This increased efficiency is a time-saving device that allows loan officers to use their time in the analysis of marginal applications.

Present and Future Use of Credit Scoring.   To implement a scoring system, a bank must have a sufficient volume of installment credit to overcome the fixed costs associated with the development and maintenance of the system. To design a system, a bank must also have sufficiently large samples of good and bad loans to develop a statistically significant discriminant model. Alternatively, a bank can employ a credit-scoring device based upon other banks' experience. Although this allows a bank with limited experience to employ credit scoring, it has limitations in the sense that a particular bank's credit policies and/or experience could differ from other banks' data bases. However, the scoring performance could be adjusted over time to reflect such differences.

Larger banks use credit-scoring devices more often than smaller banks. In 1982 approximately 40 percent of banks with deposits of $500 million or more were currently using credit-scoring models on direct loans (see Exhibit 10.7). No bank with deposits under $50 million reported using credit-scoring devices.

Based on the reported advantages, the use of credit scoring is likely to increase. For smaller banks future use will depend on the develop-

---

[18]In theory the bank wants to identify profitable and unprofitable loans, and so the charge-off criteria may not be optional. Other possibilities include classification of bad loans according to percentages of late payments or collection expenses as well as the charge-off criteria. Most reported classifications have been based on the charge-off criteria. (For a discussion see Orgler, op. cit., chap. 3.)

[19]Day, op cit., 14.

EXHIBIT 10.7   Percentage of Banks Employing Credit-Scoring Devices

Deposit Size Categories (in millions of dollars)	All Loans		Direct Loans Only	
	Currently Use	Plan to Use	Currently Use	Plan to Use
Under 25	—	—	—	4.5%
25–50	—	—	—	10.7
50–100	3.5%	6.8%	—	10.8
100–500	5.5	7.7	8.3%	10.8
500 and over	22.3	16.4	39.1	10.9

Source: *1983 Retail Bank Credit Report* (Washington, DC: American Bankers Association, 1983), 64.

ment of pooled systems because smaller banks do not have data bases large enough to develop their own systems. For larger banks advances in credit scoring are likely to focus on the refinement of models for different classes of borrowers. Examples of refinement include separate scoring models for homeowners and renters and separate models for different geographic regions.

Collections Management

The same general principal of efficiency that applies to credit administration applies to collection management—the smaller the number of employees needed to adjust consumer loans, the greater the profitability of the consumer loan portfolio. Efficient organization of collections yields a higher margin on the portfolio.

The extent and type of a bank's collection activity depends on many factors, but they are clearly related to credit standards. Easier credit standards result in more delinquent loans and therefore the necessity to use greater resources in collecting bad debts.

Most larger banking institutions employ some sort of centralized collection of consumer accounts. This organizational structure is different from the commercial lending function wherein the contact officer is typically responsible for the initial collection activity on a delinquent commercial loan. The degree of centralization and the organization of the collection function depends on the volume of installment credit and the type of banking structure involved.

Some basic organizational alternatives for the administration of collections are displayed in Exhibit 10.8. In a small unit bank, collections for all types of consumer loans may be centralized. Such an organizational structure may be more efficient because fewer specialized collections personnel can handle both routine and problem collections. In a large unit bank, routine collections can be performed in the various

EXHIBIT 10.8   Organization of Collection Management

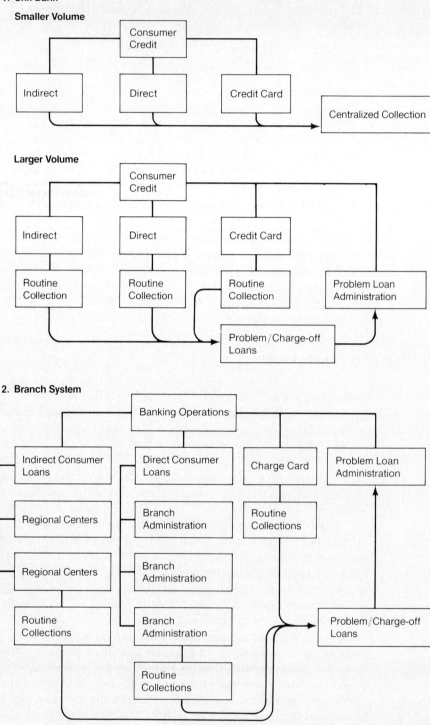

1. Unit Bank

   Smaller Volume

   Larger Volume

2. Branch System

areas (direct, indirect, and charge card). If volume is sufficient, the structure might include a specialized loan adjustment department to handle problem and charge-off loans.

In a large branch system routine collections for indirect loans and charge cards are usually organized under each of the centralized areas. Responsibility for routine collections or direct loans lies with the branch personnel. Problem loans are typically referred to a special collections unit, which may be part of the branch/regional administration or a centralized unit. In a large branch system control of collection activity is not an easy function. The better the organizational structure to assure adequate collection activity, the lower will be the delinquency on the loan portfolio.

Interest Income and Accrual Policy

Banks can write installment loans on either a simple-interest or precomputed basis. When a loan is written on a simple-interest basis, interest income is figured as follows: when a payment is received, interest is figured on a daily basis on the principal balance and interest is applied from the payment. The remainder of the payment is then applied to the principal, which reduces the principal balance for the next period.

When a loan is written on a precomputed basis, the entire amount of the loan principal and interest are booked and the bank then accrues interest income over the life of the loan. The bank has some flexibility in the method chosen to accrue interest on the loan. The method it selects affects its reported interest income and also the remaining principal balance (the payoff balance). The most commonly accepted method for accruing interest is based upon the "rule of 78s."[20] The "rule of 78s" is a sum-of-digits method for recognition of interest; the term is derived from the sum of digits on a one-year loan. The sum of digits 1 through 12 equals 78. The method of accrual assumes that the bank will earn $12/78$ of the total interest in the first month, $11/78$ of the total interest in the second month, and so on.

A simple example, displayed in Exhibit 10.9, illustrates the difference in interest income between a simple-interest and a precomputed loan. In the example we examine a one-year loan written at 24 percent, 2 percent per month. The monthly loan payment of $472.80 is calculated by using a standard present-value interest-factor table, and total payments of $5,673.60 equal 12 times the monthly payment. Total interest income for the year is thus $673.60.

---

[20]For a technical discussion of allowable methods for accruing interest, see Bank Administration Institute, *The Bank Administration Manual* (Park Ridge, IL: Bank Administration Institute, 1974), vol. 2, 897–905. This section describes alternative methods of interest accrual on precomputed loans.

EXHIBIT 10.9   Interest Accrual Example

Loan amount: $5000	Total payments: $5673.60
Installments: 12 @ $472.80	Total interest: 673.60
Annual percentage rate: 24%	

	Simple Interest	*78s*
First-month income	$ 100.00[a]	$ 103.63[b]
Payoff balance to customer	4627.20	4630.83

[a].02 × $5000 = $100.00.

[b]$\sum_{t=1}^{12} = 78$

(12/78)($673.60) = $103.63.

The interest income on a simple-interest basis is $100, whereas the interest income on the precomputed loan using the "rule of 78s" method is $103.60. The payment in Exhibit 10.9 was received and applied on the thirtieth day. In that case use of the "rule of 78s" method will result in greater interest income and a larger payoff balance to the customer than a simple-interest loan (see Exhibit 10.9). If all payments were received on the due dates, use of the "rule of 78s" would result in greater interest income in the early portions of the loan. With a precomputed loan the customer is given a grace period, typically ten days, before a late charge is added, whereas with a simple-interest loan interest is figured on the principal balance on a daily basis. If the loan payment was made within the grace period, the payoff balance would be the same on the precomputed loan but additional interest would be recorded on the simple-interest loan. Difference in reported interest earned using the simple interest and "rule of 78s" method will be larger the longer the term of the loan and the higher the interest rate.[21]

The example in Exhibit 10.9 is based on a single loan. The accrual problem for a bank is more significant in that loans must somehow be grouped according to maturity to apply the "rule of 78s" for the installment loan portfolio. Using precomputed loans requires the bank to accrue income on an estimated basis, whereas with simple-interest loans daily interest is calculated on the outstanding balance of the individual loans. Consumer advocates have expressed concern over use of the "rule of 78s" method because of the penalty to consumers on early payoffs. We shall probably witness greater movement toward simple-interest

---

[21]For a detailed comparison of simple-interest and "rule of 78s" approximation, see Dick Bonker, "The 'Rule of 78'," *Journal of Finance*, June 1976: 877–888. The author shows that the "rule of 78s" is a poor approximation for long-terms loans or for loans written at higher interest rates.

loans in the future, but in 1982 the majority of banks still did not offer simple-interest loans.

Regulation and Legislation

No area of banking has witnessed as many regulatory and legislative changes as consumer lending. Consumer protection legislation passed in the late 1960s and 1970s has placed heavy compliance burdens on bankers. Recent changes in the bankruptcy law appear to have increased risks in consumer lending, particularly in the area of unsecured credits.

Major legislation passed since the late 1960s includes:

* *The Truth-in-Lending Act:* Major provisions of this act include disclosure of interest charges using a standardized actuarial method, complete disclosure of all charges associated with the loan, and Fair-Credit Billing, which contains provisions pertaining to credit card issuance and customer liability on lost or stolen credit cards.
* *The Equal Credit Opportunity Act:* This act prohibits discrimination in the granting of credit and requires the lender to notify the credit applicant of adverse action taken on a credit request. Other provisions include reporting credit in both the husband's and wife's name for joint credit and require that any credit-scoring system be statistically sound.
* *Community Reinvestment Act:* This act requires that each bank meet the credit needs of its community. Primary emphasis here is on residential mortgage loans but general provisions also apply to all consumer loans.
* *Changes in the Holder-in-Due-Course Provisions:* Formerly, when a dealer discounted a loan with the bank, the bank was a holder in due course, which meant that the customer who purchased the automobile or other merchandise could not withhold payment on the loan because of dissatisfaction with the merchandise. Most states now restrict the holder-in-due-course provision, causing many banks to reevaluate indirect loan arrangements.

Some major changes were made in the bankruptcy laws with the enactment of The Bankruptcy Reform Act of 1978. Of particular importance to consumer credit are changes in the Chapter 13 bankruptcy requirements. Chapter 13, the so-called wage earner's plan, allows a wage earner to reschedule debt payments over three years.

The 1978 reform changed the definition of wage earner to include those persons in small businesses and the professions who have unsecured debts of less than $100,000 and secured debts of up to $350,000. The rights of unsecured creditors in approving the payout plan and obtaining reaffirmation of debts were also limited, increasing the risks of unsecured loans.[22] Since its passage bankruptcies have increased, along with losses to unsecured creditors. As losses have increased, many banks have tightened their credit standards on unsecured loans. A recent survey indicated that between 20 percent and 27 percent of total consumer credit losses were attributable to bankruptcy.[23] The percentage of such losses has been increasing.

SUMMARY

Commercial banks are the major financial institution granting most types of consumer credit. Since its introduction in the late 1920s, banks have become more and more involved in consumer credit. Today consumer loans are a major component of every bank's loan portfolio.

Major types of consumer credit include installment loans, which are made on a secured or unsecured basis, charge cards, and revolving credit lines. Organization of the consumer loan function is very important. Given the uniform nature of most consumer loans, the profitability of the overall consumer loan portfolio depends on the efficient administration of the loans.

Questions and Problems

1. Discuss the difference in relative importance of consumer loans for large and small banks.

2. Discuss the effect that the uniform nature of consumer loans has on their administration.

3. Identify the potential effects that fixed rates and terms of consumer loans have on the management of a bank's interest margin.

4. What types of collateral may be used to secure consumer loans?

5. Distinguish between direct and indirect consumer loans.

6. Briefly discuss the potential advantages of implementing credit scoring.

7. Differentiate loans written on a simple-interest basis from those written on a precomputed basis.

8. Describe the potential differences in interest income on simple-interest loans and precomputed loans when the "rule of 78s" is used to accrue interest.

---

[22]For a summary of major changes, see George T. Wruck, "Highlights of the Bankruptcy Reform Act of 1978," *The Credit World*, June-July 1979: 10–12.

[23]American Bankers Association, *1983 Retail Bank Credit Report*, op. cit., 36.

Suggested Case

Case 3, Rocky Ford National Bank. This case involves scoring charge card applications

References

Adkins, W. A., Jr. "Consumer Credit." In *Bank Credit,* ed. H. V. Prochnow, 189–218. New York: Harper & Row, 1981.

American Bankers Association. *1981 Retail Bank Credit Report.* Washington, DC: American Bankers Association, 63–64, 78, and American Bankers Association. *1983 Retail Bank Credit Report.* 23–36. Washington D. C.: American Bankers Association.

Anderson, P. S. "Costs and Profitability of Bank Functions." *New England Economic Review, Federal Reserve Bank of Boston,* March-April 1979: 43–61.

Ang, J., J. H. Chua, and C. H. Bowling. "The Profiles of Late Paying Consumer Loan Borrowers: An Expository Study." *Journal of Money, Credit, and Banking,* May 1979: 222–226.

Bank Administration Institute. *The Bank Administration Manual,* vol. 2, 897–905. Park Ridge, IL: Bank Administration Institute, 1974.

Baughn, W. H., and C. E. Walker, eds. *The Bankers' Handbook.* 2d ed. Homewood, IL: Dow Jones-Irwin, 1978.

Bonker, D. "The 'Rule of 78'." *Journal of Finance,* June 1976: 877–888.

Browning, D. D. "Bank Cards." In *The Bankers' Handbook,* 2d ed., ed. W. H. Baughn and C. E. Walker, 879–894. Homewood, IL: Dow Jones-Irwin, 1978.

Churchill, G. A., J. R. Nevin, and R. R. Watson. "Credit Scoring: How Many Systems Do We Need?" *The Credit World,* November 1977: 6–11.

Cole, R. H. *Consumer and Commercial Credit Management,* 6th ed. Homewood, IL: Dow Jones-Irwin, 1980.

Crigger, J. R. "An Ocean of 'C's'." In *Classics in Commercial Bank Lending,* ed. W. W. Sihler, 40–46. Philadelphia: Robert Morris Associates, 1981.

Day, J. "Credit Scoring: The Seattle First System for Bank Card Applicants." *The Credit World,* April 1978: 13–14.

Eisenbeis, R. A. "Pitfalls in the Application of Discriminant Analysis in Business, Finance and Economics." *Journal of Finance,* June 1977: 875–900.

Grablowsky, B. J. "Credit Scoring: New Discriminant Methodology." *Journal of Consumer Credit Management,* Winter 1979: 86–92.

Hsia, D. C. "Credit Scoring and The Equal Credit Opportunity Act." *Hastings Law Journal,* no. 2, 1978: 371–448.

Johnson, R. W. "Pricing of Bank Card Services." *Journal of Retail Banking,* June 1979: 16–22.

McNeill, W. B. "Primary Areas of Consumer Credit." In *The Bankers' Handbook,* 2d ed., ed. W. H. Baughn and C. E. Walker, 750–767. Homewood, IL: Dow Jones-Irwin, 1978.

Nelson, O. D. "Credit Scoring Outlook for the '80s." *The Credit World,* April-May 1979: 34–37.

Orgler, Y. E. *Analytical Methods in Loan Evaluation.* Lexington, MA: Lexington Books, 1975, 50–51.

Peterson, R. L. *Occupational and Employment Variations in Commercial Bank Credit Risk.* Working Paper No. 17. Lafayette, IN: Credit Research Center, Purdue University, 1978.

Peterson, R. L., and C. A. Luckett. "Determinants of Delinquency Rates, 1951–74." *Journal of Consumer Credit Management,* Fall 1978: 44–57.

Shanahan, R. B. "The Organization and Operation of a Consumer Loan Department." In *The Bankers' Handbook,* 2d ed., ed. W. H. Baughn and C. E. Walker, 862–878. Homewood, IL: Dow Jones-Irwin, 1978.

Sihler, W. W., ed. *Classics in Commercial Bank Lending.* Philadelphia: Robert Morris Associates, 1981.

Smith, J. L. "Consumer Credit Role and Concept." In *The Bankers' Handbook,* 2d ed., ed. W. H. Baughn and C. E. Walker, 741–749. Homewood, IL: Dow Jones-Irwin, 1978.

Thornhill, W. T. "Credit Cards, A Time for Changes, Parts I and II." *The Credit World,* April-May 1980: 14–18; June-July 1980: 8–12.

Wruck, G. T. "Highlights of the Bankruptcy Reform Act of 1978." *The Credit World,* June-July 1979: 10–12.

CHAPTER 11

Mortgage Loans

Mortgage lending differs in many respects from commercial and consumer lending. Although banks are the dominant financial institution in both commercial and consumer lending, they are not dominant in mortgage lending. Real estate loans, particularly residential mortgages, are not easily matched, or hedged, with a bank's sources of funds. Most mortgages are long-term fixed-rate loans. This use of funds does not match well with a bank's sources of funds, which are primarily short term with varying rates. Mortgage lending is highly specialized, and much of the emphasis in credit evaluation is placed on the appraised value of the property, which differs from the emphasis in typical commercial and consumer loans.

Even though they are not the dominant institution in mortgage lending, commercial banks are still an important institution in the overall market. As displayed in Exhibit 11.1, commercial banks' holdings of mortgage debt composed 18 percent of the total at the end of the third quarter of 1983. Of the reported $1.78 trillion in outstanding mortgage debt at the end of the third quarter of 1983, commercial banks held $324 billion. Banks' holdings of mortgage debt are concentrated in the commercial and 1–4 family residence categories. In terms of percentages, banks provide approximately one third of commercial mortgage debt, with much of the activity concentrated in construction lending. In terms of dollars outstanding, the greatest activity is in the 1–4 family residences, which comprise 59 percent of total mortgages for commercial banks. The most active institutions in the mortgage-lending area are thrift institutions, which held approximately 34 percent of total outstanding mortgage debt at the end of the third quarter of 1983.

Real estate lending, similar to commercial and consumer lending, varies in relative importance for banks of different sizes. Real estate loans tend to constitute a larger portion of total loans and assets for smaller banks than for larger banks. The differences in loan portfolios reflect larger banks' emphasis on commercial loans. In a recent study of bank holding companies, real estate loans made up 37 percent of total loans of smaller banks in the study and 16 percent of total loans for banks with assets over $5 billion.[1] Real estate loans composed 20.8 percent of total loans for the sample of bank holding companies.

---

[1] A. G. Cornyn and T. L. Zearley, "Financial Developments of Bank Holding Companies in 1980," *Federal Reserve Bulletin*, June 1981: 473–479.

EXHIBIT 11.1   Bank Holdings of Mortgage Debt for Various Categories

	Percentage of Outstanding Mortgage Debts		
	1981	**1982**	**Q3 1983**
Bank Outstandings of Total Mortgage Debt	18%	18%	18%
Categories as a Percentage of Bank Outstandings			
1–4 Family	59	59	59
Multifamily	5	5	5
Commercial	33	33	33
Farm	3	3	3

Source: Based on figures reported in the *Federal Reserve Bulletin*, November 1983: Table A39.

THE MORTGAGE MARKET

The market for mortgage loans can be segmented into two categories: construction loans and permanent loans. Construction loans are short-term loans made to developers of income and residential properties. Banks provide interim financing to assist developers in completion of projects. Banks also provide short-term loans for other financial institutions that are involved in making real estate loans. Of particular significance are loans to mortgage banking institutions, which specialize in making real estate loans for sale to investors in the secondary market. Permanent loans are secured by mortgages on property. They are long-term loans, usually amortized over the life of the loan. Permanent mortgage loans are made on single-family residences, on income-producing property such as apartments and office buildings, and on special types of property such as churches. Banks' activity in permanent lending has focused on residential mortgages rather than on mortgages on income-producing property because of the long-term nature of these loans. Mortgages on income-producing property do not produce deposit balances proportionate to their size.[2] Life insurance companies are the largest provider of funds for mortgages on income-producing property.

In contrast, banks are more active in long-term loans in the residential mortgage market for several reasons. First, residential mortgage loans are smaller and less risky than loans on income-producing property.

---

[2]H. G. Summerfield, Jr., "Commercial Bank Real Estate Lending," in *Bank Credit*, ed. Herbert V. Prochnow (New York: Harper & Row, 1981), 172.

Returns on income property such as commercial developments are more closely related to general economic conditions and are subject to greater risk. Traditionally delinquency rates on residential mortgages have been very low. Second, the service of providing residential financing provides an opportunity to sell other bank services and fits into the concept of retail-customer-relationship banking. Finally, banks must meet the needs of their communities as required under The Community Reinvestment Act. Banks can show they are serving their communities by making residential mortgages. The long-term nature of residential mortgage lending does place a limit on bank activity in permanent lending, because banks' sources of funds are shorter term.

Construction Loans

Construction loans are short-term loans made to developers for the purpose of completing proposed projects. Maturities on construction loans range from 12 months to as long as 4 to 5 years, depending on the size of the specific project. Construction loans are typically written on a floating-rate basis, often at several percentage points over prime. These loans are an attractive source of revenue for banks, but the risks involved in construction lending are commensurate with the returns.

Construction loans are specialized commercial loans that require specialized qualification and control. Construction loans typically involve large loan amounts in which an individual bank is exposed to significant risk. Many construction loans involve participations with other banks in the service area. These participation agreements serve to limit exposure to any one bank. Similar to permanent mortgage loans, construction loans meet community reinvestment requirements, but they are not as subject to interest rate risk as long-term mortgages.

Qualifying the Loan Request.   The basic steps involved in qualifying or underwriting construction loans is similar to the steps involved in credit analysis of commercial loans. The analysis involves the C's of credit, as do all requests for credit, but there is greater emphasis on the value of the underlying project than is common with other loan requests. In case of default, the bank must be able to arrange for the completion of the project to limit potential losses.

Qualifying the request for a construction loan involves four stages or steps: (1) analysis of the developer, (2) analysis of the proposed project, (3) valuation of the proposed project, and (4) evaluation of the source of loan repayment.[3]

---

[3]This section draws heavily on Summerfield, ibid., and on John R. Gallaudet, "Construction Mortgage and Real Estate Warehousing Loans," in *The Bankers' Handbook*, 2d ed., ed. W. H. Baughn and C. E. Walker (Homewood, IL: Dow Jones-Irwin, 1978), 703–718. Greater detail on the underwriting of construction loans can be found in these citations.

1. *Analysis of the developer.* The developer's character, capacity, and capital must be analyzed to determine ability to complete the project. Past performance on construction loans and general credit references are used to develop information on character. The financial statements of the developer must be analyzed to assess capacity and capital position.[4] Of special concern here is the ability of the developer to complete the proposed project. If the current project is much larger or involves a totally different type of project, special care must be taken to assess the ability of the developer to complete the project.

2. *Analysis of the proposed project.* The developer presents complete statements that detail the project. Among the most important considerations in analysis of the proposal is the estimate of costs. The loan officer must be certain that the loan will be adequate to meet the costs of construction. Cost analysis can be done internally if the bank's staff is adequate, or outside consulting may be required on large or specialized projects.

3. *Valuation of the proposed project.* To qualify the loan request, the analysis must include an appraisal of the value of the completed project. This appraisal can be done by using the income, cost, or market approach or some combination of these methods.[5] Appraisal of the completed project is necessary because if the developer fails to complete the project, the bank needs to assess the ultimate value to limit its potential loss exposure. This appraisal should be completed even if a permanent lender has been arranged because the project may not be completed and the bank may be forced to take it over.

4. *Evaluation of the source of loan repayment.* Construction loans can be written either with takeout commitments or on an open-ended basis. In a construction loan with a takeout commitment, another lender has agreed to provide permanent financing when the project is completed. In an open-ended loan, the bank looks to the developer to arrange permanent financing at some time during the completion of the project. Loans with takeout commitments are generally preferred since risk exposure is limited. The takeout commitment agreement is complex. The permanent lender agrees to provide permanent

---

[4]Statements of developers are structured somewhat differently from financial statements of other business enterprises. Analysis of the financial statement requires knowledge of how these statements may differ. See Summerfield, op. cit., 175–176.

[5]The income method involves capitalizing the potential net earnings from the completed project. The cost method involves estimating the costs of construction of the completed facility. The market method involves comparison of similar properties that have sold at market values in the service area. The most appropriate method depends on the particular project.

financing if the terms of the agreement are met. The construction lender must assess the likelihood of performance with the conditions set forth in the agreement to assess the ultimate repayment of the construction loan.[6]

Consideration of the effect of economic conditions is very important in the qualification of construction loans. Cost estimates must be analyzed for sensitivity to changes in the rate of inflation. Demand for the final product is also related to changing economic conditions. If the project in question involves residential construction, the effect that interest rates will have on demand for the houses must be assessed. If rates increase during construction, demand might be much lower than anticipated. The capital position of the developer may be more important if a restrictive economy is predicted.[7]

Control of all aspects involved with construction lending is critical. The contracts involved with construction lending are complex, and failure to ensure compliance with all of the contractual agreements may seriously affect a loan's performance. For example, if all requirements for the takeout agreement are not met, the permanent lender has cause to withdraw its commitment. The bank may experience significant losses if alternative sources of permanent financing cannot be found. The complex agreements involved in construction lending require careful documentation and monitoring. One area of special concern is the disbursement of funds on construction loans.

Disbursements.   Construction loans differ from other commercial loans in the manner in which the proceeds of the loans are disbursed. Advances are made according to the stage of completion of the particular project. Control of disbursements or advances is critical to the lender in limiting risk exposure.

The basic guiding principle involved in disbursement policy is to advance funds corresponding to the completion stage of the project. If funds are advanced beyond the appropriate stage of completion, the value of the bank's secured interest declines. The personnel requirements and monitoring costs involved in carefully controlled disbursements are extensive.

The disbursement policy must specify what percentage of the loan will be disbursed at which stage of completion. Depending on the type of project, disbursement agreements can be either standardized or designed for a particular project. Exhibit 11.2 displays a disbursement schedule for a residential construction loan. The form has three or four

---

[6]For a detailed discussion on takeout commitments, see Gallaudet, op. cit.

[7]Summerfield, op. cit., makes several references to the 1974–1975 restrictive economy and the impact that this period had on performance of construction loans.

**EXHIBIT 11.2   Sample Disbursement Schedule for a
Single-Family Residential Construction Loan**

Construction Checklist—Four-Advance Schedule

Property:

First Advance 40%

Date

_____ __   1. Foundations completed.

_____ __   2. Dwelling framed and entirely sheathed.

_____ __   3. All roof areas completely shingled.

_____ __   4. All window sash (except picture window, if any) and partition studding in place.

_____ __   5. Chimneys and fireplaces (except fireplace facings) erected.

_____ __   6. Rough flooring laid.

_____ __   7. Rough plumbing and electric complete.

_____ __   8. Heating risers in walls of one-and-a-half- and two-story dwellings.

Second Advance 30%

_____ __   9. Insulation installed.

_____ __   10. Exterior surface complete, including prime coat of paint.

_____ __   11. Cellar bottom cemented.

_____ __   12. Interior staircases installed.

_____ __   13. All exterior porches and steps in place.

_____ __   14. Plastering complete (if drywall, taped and spackled), ready for trim. Wood paneling not required at this stage.

Third Advance 15%
A completely finished unit is required with the following *exceptions:*

_____ __   15. Scraping and finishing floors.

_____ __   16. Leaders and gutters installed.

_____ __   17. Interior decorating (trim must be painted—two coats).

_____ __   18. Electric fixtures installed.

_____ __   19. Linoleum and/or floor tile installed; kitchen, halls, family room only.

_____ __   20. Finish grade, seed and shrub.

_____ __   21. Service walks and driveways installed.

_____ __   22. Plumbing fixtures except bathtub and shower stalls.

_____ __   23. Ovens and ranges installed.

Fourth Advance 15% (Final)
A completely finished dwelling, ready for immediate occupancy. Offsite construction must be finished or proof of proper bonds furnished.

EXHIBIT 11.2 *(continued)*

Fourth Advance 15% (Final)

If interior decorating and electric fixtures are left to an owner's choice, then escrows of one and one half times the cost are to be withheld. The same escrow procedure is to be followed if floors are left unfinished. Escrow $_____.

Note:

1. For 3-Advance schedule eliminate no. 3 Advance from the 4-Advance schedule.

2. If other than normal building materials are to be used (i.e., carpeting over subfloors, complete wood panel walls) or construction procedures not in accordance with the above list are contemplated, these changes must be approved prior to the granting of a commitment.

3. Minimum acceptable specifications are those approved by the Federal Housing Administration, local building codes, and this bank.

Source: J. R. Gallaudet, "Construction Mortgage and Real Estate Warehousing Loans," in *The Bankers' Handbook,* 2d ed., ed. W. H. Baughn and C. E. Walker (Homewood, IL: Dow Jones-Irwin, 1978), 709.

---

stages, depending on whether the home is presold or built on a speculative basis. Each advance is made after all items in the stage are complete.

For larger specialized structures a bank will not use a standardized form like the one shown in Exhibit 11.2. Such projects require a specialized construction-item schedule that is usually prepared by the project builder or architect. Disbursements are made upon stages of completion of the major elements of construction such as framing, masonry work, and so on.[8]

Controlled disbursements are designed to protect the bank's security interest and limit the risk of potential loss on the loan. Monitoring the disbursement plan is as important as its design. To ensure compliance someone from the bank's staff must make a proper inspection to ensure the work is completed before disbursing funds. Periodic inspection of structures even when advances are not requested may be helpful in identifying potential problems on loans. Inspection could reveal construction slowdowns or early warning of an abandoned project.[9] This early warning allows the bank to take the steps necessary to limit its exposure.

---

[8]Gallaudet, op. cit., 708–710.
[9]Ibid., 711.

Acquisition, Development, or Construction Loans as Real Estate Investments.   Certain lenders enter into transactions with borrowers for acquisition, development, or construction (ADC) of commercial projects that have characteristics of real estate investments rather than loans. These arrangements are structured to provide the lender with participation in residual profits on the projects.

Terms may be structured in several different forms. The contractual interest may be a fair market rate with expected sales prices sufficient to cover at least principal and accrued interest, and the lender shares in an agreed-upon proportion of any profits on the sale of the projects. Other variations may include an interest rate at higher than market with smaller participation in profits, an interest rate at a level sufficient to produce similar results without participation in profits, or an arrangement in which the lender shares in gross rents or net cash flow from the projects.

An ADC arrangement usually has most of the following characteristics:

- The lender commits to providing all or substantially all necessary funds to acquire the property and to complete the project. The borrower has title to, but little or no equity in, the underlying property.
- The lender funds the loan commitment or origination fees or both by including them in the amount of the loan. Often the transaction is structured to maximize the immediate or early recognition of such fees as income.
- The lender completely funds the interest during the term of the loan by adding the interest to the loan balance.
- The loan is secured only by the ADC project. The lender has no recourse to other assets of the borrower, and the borrower does not guarantee the debt.
- In order for the lender to recover the investment in the project, the property must be sold to independent third parties, the borrower must obtain refinancing from another source, or the property must be placed in service and generate sufficient net cash flow to service the debt principal and interest.
- The arrangement is structured so that foreclosure during the project's development is unlikely because the borrower is not required to fund any payments until the project is complete; therefore the loan cannot become delinquent.

Since the transaction is a real estate investment rather than a loan, income is recognized at the time of sale of the project. Loan fees associated with the project are normally recognized immediately to the extent that they exceed associated costs.

Although our discussion of construction lending has been limited in scope, we have attempted to identify the key elements involved in the management of a construction-lending function. Construction lending can be very profitable, but special risks are involved and careful credit analysis is essential. Careful credit analysis is likely to be expensive, but the size and special credit risks involved with construction lending make it necessary to spend considerable resources in qualifying a credit. Once a loan is approved and made, the bank incurs considerable administrative and monitoring costs. Specialists knowledgeable in construction and construction finance are necessary to operate a bank's construction lending program, but, properly administered, such a lending program can be highly profitable.[10]

Interim Financing of Mortgage Bankers.   Another type of loan made through a bank's real estate department is the short-term working-capital loan to mortgage bankers or other financial institutions involved in mortgage banking. This type of loan is typically referred to as a "mortgage warehouse loan."[11]

A mortgage banker acts as a middleman in the real estate lending process by originating real estate loans and selling them to permanent investors. Interim financing of mortgage bankers involves providing funds to carry the loans they have originated until the loans are sold to the permanent investors.

These loans are similar to regular working-capital loans made to nonfinancial firms; in effect, banks provide working capital for the mortgage bankers to buy and hold loans until they are resold. The interim loans are short term and secured by the mortgages that the mortgage bankers have originated. Rates charged for mortgage warehouse loans can be based upon the rates of the mortgages used as collateral or can be on a variable-rate basis set in relation to the prime rate.

The advantages to a bank in making this type of loan (beyond the interest on the secured loan) include the income earned on the compensating balances typically required and the opportunity to make additional construction loans and generate additional service-fee income. Compensating balances typically range from 10 percent to 20 percent. The bank may also have the opportunity to make construction loans on the development for which the loans are being originated.[12]

---

[10]For an analysis of the profitability of construction and residential loans, see F. P. Johnson and C. F. Muenzberg, "Can Cost Analysis Improve Your Mortgage Loan Function?" *Management Accounting*, February 1980: 22–25. The authors analyze costs and profitability of various areas of mortgage lending for a bank under $200 million in assets. Their findings show construction lending to be highly profitable.

[11]Gallaudet, op. cit.

[12]Ibid., 716.

As with all loans, qualification of the mortgage warehouse loan depends on the source of its repayment. If the mortgage banker is originating presold loans (where prior arrangements have been made for groups or "packages" of mortgages), the risk to the bank concerning the source of repayment is lower. Mortgage warehouse loans can be made when the loans are not presold, but the bank assumes greater risk in this case.

Changes in interest rates in the secondary market for mortgages affect the mortgage banker's profitability. The extreme volatility in mortgage rates during 1979 and 1980 caused great variability in profits to mortgage bankers who were dealing with loans that were not presold. Mortgage bankers, like most dealers in financial markets, are thinly capitalized, and extreme variability in rates can cause large losses that they may not be able to absorb. The risks to the banks consequently increase when rates are volatile. The banks have the security for the loans in case of default, but the value of the mortgages is lower if interest rates have risen.

Bank Participation in Construction and Mortgage Warehouse Lending.
To be an effective construction or mortgage warehouse lender, a bank must have the specialized personnel to qualify and administer these specialized loans. A bank must also have sufficient volume to produce sufficient revenue to overcome the fixed costs associated with this type of lending. Consequently the major construction lenders tend to be the larger banks.

Smaller banks are able to make construction loans through participation agreements with larger correspondent banks, which allow them to acquire these high-earning assets without the heavy investment in staff. The smaller bank must still evaluate the market and the ability of the correspondent bank to effectively administer the portfolio.

Residential Mortgage Loans

No single area of finance or banking has been more affected by the economic environment of the late 1970s and early 1980s than residential mortgage lending. High levels of inflation with accompanying high levels and variability of interest rates sent shock waves through the residential lending markets. Volatile interest rates severely affected both lenders and borrowers of mortgage funds. The traditional fixed-payment mortgage that served the market well since the 1930s would not function in an economic environment characterized by high rates of inflation and extremely volatile rates.

The main problem from the lender's point of view stems from the mismatch of maturities between the source and use of funds in mortgage lending. The traditional mortgage instrument is a fixed-rate, fixed-payment loan amortized over its maturity of from 20 to 30 years. The institution that lends funds under those terms is locked in at that rate until the loan matures or is paid off (with sale and refinancing). The sources of funds have much shorter maturities than the real estate loans. Profits deteriorate in periods of rising rates; and, if the rise in rates is large enough, negative margins result. The condition of the nation's thrift institutions in 1981 and 1982 demonstrated the risks of funding long-term loans with short-term sources. Those that survived have seen some improvement as rates declined in 1983, although the current financial condition of the nation's thrift institutions attests to the difficulty of lending long at fixed rates with funds that are borrowed for shorter terms.

As inflation increased the cost of homes and raised interest rates on mortgages, lenders made riskier loans. Mortgage loans were made with smaller-percentage down payments. This increased the loan-to-value ratio and decreased the protection offered by the collateral in case of default. Lenders also made loans with the mortgage payments requiring larger portions of the borrowers' incomes.[13]

From the borrower's perspective, the increased rate of inflation has increased both the cost of a home and the interest rate at which mortgage funds are available. The borrower's real income from which mortgage payments must be made has not kept pace with the rise in housing prices or in interest costs for mortgage funds. In 1965 approximately 15 percent of income was needed to service a typical mortgage loan, whereas in 1982 nearly 40 percent of income was needed.[14] In the current environment the demand for loans is depressed because borrowers simply cannot make the mortgage payments necessary to purchase a home.

The effect of inflation on residential mortgage lending is displayed in Exhibit 11.3, which clearly demonstrates the inverse relationship between mortgage demand and interest rates. The most striking figure is the monthly payment series (based on new conventional loans). The average monthly payment in 1982 had risen to over $850 and more than doubled since the end of 1978, when interest rates were approximately 10 percent.

In reaction, market participants have had to come up with new and innovative methods to finance the purchase of residential property. The average monthly payment of $850 requires a monthly income of $3400,

---

[13]M. T. Jones, "Mortgage Design, Inflation and Real Interest Rates," *Quarterly Review, Federal Reserve Bank of New York,* Spring 1982: 20–29; and S. E. Hein and J. C. Lamb, Jr., "Why the Medium-Priced Home Costs So Much," *Review, Federal Reserve Bank of St. Louis,* June-July 1981: 11–19.

[14]J. L. Freund, "The Housing Market: Recent Developments and Underlying Trends," *Federal Reserve Bulletin,* February 1983: 66.

EXHIBIT 11.3 Housing Prices and Interest Rates

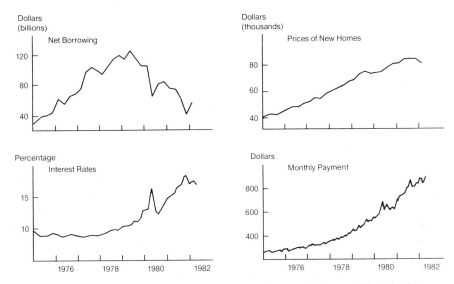

Net borrowing is at seasonally adjusted annual rates, from the household sector of the Federal Reserve quarterly flow of funds accounts. Mortgage interest rates at a sample of savings and loans are for new commitments on fixed-rate level-payment conventional loans.

The average home price is the Census Bureau series for new homes sold. The average monthly payment is on new conventional loans closed during the month and partly reflects mortgage amounts and interest rates determined earlier.

Source: C. Luckett, "Recent Developments in the Mortgage and Consumer Credit Markets," *Federal Reserve Bulletin*, May 1982: 283.

according to traditional standards employed in mortgage lending.[15] As many, indeed most, households cannot qualify for payments of this size, many sellers and buyers have had to resort to "creative financing" to sell or buy residential properties.

Many of these arrangements involve the purchaser's assuming the seller's original loan and the seller's providing some financing through second mortgage loans on the property. Although terms on second mortgage loans vary, it is typical for the purchaser to agree to repay the entire amount of the second mortgage loan in three to five years. The borrower must arrange to pay off the balance on the second loan by saving enough funds to retire it or by refinancing the loans when the second loan becomes due.

---

[15]Traditionally lenders required that the total mortgage payment, including insurance and taxes, be 25 percent of net income. Evidence indicates that this standard has been lowered by many lenders. The $3400 figure is low because it does not include the monthly provision for taxes and insurance.

Many of these deals were made in the late 1970s in anticipation of rate declines, with eventual refinancing of the entire amount borrowed through conventional financing. The anticipated decline in rates did not materialize, and many purchasers have been unable to refinance. Delinquency rates on mortgage loans and foreclosures at banks and thrift institutions increased. By 1982 over 1.5 percent of mortgage loans at savings and loan institutions were 60 days or more delinquent.[16]

Mortgages are often written with a due-on-sale clause, which allows the lender to accelerate the loan and demand that the loan be paid off if the real estate is sold. The original purpose of the due-on-sale clause was to protect against the loan's being assumed by a riskier borrower, but in the 1970s the clause was used for portfolio adjustment. With increased inflation, lenders used the clause to eliminate low-rate mortgages from their portfolios.

A problem arose with due-on-sale clauses in the late 1970s. Some states had laws that prohibited their use, and the question was raised as to whether or not a federally chartered institution could enforce a due-on-sale clause in those states. In 1978 the California Supreme Court, in the landmark case of Wellenkamp vs. Bank of America, ruled that a due-on-sale clause could not be enforced.[17] The California courts interpreted the Wellenkamp decision to apply to both state and federally chartered institutions. In June 1982 the U.S. Supreme Court ruled in favor of a federally chartered financial institution in California, allowing it to enforce a due-on-sale clause. The question of the enforceability of due-on-sale clauses was again called into question.

The ability of federally chartered institutions to enforce due-on-sale clauses appears to have been determined with the passage of the Garn-St. Germain Depository Institutions Act of 1982. The act specified federal override of state restrictions against the clause.

The long-range effect of the ability of lenders to enforce due-on-sale clauses is positive. Banks and other lenders will be able to shorten the average maturities of their mortgage loan portfolios, thereby reducing the interest rate risk associated with real estate lending. In the long run this should also serve to increase the flow of funds to residential mortgages, which will benefit borrowers.

In addition to financing arrangements that bypass financial intermediaries, alternative types of mortgages are appearing. The main developments in this area are variable-rate mortgages, which allow institutions to adjust rates as the cost of funds supporting the mortgages

---

[16]C. Luckett, "Recent Developments in the Mortgage and Consumer Credit Markets," *Federal Reserve Bulletin*, May 1982: 281–290. Luckett indicates that a major number of these balloons have not yet come due and further pressure on delinquencies could be experienced in the next several years.

[17]G. Garcia et al. "The Garn-St. Germain Depository Institutions Act of 1982," *Economic Perspectives, Federal Reserve Bank of Chicago*, March-April 1983:20. This article contains a brief summary of legislative developments relating to due-on-sale clauses.

increases, and the development of mortgages with lower initial payments to qualify marginal borrowers. Given the development of variable-rate mortgages, the significance of the Supreme Court's decision on future mortgage lending may be minimal. The effect will depend on how the fixed-rate mortgage fares in the future economic environment.

Types of Mortgage Instruments.   Following the depression of the 1930s, the standard mortgage instrument was the fixed-rate fixed-payment mortgage. The conventional mortgage was characterized by full amortization of the principal over the maturity of the loan, which could extend up to 30 years.

Although the traditional mortgage is still the most commonly used instrument, many new instruments have appeared. Changes from the standard form involve altering the rate characteristics or the amortization characteristics, or both. Exhibit 11.4 displays the characteristics of mortgage instruments currently used.

Mortgage instruments wherein the fixed rate has been changed include the adjustable-rate mortgage, the variable-rate mortgage, and the renegotiable-rate mortgage (sometimes referred to as a rollover mortgage). These mortgages allow the lender to adjust the interest rate on the mortgage within limits and therefore reduce some of the problems experienced with rising rates of interest. As the lender's cost of funds increases with rising rates, the lender is able to increase the rate charged for the mortgage. When interest rates fall, the opposite occurs.

The borrower bears interest rate risk with these types of mortgages. Of course, if interest rates decline, the rate on the loan declines, but if rates rise, the borrower must pay the higher rate. The monthly payment is adjusted for the variable-rate mortgage as interest rates change. For the adjustable-rate mortgage the maturity of the mortgage can be extended in lieu of increasing payments.

Although the variable-rate mortgage alleviates some of the interest rate risk to the lender, it merely transfers the risk to the borrower. If interest rates rise and monthly payments also rise, the risk of default or credit risk to the lender may increase. Rising payments could place serious burdens on the borrower if the borrower's income does not rise proportionately to offset the increased rate. The adjustable-rate mortgage, which allows for extension of maturity in lieu of an increase in payments, may be preferable to borrowers.[18]

Another group of mortgage instruments has evolved to assist new borrowers by creating a mortgage with lower payments in the early life of the mortgage and increased payments later. Such mortgages are referred to as "graduated-payment mortgages," and they usually include

[18]For greater detail on variable-rate mortgages, see W. C. Melton and D. L. Heidt, "Variable Rate Mortgages," *Quarterly Review, Federal Reserve Bank of New York,* Summer 1979: 23–31.

254

EXHIBIT 11.4 Varieties of Home Financing

Mortgage Type	Interest Rate	Maturity	Payments
Conventional	Fixed. May be scarce when interest rates are climbing, because lenders do not want to risk being locked into lower income.	Fixed, often 30 years.	Fixed over term of the loan.
Adjustable Rate or Variable Rate (ARM or VRM)	Indexed to a market rate (for example, 6-month Treasury bill rate). Starting rate may be lower than on conventional because borrower shares risk of rising rates with lender.	Fixed, but sometimes can be extended in lieu of increase in monthly payment when interest rate rises.	May change when interest rate changes or only at specified intervals, such as annually or every 3 to 5 years. If payments do not increase with interest rates, result may be negative amortization (see GPM below).
Graduated Payment (GPM)	Fixed.	Fixed	Low at start. Increase gradually as predetermined during first 5 or 10 years, then level out.

Because of lower starting payments, may appeal to young borrowers who anticipate increased income in future years. *Caution:* Early payments may not cover interest due. Unpaid interest is added to outstanding principal, increasing the debt. This is called *negative amortization*, and borrowers may get a shock if they decide to sell in a few years and discover reduced equity in the property. However, some GPMs may include arrangements to prevent negative amortization.

Mortgage Type	Interest Rate	Maturity	Payments
Graduated Payment Adjustable	Adjustable as in ARM or VRM.	Fixed, up to 40 years.	Similar to GPM. During first 10 years may be less than required to fully amortize loan. Adjusted within that period and every 5 years thereafter to insure full payment.

Federal savings and loans and mutual savings banks were authorized in July 1981 to offer this mortgage, which combines graduated payments with adjustable interest rates. Payment adjustments may be quite large because of these two areas of change.

Type				
Renegotiable Rate (RRM)	Fixed for 3 to 5 years, then renegotiated.	Short-term loan (3 to 5 years) but amortized over longer term, usually up to 30 years.	Payments will change as interest rate changes.	Short-term loan is automatically renewable: but if new interest rate is not acceptable, the borrower must either refinance or sell the property. The interest rate increases permitted each year and over the life of the loan may be limited.
Shared Appreciation (SAM)	Fixed.	Fixed.	Fixed.	In return for lower interest rate the borrower agrees to share with the lender a percentage of any increase in the value of the home—at specified future dates or when it is sold, whichever occurs first. This plan may appeal to first-home buyer as a way to make the purchase affordable. But remember, increase in value must be shared with the lender; sharing a *decrease* in value may or may not be part of the agreement.
Wraparound (WRAP)	Fixed.	Fixed.	Fixed.	The lender combines an existing mortgage on the property (bearing a lower rate) with a new mortgage for the balance needed (at a higher rate) to provide a lower overall cost to the borrower. This is possible only if the existing mortgage is assumable by the buyer. (All FHA and VA mortgages are assumable.)
Balloon Payment	Fixed or adjustable.	Fixed. Traditionally 5 years but may be shorter or longer.	Fixed, usually based on 20- to 30-year amortization, but at end of term debt will not be fully paid. Borrower must pay off remaining "balloon" balance or refinance at prevailing rates.	Because of short term and balloon payment, the down payment may be as little as 5 percent.
Reverse Annuity (RAM)	May be adjustable.	May be fixed with refinancing option.	Loan due when home is sold or upon death of borrower.	This plan calls for periodic payments to homeowners based on a loan against their equity in a home. It is designed to appeal to older persons who may be having difficulty living on reduced incomes.

EXHIBIT 11.4 (Continued)

Mortgage Type	Interest Rate	Maturity	Payments
"Take-Back"	Usually fixed.	Usually short term.	Usually a high down payment. May call for balloon payment at maturity.
	This is a loan by the seller of the property, who agrees to take the mortgage in order to facilitate the sale.		
Federal Housing Administration (FHA) Insured	Set by FHA. Usually more favorable because of protection afforded lender. Seller may have to pay "points," an amount to raise lender's return to market levels.	Fixed	Fixed or graduated, depending on FHA options.
	Available from lenders approved by FHA. Properties to be mortgaged must meet FHA requirements.		
Veterans Administration (VA) Guaranteed	Fixed. Lower than others but seller may have to pay points.	Fixed. Usually 25–30 years.	Fixed or graduated, depending on VA options.
	Terms are eased because of VA guarantee. No or low down payment. Veterans should check with VA for eligibility requirements and for other assistance related to housing.		
Buy-Down	Below market rate, for a specified period or for the life of the loan.	Fixed.	Fixed for term of the buy-down; usually increase thereafter.
	A seller or home builder pays an amount to a lender "up front," who then gives to buyers below-market rate loans. The borrower should realize this arrangement may increase the purchase price of the home.		

Source: *Charting Home Mortgages, Federal Reserve Bank of Philadelphia,* January 1982.

some amount of negative amortization. The payments in the early life of a loan are not large enough to cover the interest, and the remaining interest is added to the principal on the loan until the payments rise to the point of covering the interest. Traditionally these instruments were written at a fixed rate, but they are currently offered at variable rates as well. The adjustment in payments could be large with a variable-rate graduated-payment mortgage.

The advantage of the graduated-payment mortgage is that qualifying buyers for the mortgage is made easier. The credit risk to the lender may increase as payments increase, however. The increase in risk depends on whether the borrower's income required to service the loan increases commensurate with the rise in payments. For some graduated-payment mortgages, payments increase at rates in excess of 7 percent per year for approximately 5 years.[19] If income does not rise commensurately, the borrower may have difficulty in making payments.

Exhibit 11.4 describes a variety of other means of making a residential mortgage. Two of the more novel instruments that have developed in recent periods are the shared-appreciation mortgage and the reverse-annuity mortgage. The shared-appreciation mortgage permits the lender's participation in the increase in the value of the home in return for a lower interest rate. The shared-appreciation mortgage is typically written at a fixed rate with fixed payments.[20]

The reverse-annuity mortgage is designed to allow retired individuals to borrow funds against the equity in their homes. The mortgage, which increases over time, is due upon the death of the borrower or when the home is sold. This innovation is designed to ease the burden of retired individuals on fixed incomes in an inflationary environment.

A recent addition to the list of alternative mortgage instruments is the growing-equity mortgage (GEM). A GEM is a mortgage written at a fixed rate but with graduated payments that reduce the principal on the mortgage. Payments typically increase at 3 percent to 4 percent per year over the first ten years of the mortgage and then are stable thereafter.[21] The increasing payments result in an average maturity that is approximately half that of a traditional mortgage.

GEMs have been offered by financial institutions at lower rates than traditional instruments. They have lower risk because of the shorter average maturity. The primary advantage to the borrower is lower interest costs because of the growing equity (reduced principal balance). The primary disadvantage is the pressure of increased

---

[19]W. C. Melton, "Graduated Payment Mortgages," *Quarterly Review, Federal Reserve Bank of New York*, Spring 1980: 21–28.

[20]For greater detail see T. J. Parliment and J. S. Kaden, "The Shared Appreciation Concept in Residential Financing," in *Financial Markets: Instruments and Concepts*, ed. J. R. Brick (Richmond, VA: Robert F. Dame, 1980), 285–300.

[21]"Nailing Down an Affordable Mortgage," *Business Week*, Mar. 14, 1983, 152–155.

payments. If the borrower's income does not increase at a rate commensurate with the increase in the mortgage payment, the risk of default increases.

The problems of financing residences in periods with high rates of inflation are extreme. The traditional fixed-payment mortgage requires the lender to bear the risks associated with the changing rates. The variable-rate mortgage, however, may cause the borrower to experience difficulty in making mortgage payments, which in turn increases the risk to the lender.

More and more innovative mortgage instruments may evolve if inflation persists. One proposed instrument is the indexed mortgage, which allows the borrower and lender to agree on a real rather than a nominal rate of interest.[22] See Exhibit 11.4 for descriptions of other types of innovative mortgages.

Insured or Guaranteed Mortgages.   The federal government has been an active participant in the mortgage market since the depression of the 1930s. One of the federal government's major programs has been insuring or guaranteeing mortgages of individuals against default. The purpose of the insurance is to encourage residential mortgage financing, particularly for individuals with lower incomes.

Private mortgage insurance has also been available since the 1960s on conventional mortgage loans. It differs from federal government insurance in that only a portion of the mortgage is insured. Private mortgage insurance allows the borrower to obtain a mortgage loan with a lower down payment than would otherwise by required.

Federally Insured or Guaranteed Mortgages. Two government agencies insure or guarantee mortgages. The Federal Housing Administration (FHA) was the first federal government agency to offer insurance on mortgages. FHA insurance requires a premium of ½ percent to be paid on the mortgage balance and FHA insurance guarantees full payment to the lender. In addition to the insurance premium, mortgage loans insured by the FHA must meet other requirements, including a specified maximum loan amount.

Originally FHA-insured mortgages had to be fixed-rate fixed-payment mortgages that were fully amortized over their maturities. In 1974 a graduated-payment mortgage program was approved, and under current legislation FHA will insure graduated-payment mortgages under several accelerated-payment plans.[23]

The Veterans Administration (VA) guarantees residential mortgages made to military veterans. VA-guaranteed mortgages became available in 1944. The terms offered to veterans are more liberal than

---

[22]Jones, op. cit.

[23]For a detailed explanation of the various FHA graduated-payment mortgage plans that are available, see Melton, op. cit.

those offered under the FHA program, in some cases requiring no down payment. Similar to FHA-insured loans, VA mortgages include a cap on interest rates.

To be insured by the FHA or guaranteed by the VA, residential mortgages must meet all requirements set by those agencies. These requirements include extensive red tape involved in origination of the loans, specified maximum rates of interest, and maximum loan amounts. Most commercial banks are more active in conventional mortgages on which no interest rate ceilings apply (except where states have set limits).

Private Mortgage Insurance. Private insurers offer insurance on residential mortgages for up to 20 percent of the mortgage amount. The borrower pays for private mortgage insurance in the form of a higher interest rate in the early years of the mortgage. The premium for private insurance depends on what percentage of the loan is insured. The insurance applies for a limited period, typically ten years, after which the lender is willing to bear potential losses from default. The equity built up in a mortgage over that period reduces the loan-to-value ratio.

The development of private mortgage insurance has encouraged an increased flow of funds into conventional mortgages by protecting lenders against default on loans with larger loan-to-value ratios. Private mortgage insurance has also increased the marketability of conventional mortgages sold in the secondary market.

Secondary Mortgage Markets.   A key development in the residential mortgage market in the last two decades has been the extended activity in secondary mortgage markets. A secondary market transaction is the sale of mortgages originated by financial institutions to investors who hold the mortgages as investment securities. Activity in secondary markets has existed since 1938, when the Federal National Mortgage Association (FNMA) was formed, but significant volume in the secondary market did not develop until the early 1970s.

The development of secondary markets extends a bank's participation in the residential mortgage market. A bank can originate mortgages and sell them to other investors, allowing the bank to provide mortgage lending services without tying up funds in long-term assets that are mismatched with their sources of funds. Normally a bank services the mortgages sold in the secondary market and generates noninterest-fee income. Through purchases in the secondary market, a bank can also invest in mortgages without originating them.

The existence of a secondary market contributes to the residential mortgage market in several ways. First, it encourages funds to flow into residential mortgages from investors who lack the expertise to make real estate loans directly. For example, pension funds, which have long-term sources of funds, can invest in mortgages without making the loans directly. Second, banks and thrift institutions can originate the loans and, when they are sold in the secondary market, can reinvest the funds in additional mortgages. This activity provides service income, promotes the transfer of funds from investors to users, and increases the funds available for mortgage loans. Third, the secondary market enables investors to gain geographic diversification, allowing investors an opportunity to protect themselves from recessions in a particular region and, in turn, promoting the allocational efficiency of the market.

Mortgages are sold in the secondary market by using one of two types of security instruments: mortgage-backed bonds and pass-through securities. Mortgage-backed bonds are issued by an intermediary and offer interest and scheduled repayments of principal. The bonds are secured by the individual mortgages that provide the income to service the debt. Pass-through securities involve ownership interest in a pool of mortgages. Payments from the pool of mortgages, including both monthly payments and early payoffs, are passed through to the owners of the certificates.

Mortgage-backed bonds and pass-through certificates are issued by both federal government agencies and private intermediaries. The greatest volume in the secondary market involves government agencies or quasi-government agencies. The first publicly issued pass-through securities were issued by the Bank of America in 1977.[24]

Exhibit 11.5 describes the major government agencies or quasi-government agencies in the secondary market. FNMA, which was reorganized in 1968 as a privately owned institution, was the first agency involved. Other major agencies include the Government National Mortgage Association (GNMA) and the Federal Home Loan Mortgage Corporation (FHLMC). FNMA purchases mortgages using mortgage-backed bonds, whereas GNMA and FHLMC are primarily involved through pass-through securities. Differences in the pass-through securities offered by GNMA and FHLMC involve the timing of principal and interest payments and the guarantees offered.[25]

Publicly issued securities are relatively new and are just developing. Following their introduction in 1977, banks, savings and loan institutions, and private mortgage insurers have offered mortgage-backed securities. Private mortgage insurance is purchased for the pool of mortgages, providing limited protection against default.

Publicly issued securities could greatly expand a bank's accessibility to the secondary mortgage market. First, such offerings could streamline and reduce the red tape involved with the pools sponsored by federal agencies. Second, public intermediaries have greater potential

---

[24]C. M. Swesind, "Mortgage-Backed Securities: The Revolution in Real Estate Finance," *Quarterly Review, Federal Reserve Bank of New York,* Autumn 1979: 1–10.

[25]The services listed in Exhibit 11.5 are the major secondary market services offered by the agencies. For greater detail on related services and on particular characteristics of the securities, see Swesind, ibid.

EXHIBIT 11.5   Government Agencies Involved in the Secondary Mortgage Market

Agency	Description	Secondary Market Activity
Federal National Mortgage Association (FNMA)	Formed in 1938 to purchase government-guaranteed mortgages. Reorganized in 1968 as a privately owned corporation. Began purchase of conventional loans in 1971.	Issues short-term discount notes and intermediate-term debentures. Funds obtained through debt issues are used to purchase conventional and government-guaranteed loans.
Government National Mortgage Association (GNMA)	Formed in 1968 as a government corporation in the Department of Housing and Urban Development when FNMA was recharted as a private corporation. Began government-guaranteed pass-through program in 1970.	Guarantees timely payment of principal and interest on pools of mortgages backed by government-insured mortgages. Issues pass-through securities of pools of mortgages originated by financial intermediaries.
Federal Home Loan Mortgage Corporation (FHLMC)	Created by Congress in 1970. Wholly owned corporation of the Federal Home Loan Banks with primary goal of developing a national secondary market in conventional mortgages. Originally purchased conventional mortgages for its own portfolio. In 1974 emphasis shifted to pass-through certificates.	Issues pass-through certificates on conventional and government-guaranteed mortgages. Private certificates are not guaranteed. Pass-through certificates on government-insured mortgages are guaranteed by FHLMC. Interest and principal repayments are passed through on a semiannual basis rather than monthly basis as with GNMA pass-throughs.

in pooling a number of originators to allow smaller banks greater access to the secondary market. Finally, public offerings can help fill the need for greater secondary market activity in mortgage loans not insured by the federal government.

The performance of the secondary market in the late 1970s and early 1980s reflects basic underlying problems with high levels of inflation and great uncertainty about future levels of inflation. Investors were not willing to invest in long-term fixed-rate securities because of uncertainty about inflation. To date there has been very little secondary market activity in alternative mortgage instruments. To attract permanent investors, secondary market activity in variable-rate and adjustable-rate mortgages must be developed. The existence of the secondary market for fixed-rate instruments does not solve any problems for lenders if permanent investors are unwilling to invest in such securities.

Forward Commitments and the Futures Market. When a lender originates and packages mortgages for resale in the secondary market, the risk associated with the selling price of the pool of mortgages must be managed. As with any fixed-rate instrument, if market rates rise, the value of the fixed-rate mortgage falls. If a lender does not have a commitment of price for the pool of mortgages, the lender bears the risk associated with any changes in interest rates. Most market participants use some form of commitment to limit this price risk.

"Forward commitments" are available through dealers who make markets in mortgage securities, and "forward contracts" are available through the organized commodity exchanges, which offer futures contracts on GNMA pass-through certificates.

Two types of commitments are used in the secondary market: firm commitments and standby commitments. Under a firm commitment the lender makes a firm agreement to deliver the mortgages at the commitment price. Standby commitments give the lender the option of delivering the mortgages. The seller of the mortgages for a standby commitment must pay a nonrefundable fee, typically 1 percent of the mortgage pool amount. Standby commitments are commonly used on contracts with distant deliveries (often 12 months). The greatest market activity in commitments is in GNMA securities, but dealers also offer commitments for other secondary market securities.[26]

Futures contracts for GNMA securities are available through the Chicago Board of Trade, the Amex Commodities Exchange, and the Commodity Exchange, Inc. The first GNMA contract became available through the Chicago Board of Trade in 1975 and market activity has steadily increased since then. Futures contracts differ from commitments sold by dealers in that the contracts tend to be more standardized.[27] They also allow a lender to eliminate price risk because a sales price can be established in advance of delivery.

Administration of Residential Mortgages. In many ways the residential mortgage loan portfolio is similar to the installment loan portfolio. Efficient management of the portfolio requires efficient use of personnel and cost control to maintain profit margins. Areas of special concern in administration of the portfolio include the basic structural

---

[26]Swesind, ibid.

[27]For a complete description of the various GNMA contracts, see M. Arak and C. J. McCurdy, "Interest Rate Futures," *Quarterly Review, Federal Reserve Bank of New York,* Winter 1979–1980: 33–46. The authors describe the technical aspects of the various contracts.

organization for the various functions, credit analysis, compliance with consumer protection legislation, and interest margin management.

FUNCTIONAL ORGANIZATION

Most large banking organizations, whether unit or branching systems, centralize residential mortgage lending. Factors contributing to management's decision to centralize include the importance of the value of the collateral and the specialized knowledge of appraisal techniques required, the extensive documentation required in residential lending, compliance with federal and state regulations that apply to mortgage lending, and overall control of the mortgage portfolio.

In a unit organization the entire loan process—from taking the loan application to closing the loan to servicing the loan—is typically centralized in a separate physical location. In a branching organization varying degrees of centralization are possible. For example, all functions could be centralized except for taking the original application and closing the loan. The centralized department maintains control of approval and services the loan, while customer convenience is maintained through application and closing at the branch facility. Alternatively, the entire loan process could be handled through a centralized department with regional locations. The advantage of the latter type of organization is that efficiency is increased while at the same time customer convenience is maintained (although to a slightly lesser degree).

If a bank is originating loans and selling those loans in the secondary market, a highly centralized organizational structure is preferable. Selling packages of mortgages requires exact documentation and compliance with intricate regulations, and to control this activity a highly centralized structure is more efficient.

Many banks choose to participate in the mortgage market through a subsidiary of a bank holding company. The subsidiary can be used as an alternative to making mortgages through the bank or as a means of servicing additional markets. For example, five of the top ten mortgage banking firms in the United States are owned by bank holding companies.[28] The advantages to the separate-subsidiary form of organization include diversifying across geographic markets and servicing markets that cannot be serviced by the bank because of regulatory constraints.

Efficient administration of residential mortgages for multibank holding companies is possible through the formation of separate lending organizations that handle loans for separate banks in the holding company. Returns to scale are achieved since the volume of each of the

---

[28]T. W. Thompson and R. D. Edwards, *The Changing World of Banking* (Richmond, VA: Robert F. Dame, 1982), 387.

banks is not sufficient to efficiently operate separate residential mortgage functions in each bank. When the volume is centralized, greater profitability is achieved.

Credit Analysis

The basic considerations involved in credit analysis of consumer loans also apply to residential mortgage loans. The lender is concerned with character, capacity, capital, collateral, and conditions. The process of clearing the credit is similar to that described for consumer loans (see Chapter 10).

The most significant difference in credit analysis for residential mortgage loans is the greater emphasis placed on the value of the collateral. The average price of a new home is over $80,000, and with a 25 percent down payment the average borrower is still borrowing $60,000. Because its exposure to potential loss is therefore much greater, the bank must carefully assess the value of the house.

Capacity, as measured by the borrower's income available to cover the monthly mortgage payments, is also critical for the credit analysis of a residential mortgage loan. Traditional standards for evaluating capacity in mortgage lending involve comparison of the monthly mortgage payment to net income. Lenders have traditionally indicated that the mortgage payment should not exceed 25 percent of monthly income or that total monthly installment payments, including the mortgage, should not exceed 35 percent of monthly income. Because of inflation in housing prices and high nominal interest rates, many lending institutions are relaxing those standards, and some lenders are allowing the mortgage payment to be as high as 40 percent of monthly income.[29] Lenders are making loans that are riskier with respect to borrowers' cash flows, and young families are using two incomes to qualify for loans.

An additional concern for capacity arises with variable-rate mortgages and graduated-payment mortgages. If the mortgage payment increases at a pace faster than the borrower's income to support the mortgage, lenders might be faced with increased credit risk. These factors should be considered (along with loan-to-value ratios) when qualifying a mortgage loan with increasing or potentially increasing monthly payments.

Compliance with Consumer Protection Legislation

As with consumer loans, lenders in residential mortgages must comply with a variety of federal and state regulations designed to protect consumers. The purposes of these regulations are to ensure the fair disclo-

---

[29]Jones, op. cit., 22.

sure of costs associated with the loan, to ensure that lenders do not discriminate in mortgage lending, and to protect borrowers from usurious interest rates. Complying with these regulations, however, places additional administrative burdens on management.

The major regulations include:

- *The Real Estate Settlement Procedures Act* requires lenders to provide borrowers with information that describes settlement costs and to use a uniform settlement statement that meets the requirements of The Truth in Lending Act.
- *The Fair Housing Act* prohibits a lender from discrimination on the basis of age, sex, race, national origin, religion, and marital status. The act requires the lender to inform an applicant within 30 days on approval of the loan and to provide information, if requested, as to why the loan was not approved in the case of denial.
- *The Home Mortgage Disclosure Act* requires most lenders to compile information on residential mortgages that they originate or purchase. The information must be kept according to areas where the loans were made (census tract or zip code), and the information must be publicly available.
- *The Community Reinvestment Act* requires that each bank meet the credit needs of its community. The act is vague in defining credit needs, but one of the key services that regulators view as "meeting credit needs" is residential mortgage lending.[30]
- *State usury laws.* Many states have laws that prescribe a maximum interest rate on residential mortgage loans. Lenders in a given state must comply with those ceiling rates.[31]

Management of the Mortgage Loan Portfolio

The demand for housing and for residential mortgages has been and continues to be highly cyclical.[32] The volatility in the demand for mortgage loans exceeds the volatility in consumer loans and commercial loans. The cyclical nature of the demand for housing places special burdens on banks that participate in residential lending.

---

[30]For an in-depth study of the performance of The Community Reinvestment Act, see N. N. Bowsher, "The Three-Year Experience with the Community Reinvestment Act," *Review, Federal Reserve Bank of St. Louis*, February 1982: 3–10.

[31]The Depository Institutions Deregulation and Monetary Control Act of 1980 (Title V) exempted residential mortgage loans from state usury laws but gave the states the right to reinstate usury ceilings until April 1, 1983. Several states reimposed such ceilings.

[32]N. G. Berkman, "Mortgage Finance and the Housing Cycle," *New England Economic Review, Federal Reserve Bank of Boston*, September-October 1979: 54–76.

Many of the costs of personnel and administration are fixed and, given the variability of demand, the returns are highly variable. Commercial banks' activity in providing funds for residential mortgages in the 1970s fluctuated widely. Home mortgages as a percentage change in assets of commercial banks was 2 percent in 1970 and 15 percent in 1978.[33]

The performance of the secondary market in the late 1970s and early 1980s indicates that existence of the secondary market does not alleviate the problems of inflation or the cyclical nature of housing demand. The ability to sell a fixed-rate long-term instrument depends on the demand for those assets. Investors have not been willing to purchase fixed-rate assets at reasonable rates in a highly uncertain environment.

Investment in mortgage loans presents problems in the management of interest margin as well. A bank that makes a fixed-rate long-term loan has committed its resources to an uncertain future. In periods of rising rates the bank experiences declines in interest margins as its costs of funding those loans increase. Prudent management calls for limiting a bank's investments in fixed-rate mortgages and for giving special attention to the management of interest margin management (see Chapter 16).

Some of the problems of managing interest margin have been reduced by the introduction of mortgage instruments with adjustable rates. These alternative instruments have eased but not eliminated the problems; because the increase in rates is limited, they do not totally remove the risk. The variable-rate mortgage results in an increased mortgage payment and might therefore increase credit risk. The adjustable-rate mortgage, which allows the maturity of the loan to be extended, increases the interest return to the bank but postpones the cash flow.

FUTURE OF RESIDENTIAL MORTGAGE LENDING

Residential mortgage lending is a challenging endeavor in the present environment of high and volatile rates. Given all the current problems, one might conclude that this area of lending should be deemphasized in the future, but several factors point to an opposite conclusion if the long term is considered. First, the financial services industry is undergoing significant structural changes that will result in expanded competition in offering services traditionally the exclusive province of commercial banks. To be effective competitors, banks might be forced to offer more in residential mortgage services. Second, the demand for residential mortgage financing has been depressed by current market conditions,

[33]Ibid.

but the demand for mortgage financing is likely to be very strong in the long run. The demand offers commercial banks an opportunity to serve a market with great potential. Third, the notion of relationship banking must be considered. The ability to attract retail customers for related services may depend on the bank's willingness to provide residential mortgage financing. The profitability of the overall relationship, rather than the mortgage loan exclusively, must be considered. Finally, the changing regulatory environment might allow commercial banks greater freedom to provide complementary services to the mortgage loan, an opportunity that could offer banks a greatly expanded service market.

The effective servicing of this potential market requires much innovation, with the first stage the possible redesign of the mortgage instrument. The market potential for banks that can offer innovative services is promising.

The changing structure of the financial services industry will significantly affect banks' future participation in residential mortgage lending. The regulatory changes that allow thrift institutions to offer to retail customers all services that banks can offer may force banks to offer more mortgage financing to maintain customer relationships. If a customer can get all the services offered by a commercial bank at a thrift institution, why does he need a bank?[34]

As the regulatory environment eases, related services that are highly profitable could be offered, making the overall package of residential lending more profitable. Potential related services include real estate brokerage services, increased mortgage banking activity with capabilities of direct placement of mortgages with customers through investment services, additional fee-producing services such as insurance and appraisal, and related loan services such as large lines of credit offered at variable rates and secured by equity in the residences.[35] The possibility of expanded service in these areas offers great potential to commercial banks.

SUMMARY

Mortgage lending by commercial banks involves two major types of loans: wholesale and retail. Wholesale mortgage loans are specialized commercial loans made to enterprises involved in real estate development or finance. The majority of wholesale mortgage loans are construction loans in which banks lend funds to builders to complete residential

---

[34]For an interesting and detailed discussion of the potential developments in the market, see Thompson and Edwards, op. cit., and T. W. Thompson, L. L. Berry, and P. H. Davidson, *Banking Tomorrow: Managing Markets Through Planning* (New York: Van Nostrand Reinhold, 1978).

[35]Thompson and Edwards, op. cit., offer a good discussion of the concept of the mortgage as the core in the development of retail relationship banking.

or commercial developments. Commercial banks also provide working capital loans to mortgage bankers. Retail lending involves financing services for the purchase of housing.

The residential mortgage market has changed significantly in the last decade. The traditional fixed-rate mortgage is not well suited for an environment characterized by high and volatile interest rates. The lender is exposed to interest rate risk because most long-term loans are funded with short-term liabilities. When rates rise, interest margins decline and in some cases turn negative.

The most significant changes have been the development of secondary and futures markets in mortgage-based instruments and innovation in the types of mortgage instruments. The secondary market allows banks to participate in lending through origination and servicing of loans without holding the loans as investments. Doing so provides banks with service income and also allows banks to service the needs of their communities without a long-term commitment of funds. Many alternative mortgage instruments have been developed. A common provision of these alternative instruments is a variable-interest rate, which allows a bank to increase the interest rate on a loan if inflation increases. Although these instruments do not eliminate interest rate risk, they do minimize some of its effects.

The organization and management of the mortgage lending function involve a combination of the principles of commercial and consumer loan management. Wholesale lending is similar to commercial lending, and the retail area is similar to the consumer lending function. Procedures common to the areas are securing title and valuing the real estate used to secure the loans.

Questions and Problems

1. List and briefly describe the steps involved in qualifying a construction loan.

2. Discuss the significance of setting up controls for construction loans.

3. Describe mortgage warehouse loans.

4. What are the problems that the long maturity and fixed rate of the traditional mortgage instrument present to lenders?

5. Define a *due-on-sale clause* and discuss the effect of such a clause on the risk of making residential mortgage loans.

6. Define the following types of mortgage instruments: (1) adjustable or variable rate, (b) graduated payment (fixed rate), (c) graduated payment (variable rate), and (d) renegotiable rate.

7. Briefly describe FHA and VA mortgages.

8. Describe how the secondary mortgage market extends a bank's options for participation in mortgage loans.

9. Describe mortgage-backed bonds and pass-through securities.

10. Describe the potential effects that changes in the structure of the financial services industry have on banks' participation in the residential mortgage market.

References

Anderson, P. S. "Costs and Profitability of Bank Functions." *New England Economic Review, Federal Reserve Bank of Boston,* March-April 1979: 43–61.

Arak, M., and C. J. McCurdy. "Interest Rate Futures." *Quarterly Review, Federal Reserve Bank of New York,* Winter 1979–1980: 33–46.

Berkman, N. G. "Mortgage Finance and the Housing Cycle." *New England Economic Review, Federal Reserve Bank of Boston,* September-October 1979: 54–76.

Bowsher, N. N. "The Three-Year Experience with the Community Reinvestment Act." *Review, Federal Reserve Bank of St. Louis,* February 1982: 3–10.

Brockschmidt, P. "The Secondary Market for Home Mortgages." *Monthly Review, Federal Reserve Bank of Kansas City,* September-October 1977: 11–20.

Cornyn, A. G., and T. L. Zearley. "Financial Developments of Bank Holding Companies in 1980." *Federal Reserve Bulletin,* June 1981: 473–479.

Freund, J. L. "The Housing Market: Recent Developments and Underlying Trends." *Federal Reserve Bulletin,* February 1983: 61–69.

Gallaudet, J. R. "Construction Mortgage and Real Estate Warehousing Loans." In *The Bankers' Handbook,* 2d ed., ed. W. H. Baughn and C. E. Walker, 703–718. Homewood, IL: Dow Jones-Irwin, 1978.

Garcia, G., et al. "The Garn-St. Germain Depository Institutions Act of 1982." *Economic Perspectives, Federal Reserve Bank of Chicago,* March-April 1983: 1–30.

Gilbert, R. A. "Will the Removal of Regulation Q Raise Mortgage Interest Rates?" *Review, Federal Reserve Bank of St. Louis,* December 1982: 3–12.

Hein, S. E., and J. C. Lamb, Jr. "Why the Medium-Priced Home Costs So Much." *Review, Federal Reserve Bank of St. Louis,* June-July 1981: 11–19.

Johnson, F. P., and C. F. Muenzberg. "Can Cost Analysis Improve Your Mortgage Loan Function?" *Management Accounting,* February 1980: 22–25.

Jones, M. T. "Mortgage Design, Inflation and Real Interest Rates." *Quarterly Review, Federal Reserve Bank of New York,* Spring 1982: 20–29.

Kearl, J. R. "Mortgage Innovation: The Issues and Some Evidence." *The Journal of Consumer Credit Management,* Spring 1979: 103–115.

Luckett, C. "Recent Developments in the Mortgage and Consumer Credit Markets." *Federal Reserve Bulletin,* May 1982: 281–290.

Melton, W. C. "Graduated Payment Mortgage." *Quarterly Review, Federal Reserve Bank of New York,* Spring 1980: 21–28.

Melton, W. C., and D. L. Heidt. "Variable Rate Mortgages." *Quarterly Review, Federal Reserve Bank of New York,* Summer 1979: 23–31.

Miller, G. H. "The Affordability of Home Ownership in the 1970s." *Economic Review, Federal Reserve Bank of Kansas City,* September-October 1980: 17–23.

"Nailing Down an Affordable Mortgage." *Business Week*, Mar. 14, 1983, 152–155.

Parliment, T. J., and J. S. Kaden. "The Shared Appreciation Concept in Residential Financing." In *Financial Markets: Instruments and Concepts*, ed. J. R. Brick, 285–300. Richmond, VA: Robert F. Dame, 1980.

Summerfield, H. G., Jr. "Commercial Bank Real Estate Lending." In *Bank Credit*, ed. Herbert V. Prochnow, 168–188. New York: Harper & Row, 1981.

Swesind, C. M. "Mortgage-Backed Securities: The Revolution in Real Estate Finance." *Quarterly Review, Federal Reserve Bank of New York*, Autumn 1979: 1–10.

Thompson, T. W., and R. D. Edwards. *The Changing World of Banking*. Richmond, VA: Robert F. Dame, 1982, 387.

Thompson, T. W., L. L. Berry, and P. H. Davidson. *Banking Tomorrow: Managing Markets Through Planning*. New York: Van Nostrand Reinhold, 1978.

Walsh, J. M. "Mortgage Lending: Income Producing Property." In *The Bankers' Handbook*, 2d ed., ed. W. H. Baughn and C. E. Walker, 729–740. Homewood, IL: Dow Jones-Irwin, 1978.

Walsh, J. M. "Residential Mortgage Loans." In *The Bankers' Handbook*, 2d ed., ed. W. H. Baughn and C. E. Walker, 719–728. Homewood, IL: Dow Jones-Irwin, 1978.

CHAPTER 12

Investments

Although banks employ the majority of their funds in loans, some funds are also employed in marketable securities. These investments consist of short-, intermediate-, and long-term debt securities. Regulations allow banks to invest in debt securities that are issued by governmental units and corporations, but with a few exceptions banks are not allowed to invest in equity securities for their own accounts. Although regulations allow banks to invest funds in corporate bonds, as a matter of practice few banks do so. Banks are able to shelter income from income taxes through the purchase of municipal securities, whereas corporate and federal bond income is subject to income taxes. Most commercial bank investments are concentrated in federal government, federal government agency, and state and local government securities.

Since loans generally earn a higher rate of interest than marketable securities, banks could maximize interest income by employing all of their funds in loans. But that is not possible for two reasons. First, loan demand is cyclical. During some periods demand for new loans falls short of available loanable funds. Second, since banks are not able to predict deposit flows with perfect accuracy, they are not able to employ all funds in loans. Marketable securities provide backstop liquidity so that if customers draw down deposits, these securities can be sold in the secondary market to provide funds to meet the deposit outflow. Therefore funds are employed in marketable investments to generate interest income and to provide liquidity for unexpected fund outflows.

The importance of the investment portfolio in meeting short-term liquidity demands has declined over the last two decades. Banks have increasingly relied on liability adjustments to provide liquidity to meet a temporary or short-term demand for funds. Use of the investment portfolio to provide day-to-day liquidity needs has declined, but the portfolio is still important in meeting longer-term and cyclical demands for liquidity.

The change in reliance on marketable securities to meet liquidity needs has resulted in changes in the composition of investment portfolios, with investment managers placing greater emphasis on return characteristics of securities. In the last three decades banks have increased holdings of higher-return and less marketable securities over the most liquid types of securities. Banks have emphasized returns from the investment portfolio rather than liquidity characteristics.

Exhibit 12.1 displays holdings of marketable securities by commercial banks in 1950 and 1979. The holdings display the change in primary

EXHIBIT 12.1   Commercial Bank Investment Portfolio Holdings

	1950		1979	
Security	$ Billion	Percent	$ Billion	Percent
U.S. Treasury	62.6	84	97.2	34
Federally sponsored agency	1.9	3	51.0	18
State and local government	8.2	11	135.9	48

Source: David M. Darst, *The Handbook of the Bond and Money Markets* (New York: McGraw-Hill, 1981), 217.

emphasis from liquidity to income. In 1950, 86 percent of commercial banks' investment portfolios were made up of U.S. Treasury securities, whereas in 1979 that figure had dropped to 34 percent. In today's environment banks place a greater amount of investment funds in agency and municipal securities.

Our emphasis in this chapter is on return characteristics and structuring of the investment portfolio to maximize returns rather than on the use of marketable securities for day-to-day liquidity management. Shorter-term liquidity management is discussed in Chapter 13.

SETTING INVESTMENT OBJECTIVES

The major goal of investment portfolio management is to maximize returns from investments while controlling the basic elements of risk. Secondary goals include providing backstop liquidity and meeting the needs of the community that is serviced by the bank. To develop the background necessary for evaluating investment strategies, we first need to investigate the basic elements of risk and return of the investments included in the portfolio.

Return Characteristics

Fixed-income securities in which banks invest generate two components of returns: periodic interest income and capital appreciation/depreciation. Periodic interest income includes semiannual interest payments on bonds and repayment of principal on discount instruments such as Treasury bills.[1] Capital appreciation/depreciation is determined by changes in the market value of a security as a result of changes in

---

[1]We assume a basic understanding of bond pricing in our discussion of investment strategies. An overview of bond pricing is included in Appendix 12.1, which includes a discussion of Treasury bill pricing.

bond yields over the maturity of the security. Increases in interest rates and bond yields following issuance reduce current market values, whereas decreases in interest rates and yields increase market values.

The return that is earned on a bank's investment portfolio depends on the gains or losses realized and on the interest earned on reinvestment of periodic interest payments. If bonds are sold in advance of maturity, any changes in bond yield will result in increases or decreases in market values. Realized gains or losses can have a very large impact on returns for commercial banks.[2] If periodic interest payments are reinvested in marketable securities, returns are affected by the reinvestment rates.

Elements of Risk

Risk involved with investment can be measured by the extent to which return that is realized turns out to be lower than expected. Realized return can vary from expected return because of a variety of factors. The bank has some control over some of the factors that could cause returns to be lower, but other factors such as general economic performance cannot be controlled. Portfolio construction determines the elements of risk that are most significant for a given portfolio.

The specific elements or sources of risk that have an effect on returns are described in Exhibit 12.2. Most of these elements are controllable to some extent, although to the investment portfolio manager some elements represent trade-offs.

One of the key elements causing variation in return is changes in interest rates. Changes in interest rates cause variation in return from two interrelated factors—price risk and reinvestment risk. Price risk refers to the variation in return caused by the change in the value of a bond resulting from changes in market rates or yields. Generally longer-term bonds with low coupon rates will change more in value with a given change in yield. Reinvestment risk refers to the variation in return caused by reinvesting intermediate payments at rates different from the bond's yield at the time of purchase (promised yield). Shorter-term bonds and bonds with larger intermediate interest payments are generally subject to greater reinvestment risk.

The level of risk involved in a portfolio depends to a significant extent on the planned investment horizon, or holding period. Two identical portfolios will possess different risk levels if the holding periods for the two investors are different. Price risk is relevant only if the bond is sold before maturity. If an investor's holding period is equal to maturity (assuming no default risk), the investor will be assured of receiving the

---

[2]Banks can use various strategies or trading tactics to use gains and losses for tax purposes and smoothing of income considerations. We shall discuss such tactics later in the chapter.

EXHIBIT 12.2   Basic Elements of Risk in Fixed-Income Instruments

Element of Risk	Description	Characteristics of Securities
Interest rate risk	Variation in return caused by fluctuations in interest rates.	
Price risk	Variation in return caused by change in the market value of the securities.	Generally, longer-term bonds with lower coupon rates will vary more in price with a given change in interest rates.
Reinvestment risk	Variation in return caused by reinvesting intermediate payments at a rate different from the promised yield.	Generally, bonds with larger coupon rates will have a higher degree of reinvestment risk.
Credit risk	Variation in return caused by default on interest payments or repayment of principal.	U.S. Treasury securities and federal government agency securities are free of credit risk for all practical purposes. Municipal securities are subject to various degrees of credit risk, depending on quality.
Purchasing power risk	Variation in real rate of return caused by generalized inflation.	All fixed-income securities are subject to purchasing power risk.
Marketability risk	Variation in return caused by selling costs when bonds are sold before maturity.	Depends on the trading characteristics of the particular issue. U.S. Treasury securities are the most marketable, agency securities are generally less marketable, and municipal securities are generally the least marketable, although marketability characteristics of these securities vary widely among issuers.

principal payment upon maturity. If the bond is sold in advance of maturity, the sale price will depend on changes in the level of rates. If market yields rise, the bond's market value will be lower and the lower sale price serves to lower the realized return.

The lower return experienced by the sale in the above example would probably be offset to some extent by larger returns on the periodic reinvestment of coupon payments. If rates rose following the purchase, the intermediate coupon payments could be reinvested at higher rates, which would offset the lower price received. The total return would depend on when the bond was sold and the extent of the changes in market rates. The second element of interest rate risk acts to offset price risk.

The elements of price risk and reinvestment risk can be controlled if the investment holding period can be specified. In that case it is possible to set up a portfolio that has the characteristic of offsetting price and reinvestment risk, resulting in what is termed an "immunized portfolio." This is accomplished through the use of the concept of duration, which is described in greater detail in Appendix 12.2. The duration of a bond or a bond portfolio is a measure of the weighted average maturity, which weights all intermediate payments as well as the final principal repayment. By setting the duration equal to the holding period, the elements of price and reinvestment risk can be offset, resulting in a realized return that is immunized from changes in interest rates. Such a result is possible only if the investment holding period can be specified.[3]

Credit or default risk is the variability in return that is caused by a bond issuer failing to make principal or interest payments according to the promised schedule. Given that most banks restrict their investments to U.S. government, U.S. government agency, and municipal series, risk of default is generally quite low on most portfolios. The only issues subject to any significant default risk are municipal issues.

Municipal securities vary in quality depending on the issuer and the type of obligation. General obligation bonds are backed by the full taxing authority of the issuer, and revenues for repayment are not tied to any particular project. Revenue bonds, on the other hand, have a limited source of repayment in that revenues from a particular project are used to make interest and scheduled principal repayments. Revenue bonds have characteristics similar to term loans in that the purchasing bank has to assess the revenues available to cover the debt service. Therefore general obligation bonds are viewed as having lower default risk than most revenue bonds.

As a rule, there has been limited default in the municipal bond markets, but there are a few glaring exceptions. The failure of New York City to roll over maturing debt in August of 1975 sent shock waves through the municipal markets.[4] Following the default of New York City, ratings on the general obligations of some cities and states were

---

[3]The ability to immunize bond portfolio returns by setting the duration equal to the planned investment horizon depends on the shape of the yield curve and changes in the structure of rates. Strict immunization is possible by using the simple definition of duration under flat yield curves. If the term structure changes as well as the levels of rates, variation in return will occur. Alternative measures of duration that will result in immunized returns for specified changes in rate structures are also possible. Results from empirical research show that a duration strategy based on the simple duration definition yields realized returns that are closer to promised returns than a maturity-matching strategy. See G. O. Bierwag, G. G. Kaufman, and A. Toevs, "Duration: Its Development and Use in Bond Portfolio Management," *Financial Analysts Journal*, July-August 1983: 15–35.

[4]D. L. Hoffman, "The 'New York City Effect' in the Municipal Bond Market," *Financial Analysts Journal*, March-April 1977: 36–39.

changed to reflect larger credit risks. More recently the municipal bond market has been affected by the largest default in history. In July 1983 the Washington Public Power Supply System (WPPSS, appropriately referred to as "Whoops" in the financial press) defaulted on $2.25 billion in bonds.[5] The bonds were issued to obtain funding for construction of two nuclear power plants that were later canceled. WPPSS is currently not in default on $6 billion of additional bonds used to finance three other plants, but suits and judgments related to the unfinished plants could cause default on these issues as well.

Credit risk can be controlled through diversification and by limiting the proportion of funds committed to lower-quality revenue bonds. A bank can increase the expected return from its bond portfolio through acquisition of riskier bonds, but such action will also increase the variance in returns. Recent evidence shows that municipal bonds are not default-free.

Purchasing power risk is present in all fixed-income investments. An investor purchasing a bond with an 11 percent yield will earn less than 11 percent if inflation is present. If inflation turns out to be 6 percent over the holding period of the investment, the real rate of return will be 5 percent. Variations in real rate of return will depend on how correctly inflation is anticipated and incorporated into bond yields.[6]

The final element of risk involved in the investment portfolio is marketability risk. The importance of marketability risk depends on the trading activity of the portfolio and on the degree to which the investment portfolio is used for liquidity purposes. The marketability characteristics of issues in the portfolio are of greater importance when trading is extensive.

The portfolio manager must balance the risk and return characteristics of the portfolio. It is possible to achieve higher rates of return by assuming higher levels of risk, but so doing will result in greater variation or volatility in returns. The portfolio manager must assess the risk characteristics as well as the return expected from the portfolio.

Interrelationship of Investments and Other Earning Assets

In establishing strategy and specific investment objectives, management should consider the level of risk of other earning assets and the liquidity position of the bank. Key factors that should be considered include the quality of the loan portfolio and the short-term borrowed-funds position.

---

[5] L. Asinof, "WPPSS Begins to Cause Pain for Investors," *The Wall Street Journal*, Dec. 28, 1983, 15. Numerous suits have been filed on the WPPSS default and according to lawyers involved in some of the suits, the cases will not reach trial until the summer of 1985.

[6] Real rates of return that are earned on a fixed-income portfolio depend on tax factors as well as on expected or anticipated rates of inflation. Because of larger taxes, market yields must actually exceed the rate of inflation in order to generate a given real rate of return.

If larger portions of a bank's funds are employed in medium- or lower-quality loans, it may be prudent to limit credit risk in the investment portfolio. If a bank has significant concentration in longer-term loans, it may be prudent to place maturity limits on the investment portfolio. Failure to do so could have a significant impact on the bank's earnings in periods of rising rates. The level of interest rate risk in the loan portfolio should be coordinated with such risk in the investment portfolio.

The liquidity position of the bank must also be coordinated with investment strategy. The bank's borrowed-funds position is critical in this regard. If the bank has borrowed significant amounts of funds in the market to meet liquidity needs, marketability considerations of the investment portfolio become more important. Prudent management may call for greater investment in short-term Treasury securities if the bank has used much of its borrowing capacity. The backstop liquidity aspect is more important because of the constrained borrowing position.

Tax Considerations

To this point in our discussion we have been concentrating on pretax yields on bonds. Tax considerations play a very important role for commercial banks in setting investment objectives and in management of portfolios. Tax factors incorporated into the investment policy include the breakdown of the portfolio into taxable and tax-exempt issues and the timing decision on realizing gains or losses.

Tax-Exempt Securities.   Interest income on municipal securities is not subject to federal income taxes.[7] The relative advantage of tax-exempt over taxable securities depends on a bank's marginal tax rate. Banks with large earnings in higher tax brackets can use tax-exempt municipal securities to earn higher after-tax yields.

To compare yields on municipal securities with yields on Treasury and agency securities, the yield on municipals must be adjusted for tax effects. An equivalent taxable yield is determined as:

$$\text{Equivalent taxable yield} = \frac{\text{Municipal yield}}{(1 - \text{Tax rate})}$$

As an example, assume that a municipal security offers a 9 percent yield and a bank's marginal tax rate is 40 percent. If all other risk factors

---

[7]In addition, some municipal securities are exempt from state income taxes. It is important to note that only interest income and not realized gains or losses from changes in market value are exempt from taxes. Realized gains and losses are subject to taxes.

involved in comparable issues were constant, a 9 percent tax-exempt yield would be equivalent to a taxable yield of 15 percent:[8]

$$\text{Equivalent taxable yield} = \frac{0.09}{(1 - 0.40)} = 0.15$$

As we have indicated, banks have invested larger amounts of funds in tax-exempt securities in recent periods. Yields offered on municipal securities have been attractive relative to taxable Treasury and agency securities. The relative advantage depends on marginal tax brackets. Smaller banks in lower brackets will invest less in tax-exempt securities.

Trading and Tax Considerations.   Under recently changed regulations, gains and losses from trading in investment securities are reported as operating earnings for banks. Formerly such transactions were separately reported in the income statement following operating earnings. This action may make it a little more difficult to interpret earnings.[9] Regardless of how they are reported, securities gains and losses affect earnings per share, and tax liability and tax considerations play an important role in investment strategy.

To see how tax considerations influence trading, consider a bank that has had a very profitable year and has at the same time experienced reduction in the value of some of its investment securities because of rising interest rates. The bank could sell bonds that have decreased in value and realize the loss. This will reduce the tax liability of the bank and at the same time allow the bank to reinvest a larger amount of funds in additional securities at higher yields. Exhibit 12.3 illustrates such a transaction.

The opposite type of transaction could be undertaken if the bank experienced operational losses and lower marginal tax rates in a given year. Gains on securities could be realized and the taxes paid on such gains would be lower than taxes on a similar transaction in a very profitable year. This type of trading also results in smoothed reported earnings per share, which may be important to shareholders of the bank.

Constraints on Investment Policy.   Among the constraints that apply to a bank's investment policy are community reinvestment considerations, specific regulations imposed by national and state regulatory agencies, and pledging requirements that apply to deposits of

---

[8]The equivalent taxable yield considers only the tax factors. Other elements of risk, particularly credit and marketability, must also be considered in order to have totally comparable yields.

[9]For a discussion of the issues surrounding the reporting change, see D. Hertzberg, "Bank Profit Reports Are Distorted by New SEC Rules, Other Changes," *The Wall Street Journal*, Jan. 19, 1984, 32.

EXHIBIT 12.3   Tax Swap Transaction

Bond X: Purchase price and par value $1000
Current market value $ 700
Bank's marginal tax bracket   40%

Sales transaction: Sell the bond at current market value and realize the loss.

Proceeds from the sale: $ 700   Sales price
$ 120   Tax reduction ($300 loss × 40%)
Net proceeds: $ 820

Reinvestment transaction: The bank can reinvest $820 in higher-yielding securities, resulting in greater interest income.

---

governmental units. In managing its investment portfolio, the bank must satisfy these constraints.

Community reinvestment considerations require the bank to satisfy the needs of the community it services. One of the ways community reinvestment requirements can be satisfied is through the purchase of municipal securities of local issuers. As part of servicing its customer relationships, banks purchase local issues. This constraint must be balanced against undue concentration. If the local area suffers an economic recession, the bank could experience larger losses than if adequate diversification exists.

Regulation of Investment.   The regulatory agencies limit banks' investments in securities in terms of quality and liquidity. Although many banks view the investment function predominantly as a function separate from liquidity management, the regulators still place emphasis on liquidity requirements. In the introductory section of the *Comptroller's Handbook for National Bank Examiners*, the liquidity characteristics are emphasized: "Bank management must recognize that the investment account is primarily a secondary reserve for liquidity rather than a vehicle to generate speculative profits. Speculation in marginal securities to generate more favorable yields is an unsound banking practice."[10]

The basic strategy employed by regulators in attempting to control risk involves limiting the type of securities a bank may purchase, plac-

---

[10]Comptroller of the Currency, Administrator for National Banks, *Comptroller's Handbook for National Bank Examiners* (Englewood Cliffs, NJ: Prentice-Hall, 1979), sec. 203.1.

ing limits on the investments in riskier types of securities, and examining the bank's investment policy to make sure that it is consistent with sound banking practice. Some of the general requirements that regulators impose include adequate liquidity, adequate diversification, and an established policy concerning maturities of investment securities. On riskier issues such as municipal bonds, regulators stress that it is the bank's responsibility to maintain adequate credit files and investigate the ability of the issuers to pay the obligations.

Specific regulations concerning type involve classification into risk classes. Type I securities include obligations of the U.S. government or its agencies and general obligations of states and political subdivisions. No restrictions apply to the amount of Type I securities that a bank may hold with the exception of the exercise of prudent banking judgment. All other eligible securities, including revenue bonds and corporate obligations, are classified as Type II or Type III. For these securities a limitation of 10 percent of capital and surplus applies to the purchase of securities of any one issuer when the purchase is based on adequate evidence on the maker's ability to perform. A 5 percent limitation applies to new-issuer obligations when the purchase is based on reasonable estimates of the ability to perform. The 5 percent limitation applies in cases in which the issuer does not have an adequate record of performance.[11]

For securities that are rated by the national rating services, banks are limited to the purchase of investment-grade securities. Investment-grade securities are those in the top four rating classes (see Exhibit 12.4). Banks can also purchase nonrated municipal issues but are required to maintain credit files and perform credit analyses to satisfy the requirements for sound banking practice. It is not uncommon for banks to acquire nonrated issues of municipalities.

In general, banks may not acquire stock for their investment accounts. Exceptions to this regulation are made for corporate ownership positions that are related to the delivery of banking services. Common examples include stock of Federal Reserve banks, small-business investment corporations, and foreign banking corporations.[12] Occasionally a bank will hold stock that has been acquired because of a loan default in its investment account. The bank is expected to dispose of such stock within a reasonable time period.

Pledging Requirements. Deposits of most governmental units in excess of the amount insured by the FDIC must be backed by eligible collateral. The purpose of the pledging requirements is to protect the public's funds in the event of a bank failure. If a bank holds deposits in

---

[11]Ibid., 2.

[12]Ibid., 24.

EXHIBIT 12.4   Acceptable Rating Classifications

Standard & Poor's	Moody's	Description
Bank Quality Investments		
AAA	Aaa	Highest grade obligations.
AA	Aa	High grade obligations.
A	A-1, A	Upper medium grade.
BBB	Baa-1, Baa	Medium grade, on the borderline between definitely sound obligations and those containing predominantly speculative elements. Generally, the lowest quality bond that may qualify for bank investment.
Speculative and Defaulted Issues		
BB	Ba	Lower medium grade with only minor investment characteristics.
B	B	Low grade, default probable.
D	Ca, c	Lowest rated class, defaulted, extremely poor prospects.
Provisional or Conditional Rating		
Rating—P	Con. (Rating)	Debt service requirements are largely dependent on reliable estimates as to future events.

Source: Comptroller of the Currency, Administrator for National Banks, *Comptroller's Handbook for National Bank Examiners* (Englewood Cliffs, NJ: Prentice-Hall, 1979), sec. 203.1, 5.

---

excess of the insured amounts, investment securities must be pledged if required for the particular governmental unit.

Federal government deposits must be backed by either Treasury securities, federal government agency securities, or municipal securities. Under current regulation collateral values of 100 percent for Treasury and agency securities, 90 percent for state obligations, and 80 percent for other political subdivisions are allowed to back federal government deposits.[13]

In addition, most states also have pledging requirements that apply to deposits of state and local governments and other political subdivisions. State pledging requirements vary with respect to what is eligible collateral to back deposits and what percentage value of public deposits must be pledged. A great deal of variability is present in pledging requirements of states. For example, South Dakota has a pledging requirement of 5 percent on public deposits, whereas California requires a 110 percent backing. Many states have eligible collateral similar to the fed-

---

[13]Ronald A. Ratti, "Pledging Requirements and Bank Asset Portfolios," *Economic Review, Federal Reserve Bank of Kansas City,* September/October 1979: 13–23.

eral requirement, but some states also include other assets such as first mortgages as eligible collateral.[14]

If a bank holds public deposits in excess of the insured amount and pledging requirements apply, then a constraint is placed on the bank's investment portfolio. Pledging requirements may lead to a reduced liquidity position for the portfolio as well, since pledged securities may not be liquidated to accommodate loans or deposit withdrawals.[15]

INVESTMENT STRATEGIES

Banks employ a variety of trading strategies to meet goals and objectives of investment policy. In this section we shall examine some specific types of trading strategies along with a discussion of bond-swapping techniques that are employed by banks. We begin with a discussion of the most fundamental decision in implementing a strategy—how aggressively to trade the investment portfolio.

Aggressive or Passive Management?

The most fundamental decision that management must make is the decision to pursue either an active or a passive management style related to investments. Passive management involves a buy-and-hold type of strategy in which securities in the portfolio are not actively traded. With a passive management style, transaction, administrative, and personnel costs involved with the investment portfolio are minimized.

An active management style involves frequent trading of securities with the goal of maximizing the returns from the portfolio. Active management may involve trading to take full advantage of expected movements in interest rates, attempting to profit from temporary imbalances in securities pricing, and using sophisticated swapping techniques. Active management will result in greater transaction, administrative, and personnel costs. The increase in expected returns must be balanced against these increased costs. In addition, active management frequently involves increased risk since the portfolio may be restructured to take on expected interest rate moves.

Three major factors will influence a bank's choice of management style: size, accessibility to markets, and personnel qualifications. For efficiency in active trading, a bank's investment portfolio must be of

---

[14]Ibid.

[15]Ibid. Ratti examines the impact of pledging requirements on bank liquidity and lending practice for a limited number of states. His findings indicate that pledging requirements tend to reduce bank liquidity and in some cases may reduce loans made to nongovernmental customers.

sufficient size. Small banks with limited portfolio size are not likely to be able to overcome the added costs associated with active trading. They are also not likely to have the same degree of accessibility to the bond markets as large money-center banks. To maintain actively traded port-folios, banks must employ specialized personnel. Small banks with lim-ited resources cannot efficiently employ such personnel. Therefore ac-tive management styles are most often observed in large banks.

The decision to actively trade the portfolio is not an automatic one for large banks. Management must evaluate whether the additional re-turn generated by the active style is sufficient to overcome the addi-tional costs and possibly the added risk involved with maturity modifi-cation.

Maturity Strategies

A key element in the management of an investment portfolio is the maturity composition. A maturity decision must be made regardless of whether an active or passive strategy is adopted. We shall discuss ma-turity strategies involved with very active management styles in the following section. Our discussion here is limited to less actively man-aged portfolios.

The maturity composition of a portfolio involves the breakdown of securities according to varying years to maturity. The decision involves both the maximum maturity in which the bank is willing to invest and the distribution of funds over the selected maximum maturity. For ex-ample, a bank could select a maximum maturity of 10 years and decide that it would concentrate a portion of its funds in 1-year maturities with the remainder in 10-year maturities. The maturity composition will af-fect the price and reinvestment risks of the portfolio. Two strategies used by banks in selecting maturity composition are a laddered portfolio approach and a barbell portfolio approach. Both require limited manage-ment, but the barbell approach is slightly more active.

Laddered Approach.   The laddered approach is a very simple approach to apply. A bank must specify a maximum maturity and once that is specified, investment funds are distributed equally in maturity seg-ments up to the maximum maturity. As the securities mature, funds are used to purchase securities at the maximum maturity. This results in a portfolio with equal percentages of funds spaced over the maximum specified maturity. This type of portfolio is illustrated in Exhibit 12.5.

In the laddered portfolio in Exhibit 12.5, 10 percent of the total investment portfolio is invested in each security segment from 1 to 10 years. As the short-term securities mature, funds are used to purchase securities with 10-year maturities.

Transaction costs are minimal in this type of strategy. The goal of a laddered approach is to minimize administrative costs and at the same

EXHIBIT 12.5   Laddered Portfolio Structure

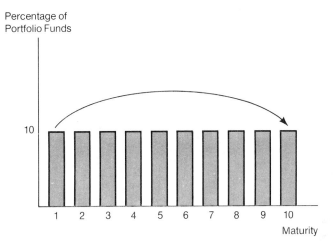

time earn average yields. Since the portfolio is distributed equally over various maturities, the strategy should result in an average rate of return.[16]

Barbell Approach.   Another maturity strategy is the barbell (or dumbbell) approach. The strategy calls for investing in short-term and long-term securities with no investment in intermediate-term securities. When the portfolio is displayed by maturities, investment is concentrated on the short and long ends of the maturity spectrum, giving the appearance of a barbell and hence the name. A sample barbell maturity strategy is illustrated in Exhibit 12.6.

The portfolio in Exhibit 12.6 is split with 50 percent of funds in the short-term sector and 50 percent in the long-term sector. The short-term sector is limited to 5-year maturities with 10 percent of the total portfolio in each year in 1- to 5-year securities. As the short-term securities mature, the funds are invested in 5-year securities. In the long sector 5 percent of the total portfolio is invested in securities in each maturity segment from 16 to 25 years. As the securities reach 15 years to maturity, they are sold in the secondary market and the proceeds are invested in securities with maturities of 25 years. The example is illustrative and is not meant to imply any optimal mix.

---

[16]For greater detail, see George H. Hempel, ''Basic Ingredients of Commercial Banks' Investment Policies,'' in *Funds Management Under Deregulation* (Washington, DC: American Bankers Association, 1982), 381–396.

EXHIBIT 12.6   Barbell Portfolio Approach

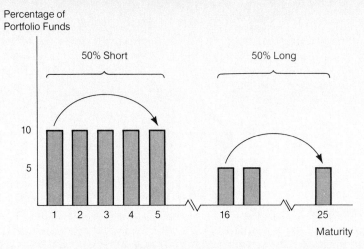

The strategy calls for selling the long-term bonds as they reach intermediate term and investing the proceeds in long-term bonds at the end of the maturity segment. As the short-term securities mature, the proceeds are reinvested at the end of the short-term maturity segment.

The superior returns generated from the barbell strategy are dependent to some degree on the term structure of interest rates over the particular holding period.[17] Research indicates that the barbell approach outperformed the laddered strategy in the period from 1950 to 1970. The results are attributable in part to the particular term structure observed during the period. The predominant term structure observed in the 1950 to 1970 period was upward sloping. Since 1970 we have experienced periods when short-term rates have exceeded long-term rates. Under the alternative term structure a barbell strategy would not generate larger returns.[18]

---

[17]The *term structure of interest rates* refers to the relationship between interest rates and maturity. Over much of the period from 1950 to 1970 long-term rates exceeded short-term rates. In recent periods that has not been the case—short-term rates have exceeded long-term rates. For an explanation of term structure and a discussion of the theories and evidence concerning term structure relationships, see James C. Van Horne, *Financial Market Rates and Flows* (Englewood Cliffs, NJ: Prentice-Hall, 1978), chap. 4 and 5.

[18]Hempel, op. cit. The research on performance of barbell strategies has also been criticized on other grounds. See H. R. Tagler, W. A. Groves, and J. G. Richardson, "Bond Portfolio Strategies, Returns and Skewness: A Note," *Journal of Financial and Quantitative Analysis*, March 1977: 127–140. Using a holding-period-return criterion, the authors demonstrate that a buy-long-and-hold strategy outperformed a barbell strategy.

Trading Tactics and Swaps

The managers of bond portfolios that are actively traded to secure superior returns use a variety of trading techniques and strategies. The goal of superior returns can be accomplished by positioning the portfolio to take advantage of movements in interest rates and by capitalizing on any inefficiencies in pricing of bonds that may occur on a temporary basis. To undertake the strategies discussed in this section, the bank must have qualified personnel with expertise in prediction of interest rate movements and bond-pricing relationships. These trading strategies are usually employed only by larger banks.

Playing the Interest Rate Cycle.   If management is able to predict movements in the level of interest rates, it is possible to secure high rates of returns by adjusting the maturity composition of the portfolio. The basic strategy involved is very similar to the strategy involved in gap management, which was discussed in Chapter 5. The major difference is that instead of adjusting loan maturities, the maturities of the bond portfolio are adjusted to profit from movements in rates.

The basic goal is to shorten or lengthen the maturity of the portfolio in line with predicted interest rate movements. If interest rates are predicted to decline, superior returns can be generated by purchasing long-term bonds. As rates fall, the prices of these bonds rise and trading profits result. If rates are predicted to increase, the maturity of the portfolio is shortened to avoid price depreciation in longer-term bonds and to capture increased return as funds are invested in short-term securities.

If the predicted-rate scenario materializes, returns from the portfolio will be larger than comparable returns from a laddered or barbell approach. Such a strategy increases the risk involved and if the predicted movement in rates does not occur, large losses could result. For example, if maturities are lengthened in expectation of a decline in interest rates and the rates increase, then large losses will result. If maturities are shortened in anticipation of an increase in rates and the rates decline, then the bank will experience lower rates of return. Thus trading against interest rate cycles increases the risks involved with the investment function.

The concept of duration can also be used in active management strategies to profit from changes in interest rates. When rates are predicted to decline, the strategy calls for lengthening or increasing the duration of the bond portfolio. Duration takes into account price and reinvestment characteristics and is therefore a more exact measure of expected price volatility.[19]

---

[19]See Bierwag, Kaufman, and Toevs, op. cit., for discussion.

The ability to profit from trading against interest rate cycles depends on the ability of management to predict interest rate movement. As we indicated in our discussion of gap management, rates have become increasingly volatile in recent years. This makes it more difficult to time interest rate movements and increases the risk involved in an incorrect prediction of rates.

Exhibit 12.7 displays recent yearly fluctuations in interest rates on selected U.S. Treasury and municipal securities. Since 1979 rates have been quite volatile, although 1983 was characterized by relative stability. The most volatile years were 1980 and 1981. In 1980 the Treasury bill rate displayed a range of over 8 percent. In 1980 the Treasury bill rate actually displayed two cyclical moves, rising from 12 percent to 15.20 percent in the first quarter, then falling to 7.07 percent in June and rising to 15.49 percent in December.

To trade against this degree of volatility requires extremely accurate predictive ability and the ability to adjust the maturity of the portfolio very quickly. The risk involved if the portfolio is incorrectly positioned is also extreme. Trading discussed to this point has pertained to trading on level interest rates. It is also possible to trade on movements in interest rates related to term structure. If predictable, movements in interest rates related to maturity can be traded against to generate superior returns.

One such strategy is referred to as "riding the yield curve." The strategy is based upon the fact that historically long-term rates usually exceed short-term rates. As shown in Exhibit 12.8, the yield curve in that instance is upward sloping. The tendency is for yields to fall as longer-term securities approach maturity.

With relatively stable interest rate levels and long-term rates exceeding short-term rates, as a longer-term security approaches maturity the yield tends to decline. It is possible in such a case to profit by purchasing a longer-term security and selling it as it approaches maturity. Profit results from a higher coupon rate on the longer-term security and from price appreciation as the yield declines.[20] The term *riding the yield curve* derives from the concept of owning a security while the market yield decreases as maturity approaches.

The profitability of the sample yield curve ride depends on the stability of the general level of interest rates. If interest rates increase, the bond price will decrease and the strategy could result in lower profits (possible losses if the rate increase is large).

Bond-Swapping Strategies.   The term *bond swapping* refers to a sophisticated trading practice in which bonds that are currently owned are

---

[20]An example of riding the yield curve can be found in David M. Darst, *The Complete Bond Book* (New York: McGraw-Hill, 1975), 295.

EXHIBIT 12.7 High and Low Rates on Selected Securities from 1979 through 1983

	1979[a]		1980		1981		1982		1983	
	High	**Low**	**High**	**Low**	**High**	**Low**	**High**	**Low**	**High**	**Low**
3-Month Treasury Bills	12.04%	9.06%	15.49%	7.07%	16.30%	10.85%	13.48%	7.71%	9.34%	7.86%
6-Month Treasury Bills	11.84	9.06	15.03	7.30	15.52	11.37	13.61	8.16	9.51	7.93
5-Year Treasury Bonds	10.93	8.85	13.25	9.21	15.93	12.77	14.65	10.22	11.63	10.03
10-Year Treasury Bonds	10.65	8.91	12.84	9.78	15.32	12.57	14.59	10.54	11.85	10.46
Moody's Aaa Municipal Bonds	6.50	5.54	7.11	9.44	12.05	8.98	12.30	9.34	9.04	8.28

[a]Rates are average monthly rates as reported in the *Federal Reserve Bulletin*.

EXHIBIT 12.8   Upward-Sloping Yield Curve

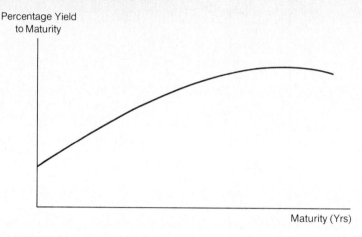

sold and the proceeds of the sale are used to purchase other bonds. The term *swap* derives from the exchange of one bond for another bond.

Swaps are undertaken for a variety of reasons, ranging from tax considerations to profiting from perceived disequilibrium in the market prices of debt securities. Exhibit 12.9 outlines commonly used bond swaps.[21]

We described the strategies involved in the tax swap and the rate anticipation swap in earlier sections of this chapter. Motivation for the tax swap is to use a gain or loss to tax advantage while reinvesting the proceeds from the sale in similar types of bonds. Motivation for the rate anticipation swap is to profit from expected changes in interest rates.

Motivation for the substitution and sector swaps involves disequilibrium pricing in the market. A substitution swap is considered when two similar issues (substitutes) that should be similarly priced are priced differently. The swap involves the sale of the higher-priced security and the purchase of the lower-priced security. The trade results in obtaining a similar issue at a lower price to increase yield. Motivation for a sector swap is similar except that there is some difference in the bond issues. Although the prices or yield relationships are not expected to be the same, a relationship-yield differential is expected. For example, the

[21]Bond-swapping strategies are very complex types of trades. Our purpose is to overview these strategies. Greater detail, including numerous examples of swaps, is available in David M. Darst, *The Handbook of the Bond and Money Markets* (New York: McGraw-Hill, 1981), chap. 14; and Sidney Homer and Martin L. Liebowitz, *Inside the Yield Book* (New York: Prentice-Hall and The New York Institute of Finance, 1972).

EXHIBIT 12.9   Bond Swaps

Type of Swap	Motivation	Example
Tax Swap	To realize a gain or loss to take advantage of tax rate considerations.	Sell a security that is selling at a price lower than purchase price. Use the loss to reduce current taxes and reinvest the proceeds in a similar issue.
Rate Anticipation Swap	To alter the maturity structure of the portfolio to profit from expected movements in interest rates.	Sell a short-term security and use the proceeds to purchase a long-term security in anticipation of a decrease in interest rates.
Substitution Swap	To profit by trading on a market disequilibrium of two similar or substitute securities.	Sell a municipal bond of X maturity at a higher price and purchase a lower-priced but similar-risk municipal bond.
Sector Swap	To profit by trading on a market disequilibrium involving securities that are not perfect substitutes.	Sell a low-yield Treasury security and use the proceeds to purchase a higher-yielding agency security. Trade is motivated by a differential in yield that is larger than expected.
Yield Pickup Swap	To switch from a lower-yielding security to a higher-yielding security.	Sell 2-year Treasury bonds and purchase 5-year Treasury bonds to gain a higher yield.

trader believes that a difference of 0.25 percent in yield should be observed for an agency security over a Treasury security. If the observed difference in yields varies from the predicted difference, a swap can be made to profit on the incorrect pricing. Implicit in this type of swap is the assumption that the market prices are incorrect and that subsequent to the swap the relative prices will readjust.

The final type of swap described in Exhibit 12.9 is the pure yield pickup swap. This type of swap does not involve a perceived market disequilibrium but rather involves the sale of a lower-yielding security and the purchase of a higher-yielding security—for example, selling a Treasury bond and purchasing a similar agency bond that offers a higher coupon rate and yield. This type of swap involves an internal adjustment in the portfolio and is not motivated by any perceived disequilibrium pricing.

As our discussion indicates, swapping strategies are very sophisticated techniques that require sophisticated administration. These techniques require a large investment portfolio and accessibility to bond markets. Administrative and transaction costs are higher for these actively traded portfolios. For the portfolio to be profitable, the returns generated must be large enough to offset the higher costs.

SUMMARY

Banks' holdings of investment securities generate additional interest income and also provide backstop liquidity to meet unexpected demand for funds. The investment portfolios of most commercial banks are composed of U.S. Treasury, federal agency, and municipal securities.

We examined strategies that banks can employ in the management of investment portfolios and examined the elements of risk and return associated with the management of fixed income securities. The goal in managing an investment portfolio is to maximize returns while limiting and controlling the involved elements of risk.

A variety of strategies, ranging from those used for very passively managed portfolios to those used for very actively managed portfolios, were examined. Primary determinants of the type of strategy a bank will employ in managing its investment portfolio are the size of the bank and the expertise of its personnel. The returns generated through active management strategies must be sufficient to overcome the costs involved with such management. Active management strategies were found to be more appropriate for larger banks with large portfolios and adequate managerial talent.

Questions and Problems

1. Describe the difference in the construction of the typical bank's investment portfolio as a result of banks' reliance on liability management for liquidity.

2. Identify the two components of return earned on an investment portfolio.

3. Identify and briefly describe the major elements of risk involved in the investment of fixed-income securities.

4. What is the potential effect that pledging requirements have on the liquidity of an investment portfolio?

5. Differentiate between a laddered and a barbell maturity strategy.

6. Differentiate between aggressive and passive management of an investment portfolio.

7. Define *bond swap.*

8. Describe the basic types of bond swaps discussed in this chapter.

References

Asinof, L. "WPPSS Begins to Cause Pain for Investors." *The Wall Street Journal*, Dec. 28, 1983, 15.

Bierwag, G. O., G. G. Kaufman, and A. Toevs. "Duration: Its Development and Use in Bond Portfolio Management." *Financial Analysts Journal*, July-August 1983: 15–35.

Bildersee, J. S. "U.S. Government and Agency Securities: An Analysis of Yield Spreads and Performance." *Journal of Business*, July 1978: 499–520.

Comptroller of the Currency, Administrator for National Banks. *Comptroller's Handbook for National Bank Examiners.* Englewood Cliffs, NJ: Prentice-Hall, 1979, sec. 203.1.

Cook, T. Q. "Determinants of Individual Tax-Exempt Bond Yields: A Survey of the Evidence." *Economic Review, Federal Reserve Bank of Richmond*, May-June 1982: 14–39.

Darst, D. M. *The Complete Bond Book.* New York: McGraw-Hill, 1975.

Darst, D. M. *The Handbook of the Bond and Money Markets.* New York: McGraw-Hill, 1981.

"The Fallout from 'Whoops'." *Business Week*, July 11, 1983, 80–87.

Gushee, C. S. "How to Hedge a Bond Investment." *Financial Analysts Journal*, March-April 1981: 44–51.

Hayes, D. A. "Bank Portfolio Management: Revolution in Portfolio Policies." In *Funds Management Under Deregulation*, ed. G. H. Hempel, 433–439. Washington, DC: American Bankers Association, 1981.

Hempel, G. H. "Basic Ingredients of Commercial Banks' Investment Policies." In *Funds Management Under Deregulation*, ed. G. H. Hempel, 381–396. Washington, DC: American Bankers Association, 1981.

Hertzberg, D. "Bank Profit Reports Are Distorted by New SEC Rules, Other Changes." *The Wall Street Journal*, Jan. 19, 1984, 32.

Hoffland, D. L. "A Model Bank Investment Policy." *Financial Analysts Journal*, May-June 1978: 64–67.

Hoffman, D. L. "The 'New York City Effect' in the Municipal Bond Market." *Financial Analysts Journal*, March-April 1977: 36–39.

Homer, S., and M. L. Liebowitz. *Inside the Yield Book.* New York: Prentice-Hall and The New York Institute of Finance, 1972.

Monhollon, J. R. "Treasury Bills." In *Bank Management: Concepts and Issues*, ed. J. R. Brick, 157–163. Richmond, VA: Robert F. Dame, 1980.

Nelson, J. F. "Federal Agency Securities." In *Bank Management: Concepts and Issues*, ed. J. R. Brick, 165–181. Richmond, VA: Robert F. Dame, 1980.

Ratti, R. A. "Pledging Requirements and Bank Asset Portfolios." *Economic Review, Federal Reserve Bank of Kansas City*, September-October 1979: 13–23.

Reilly, F. K., and R. S. Sidhu. "The Many Uses of Bond Duration." *Financial Analysts Journal*, July-August 1980: 58–72.

Tagler, H. R., W. A. Groves, and J. G. Richardson. "Bond Portfolio Strategies, Returns and Skewness: A Note." *Journal of Financial and Quantitative Analysis*, March 1977: 127–140.

Van Horne, J. C. *Financial Market Rates and Flows.* Englewood Cliffs, NJ: Prentice-Hall, 1978, Chaps. 4 and 5.

Watson, D. D. "Bank Bond Management: The Maturity Dilemma." *Business Review, Federal Reserve Bank of Philadelphia*, March 1972: 23–29.

APPENDIX 12.1

Basics of Bond Pricing

BASIC VALUATION

The basic valuation equation used in the valuation of bonds is

(12.1)
$$V_B = I \sum_{t=1}^{N} \left(\frac{1}{1+i}\right)^t + P_N \left(\frac{1}{1+i}\right)^N$$

where

V_B = market value of the bond
I = interest payments that are determined by the coupon rate and the par value; payments are usually fixed for each of the periods
P_N = principal repayment due on maturity
i = yield to maturity
N = years to maturity

Bonds are commonly valued using semiannual compounding. The holder of the bond is promised semiannual interest payments, and these payments are discounted by one half the annual yield rate. For example, a bond with a par value of $1000, a maturity of 10 years, a coupon rate of 10 percent, and selling at a yield to maturity of 12 percent would have a market value, using Equation 12.1, of

$$V_B = 50 \sum_{t=1}^{20} \left(\frac{1}{1.06}\right)^t + \$1000 \left(\frac{1}{1.06}\right)^{20}$$

where

$$V_B = \$50(11.4699) + \$1000(0.3118)$$
$$V_B = \$885.30$$

In this example the bond would pay $100 in annual interest payments, which would actually be paid in $50 installments every 6 months. In the example the bond sells at a discount, since similar new bonds are offering $120 in annual interest per $1000 bond. The difference in yield is made up in the form of capital appreciation.

Equation 12.1 is the bond valuation equation that applies to a bond with an even number of years to maturity. For bonds with maturities not exactly equal to an even number of years, Equation 12.1 does not precisely apply. In general, the equation is modified to include the sub-periods in days.

The general bond formula in Equation 12.1 applies to most long-term debt instruments. With Treasury bills, which are sold at a discount, all income comes in the form of capital appreciation rather than in the form of periodic interest payments. The value of a Treasury bill is found by using Equation 12.2:

(12.2)
$$V_{TB} = \$10,000 - \left(\begin{array}{c} \text{Discount rate} \\ \text{in basis points} \end{array} \times \begin{array}{c} \text{Days to} \\ \text{maturity} \end{array} \times \$0.00277778 \right)$$

In the above formula $0.00277778 is the value of 1 basis point per day for $10,000. Each percent yield or discount is composed of 100 basis points.

For example, a Treasury bill with 90 days to maturity selling at a discount rate of 12 percent would have a value of

$$V_{TB} = \$10,000 - (12,000 \times 90 \times \$0.00277778)$$
$$V_{TB} = \$9,700.00$$

The discount yield of 12 percent in the above example is based on a 360-day year, whereas equivalent bond yields are on the basis of a 365-day year. An equivalent bond yield can be found by using Equation 12.3, in which the discount yield is adjusted to reflect the difference in days:

(12.3)
$$\begin{array}{c} \text{Equivalant bond} \\ \text{yield} \end{array} = \frac{365 \times \text{Discount yield rate}}{360 - (\text{Discount yield rate} \times \text{Days to maturity})}$$

In our example the equivalent bond yield for the 12 percent discount rate would be

$$\frac{365 \times 0.12}{360 - (0.12 \times 90)} = \frac{43.80}{349.20} = 0.1254 \text{ or } 12.54\%$$

BOND PRICES, YIELDS, AND RETURNS

Bond prices and yields are inversely related. If the yield on a given bond rises following acquisition, the market value of the bond will decrease. In general, the longer the maturity of the bond, the greater will be the change in price for a given change in yield.[22] Longer-term bonds have greater price risk than shorter-term bonds.

---

[22]The relationship between yield and maturity also depends on the coupon rate on the bond. In general, longer-term bonds will experience greater price volatility, but the extent of volatility is also dependent on the level of periodic interest payments. For a discussion see Appendix 12.2.

The actual realized return from a bond will not necessarily equal the yield to maturity or promised yield at the time of purchase. Actual yield depends on the rate at which intermediate interest payments are reinvested. Only in the case in which all periodic interest payments are invested at the yield to maturity will the realized yield equal the promised yield.[23] This is true even when the bond is held to maturity.

If the bond is sold before maturity, realized return will vary from the promised yield if market yields have fluctuated from the yield at the time of purchase. If yields have increased, bond prices will be lower and realized returns will also likely be lower. If yields have decreased, bond prices will have risen and will likely result in increased realized returns.[24]

Our discussion of bond pricing and bond yields has been limited to very basic concepts. Complete discussions of the factors affecting bond prices can be found in Darst, *The Complete Bond Book* and *The Handbook of the Bond and Money Markets,* and a complete discussion of the mathematics of bond yields and swapping strategies can be found in Homer and Leibowitz, *Inside the Yield Book* (see References).

---

[23]Homer and Leibowitz, op. cit., chap. 15.

[24]This statement in general is correct, but return is also affected by interest earned on the periodic interest payments on the bond. If market yields rise, coupon payments will likely be reinvested at higher rates, which will offset some of the decrease in return caused by the lower sales price.

APPENDIX 12.2

Duration

The concept of duration, developed in 1938 by Frederick Macauley, has become widely used in recent years.[25] *Duration* is a more complete measure of length or average maturity of a bond with intermediate payments than is the *term to maturity*. The concept can be used in active and passive investment strategies to improve return or reduce risk. Potentially duration can be used in interest margin management as well. The concept of duration more correctly describes the average life of the asset and liability portfolios and can be used in gap management.

The concept of duration is related to the elements of price and reinvestment risk and is not directly related to default risk. For the remainder of this discussion we shall assume investment in securities that are free of default risk. This is not to say that the concept has no application for bonds subject to default risk, but rather that the extension to bonds subject to default risk requires consideration of additional elements.[26]

DURATION MEASUREMENT

Duration of a bond is defined as

$$D = \frac{\displaystyle\sum_{n=1}^{m} \frac{nC_n}{(1+i)^n} + \frac{mA_m}{(1+i)^m}}{\displaystyle\sum_{n=1}^{m} \frac{C_n}{(1+i)^n} + \frac{A_m}{(1+i)^m}}$$

where

C = Coupon payment at the end of period n
A = Principal payment at maturity (m)
i = Yield to maturity

Duration is measured in units of time, e.g., in years to maturity. The duration of a bond will be less than the term to maturity for all

---

[25]This appendix draws heavily on the excellent article summarizing duration: Bierwag, Kaufman, and Toevs, op cit., 15–35.

[26]Ibid., 26.

bonds except zero coupon bonds. For these discount instruments, the term to maturity equals the duration.

A sample duration calculation (based on annual compounding) for a bond with 5 years to maturity, a coupon rate of 8 percent, a par value of $1000, and selling to yield 12 percent (yield to maturity) is displayed below:

$$D = \frac{\displaystyle\sum_{n=1}^{m} \frac{n80}{(1.12)^n} + \frac{(5)1000}{(1.12)^5}}{\displaystyle\sum_{n=1}^{m} \frac{80}{(1.12)^n} + \frac{1000}{(1.12)^5}} = \frac{3637.28}{855.78} = 4.25$$

For the sample bond the duration is 4.25 years. As expected, the duration is less than the term to maturity. The exact relationship between a bond's duration and its maturity is not easily described. The relationship depends on whether the bond is selling at a premium or a discount and on the number of years to maturity.[27]

POTENTIAL USES OF DURATION IN INVESTMENT POLICY

The concept of duration can be employed to construct investment portfolios that are subject to less variance in realized return from promised return. The concept can also be used in aggressive trading strategies to capture higher returns from trading on predicted movements in interest rates.

Immunization Strategy

An immunization strategy is a defensive strategy that can be used to reduce variance in return. It is accomplished by constructing a portfolio for which the duration equals the holding period. The term *immunization strategy* derives from the fact that when the duration is equal to the holding period, price risk and reinvestment risk tend to be offsetting. Such a strategy results in the realized return equaling the promised return (the yield that the portfolio is currently offering), and the investor is immunized against changes in interest rates.

The extent to which reinvestment risk and price risk are offsetting depends on characteristics of the change or shift in interest rates. For example, if the yield curve is flat and remains so after the change in rates, realized yield will equal promised yield when the duration of the

---

[27]Ibid., 18.

bond portfolio equals the holding period. Price risk and reinvestment risk will exactly offset each other. If the yield curve is not flat or if the change in interest rates is also accompanied by a change in term structure, exact immunization will not occur. Some variance in promised and realized returns will be observed.

Empirical investigations of the relationship between promised return and realized return indicate that duration strategies (setting the duration equal to the holding period) outperform maturity strategies (setting the maturity equal to the holding period). Bierwag, Kaufman, and Toevs examined the performance of duration and maturity strategies for bond returns from 1925 through 1978.[28] Their results show that realized returns are much closer to promised returns for duration strategies. The variance in realized return from promised return is consistently smaller for duration strategies than it is for maturity strategies.

Active Duration Strategies

Although the immunization strategy is a defensive strategy, duration can also be used in active or aggressive trading strategies. Since duration is a more complete measure of length or average maturity, it can be used to simplify bond pricing characteristics. Bond pricing is directly related to duration and it is not directly related to maturity. The greater the duration of a bond or a bond portfolio, the greater the price volatility for a given change in yield to maturity.

If an investor believes that interest rates are going to decline, a return-maximizing strategy would involve construction of a bond portfolio made up of bonds that would have the greatest price appreciation. The longest-maturity bonds are not necessarily the bonds that will appreciate the most in price. The price appreciation also depends on the intermediate coupon payments of the bonds. By maximizing the duration of the portfolio, one can maximize the price appreciation because price volatility is proportional to duration.

By comparing the active and immunized strategies, some general trading rules can be developed for profiting from changes in interest rates. If rates change as predicted, the active strategies will outperform the immunization strategy. If the investor predicts interest rates to rise, additional returns can be secured by setting the duration less than the holding period. The returns from reinvestment of larger intermediate cash flows will be greater than the price decline associated with the rise in rates. If the investor predicts interest rates to decline, additional returns can be earned by setting the duration to exceed the holding period. If the prediction is correct, the price appreciation will exceed the loss in reinvestment return from the decline in rates.

---

[28]Ibid., 28–30.

CHAPTER 13

Funds Management– The Balancing Act

The process of short-term funds management is a delicate procedure. It requires the funds manager to react to inflows and outflows of funds over which the bank has little control in the short run. On a daily basis funds are needed to meet reserve requirements and demands for loans by customers of the bank. To meet a liquidity need, assets must be liquidated or funds must be borrowed. If surplus funds become available, these funds must be employed in interest-earning assets to maintain profit margins. The funds manager must react to uncertain funds flows in order to maintain profits and at the same time reduce risk. In short, he must perform a delicate balancing act.

GOALS OF FUNDS MANAGEMENT

A bank must meet a variety of goals related to its short-term funds management. The first and primary goal is that of meeting reserve requirements within the allowable range. Second, a bank must maintain sufficient liquidity or flexibility to meet the liquidity needs of its customers. Finally, funds must be managed in a manner to assist in satisfying such longer-term goals as structuring the investment and loan portfolios and funding the targeted gap position.

Failure to maintain the minimum required reserves exposes a bank to penalties that are assessed on shortages. In addition, a bank may experience greater interference from regulators if the required reserves are not met with regularity. If a bank maintains larger reserves than are required, it suffers an opportunity loss. Reserves are nonearning assets, and if a bank carries excess reserves, its overall return will be lower. A bank is therefore penalized for any inefficiency in its reserve management.

The secondary goal of meeting the needs of its customers is also of critical importance. The competitive nature of the banking industry requires that a bank maintain sufficient flexibility to meet the needs of its customers. Failure to accommodate the demands of its customers may impose the penalty of losing the customers to other banks or financial institutions that will service their needs.

Demands for liquidity arise from both demand for loans and investment of excess funds. Demand for loans can be expected or unexpected. If expected, a bank can plan for acquisition of funds to meet the loan requests. If unexpected, the bank will have to accommodate the demand for liquidity by liquidating other earning assets or by borrowing funds. Conditions in the market for short-term funds may result in lower interest margins. Customers of the bank may have excess funds that they want to invest. The bank must be ready to meet a demand for investment of funds as well.

Funds management must also be consistent with the longer-term goals being pursued by management. After all, the long run is merely the summation of actions taken in the short run. If the bank has a long-range goal of restructuring the investment portfolio, the short-term adjustment process should explicitly attempt to satisfy the longer-range objective. If a goal has been set to improve the liquidity of the asset portfolio through increases in holdings of Treasury securities, the option of liquidating such securities to meet a funds shortage is constrained. Actions taken in the short run need to contribute to long-run objectives.

RESERVE MANAGEMENT

As in many areas of banking, regulations in the area of reserve requirements are undergoing significant changes. Distinctions between state and federally chartered banks concerning required reserves will eventually disappear. The system of lagged-reserve accounting (LRA), which had been in place since 1968, was changed back to contemporaneous reserve accounting (CRA) in 1984.

Required Reserves: A Historical Perspective

Under our dual banking system, banks can be chartered under a federal or state charter. If federally chartered, a bank is required to be a member of the Federal Reserve System. A bank that is state chartered can elect to become a member of the Federal Reserve System but is not required to be a member. Member banks are required to meet the Federal Reserve System reserve requirements and were able to secure the services provided by the Federal Reserve System at no additional costs. With the passage of the DIDMCA and its subsequent uniform reserve requirements, the question of membership election became moot since all depository institutions will eventually be subject to the same reserve requirements and will have access to the services of the Federal Reserve System on a fee basis. To gain an understanding of some of the reasoning behind the 1980 act, it is useful to compare state and member-bank reserve requirements from a historical perspective.

State vs. Member-Bank Reserve Requirements. Reserve requirements imposed by states were generally less binding than those imposed by the Federal Reserve System on its members. First, the percentages that were required to be held as reserves were often smaller; second, and even more significant, different assets could be counted as reserves for state requirements. Most states counted balances due from correspondent banks as eligible assets to meet reserve requirements where these are not eligible under the Fed's requirements. State banks used correspondent balances to gain most of the services offered by the Fed, and so these assets were earning assets for nonmember banks. Furthermore, many states counted investment securities in meeting reserve requirements, and so banks earned an explicit interest rate on other portions of their reserves as well.

Members of the Fed were required to meet reserves with vault cash and balances held at the Federal Reserve banks. The key difference in the requirements is that reserves had to be met with nonearning balances. The benefits of membership included the availability of services such as check clearing, wire funds transfer, currency services, and access to the discount window. Because most of the same services were available through the correspondent bank system, when the reserve requirements were considered many banks found it more profitable to elect out of membership.[1]

The effect of the different requirements was that membership in the Federal Reserve System began to decline. New banks often elected state chartering and chose not to become members. From 1968 through 1978 at least 41 banks annually elected to withdraw from the Federal Reserve System. In the first half of 1978, 37 banks withdrew from membership.[2] The importance of member deposits as a percentage of total bank deposits continually declined, and this decline was directly related to the burdensome member reserve requirements. Exhibit 13.1 displays the decline in the percentage of member bank deposits.

The significance of the decline in membership can be understood by considering the reason for requiring banks to hold reserves. Three possible roles for reserve requirements exist. First, it was originally thought that by requiring banks to hold reserves it was possible for the regulatory authorities to improve bank liquidity. Second, reserves that were required to be held as deposits in the Federal Reserve banks serve as a tax on banks. Third, and most significant in contemporary analysis, reserves play an important role in facilitating monetary control. As more and more banks left the system and new banks elected state charters without membership, the decline in members deposits led to less control of monetary aggregates by the monetary authorities.[3] This

---

[1] Numerous studies have addressed the issues of costs and benefits of Federal Reserve membership. For example, see C. M. Gambs, "Federal Reserve Membership and the Role of Nonmember Bank Reserve Requirements," *Economic Review, Federal Reserve Bank of Kansas City*, February 1979: 3–14; and B. J. Summers, "Correspondent Services, Federal Reserve Services, and Bank Cash Management Policy," *Economic Review, Federal Reserve Bank of Richmond*, November-December 1978: 29–38.

[2] Gambs, op. cit.

[3] For development of the role of reserves, see Gambs, op. cit.

EXHIBIT 13.1   Percentage of Total Demand Deposits at Federal Reserve Member Banks

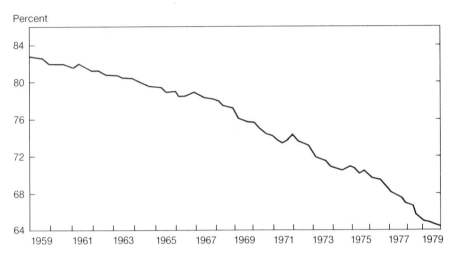

Source: J. A. Cacy and S. Winninghan, "Reserve Requirements Under the Depository Institutions Deregulation and Monetary Control Act of 1980," *Economic Review, Federal Reserve Bank of Kansas City*, September-October 1980: 8.

decline in member deposits and the subsequent loss of control over reserves by the monetary authorities were significant motivating forces behind the passage of the DIDMCA.

The Depository Institutions Deregulation and Monetary Control Act of 1980.   This landmark piece of legislation has and will continue to have a profound effect on the structure and operation of banks. The DIDMCA served two main purposes: (1) to help the monetary authorities gain control of the money supply, and (2) to make the regulatory environment more competitive for depository financial institutions. Its major provisions included creating similar reserve requirements for all depository institutions, making Federal Reserve System services available to all banks and changing the services to a fee-based system, and eventual elimination of Regulation Q, which will allow banks to compete for funds with financial institutions that are not as regulated as deposit institutions.

The changes in reserve requirements mandated by the DIDMCA are being phased in so that banks can plan for the modifications that are required. The phase-in period for nonmember depository institutions is eight years. For member banks the phase-in period is three and a half years. For new institutions the phase-in period is two years. (See Exhibit 13.2 for details.)

EXHIBIT 13.2   Depository Institutions Reserve Requirements[1] (Percent of Deposits)

Type of Deposit, and Deposit Interval in Millions of Dollars	Member Bank Requirements before Implementation of the Monetary Control Act		Type of Deposit, and Deposit Interval[5]	Depository Institution Requirements after Implementation of the Monetary Control Act[6]	
	Percent	Effective Date		Percent	Effective Date
Net demand[2]			*Net transaction accounts*[7,8]		
0–2	7	12/30/76	$0–$26.3 million . . .	3	12/30/82
2–10	9½	12/30/76	Over $26.3 million. . .	12	12/30/82
10–100	11¾	12/30/76			
100–400	12¾	12/30/76	*Nonpersonal time deposits*[9]		
Over 400	16¼	12/30/76	By original maturity		
			Less than 2½ years . . .	3	3/31/83
Time and savings[2,3]			2½ years or more . . .	0	3/31/83
Savings	3	3/16/67			
			Eurocurrency liabilities		
Time[4]			All types	3	11/13/80
0–5, by maturity					
30–179 days . . .	3	3/16/67			
180 days to 4 years . .	2½	1/8/76			
4 years or more . . .	1	10/30/75			
Over 5, by maturity					
30–179 days . . .	6	12/12/74			
180 days to 4 years . .	2½	1/8/76			
4 years or more . . .	1	10/30/75			

1. For changes in reserve requirements beginning 1963, see Board's *Annual Statistical Digest, 1971–1975* and for prior changes, see Board's *Annual Report* for 1976, table 13. Under provisions of the Monetary Control Act, depository institutions include commercial banks, mutual savings banks, savings and loan associations, credit unions, agencies and branches of foreign banks, and Edge Act corporations.

2. Requirement schedules are graduated, and each deposit interval applies to that part of the deposits of each bank. Demand deposits subject to reserve requirements were gross demand deposits minus cash items in process of collection and demand balances due from domestic banks.

The Federal Reserve Act as amended through 1978 specified different ranges of requirements for reserve city banks and for other banks. Reserve cities were designated under a criterion adopted effective Nov. 9, 1972, by which a bank having net demand deposits of more than $400 million was considered to have the character of business of a reserve city bank. The presence of the head office of such a bank constituted designation of that place as a reserve city. Cities in which there were Federal Reserve Banks or branches were also reserve cities. Any banks having net demand deposits of $400 million or less were considered to have the character of business of banks outside of reserve cities and were permitted to maintain reserves at ratios set for banks not in reserve cities.

Effective Aug. 24, 1978, the Regulation M reserve requirements on net balances due from domestic banks to their foreign branches and on deposits that foreign branches lend to U.S. residents were reduced to zero from 4 percent and 1 percent respectively. The Regulation D reserve requirement of borrowings from unrelated banks abroad was also reduced to zero from 4 percent.

Effective with the reserve computation period beginning Nov. 16, 1978, domestic deposits of Edge corporations were subject to the same reserve requirements as deposits of member banks.

3. Negotiable order of withdrawal (NOW) accounts and time deposits such as Christmas and vacation club accounts were subject to the same requirements as savings deposits.

The average reserve requirement on savings and other time deposits before implementation of the Monetary Control Act had to be at least 3 percent, the minimum specified by law.

4. Effective Nov. 2, 1978, a supplementary reserve requirement of 2 percent was imposed on large time deposits of $100,000 or more, obligations of affiliates, and ineligible acceptances. This supplementary requirement was eliminated with the maintenance period beginning July 24, 1980.

Effective with the reserve maintenance period beginning Oct. 25, 1979, a marginal reserve requirement of 8 percent was added to managed liabilities in excess of a base amount. This marginal requirement was increased to 10 percent beginning Apr. 3, 1980, was decreased to 5 percent beginning June 12, 1980, and was eliminated beginning July 24, 1980. Managed liabilities are defined as large time deposits, Eurodollar borrowings, repurchase agreements against U.S. government and federal agency securities, federal funds borrowings from nonmember institutions, and certain other obligations. In general, the base for the marginal reserve requirement was originally the greater of (a) $100 million or (b) the average amount of the managed liabilities held by a member bank, Edge corporation, or family of U.S. branches and agencies of a foreign bank for the two reserve computation periods ending Sept. 26, 1979. For the computation period beginning Mar. 20, 1980, the base was lowered by (a) 7 percent or (b) the decrease in an institution's U.S. office gross loans to foreigners and gross balances due from foreign offices of other institutions between the base period (Sept. 13–26, 1979) and the week ending Mar. 12, 1980, whichever was greater. For the computation period beginning May 29, 1980, the base was increased by 7½ percent above the base used to calculate the marginal reserve in the statement week of May 14–21, 1980. In addition, beginning Mar. 19, 1980, the base was reduced to the extent that foreign loans and balances declined.

5. The Garn–St Germain Depository Institutions Act of 1982 (Public Law 97–320) provides that $2 million of reservable liabilities (transaction accounts, nonpersonal time deposits, and Eurocurrency liabilities) of each depository institution be subject to a zero percent reserve requirement. The Board is to adjust the amount of reservable liabilities subject to this zero percent reserve requirement each year for the next succeeding calendar year by 80 percent of the percentage increase in the total reservable liabilities of all depository institutions, measured on an annual basis as of June 30. No corresponding adjustment is to be made in the event of a decrease. Effective Dec. 9, 1982, the amount of the exemption was established at $2.1 million. In determining the reserve requirements of a depository institution, the exemption shall apply in the following order: (1) nonpersonal money market deposit accounts (MMDAs) authorized under 12 CFR section 1204.122; (2) net NOW accounts (NOW accounts less allowable deductions); (3) net other transaction accounts; and (4) nonpersonal time deposits or Eurocurrency liabilities starting with those with the highest reserve ratio. With respect to NOW accounts and other transaction accounts, the exemption applies only to such accounts that would be subject to a 3 percent reserve requirement.

6. For nonmember banks and thrift institutions that were not members of the Federal Reserve System on or after July 1, 1979, a phase-in period ends Sept. 3, 1987. For banks that were members on or after July 1, 1979, but withdrew on or before Mar. 31, 1980, the phase-in period established by Public Law 97–320 ends on Oct. 24, 1985. For existing member banks the phase-in period is about three years, depending on whether their new reserve requirements are greater or less than the old requirements. All new institutions will have a two-year phase-in beginning with the date that they open for business, except for those institutions that have total reservable liabilities of $50 million or more.

7. Transaction accounts include all deposits on which the account holder is permitted to make withdrawals by negotiable or transferable instruments, payment orders of withdrawal, and telephone and preauthorized transfers (in excess of three per month) for the purpose of making payments to third persons or others. However, MMDAs and similar accounts offered by institutions not subject to the rules of the Depository Institutions Deregulation Committee (DIDC) that permit no more than six preauthorized, automatic, or other transfers per month of which no more than three can be checks—are not transaction accounts (such accounts are savings deposits subject to time deposit reserve requirements.)

8. The Monetary Control Act of 1980 requires that the amount of transaction accounts against which the 3 percent reserve requirement applies be modified annually by 80 percent of the percentage increase in transaction accounts held by all depository institutions determined as of June 30 each year. Effective Dec. 31, 1981, the amount was increased accordingly from $25 million to $26 million; and effective Dec. 30, 1982, to $26.3 million.

9. In general, nonpersonal time deposits are time deposits, including savings deposits, that are not transaction accounts and in which the beneficial interest is held by a depositor that is not a natural person. Also included are certain transferable time deposits held by natural persons, and certain obligations issued to depository institution offices located outside the United States. For details, see section 204.2 of Regulation D.

Note: Required reserves must be held in the form of deposits with Federal Reserve Banks or vault cash. After implementation of the Monetary Control Act, nonmembers may maintain reserves on a pass-through basis with certain approved institutions.

Source: *Federal Reserve Bulletin*, May 1983.

When all the provisions of the DIDMCA are completely phased in, most member banks' reserves will be lower than they were under the old requirements. Personal savings and time deposits will not be subject to reserves, as was the case under the old requirements. In addition, some exempt deposits, such as Eurodollar deposits, will now be subject to reserve requirements.

The changes taking place in reserve requirements make it difficult to describe with precision the procedure for measuring deposits and meeting reserve requirements. All depository institutions are in some phase-in or phase-down process. At this point no bank is under the exact DIDMCA requirements.

Lagged Reserve Accounting. In 1968 the Federal Reserve System changed the procedure used in reserve accounting. Prior to 1968 mem-

---

Reserve Accounting and Monetary Policy

Prior to 1968 banks were required to hold reserves against deposits on a contemporaneous reserve accounting (CRA) basis. Under CRA changes in current deposit levels have an immediate impact on required reserves, and since banks could not be certain of short-term changes in their deposit levels, they were forced to hold excess reserves.

In 1968 the Federal Reserve Board moved to a lagged reserve accounting (LRA) procedure and liberalized the carryover provision. The presumption was that this would improve monetary control and reduce the volatility of the federal funds rate. Because banks felt the need to hold excess reserves under CRA, the federal funds market became quite volatile at the end of each reserve period. Banks with surplus reserves were trying to place them, and banks with reserve shortages were scrambling to borrow. The problem was exacerbated by the fact that the pre-1968 rules did not allow a bank to move excess reserves forward into the next reserve period. The resulting volatility made it more difficult for the Fed to enact monetary policy because it required larger adjustments to counteract the activity of banks.

Following the changes made in 1968, empirical evidence indicated that the federal funds rate was more volatile than it was under CRA. Furthermore, it was found that the level of Fed activity in open market operations exceeded the pre-1968 levels. Later investigations revealed that the volatility in the federal funds rate was basically unaffected by the change, but the level of open market operations was higher under the new policy. In short, the opposite of what was expected resulted from the change.

ber banks were required to hold reserves against current deposits. This procedure made it difficult for banks to meet reserve requirements because banks did not have the ability to measure the level of deposits with precision. To avoid failure to meet required reserves, banks were forced to hold excess reserves. The monetary authorities believed that this practice led to greater volatility in the money markets.

We shall describe reserve calculation and management under the LRA procedure because it facilitates an understanding of the new CRA procedure. Furthermore, some deposits will continue to be lagged under the CRA system.

Under the LRA system the computation period and settlement period were one-week periods. The computation period began on Thursday and ended on the following Wednesday. A bank's closing deposit figure for each of the days in that week was used to determine the deposits

The reasons for changing from lagged back to contemporaneous reserve accounting in 1979 were the same as those for the original change—improved monetary control and a reduction in the variability of the federal funds rate. The line of reasoning had changed, however, because the Federal Reserve had changed its operating targets. Prior to October 1979 the Fed operated on the federal funds rate as its primary target. The Fed attempted to keep the federal funds rate in a target range thought to be consistent with the money supply target. Since October 1979 the money supply has been the primary target, with interest rates as a secondary target. The Fed has attempted to meet the money supply target by controlling the level of reserves in the banking system.

It is impossible for the Fed to meet its reserve target on a short-run basis under LRA. Because of the lag, required reserves are not immediately affected by open market operations. If the Fed acts to reduce (increase) reserves by undertaking purchases (sales), under LRA there is no simultaneous change in required reserves. Under LRA the Fed is unable to make an immediate adjustment in reserves for the system.

Under CRA excess reserves for the system are affected by open market sales and purchases because required reserves are a function of current deposits. Open market operations have an immediate impact and, in theory, should improve the ability of the Fed to meet its monetary aggregates target. Thus the change in operating targets mandated the change in the reserve accounting procedure.

against which reserves must be held. The reserve settlement week, which also ran from Thursday through Wednesday, was the period during which reserves must have been held for deposits measured two weeks earlier. This process is illustrated in Exhibit 13.3, which shows the lagged process. The bank knew well in advance the deposit amounts against which reserves must be held, but the actual reserves that were to be held could not be determined until the end of the previous settlement week because of the carryover provision.

Under the DIDMCA reserve requirements, reserves were to be held against three classes of deposits: net transaction accounts, nonpersonal time and savings deposits, and Eurocurrency liabilities. Net transaction accounts include demand deposits, NOW accounts, and any accounts on which the account holder is permitted to make three or more withdrawals by negotiable or transferable instruments.[4] These deposits are net of cash items in the process of collection. Reserve percentages were graduated, with 3 percent on the first $26.3 million in deposits and 12 percent on deposits in excess of $26.3 million.[5] Nonpersonal time deposits are any time or savings deposits in which the beneficial owner is not a natural person.

Two assets counted as reserves for member banks: (1) vault cash and (2) reserve balances held at the Federal Reserve Bank. Vault cash held during the measurement week counted toward meeting reserves for the settlement week. Reserves not met by vault cash were required to

---

EXHIBIT 13.3   Measurement and Settlement Weeks under LRA

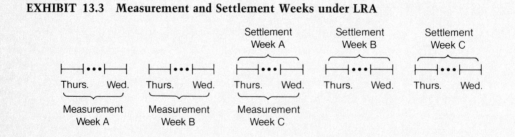

---

[4]One exception to the three-transfers limit is the new money market deposit account, which was authorized in December 1982. On these accounts no more than six preauthorized transfers can take place per month. (See notes in Exhibit 13.2.)

[5]The Garn-St. Germain Depository Institutions Act placed one further change in reserve requirements. It established a zero percent reserve requirement on the first $2 million of reservable liabilities. It further directed the Federal Reserve Board to adjust the reservable liabilities subject to a zero percent reserve requirement by 80 percent of the increase in the total reservable liabilities of all depository institutions starting in June 1982. The initial exemption was set at $2.1 million on December 9, 1982. (See notes in Exhibit 13.2.)

be held in the bank's account at the Federal Reserve Bank. Nonmember institutions were permitted to hold reserves on a pass-through basis with approved institutions.

An example of the actual calculation of reserves under LRA for a bank is displayed in Exhibit 13.4. The procedure involved calculating the daily average deposits in the various categories. The reserve percentages were then applied to the appropriate balances and the total amount of required reserves was determined.

Deposits in the various categories were totaled and then averaged for the measurement week. The graduated percentages that apply to transaction accounts were then applied to the daily average deposits in the various categories. For our sample bank, which had total daily

EXHIBIT 13.4 Sample Calculation of Reserves

Day	Net Transaction Accounts	Nonpersonal Time Deposits, Less than 2½ Years	Eurocurrency Liabilities	Vault Cash
		Deposits[a]		
Thursday	.	.	.	.
Friday	.	.	.	.
Saturday	.	.	.	.
Sunday	.	.	.	.
Monday	.	.	.	.
Tuesday	.	.	.	.
Wednesday	.	.	.	.
Week's totals	$3,500,000	$700,000	$350,000	$70,000
÷ 7				
Daily average	$500,000	$100,000	$50,000	$10,000

Reserve Calculation

Account	$ Million	Reserve Percentage	Deposit Amount	Required Reserves
Net transaction accounts	0–26.3	3%	$ 26,300	$ 789
	Over 26.3	12	473,700	56,844
Nonpersonal time deposits, less than 2½ years		3	100,000	3,000
Eurocurrency liabilities		3	50,000	1,500
Total daily required reserves				$62,133
Cumulative reserves: Daily reserves × 7 = $434,931				

[a]All dollar amounts are in thousands.

average reservable deposits of $650 million, the daily required reserves for the settlement week, two weeks later, were $62,133,000.

The next step in the procedure was to figure the actual average balances that must be held in the reserve accounts. Vault cash for the measurement period was subtracted from the total required reserves to arrive at the daily average figure that must be held in the reserve accounts. For our sample that figure is $52,133,000 (daily required reserves minus daily average vault cash).

In practice, the funds manager targeted on the cumulative reserve figure for the settlement week. In our example the cumulative balance held at the Fed and lagged vault cash must total $434,931,000. The bank could have excess or deficit amounts on a daily basis, but total cumulative reserves must equal the total figure with the exception of the carryover provision, which we shall now discuss.

The carryover provision under LRA allowed a bank to carry to the next reserve settlement period a maximum of ±2 percent of required reserves. The calculation of the carryover is shown in Exhibit 13.5. For our example the acceptable range of cumulative reserves that was to be held in the reserve account was between $356,232,380 and $373,629,620.

If a bank incurred a deficit of up to 2 percent, that deficit was required to be cleared in the next settlement period. The Fed assessed penalties for deficits in excess of 2 percent. If a bank was over its requirements by an amount up to 2 percent, that surplus could be carried forward to the next settlement week. If a bank carried more than a 2

EXHIBIT 13.5   Reserves to Be Held during Settlement Week

Total cumulative required reserves	$434,931[a]
Less cumulative vault cash	70,000
Cumulative reserve balances	$364,931

Carryover Provision[b]

2% of cumulative required reserves

$0.02 \times \$434,931 = \$8,698.62$

Acceptable Range on Cumulative Balances Held in Reserve Account

	Required Reserves		2% Carryover		Vault Cash		Reserve Account
Low	$434,931	−	8,698.62	−	70,000	=	$356,232.38
High	$434,931	+	8,698.62	−	70,000	=	$373,629.62

[a]All dollar amounts are in thousands.
[b]The calculation of acceptable range assumes that the bank had no previous surplus or deficit.

percent surplus for any settlement period, it lost the benefit of the excess, which means that the bank would have tied up funds in a nonearning asset over the amount that could be used in the following period.

Strategies for Using the Carryover Provision under LRA.   The goal pursued by the funds manager was to fully utilize the carryover provision. The bank minimized the cost of meeting its reserve requirements by carrying no excess (over the carryover) reserves and avoiding the penalties assessed for deficits in excess of the allowable ranges. In this regard a basic strategy was to alternate surpluses and deficits and to set up target ranges of minimums and maximums.[6]

To see how this works, consider our sample bank with cumulative required reserves for the first settlement week of $434,931,000. Assume that the bank incurred the maximum deficit in this settlement week of $8,698,620. Further assume that deposits during the next measurement period declined slightly so that the required reserves for the second settlement week were $400,000,000.

As shown in Exhibit 13.6, since the deficit from the first week must be cleared up, the minimum amount of reserves for the second settlement week would be $408,698,620. Any amount less than that

---

EXHIBIT 13.6   Target Range of Cumulative Reserves with Previous Carryover

Maintenance Week		Reserves[a]		Carryover
1		$434,931.00[b]		($8,698.62)
2		408,698.62[b]		

Required reserves	+	Deficit	=	New required reserves
$400,000	+	$8,698.62	=	$408,698.62

Target Range of Cumulative Reserves for Maintenance Week 2

Minimum level	=	Required reserves	+	Deficit
$408,698.62	=	$400,000	+	$8,698.62

Maximum level	=	Minimum level	+	2% surplus
$416,698.62	=	$408,698.62	+	$8,000

[a]All dollar amounts are in thousands.
[b]These amounts are cumulative reserves and not the actual balances that must be carried in the reserve account. Lagged vault cash is counted as meeting required reserves.

---

[6]This section draws heavily on R. E. Knight, "Guidelines for Efficient Reserve Management," *Monthly Review, Federal Reserve Bank of Kansas City,* November 1977: 11–23. The article contains several sample calculations with surplus and deficit carryovers.

figure would subject the bank to possible penalties. The maximum amount that should be carried as total reserves is $416,698,620. The bank would incur an opportunity loss if total cumulative reserves exceeded $416,698,620 because the carryover would exceed 2 percent. For example, if the bank maintained $426,698,620 in the reserve account, it would have tied up an extra $10 million (on a cumulative basis) in nonearning assets. The bank could not regain the lost revenue on the surplus because it exceeded the maximum allowable carryover.

Efficient reserve management called for the bank to alternate surpluses and deficits as the example shows. With the introduction of lagged-reserve accounting in 1968 and the carryover provisions associated with reserve requirements, banks were able to greatly reduce the level of excess reserves. Furthermore, evidence indicates that most banks used the carryover position as we have described with alternating surplus and deficit positions.[7]

Contemporaneous Reserve Accounting

In February 1984 banks with deposits in excess of $15 million were required to switch from lagged-reserve accounting to contemporaneous-reserve accounting (CRA). CRA means that the measurement and settlement periods will coincide. Actually, there is a two-day lag for most deposits instead of the current two-week lag. The measurement and maintenance periods have also been changed to two weeks. The change to CRA will pose greater measurement problems and will also reduce a bank's ability to keep reserves at the lowest possible minimum.

Motivation for the Federal Reserve System's switching back to CRA from the current LRA system is tied to monetary policy considerations. The change to LRA in 1968 was expected to enhance the monetary authorities' ability to control the money supply through controlling bank reserves. The change was also expected to reduce the volatility in the short-term money markets. Evidence indicates that neither objective was accomplished.[8] To improve control of the money supply, the decision was made to return to CRA.

The costs of returning to a CRA system will include costs to individual banks in changing their reserve management and information systems and the costs to the Federal Reserve System in changing its

---

[7] D. C. Beek, "Excess Reserves and Reserve Targeting," *Quarterly Review, Federal Reserve Bank of New York*, Autumn 1981: 15–22.

[8] For detailed discussion, see R. A. Gilbert, "Lagged Reserve Requirements: Implications for Monetary Control and Bank Reserve Management," *Review, Federal Reserve Bank of St. Louis*, May 1980: 7–20; and D. S. Jones, "Contemporaneous vs. Lagged Reserve Accounting: Implications for Monetary Control," *Economic Review, Federal Reserve Bank of Kansas City*, November 1981: 3–19.

monitoring system. Some have questioned whether the changes will be economically efficient—will the gain in control offset the costs?[9]

The major changes in reserve accounting are summarized in Exhibits 13.7 and 13.8. All depository institutions with deposits in excess of $15 million have switched to CRA. CRA will apply to transaction accounts that include checking, NOW, automatic transfer, and share draft accounts. Reserve requirements on nontransaction accounts will

---

EXHIBIT 13.7 Summary of Changes in Reserve Requirements under Contemporaneous Reserve Accounting

1. Contemporaneous reserve requirements (CRR) will apply only to institutions reporting their deposits on a weekly basis. (Certain institutions with $15 million or less in total deposits report deposits and calculate required reserves quarterly, and certain others, with reservable liabilities under $2 million, are exempt from reserve requirements.)
2. Reserves will be maintained over two-week periods that will continue to end on a Wednesday.
3. All institutions subject to CRR will settle their reserve accounts on the same day.
4. Required reserves will be *computed* on the basis of average deposits over a two-week computation period ending on Monday. Reserves required to be posted against transaction accounts will be *maintained* in the two-week period ending on Wednesday, two days after the end of the computation period. The two-day interval provides time for calculation of required reserves.
5. Required reserves for other liabilities against which reserves must be held—such as certain kinds of time deposits—will also be computed on the basis of average deposits over a two-week period ending on Monday, but the reserves required will be posted in the two-week maintenance period beginning 17 days later, on a Thursday.
6. Vault cash eligible to be counted as reserves will be equal to vault cash holdings during the computation period ending 17 days before the beginning of the maintenance period.
7. To assist depository institutions in implementing CRR, the Board adopted transition periods for the carryover of reserve balance deficiencies or surpluses. During the first six months following the start of CRR, reserve surpluses or deficiencies that may be carried over into the next reserve period will equal the greater of 3 percent of the daily average level of required reserves (including required clearing balances) or $25,000. During the next six months, the permissible carryover will equal the greater of 2½ percent of daily average required reserves or $25,000. Thereafter, the carryover is the greater of 2 percent of daily average required reserves or $25,000.

Source: Board of Governors of the Federal Reserve, press release, October 5, 1982.

---

[9]T. Herman and E. P. Foldessy, "Fed's New Rules for Setting Bank Reserves Could Cause Large Swings in Interest Rates," *The Wall Street Journal*, Feb. 16, 1984, 31; Jones, op. cit.; and R. D. Laurent, "Comparing Alternative Replacements for Lagged Reserves: Why Settle for a Poor Third Best?," *Staff Memoranda 83-2, Federal Reserve Bank of Chicago*, 1–23.

EXHIBIT 13.8   Reserve Computation and Maintenance Cycle under CRR Weekly Reporters

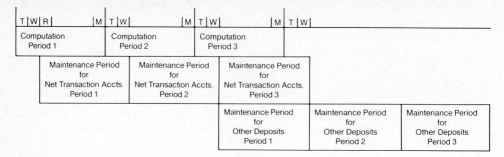

Reserves on net transaction accounts are maintained on a near contemporaneous basis; reserves on all other deposits (time and saving deposits, eurocurrency liabilities and vault cash) and clearing balances are maintained on a lagged basis.

Source: *Reserve Maintenance Manual, Federal Reserve Bank of Kansas City*, 7.

continue to be met on a lagged basis. In addition, there is a phase-in period with larger carryover provisions.

From a management standpoint, meeting reserves under CRA requires closer monitoring, especially for banks with volatile deposits. The key difference is less certainty about the exact level of reserves that will have to be held. Large inflows or outflows to the reserve account near the end of the measurement and maintenance periods could cause a bank to make larger adjusting transactions.

In one sense the change to CRA reduces the problems in managing the reserve account. For a bank that clears through its Federal Reserve account, under LRA no simultaneous change in reserve requirements accompanied a change in deposits. A reduction in reserves as checks clear simultaneously lowers required reserves under CRA, resulting in a smaller deficiency than under LRA.[10]

It is difficult to assess the problems with measurement that will arise with the change to CRA, but such problems should be much less significant than before 1968. Advancements in technology should improve the ability of banks to measure deposits. Even so, some problems will undoubtedly be encountered in the initial stages of the switch.

Reserve Calculation under Contemporaneous Reserve Accounting.   Illustrations of reserve calculation under CRA are shown in Exhibits 13.9, 13.10, and 13.11. Exhibit 13.9 displays calculation of reserves for transaction accounts. The daily reserves must be held with a two-day lag.

---

[10]For illustrations of changes in deposits and reserves under LRA and CRA, see Gilbert, op. cit., appendix.

EXHIBIT 13.9 Reserve Calculation for Transaction Accounts under Contemporaneous Reserve Accounting

Day	Transaction Accounts	Daily Required Reserves[a]		Maintenance Period for Transaction Accounts	
				Daily	Cumulative
Tues. 1	$200,000	$0–26.3 million	3%		
		Over $26.3 million	12% ⟶ $21,633		
Wed. 2	$250,000	$0–26.3 million	3%		
		Over $26.3 million	12% ⟶ $27,633		
Thurs. 3	$225,000	$0–26.3 million	3%		
		Over $26.3 million	12% ⟶ $24,633	⟶ $21,633	
Fri. 4	.		.	⟶ $27,633	$49,266
Sat. 5	.		.	⟶ $24,633	$73,899
.	.		.	.	.
.	.		.	.	.
Mon. 14	.		.	.	.
Tues. 15			.	.	.
Wed. 16				.	.

[a]All dollar amounts are in thousands.

EXHIBIT 13.10   Calculation of Reserves with Lagged and Transaction Accounts under Contemporaneous Reserve Accounting

Lagged vault cash (daily average)	= 56,000 ÷ 14 = 4,000[a]
Nontransaction accounts (daily average)	= 3,150,000 ÷ 14 = 225,000
Nontransaction daily reserves	= 225,000 × .03 = 6,750

Maintenance Period	Nontransaction Lagged Reserves	Transaction Contemporaneous Reserves	Required Reserves	Vault Cash	Required Reserve Account Balance
1 Daily	$ 6,750	$21,633	$28,383	$ 4,000	$24,383
2 Daily	6,750	27,633	34,383	4,000	30,383
Cumulative	13,500	49,266	62,766	8,000	54,766
3 Daily	6,750	24,633	31,383	4,000	27,383
Cumulative	20,250	73,899	94,149	12,000	82,149
4	. . . . .	. . . . .	. . . . .	. . . . .	. . . . .

[a]All dollar amounts are in thousands.

EXHIBIT 13.11 Reserve Maintenance under Contemporaneous Reserve Accounting

Maintenance Period	Required[a] Reserves	Carryover Allowance at 3%	Minimum Total Reserves (deficit carryover)	Maximum Total Reserves (surplus carryover)	Minimum Reserve Balance (less vault cash)[b]	Maximum Reserve Balance (less vault cash)[b]
1 Daily	$28,383	$ 851.49	$27,531.51	$29,234.49	$23,531.51	$25,234.49
2 Daily	34,383	1,031.49	33,351.51	35,414.49	29,351.51	31,414.49
Cumulative	62,766	1,882.98	60,883.02	64,648.98	52,883.02	56,648.98
3 Daily	31,383	941.49	30,441.51	32,324.49	26,441.51	28,324.49
Cumulative	94,149	2,824.47	91,324.53	96,973.47	79,324.53	84,973.47
.	.	.	.	.	.	.
.	.	.	.	.	.	.
.	.	.	.	.	.	.
14						

[a]All dollar amounts are in thousands.

[b]Lagged vault cash is $4,000.

In the example the bank would have to hold reserves of $21,633,000 on Thursday for the transaction accounts of Tuesday.

Exhibit 13.10 displays the calculation of reserves that must be maintained in the reserve account for all reservable deposits. In the example nontransaction accounts average $225,000,000 per day, which requires reserves of $6,750,000. Reserves for these liabilities are based on a two-week lag. Total required reserves for the maintenance period are equal to the total of transaction accounts (lagged two days) and the daily average for nontransaction accounts (lagged two weeks). Since lagged vault cash counts as meeting reserve requirements, the actual amounts that must be carried in the reserve account are displayed in the last column of Exhibit 13.10. The most significant difference between CRA and LRA requirements is that the reserves for transaction accounts under CRA cannot be calculated until two days before they are required to be maintained.

The final step in measuring the reserve requirement involves incorporation of the carryover allowance. Under LRA the carryover allowance was based on lagged deposits; thus the exact dollar range of required reserves could be assessed in advance. Under CRA the target range of reserves will change with any change in the transaction accounts. A sample calculation is displayed in Exhibit 13.11. Notice how the range of reserves changes with variation in the transaction account levels.

Under CRA the maintenance period is twice as long as it was under LRA. In addition, during the phase-in period the carryover allowance percentage has been increased to 3 percent. The range of allowable reserves will be much larger under CRA than it was under LRA. The actual dollar amounts of allowable carryovers (based on cumulative reserves) will be twice as large after the phase-in period, when the allowance returns to the 2 percent level.

MANAGEMENT OF DAILY FUNDS FLOW

The overriding goal in managing the money desk is to simultaneously satisfy the goals of meeting reserve requirements, meeting other liquidity needs, and meeting investment needs while minimizing transaction costs. In minimizing costs, the funds manager must avoid needless or superfluous transactions, attempt to make sales and purchases in units that minimize transaction costs and maximize interest income or that minimize interest expense on adjusting transactions. All of this must be accomplished in an environment in which the manager is uncertain of flows and liquidity needs.

An overview of the management process is displayed in Exhibit 13.12. The inflows and outflows to the reserve account are netted, and

EXHIBIT 13.12   Daily Funds Management

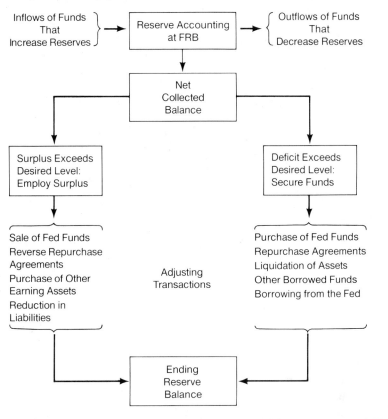

the net addition to the collected balance of the reserve account will change with any imbalances in the flows. If a surplus occurs, then the manager must decide whether to employ the surplus funds in earning assets or to use the funds to reduce existing liabilities. If a deficit or net outflow occurs, the manager must decide whether to cover the outflow by borrowing funds or by liquidating assets.

The decision to employ or secure funds for an imbalance depends on the size of the imbalance and on whether the imbalance is out of line with projections. If the imbalance is small, from a cost minimization standpoint it may not be feasible to make an adjusting transaction. The transaction costs involved with a small-denomination transaction may make it too costly. With a small imbalance the manager may want to let the surplus or deficit accumulate until the funds are large enough to be employed or borrowed in an efficient fashion.

Reserve Maintenance under CRA

Exhibit 13.13 displays a worksheet that can be used to manage the reserve position during the maintenance period. The figures used in the worksheet are based on the sample reserve calculations in Exhibits 13.9, 13.10, and 13.11. For each day the minimum and maximum levels of daily reserves and cumulative reserves that are to be carried in the reserve balance are displayed. The fifth column is used to record adjusting transactions.

In the example we have recorded adjusting transactions that could be used by the funds manager to keep reserve levels within the target range. Since the net collected balance in the reserve account exceeds the maximum for the first day of the maintenance period, the funds manager employs the surplus funds by selling $2 million in federal funds, earning one day's interest on $2 million. The transaction results in an ending reserve balance of $24 million, which is within the target range. On the second day the funds manager sells $1 million in federal funds to keep the reserve balance within the target range. On the third day the net collected balance is less than the minimum, and so the funds manager purchases $2 million in federal funds to bring the cumulative reserve level back within the target range.

For the adjustment transactions the funds manager kept cumulative reserves within the target range each day during the maintenance period. This strategy results in potentially excessive transactions cost and potentially greater variability in return. As exhibited by the second and third days' transactions, one day's interest income was gained on the second day, but the funds manager had to borrow funds on the third day to cover a deficit larger than the amount within the acceptable range. The offsetting pattern in the reserve balances in the second and third days would have resulted in the cumulative balance being within the acceptable range without any adjustment transactions. The interest expense could also be larger than the interest income, depending on the volatility of the federal funds rate.

The imbalance may be in line with projected flows later in the reserve period. For example, if a deficit occurs, the funds manager may be projecting larger than average inflows later in the period that would offset the deficit. Large amounts of credit from deferred items may be coming available or large inflows to the reserve account from the sale of investments may be expected. By waiting for projected inflows later in the period, unnecessary adjusting transactions may be avoided.

Uncontrollable Flows

Exhibit 13.14 presents a summary of the major flows affecting reserve balances over which a bank has very little or no control. Clearings are the major flow affecting the reserve balance. A bank has no control over

EXHIBIT 13.13   Sample Reserve Maintenance Worksheet

Maintenance Period	Minimum[a,b] Reserve Balance	Maximum[a] Reserve Balance	Net Collected Balance	Adjusting Transactions	Ending Reserve Balance
1 Daily	$23,531.51	$25,234.49	$26,000	−$2,000 (Sale of Fed Funds)	$24,000
2 Daily	29,351.51	31,414.49	28,000	+ 2,000 (Repayment of Fed Funds) − 1,000 (Sale of Fed Funds)	29,000
Cumulative	52,883.02	56,648.98			53,000
3 Daily	26,441.51	28,324.49	24,000	+ 1,000 (Repayment of Fed Funds) + 2,000 (Purchase of Fed Funds)	27,000
Cumulative	79,324.53	84,973.47			80,000

[a]This exhibit assumes that no previous carryover surplus or deficit exists. If a previous carryover exists, the minimum and maximum reserve balance figures would have to be adjusted to reflect the carryover.
[b]All dollar amounts are in thousands.

EXHIBIT 13.14   Uncontrollable Flows That Affect Reserve Balances

Item	Inflows	Outflows
Deposit Transactions	Transaction items presented by the bank for clearing; funds become available on predetermined schedule	Checks presented by other banks for payment
		Returned items presented by other banks
	Returned items from clearing	
Investment Transactions	Proceeds of sales of investments or funds from maturing securities	Purchase of investment securities
	Periodic interest payments on securities	
Loan Transactions	Decrease in loan balances	Increase in loan balances
Miscellaneous Transactions	Decreases in due-from-correspondent balances	Increases in due-from-correspondent balances
	Increases in due-to-correspondent balances	Decreases in due-to-correspondent balances
	Deposits in Treasury tax and loan accounts	Call by the Treasury of Treasury tax and loan balances

clearing items presented for payment by other banks. A bank has limited control over inflows that result from items it presents for payment since it can select the method to clear its items. Once the method of clearing is selected and is in place, it is not changed on a short-term basis to adjust money management operations. Inflows and outflows to the reserve account just happen and management must react to these uncertain flows.

One exception may be the clearing process of large nonroutine items. The funds manager may set up a system that identifies large checks presented for payment. These items may then be routed to obtain use of the funds in the most efficient fashion.

Other flows that affect the reserve balances include investment and loan transactions. In large banks the money desk and investment functions are separated. The investment managers may undertake transactions that will affect reserve balances and the money desk manager must react to these transactions. In smaller banks the investment and funds management functions are normally combined. In this case both of the activities can be coordinated by a single manager.

Loan activity will also have an impact on reserves and the money desk. To examine the impact that loan demand may have on the daily flows, consider the loan transaction displayed in Exhibit 13.15. A

EXHIBIT 13.15   Loan Transaction Effect on Reserves

Condition 1:
Customer "takes down" line and transfers funds by wire.

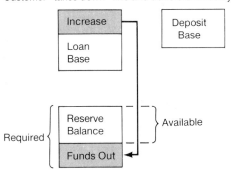

Pressure: Direct reduction in reserve balance and creation of an immediate deficit.

Condition 2:
Customer "takes down" line and proceeds are deposited into the customer's demand-deposit account.

Initial Effect

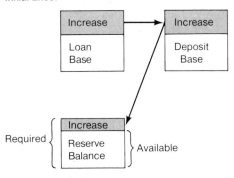

Delayed Effect
When customer uses proceeds and the check clears, reducing the reserve balance.

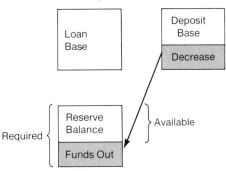

customer who "takes down" a credit line creates an earning asset. The immediate affect that such a transaction has on reserves and daily funds flow depends on how the customer receives the proceeds from the loan.

Under Condition 1 the customer requests that the proceeds be transferred by wire to another bank. In this case the immediate effect is a reduction in reserve balances by the amount of the proceeds of the loan. Assuming that no excess reserves were carried prior to the transaction, a deficit is created.[11] If a loan customer repaid an outstanding loan in the same fashion, an immediate surplus would be created.

Condition 2 displays the effect if proceeds of the loan are deposited to the customer's demand deposit account. The reserve requirements for the bank will increase by the amount of the required percentage times the deposit amount (a two-day lag applies). This results in a deficit since funds in the reserve account are less than required.

If the customer uses the proceeds to issue a check to a customer of another bank, the delayed effect will be identical to Condition 1. Required reserves would decline to the pretransaction level. When the check clears, the reserve balance would decline by the amount of the check, leaving the bank with a deficit. If the customer issues the check to a customer of the lending bank, the effect remains identical to the initial effect under Condition 2 until the funds escape the lending bank. If the customer merely leaves the loan proceeds on deposit, the initial effect under Condition 2 would be permanent.[12]

The loan transactions in Exhibit 13.15 indicate the complexity of the process involved in managing uncontrollable flows. If we consider all of the various inflows and outflows on a simultaneous basis, the complexity in managing the money desk becomes apparent. In the following section we shall consider the controllable flows that compose the adjusting transactions used by the funds manager in the balancing act.

Adjusting Transactions

The funds manager must balance uncertain and uncontrollable flows by means of adjusting transactions that are controllable flows. The choice of how deficits are covered or how surpluses are employed is based on the cost-minimization and return-maximization principle. If a surplus occurs, the funds manager will evaluate the relative rates of return on various instruments that can be purchased. The appropriate maturity is also selected in accordance with prediction of the length of time for

---

[11]The immediate effect of this transaction would also differ if the loan proceeds were disbursed in the form of a cashier's check.

[12]The effect of the transaction under Condition 2 would have been different under LRA. The transaction would have had no initial effect because of the lag of two weeks. For a complete discussion, see Gilbert, op. cit.

which the surplus will be available. If a deficit occurs, the funds manager seeks the funds that can be secured for the desired maturity at the lowest total cost.

The primary instruments used in the reserve adjustment process are listed in Exhibit 13.16. The majority of reserve-balancing transactions employ either Fed funds or repurchase agreements. Both of these instruments are settled in "immediately available funds," which makes them ideal for short-term adjustment.[13] Fed funds or repurchase agreements are commonly negotiated on an overnight or single-day maturity basis. The funds manager can secure or employ funds for a single day and can therefore fine-tune the adjustment process.

Because the market for Fed funds and repurchase agreements is very active, search and transaction costs are reduced. Rates on Fed funds and repurchase agreements are highly volatile because of their extensive use in the short-term adjustment process. The volatility in rates is particularly extreme in the last few days of the maintenance period. If large numbers of banks are experiencing deficits, the demand for funds can drive rates very high. If many banks are experiencing surpluses, the opposite can occur.

Secondary instruments used in the reserve adjustment process are also listed in Exhibit 13.16. Key differences in the secondary instruments include greater variability in marketability characteristics, settle-

EXHIBIT 13.16 Instruments That Can Be Purchased or Sold to Effect Adjusting Transactions

Primary Adjusting Instruments	Key Characteristics
Federal funds	Very short maturities, often overnight
Repurchase agreements	Settled in immediately available funds
	Large active markets with low transaction costs

Secondary Adjusting Instruments	Key Characteristics
Treasury and agency securities	Maturities vary but are typically longer than those of primary instruments
Negotiable CDs	
Eurodollar deposits	Settlement also varies but usually not in immediately available funds
Bankers' acceptances	Generally active markets but some variability in degree of activity
Commercial paper	

---

[13]For a discussion, see C. M. Lucas, M. T. Jones, and J. Thurston, "Federal Funds and Repurchase Agreements," *Quarterly Review, Federal Reserve Bank of New York,* Summer 1977: 33–48.

ment in funds that may not be immediately available, and more varied maturities.

Treasury bills were the primary adjusting instruments prior to the development of the Fed funds market. In the current market these instruments continue to be important but from a different standpoint. Treasury securities are used in repurchase agreements. The sale or purchase of Treasury bills, though a viable option, may be more appropriate for permanent rather than short-term adjustments because of their longer maturities.

The remaining instruments may be more appropriate for longer-term adjustments. If the funds manager anticipates needing funds for longer periods, using instruments such as negotiable CDs may be more efficient.[14]

The final option available to meet a reserve deficiency is to borrow from the Fed through the discount window. This option, formerly available only to members, became available to all banks with the passage of the DIDMCA. The Fed provides three types of credit through the discount window: adjustment, seasonal, and emergency.[15] Adjustment credit, pertinent to our discussion, is available for a bank to borrow on a short-term basis to meet a reserve deficiency. Seasonal credit is available to smaller banks that experience a persistent need for funds related to seasonal fluctuations in deposit levels.[16] Larger banks have access to the money market and therefore have greater ability to make adjustments. Emergency credit is made available to banks experiencing severe financial difficulties. It is through emergency credit that the Fed is fulfilling its role as the lender of last resort to maintain confidence in the banking system.

Adjustment credit is made available to meet unexpected or temporary credit needs caused by unexpected outflows. The Fed discourages banks from persistent borrowing, and regulations explicitly prohibit a bank's borrowing to profit on rate differentials. The Fed on occasion has initialed a surcharge for banks that borrow too frequently.[17] The individual Federal Reserve banks are responsible for judging the appropriateness of adjustment borrowing, and they occasionally will deny requests.

---

[14]For a discussion on how the anticipated duration of the funds deficit or surplus would affect the choice of instrument, see D. G. Luckett, "Approach to Bank Liquidity Management," *Economic Review, Federal Reserve Bank of Kansas City,* March 1980: 11–27.

[15]For complete discussions on discount-window credit, see R. A. Gilbert, "Benefits of Borrowing from the Federal Reserve When the Discount Rate Is Below Market Interest Rates," *Review, Federal Reserve Bank of St. Louis,* March 1979: 25–32; and J. Parthemos and W. Varvel, "The Discount Window," in *Instruments of the Money Market,* 5th ed., ed. T. Cook and B. Summers (Richmond, VA: Federal Reserve Bank of Richmond, 1981), 59–72.

[16]A bank must need the funds for a four-week period in order for its request to qualify as a persistent need. See Parthemos and Varvel, op. cit., 62.

[17]For example, in March 1980 the Fed imposed a 3 percent surcharge on adjustment credit for member banks with deposits in excess of $500 million when adjustment borrowing occurred in two or more consecutive reserve maintenance weeks or when the bank borrowed for more than four weeks in a calendar quarter. Ibid., 64–65.

EXHIBIT 13.17   Discount Window Borrowing Compared with Federal Funds and Discount Rate Differentials

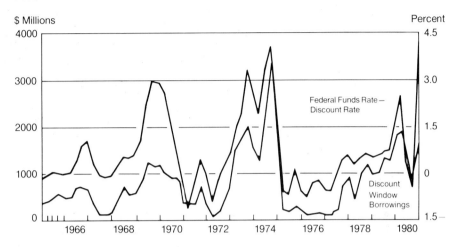

Source: J. Parthemos and W. Varvel, "The Discount Window," in *Instruments of the Money Market*, 5th ed., ed. T. Cook and B. Summers (Richmond, VA: Federal Reserve Bank of Richmond, 1981).

Most banks make adjustments in the open market rather than borrow from the Fed. This is true even when the discount rate is lower than the rate available on federal funds. A study on borrowing practices indicated that fewer than 25 percent of member banks borrowed from the Fed even when a large differential in rates existed.[18]

The level of borrowing, even though a minority of banks borrow, is higher when the discount rate is lower than the rate on funds available in the open market. Exhibit 13.17 indicates the positive relationship between borrowing and rate differentials. Banks can save on interest expense when the discount rate is lower than the federal funds rate, and more banks borrow when rate differentials are larger.[19]

SUMMARY

In this chapter we have examined the process of short-term funds management. A bank must attempt to satisfy a variety of goals in short-term funds management. The primary goal entails meeting reserve requirements in an efficient fashion. Secondary goals include meeting customer demand for loan and deposit services and meeting the longer-term investment goals of the bank.

---

[18]Gilbert, op. cit.

[19]Ibid. Gilbert demonstrates that the interest savings for some banks can be substantial. One bank in his study saved over $1 million by borrowing from the Fed rather than obtaining funds in the federal funds market.

Reserve management under the new contemporaneous reserve accounting and previous lagged reserve accounting were examined. Methods for measuring reserve requirements for both contemporaneous and lagged accounts were described, along with strategies for optimal use of funds in meeting those requirements. Reserve accounting and maintenance under contemporaneous requirements were found to be more complex than under previous requirements.

The actual management of the money desk requires balancing uncontrollable flows of funds with controllable adjusting transactions. The goal in balancing these flows is to minimize the costs involved in meeting the daily funds requirements.

Questions and Problems

1. List and briefly explain the major goals of short-term funds management.

2. Compare and contrast lagged and contemporaneous reserve accounting with respect to measurement and maintenance periods.

3. Define *carryover provision*.

4. Compare and contrast the use of carryover provisions under lagged and contemporaneous reserve accounting.

5. How is vault cash used to meet reserve requirements?

6. List the major uncontrollable flows that have an effect on the reserve balance account.

7. Identify the primary adjusting transactions used by a funds manager.

8. In managing the reserve account, how must a funds manager balance excessive transaction costs against opportunity costs associated with not keeping reserves at minimum levels?

9. Refer to Exhibits 13.4, 13.5, and 13.6. The minimum and maximum reserves calculated in Exhibit 13.6 represent the case in which the bank had the largest allowable deficit carryover from the previous maintenance period. Suppose that the bank in question had the same level of deposits in the two measurement periods and therefore the same level of required reserves without consideration of the carryover provision. Calculate the minimum and maximum reserve balances similar to those in Exhibit 13.6 under the assumption that the bank had carried over the maximum allowable surplus of $8,698,620 in the previous week instead of the deficit illustrated.

References

Beek, D. C. "Excess Reserves and Reserve Targeting." *Quarterly Review, Federal Reserve Bank of New York*, Autumn 1981: 15–22.

Board of Governors of the Federal Reserve System. Press release, Oct. 5, 1982.

Brutsche, E. W. "Managing Liquidity on a Global Basis." In *Funds Management Under Deregulation*, ed. G. H. Hempel, 285–297. Washington, D.C.: American Bankers Association, 1981.

Cacy, J. A., and S. Winninghan. "Reserve Requirements Under the Depository Institutions Deregulation and Monetary Control Act of 1980." *Economic Review, Federal Reserve Bank of Kansas City*, September-October 1980: 3–18.

Federal Reserve Bank of Chicago. *Depository Institutions Deregulation and Monetary Control Act of 1980: A Summary.* Chicago: Federal Reserve Bank, March 1980.

Gambs, C. M. "Federal Reserve Membership and the Role of Nonmember Bank Reserve Requirements." *Economic Review, Federal Reserve Bank of Kansas City*, February 1979: 3–14.

Gilbert, R. A. "Benefits of Borrowing From the Federal Reserve When the Discount Rate Is Below Market Interest Rates." *Review, Federal Reserve Bank of St. Louis*, March 1979: 25–32.

Gilbert, R. A. "Benefits of Borrowing From the Federal Reserve When the Discount Rate Is Below Market Interest Rates." *Review, Federal Reserve Bank of St. Louis*, March 1979: 25–32.

Gilbert, R. A. "Lagged Reserve Requirements: Implications for Monetary Control and Bank Reserve Management." *Review, Federal Reserve Bank of St. Louis*, May 1980: 7–20.

Herman, T., and E. P. Foldessy. "Fed's New Rules for Setting Bank Reserves Could Cause Large Swings in Interest Rates. *The Wall Street Journal*, Feb. 16, 1984, 31.

Jones, D. S. "Contemporaneous vs. Lagged Reserve Accounting: Implications for Monetary Control." *Economic Review, Federal Reserve Bank of Kansas City*, November 1981: 3–19.

Kaufman, D. J., Jr., and D. R. Lee. "Planning Liquidity: A Practical Approach." *The Magazine of Bank Administration*, March 1977: 55–63.

Knight, R. E. "Guidelines for Efficient Reserve Management." *Monthly Review, Federal Reserve Bank of Kansas City*, November 1977: 11-23.

Kreuker, L. L. "Eurodollar Arbitrage." *Quarterly Review, Federal Reserve Bank of New York*, Summer 1982: 10–21.

Laurent, R. D. "Comparing Alternative Replacements for Lagged Reserves: Why Settle for a Poor Third Best?" *Staff Memoranda 83-2, Federal Reserve Bank of Chicago*, 1–23.

Lucas, C. M., M. T. Jones, and J. Thurston. "Federal Funds and Repurchase Agreements." *Quarterly Review, Federal Reserve Bank of New York*, Summer 1977: 33–48.

Luckett, D. G. "Approaches to Bank Liquidity Management." *Economic Review, Federal Reserve Bank of Kansas City*, March 1980: 11–27.

Parthemos, J., and W. Varvel. "The Discount Window." In *Instruments of the Money Market*, 5th ed., ed. T. Q. Cook and B. J. Summers, 59–72. Richmond, VA: Federal Reserve Bank of Richmond, 1981.

Pierce, J. L. "Commercial Bank Liquidity." *Federal Reserve Bulletin*, August 1966: 1093–1101.

Ratti, R. A. "Pledging Requirements and Bank Asset Portfolios." *Economic Review, Federal Reserve Bank of Kansas City*, September-October 1979: 13-23.

Summers, B. J. "Correspondent Services, Federal Reserve Services, and Bank Cash Management Policy." *Economic Review, Federal Reserve Bank of Richmond*, November-December 1978: 29–38.

CHAPTER 14

Capital

Traditionally defined, capital represents the owners' interest in a business. On a book value basis, capital is defined as net worth that is equal to the book value of assets minus the book value of liabilities.

The issue of how much capital a bank should have and what the composition of a bank's capital should be is a highly debated issue. Different parties with different interests in the operation of a specific bank can have different views on the importance and functions of capital. Regulators and large uninsured depositors view capital's primary function as protection against failure or insolvency. Net worth acts as a buffer to absorb loan losses and other operating losses and protects depositors against failure of the bank to perform.

The owners may have a conflicting view of the function that capital serves. Owners can earn a higher rate of return on investment by limiting that investment. That is, return on equity can be increased by earning the same level of net income over a smaller equity investment. Although owners are also interested in the solvency of the bank, higher levels of capital reduce their relative profits.

Regulatory considerations involved with capital are very complex. Such considerations are complicated by a variety of factors, with the central issue being deposit insurance. The FDIC insures deposits up to $100,000. The FDIC can protect itself against depositor claims by making sure that banks have large capital cushions to absorb losses. Large capital cushions protect the insurance fund from claims. In a recent address William Isaac notes that many bankers really believe that FDIC stands for "Forever Demanding Increased Capital."[1]

Although conflicts concerning capital adequacy exist, all parties share a common concern. Regulators, owners, managers, and depositors of a bank all have in their best interest seeing the bank continue as a profitable enterprise. Regulators' concern for high levels of capital is tempered with concern for bank profitability. The long-range ability of a bank to grow depends on its ability to attract adequate capital from the market, which in turn depends on the relative return provided to the suppliers of that capital. Regulators, owners, and depositors all share

---

[1]W. M. Isaac, "The World Would Sleep (Or, All You Would Ever Care to Hear About Capital Adequacy)," in *Funds Management Under Deregulation*, ed. G. H. Hempel (Washington, DC: American Bankers Association, 1981), 453.

that interest. In this sense the conflict is not really as significant as it may appear.

Given the regulatory view, capital management is an important issue to the managers of a bank. The central issue involves the constraint that capital adequacy requirements place on a bank's ability to grow. To support higher levels of assets and deposits, that bank must have adequate capital. To increase the capital base, the bank must retain larger proportions of earnings, earn higher rates of return on its assets, or obtain additional capital by selling securities in the capital markets. Each of these options presents unique problems to management. For example, increasing rates of return on assets usually entails increasing risk. Increased risk in the asset portfolio increases the probability of losses, which in turn may result in a demand from regulators for additional capital.

FUNCTIONS AND SOURCES OF BANK CAPITAL

The determination of an appropriate source of capital is based on the particular functions to be served by capital. For example, if capital is to serve as protection against failure of the bank, equity capital is the only appropriate source. The equity capital cushion serves to absorb losses and the adequacy of that cushion is critical to the solvency of the bank. If losses exceed net worth, liquidation must occur.

In contrast, if capital is to serve as protection of depositors' claims, subordinated notes and debentures as well as equity capital function as capital. If losses exceed the equity capital base, the bank must be liquidated but the funds supplied by the owners of the subordinated notes and debentures serve as a cushion to protect the value of depositor funds. Debt capital does not directly protect against the failure of the bank.[2]

Functions

Capital serves three functions. First, it serves as a cushion to absorb operating and other losses. In this function capital protects against failure and protects the depositors of the bank. Capital also serves a secondary function of being the base on which lending limits are established. This is just one step removed from the primary function in that it is an operational consideration for regulators to limit the amount of loans to any individual borrowing entity. By imposing lending limits, regulators force banks to diversify their lending and thereby protect against non-

---

[2]In an indirect sense debt may protect against future failure by improving liquidity and increasing longer-run return on equity. See D. S. Howard and G. M. Hoffman, *Evolving Concepts of Bank Capital* (New York: Citicorp, 1980).

performance on a single loan. For example, national banks are limited to lending a maximum of 15 percent of total capital to any borrowing entity. Finally, capital also serves as a base on which market participants can evaluate relative profitability. Return on the owner's investment is assessed by comparing net income with equity. Market participants compare return on investment among banks.

To understand how capital serves the primary function of absorbing loan losses, we must understand how capital serves to absorb loan and other operating losses. Capital serves to protect against losses that flow to the bank through the income statement. For example, a bank can experience defaults on loans and capital serves as a buffer to absorb those losses. Additionally, a bank can experience losses related to liquidity problems. An unanticipated decline in deposits could result in losses. Assets may have to be liquidated at losses or additional funding may have to be acquired at higher rates. If operating losses result, the owners' investment (capital) serves to absorb the losses that flow through the income statement.

No amount of capital can take care of a prolonged liquidity problem. In such cases capital applies only in liquidation of the bank. If assets must be liquidated at values less than the book value in a quick sale to meet a liquidity need, capital must be adequate as a buffer to absorb the loss in value.

The primary function of capital in serving as a buffer against losses arises because of the nature of banking as an enterprise and the nature of a bank's financial statements. The solvency of banks and the strength and soundness of the banking industry are central to the performance of the entire economy. Without a sound and efficiently functioning banking system, the economy cannot function. Solvency of banking as an enterprise extends beyond solvency considerations for almost all other enterprises. The importance of banking to the entire economic system requires that capital's primary function be to serve to protect against insolvency.

The financial structure of the banking industry dictates that the primary function of capital be to absorb losses as well as to protect against failure. The degree of financial leverage employed by banks far exceeds the leverage employed by other enterprises. A typical bank is financed with 90 percent to 95 percent borrowed funds. If we compare the financing of a bank with that of a nonfinancial enterprise, such as a manufacturing firm in which 30 percent to 40 percent of the capital supporting the firm's assets is in the form of debt, the significance of capital serving as a cushion to absorb losses is obvious. The claims of a bank's creditors are relatively far more significant and the small cushion to absorb losses to protect those claims becomes critical.

To see how capital serves to protect creditors from potential loan losses, we must consider how unusual loan losses affect the bank. In its operation a bank sets up a reserve to absorb losses in the loan portfolio.

The reserve must be adequate to absorb normal or expected losses as well as some additional or unplanned losses.

If the valuation reserve set up for loan losses is inadequate, the bank has created illusionary profits. If loan losses exceed or dramatically reduce the provision for such losses when the nonperforming loans are written off, the provision for loan losses must be restored. Restoration of the loan loss provision results in a reduction in net income, which in turn reduces capital.

A bank is able to operate safely on a small equity cushion if it restricts its lending policy. Two characteristics are important in this regard. First, smaller capital cushions are necessary if low-risk loans are made. Second, smaller capital cushions are necessary if loans are highly liquid. Short-term loans that possess underlying natural liquidity serve to reduce potential liquidity crises.

Although a bank can experience profitability problems from unplanned loan losses, such problems can also result from mismanaged gap positions. If the bank has funded long-term loans with short-term funds and the rates on short-term funds rise above the rates on the long-term loans, the bank will experience a margin squeeze. As we have indicated, no amount of capital will solve this problem, but capital acts as a buffer, absorbing losses if assets are liquidated at losses to raise the funds necessary to cover the outflow. If the problem is prolonged, liquidation will occur, and the equity base serves the function of absorbing losses in such a liquidation. The capital cushion that is adequate to absorb potential losses from a liquidity crisis is a function of the level of interest rate risk assumed by the bank.

The level of capital that is adequate to absorb losses from bank operations basically boils down to earnings quality. The higher the quality of earnings, the smaller the capital base must be to protect depositor claims.

Sources

There are two major sources of capital. The first and most significant source of capital is equity, which comprises both common stock and preferred stock. The second source is debt capital in the form of subordinated notes and debentures.

Equity Capital.   When sources of capital are defined and discussed, it is important to make a distinction between book value definitions and market value additions to capital. From a historical standpoint the book value definition is important in that it defines the equity base at a given point in time. From a planning perspective the market value of additions to the capital base is important.

A bank's common equity capital is defined or measured on a book value basis as the sum of the common equity accounts and the reserve for loan losses account. The common stock accounts are composed of three accounts: the Common Stock Par Value Account, the Surplus or Additional Paid-in Capital Account, and the Retained Earnings or Undivided Profits Account.[3]

A bank can make additions to its common equity capital base in two ways. First, additions arise from earnings that are not paid out to the stockholders in the form of dividends. For many banks this is the only practical source of new equity capital, and for all banks retained-earnings additions are the most important source of equity capital on an ongoing basis. Second, a bank can make additions to its common equity base through the sale of additional shares of common stock. This source of equity capital is generally limited to larger banks whose stock trades in active markets. The market value of the common stock is important in determining the desirability of this source of capital.

The *additions* to the common equity accounts are important to bank management from the perspective of supporting growth. From a planning standpoint, then, our main concern is with additions to the capital base.

Banks can also raise equity capital through the sale of preferred stock. Preferred stock has characteristics of both common stock and debt. Preferred shareholders are entitled to a fixed-dividend payment and have a priority claim over common shareholders to assets in the case of liquidation. The claim of preferred shareholders is subordinated to creditors and depositors of the bank with respect to priority of periodic payments and rights to assets in dissolution.

Since the dividend on preferred stock is fixed, such stock has some leverage aspects that are similar to debt. If a bank earns net income in excess of the fixed dividend, the surplus is available to the common shareholders. The fixed dividend is generally more costly than similar interest payments on debt, since the dividend on preferred stock is not tax deductible.

Although preferred stock is an option available to the bank, such capital is an insignificant portion of total capital. It has the disadvantages of debt associated with the fixed payment, and it does not have the tax subsidy that interest on debt enjoys.

Subordinated Notes and Debentures. Since 1962 national banks have been allowed to use a limited amount of debt as a form of capital. Before the 1962 ruling by the Comptroller of the Currency that permits subor-

---

[3]The reserve for loan losses is sometimes incorrectly discussed as a source of equity. Technically the valuation portion of the loan loss reserve is an asset valuation reserve and not an equity reserve. For establishment of loan limits and capital adequacy considerations, regulators may use gross loans and consider reserves as capital; but in the sense that we are discussing capital here, loan loss reserve is not equity capital. See G. H. Hempel, "Bank Capital: Evaluating the Recent Trends," in G. H. Hempel, ed., *Funds Management Under Deregulation* (Washington, D.C.: American Bankers Association, 1981), 461.

dinated notes and debentures to be included as part of the capital base, such debt was used as distress financing. Following the ruling on national banks, many states changed their laws and allowed state-chartered banks to include a limited amount of debt as capital.[4]

To be included in the capital base, debt must meet certain characteristics. When issued, its maturity must exceed seven years. The debt must be subordinated to depositors' claims. FDIC approval is also required before repayment of any subordinated notes and debentures. This approval gives the FDIC some protection against a bank's reducing its liquidity position, which may impair depositor funds.

Subordinated notes and debentures represent longer-term and more permanent sources of financing for a bank. The ability of this type of capital to absorb losses differs from that of equity capital. Debt capital does protect depositors' claims, but to absorb losses the bank must be liquidated. Unlike equity, for which dividend payments can be passed, interest payments on debt must be made on a regular basis.[5] Failure to make an interest payment can cause a bank to fail. The use of debt increases the risk involved with the operation of the bank because of this added fixed payment.

The advantages and disadvantages of debt compared with common equity are summarized in Exhibit 14.1. The key factors that differentiate debt and equity as sources of capital are the cash flow, leveraging, and issue characteristics. It is important to emphasize that although the use of debt does provide permanent financing and may increase expected returns to the bank, it also increases risk.

One additional concern that may attach to the use of debt is liquidity if the issue has a sinking-fund requirement. A sinking-fund requirement calls for a bank to set aside funds to retire the debt issue on a periodic basis. This reduces the risk that the bank will be unable to repay the issue at maturity, but it also increases the liquidity risk in that the sinking-fund payments must also be made.

The long-range effect that the use of debt capital can have on a bank's capital position is a complex issue. If a bank can earn sufficient return on its capital, excess returns over the interest payments will flow to the owners of the bank. Since some portion of the earnings will be retained by the bank, use of debt capital in the long run may also increase the equity capital base.

In addition to standard debt instruments, a bank may also issue convertible bonds. The advantage of using such instruments is that issuing bonds that may eventually be converted into common stock does not immediately dilute earnings per share to present shareholders. The

---

[4]For a discussion of state member bank requirements, see *Federal Reserve Bulletin*, July 1976: 601–604.

[5]R. D. Watson, "Banking on Debt for Capital Needs," *Business Review, Federal Reserve Bank of Philadelphia*, December 1974: 17–28; and Howard and Hoffman, op. cit.

**EXHIBIT 14.1   Advantages and Disadvantages of Debt
Compared with Equity as a Source of Capital**

Advantages	Disadvantages
Cash Flow Characteristics	
Interest payments on debt are tax deductible, and the cash-servicing costs of debt may be less than the cash-servicing costs of dividends with common equity.	The fixed-interest payment may cause liquidity problems; failure to make an interest payment results in default and may cause liquidation.
Leveraging Effects	
Use of debt increases bank leverage. As long as earnings on capital exceed the interest costs on an aftertax basis, surplus profits accrue to the bank. This in turn will serve to increase the capital base in future years.	Leverage is a two-edged sword: increased use of debt increases risk as well. If earnings are not adequate, future reductions in the capital base are possible.
Issue Characteristics	
The costs associated with issuance of debt are usually lower than similar costs of equity. With debt there is no loss of control or immediate dilution of earnings as there is with an equity issue.	Debt has a maturity and therefore must be refunded or paid off from equity earnings. At maturity liquidity problems could occur. Equity capital is permanent.

---

yield offered on convertibles is usually less than the yield offered on similar nonconvertible issues, thereby decreasing the cost to the issuing bank. The conversion price equivalent for common stock of a convertible bond issue also exceeds the price at which a bank could directly issue common stock.[6]

LEVELS AND TRENDS IN BANK CAPITAL

A variety of measures can be used to assess the level of bank capital. Capital is commonly measured relative to the assets it supports, with some measures emphasizing only the risky assets in a bank's portfolio.

Two frequently used ratios are the capital-to-assets ratio and the capital-to-risk-assets ratio. *Risk assets* are defined as total assets minus reserves and other cash assets and Treasury and agency securities.[7] The

---

[6]For a complete discussion of the advantages and disadvantages associated with convertible debt, see Hempel, op. cit., part III, 479.

[7]Alternative definitions of capital adequacy are often employed. Capital plus reserves is sometimes employed in lieu of sole consideration of capital. A direct comparison of ratios with alternative definitions of capital is not possible.

second ratio is thought to be a better measure of capital adequacy because it relates the level of capital to those assets that are subject to potential loss.

Trends

As illustrated in Exhibit 14.2, the trend in the capital-to-assets and capital-to-risk-assets ratios has declined since the mid-1930s. The decline in the capital-to-risk-assets ratio has been the most severe, with the only period in which the ratio did not decline being the early to middle 1940s. This was due to the financing of the war and the consequent increase in bank holdings of government issues.

The decline in capital-to-risk-assets ratio compared with the relative decline in the capital-to-total-assets ratio can be explained by the change in banks' investment policies. Banks have placed more funds in loans and higher-earning investments and have relied on liabilities to meet liquidity needs. The combined effect of increased risk in the asset portfolio and decreased amount of capital has caused the larger relative decline in the capital-to-risk-assets ratio.[8]

Since the mid-1970s the capital ratios have continued to decline. Currently the capital-to-risk-assets ratio is nearly 8 percent for all commercial banks.

The decline in capital adequacy ratios has caused alarm among regulators. It is unlikely that regulators will allow any further decline in capital ratios. In the future, capital requirements will clearly place constraints on the levels of growth that banks will be able to assume. The ability of a bank to grow at levels that have been experienced in the past will depend on the bank's ability to attract external capital. Current levels of retained earnings are not adequate to support recent growth rates.

Inflation has significantly complicated the capital adequacy problem. With high rates of inflation, a bank's portfolio of assets grows artificially. Even if the bank is able to earn the same rate of return on its inflated assets, the tax burden increases, making it impossible for the bank to maintain its capital ratios unless it earns a still higher rate of return. With real growth the constraints are even more severe. As in many areas of finance and business, inflation has had a serious impact.[9]

---

[8]The median capital ratios have declined more than the mean ratios that are displayed in Exhibits 14.2 and 14.3. In comparing 1960 and 1975 distributions of capital ratios, larger percentages of banks were found to have ratio measures that were lower than the mean. See R. A. Taggert, Jr., "Regulatory Influences on Bank Capital," *New England Economic Review, Federal Reserve Bank of Boston,* September-October 1977: 37–46.

[9]Inflation may have a serious impact on bank profits and the level of capital. When bank profits are adjusted for inflation, the real or adjusted value of capital may be even lower than reported in recent studies. See H. C. Wallich, "Bank Profits and Inflation," *Economic Review, Federal Reserve Bank of Richmond,* May-June 1980: 27–30.

EXHIBIT 14.2   Capital Ratios of Insured Commercial Banks

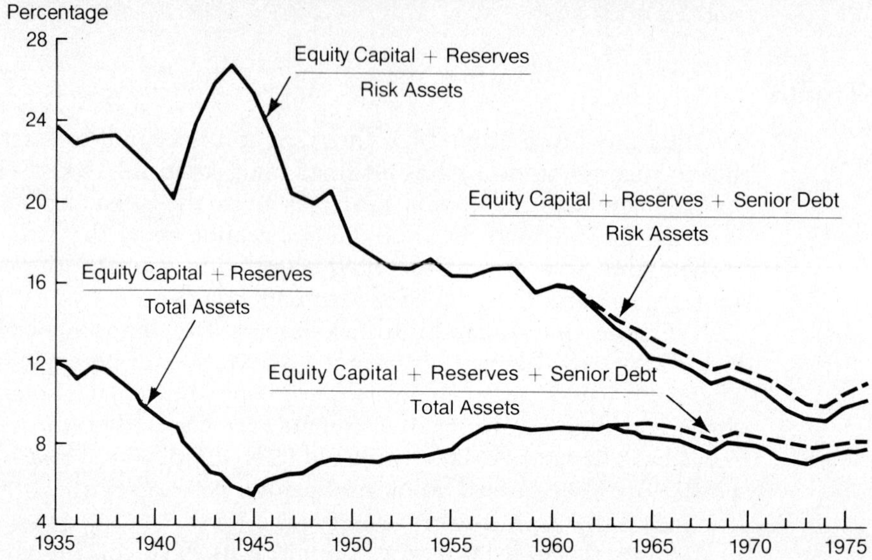

Percentage

Source: Bruce J. Summers, "Bank Capital Adequacy: Perspectives and Prospects," *Economic Review, Federal Reserve Bank of Richmond*, July-August 1977: 4.

Capital and Bank Size

Systematic differences exist in the levels of capital to assets for large and small banks. As shown in Exhibit 14.3, smaller banks have larger capital ratios than do larger banks. Regulators have required large capital-to-assets ratios for small banks.

The justification for large banks having smaller capital ratios is related to the size of the pool of capital and to management efficiency. Even though the ratios are smaller for large banks, the pools of capital are larger for large banks. Large banks are also thought to employ more sophisticated management techniques and, because of access to financial markets, possess superior liquidity management capabilities. Larger banks also have greater access to the money markets, which provides them with more flexibility in meeting a demand for liquidity.

The difference in capital ratios also arises because of differences in the loan portfolios of large and small banks. The loan portfolios of larger banks are composed of greater proportions of short-term commercial loans, which have shorter maturities and therefore are more liquid than the loan portfolios of smaller banks. Larger banks have greater diversi-

EXHIBIT 14.3   Comparative Capital Ratios of Large and Small Commercial Banks

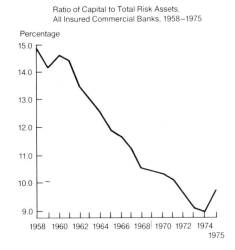

Ratio of Capital to Total Risk Assets,
All Insured Commercial Banks, 1958–1975

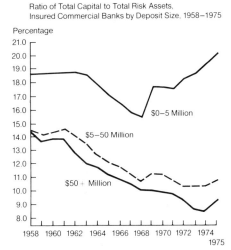

Ratio of Total Capital to Total Risk Assets,
Insured Commercial Banks by Deposit Size, 1958–1975

Source: Robert A. Taggert, Jr., "Regulatory Influences on Bank Capital," *New England Economic Review, Federal Reserve Bank of Boston,* September-October 1977: 38–39.

fication in both loan types and geographic locations of borrowers. Systematic differences in the loan portfolios of large and small banks lead to smaller capital requirements for large banks.

Because evidence indicates that larger banks do experience fewer failures, the justification may be valid. In recent years, however, we have witnessed failures of some very large banks, which indicates that size alone is no assurance of success.[10]

Exhibit 14.3 illustrates the differences in capital ratios between large and small banks, with large banks being defined as banks with deposits in excess of $50 million. Exhibit 14.4 displays capital ratios for larger banks of various sizes. For banks with assets in excess of $100 million, the capital-to-risk-assets ratio has declined to slightly over 6 percent. Among banks with larger assets we find similar capital ratios. For very large banks with assets in excess of $5 billion, the capital-to-risk-assets ratio was approximately 5.7 percent at the end of 1982.

---

[10]Size may create additional adminstrative problems as well. Size allows greater geographic diversification, but control problems associated with participation loans are significant. See Isaac, op. cit.

EXHIBIT 14.4   Selected Capital Ratios, 1980–1982

Size Class	Equity to Assets[a]			Equity to Risk Assets[b]		
	1980	1981	1982	1980	1981	1982
Universe	4.67%	4.76%	4.92%	6.35%	6.21%	6.33%
$100 Million to $1 Billion	6.49	6.49	6.50	8.58	8.63	8.72
$1 Billion to $5 Billion	6.10	6.09	6.12	8.18	8.18	8.23
$5 Billion or More	4.14	4.30	4.49	5.69	5.53	5.67

[a]Total stockholders' equity plus minority interest in equity accounts of consolidated subsidiaries divided by total assets.
[b]Total stockholders' equity plus minority interest in equity accounts of consolidated subsidiaries divided by total assets less cash and due from depository institutions, U.S. Treasury securities, and obligations of U.S. government agencies and corporations.

Source: Anthony G. Cornyn, "Financial Developments of Bank Holding Companies in 1982," *Federal Reserve Bulletin*, July 1983: 514.

Regulation of Bank Capital

The regulatory agencies are charged with maintaining the stability of the banking system. One element involved in stability is limiting the number of bank failures. Regulators employ a variety of methods to protect against bank failures, including limiting the risk that a bank may assume in its assets and placing restrictions on the types of liabilities that it can issue. Another important element in protecting against bank failures is making sure that banks have adequate capital. A larger cushion of capital serves to protect against insolvency.

In theory the level of capital necessary to protect against insolvency is a function of the riskiness of the particular bank. Risk could be related to default on loans, liquidity problems, or funding mismatches. The adequacy of the bank's level of capital would depend on each of these individual elements of risk.

As a matter of practice, regulators do not attempt to assess risk and capital levels on an individual basis. The amount of supervision time required for individual assessment would be too great. Furthermore, to assign unique levels of capital would require regulators to predict loan and other operating losses much more accurately than they are able to predict. Regulators attempt to regulate capital by requiring banks to maintain capital-to-assets ratios according to percentage guidelines. In theory, some attempt is made to implement risk-adjusted levels of capital by requiring larger capital-to-assets ratios for smaller banks.

Historical Regulation of Capital

Historically each of the three regulatory agencies supervised capital according to its own perceptions. Regulations were similar in that capital expressed as a ratio of assets or risk assets was used as a measure of capital adequacy and that different ratios were required for different-sized banks. Regulations differed in what counted as capital and in how target or minimum ratios were set.[11]

The FRS and FDIC grouped banks into categories according to size. For each category a minimum and target capital-to-assets ratio was established. The FRS allowed banks to count a limited amount of debt as capital, whereas the FDIC did not count debt as capital.

The Office of the Comptroller of the Currency (OCC) took a slightly different approach. The OCC grouped banks into homogeneous classes based on size of branches and degree of competition. Each bank was assigned to a peer group and was expected to maintain capital ratios consistent with the average ratios of the banks in the peer group. Larger banks started with lower capital ratios and therefore were required to hold less capital. This OCC policy also failed to stem the decline in capital ratios, and the capital maintenance policy was changed in 1981.

New Capital Adequacy Requirements

In December 1981 each of the regulatory agencies made specific policy statements concerning its regulation of capital. Capital requirements for each of the regulatory agencies are displayed in Exhibit 14.5. The most significant element of change involved the OCC's abandoning its peer group policy in favor of set capital ratios.

EXHIBIT 14.5   Percentage Capital Requirements under the December 1981 Guidelines

| | Federal Reserve–Comptroller[a] | | FDIC[b] |
Zones	Regional Banks	Community Banks	All Banks
1. Acceptable	6.5 or more[c]	7.0 or more[d]	6.0 or more
2. Possibly undercapitalized	5.5 to 6.5	6.0 to 7.0	5.0 to 6.0
3. Undercapitalized	Less than 5.5	Less than 6.0	Less than 5.0

[a]May include debentures and limited-life preferred stock.
[b]May not include debentures or limited-life preferred stock.
[c]Primary capital must be greater than 5.0 percent of assets.
[d]Primary capital must be greater than 6.0 percent of assets.

Source: R. M. Baker, "Sources of Bank Capital: An Issue for the 80s," *Economic Review, Federal Reserve Bank of Atlanta*, December 1982: 66.

---

[11]For a complete discussion of differences in regulations, see R. M. Baker, "Sources of Bank Capital: An Issue for the 80s," *Economic Review, Federal Reserve Bank of Atlanta*, December 1982: 65–73; and A. A. Heggestad and B. F. King, "Regulation of Bank Capital," *Economic Review, Federal Reserve Bank of Atlanta*, March 1982: 35–43.

The FRS and OCC issued joint guidelines and now have identical capital adequacy requirements. The FDIC issued separate guidelines, and its policy differs from the FRS and OCC policy in the percentages required and in what is counted as capital. The FRS and OCC policy allows a limited amount of subordinated debt and limited-life preferred stock to count as capital, whereas the FDIC counts only equity capital.[12] The difference in FDIC requirements is not all that significant since the FDIC regulates smaller banks, which, as a matter of practice, do not use debt and preferred stock as regular sources of capital.

The FRS and OCC policy involves separating banks into three size categories and setting up zones according to the capital-to-assets ratios. The size categories are community banks, those with assets of less than $1 billion; regional banks, those with assets of from $1 billion to $15 billion; and multinational banks, those with assets in excess of $15 billion. The last group contains the 17 largest banks in the United States. Immediate guidelines were not set for the largest banks, but in June 1983 the regulators established the minimum guideline that primary capital be 5 percent of assets.[13]

For the community and regional banks three zones were established: acceptable level, possibly undercapitalized, and undercapitalized. In addition, the FRS and OCC set minimum ratios for primary capital, which does not include limited-life preferred or subordinated debt issues. Following the traditional policy, larger capital-to-assets ratios are required for smaller banks.

The FDIC followed the other regulators in establishing zones but did not make a distinction on size. The FDIC policy is not that different, because all the banks it supervises have assets of less than $1 billion. The standards are similar to the other regulators' requirement that primary capital must exceed 6 percent of assets for community banks.

Banks that have capital ratios in Zone 2 (possibly undercapitalized) are subject to greater regulation and are required to submit plans to improve their capital positions. Those in Zone 3 (undercapitalized) are subject to continuous supervision.

Exhibit 14.6 displays a breakdown of regional and community banks in the FRS-OCC zones on the basis of their December 31, 1980 capital ratios. As the exhibit indicates, fewer than 3 percent of all banks were in the undercapitalized zone. On the basis of 1980 capital levels, 21 percent of regional banks were classified in Zone 2. For the multinational banks, only four of the major banks were below the 5 percent level in March 1983. The capital level for the major banks has improved

---

[12]Debt and limited-life preferred stock are classified as secondary capital, and the new guidelines limit bank-issued secondary capital to 50 percent of primary capital.

[13]"Minimum Capital Guideline Amendments," *Federal Reserve Bulletin*, July 1983: 539–540. Minor changes were also made in secondary capital requirements that allow more extensive use of debt issued by an affiliate of the bank or the bank holding company.

**EXHIBIT 14.6   Distribution of Banks within the December 1981
Revised Capital Standards of the FRS and OCC**

	Regional	Community
Primary Capital	95%[a]	97%[b]
Total Capital		
Zone 1	76	93
Zone 2	21	5.5
Zone 3	3	1.5

[a]Primary capital must be greater than 5.0 percent of assets.
[b]Primary capital must be greater than 6.0 percent of assets.

Sources: Office of the Comptroller of the Currency, and R. M. Baker, "Sources of Bank Capital: An
Issue for the 80s," *Economic Review, Federal Reserve Board of Atlanta,* December 1982: 67.

---

since December 1980, when the average capital-to-assets ratio was 4.6
percent. Regulators gave the large banks additional time to get the ratio
up to the standard of 5 percent.

Whether the increased capital ratios required by the regulators will
significantly reduce future bank failures is subject to debate. Capital can
only serve as a primary buffer to absorb temporary loan and operating
losses. It cannot solve a long-term problem. Increased capital-to-assets
ratios will constrain growth in assets that may provide longer-term stability. The growth constraint will have an effect on banks' ability to
manage their capital position.

MANAGEMENT OF BANK CAPITAL

The basic decisions that management must make concerning capital involve the mix of capital to employ and the appropriate level of capital
to employ. The decision on mix involves the breakdown between debt
and equity and the breakdown between retained earnings and new equity sales. The decision on what level of total capital to employ involves
consideration of regulatory constraints and basic risk factors. Management must decide what level of capital is necessary to satisfy regulators
and then decide whether that level is adequate to absorb potential
losses.

Once the decisions on appropriate mix and level are made, management must then plan for asset growth in line with these targets. The
impact of projected asset growth must be assessed and the acquisition
of any additional required capital must be planned for. As we shall see,
capital constraints limit the ability of many banks to grow.

Flows of Capital

Exhibit 14.7 displays the flow of capital through a cycle. The exhibit is constructed on the basis of total capital being composed only of equity capital. We shall later expand the source of capital to include subordinated notes and debentures.

EXHIBIT 14.7   Capital Cycle with Total Capital Composed of Common Stock

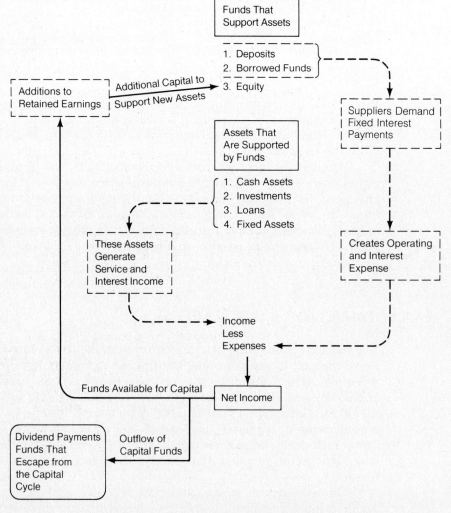

Suppliers of equity capital (owners of the bank) have a residual claim to net income. Service and interest income on assets that exceed operating and interest expense belong to the owners. The retained portion of net income cycles back to the capital account and supports additional assets.

Funds that support assets are made up of deposits, other borrowed funds, and the owner's equity. Depositors and creditors agree to provide their funds for a promised rate of return in the form of interest payments and services provided by the bank. The owners provide their funds for a residual payment of what is left after depositors and creditors have been paid.

Assets that are acquired with the funds generate interest and service income. From that gross income, interest and operating expenses must be paid. The residual payment to the owners, net income, is either distributed in the form of dividends or retained to support the acquisition of additional assets.

The cycle is depicted in Exhibit 14.7 identifies two important points concerning asset growth. First, owners must make some contribution to support asset growth. Other factors being constant, the larger the percentage of earnings retained, the greater will be the ability of the bank to grow. Second, income generation is critical for asset growth. The larger the return on assets, the greater will be the ability of the bank to grow.

Exhibit 14.8 displays a similar capital cycle with the inclusion of debt capital. These suppliers of capital require a promised rate of return in the form of interest payments, as do depositors. The only significant difference in these claims is that subordinated notes and debentures have distant maturities compared with most deposits, and thus they are a more permanent form of funding.

To be of benefit to the owners, returns generated on the assets supported by long-term debt must generate returns sufficient to cover the returns required by these suppliers of funds. If returns on assets supported by debt exceed the costs associated with the debt, because of the leverage factor, greater earnings will be available to the owners of the bank.[14]

A strong argument can be made in favor of using subordinated notes and debentures as capital when the long-range effects are considered. As long as earnings on assets supported by the debt exceed the cost of the debt, the net income to the bank will be increased. Since the bank retains a substantial portion of those additional earnings, the long-range effect is to bolster equity capital. Use of debt does increase default risk, but in the long run it may well reduce risk of failure because of increased equity. Since debt has a longer term than other borrowed funds, use of debt may well improve the liquidity of the bank.[15]

---

[14]Returns on assets supported by debt must cover both the explicit and implicit costs associated with that debt. The explicit cost on the debt is the aftertax interest cost on the debt. The implicit costs of higher required returns on equity and uninsured deposits could also be associated with the use of debt because of higher perceived risk.

[15]For a complete development, see Howard and Hoffman, op. cit., chaps. 4 and 5.

**EXHIBIT 14.8   Capital Cycle with Total Capital Composed of
Long-Term Debt and Common Stock**

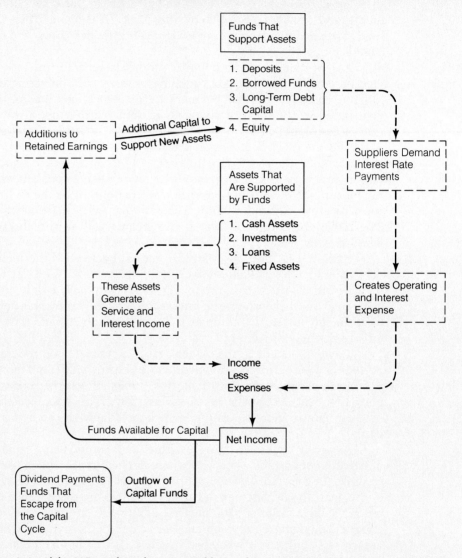

As in exhibit 14.7, suppliers of equity capital have a claim to net income. The addition of long-term debt capital increases the bank's fixed interest expense and financial leverage. If the income on the new assets supported by the long-term debt exceeds the interest cost, additional net income is available to the owners. The portion of the additional income that is retained cycles back to the equity capital account and is available to support additional assets. Through the leveraging effect, use of long-term debt will also increase the equity capital.

Capital Constraints and Growth

The level of capital relative to assets places a constraint on the ability of a bank to grow. Sufficient additions to equity capital must be made as assets grow or the capital ratios will suffer a decline. As we saw in the previous section, capital ratios have declined in the banking system. Growth in capital has failed to keep pace with growth in assets.[16]

To identify the constraint of capital requirements on asset growth, consider the sample bank in Exhibit 14.9. This small bank starts with initial capital at 8 percent of total assets. We assume that the bank earns 1 percent on assets and pays out 40 percent of its earnings in the form of dividends. Given these constraints, the impact of various rates of growth in assets is examined.

Consider the case of asset growth at 10 percent. The addition to retained earnings in that case is insufficient to maintain the capital-to-assets ratio at the 8 percent level. Even though the bank's return-on-assets ratio and dividend-payout ratio are unchanged, the addition to retained earnings falls short. If the capital-to-assets ratio is viewed as a minimum target level, the bank will be unable to grow at 10 percent unless the other financial variables are altered. To leave the capital ratio unaffected, the bank must pay out a smaller percentage of earnings in the form of dividends, earn a higher rate of return on assets, secure additional equity capital by selling additional shares of stock, or alter some combination of these variables.

EXHIBIT 14.9 Effect of Asset Growth on Capital Position

Beginning Assets: $2,000,000
Return on Assets: 1%
Dividend Payout Ratio: 40%
Beginning Equity Capital: $160,000
Beginning Capital/Assets: 8%

Asset growth (%)	6	8	10	12
Assets ($)	2,120,000	2,160,000	2,200,000	2,240,000
Net income ($)	21,200	21,600	22,000	22,400
Dividends ($)	8,480	8,640	8,800	8,960
Additions to retained earnings ($)	12,720	12,960	13,200	13,440
Total equity capital ($)	172,720	172,960	173,200	173,440
Capital/assets (%)	8.15	8.01	7.87	7.74

---

[16]R. C. Kimball and R. L. McDonald, "Inflation and the Capital Financing of New England Commercial Banks in the 1980s," *New England Economic Review, Federal Reserve Bank of Boston,* September-October 1979: 5–24.

The first alternative involves a reduction in the dividend-payout ratio. If cash dividends were reduced to $6000, adequate retained earnings would be available to leave the capital ratio unaffected. This action would reduce the payout ratio to 27 percent from its current level of 40 percent. Such a reduction could be viewed as unfavorable by the owners.

Alternatively, the bank could attempt to increase its return on assets. If the dividend-payout ratio remains at 40 percent, $26,667 in net income is necessary to leave the capital-to-assets ratio at 8 percent. This would mean increasing the return-on-assets ratio to 1.21 percent from its current level of 1 percent. Assuming reasonably competitive markets, the bank would probably have to increase the riskiness of its asset portfolio in order to generate the higher required return. This action may reduce the cushion provided by equity to absorb losses.[17]

Finally, the bank could maintain its dividend-payout and return-on-assets ratios and secure the needed capital by selling additional stock. This alternative is not likely to be a realistic possibility for a small bank. Small banks just do not have the access to capital markets necessary to make this a viable option. For large banks the sale of additional stock may be a possibility.

Sale of additional stock is also not without problems. The amount of capital secured from such a sale is dependent on the current market value of the bank's stock. In recent years the market values of bank stocks have been depressed.[18] The sale of additional shares may also have a temporary dilution effect on the earnings per share of the current shareholders. The registration and selling costs associated with the sale of common stock are very large. These factors usually lead to the conclusion that retention of earnings is preferable to sale of new stock.[19]

Expanded Model to Simulate Capital Needs.   David G. Bernon, in his 1978 article on capacity for asset growth, expands the basic model that we have discussed to simulate the effect that capital adequacy has on asset growth.[20] The basic model is defined as

(14.1)
$$\Delta E/E = (TA/E \times NI/TA) \times (1 - D/NI)$$

---

[17]We are using the capital-to-total-assets ratio in our example. If we were to use the capital-to-risk-assets ratio, the constraint could be affected differently. If Treasury securities were reduced and more funds were employed in loans, the capital-to-risk-assets ratio would decline. The increase in earnings would have to be large enough to offset this decline.

[18]Wallich, op. cit.

[19]Retained earnings are often incorrectly perceived as being a free source of funds. The additions to retained earnings represent an increased investment by the owners of the bank. The bank must earn the return required by these owners for risking their capital.

[20]D. G. Bernon, "Capacity for Asset Growth Model: A Tool for Internal Bank Management and External Bank Analysis," *The Magazine of Bank Administration,* August 1978: 36–39.

where

$\Delta E/E$ = Percentage addition to current equity
TA/E = Total assets divided by equity (equity multiplier)
NI/TA = Return on assets
D/NI = Dividend-payout ratio

Working with TA/E, NI/TA, and D/NI as constraints, Bernon simulates the rates of return on assets necessary to meet a dividend-payout constraint and an equity-multiplier constraint. Results from a simulation imposing capital to assets at 6 percent are displayed in Exhibit 14.10.

As shown in this exhibit, for the sample bank with an asset growth rate of 7 percent, a dividend-payout ratio of 35 percent, and a capital-to-assets ratio of 6 percent, a return-on-assets ratio of 0.56 percent is necessary to meet the imposed constraints. The simulation demonstrates the constraints that are imposed on asset growth. To meet capital needs internally, at higher rates of growth the bank must secure additional capital either through larger retentions or through higher returns on assets. It may be very difficult to accomplish either of these tasks.

For the sample bank used in the simulation, the growth rate in assets that meets the current constraints of dividend policy, return on assets, and capital to assets is less than 3 percent. That is, if dividends are maintained at 75 percent of earnings, return on assets is maintained at 0.51 percent, and capital is maintained at 6 percent of assets, the bank cannot accommodate growth in assets in excess of 3 percent. The historical rate of growth of the sample bank has been 13 percent. It is clear that this bank needs to revise its policies drastically or plan its growth at a much lower rate. At 13 percent growth in assets, even if the bank were to retain 100 percent of its earnings at its current return on assets, its capital-to-assets ratio would fall below 6 percent.

Management of the capital position of a bank is a complicated process requiring managers to simultaneously consider return on assets, distribution of earnings, and growth in assets. Given the views of regulators, it seems unlikely that further deterioration of capital ratios will be allowed. To meet the constraint of no further deterioration in capital ratios, bank managements will have to either limit their asset growth or secure additional equity capital through greater retention of earnings or through sale of additional stock.

Acquisition of External Capital

As we have seen, the ability of banks to grow is clearly constrained by capital requirements. Without further reduction in capital ratios, which is not likely to be allowed given the current levels of capital, any significant levels of growth will require additions of external capital.

EXHIBIT 14.10 Capacity for Asset Growth

Historical Information of Sample Bank

	1975	1974	1973	1972	3-Year Compound Growth Rate
Average Total Assets	982,000[a]	954,200	787,800	675,100	13.30%
Average Equity	59,200	55,300	47,700	38,800	15.13%
Dividend Payout	75.1%	42.3%	51.3%	42.1%	—
Return on Average Total Assets	.51%	.75%	.74%	.73%	—
Leverage Ratio	16.6×	17.3×	16.5×	17.4×	—

Capacity for Asset-Growth Matrix for Sample Bank[b] (Assuming 16.6× Leverage Ratio)

Dividend Payout			Asset Growth Rate			
	5%	7%	8%	9%	13%
35%	.40%	.56%	.64%	.72%	1.02%
40	.43	.61	.70	.78	1.11
45	.47	.67	.77	.85	1.21
50	.52	.73	.84	.94	1.33
55	.57	.81	.93	1.04	1.48
60	.65	.91	1.04	1.17	1.66

[b]The matrix is calculated by solving Equation 14.1 for net income (NI), by assuming different asset-growth and dividend-payout rates, and given a desired leverage ratio. A step-by-step calculation is outlined below.

Calculating Required Return on Average Total Assets for the Capacity for Asset-Growth Matrix

Step in Calculation	Sample Bank	Comment
1. Calculate average total assets, assuming an asset-growth rate.	$\dfrac{982{,}000 \times 1.07}{1{,}050{,}740}$	Assumed 7% asset-growth rate.
2. Calculate required level of average equity in order to keep leverage ratio constant with assumed asset-growth rate.	$\dfrac{1{,}050{,}740 \times .06}{63{,}044}$	Constraint #1 was the assumption to keep the leverage ratio at 16.6×, which is the same as saying average equity is 6% of average total assets. (Varying constraint #1 will generate other matrices.)
3. Calculate dollar change in equity necessary to keep the leverage ratio constant.	$\dfrac{63{,}044 - 59{,}200}{3{,}844}$	
4. Calculate dollar level of net income, given an assumed dividend-payout ratio, necessary to generate the required addition to average equity.	$\dfrac{3{,}844}{1 - .35} = 5{,}914$	Constraint #2 was the dividend-payout ratio; here it was assumed to be 35%. (The denominator in this step of the calculation is the complement of the assumed dividend-payout ratio.)
5. Calculate the required return on average total assets that will allow the leverage ratio to remain constant, given an assumed asset-growth rate and dividend-payout ratio.	$\dfrac{5{,}914}{1{,}050{,}740} = .56\%$	Constraint #3 was earnings, measured by return on average total assets. In the matrix, a 7% capacity for asset growth is consistent with a 16.6× leverage factor if the dividend-payout ratio is 35% and the return on average total assets is .56%

[a]All dollar amounts are in thousands.

Source: David G. Bernon, "Capacity for Asset Growth Model: A Tool for Internal Bank Management and External Bank Analysis," *The Magazine of Bank Administration*, August 1978.

In regard to sources of external capital, a clear distinction exists between large and small banks. Large banks can plan capital acquisition through registered public offerings of securities. Most large banks' stock trades in active public markets, and it is possible for these organizations to attract additional capital through public offerings.

Raising external capital is a more formidable problem for smaller banks with no direct access to public financial markets. Sale of additional stock on subordinated notes and debentures for smaller banks is limited to private placements. The cost associated with a public offering is too large relative to the size of the offering to make a public sale viable. Furthermore, there is no adequate market demand for the stock or bonds of such banks.

Private placements are made to a limited number of sophisticated offerees and require that the securities be purchased without intent to redistribute the securities to the investing public. The bank must make the same type of information available to the offerees in a placement as would be available to investors in public offerings, but the costs associated with providing the information are far lower.[21]

Most placements are made to institutional investors such as insurance companies or investment trusts. A bank with a need for external capital may be able to raise the capital through such a placement with an institution at far lower costs. The price at which the stock can be sold (or the yield on bonds) will likely be lower (higher) because of the resale restrictions that apply to such investments.

Direct-placement, or Regulation A, small public offerings can be made directly to individual investors as well. A bank may be able to attract sufficient capital from a limited number of individuals. The most likely prospects for this type of sale will be individuals who are located in the service area and/or are customers of the bank.

Faced with the capital constraint, many small banks elect to seek new ownership through affiliation with a bank holding company. The bank holding company, because of its size, will have access to regional or national markets. Through affiliation the small bank can gain access to external capital it otherwise could not achieve. Many small banks have elected to meet the capital constraint in this fashion.

SUMMARY

Bank capital serves a primary function of protection of depositor claims by acting as a buffer to absorb loan and other operating losses. In that function both long-term subordinated debt and equity capital serve as buffers to absorb losses.

---

[21]For example, a certified audit of financial statements is required with a public offering. In a private placement such an audit is not required unless the private placement purchasers require it. A private placement requires far less administrative time and can be completed in a matter of days, whereas a public offering may take as long as six months to complete.

Capital as a percentage of assets or risk assets has declined in recent years and is currently at its lowest level since the 1930s. The decline in capital ratios is the result of both a reduction in capital and more aggressive investing by commercial banks. Today's bank has a much larger percentage of its funds in loans and higher-earning municipal securities. The decline in capital ratios has caused concern among regulators.

From a management standpoint, capital constrains the ability of the bank to grow, and capital management requires careful analysis of the impact of growth on capital ratios. Given the present regulatory concern over the current low levels of capital, the future ability of banks to grow without acquiring additional capital from outside sources is likely to be even more constrained.

Questions and Problems

1. Identify and briefly discuss the functions of bank capital.

2. List the two major sources of capital.

3. List the requirements of the Comptroller of the Currency for debt to be included in the capital base.

4. Explain how judicious use of limited long-term debt could also increase the equity capital base.

5. Compare and contrast capital adequacy from the viewpoints of depositors, borrowers, owners, and regulators.

6. Describe the long-term trend in the capital-to-risk-assets ratio.

7. Suppose you were analyzing two banks and you found the capital-to-assets ratio of Bank 1 to be 0.04, and the capital-to-assets ratio of Bank 2 to be 0.09. Other factors being constant, which of these banks would you expect to be a large bank? Explain.

8. Describe the effect that dividends have on the ability of a bank to grow and at the same time to maintain its capital ratios.

9. a. Reconstruct Exhibit 14.9 under the assumption that return on assets falls to 95 percent and the dividend-payout ratio increases to 50 percent.   **b.** Compare your results with those in Exhibit 14.9.
c. What general conclusions do your findings allow you to draw?

References

Baker, R. M. "Sources of Bank Capital: An Issue for the 80s." *Economic Review, Federal Reserve Bank of Atlanta,* December 1982: 65–73.

Bernon, D. G. "Capacity for Asset Growth Model: A Tool for Internal Bank Management and External Bank Analysis." *The Magazine of Bank Administration,* August 1978: 36–39.

"Capital Rules for Big Banks Set by Regulators." *The Wall Street Journal,* June 10, 1983, 3.

Cornyn, A. G. "Financial Developments of Bank Holding Companies in 1982." *Federal Reserve Bulletin,* July 1983: 508–514.

DeBussey, F. W. "Double Leverage in Bank Holding Companies." In *Funds Management Under Deregulation,* ed. G. H. Hempel, 510–517. Washington, DC: American Bankers Association, 1981.

Federal Reserve Bulletin, July 1976: 601–604.

Field, A. H., and C. Field. "Direct Equity Marketing for Banks." In *Funds Management Under Deregulation,* ed. G. H. Hempel, 518–526. Washington, DC: American Bankers Association, 1981.

Flannery, M. H. "Deposit Insurance Creates a Need for Bank Regulation." *Business Review, Federal Reserve Bank of Philadelphia,* January-February 1982: 17–27.

Heggestad, A. A., and B. F. King. "Regulation of Bank Capital." *Economic Review, Federal Reserve Bank of Atlanta,* March 1982: 35–43.

Hempel, G. H. "Bank Capital: Evaluating the Recent Trends—A Four-Part Series." In *Funds Management Under Deregulation,* ed. G. H. Hempel, 460–503. Washington, DC: American Bankers Association, 1981.

Howard, D. S., and G. M. Hoffman. *Evolving Concepts of Bank Capital.* New York: Citicorp, 1980.

Isaac, W. M. "The World Would Sleep (Or, All You Would Ever Care to Hear About Capital Adequacy)." In *Funds Management Under Deregulation,* ed. G. H. Hempel, 453–459. Washington, DC: American Bankers Association, 1981.

Kimball, R. C., and R. L. McDonald. "Inflation and the Capital Financing of New England Commercial Banks in the 1980s." *New England Economic Review, Federal Reserve Bank of Boston,* September-October 1979: 5–24.

"Minimum Capital Guideline Amendments." *Federal Reserve Bulletin,* July 1983: 539–540.

Sharpe, W. F. "Bank Capital Adequacy, Deposit Insurance and Security Values." *Journal of Financial and Quantitative Analysis,* November 1978: 701–718.

Summers, B. J. "Bank Capital Adequacy: Perspectives and Prospects." *Economic Review, Federal Reserve Bank of Richmond,* July-August 1977: 3–8.

Taggert, R. A., Jr. "Regulatory Influence on Bank Capital." *New England Economic Review, Federal Reserve Bank of Boston,* September-October 1977: 37–46.

Talley, S. H. "Bank Capital Trends and Financing: Study Summary." *Federal Reserve Bulletin,* February 1983: 71–72.

Wallich, H. C. "Bank Profits and Inflation." *Economic Review, Federal Reserve Bank of Richmond,* May-June 1980: 27–30.

Watson, R. D. "Banking on Debt for Capital Needs." *Business Review, Federal Reserve Bank of Philadelphia,* December 1974: 17–28.

Watson, R. D. "Banking's Capital Shortage: The Malaise and the Myth." *Business Review, Federal Reserve Bank of Philadelphia,* December 1974: 3–13.

"Why Bank Loans Could Be Harder to Get." *Business Week,* July 18, 1983, 148–149.

PART THREE

♦

Analysis of
Performance and Planning

CHAPTER 15

Analyzing Bank Performance

The purpose of bank performance analysis is to evaluate progress toward meeting the goals and objectives set forth by management and to compare the performance of the bank relative to that of similar banks. The evaluation of performance involves analysis of the basic financial statements and construction of the ratios that identify the key components of performance. The goal of performance analysis is to highlight strengths and weaknesses so that management can take appropriate action to strengthen the weak areas and maintain performance in the strong areas.

TRENDS IN BANK PERFORMANCE

In a recent study undertaken by Olson Research Associates, 130 commercial banks were surveyed. These banks represented different geographic areas, unit banks, branch banks, holding company banks, independent banks, and banks of various sizes ranging from less than $10 million to more than $6 billion in total assets. The sample represented over 6 percent of the assets held by all U.S. commercial banks.

As indicated in Exhibit 15.1, gross loans remained fairly stable over the ten-year period, while investment securities declined with compensating increases in short-term investments. The trend reflects banks' reliance on short-term money management to maximize income potential while minimizing short-term interest-rate risk on portfolio decisions. These changes resulted principally from favorable changes in the interest sensitivity of short-term investments to market rates and from increases in time and interest-bearing deposits with lower reserve requirements.

The composition of income remained constant; however, interest expense increased significantly over the ten-year period. Other expenses declined, reflecting greater operating efficiencies. Net income in 1982 was approximately half the level in 1973 as a result of narrowed interest margin. The trends derived from the study suggest that profits will continue to erode due mainly to higher interest expense. These increases in interest expense may be offset with greater fee income and greater control of operating expenses.

EXHIBIT 15.1 Percent Distribution, Combined Financial Information of 130 Commercial Banks

	1973	1974	1975	1976	1977	1978	1979	1980	1981	1982
Statement of Condition										
Gross loans	56.7	57.6	53.8	52.6	53.8	56.3	57.4	56.2	55.3	55.7
Securities portfolio	24.0	22.3	24.2	24.7	23.6	22.2	21.0	20.7	20.1	18.5
Short-term investments	3.4	4.2	6.0	6.9	7.5	6.4	6.3	7.8	9.3	10.8
Total earning assets	84.2	84.0	84.0	84.2	84.9	84.9	84.6	84.6	84.7	85.1
Cash	12.5	12.2	11.9	11.9	11.3	11.3	11.2	10.9	10.1	9.2
Fixed and other assets	4.0	4.4	4.8	4.5	4.4	4.4	4.7	5.1	5.8	6.4
Reserve for loan losses	−0.7	−0.7	−0.7	−0.6	−0.6	−0.6	−0.6	−0.6	0.7	0.7
Total assets	100.0	100.0	100.0	100.0	100.0	100.0	100.0	100.0	100.0	100.0
Noninterest demand deposits	37.2	34.1	33.3	32.8	31.7	30.8	28.8	27.3	23.7	21.2
Core interest-bearing deposits	31.9	30.7	31.5	34.2	35.7	33.8	32.8	33.6	35.1	36.5
Other time (purchased CDs)	14.1	16.8	17.0	14.8	13.8	16.5	18.2	17.6	18.5	18.6
Total deposits	83.2	81.6	81.8	81.8	81.2	81.1	79.9	78.5	77.3	76.2
Borrowed funds	6.9	8.4	8.2	8.4	9.2	9.1	10.2	11.1	12.1	13.0
Other liabilities	2.2	2.3	2.0	1.8	1.8	2.0	2.4	2.8	3.2	3.5
Long-term debt	1.2	1.3	1.3	1.3	1.3	1.3	1.2	1.1	1.0	0.9
Equity	6.5	6.4	6.7	6.7	6.5	6.4	6.4	6.4	6.4	6.3
Total liabilities and capital	100.0	100.0	100.0	100.0	100.0	100.0	100.0	100.0	100.0	100.0
Statement of Income										
Total interest income	89.2	90.3	89.1	88.0	88.5	89.6	90.4	90.9	91.3	90.3
Noninterest income	10.8	9.7	10.9	12.0	11.5	10.4	9.6	9.1	8.7	9.7
Total income	100.0	100.0	100.0	100.0	100.0	100.0	100.0	100.0	100.0	100.0
Interest expense	44.2	50.2	44.6	43.1	43.5	46.2	52.4	56.8	62.4	59.8
Loan loss provision	2.1	3.0	4.8	4.4	3.5	3.3	3.0	2.9	2.5	3.6
Other expenses	38.4	34.9	39.8	41.4	40.3	37.1	32.7	30.2	26.6	28.7
Total expenses	84.7	88.1	89.2	88.9	87.2	86.6	88.1	89.9	91.5	92.1
Net before taxes	15.3	11.9	10.8	11.1	12.8	13.4	11.9	10.1	8.5	7.9
Income taxes	3.3	2.1	1.2	1.5	2.4	3.0	2.3	1.4	1.1	0.7
Net before security gains and losses	12.0	9.9	9.5	9.6	10.4	10.4	9.6	8.7	7.4	7.3
Security gains and losses	−0.3	−0.2	−0.1	0.1	0.0	−0.3	−0.4	−0.4	−0.6	−0.5
Net income	11.6	9.6	9.5	9.8	10.4	10.1	9.2	8.3	6.9	6.8

Source: Olson Research Associates, *Bank Performance Report 1983*, (Greenbelt, MD: Olson Research Associates, 1983).

HIGH-PERFORMANCE BANKING

In recent years bankers have been introduced to the concept of high-performance banking. High-performance banking is simply high-profitability banking. In a study of the top 1000 U.S. banks in return on assets, several key characteristics common to the high-performance banks were found, including:

1. Maximization of revenues

   High loan income attained through appropriate pricing and avoidance of nonaccruing loans, rather than relatively high volume.

   Maximization of income from tax-exempt securities.

   Maintenance of sufficient flexibility in asset structure to take advantage of changes in interest rates.
2. Expense control

   Low investment in fixed assets, lower occupancy expense.

   Proper control of overhead and discretionary costs, such as "Other Operating Expense."

   Minimization of loan losses through proper credit analysis.

   Control of personnel expense through efficient use of fewer employees, rather than through low salaries.
3. Consistently good management

   Large comparative advantages in the management of smaller, controllable factors.

   Smaller comparative—but large absolute—advantages in management of larger, less controllable factors.[1]

The authors identify specific differences in high performance among banks. High-performance banks concentrated more of their investments in tax-exempt securities and earned higher yields on these tax-exempt securities. High-performance banks had lower ratios of loans to total assets but were able to earn higher yields on loans and experienced smaller loan losses. High-performance banks operated with slightly less capital and displayed excellent control of overhead, including austere facilities and fewer employees (but with higher than average salaries).

Factors depressing profitability included extensive branching, high proportions of fixed assets to total assets, and competition from the thrifts. The authors found significantly lower performance in areas in which competition from thrift institutions was more pronounced.

---

[1]See W. F. Ford and D. A. Olson, "How 1000 High Performance Banks Weathered the Recent Recession," in *Bank Management: Concepts and Issues*, ed. J. R. Brick (Richmond, VA: Robert F. Dame, 1981), 493.

The study was summarized with the statement: "As we reviewed all the various factors that distinguish high-performance banks, each could be classified into three functional areas: planning, organizing, and controlling. These functions—at least according to our textbook—are the definition of management."[2]

The achievement of high-performance banking in today's environment is a difficult task. With increased competition from nonbanking institutions and increased pressures on interest margins, banks must move toward selective packaging and pricing of profitable products. For banks to achieve high performance, products offered under the full-service concept in a less competitive environment must be reevaluated.

FINANCIAL STATEMENT ANALYSIS

Certain analytical techniques are unique to financial institutions, specifically the use of interest yield and variance analyses. The common analyses used by financial institutions include:

1. Comparative statements from period to period.
2. Common-size statements relating each asset item and liability and capital items to total assets and each income statement item to total operating income.
3. Indexed financial statements that measure growth or contraction in key financial accounts.
4. Ratio analyses that develop meaningful relationships between accounts.

The analytical techniques discussed below are formulated from an internal rather than an external viewpoint. External analysis, such as an analysis performed by a bank stock analyst, depends on the use of available public data. Bank management has information that is not available to outside analysts; therefore more detailed analysis is possible.

Procedures for generating bank operating statistics include the development of comparative spread sheets leading to the preparation of common-size statements and index comparisons, preparation of financial ratios, development of maturity and yield schedules, and analysis of changes in specific accounts such as allowance for loan losses and capital.

Comparative statements illustrate absolute dollar changes in accounts from one period to another, which explain certain results of bank operations. This analysis serves to pinpoint major areas that require additional analysis to explain significant trends. Since comparative statements indicate absolute dollar changes, the analysis gives the observer

---

[2]Ibid, 483.

a quick indication of significant changes within the balance sheet and income statement but does not present the degree of significance of the change.

Common-size statements express individual balance sheet accounts as a percentage of total assets and individual income statement accounts as a percentage of total operating income. These relationships measure composition or mix expressed as a percentage distribution. If a change in proportion represents a departure from current or past trends, we should trace the events that may have led to change. For example, we would expect a continued reduction in demand deposit accounts and an increase in interest-bearing deposits because of deregulation. If the increase in interest-bearing deposits did not occur, we should examine how the bank obtained funds to support the asset base and what might be the present and future impact on bank earnings. The purpose of common-size statement analysis is to narrow the analyst's review to the key areas impacting profits, return on assets, and return on equity. An example of a common-size spread sheet format is found in Exhibit 15.2.

Indexed financial statements identify the magnitude of increases or decreases in individual balance sheet and individual income statement accounts. The analyst compares the actual results expressed as percentage increases or decreases to planned or expected results. Accounts that did not perform according to plan or expectation are subjected to further detailed analyses. The additional analyses may include ratio analysis or analyzing the specific transactions that produced the unexpected results. Exhibit 15.3 is an example of an indexed financial statement format.

Common-size statements form a vertical analysis and indexed financial statements form a horizontal analysis. When considered together, a change in composition may explain the degree of increase or decrease in an account balance. If the change in composition is desirable, then a significant change in trend for the account may not be meaningful. However, if the change in composition is unexpected or not within a range acceptable to management, then an examination of the trend becomes important. Even if a composition change appears to be material, the trend may not be significant enough to warrant further attention. Therefore, a significant change in composition should be confirmed by a significant change in the trend. If not confirmed, then the scope of analysis becomes limited. Limiting the scope of analysis assists the analyst in determining the extent and type of additional analyses necessary to explain the significance of the account change.

Ratio Analysis

Ratio analysis extends the overall analysis into greater detail for examining account relationships presented in the balance sheet and income statement. Overall measures of performance are condensed into two

EXHIBIT 15.2   Statement Analysis—Common-Size Statements

Format for Spread Sheet: Balance Sheet

	Year ×4	% of Total Assets	Year ×3	% of Total Assets
Assets	_____	_____	_____	_____
Total Assets	_____	100.00	_____	100.00
Liabilities				
Capital Accounts	_____	_____	_____	_____
Total Liabilities and Equity	_____	100.00	_____	100.00

Format for Spread Sheet: Income Statement

	Year ×4	% of Total Operating Income	Year ×3	% of Total Operating Income
Interest Income				
Interest Expense	_____	_____	_____	_____
Net Interest Income				
Provision for Loan Losses				
Other Income				
Other Expense	_____	_____	_____	_____
Income before Taxes				
Income Taxes	_____	_____	_____	_____
Net Income	_____	_____	_____	_____

Note: Total operating income = Total interest income + Other income = 100.00%. Alternative comparisons include comparing each item with total interest income or net interest income. Total operating income and interest income comparisons will produce the most consistent results between periods. Net interest margin comparisons can produce volatile relationships and are more difficult to interpret.

basic measures—return on assets (ROA) and return on equity (ROE). Many factors compose performance. Consequently ROA and ROE serve as targets for comparisons within the industry.

From a shareholder's viewpoint, ROA and ROE are two key measures of performance. Uninsured depositors are directly concerned with safety and liquidity and indirectly concerned with ROA and ROE as they relate to equity increases for depositor protection. Imprudent investments in securities and loans eventually affect ROA, ROE, safety, and liquidity. Regulators are concerned with depositor safety and emphasize capital adequacy and liquidity. From an analytical viewpoint, each of these interests must be given attention.

EXHIBIT 15.3   Statement Analysis—Indexed Financial Statements

Format for Indexed Statements: Balance Sheet

	Year ×4	Year ×3	Year ×4 Divided by Year ×3	Year ×2	Year ×3 Divided by Year ×2
Assets					
Total Assets					
Liabilities					
Capital Accounts					
Total Liabilities and Equity					

Format for Indexed Statements: Income Statement

	Year ×4	Year ×3	Year ×4 Divided by Year ×3	Year ×2	Year ×3 Divided by Year ×2
Interest Income					
Interest Expense					
Net Interest Income					
Provisions for Loan Losses					
Other Income					
Other Expense					
Income before Taxes					
Income Taxes					
Net Income					

Exhibit 15.4 outlines the primary factors that are controllable by management and defines the general and specific measures that may be used to measure performance on each factor. The controllable factors are business mix, income production including expense control, loan quality, safety, and liquidity. Several measures or analyses interrelate these factors. For example, business mix defines the components of interest margin, and these components of interest margin define the quality of income production.

The analysis of income production requires examination of the major components of the income statement, taking into consideration associated balance sheet accounts, which culminates in determining how ROA and ROE were generated. Interest-margin variance analysis is used to measure performance of the controllable factors of volume and mix

---

EXHIBIT 15.4   Analysis of Overall Performance

	General Measure	Specific Ratio or Analysis	Factors Determined
Business Mix			
1. Assets	Asset composition Indexed balance sheet	Investment ratios	Resource level and utilization Mix Trend
2. Liabilities and equity	Liability and equity composition Indexed balance sheet	Funding and leverage ratios	Resource level and utilization Mix Trend
3. Interest margin	Income statement composition Indexed income statement	Yield analysis Interest-margin variance analysis	Yield Rate, volume, mix variances Trend
Income Production			
1. Interest margin	Income statement composition Indexed financial statement	Yield analysis— interest spread Interest-margin variance analysis Net interest margin	Degree of taxable interest income Yield Rate, volume, mix variances Average rates earned and paid on assets and liabilities, respectively Income generation from average earning assets

(continued)

EXHIBIT 15.4   *(continued)*

	General Measure	Specific Ratio or Analysis	Factors Determined
2. Provision for loan losses	Income statement composition	Loan loss ratios— loan loss provision divided by average loans	Recognition of changes in loan quality that impact earnings
3. Noninterest expenses	Income statement composition Indexed income statement	Comparison with average assets Breakeven yield Employee productivity ratios	Degree of expense control Expense levels related to type of bank (wholesale, retail) Net yield on average assets required to cover net noninterest expenses Economies of scale evidenced by employee levels required to perform operational tasks Trend
4. Other income	Income statement composition Indexed income statement	Breakeven yield	Fee income from services not requiring portfolio balances Fee income from deposit services Net yield on average assets required to cover net noninterest expenses Trend
Securities gains and losses	Income statement composition Indexed income statement	Yield analysis Mix and maturity of investment securities	Current portfolio changes and potential changes due to investment policies to improve yields or alter taxable income

(continued)

EXHIBIT 15.4   *(continued)*

	General Measure	**Specific Ratio or Analysis**	**Factors Determined**
5. Income taxes	Income statement composition Indexed income statement	Mix of investment securities Comparison to statutory tax rates Comparison of current taxes and deferred taxes payable	Degree to which bank employs tax-planning techniques in minimizing or deferring income taxes
6. Net income	Income statement composition Indexed income statement	***Return on assets*** ***Return on equity*** Capital formation ratio Dividend payout ratio	***Overall performance*** Growth potential Cash returns to shareholders
Loan Quality		Loan mix Loan maturity Loan loss ratios Yield analysis	Degree to which loans bear risk and whether additions to allowance reflect characteristics of portfolio and loan policies Degree to which loan yields reflect significantly higher yields than competition, which may reflect larger potential loan losses from riskier loans providing higher yields
Safety and Liquidity	Balance sheet composition Indexed balance sheet	Liquidity ratios Capital adequacy ratios Funding and leverage ratios Earning assets ratio	Degree to which bank can meet unforeseen demands for reserve balances or meet financial claims

(continued)

EXHIBIT 15.4   *(continued)*

	General Measure	Specific Ratio or Analysis	Factors Determined
			Degree to which capital is minimized, placing importance on acquiring and maintaining high-quality assets
			Degree to which liquidity in nonearning assets is minimized to maximize earning assets potential
Peer Bank Analysis			
	Balance sheet composition	Ratios	Competitive position among peer banks
	Indexed balance sheet		Competitive success among similar banks or banks in trade area
	Income statement composition		
	Indexed income statement		

of assets and deposit resources. Interest rate levels are not controllable because they are market determined. The rate variance therefore measures the bank's performance in responding to interest rate changes and policies directed toward minimizing rate adjustments on bank income.

A final step in the analytical process is the selection of peer banks for comparison. The analyst should carefully select those banks that display similar characteristics for peer group analysis. Additionally, a useful analysis is to compare other banks in the same geographic or trade area to identify strengths and weaknesses of competitive banks. Any weakness in serving the market area may be exploited by a change in marketing strategy, resulting in a change in business mix.

With the advent of deregulation, few precise standards exist as a norm of the industry. The analyst must be concerned with first identifying the type of bank—wholesale vs. retail, money-center, regional vs. small bank. Several ratios will assist in characterizing the bank and its appropriate peer group. Loan and deposit mix with concentrations of commercial loans, large certificates of deposits, large amounts of borrowed funds, and interest spreads of less than 3 percent typically identify the wholesale, money-center, or regional bank. Consumer-oriented loans and deposits with interest spreads of approximately 3 to 6 percent normally identify a retail bank.

Exhibit 15.4 presents a basic framework for analyzing ROA and ROE. Exhibit 15.5 presents certain ratios and analyses in greater detail and should be used in conjunction with Exhibit 15.4. The ratios are explained in sufficient detail to complete most of the elements outlined in Exhibit 15.4. Interest-margin variance analysis is more complex and is described in detail on page 368.

Interest-Margin Variance Analysis.   A more sophisticated technique used to analyze interest income on earning assets is interest-margin variance analysis. Variance analysis involves breaking down the changes in interest margin over two periods into three factors: changes in rates, volume, and mix. Interest-margin variance analysis can be performed on specific earning assets, on interest-bearing liabilities, or on the bank's overall portfolio of earning assets and interest-bearing liabilities.

The rate variance identifies the effect of rate changes on interest income and expense from the prior period to the current period. Volume variances measure the change in the resource level from the prior period to the current period and indicate the effect of volume changes on interest income and expense for the current period. The mix variance refers to the percentage composition of assets and liabilities for the prior period compared to the current period and explains the impact on interest income and expense for the current period. However, the mix variance is not so well defined as the volume and rate variances since the resulting mix variance is a residual. It results as a part of the volume change and is affected by interest rate changes.

The variances where M is the mix, V is the resource volume level, R is the rate, and the subscripts 1 and 2 indicate the prior period and current period, respectively, may be stated as follows:

$$\text{Rate variance } (R_2 - R_1)V_1 = R$$

$$\text{Volume variance } (V_2 - V_1)R_1 = V$$

$$\text{Mix variance } (R_2 - R_1)(V_2 - V_1) = M$$

EXHIBIT 15.5 Ratio Analysis

Liquidity Ratios

Indicate amounts of deposits required to meet reserve requirements and cash operating funds for transactions and processing clearings. Reduce cash by net borrowed funds and securities sold under repurchase agreements to reflect cash obtained by borrowing. Short-term government securities should be reduced by amounts of short-term securities pledged for public deposits.

Average cash divided by average demand deposits

Average cash divided by average total deposits

Cash and short-term U.S. government securities divided by average total deposits

Investment Policies

Indicate income potential and investment policies.

Earning assets ratio: Indicates percentage of assets used in interest-earning assets.

Average earning assets divided by average total assets

Loans-to-deposits ratio: Indicates percentage of deposits used in loans that are generally less liquid than higher income-yielding assets. A ratio greater than 75% indicates an aggressive loan strategy, whereas lower than 65% indicates a very conservative loan strategy.

Average loans divided by average deposits

Loans-to-total-purchased-funds ratio: Indicates extent that bank relies on interest-sensitive funds to support loan portfolio. Purchased funds include time deposits, federal funds sold, and securities sold under repurchase agreements.

Average loans divided by average total purchased funds

Securities mix: Indicates percentage of each type of security in investment portfolio. A high proportion of U.S. government and agency securities indicates policies emphasizing liquidity and income stability. A high proportion of municipal securities indicates policies emphasizing minimization of federal income tax expense.

Format:

	Average Amount	Percent
U.S. government	$.	.
U.S. government agencies	.	.
Municipals	.	.
Other	.	.
Total	$.	100.00

Securities maturity distribution: Indicates strategy to emphasize liquidity, stabilize income, and/or minimize income taxes over relevant time periods. The analysis may indicate current or potential problems in a time period because of high or low proportions of each type of security.

Format:

	Amount (Period-End Balance)				
	Under 1 Year	1–5 Years	5–10 Years	Over 10 Years	Total
U.S. government	$.	$.	$.	$.	$.
U.S. government agencies	.	.	.	.	.
Municipals	.	.	.	.	.
Other	.	.	.	.	.
Total	$.	$.	$.	$.	$.

Loan mix: Indicates proportions of each type to total loans. The proportions may indicate bank's role as a retail bank (higher proportion of consumer and/or mortgage loans) or wholesale bank (higher proportion of commercial loans). Key factors to assess include risk, liquidity, profitability, absence of concentration, and conformity to loan policy.

Format:

	Average Amount	Percent
Commercial	$.	.
Consumer	.	.
Mortgage	.	.
Agricultural	.	.
Total	$.	100.00

EXHIBIT 15.5 (continued)

Loan maturity distribution: Indicates the balance, liquidity, concentration, and conformity to loan policy by time period. Comparisons should be made with deposit maturities to assess matching of time periods regarding investment and funding decisions.

Format:

	Amount (Period-End Balance)			
	Under 1 Year	1–5 Years	Over 5 Years	Total
Commercial	$ . .	$ . .	$ . .	$ . .
Consumer	. .	. .	. .	. .
Mortgage	. .	. .	. .	. .
Agriculture	. .	. .	. .	. .
Total	$	$	$	$

Funding and Leverage Ratios

Deposit mix: Indicates amount of core deposits versus purchased funds (interest sensitive).

Format:

	Average Amount	Percent
Demand	$ . .	. .
Savings	. .	. .
Time in denominations:		
Under $100,000	. .	. .
$100,000 and over	.	.
Total	$	100.00

Deposit maturity distribution: Indicates proportions of deposits by time period and trends toward reliance on purchased funds over extended periods.

Format:

	Amount (Period-End Balance)			
	Under 1 Year	1–5 Years	Over 5 Years	Total
Savings	$ . .	$ . .	$ . .	$ . .
Time in denominations:				
Under $100,000	. .	. .	. .	. .
$100,000 and over	. .	. .	. .	. .
Total	$	$	$	$

Leverage ratios: Indicate relationship between deposits, borrowed funds, and permanent capital in financing loans and investments. Should be compared with regulatory and industry standards for size and geographic location for similar banks.

Average deposits divided by average capital
Average borrowed funds divided by average capital

Capital Adequacy Ratios

Indicate period-end balance relationships of assets and equity. Ratios are general indications of loans funded by shareholders and protection provided to depositors. The capital-to-asset ratio should approximate 7% for most banks, as suggested by Federal Reserve Board guidelines, but 5–6% is considered adequate for money-center and regional banks.

Risk assets divided by capital
Capital divided by assets

Income Statement Relationship

Compared with average assets: Indicates relative income earning and expense incurrence-to-asset levels to determine operating trends. Comparisons should be made to peer banks. Typical relationships for net income divided by average assets are

Bank Size	Percent
$500 million and below	1.25–1.50
$500 million–$2 billion	1.00–1.25
Over $2 billion	0.50–1.00

Interest income divided by average assets
Interest expense divided by average assets
Net interest income divided by average assets
Loan loss provision divided by average assets
Noninterest income divided by average assets
Salaries and benefits divided by average assets
Occupancy, furniture, and equipment expense divided by average assets
Other noninterest expense divided by average assets
Securities gains (losses) divided by average assets
Tax provision divided by average assets
Net income divided by average assets

(continued)

EXHIBIT 15.5 *(continued)*

Compared with gross average earning assets: Indicates key income expense relationships on earning assets. Net interest income divided by average earning assets is termed net interest margin. A low net interest margin of approximately 3% indicates that the bank is wholesale in nature, while a high margin of approximately 6% indicates that the bank is a retail bank. A low margin may also indicate that the bank has investments in low-yield riskless assets or has significant nonaccrual loans. A high ratio may also indicate a high ratio of core deposits or a bank with high-yielding risky loans.

Interest income divided by gross average earning assets

Interest expense divided by gross average earning assets

Net interest income divided by gross average earning assets

Return on Equity
Indicates rate of earnings on invested capital. A return of 13%–16% is considered adequate.

Net income divided by average capital

Loan Loss Ratios
Indicate adequacy of allowance and trends in collection and performance in loan portfolio.

Allowance for loan losses divided by loans (year-end)

Net charge-offs divided by average loans

Loan loss provision divided by average loans

Employee Productivity
Indicates relative number of employees required to perform key bank operations.

Income before taxes and securities gains (losses) divided by full-time equivalent employees (FTE)

Average assets divided by FTE employees (in millions)

Average deposits divided by FTE employees (in millions)

Dividend-Payout Ratio
Indicates rate of cash income returned to shareholders. Typical ratios range from 30% to 40%.

Cash dividends divided by net income

Capital Formation Ratio
Indicates proportion and trend of internally generated capital.

Net income minus cash dividends divided by beginning capital

Breakeven Yield
Indicates minimum rate of return on assets to cover noninterest income less noninterest expense.

Noninterest income minus noninterest expense divided by average assets

Yield Analysis
Indicates average rates earned or paid on assets and liabilities for the period.

Interest and fees on loans divided by average gross loans
Interest on U.S. Treasuries divided by average U.S. Treasuries
Interest on U.S. agencies divided by average U.S. agencies
Interest on municipals divided by average municipals
Earnings on other securities divided by average other securities
Interest on federal funds sold divided by average federal funds sold
Interest on savings divided by average savings
Interest on time deposits divided by average time deposits
Interest on federal funds purchased divided by average federal funds purchased
Interest on long-term debt divided by average long-term debt

EXHIBIT 15.6 Yield Analysis

	1980			1979		
	Average Balance ($)	Interest Income or Expense ($)	Average Yields or Rates (%)	Average Balance ($)	Interest Income or Expense ($)	Average Yields or Rates (%)
U.S. Treasury	38,405	4,147	10.79	29,654	2,573	8.68
Municipals[a]	89,203	9,278	10.40	76,280	6,949	9.11
Other	1,759	44	2.50	1,235	30	2.43
Total	129,367	13,469	10.41	107,169	9,552	8.91
Federal Funds Sold	33,510	4,609	13.75	20,694	2,425	11.72
Loans (Net of Unearned Income)	281,591	39,534	14.04	282,394	34,667	12.28
Total Earning Assets	444,468	57,612	12.96	410,257	46,644	11.37
Savings Deposits	77,740	4,066	5.23	81,222	4,144	5.10
Time Deposits	204,162	21,203	10.39	179,715	15,232	8.48
Federal Funds Purchased	4,642	558	12.02	4,458	469	10.52
Other Short-Term Debt	6,301	881	13.98	7,985	860	10.77
Long-Term Debt	16,127	1,393	8.64	15,575	1,349	8.66
Total Interest-Bearing Liabilities	308,972	28,101	9.09	288,955	22,054	7.63
Net Interest Income		29,511			24,590	
Yield Spread			3.87			3.74
Net Interest Income to Earning Assets			6.64			5.99

[a]Tax equivalent rate = 46%.

Source: Wyoming Bancorporation, *1980 Annual Report* (Cheyenne, WY: Wyoming Bancorporation, 1981), 56–57.

Exhibit 15.6 provides basic data for conducting variance analysis of federal funds sold. The yield analysis includes the dollar amounts for balance sheet and related income statement accounts and the average rates earned or paid. For federal funds sold the computations are as follows:

			Amount	Percent of Total Variance
$R = (0.1375 - 0.1172)(20,694)$		=	\$ 420	19%
$V = (33,510 - 20,694)(0.1172)$		=	1,502	69
$M = (13.75 - 11.72)(33,510 - 20,694)$		=	260	12
Total variance			\$2,182	100%

Exhibit 15.7 summarizes the major data and changes for federal funds sold and earning assets. If we examine the change in total earning assets, where the average of earning assets for 1979 was \$410,257 and for 1980 was \$444,468, the increase was 8.3 percent. The increase in volume for federal funds sold was 61.9 percent. In this case the volume variance explains the majority of the total variance. Correspondingly, the average rate earned on earning assets increased 14 percent, whereas the rate on federal funds sold increased 17.3 percent and accounted for 19 percent of the total variance. The remaining 12 percent is the mix, or the unexplained, variance since it involves combinations of rate and volume changes. However, if we examine the percentage distribution of federal funds sold to earning assets, we find that in 1979 it accounted for 5 percent of earning assets compared to 7.5 percent in 1980, which indicates an adjustment of small magnitude in the composition of the earning assets.

A very simple technique that can be applied to determine the change in interest margin is to compare the rate of change in interest

EXHIBIT 15.7   Analysis of Federal Funds Sold and Earning Assets

	1980	1979	Percent Increase
Rate of Federal Funds Sold	13.75%	11.72%	17.3%
Volume of Federal Funds Sold	\$ 33,510	\$ 20,694	61.9
Earning Assets	\$444,468	\$410,257	8.3
Interest Income	\$ 57,612	\$ 46,644	23.5
Yield on Earning Assets	12.96%	11.37%	14.0
Interest Expense	\$ 28,101	\$ 22,054	27.4
Net Interest Income	\$ 29,511	\$ 24,590	20.0
Federal funds sold / Earning assets	7.5%	5.0%	

income to the rate of change in interest expense. In Exhibit 15.7 interest income increased 23.5 percent and interest expense increased 27.4 percent, whereas net interest income increased only 20 percent.

By computing the rates of change for each income or expense account, the magnitude of growth or contraction in the amount of income or expense can be isolated and analyzed by using rate, volume, and mix variances to further explain the reasons behind the change. In the example it may be well to examine why interest income accounts did not keep pace with interest expense accounts. This may require analyzing the percentage distribution of assets and liabilities for adjusting the composition of assets and liabilities.

Variances may be defined by using the prior period (past to present) or current period (present to past) as the base period for analysis. The approach used here utilizes prior-period relationships as the base. Other authors have chosen the current period or a combination of the current and prior periods as the base period to define the variances. Therefore the results of computing variances will differ among analysts, depending on which period is the base period. In defining variances, the important consideration is to apply a consistent approach that is commonly understood and accepted.

Sources of Comparative Data

Comparative data is available through the Federal Deposit Insurance Corporation, district Federal Reserve Banks, the Bank Administration Institute, and professional consulting firms. The FDIC publishes statements of condition and income statements in its *Annual Report.* Bank data are categorized by bank size. Quarterly and annual data for specific banks are available. However, the data are in the form of photocopies of computer printouts and are difficult to use since the data must be referenced to call report formats. The FDIC makes its computer tapes available, and these can be processed and analyzed for creating bank statistics. Certain district Federal Reserve Banks prepare statistics by bank size within the district and by state. These statistics more closely approximate data that model the attributes of the bank's market.

Uses of Comparative Data

Comparative data assist in identifying high-performance banks among a specific bank's competitors. Examination of the data provides insight into successful operations, into how performance was attained, and into how well the bank performs against its competitors. The data are useful in analyzing bank markets, including deposit and loan penetration. Realistic market goals and objectives for internal budgeting may be set, including quantitative targets. Internal budgeting will be discussed more fully in Chapter 17.

SUMMARY

The periodic analysis of operations is important in tracking a bank's performance against its policies and objectives. Comparisons with peer banks relates a bank's performance to that of its peers and indicates potential markets that may be explored. Many elements of analysis are contained in the discussion of the United American Bank failure found in Appendix 15.1. This failure provides insight into the bank policies and procedures that can lead to poor bank performance.

The case problem and questions in Part Five are designed to lead one through a basic analysis of bank operations. Certain data are purposely excluded from the case materials, so that one is forced to examine the limitations of the analysis and to identify the need for additional information either to explain variances in operating data or to arrive at sound conclusions regarding the analytical results.

Questions and Problems

1. What are the key characteristics of high-performance banks?

2. Describe the purpose of interest-margin variance analysis.

3. Describe the construction of the volume, rate, and mix variances.

4. What major balance sheet and income statement factors contribute to impact return on assets and return on equity?

5. Describe how an analysis of net interest margin may be conducted. Relate the process outlined in Exhibit 15.4 to the applicable ratios described in Exhibit 15.5 and interest-margin variance analysis.

6. Describe the relationships that identify a wholesale bank and a retail bank.

7. What key factors are examined in an analysis of loan mix?

8. What relationships or problems may be identified in comparing key income or expenses with gross average earning assets?

9. When are average balances for balance sheet accounts more appropriate than period-end balances in an analysis?

10. Using Exhibit 15.6, construct an interest variance analysis for time deposits.

Suggested Cases

Case 4, Analysis of Bank Performance; Laramie County Bank.
Case 5, Projection of Bank Performance; Laramie County Bank.

References

Ford, W. F., and D. A. Olson. "How 1000 High Performance Banks Weathered the Recent Recession." In *Bank Management: Concepts and Issues*, ed. J. R. Brick, 481–493. Richmond, VA: Robert F. Dame, 1981.

Garcia, F. L. *How to Analyze a Bank Statement*. Boston: Bankers Publishing, 1974, 163–206.

Olson Research Associates. *Bank Performance Report 1983*. Greenbelt, MD: Olson Research Associates, 1983.

U.S. Congress. House. *Federal Supervision and Failure of United American Bank in Knoxville, Tenn., and Affiliated Banks*. Twenty-Third Report by the Committee on Government Operations Together with Dissenting Views. 98th Cong., 1st sess., 1983. H.R. 98–573:7.

Wyoming Bancorporation. *1980 Annual Report*. Cheyenne, WY: Wyoming Bancorporation, 56–57.

APPENDIX 15.1

Failure of United American Bank, Knoxville, Tennessee

In a report to the House of Representatives, the House Committee on Government Operations criticized the FDIC in its handling of the events leading to the failure of United American Bank (UAB) on February 14, 1983. The report stated: "Every FDIC examination report between 1977 and 1982 criticized virtually the identical categories of bank operations, policies and procedures that had been criticized in previous reports: Document exceptions, quality of assets, overdue loans, capital inadequacy, excessive insider lending, insufficient earnings, excessive reliance on large denomination financial instruments, overdrafts, lack of lending guidelines, concentration of credit, weaknesses in the securities portfolio, and violations of various laws and regulations".[3]

The insolvency of UAB is the third largest single bank failure after the failure of Franklin National Bank in 1973. However, in addition to UAB, which was controlled by Jake Butcher and his brother C. H. Butcher, eight other Butcher banks in Tennessee failed and eleven banks in Tennessee and Kentucky in which the Butchers had interests were either sold or merged. Collectively, these banks represent the largest commercial bank failure in U.S. history. In terms of losses to the FDIC insurance fund, UAB alone is the nation's largest bank failure.

The FDIC uses a rating system for all insured banks (Uniform Financial Institutions Rating System). Each bank is classified according to CAMEL classes (C = Capital adequacy, A = Asset quality, M = Management, E = Earnings, and L = Liquidity). The numerical ratings for each factor range from 1—best to 5—worst. Composite ratings of the five factors indicate the overall bank quality as follows:

- 1—Basically sound.
- 2—Fundamentally sound, but weaknesses are correctable in the normal course of business.
- 3—Institution has a combination of financial and operational weaknesses ranging from moderately severe to unsatisfactory. Failure is a remote possibility.

---

[3]U.S. Congress, House, *Federal Supervision and Failure of United American Bank in Knoxville, Tenn., and Affiliated Banks,* Twenty-Third Report by the Committee on Government Operations Together with Dissenting Views, 98th Cong., 1st sess., 1983, H.R. 98–573:7.

379

- 4—Immoderate volume of serious financial weaknesses or combination of other unsatisfactory conditions. Requires close supervision.
- 5—Extremely high immediate or near-term probability of failure.

In the course of regulatory examinations, CAMEL ratings for UAB were established as follows:

- May 8, 1978   2/2/2/3/2:2
- January 15, 1979   3/3/3/3/3:3
- June 9, 1980   2/2/3/4/2:2
- November 13, 1981   3/3/3/3/4:3
- November 30, 1982   5/5/5/5/5:5

A major criticism of the FDIC by the committee was that its supervisory reports failed to indicate the severity of the bank's problems and that these problems were not fully reflected in the CAMEL ratings. Additionally, the FDIC failed to obtain prompt corrective action by management. A synopsis of comments from the supervisory reports over the six-year period are presented in Exhibit 15.8. These comments represent a cross section of problems, each in its own respect contributing to UAB's failure.

The facts outlined in the UAB case strongly support the need for periodic comprehensive analyses of operations. Importantly, management must take corrective action. One can only speculate whether UAB would have survived if the FDIC had removed management or if management had taken appropriate corrective measures.

EXHIBIT 15.8   Criticisms of UAB Quoted from Examination Reports

Date	Loan Status	Insufficient Earnings	Insider Loans	Capital Adequacy
4-18-77	Overdue loans at 7.5 percent of total loans are heavy, and these delinquent debts merit special supervision by management.		There is no objection to director's borrowings as such but such loans should be in responsible proportion to capital funds and total loans.	. . . UAB's adjusted capital is well below both state and national averages.
5-8-78	The most significant factor noted in the analysis of the loan portfolio is the inordinately high volume of loans in delinquent status.	Bank operations have not generated sufficient retained earnings to support . . . growth and net operating income; .33 percent of average total assets for 1977 is well below the .80 percent for banks of this size in the same general geographic area.	. . . inordinately high volume of loans in delinquent status.	Bank operations have not generated sufficient earnings to support this growth.
1-15-79	. . . in the case of several of the loan classifications, weak lending policies have directly contributed to the unsatisfactory status of the loans.	The bank's earning performance compares quite unfavorably to other banks in its peer group composed of similar-sized banks in Tennessee and Arkansas. . . . The crux of the earnings problem is the bank's heavy reliance on large denomination liabilities consisting of CD's greater than $100,000, funds borrowed from other banks, and net borrowings under securities repurchase	Both ratios (insider loans to adjusted equity capital) are quite excessive. . . .	For any bank to earn its way out of a substantial capital deficiency will occur rarely, if ever.

(continued)

EXHIBIT 15.8 *(continued)*

Date	Loan Status	Insufficient Earnings	Insider Loans	Capital Adequacy
		agreements. . . . Another significant earnings depressant is the bank's investment portfolio. The yield . . . is quite low and the maturity distribution is long, so the effects of previous investment policy miscalculations will be felt for many years. . . . It is strongly recommended that the bank's investment policy provide exclusively for short-term investments. . . .		
6-9-80	This ratio (35.6 percent criticized assets to total assets) reflects a favorable trend . . . but little comfort can be derived . . . because of the continuation of the negatively high volume of loss classification and the higher than usual potential for loss within those assets classified Substandard. . . .			The bank has a capital formation ratio of 3.06 percent while the 485 insured commercial banks of over $300 million in assets have a ratio of 8.55 percent. This same ratio for all the 350 state-insured commercial banks is 9.68 percent and the 76 banks within a 53-county Bureau of Economic Analysis area reflect a 10.40 percent ratio. The bank's adjusted total capital . . . remains low.

11-31-81	Loans in overdue status, 6.4 percent of total loans . . . are considered high . . . with 1.7 percent of the portfolio delinquent more than 6 months. . . . The bank's loan valuation reserve appears inadequate in view of the quality and volume of the loan portfolio.	The bank's net operating income equals only 0.51 percent of average total assets for 1980. This ratio may be compared with a 0.94 percent ratio for the 153 banks with assets between $500 million and $1 billion dollars throughout the nation. The bank has an inordinate volume of high-denomination, interest-sensitive deposits and other liabilities. In addition, the bank has invariably paid substantially more for these funds than the peer group used for comparison.	The bank's adjusted equity capital and reserves, 4.7 percent of total adjusted assets, is considered well below the level of adequacy. It is noted that the bank has suffered from a low equity capital continually for many years without sufficient retained earnings to improve the condition. . . . Exacerbating the adequacy problem is the constant lack of income from operations, a significant decline in asset quality. . . .
11-1-82	Adversely classified loans account for an overwhelming majority of total classifications with a staggering 65.48 percent of the portfolio subject to criticism. . . .	The bank's earnings have been historically weak, ranking near the bottom of peer group indicators. There is overwhelming evidence to support the fact that the bank has extended an awesome volume of loans to relatives, friends, and business associates of Chairman of the Board Butcher and his brother, C. H. Butcher, Jr. Many of these loans have resulted in concentrations of credit and most are adversely classified.	The bank is insolvent and in imminent danger of failing unless massive amounts of new capital can be injected immediately.

Source: U.S. Congress, House, *Federal Supervision and Failure of United American Bank in Knoxville, Tenn., and Affiliated Banks,* Twenty-Third Report by the Committee on Government Operations Together with Dissenting Views, 98th Cong., 1st sess., 1983, H.R. 98–573:7.

CHAPTER 16

Managing Interest Margin

In Chapter 5 we discussed the concepts of asset/liability and gap management. Managing interest margin is concerned with implementing asset/liability and gap strategies under varying interest rate conditions. Since deposit deregulation is almost complete, banks and other financial institutions are likely to face strong possibilities of decreased interest margin. If interest margin declines with no compensating decreases in loan losses and expenses or increases in other income, net income will decline.

As we indicated in the previous chapter, a bank can control certain factors—business mix, volume, loan losses, and expenses. In Chapter 9 we outlined systems and procedures for controlling loan losses. In this chapter we shall be concerned with business mix, volume, and interest rates. In the following chapters we shall address cost control, pricing, and business expansion to complete our "walk" through the financial statements.

DYNAMICS OF INTEREST MARGIN

The terms *floating, variable,* and *interest-sensitive* have been applied to rates that vary according to market rates of interest. A *floating rate* is defined for this analysis as a rate that changes frequently, the basis for classification being the rate on the rollover or repricing date regardless of final maturity. *Fixed rates* are defined as rates that remain unchanged for at least one year.

The primary factors that affect a bank's interest-differential earnings are:

- Asset mix, particularly changing relationships between fixed-rate and floating-rate assets.
- Liability mix, particularly changing relationships between fixed-rate sources, such as demand and savings deposits, and capital and floating-rate liabilities, such as purchased funds.
- Level and direction of interest rates.
- Liability strategy and funding costs.

♦ Asset-pricing strategy: fixed rate versus floating rate; spread over or under base rate.[1]

To place each of these factors in proper perspective, let us examine the funding implications of floating- or fixed-rate liabilities as related to asset pricing. Exhibit 16.1 illustrates several alternative financing structures that affect earnings. Item 1 of the exhibit illustrates an asset structure broken into floating- and fixed-rate components and the liabilities and equity broken into floating- and fixed-rate components that fund those assets. A mismatch in the funding exists: floating-rate assets are funded with fixed-rate sources. This mismatch is the portion of the business that is subject to interest rate risk and is referred to as the "gap." The magnitude of the gap and the volatility and range of the interest rate changes create potentially substantial risk and affect interest margin and profits.

The earnings dynamics of floating-rate assets funded with floating-rate liabilities (Item 2) describe the portion of the balance sheet in which floating-rate assets are matched with floating-rate sources. Assuming that these assets and liabilities are perfectly matched by maturity and that the market rates that floating-rate assets follow move simultaneously with the market rates that floating-rate liabilities follow, a change in interest rate levels will produce the same interest margin before and after the market interest rate change.

The earnings dynamics of fixed-rate assets funded with fixed-rate liabilities (Item 3) are unaffected by interest rate changes. The amounts earned and paid remain constant and interest margin and profits remain unchanged.

When floating-rate assets are funded with fixed-rate liabilities or when fixed-rate assets are funded with floating-rate liabilities, interest margin is subjected to risk, depending on the direction, velocity, and duration of the interest rate change. Item 4 identifies a positive gap in which floating-rate assets are funded with fixed-rate liabilities. Item 5 portrays a negative gap in which fixed-rate assets are funded with floating-rate liabilities.

In a rising interest rate environment and a positive gap position, the amount earned increases while the amount paid remains constant and interest margin increases. A negative gap under the same circumstances produces a decrease in interest margin because amounts paid increase while amounts earned remain constant.

With declining rates and a positive gap, amounts earned and interest margin decline while amounts paid remain constant. A negative gap

[1]D. S. Howard, "Dynamics of Interest Differential Earnings," in *Funds Management Under Deregulation*, ed. G. H. Hempel (Washington, DC: American Bankers Association, 1981), 554.

EXHIBIT 16.1   Interest Rate Dynamics

1. Business Subject to Rate Risk—GAP

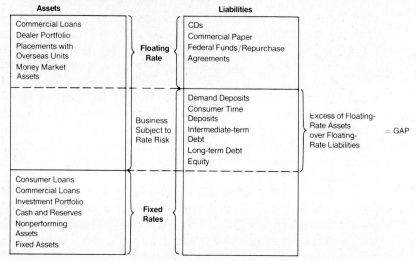

2. Floating-Rate Assets Funded with Floating-Rate Liabilities

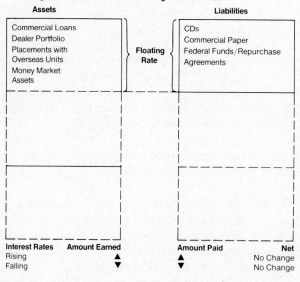

EXHIBIT 16.1 *(continued)*

3. Fixed-Rate Assets Funded with Fixed-Rate Liabilities

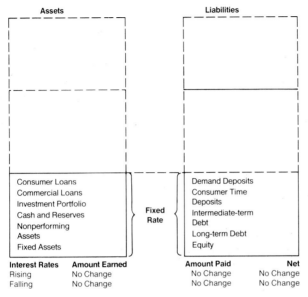

Interest Rates	Amount Earned	Amount Paid	Net
Rising	No Change	No Change	No Change
Falling	No Change	No Change	No Change

4. Floating-Rate Assets Funded with Fixed-Rate Liabilities

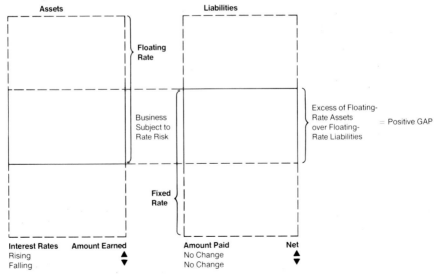

Interest Rates	Amount Earned	Amount Paid	Net
Rising	▲	No Change	▲
Falling	▼	No Change	▼

EXHIBIT 16.1 *(continued)*

5. Fixed-Rate Assets Funded with Floating-Rate Liabilities

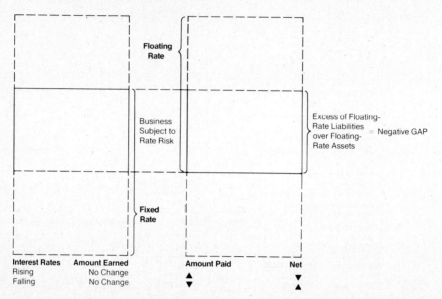

Source: Modified and extracted from D. S. Howard, "Dynamics of Interest Differential Earnings," in *Funds Management Under Deregulation*, ed. G. H. Hempel (Washington, DC: American Bankers Association, 1981), 555–557.

produces decreased amounts paid and increased interest margin because amounts earned remain constant.

INTEREST MARGIN COMPONENTS BY BANK SIZE

Although the dynamics of interest margin affect all banks, changes in market interest rates impact banks of varied sizes differently. Exhibit 16.2 identifies the components of interest margin and the rates paid and earned by three classes of banks—those with average assets of below $100 million, those with assets of $100 million to $1 billion, and 13 money-center banks. For the money-center banks net interest margin is significantly lower than that for the banks of under $100 million in assets. Although interest income of all three classes is approximately the same, a wide variance in interest paid accounts for the variance in net interest margin. In part, these differences relate to the retail versus wholesale characteristics of the three classes of banks and to the reliance upon borrowed funds versus core liabilities.

Many of these characteristics are displayed in Exhibit 16.3. The components of money-center bank assets indicate a larger proportion of

EXHIBIT 16.2   Components of Interest Margin

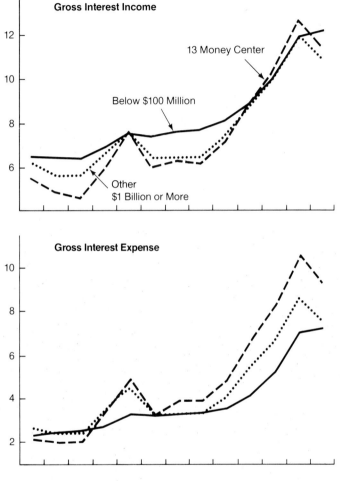

Percentage of
Average Assets

Gross Interest Income

13 Money Center

Below $100 Million

Other
$1 Billion or More

Gross Interest Expense

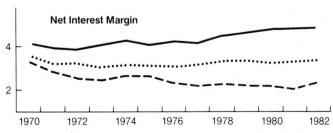

Net Interest Margin

1970   1972   1974   1976   1978   1980   1982

Source: B. N. Opper, "Profitability of Insured Commercial Banks in 1982," *Federal Reserve Bulletin,*
July 1983: 490.

EXHIBIT 16.3 Key Statistics by Bank Size, 1982: Percentage of Average Assets

	All Banks	Banks with Assets of Less than $100 Million	Banks with Assets of $100 Million to $1 Billion	13 Money-Center Banks
Earning Assets	85.1	91.0	89.0	81.4
Loans	56.1	52.5	53.4	61.0
Commercial loans	22.8	12.9	16.9	33.6
Real estate	14.2	18.4	19.4	8.1
Personal	9.2	12.9	13.2	4.3
Other including agriculture, foreign	9.9	8.3	3.9	15.0
Securities	16.6	29.6	25.3	6.3
Federal funds sold	4.4	6.4	5.9	2.4
Interest-bearing deposits	8.1	2.6	4.4	11.7
Financial Claims	88.8	89.5	90.6	87.2
Demand deposits	17.4	19.0	21.3	11.1
Interest-bearing claims	70.9	70.3	69.2	74.8
Money market liabilities	41.0	12.8	46.0	67.1
Interest-bearing core liabilities	29.9	57.5	23.2	7.7
Interest income	11.19	11.71	11.05	11.50
Interest expense	8.02	7.33	7.13	9.40
Net interest margin	3.17	4.38	3.92	2.11
Net interest margin (taxable equivalent)	3.55	4.95	4.47	2.27
Return on Assets	.71	1.08	.85	.50[a]
Return on Equity	12.2	12.7	12.0	12.3[a]

[a] All money-center banks.

Source: B. N. Opper, "Profitability of Insured Commercial Banks in 1982," *Federal Reserve Bulletin,* July 1983: 503–506.

commercial loans to total loans, significantly less investment in securities, and greater investment in interest-bearing deposits placed by these banks in other financial institutions when compared to the other size classes. More significant is the level of money market liabilities where money-center banks have approximately two thirds of their liabilities as compared to small banks that have approximately 60 percent of their liabilities in core liabilities. Small banks generate larger net interest margins and returns on assets, yet their returns on equity are approximately the same as money-center banks.

During the period from 1978 to 1982 market interest rates fluctuated significantly, yet both large and small banks were apparently able to weather these fluctuations without substantial impact on their returns on equity. The following table gives the average returns on equity over this period:

	Return on Equity				
	1978	**1979**	**1980**	**1981**	**1982**
All Banks	12.9%	13.9%	13.7%	13.2%	12.2%
Less than $100 Million	13.2	14.1	14.2	13.6	12.7
$100 Million to $1 Billion	13.2	13.9	13.7	12.8	12.0
Money-Center Banks	12.8	14.0	14.4	13.4	12.3

In two independent studies it was found that the level of interest rates had no material impact on profits and return on equity for 15 money-center banks and 60 banking firms with less than $1 billion in assets.[2] Small banks were found to be no more susceptible to interest rate fluctuations than larger banks. The principal conclusion was that both money-center and smaller banks have matched fixed- and variable-rate assets and liabilities by maturity.

We are concerned here with how banks manage interest margins to maintain profits and return on equity. The techniques that banks engage in include:

+ Gap management—the management of levels of interest-sensitive assets and liabilities on the balance sheet.

---

[2]M. J. Flannery, *The Impact of Market Interest Rates on Small Commercial Banks* (Philadelphia, PA: Federal Reserve Bank of Philadelphia, 1981), 22–24; "Market Interest Rates and Commercial Bank Profitability: An Empirical Investigation," *Journal of Finance*, December 1981: 1098–1099.

- Spread management—the management of yields on earning assets and amounts paid on interest-sensitive liabilities to maintain or increase interest spread.
- Interest margin management—the management of net interest income components related to their balance sheet components.

The tools that banks use to manage these three interrelated financial targets include interest-sensitivity analysis and identification of the characteristics of gap, spread, and margin over varied maturities.

INTEREST-SENSITIVITY ANALYSIS

Sensitivity analysis involves planning from a given point in time and using "what if" questioning to determine what changes will be induced in the income statement if certain characteristics in the balance sheet are changed. For a bank the projection of a plan using "what if" questioning is a beginning point in the development of a profit plan. Interest-sensitivity analysis addresses the changes in rate, volume, and mix of assets and liabilities in defining interest income and expense and in analyzing the effects of change on interest spread and margin. Interest-sensitivity analysis is developed from a gap management framework in which interest-sensitive assets and liabilities are distinguished from fixed-rate assets and liabilities.

Framework of Analysis

The concept of interest-sensitivity analysis is simple, but its application can be very complex. If we model certain changes in the balance sheet over the next one-year period, we can trace the effects that impact income, spread, and net interest margin. Let us assume that the following conditions exist in our balance sheet (see Exhibit 16.4 on page 394, Base columns):

- Earning assets are equal to liabilities (a condition not normally present in a bank's balance sheet).
- One half of assets and liabilities, respectively, are variable rate.
- The bank is perfectly matched; therefore there is no gap.
- Rate spread and net interest margin are equal for variable-rate, fixed-rate, and total components.
- All variable-rate assets and liabilities vary according to the bank's prime rate, which may lag or precede the general market interest rates.

Our model assumes that the base case represents the portfolio of interest-bearing assets and liabilities as of today. If we assume that a repricing decision must be made today regarding certain amounts of assets or liabilities that can be converted from fixed-rate to variable-rate instruments, we will change the gap position. In order to analyze the impact on rate spread and net interest margin for assumed market interest rate increases and changing gap positions, we have constructed six case situations. These cases are compared to our present position and take a stepwise analytical approach.

For illustration we have separated asset changes from liability changes to create different gap positions and to isolate what happens to rate spread and net interest margin when the repricing rate is applied only to the change in gap and then to all other variable-rate assets or liabilities. The analysis of each case situation is displayed in Exhibits 16.4, 16.5, and 16.6. The following chart summarizes the results of the analysis.

Gap Created by	Repricing Rate	Case	Changes in Rate Spread and Net Interest Margin
Converting $100 of fixed-rate assets to variable-rate assets. Liability characteristics remain unchanged. Gap is positive.	Increases	1	Increases due to change in gap at higher marginal rate.
		2	Increases over Case 1 result because all other variable-rate assets are repriced at higher marginal rate.
Converting $100 of fixed-rate liabilities to variable-rate liabilities. Asset characteristics remain unchanged. Gap is negative.	Increases	3	Decreases due to change in gap at higher marginal rate.
		4	Decreases more than Case 3 because all other variable-rate liabilities are repriced at higher marginal rate.
Expanding total assets and liabilities with $100 variable-rate assets and $100 fixed-rate liabilities. Gap is positive.	Increases	5	Increases due to change in gap at higher marginal rate.
		6	Increases due only to change in gap because all repricing rates on variable-rate assets and variable-rate liabilities are assumed to increase concurrently and symmetrically.

EXHIBIT 16.4 Asset Changes

	Base			Case 1			Case 2		
	Var. Rate	Fixed Rate	Total	Var. Rate	Fixed Rate	Total	Var. Rate	Fixed Rate	Total
Earning Assets	500	500	1000	500	500	1000	500	500	1000
Asset Change	0	0	0	100	-100	0	100	-100	0
Total Assets	500	500	1000	600	400	1000	600	400	1000
Liabilities	500	500	1000	500	500	1000	500	500	1000
Liability Change	0	0	0	0	0	0	0	0	0
Total Liabilities	500	500	1000	500	500	1000	500	500	1000
Gap	0	0	0	100	-100	0	100	-100	0
Net Interest Income									
Interest Revenue	60	50	110	73	40	113	78	40	118
Interest Expense	45	35	80	45	35	80	45	35	80
Net Interest Income	15	15	30	28	5	33	33	5	38
Spread									
Yield	.1200	.1000	.1100	.1217	.1000	.1130	.1200	.1000	.1180
Rate	.0900	.0700	.0800	.0900	.0700	.0800	.0900	.0700	.0800
Rate Spread	.0300	.0300	.0300	.0317	.0300	.0330	.0400	.0300	.0380

	Base			Case 1			Case 2		
Interest Margin									
Yield	.1200	.1000	.1100	.1217	.1000	.1130	.1300	.1000	.1180
Cost	.0900	.0700	.0800	.0750	.0875	.0800	.0750	.0875	.0800
Net Interest Margin	.0300	.0300	.0300	.0467	.0125	.0330	.0550	.0125	.0380
Asset Rate	.1200	.1000		.1200	.1000		.1300	.1000	
Liability Rate	.0900	.0700		.0900	.0700		.0900	.0700	
New Asset Rate	0	0		.1300	.1000		.1300	.1000	
New Liability Rate	0	0		0	0		0	0	

Base	Case 1	Case 2
Earning assets = Liabilities. Variable-rate assets = Variable-rate liabilities. Gap = 0.	Create positive gap. Anticipating increase in variable rate, increase rate on reinvested assets. Gap = 100. Rate spread and net interest margin increase from base.	Create positive gap. All assets at variable rates but liability rates held constant. Gap = 100. Rate spread and net interest margin increase over base and Case 1.

EXHIBIT 16.5 Liability Changes

	Base			Case 3			Case 4		
	Var. Rate	Fixed Rate	Total	Var. Rate	Fixed Rate	Total	Var. Rate	Fixed Rate	Total
Earning Assets	500	500	1000	500	500	1000	500	500	1000
Asset Change	0	0	0	0	0	0	0	0	0
Total Assets	500	500	1000	500	500	1000	500	500	1000
Liabilities	500	500	1000	500	500	1000	500	500	1000
Liability Change	0	0	0	100	−100	0	100	−100	0
Total Liabilities	500	500	1000	600	400	1000	600	400	1000
Gap	0	0	0	−100	100	0	−100	100	0
Net Interest Income									
Net Interest Revenue	60	50	110	60	50	110	60	50	110
Interest Expense	45	35	80	55	28	83	60	28	88
Net Interest Income	15	15	30	5	22	27	0	22	22
Spread									
Yield	.1200	.1000	.1100	.1200	.1000	.1100	.1200	.1000	.1100
Rate	.0900	.0700	.0800	.0917	.0700	.0830	.1000	.0700	.0880
Rate Spread	.0300	.0300	.0300	.0283	.0300	.0270	.0200	.0300	.0220

Interest Margin	Base		Case 3			Case 4		
Yield	.1100	.1000	.1200	.1000	.1100	.1200	.1000	.1100
Cost	.0800	.0700	.1100	.0560	.0830	.1200	.0560	.0880
Net Interest Margin	.0300	.0300	.0100	.0440	.0270	0	.0440	.0220
Asset Rate	.1200	.1000	.1200	.1000		.1200	.1000	
Liability Rate	.0900	.0700	.0900	.0700		.1000	.0700	
New Asset Rate	0	0	0	0		0	0	
New Liability Rate	0	0	.1000	.0700		.1000	.0700	

Base	**Case 3**	**Case 4**
Earning assets = Liabilities. Variable-rate assets = Variable-rate liabilities. Gap = 0.	Create negative gap. With increase in variable rate, maturing liabilities renewed at increased rates. Gap = −100. Rate spread and net interest margin decrease from base.	Create negative gap. All liabilities adjusted to variable rate but asset rates held constant. Gap = −100. Rate spread and net interest margin decrease from base and Case 3.

EXHIBIT 16.6 Asset and Liability Changes

	Base			Case 5			Case 6		
	Var. Rate	Fixed Rate	Total	Var. Rate	Fixed Rate	Total	Var. Rate	Fixed Rate	Total
Earning Assets	500	500	1000	500	500	1000	500	500	1000
Asset Change	0	0	0	100	0	100	100	0	100
Total Assets	500	500	1000	600	500	1100	600	500	1100
Liabilities	500	500	1000	500	500	1000	500	500	1000
Liability Change	0	0	0	0	100	100	0	100	100
Total Liabilities	500	500	1000	500	600	1100	500	600	1100
Gap	0	0	0	100	−100	0	100	−100	0
Net Interest Income									
Interest Revenue	60	50	110	73	50	123	78	50	128
Interest Expense	45	35	80	45	42	87	50	42	92
Net Interest Income	15	15	30	28	8	36	28	8	36
Spread									
Yield	.1200	.1000	.1100	.1217	.1000	.1118	.1300	.1000	.1164
Rate	.0900	.0700	.0800	.0900	.0700	.0791	.1000	.0700	.0837
Rate Spread	.0300	.0300	.0300	.0317	.0300	.0327	.0300	.0300	.0327

	Base			Case 5			Case 6		
Interest Margin									
Yield	.1200	.1000	.1100	.1217	.1000	.1118	.1300	.1000	.1164
Cost	.0900	.0700	.0800	.0750	.0840	.0791	.0833	.0840	.0837
Net Interest Margin	.0300	.0300	.0300	.0467	.0160	.0327	.0467	.0160	.0327
Asset Rate	.1200	.1000		.1200	.1000		.1300	.1000	
Liability Rate	.0900	.0700		.0900	.0700		.1000	.0700	
New Asset Rate	0	0		.1300	.1000		.1300	.1000	
New Liability Rate	0	0		.1000	.0700		.1000	.0700	

Base

Earning assets = Liabilities.
Variable-rate assets = Variable-rate liabilities.

Gap = 0.

Case 5

Create positive gap with variable-rate asset increase funded by fixed-rate liability increase.

New assets invested at variable rates higher than base with liabilities obtained at existing fixed-rate level.

Gap = 100.

Rate spread and net interest margin increase over base.

Case 6

Create positive gap.

All assets and liabilities adjusted to new variable-rate levels.

Gap = 100.

Rate spread and net interest margin increase over base but are equal to Case 5.

Factors Impacting Interest-Sensitivity Analysis

Asset and Liability Mix.   The examples above disregarded differences in earning assets such as loans and investments and differences in liabilities such as demand, savings, and time deposits and borrowed funds. These accounts have different characteristics such as rate earned or paid, maturity, response to market conditions, and fixed-rate vs. variable-rate instruments. Through marketing promotions and pricing incentives, for example, a bank may attract certain types of deposits that may impact the gap by changing the mix, fixed versus variable rate, and time period of maturity.

We should also note that asset decisions may be made without regard to funding sources. For example, an increment of variable-rate assets may be funded by a mix of variable- and fixed-rate liabilities or vice versa. This complexity requires that bank management be kept apprised of portfolio changes on a timely basis, so that implications of actual changes in portfolio mix, maturity, variable- or fixed-rate components, and rates may be measured.

Rate Spread.   Movements in variable rates on assets and liabilities do not occur simultaneously. Asset rates may be tied to market rates (prime, for example), whereas liability rates may be tied to other indicators (Treasury bill rates, for example). This disparity in rate and timing impacts the effectiveness of interest-sensitivity analysis. For our purposes it is best to assume that liability rate changes will precede asset rate changes—a conservative approach. Examination of changes in prime rate and changes in other market rates such as the negotiable CD rate supports the assumption that liability rate changes precede asset rate changes.

Maturity.   If we expand our base case example as shown below, we see that the bank may have a zero gap in the aggregate but have positive and negative gaps in certain maturity periods:

	Period 1	Period 2	Period 3	Total
Variable-Rate Assets	100	100	300	500
Variable-Rate Liabilities	200	100	200	500
Gap	−100	0	100	0

When assets and liabilities mature in Period 1, the bank may reposition its liability structure to create a positive gap overall. To do so, the bank should prepare an interest-sensitivity analysis for the proposed changes to Period 1 conditions and their impact on Periods 2, 3, and beyond.

In preparing an interest-sensitivity analysis by maturity, assets and liabilities should be placed in time periods according to their repricing dates rather than their final maturities. Certain assets and liabilities may be considered demand instruments and assumed to be all due in the shortest period. However, these funds may have both short- and long-run characteristics and should be divided among periods based on the bank's history of renegotiation and the base levels of assets and liabilities maintained over several periods. Additionally, an installment repayment should be placed in the period in which the installment is to be received.

Proportions between Variable-Rate Assets and Liabilities. In the base case the amounts of variable-rate assets and liabilities were equal. In Case 2 a $100 positive gap produced a ratio of 1.2 variable-rate assets to 1.0 variable-rate liabilities. An important question is how large a gap (positive or negative) can be managed without submitting the bank to substantial interest margin risk—the risk that any change in market interest rates will have an adverse effect upon the total interest margin.

If the proportion of variable-rate assets compared to total earning assets is relatively small, then the bank could enlarge a positive gap and the ratio of variable-rate assets to variable-rate liabilities without severely impacting total interest margin in a declining rate scenario. If the proportion of variable-rate assets compared to total earning assets is relatively large, greater risk of a material decline in interest margin exists in a declining rate scenario because absolute amounts of interest income from variable-rate assets will outweigh any earnings from fixed-rate assets. In a rising rate scenario the rewards of a large positive gap and higher proportions of variable-rate assets to total assets will be substantial. However, there is substantial risk introduced in managing interest margin.[3]

Matching Alternatives. When we relax the assumptions in the analysis and plan for changes in several assets and liabilities, significant complexity is introduced. A basic problem is identifying how matching should be accomplished. At least two alternatives exist. One is matching on an aggregate basis, and the second is specific identification of the assets and liabilities to be matched. To illustrate the first alternative, consider matching by maturity. Appendix 16.1 is a schedule proposed by the Comptroller of the Currency to be included in the call report. The report is divided into five gap maturity ranges from 0–3 months to 5 years and over. The instructions accompanying the report include the following:

> Assets and liabilities should be recorded in the time intervals according to final maturity date or next date when an adjustment to market rate could occur including contractual amortization. If there exist limitations (caps, floors, etc.) to the repricing, adjustments should be reported on the line for "adjustment for partial

---

[3]For a complete discussion of net interest margin risk, see B. L. Binder, "New Initiatives in Asset/Liability Management," *The Magazine of Bank Administration*, December 1978: 56–64.

repricing." When market rates exceed the adjustable range, the asset or liability should be recorded at its final maturity date. Market rate is defined as the current rate which the bank would quote/accept for a similar instrument.[4]

The purpose of the report is to indicate the ability of a bank to make adjustments in rates during certain maturity periods. The report is a mixture of fixed- and variable-rate components and is designed for computer analysis by the regulatory agency to determine interest margin and spread by time period. For internal management purposes, the report is not in a format that can be easily used. However, it does provide the basic data needed to prepare a detailed gap interest-sensitivity report.

Many large banks are now structuring internal data bases to gather the required information. Essentially, the data required from each subsidiary system are provided by a "runoff" analysis or an aging schedule that identifies assets and liabilities by maturity. Small and medium-sized banks typically do not have data base management tools available to prepare even the simplest analysis. Recognition of this fact has led the FDIC and the Federal Reserve Bank to oppose the reporting of certain information by bank size (exclude banks under $1 billion in assets) and the gathering of certain detailed information.

Specific identification may be an alternative for the smaller bank. This approach attempts to match certain assets with a specific funding source. Our example of interest-sensitivity analysis with minimal assumptions may be the best alternative for planning until the proper data base management tools are in place. A compromise to specific identification is the management of assets individually and the use of a pooled-funds approach for liabilities. Pooled funds include either all sources of funds priced at a weighted average rate or, more appropriately, the fund balances priced at a weighted average of current market rates. Whatever approach is taken, the bank must take steps to set the stage for more frequent analysis of gap and its earning position in time periods of less than one year.

Runoff analysis is important in identifying the gap currently and in short future periods. The gap in certain of the short periods may be positive, balanced, or negative. Different strategies will be required to bring the composite gap to the expected gap for the budget year. The various period gaps will also illustrate past decisions and their layering effects on asset and liability volumes by fixed- and variable-rate categories that are affecting current and near-term interest margin. A possible gap report format is presented in Exhibit 16.7. Each period's gap represents a different degree of risk and a different exposure to interest rate changes.

---

[4]Comptroller of the Currency, *The Call Report: Schedule J,* June 30, 1983.

EXHIBIT 16.7 Funds Gap, Spread, and Margin Summary, Actual as of _____

	Due in 0–90 Days	Due in 91–180 Days	Due in 181–270 Days	Due in 271–365 Days	Due in Over 1 Year	Total
Variable Rate						
Securities	$	$	$	$	$	$
Short-term investments						
Net loans	___	___	___	___	___	___
Total						
Time deposits						
Borrowed funds	___	___	___	___	___	___
Total						
Funds gap	$	$	$	$	$	$
Fixed and Nonrate						
Cash and due from banks	$	$	$	$	$	$
Securities						
Net loans						
Other assets	___					___
Total						
Demand deposits						
Time deposits						
Borrowed funds						
Other liabilities						
Capital	___					___
Total						
Total earning assets	___					___
Variable-rate assets/earning assets						
Variable-rate funds/earning assets						
Sensitivity ratio (RSA/RSL)	___					___
Spread						
Margin						

Note: For management purposes, each of the above assets and liabilities should be broken down into finer categories for decisions regarding policy direction in the management of gap, spread, and margin.

GAP STRATEGIES

The keys to managing gap lie in three basic strategies. First, assets should be acquired in resalable lots. For example, securities should be purchased in blocks with different maturities and rates to avoid over-concentration and future liquidation problems. This strategy ensures that one poor decision will not severely impact all operations and ensures an orderly process in new purchases and sales of assets. Second, a plan of action should be designed for specific assets and liabilities during specific phases of the interest rate cycle. The plan should indicate specific actions to be taken when rates meet certain levels. The final strategy is to avoid interpreting each change in interest rates as a new cycle. Using a controlled approach in taking action, although conservative, will assure the true direction of the cycle rather than trading the minor fluctuations, which are purely speculative in nature.[5]

Gap management provides three options for matching rate-sensitive assets to rate-sensitive liabilities. The first is a balanced approach in which rate-sensitive assets (RSA) equal rate-sensitive liabilities (RSL), expressed in the ratio RSA/RSL = 1. The second option is to have an asset-sensitive ratio that will exceed 1 (RSA/RSL > 1). This simply means that the rate-sensitive assets are being supported by fixed-rate liabilities. The third option is the ratio RSA/RSL < 1, which indicates that rate-sensitive liabilities exceed rate-sensitive assets. A ratio in excess of 1 is the preferable unmatched position in a situation where interest rates are rising and the amount of assets that are rate sensitive produce a larger gap and increase interest margin. The RSA/RSL < 1 option may be preferable in situations where interest rates are declining, the majority of assets employed are fixed rate, and these assets are supported by rate-sensitive liabilities. The essence of this option is that rates will decline on liabilities while a floor has been set on the decline in income from interest-earning assets.

The strategies that may be employed in the various phases of the interest rate cycle are illustrated in Exhibit 16.8. The low-rate phase is a period of evaluation in anticipation of the rising-rate phase. Actions should be taken to ensure loan quality by purging the existing credit lines of borrowers whose relationships are marginal—for example, the customer who does not provide deposits or the company that is in a nongrowth industry. Fixed-rate liabilities, including long-term debt, should be obtained and their maturities lengthened. Loan rates should become variable so that they will follow interest rate increases. Theoretically, if these actions are taken during the low-rate phase, the gap

---

[5]The prediction of absolute interest rate levels is difficult and imprecise. In managing gap, anticipation of the direction of interest rate changes is more important than targeting the level of rates. Depending on the theory of the yield curve that one holds, the direction of rates may be derived by examining the appropriate yield curves and planning portfolio adjustments accordingly.

EXHIBIT 16.8   Rate Cycle Phases

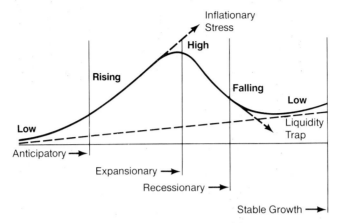

Asset/Liability Management Action Guidelines

Low-rate phase
Purge credit lines
Lengthen funds maturities
Shorten investment maturities
Raise long-term debt
Restrict fixed-rate loans
Update loan pricing policy
Sell investments
Plan diversification

High-rate phase
Replenish credit lines
Shorten funds maturities
Lengthen investment maturities
Upgrade investment quality
Expand fixed-rate loans
Plan investment sales
Acquire investments
Execute diversification

Transitional—Rising
Gradually: increasing emphasis on
   high side
Shorten funds maturities
Lengthen investment maturities
Expand fixed-rate loans
Acquire investments
Execute acquisitions

Transitional—Falling
Gradually: increasing emphasis on
   low side
Lengthen funds maturities
Shorten investment maturities
Restrict fixed-rate loans
Sell investments
Plan acquisitions

Source: J. T. Clifford, "A Perspective on Asset-Liability Management: Part II," in *Bank Management, Concepts and Issues*, ed. J. R. Brick, (Reston, Va.: Reston Publishing Co., 1980), 364. Reprinted with permission of Reston Publishing Co., a Prentice-Hall, company 11480 Sunset Hills Road, Reston, VA 22090.

will widen during the rising-rate phase and be maximized at the top of the cycle.

During the rising-rate phase and a period of expansion of assets and liabilities, assets will be added at higher rates and will tend toward fixed rates in anticipation that the highest rate will soon be reached. Funds will be acquired at higher rates but will have shorter maturities. These activities set the stage for the falling-rate phase in which asset-earning rates are set at different floors and actual declining rates may drop below the fixed-rate levels. Correspondingly, liabilities in the declining phase will follow actual rates as liabilities mature and are replaced at the lower market rates and longer maturities.

At the top of the high-rate phase, loans should be expanded with loan rates at market. Investment securities that mature may be replaced at equal or higher rates with an improvement in investment grade. During the declining phase a positive gap will begin to decrease due to the timing of changes in asset-earning rates. It is also likely that asset-repricing decisions will occur more frequently than liability-repricing decisions because many liability instruments have specific maturities related to specific rates paid and these maturities tend to be longer than the maturities of funded assets.

IMPROVING INTEREST MARGIN

In the future improving interest margin is likely to be one of banking's highest priorities. What banks are able to control in improving margins, though limited, is important. Rates are not controllable because market rates are cyclical and competition must be met. Mix relationships can be controlled more directly, particularly in a period of expansion. However, in a no-growth environment the ability to reinvest maturing assets in a different mix may be limited.

The policies established for loan and investment volumes and pricing can influence mix. Many banks are going through a restructuring period and are planning to attract specific market segments such as wholesale operations for middle market companies. These plans take time to implement. Simultaneously banks are faced with market decisions regarding rates. The coordination of an induced change in mix and the maintainance and improvement of interest margin is extremely complex. Therefore the employment of a working asset/liability management group takes on added importance in achieving this goal.

Aggressiveness is required in leading the market in the face of competition in converting traditional fixed-rate assets such as mortgage, installment, and charge card loans to variable rates. Customer resistance may set in; however, diminished demand for certain interest-bearing products may provide increased incentive for banks to seek out specific markets. Such markets would provide the banks with the "right" mix of products and customers and the opportunity to be rewarded commensurately.

If interest margin can only be maintained, then risk control of nonperforming loans and control of operating expenses take on greater importance. If interest margin diminishes, the bank must look to other alternatives, possibly outside the traditional banking environment. One such alternative employed by banks is the use of financial futures to minimize the market interest fluctuations that impact interest margin.

HEDGING WITH INTEREST RATE FUTURES

The futures market is a mechanism that transfers risk. In granting a commercial loan, a bank takes on a credit risk—the risk that the customer will not repay. In today's interest rate environment, the bank probably will set a floating rate on the loan. If the customer resists the idea of unlimited increases in rate, he may request a cap on the loan. The bank in turn may set a floor on rate decreases. Thus each party has transferred some interest rate risk to the other party. The bank has an additional problem if the source of funds has no upper rate limit. How does the bank compensate for the mismatch between the asset and liability? The answer lies in hedging on the transfer of risk in the event that the loan is capped and market interest rates continue past the cap.

Hedging Concepts

Several concepts or definitions are required to understand hedging. The cash market consists of the normal transactions executed by a bank such as buying or selling securities for its portfolio. The futures market is a formal market in which contracts for future delivery of a physical commodity or financial instrument are negotiated through brokers.

The Chicago Board of Trade, a central commodity exchange, described hedging and futures markets as follows:

> A unique feature of futures markets is that the physical commodity need not change hands in a futures transaction. A futures contract to sell can be settled by a 'buy' transaction as well as by delivering the commodity against the contract.
>
> This enables users of financial markets to protect their cash positions by hedging. In commodity marketing, hedging is the act

of taking equal and opposite positions in the cash and futures markets, with the hope that the net result will prevent a loss due to price fluctuations.[6]

Additional definitions of hedges are:

Selling Hedge: The objective of the selling hedge is to protect value of existing inventory and to earn a storage return if possible. In the selling hedge the first transaction in the futures market is selling. The hedger owns or purchases the actual (cash) commodity, and he subsequently or simultaneously sells an equivalent quantity of the commodity on the futures market so that an adverse price move will be approximately offset. Another term which is equivalent to selling hedge is short hedge.

Buying Hedge: The buying hedge involves the purchase of futures as a hedge to protect against a possible price increase of the actual commodity prior to its purchase. In the buying hedge, the first transaction in the futures market is a purchase rather than a sale. Another term which is equivalent to buying hedge is long hedge.[7]

In hedging bank transactions it is important to note that futures transactions are quoted in terms of price. Therefore if interest rates increase, prices decline. If the bank expects to enter into a transaction in the future and if the current rate is below the future expected interest rate, it will execute a short hedge. If rates actually increase, the price of the futures contract will decline. Theoretically, if the cash transaction is matched perfectly with the futures transaction, the upward interest rate movement in the cash transaction will be exactly mirrored in the futures market by a price decline.

When the short hedge is executed, the bank's trading account with the broker is credited with the sale proceeds (the option price times the quantity of contracts). When the hedge is closed, the bank buys an equal amount of contracts at the option price, which is less than the amount credited to the bank's trading account (assuming a rate increase). The net difference between the initial amount received and the amount subsequently paid is the profit on the futures transaction. Theoretically the profit on the futures transaction should equal the amount of interest lost in the cash transaction. The hedge is successful and the bank has avoided future interest rate risk.

---

[6]*Introduction to Hedging* (Chicago: Chicago Board of Trade, 1978), 1.
[7]Ibid., 3–24.

Regulatory Status of Using Interest Rate Futures

A bank cannot speculate in futures. Under the National Banking Act futures do not involve the purchase of "investment securities." The Comptroller of the Currency has set forth certain allowable hedging transactions:

1. For *investment portfolio* or *nondealer operations* in fixed-rate assets, banks should evaluate the interest rate risk exposure resulting from their overall investment activities to insure that the positions they take in futures, forwards and standby contract markets will *reduce* their risk exposure. Short positions in futures and forward contracts should reasonably relate to existing or anticipated cash positions, and should be used to enhance liquidity of the portfolio. Rather than using short hedges against portfolio holdings for purposes of income generation, we would expect, where practicable, that contract gains would be used to offset losses resulting from the sale of portfolio securities as asset yields are upgraded. Long positions in futures and forwards should reasonably reflect the bank's investment strategy and ability to fulfill its commitment.

2. *Asset-liability management* involves the matching of fixed-rate and interest-sensitive assets and liabilities in order to maintain liquidity and profitability. Futures and forward contracts may be used as a general hedge against the interest rate exposure associated with undesired mismatches in interest-sensitive assets and liabilities. Long positions in contracts could be used as a hedge against funding interest-sensitive assets with fixed-rate sources of funds; short positions in contracts could be used as a hedge against funding fixed-rate assets with interest-sensitive liabilities.

3. *Dealer-bank trading activities* that employ futures, forwards and standby contracts should be in accordance with safe and sound banking practices reasonably related to the bank's legally permitted trading activities.[8]

To participate in futures transactions, a bank must receive prior regulatory approval. For national banks proposals to participate in the market must include the following information:

1. The background and experience of all persons authorized to buy and sell futures contracts (traders).

---

[8]R. C. Tower and S. W. Ryan, "Futures Trading by National Banks," in *Interest Rate Futures: Concepts and Issues*, ed. G. D. Gay and R. W. Kolb (Richmond, VA: Robert F. Dame, 1982), 430–431.

2. The trading limits to be imposed on traders.
3. The conditions, if any, which permit deviations from those limits.
4. The bank personnel responsible for authorizing such deviations.
5. The procedures developed to prevent unauthorized trading.
6. The scope and frequency of internal audit and control procedures.
7. Copies of forms, in blank, which inform management of the daily futures contracts activity.
8. Copies of internal recordkeeping forms, in blank, which reflect the bank's daily futures contracts activity with regard to a) the maturity of each outstanding futures contract and the type and value of the corresponding cash transactions; b) the maturity date of each futures contract; c) the current market price and value of each futures contract; d) the outstanding gross futures position; e) the open position; f) the amount of money held in margin accounts; g) any maturity gaps between the maturity date of the futures contract and the completion dates of the corresponding cash transaction; h) the profit or loss for each corresponding cash and futures transaction; i) the aggregate profit or loss for all relevant cash and futures transactions; and j) the type and amount of each expected cash transaction that did not materialize.[9]

Banks that want to use hedging as a vehicle for protection against interest rate fluctuation may create hedging departments or seek outside professional consultants. In either circumstance the bank must seek prior approval from the appropriate regulatory authority.

The Comptroller has issued certain guidelines for accounting for hedged transactions. Currently the Financial Accounting Standards Board (FASB) is reviewing generally accepted accounting principles for hedged transactions for financial institutions. When the final principles are approved, the accounting for gains and losses may be adopted as the regulatory reporting practice also. The accounting aspects are beyond the scope of this book, but it is important that a bank's management consider them before undertaking hedging transactions.

Hedging Spreads

Hedging may be applied at the transactional level (the matching of individual assets and liabilities) or to a short-term gap. It should be noted that the mix of assets and liabilities must be considered in applying

---

[9]M. F. Polanis and D. C. Fisher, "Banking on Interest Rate Futures," in *Funds Management Under Deregulation*, ed. G. H. Hempel (Washington, DC: American Bankers Association, 1981), 645.

hedging. The reason for this is that certain assets and liabilities correlate differently to different interest rate futures contracts. According to a study made of comparative rates, certain money market rates correlate well with other money market instruments. For example, domestic CDs match very closely with commercial paper and Eurodollar CDs and less so with the prime rate. Prime correlates better with the Eurodollar CD market.[10] An important consideration in hedging is the choice of a financial future that closely follows the type of asset or liability to be hedged. Exhibit 16.9 illustrates these correlations.

Futures contracts may be written in GNMA certificates, Treasury bonds, Treasury bills, bank CDs, and commercial paper. The amounts of a contract vary; however, the underlying future contract is standardized for the term of the instrument.

Exhibit 16.10 presents an example in which $1000 of variable-rate funds requires rollover from 0–90 days to future periods. It is assumed that $500 of assets matched with $500 of liabilities will roll over and will continue to be matched. Therefore the net exposed position is $1000. If the bank intends to maintain the current spread, it must roll over the $1000 at the current fund rate regardless of the market rates at the rollover date. However, since the bank must be competitive, it will pay the market rate at the rollover date. If the market rate at rollover is higher than the current rate, the bank's spread will decrease. To protect itself against higher market interest rates at the rollover date, the bank can initiate a futures contract.

Exhibit 16.9   Correlation Matrix: January 1977 to July 1981

	(0)	(1)	(2)	(3)	(4)	(5)	(6)	(7)
(0) Domestic CDs	1.000							
(1) Bankers' Acceptances	0.997	1.000						
(2) Commercial Paper	0.999	0.998	1.000					
(3) Eurodollar CDs	0.999	0.997	0.998	1.000				
(4) Treasury Bills	0.994	0.989	0.993	0.991	1.000			
(5) Prime Rate	0.966	0.973	0.966	0.970	0.962	1.000		
(6) Overnight Repo	0.977	0.979	0.978	0.973	0.975	0.969	1.000	
(7) Treasury Bill Futures Yield	0.982	0.975	0.981	0.981	0.989	0.935	0.947	1.000

Source: R. Shulman, "The New CD Futures—What They Can Do," *Bankers Monthly*, Oct. 15, 1981: 16.

[10]R. Shulman, "The New CD Futures—What They Can Do," *Bankers Monthly*, Oct. 15, 1981: 13–18.

EXHIBIT 16.10   Maturity Schedule

| | Interest Sensitive | | | | | |
	0–90 Days	91–180 Days	181–270 Days	271–365 Days	Non-sensitive	Total
Assets	$ 500	$600	$1000	$1200	$ 200	$3500
Liabilities	1500				2000	3500
Gap	($1000)	$600	$1000	$1200	($1800)	$ 0

Situation: Bank has $500 of interest-sensitive assets financed with $1500 of interest-sensitive liabilities. Assuming $500 of assets and liabilities will rollover to the next 90 day period, $1000 of liabilities must be refinanced. In the second rollover period (91–180 days) after refinancing, $600 of assets can be matched with $600 of the $1000 excess sensitive liabilities, with the remaining $400 becoming matched in the third rollover period (181–270 days). The $1000 and $400 subject to refinancing create interest rate exposure in each respective period.

Hedging: Sell $1000 of 90-day T-bill futures with delivery in the 91–180 day period. Sell $400 of 90-day T-bill futures with delivery in the 181–270-day period.

Time	Cash Market	Futures Market
Loan origination and flotation of first CD	Anticipated CD costs: 10% (10%)($1000) = $100	Sell $1000 T-bill contract (1 − 0.10)($1000) = $900
Rollover of CD	Actual CD cost: 11% (11%)($1000) = $110 Loss = $110 − $100 = $10	Buy $1000 T-bill contract (1 − 0.11)($1000) = $890 Gain = $900 − $890 = $10
	Net result = 0	

Source: Extrapolated from Robert W. McLeod and George M. McCabe, "Hedging for Better Spread Management," in *Interest Rate Futures: Concepts and Issues,* eds. G. D. Gay and R. W. Kolb (Richmond, VA: Robert F. Dame, 1982).

If we examine the bank's schedule of interest-sensitive assets and liabilities and assume that maturing assets and liabilities will be rolled over to the next 90-day period, the following positions will result:

| | First Rollover | Pro Forma Maturity Schedule after Rollover | | |
	0–90 Days	91–180 Days	181–270 Days	271–365 Days
Assets	$ 500	$ 600	$1000	$1200
Liabilities	1500			
Gap	($1000)	$ 600	$1000	$1200
	Second Rollover			
	0–90 Days	91–180 Days	181–270 Days	271–365 Days
Assets	$1100	$1000	$1200	$0
Liabilities	1500			
Gap	($ 400)	$1000	$1200	$0
	Third Rollover			
	0–90 Days	91–180 Days	181–270 Days	271–365 Days
Assets	$2100	$1200	$0	$0
Liabilities	1500			
Gap	$ 600	$1200	$0	$0

The first rollover has $1000 and the second rollover has $400 in liabilities subject to interest rate risk. At the third rollover, the bank has $600 in assets subject to interest rate risk. In the absence of any hedging, the bank's spread will be subject to variability if interest rates change.

The bank may use futures contracts to eliminate interest rate risk exposure. To hedge the liability-sensitive elements the bank therefore sells $1000 of 90-day T-bill futures with delivery in the 91–180-day period to cover the first rollover and $400 of 90-day T-bill futures with delivery in the 181–270-day period to cover the second rollover. Any loss experienced in the rollover is offset by a gain in the futures market, assuming that the rates for repricing the funds correspond directly to the T-bill rates.

Hedging may find more prominence in asset/liability management. However, hedging remains an activity requiring the expertise of experienced professionals. A bank must be able to produce runoff schedules to assist the hedging activity. Without this information the bank is limited to hedging individual transactions.

SUMMARY

The management of interest margin and the tools for planning portfolio changes are an evolving art. Asset/liability, gap, and spread management provide important concepts in managing interest margin. The realities and dynamics of banking pose significant problems and opportunities in implementing these concepts. New techniques such as hedging to minimize risk are becoming important in day-to-day bank management. As bankers gain more experience with the available tools and techniques and as new techniques are developed, interest margin may become truly manageable in an interest-sensitive world.

Questions and Problems

1. What is the purpose of an asset/liability committee?

2. List the primary factors that affect interest-differential earnings or interest margin.

3. Discuss the earnings dynamics of alternative asset/liability structures under a rising-rate scenario.

4. Discuss the earnings dynamics of alternative asset/liability structures under a declining-rate scenario.

5. Describe three alternative gap strategies and the implications of each strategy in (a) a rising-rate scenario and (b) a declining-rate scenario.

6. Briefly describe how futures may be used to hedge a transaction in which a fixed-rate asset is funded by floating-rate liabilities and market interest rates are expected to rise.

Suggested Case

Case 6, Interest Margin Planning, Eighth National Bank of Denver.

References

Arak, M., and C. T. McGurdy. "Interest Rate Futures." In *Funds Management Under Deregulation*, ed. G. H. Hempel, 605–629. Washington, DC: American Bankers Association, 1981.

Bacon, P. W., and R. E. Williams. "Interest Rate Futures: New Tool for the Financial Manager." In *Interest Rate Futures: Concepts and Issues*, ed. G. D. Gay and R. W. Kolb, 241–252. Richmond, VA: Robert F. Dame, 1982.

Binder, B. L. "Asset/Liability Management, Parts I and II." *The Magazine of Bank Administration*, December 1980: 31–35, and November 1981: 42–48.

Binder, B. L. "New Initiatives in Asset/Liability Management." *The Magazine of Bank Administration*, December 1978: 56–64.

Clifford, J. T. "A Perspective on Asset-Liability Management, Parts I and II." In *Funds Management Under Deregulation*, ed. G. H. Hempel, 666–682. Washington, DC: American Bankers Association, 1981.

Comptroller of the Currency. *The Call Report: Schedule J*, June 30, 1983.

Flannery, M. J. *The Impact of Market Interest Rates on Small Commercial Banks.* Philadelphia, PA: Federal Reserve Bank of Philadelphia, 1981, 22–24.

Flannery, M. J. "Market Interest Rates and Commercial Bank Profitability: An Empirical Investigation." *Journal of Finance*, December 1981: 1098–1099.

Howard, D. S. "Dynamics of Interest Differential Earnings." In *Funds Management Under Deregulation*, ed. G. H. Hempel, 554–561. Washington, DC: American Bankers Association, 1981.

Introduction to Hedging. Chicago: Chicago Board of Trade, 1978, 1.

Jacquette, F. L. "Bank Balance Sheet Planning for the 1980's." In *Funds Management Under Deregulation*, ed. G. H. Hempel, 724–728. Washington, DC: American Bankers Association, 1981.

McLeod, R. W., and G. M. McCabe. "Hedging for Better Spread Management." In *Interest Rate Futures: Concepts and Issues*, ed. G. D. Gay and R. W. Kolb, 255–263. Richmond, VA: Robert F. Dame, 1982.

Olson, R. L., D. G. Simonson, S. R. Reber, and G. H. Hempel. "Management of Bank Interest Margins in the 1980's, Parts I, II, III, and IV." In *Funds Management Under Deregulation*, ed. G. H. Hempel, 562–599. Washington, DC: American Bankers Association, 1981.

Picon, G. "Managing Interest Rate Risk with Interest Rate Futures." *Bankers Magazine*, May-June 1981: 76–81.

Polanis, M. F., and D. C. Fisher. "Banking on Interest Rate Futures." In *Funds Management Under Deregulation*, ed. G. H. Hempel, 643–651. Washington, DC: American Bankers Association, 1981.

Opper, B. N. "Profitability of Insured Commercial Banks." *Federal Reserve Bulletin*, September 1981: 657–669; "Profitability of Insured Commercial Banks." *Federal Reserve Bulletin*, August 1982: 453–465; "Profitability of Insured Commercial Banks in 1982." *Federal Reserve Bulletin*, July 1983:489–507.

Schweser, C., J. Cole, and L. D'Antonio. "Hedging Opportunities in Bank Risk Management Programs." In *Funds Management Under Deregulation*, ed. G. H. Hempel, 630–642. Washington, DC: American Bankers Association, 1981.

Shulman, R. "The New CD Futures—What They Can Do." *Bankers Monthly*, Oct. 15, 1981: 13–18.

Tower, R. C., and S. W. Ryan. "Futures Trading by National Banks." In *Interest Rate Futures: Concepts and Issues*, ed. G. D. Gay and R. W. Kolb, 430–431. Richmond, VA: Robert F. Dame, 1982.

APPENDIX 16.1

Schedule J
(Foreign and Domestic)

INTEREST RATE SENSITIVITY REPORT (FOR ALL BANKS, SIZE CUTOFF YET TO BE DETERMINED)[a]

	0–3 Mos.	Rate	3–6 Mos.	Rate	6 Mos.–1 Yr.	Rate	1–5 Yrs.	Rate	Over 5 Yrs.	Rate
1. Interest-bearing component of cash and due from depository institutions	XXX	XX	XXX	XX	XXX	XX	XXX	XX	XXX	XX
2. Securities purchased under agreement to resell (over 1-day maturity to under 1-year maturity)	XXX	XX	XXX	XX	XXX	XX	N/A	N/A	N/A	N/A
3. Securities										
a. U.S. Treasury securities and U.S. government agency and corporation obligations	XXX	XX	XXX	XX	XXX	XX	XXX	XX	XXX	XX
Adjustments for full repricing	XXX	XX	XXX	XX	XXX	XX	XXX	XX	XXX	XX
Adjustments for partial repricing	XXX	XX	XXX	XX	XXX	XX	XXX	XX	XXX	XX
All other adjustments[b]	XXX	XX	XXX	XX	XXX	XX	XXX	XX	XXX	XX
b. Securities issued by states and political subdivisions of the U.S.	XXX	XX	XXX	XX	XXX	XX	XXX	XX	XXX	XX
Adjustments for full repricing	XXX	XX	XXX	XX	XXX	XX	XXX	XX	XXX	XX
Adjustments for partial repricing	XXX	XX	XXX	XX	XXX	XX	XXX	XX	XXX	XX
All other adjustments[b]	XXX	XX	XXX	XX	XXX	XX	XXX	XX	XXX	XX
c. All other debt securities	XXX	XX	XXX	XX	XXX	XX	XXX	XX	XXX	XX

Appendix 16.1 (continued)

	0–3 Mos.	Rate	3–6 Mos.	Rate	6 Mos.–1 Yr.	Rate	1–5 Yrs.	Rate	Over 5 Yrs.	Rate
Adjustments for full repricing	XXX	XX	XXX	XX	XXX	XX	XXX	XX	XXX	XX
Adjustments for partial repricing	XXX	XX	XXX	XX	XXX	XX	XXX	XX	XXX	XX
All other adjustments[b]	XXX	XX	XXX	XX	XXX	XX	XXX	XX	XXX	XX
4. Loans & leases										
a. Real estate										
Adjustments for full repricing	XXX	XX	XXX	XX	XXX	XX	XXX	XX	XXX	XX
Adjustments for partial repricing	XXX	XX	XXX	XX	XXX	XX	XXX	XX	XXX	XX
All other adjustments[b]	XXX	XX	XXX	XX	XXX	XX	XXX	XX	XXX	XX
b. To individuals for personal, household, and other family obligations										
Adjustments for full repricing	XXX	XX	XXX	XX	XXX	XX	XXX	XX	XXX	XX
Adjustments for partial repricing	XXX	XX	XXX	XX	XXX	XX	XXX	XX	XXX	XX
All other adjustments[b]	XXX	XX	XXX	XX	XXX	XX	XXX	XX	XXX	XX
c. All other loans and leases										
Adjustments for full repricing	XXX	XX	XXX	XX	XXX	XX	XXX	XX	XXX	XX
Adjustments for partial repricing	XXX	XX	XXX	XX	XXX	XX	XXX	XX	XXX	XX
All other adjustments[b]	XXX	XX	XXX	XX	XXX	XX	XXX	XX	XXX	XX

	0–1 Yr.	1–2 Yrs.	2–3 Yrs.	3–4 Yrs.	4–5 Yrs.	Over 5 Yrs.
5. Interest-bearing time deposits						
a. Time certificates of deposit of $100,000 or more	XXX	XXX	XXX	XXX	XX	XX
b. All other time deposits	XXX	XXX	XXX	XXX	XX	XX
c. Deposits in foreign offices	XXX	XXX	XXX	XXX	XX	XX
6. Securities sold under agreements to repurchase (over 1-day maturity to under 1-year maturity)	XXX	XXX	XXX	N/A	N/A	N/A
7. Other borrowed money	XXX	XXX	XXX	XXX	XX	XX
Adjustments for full repricing	XXX	XXX	XXX	XXX	XX	XX
Adjustments for partial repricing	XXX	XXX	XXX	XXX	XX	XX
All other adjustments[b]	XXX	XXX	XXX	XXX	XX	XX
8. Subordinated notes & debentures and limited-life preferred stock	XXX	XX	XXX	XX	XXX	XX

Assets and liabilities should be recorded in the time intervals according to final maturity date or next date when an adjustment to market rate could occur, including contractual amortization. If there exist limitations (caps, floors, etc.) to the repricing, adjustments should be reported on the line for "adjustments for partial repricing." When market rates exceed the adjustable range, the asset or liability should be recorded at its final maturity date. Market rate is defined as the current rate that the bank would quote/accept for a similar instrument.

[a]FRB objects to collection of rates and adjustment lines; FDIC objects to collecting rates from banks with assets of under $1 billion.

[b]Adjustments for expected prepayments, sales, etc.

Source: Comptroller of the Currency, *The Call Report: Schedule J*, June 30, 1983.

CHAPTER 17

The Costs and Pricing of Bank Services: Part 1

Until the mid-1960s banks ignored the costs of their operations. Pricing decisions were based upon what the competition was doing. As inflation began to accelerate increases in operating costs, banks could no longer ignore expense control.

Although technology has played an important role in increasing costs, it has also contributed to efficiency in processing the vast amount of daily transactions. The computer has changed banks' operating structures in regard to costs and personnel expertise. Personnel are no longer in cheap supply. The substitution of machines such as automated teller machines (ATMs) for tellers is one example of the change in service delivery aimed at counteracting increases in personnel numbers and costs. Banks have adopted ways of reducing customer contacts with bank personnel and will continue to examine alternatives for operations to keep costs under control.

Interestingly, few banks actually engage in significant cost accounting efforts. Although many banks with under $100 million in assets participate in the Federal Reserve Bank Functional Cost Analysis, cost accounting is principally a large-bank activity. Functional cost accounting is an aggregate costing activity that relates major funds-using functions with funds-providing functions. At a disaggregative or micro level a customer relationship can be examined through customer profitability analyses. Finally, pricing and portfolio allocation decisions can be made with greater knowledge of the underlying cost structure. In this chapter we shall examine bank-developed cost systems, responsibility accounting, and budgeting. In Chapter 18, "The Costs and Pricing of Bank Services: Part 2," we shall discuss customer profitability analysis and pricing decisions.

COST ACCOUNTING

Cost accounting assists management in improving bank profitability and thus in achieving the goals of maximum return on invested capital for bank shareholders and efficient and expanding service for bank customers. Cost accounting is not independent of the bank's financial statement accounting but is an extension of that accounting.

The importance and role of cost accounting can be illustrated by examining a conventional bank income statement and describing the information that cannot be obtained directly from it. The income statement shows bank expenses by category but does not show salary totals for specific departments. Profitability as a whole is shown but the profitability of funds-using functions such as loans, funds-providing functions such as deposits, and non-funds functions such as safe deposit are not shown. Unit costs of services such as check cashing and collection, which may assist in setting service charge schedules, cannot be found.

The need for cost data has increased as a result of the following recent developments:

1. Decreasing "spreads" between the cost of obtaining funds and the return on use of funds.
2. Competition for demand deposits requiring proper pricing of the services.
3. The proliferation of non-fund activities such as computer services.
4. The development of EFTS and the trend toward interest-bearing demand accounts such as NOW accounts.[1]

The benefits of cost accounting are:

1. To assign specific cost center goals and objectives in the budgetary process and to quantify those goals and objectives for performance evaluation.
2. To provide sufficient information to improve services, to price services, and to assist in determining cost based marketing objectives.
3. To enhance operational controls such as improving personnel productivity, identifying work flow problems, and improving general management of all work centers.
4. To identify potential internal control problems for internal audit review.
5. To provide a more informative vehicle for identifying interactive relationships, in other words, to make managers more aware of the impact of administrative and financial decisions within their control upon other cost centers. This implies that an improvement in efficiency and costs in one cost center may increase costs and decrease efficiency in another cost center.

---

[1]Bank Administration Institute, *A Financial Information System for Community Banks, Part 4, Cost Accounting* (Park Ridge, IL: Bank Administration Institute, 1977), 2.

6. To derive net functional costs after assignment of cost of money and cost of capital. In this manner, management may ascertain rates of return on each portfolio.[2]

Control Systems and Concepts

Responsibility Accounting. Banks can control expenses through accounting reporting systems. In previous chapters we examined the major financial statements and determined the aggregate results of operations concerning bank profitability. Expense or cost control is accomplished by assigning the responsibility for revenues and/or expenses to various levels of management. A system that classifies revenues, costs, and changes in levels of assets and liabilities according to responsibility centers is known as responsibility accounting. A responsibility center can be defined as the area in which a person is held accountable for the achievement of planned objectives.[3]

A responsibility center can be either a cost or a profit center. A cost center incurs costs that normally exceed any offsetting revenue. A profit center generates revenue, incurs costs, and is expected to be profitable. Importantly, only those revenues and costs are assigned that are directly controllable by the responsibility center.

Responsibility centers generally follow the organizational structure. A pyramiding concept is utilized in designing the reporting structure. The lowest management level receives detailed reports of actual operations compared to planned operations or budgets. At the next management level all lower-level reports are summarized into a single report. The process continues upward through all management levels.

Control of a bank's revenues and expenses is accomplished through comparison with the bank's profit plan. By assigning responsibility for revenues and/or costs to individuals, management can demand performance that may be measured by minimization of expense or maximization of profit.

Centers are also assigned responsibility for producing the desired changes in assets and liabilities. To achieve the results wanted in revenues, expenses, and asset and liability levels, general ledger accounts must be integrated with the organizational structure. Each transaction generated by a responsibility center must be coded with a number that identifies the originator. All transactions are accumulated for reporting monthly performance.

Functional Cost Analysis. Functional cost analysis differs from responsibility accounting in several respects. Responsibility accounting pin-

---

[2]F. P. Johnson, *Systems and Techniques for Analyzing Bank Costs and the Pricing of Bank Services* (New York: American Institute of Certified Public Accountants, to be published in 1985), 5.

[3]Bank Administration Institute, op. cit., 57.

points responsibility for certain costs and revenues, with each responsibility center being a part of a larger process or activity. A function, on the other hand, is a natural division of operations according to a major activity, such as commercial lending or demand deposits. The process of accumulating costs for demand deposits, for example, includes segregating the demand deposit activity and accumulating the costs of deposits and checks from each cost center until the total cost is accumulated. The cost centers include teller operations, cash items, data processing, bookkeeping, and other operations. Revenue is accumulated and matched with costs at the functional level.

Some functional cost systems segregate asset functions from liability functions and assign a cost or an income to the funds used or provided. In this manner each function is evaluated for profitibility. Other systems transfer the cost of funds-providing functions to funds-using functions to determine the profitability of the funds-using functions, including funds cost. These different concepts are discussed in more detail below.

Full-Absorption Costing Approach.   Under a full-absorption costing approach all direct, indirect, fixed, and variable costs are accounted for in the costing process. In banking, as in other industries, certain general overhead costs, such as those incurred by administrative departments, do not contribute directly to a functional activity. The assignment or allocation of overhead costs therefore becomes very subjective. As an example, a bank's president administers various aspects of the bank's activity. Under full-absorption costing the cost of the president's department would be allocated on some basis to all of the bank's activities. The end result is that all revenues and costs are accounted for in the costing exercise. For pricing purposes the price of a given activity must be sufficient to cover the allocated overhead costs.

Contribution Approach..   The contribution approach is an alternative to the full-absorption approach.[4] The contribution approach includes the direct costs and revenues of a specific function and excludes general overhead costs. This approach presents the net revenue available to pay for or cover all of the general overhead costs. For decision making regarding the relative profitability of a specific function, many banks use the contribution approach. The reason for excluding general overhead costs is the belief that the allocation of general overhead costs is arbitrary and adds little to the costing exercise. In cost accounting terminology the contribution approach is also called *direct costing*.

---

[4]Certain costing systems use full-absorption costing techniques. An intermediate step in the full-absorption costing system may or may not include contribution margin concepts.

Activity Measures.   It is important to measure the amount of activity in which a bank engages. The number and types of items processed are indicators of the amount of effort expended to produce bank services. The number of items indicate staffing-level needs and the degree of operational efficiency. For costing purposes, per-unit costs relate total dollar amounts and total activity levels into a single measure that serves as an index of operating performance. In addition, per-unit costs assist in pricing decisions for each service.

Gathering activity data may be difficult if the bank does not capture the statistics as part of normal operating statistics. If data do not exist, then the bank may use sampling techniques to estimate activity levels. Exhibit 17.1 illustrates the type of activity counts necessary for cost accounting, the source of the required data, and how to obtain the data.

Budgets.   Budgets are an important ingredient in a responsibility accounting system. They serve as a target that is assumed to be attainable over a relevant time period. Comparisons of actual performance to planned performance produce variances for review. The review should examine material variances to determine why performance is deviating from the plan. The review might include examining staffing levels, individual expenses, and activity measures that indicate variances due to peak periods or changes in operating conditions. The pyramiding approach for reporting provides each manager with sufficient information to address measures for returning to the plan or modifying the plan to compensate for changes in the operating environments. Techniques for budgeting are more fully discussed later in this chapter.

Customer Profitability Analysis.   Good customer relationships are important. What is good for a bank's customers, however, is not necessarily good for the bank. As customers have become more sensitive to interest rates, they have begun to minimize their nonearning demand deposit balances. As a result the use of bank services has changed. The examination of the total customer relationship, including loans, deposits, and other services, from a profitability viewpoint is called *customer profitability analysis.* This analysis is generally limited to a bank's largest customers. Because unit cost information is required for this analysis, a bank usually will have performed a functional cost analysis before engaging in the analysis of individual customer relationships.

In setting loan rates, banks historically emphasized the compensating deposits provided by the customer. As customers minimize their deposit balances, it has become very important to examine the various aspects of the total customer relationship and to price services accordingly. The techniques of analyzing customer profitability are discussed in Chapter 18.

EXHIBIT 17.1 Basic Data Requirements for Cost Accounting

Type of Data	Suggested Source	How to Obtain Data
Accounting Data:		
Average balance sheet	General ledger	Divide sum of month-end balances by 12.
Annual operating income statement	General ledger	Obtain subtotals from the general ledger for the various income and expense account groups.
Significant expenses by organizational unit, including:		
Salaries	Payroll system, sample	For employees working in more than one organizational unit, develop the time distribution based on the sample or other estimate.
Depreciation—furniture, fixtures, and equipment	General ledger, property records	If data are not available in property records, estimate the value of furniture, etc., in each unit and distribute depreciation proportionally.
Other furniture and equipment expense	General ledger, invoices	Analyze invoices or distribute in proportion to the value of furniture, etc., in each unit.
Stationery, supplies, and printing	General ledger, invoices	Analyze invoices.
Telephone and telegraph	Monthly bills	Analyze bills and separate long-distance and regular charges.
Postage, express, and freight	General ledger, postage meters, invoices	Obtain directly from postage meters or analyze invoices.
Data-processing fees	General ledger, invoices	Analyze invoices.
Advertising and public relations	General ledger, invoices	Analyze invoices.
Employees' and officers' travel	Expense reports	Analyze reports.

EXHIBIT 17.1 *(continued)*

Type of Data	Suggested Source	How to Obtain Data
Activity (Statistical) Counts:		
Checks "on us" cashed	Automated applications, miscellaneous bank reports, or sample	If data are not available from existing reports or applications, develop an estimate based on the sample.
Demand deposits— checks only	"	"
Demand deposits— with cash	"	"
Demand accounts opened	"	"
Collections	"	"
Savings deposits	"	"
Savings withdrawals	"	"
Total savings accounts	"	"
Savings accounts opened	"	"
Savings accounts closed	"	"
Real estate loans—new —payments	Loan department reports, automated applications, or sample	If data are not available from existing reports or applications, develop an estimate based on the sample.
Commercial loans—new —payments	"	"
Installment loans—new —payments	Miscellaneous reports, sample	"
Drafts issued	Automated applications, sample	"
Certified checks	Serial numbers	Subtract the first serial number from the last number used in the cost year.
Cashier's checks	Miscellaneous reports, sample	If data are not available from reports, develop an estimate based on the sample.
E-bond redemptions		

Money orders	Serial numbers	Subtract the first serial number from the last number used in the cost year.
Traveler's checks	Serial numbers	"
Checks cashed—other	Automated applications, sample	If data are not available from reports or applications, develop an estimate based on the sample.
Clearinghouse checks	Automated applications, sample	"
Transit checks	Automated applications, sample	"
Return items—bookkeeping	Sample	"
Checks "on us" posted, etc.	Automated applications, sample	"
Deposits posted, etc.	"	"
Return items—proof and transit	Sample	"
Overdrafts	Miscellaneous reports, sample	"

Distribution (Redistribution) Data:

Square feet by organizational unit	Bank building floor plans	Calculated from plan dimensions if data are not directly indicated.
Number of employees by organizational unit	Personnel, payroll, survey	Survey organizational units if data are not otherwise available.
Loans and deposit balances as a percentage of total loans	Average balance sheet	Sum loan and deposit balances and calculate for each type the percent of this total.
Loan balances by type as a percentage of total loans	Average balance sheet	Sum all loan balances and calculate for each type of loan the percent of total loans.
Number of telephones by organization unit	Telephone company, survey	If data are not available, survey each organizational unit.

Miscellaneous Data:

Market-oriented interest rate	*Wall Street Journal* and other publications	For each type of security selected for use in costing (e.g., 90-day T-bills, CDs, etc.), calculate the average rate for the year by summing month-end rates and dividing by 12.

Source: Bank Administration Institute, *A Financial Information System for Community Banks, Part 4: Cost Accounting* (Park Ridge, IL: Bank Administration Institute, 1977), 7–8.

Functional Cost Systems

A functional profitability program involves three input possibilities—cost center accountability through responsibility reporting, a cost allocation system, and work measurement integration. Work measurement involves weighing each activity measurement on the basis of the standard time required to perform the activity. Work measurement may be viewed as "fine tuning" cost allocation parameters. It is an activity usually engaged in only by very large banks.

Exhibit 17.2 illustrates the three input elements mentioned above and the three output benefits of standard unit-cost derivation, fee and rate determination, and customer account profitability analysis. The inputs produce the bank's overall functional cost analysis, and the three outputs are extensions of the basic functional profitability program.

Conceptually, the functional cost routine segregates revenues and expenses. Revenues are accounted for at the functional level, i.e., they are removed from the profit centers that have responsibility for generating revenue. Expenses are segregated into at least two categories—controllable expenses at the cost center level and noncontrollable or general expenses attributable to the function. In effect, every operating department becomes a cost center that is allocated or transferred to the functional level. At the cost center level the cost allocation system transfers cost center costs to functions. At the functional level the transferred cost center costs are added to functional expenses and subtracted from functional revenues. Functional profitability is determined for each functional activity. A further refinement is the matching of funds-using activities with funds-providing activities to determine net functional revenues.

Exhibit 17.2   Interrelationships of Functional Cost Accounting

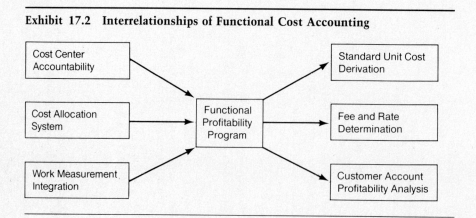

Cost Allocation Systems. There are three basic allocation methods employed by banks. The direct allocation method transfers costs directly from cost centers to the functional level. This method ignores the specific process in which each activity occurs and the interaction among cost centers in providing mutual support.

The second method is the simultaneous equation method. Functional cost is expressed in a series of equations segregating the activity relationships among cost centers that produce specific bank services. The simultaneous equation method is complex, requiring significant mathematical manipulations. For this reason the system is usually implemented through the use of a computer.

The third method is the step allocation or sequential close-out method. Activity relationships within each cost center must be defined. Reciprocal or interactive relationships among cost centers are ignored. From the activity data a priority scheme is determined. Cost centers that provide the most service to other cost centers are allocated first and those providing less service follow. All cost centers are ranked according to services provided until all costs have been allocated to functions.

Service department costs create allocation difficulties in an allocation process. For example, the personnel department provides services such as personnel selection and benefits management to all departments. The accounting department provides certain services to all departments including personnel. The simultaneous equation method can consider the interaction of services among departments. The step and direct allocation methods ignore the interaction. An alternative commonly employed is to use the direct allocation method to distribute service department costs and to use the step allocation method for cost centers involved in providing service as part of a total process of accounting for an activity. The process of accounting for demand deposits and the processing of checks was discussed in Chapter 6. The specific costs of this processing would be accumulated at the functional level from the costs allocated from each cost center involved.

Cost Allocation Parameters. Exhibit 17.1 indicated the types of activity measures used in a cost allocation process. The total number of items processed by a cost center are accumulated. Without regard to the time required to process each type of transaction, each specific item represents a percentage of cost center's effort. Depending on the process involved in accounting for each type of item, costs will be prorated to determine the cost of processing for each cost center. Unweighted activity ignores the differences in complexity and time to process each type of transaction. Unweighted activity is useful data for dividing costs if the relative time for processing is similar. If processing-time differences are significant, the activity data should be weighted. The cost allocation parameters serve each type of cost allocation system. The manner in which each system operates dictates how the parameters will be used.

The basic steps in the costing process are:

1. Distribute expenses to cost centers.
2. Distribute cost center costs to functions and activities.
3. Distribute income to functions.
4. Determine cost of funds.
5. Determine contribution margins of various functions.
6. Calculate unit costs.[5]

The distribution of expenses is accomplished by using parameters applicable to the type of expense. Salary and benefit distributions are based on time of personnel in each cost center. Depreciation and rental expense should be charged to the cost centers which utilize equipment, furniture, and fixtures. Occupancy expense may be distributed using floor space occupied by each cost center. It should be recognized, however, that various floor spaces have different fair values. For example, space on the main floor usually is more expensive than upper floors. Occupancy distributions should recognize these differences. Telephone expenses may be a combination of distributions. Base telephone charges may be charged directly to each cost center based on the number of telephone units. Long distance charges should be charged to the cost center of the caller. Most other expenses are charged to the cost center utilizing the specific service and incurring the expenses.

Illustrative Example

The Bank Administration Institute has developed a cost accounting system that can be employed by small to medium-sized banks. The system, which employs the steps described above, is fairly simple and is useful for the illustration of basic concepts. Several important concepts are employed in the system. First, the system follows a contribution approach and is not a full cost absorption model. Second, it employs a market rate for fund costs that treats the interest on average fund balances as income to funds-providing functions and transfers interest expense (cost of funds) to funds-using functions. A discussion of cost-of-funds pricing follows this example.

Exhibit 17.3 is a flowchart of the costing process. The distribution and allocation parameters are those found in Exhibit 17.1. From the income statement expenses are distributed to cost centers (Step 1). Cost centers are divided into direct and indirect centers. The purpose of this

---

[5]Bank Administration Institute, op. cit., 5.

Exhibit 17.3   Flowchart of the Costing Process

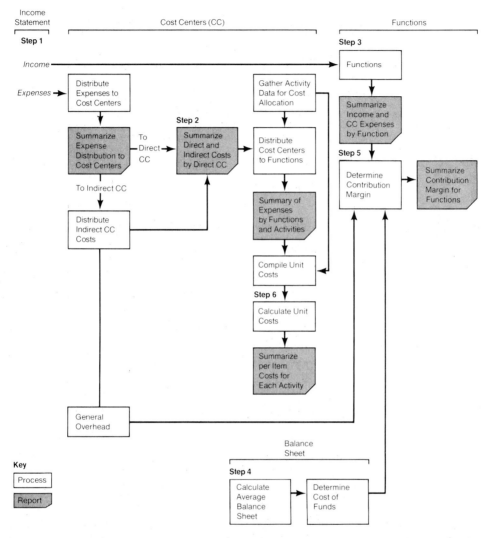

Source: Based on Bank Administration Institute, *A Financial Information System for Community Banks, Part 4: Cost Accounting* (Park Ridge, IL: Bank Administration Institute, 1977).

division is to identify those centers that contribute directly to a process involved in producing a specific service or activity and those centers that provide indirect support to the direct cost centers. The expenses of some indirect cost centers, such as the president's department, are considered general bank overhead and are not distributed to cost centers because measurable activity data are not available. The separation of cost centers into direct and indirect centers is shown below:

Direct Cost Centers

Branch offices (if any)	Real estate loan
Tellers	Installment loan
Bookkeeping	Investment
Proof and transit	Trust
Demand deposits	Safe deposit
Savings deposits	Capital funds
Commercial loan	

Indirect Cost Centers

Building	Credit
Computer services	General and administrative
Personnel	Finance and control
Advertising and public relations	

The results of expense distribution are illustrated in Exhibit 17.4. Each expense classification is spread to cost centers based upon direct assignment. Salaries are distributed to the centers where the employees are located. Employers' taxes are distributed in relation to the salary distributions. Other expenses are distributed according to usage. Step 1 (Exhibit 17.3) also involves the separation and redistribution of indirect cost center expenses to direct cost centers and to unallocated indirect costs. Unallocated indirect costs are not allocated to functions but are considered at the highest aggregate level of reporting. Indirect cost center expenses are redistributed to the following functions:

Funds-Providing	Funds-Using	Nonfund
Demand deposits	Real estate loans	Trust
Savings deposits	Commercial loans	Safe deposit
Capital funds	Installment loans	Computer services
	Investments	Other services

Exhibit 17.4 (on page 434) illustrates the results of the distribution of cost center expenses to functions. Note that unallocated indirect costs remain unallocated to functions.

Income is distributed directly to functions (Step 3). In this system interest income on tax-exempt securities is "grossed up" to reflect a tax-equivalent basis. Interest income from tax-exempt securities is divided by (1 − tax rate) to compute the gross income for comparative purposes. The general ledger classifications facilitate the direct allocation to the various functions. If the system were expanded to analyze specific types of real estate loans, for example, interest income on real estate loans would be divided among the types. Subsidiary loan records would be required for separation according to commercial, residential, and construction loans.

The next phase of the costing process is computation of the average balance of each balance sheet account. These average balances are to be used for computing gross yields and net returns on each asset or liability. The functions outlined above do not include cash and due from banks, bank premises, and other assets that reduce capital in the determination of net investable funds.

Following banking theory, cash and due from banks serve two purposes—to meet reserve requirements and to accommodate operating cash needs primarily in meeting depositor withdrawals, satisfying loan demand, and processing depositor transactions. Since these purposes are mainly related to deposit generation, only the net deposits are available for loans and investments. Similarly, capital that is a long-term source of funds is used to finance premises and other nonearning assets. Any excess capital may be invested in loans and investments. Exhibit 17.5 (on page 436) shows the calculation of net investable funds.

Exhibit 17.6 (on page 436) demonstrates the calculation of contribution margin by function. Where applicable, the average and investable balances are shown to indicate the available balances and their relative rate of return. The income and expenses are transferred from the distribution reports to the contribution report.

The contribution margin in dollars for this report is defined as:

- For funds-providing functions, the net cost of obtaining funds (income less expense) *plus* a credit for net funds provided based on the market-oriented interest rate applied to net investable funds.
- For funds-using functions, the net income (income less expense) *less* a charge for funds used based on the market-oriented interest rate applied to the funds used.
- For service (nonfund) functions, the net income or expense of the respective functions.[6]

The market rate of interest can be based upon rates for Treasury bills or certificates of deposit. In this system the sum of the credits and charges net to zero. The purpose of the market rate is to give value as earnings to funds-providing functions and to transfer to funds users the cost of funds provided. The contribution margin of each function

---

[6]Ibid., 39.

EXHIBIT 17.5   Calculation of Net Investable Funds

Source of Funds	Average Balance	Cash Plus Reserve Account[a]	Cash Items	Due from Banks	Bank Premises	Other Assets	Investable Funds
Demand Deposits	$22,300,000	$3,000,000	$200,000	$1,860,000			$17,300,000
Savings Deposits	45,200,000	2,000,000					43,200,000
Capital Funds[b]	6,000,000				$1,300,000	$1,200,000	3,500,000
	$73,500,000	$5,000,000	$200,000	$1,860,000	$1,300,000	$1,200,000	$64,000,000

[a]Distribute the sum of cash plus the reserve account with the Federal Reserve to demand deposits and time deposits in proportion to required reserves for each deposit type as a percent of the total required reserves.

[b]Total liabilities and capital less deposits plus reserve for loan losses.

Source: Bank Administration Institute, *A Financial Information System for Community Banks, Part 4: Cost Accounting* (Park Ridge, IL: Bank Administration Institute, 1977), 38.

EXHIBIT 17.6   Calculation of Contribution Margin by Function

Line No.		Funds-Providing Functions				Funds-Using Functions	
		Demand Deposits	Savings Deposits	Capital Funds	Total	Real Estate Loans	Commercial Loans
1	Average balances	$22,300,000	$45,200,000	$6,000,000	$73,500,000	$4,000,000	$22,000,000
2	Investable funds	17,300,000	43,200,000	3,500,000	64,000,000	4,000,000	22,000,000
3	Total income	150,000	X	X	150,000	330,000	2,010,000
4	Total expense	614,263	2,884,782	62,000	3,561,045	93,555	216,373
5	Operating income (expense) Lines 3−4	$ (464,263)	$ (2,884,782)	$ (62,000)	$ (3,411,045)	$ 236,445	$ 1,793,627
	Percent of Line 2	(2.7%)	(6.7%)	(1.8%)	(5.3%)	5.9%	8.2%
6	Market-oriented interest Cost of funds (percent) = 4.75%	X	X	X	X	X	X
7	Credit (charge) for funds provided (used) (Line 6 × Line 2)	$ 821,750	$ 2,052,000	$ 166,250	$ 3,040,000	$ (190,000)	$ (1,045,000)
8	Contribution margin (Line 5 + Line 7)	$ 357,487	$ (832,782)	$ 104,250	$ (371,045)	$ 36,445	$ 748,627
	Percent of Line 2	2.1%	(1.9%)	3.0%	(0.6%)	1.2%	3.4%

Source: Bank Administration Institute: *A Financial Information System for Community Banks, Part 4: Cost Accounting* (Park Ridge, IL: Bank Administration Institute, 1977), 40–41.

| Funds-Using Functions | | | Nonfund Functions | | | | | | |
Installment Loans	Investments	Total	Trust	Safe Deposit	Computer Services	Other Services	Total	Overall Total
$8,000,000	$30,000,000	$64,000,000	X	X	X	X	X	X
8,000,000	30,000,000	64,000,000	X	X	X	X	X	X
920,000	3,000,000	6,260,000	$170,000	$ 15,000	$15,000	$ 30,000	$230,000	$6,640,000
145,219	34,800	489,947	114,400	43,900	X	52,508	210,808	4,261,800
$ 774,781	$ 2,965,200	$ 5,770,053	$ 55,600	$(28,900)	$15,000	$(22,508)	$ 19,192	$2,378,200
9.7%	9.9%	9.0%	X	X	X	X	X	X
X	X	X	X	X	X	X	X	X
$ (380,000)	$ (1,425,000)	$ (3,040,000)	X	X	X	X	X	X
$ 394,781	$ 1,540,200	$ 2,730,053	$ 55,600	$(28,900)	$15,000	$(22,508)	$ 19,192	$2,378,200
4.9%	5.1%	4.2%	X	X	X	X	X	3.7%

Less: Unallocated indirect cost $ 521,200

Tax-equivalent adjustment 500,000

Net operating income $1,357,000

EXHIBIT 17.4 Cost Centers

Amount No.	Account Description	Total Expenses	Building	Computer Services	Personnel	Advertising and Public Relations	Credit	General Administrative	Finance and Control	Branch Office
7010	Officers' salaries									
7020	Employees' salaries	$ 791,000	$ 64,000	$ 24,000	$30,000	$40,000	$30,000	$ 60,000	$46,000	$47,000
7030	Employees' overtime									
7040	Employer's FICA									
7050	Unemployment taxes									
7060	Workmen's compensation	186,000	15,000	5,000	7,000	9,000	7,100	14,000	11,000	11,000
7070	Employee group insurance									
7160	Employee relations and activities									
7201– 7219	Interest expense on savings deposits	832,000								
7220	Interest expense on savings certificates									
7231– 7249	Interest expense on certificates of deposit	1,915,000								
7251– 7259	Interest expense on other time deposits									
7260	Interest on Federal funds, etc.									
7271– 7279	Interest on liabilities for borrowed money	62,000								
7290	Interest on subordinated notes and debentuers									
7301– 7499	Occupancy expense	175,000	175,000							
7510	Depreciation—furniture, fixtures, and equipment									
7540	Furniture and equipment rental expense									
7550	Furniture and equipment repairs	63,000	5,000	2,000	2,000	3,000	2,000	5,000	4,000	4,000
7560	Furniture and equipment maintenance contract expense									
7570	Personal property taxes									
7600	Provision for possible loan losses	78,000								
7710	Stationery, supplies, and printing									
7720	Telephone and telegraph	134,000	12,000	4,000	4,000	6,000	4,000	11,000	8,000	9,000
7730	Postage, express, and freight									
7751	Legal fees	30,000						30,000		
7752	Audit, tax, and accounting fees	15,000						15,000		
7753	Examination fees									
7754	Data processing fees	117,000		117,000						
7759	Other outside service fees	15,000						15,000		
7770	Advertising and public relation expense	75,000				75,000				

Universal Tellers	Book-keeping	Proof and Transit	Demand Deposits	Savings Deposits	Commercial Loan	Real Estate Loan	Installment Loan	Investment	Trust	Safe Deposit	Capital Funds
$86,000	$110,000	$38,000			$60,000	$33,000	$41,000	$16,000	$50,000	$16,000	——
20,000	26,000	8,900			14,000	8,000	10,000	4,000	12,000	4,000	——
				$ 832,000							
				1,915,000							
											$62,000
7,000	9,000	3,000			5,000	3,000	3,000	1,000	4,000	1,000	——
					42,000	6,000	30,000				
16,000	19,000	6,000			11,000	6,000	6,000	2,000	8,000	2,000	——

indicates the relative amount and percent of profits available to cover unallocated indirect costs and the tax-equivalent adjustment (from "grossing-up" nontaxable securities).

The rate of return of operating income to investable funds can be compared to the contribution margin by percent. The market rate converts gross return to a net return concept. The decisions that emanate from this report identify the specific services to be emphasized in order to increase the size of a function's contribution margin.

In retrospect, one can trace the operating income (expense) through the distribution reports to determine why the income or expense is high or low in comparison to other functions and to identify ways to improve operating efficiency or income generation. However, absolute dollar values give little insight into operations unless those values are related to other periods or are related to the average investable balances by percent, thereby providing an index of each item to all income or costs of each function. Another measure of efficiency is the calculation of unit costs and their comparison to prior periods to determine trends. The importance of computing unit costs is that the computation takes into consideration activity volumes that affect cost levels.

The individual costs incurred by each cost center are summed to give the total cost of processing an activity. The total cost is divided by the activity count and a unit cost is determined. Exhibit 17.7 presents a report identifying unit cost data. A period-to-period comparison is important to indicate areas of investigation. This comparison assists in pinpointing specific cost centers where costs require additional review. If unit costs appear to be materially different, the expense distribution of each cost center should be examined and individual unit costs should be determined for each cost center contributing to the item processing.

The Uses of Cost Information.   The purpose of cost accounting is to provide information regarding the least-cost sources of funds and the most profitable uses of funds. This cost allocation system provides basic cost data to analyze functional contribution to profits. It can be expanded by subdividing functions.

Unit cost information can be analyzed by comparing current and prior-year activity expenses. Unit cost data serve as guides to pricing. Services must be priced to cover unallocated expenses. Some services will be offered at losses simply because of competitive factors. Cost data produce measures of the degree of profit or loss. In the aggregate, pricing should cover direct and unallocated expenses. Activity costs establish a floor or minimum price that should be charged for services. With sound cost data it is possible to know what costs are not being covered by the services.

Cost of Funds.   The example presented in the preceding pages employed the market rate for funds costs. A weakness of this method lies in the selection of an appropriate rate. In the example, if the market rate

EXHIBIT 17.7   Calculation of Unit Costs

Activity	1 Teller Expense	2 Branch Office A Expense	3 Bookkeeping Expense	4 Proof and Transit Expense	5 Real Estate Loan Expense	6 Commercial Loan Expense	7 Installment Loan Expense	8 Total Activity Expense	9 Total Activity Count	10 Per-Item Cost
"On us" checks and debits	$ 37,867		$129,470	$ 52,362				$ 181,832	1,900,000	$ .10
"On us" checks cashed		$ 33,354						71,221	280,000	.25
Checking account deposits:										
Checks only	33,682	21,114	22,784	9,228				86,808	335,000	.26
With cash	25,311	26,622	10,126	4,185				66,244	150,000	.44
Checking accounts opened	6,776	4,437						11,213	1,700	6.60
Statement preparation			60,275					60,275	120,000	.50
Clearinghouse checks										
Transit checks				41,418				41,418	1,500,000	.03
Return items			10,126	107				10,233	5,000	2.05
Overdrafts			8,319					8,319	4,000	2.08
Collections										
Savings deposits	18,136	15,912						34,048	67,000	.51
Savings withdrawals	21,923	17,289						39,212	39,000	1.01
Savings accounts opened	8,370	6,273						14,643	2,200	6.66
Savings accounts closed	4,584	2,295						6,879	1,700	4.05
Real estate loans:										
New loans	199				$87,495[a]			87,694	150	584.63
Payments	797	459			4,605			5,861	2,800	2.09
Commercial loans:										
New loans	2,989					$187,920[a]		190,909	3,500	54.55
Payments	4,584					20,880		25,464	11,000	2.31
Installment loans:										
New loans	2,193						$110,720[a]	112,913	2,500	45.17
Payments	2,790	1,836					27,680	32,306	28,000	1.15
Drafts issued	3,986	1,377						5,363	8,500	.63
Certified checks	598	612						1,210	1,750	.69
Cashier's checks	4,385	3,060						7,445	11,500	.65
E-bond redemptions	1,395	918						2,313	3,600	.64
Money orders	399	1,377						1,776	3,800	.47
Traveler's checks	598	612						1,210	800	1.51
Checks cashed—other	17,738	15,453						33,191	130,000	.26
Total expense	$199,300	$153,000	$241,100	$107,300	$92,100	$208,800	$138,400	$1,140,000		

Plus:

FDIC assessment and advertising expense—demand deposits	$ 76,700
Interest and advertising expense on savings deposits plus FDIC assessment	2,790,000
Investment	96,800
Trust	114,400
Safe deposit	43,900
Capital funds	
Unallocated indirect costs	521,200
Total operating expense	$4,783,000

[a]Cost center expenses relating to real estate, commercial, and installment loans have been split between new loans and payments, with payments accounting for 5%, 10%, and 20%, respectively.

Source: Bank Administration Institute, *A Financial Information System for Community Banks, Part 4: Cost Accounting* (Park Ridge, IL: Bank Administration Institute, 1977), 44.

is the marginal rate for funds, a rate higher than average cost may produce higher returns on funds-providing functions and lower rates on funds-using units. Since the rate is the same across all functions, no weight is given to the type of funds.

For example, real estate loans usually have an average life of approximately seven years and theoretically should be financed with funds having a seven-year maturity. Installment loans have a shorter life and should be matched with funds of similar maturities. Each type of funds has different market rates associated with the respective maturities. An alternative to a single market rate is the employment of rates according to the maturities of the funds-providing functions.

Certain cost systems employ book cost of funds and allocate funds cost directly to funds-using functions. In our example the operating expense of demand deposits would be transferred to a funds-using function. Two allocation methods predominate. The pooled-cost method aggregates all expenses of funds-providing functions. The cost is divided by the sum of investable balances to derive a cost per dollar of funds. That cost is multiplied by the investable balances of funds-using functions. The balance after deducting funds cost is the contribution margin based upon an average book cost of funds.

The specific-allocation method assigns specific funds-providing sources to specific funds-using functions. This method is preferable to the pooled-cost method because the contribution margin reflects a more technically correct assignment of funds. Both methods reflect average book cost of funds, which is useful in analyzing past costs. For planning purposes the marginal cost of funds (market rate) is preferable for projecting future costs and profits.

BUDGETS

The analysis of cost data assists in the preparation of budgets. Following the costing framework outlined above, management can make projections of balance sheet accounts and translate dollar levels into revenue and expense projections by cost center. If the budgeting process begins at the highest level of the bank and is disseminated to management at the cost center level, the process is termed a "top-down" approach. Correspondingly, if cost center managers are asked to make projections of assets, liabilities, revenues, and expenditures and the results are aggregated at the highest bank level, the process is called a "bottom-up" approach. The bottom-up approach produces more direct involvement of unit managers in setting operating goals and objectives for the budget period. Also, managers are more accountable for their projections if they have actively participated in the budgeting process.

There are two basic types of budgets. The fixed budget is prepared for a single level of activity. All expenses and income are budgeted based upon the single volume. The fixed budget is easy to install, works well when activity volume can be reasonably predicted, and provides a single target for the organization. Its disadvantages are that the budget may need more frequent revision if activity forecasts are not accurate and volume effects may make the analysis of variances more difficult.

A variable budget recognizes that activity volumes may vary. The variable budget acknowledges both the fixed nature of certain expenses that do not vary with volume and the variable nature of those expenses that, wholly or in part, vary with different activity levels. The variable budget does not require frequent revision and eliminates the differences in activity levels in analyzing the results. Its disadvantages are that the budget plan is a moving target and may make assessment of progress toward bank goals more difficult. It is also more complex to install. If budgeting emanates from the costing process, the fixed and variable components of cost must be segregated.

The primary approach to introducing budgeting as a control measure is to adopt the fixed budget initially. As bank personnel gain experience in analyzing budget variances, the variable budget may be introduced as a refinement to the basic system.

Budget Process

The installation of a fixed budget employs the bottom-up approach and consists of several steps:

Step	Management Level
1. Formulate the overall objectives for the coming year and communicate them to the personnel involved in the budgeting process.	Senior management
2. Make detailed estimates for each category of income, expense, asset, and liability.	Profit/cost center managers
3. Summarize the budget and compute the budgeted net income.	Bank financial management
4. Review and revise the budget if the objectives are not met.	Senior management

The preparation of detailed estimates for each category of income, expense, asset, and liability account requires the use of several worksheets. Senior management may provide general or specific guidelines, including interest rate expectations, target ranges for asset and liability average balances, and limits on expenses such as compensation increases. Profit/cost center managers translate these objectives into income and expenses based upon the projected activity level for bank operations.

Exhibits 17.8 and 17.9 are examples of results that may be obtained for the total bank. The income and expense budget may be divided

EXHIBIT 17.8   A Balance Sheet Budget

Account Number(s)	Account Name	First Quarter	Second Quarter	Third Quarter	Fourth Quarter	Annual Average	Estimated Prior-Year Average	Percent Change
Assets								
1000–1099	Cash accounts							
1101–1199	Due from banks	$ 7,200,000	7,400,000	7,600,000	7,800,000	7,500,000	7,000,000	7.1%
1200	Reserve account							
1301–1319	U.S. Treasury securities	5,750,000	5,850,000	5,900,000	5,800,000	5,825,000	5,500,000	5.9
1321–1339	Obligations of other U.S. government agencies	4,400,000	4,300,000	4,400,000	4,500,000	4,400,000	4,500,000	(2.2)
1341–1359	Obligations of states and political subdivisions	12,500,000	12,750,000	13,000,000	12,800,000	12,763,000	12,000,000	6.4
1361–1379	Other bonds, notes, and debentures	5,200,000	5,250,000	5,200,000	5,000,000	5,162,000	5,000,000	3.2
1400	Federal funds sold and securities purchased under agreements to resell	2,384,000	2,809,000	2,804,000	2,967,000	2,741,000	3,000,000	(8.6)
1501–1519	Commercial loans	23,500,000	24,500,000	25,600,000	27,600,000	25,300,000	22,000,000	15.0
1521–1539	Installment loans	8,100,000	8,350,000	8,500,000	8,600,000	8,388,000	8,000,000	4.8
1540	Real estate loans	4,200,000	4,150,000	4,100,000	4,050,000	4,125,000	4,000,000	3.1
1561–1589	Other loans	2,450,000	2,450,000	2,450,000	2,500,000	2,450,000	2,300,000	6.5
1590	Reserve for possible loan losses	(750,000)	(775,000)	(785,000)	(790,000)	(775,000)	(700,000)	10.7
1701–1799	Bank premises, furniture, fixtures, and equipment—net	766,000	776,000	786,000	788,000	779,000	800,000	(2.6)
1830	Customers' liability to this bank on acceptances outstanding	0	0	0	0	0	0	1.0
1901–1999	Other assets	1,250,000	1,150,000	1,225,000	1,225,000	1,212,000	1,200,000	7.1
	Total assets	$76,900,000	78,960,000	80,780,000	82,840,000	79,870,000	74,600,000	7.1
Liabilities and Capital								
2000–2199	Demand deposits	$22,500,000	22,750,000	23,000,000	23,250,000	22,875,000	22,000,000	4.0
2201–2299	Savings deposits	18,000,000	19,000,000	20,000,000	21,000,000	19,500,000	16,640,000	17.2
2301–2379	Certificates of deposit	26,800,000	27,500,000	27,950,000	28,650,000	27,725,000	26,360,000	5.2
2381–2399	Other time deposits	2,200,000	2,250,000	2,300,000	2,350,000	2,275,000	2,000,000	13.8
2400	Federal funds purchased and securities sold under agreements to repurchase	0	0	0	0	0	0	
2501–2599	Liabilities for borrowed money	900,000	800,000	700,000	600,000	750,000	1,200,000	(37.5)
2710	Acceptances executed by or for accounts of this bank and outstanding	0	0	0	0	0	0	
2801–2999	Other liabilities	850,000	900,000	950,000	1,000,000	925,000	900,000	2.8
3000	Subordinated debt	0	0	0	0	0	0	
4100	Preferred stock	0	0	0	0	0	0	
4200	Common stock	1,500,000	1,500,000	1,500,000	1,500,000	1,500,000	1,500,000	
4300	Surplus	1,500,000	1,500,000	1,500,000	1,500,000	1,500,000	1,500,000	
4400	Undivided profits	2,350,000	2,450,000	2,550,000	2,650,000	2,500,000	2,200,000	13.6
4501–4599	Reserve for contingencies and other capital reserves	300,000	310,000	330,000	340,000	320,000	300,000	6.7
	Total liabilities and capital	$76,900,000	78,960,000	80,780,000	82,840,000	79,870,000	74,600,000	7.1

Source: Bank Administration Institute. *A Financial Information System for Community Banks. Part 5: Budgeting* (Park Ridge, IL: Bank Administration Institute, 1977), 12.

into profit/cost center budgets, thereby disseminating the operating objectives for the next budget period. Each manager is given the responsibility of meeting the budget objectives and is held accountable for performance.

Monitoring and Evaluating Performance

For each budgeted period an analysis of the progress toward the period objectives should be performed. This is accomplished by comparing actual performance with the budget. A system of reports for the analysis of each category of income and expense may include:

+ Current-period actual
+ Current-period budget
+ Current-period variance (actual minus budget)
+ Current period, prior-period actual
+ Year-to-date actual
+ Year-to-date budget
+ Year-to-date variance
+ Prior year, current year-to-date actual

Interest rate variances should be performed for the period and analyzed, as previously described in Chapter 16. For material variances each manager should prepare a report outlining the reasons for the positive and negative variances and what impact the current-period negative variances, if any, will have on the annual plan. The report should also include the action the manager plans to take to correct the variances and return to the plan. An example of a summary budget variance report is shown in Exhibit 17.10. At the profit/cost center level the components of the major income and expense accounts are detailed. This pyramiding approach for reports allows each level of management to pinpoint responsibility for correcting material variances in the next lower managerial level.

The budgeting process, together with associated reports, should accomplish the following:

+ Translation of senior management's objectives into specific performance targets for income and expense.
+ Communication of performance targets to bank employees, if responsibility is delegated below the level of president.
+ Comparison of actual performance with the targets.
+ Identification of significant deviations from target performance.
+ Correction of unfavorable performance trends, when possible.[7]

---

[7]Bank Administration Institute, *A Financial Information System for Community Banks, Part 5: Budgeting* (Park Ridge, IL: Bank Administration Institute, 1977), 2.

EXHIBIT 17.9 A Budgeted Income Statement

	First Quarter	Second Quarter	Third Quarter	Fourth Quarter	Annual Average	Estimated Prior-Year Average	Percent Change
Interest and fees on loans							
Commercial	$ 514,060	529,815	550,400	593,400	2,187,675	1,980,000	10.5%
Installment	247,050	255,720	261,375	264,450	1,028,595	960,000	7.1
Real estate	85,050	84,555	84,050	83,530	337,185	320,000	5.4
Other	63,000	64,310	64,310	65,625	257,245	240,000	7.2
Other service charges and fees	14,500	14,500	14,500	13,500	57,000	60,000	(5.0)
Total interest and fees on loans	923,660	948,900	974,635	1,020,505	3,867,700	3,560,000	8.6
Interest income on investment securities							
U.S. Treasury securities	103,500	104,570	105,460	102,950	416,480	409,000	1.8
Obligations of other U.S. government agencies	76,450	74,710	75,900	77,625	304,685	315,000	(3.3)
Obligations of states and political subdivisions (fully taxable equivalent basis)	420,675	422,960	428,125	418,460	1,690,220	1,684,615	.3
Other bonds, notes, and debentures	115,700	116,155	114,400	110,000	456,255	450,000	1.4
Total interest income on investment securities	716,325	718,395	723,885	709,035	2,867,640	2,858,615	.3
Income on federal funds sold and securities purchased under agreements to resell	29,500	34,410	34,000	35,975	133,885	150,000	(10.7)
Interest income on balances with banks	0	0	0	0	0	0	
Total interest income	1,669,485	1,701,705	1,732,520	1,765,515	6,869,225	6,568,615	4.6
Interest expense							
Savings deposits	225,000	237,500	250,000	262,500	975,000	832,000	17.2
Certificates of deposit	452,250	460,625	464,670	476,305	1,853,850	1,790,000	3.6
Other time deposits	34,375	35,155	35,940	36,720	142,190	125,000	13.8

Federal funds purchased and securities sold under agreements to repurchase	0	0	0	0	0	0	——
Liabilities for borrowed money	11,700	10,400	9,100	7,800	39,000	62,000	(37.1)
Total interest expense	723,325	743,680	759,710	783,325	3,010,040	2,809,000	7.2
Net interest income	946,160	958,025	972,810	982,190	3,859,185	3,759,615	2.6
Less: provision for loan losses	18,000	20,000	24,000	28,000	90,000	78,000	15.4
Adjusted net interest income	928,160	938,025	948,810	954,190	3,769,185	3,681,615	2.4
Noninterest income:							
Service charges on deposit accounts	40,000	42,000	43,000	40,000	165,000	150,000	10.0
Trust department income	55,000	45,000	50,000	40,000	190,000	170,000	11.8
Other service charges, commissions, and fees	5,600	6,000	6,700	6,100	24,400	23,000	6.1
Other income	9,900	10,000	10,800	9,900	40,600	37,000	9.7
Total noninterest income	110,500	103,000	110,500	96,000	420,000	380,000	10.5
Total adjusted net interest and noninterest income	1,038,660	1,041,025	1,059,310	1,050,190	4,189,185	4,061,615	3.1
Noninterest expense							
Salaries and employee benefits	254,390	264,340	269,200	283,155	1,071,085	977,000	9.6
Occupancy expense	49,205	48,675	49,180	50,780	197,840	175,000	13.1
Furniture and equipment expense	16,400	16,950	17,275	17,850	68,475	63,000	8.7
Other expenses	177,265	185,380	187,520	197,135	747,300	681,000	9.7
Total noninterest expense	497,260	515,345	523,175	548,920	2,084,700	1,896,000	10.0
Income before income taxes and securities gains (losses)	541,400	525,680	536,135	501,270	2,104,485	2,165,615	(2.8)
Less: provision for federal income taxes	246,100	238,860	243,675	227,610	956,245	984,415	(2.9)
Less: provision for state income taxes	21,655	21,025	21,450	20,050	84,180	86,625	(2.8)
Income before securities gains (losses)	273,645	265,795	271,010	253,610	1,064,060	1,094,575	(2.8)
Securities gains (losses)—net of income taxes	10,000	10,000	10,000	10,000	40,000	35,000	14.3
Net income	$ 283,645	275,795	281,010	263,610	1,104,060	1,129,575	(2.3)

Source: Bank Administration Institute, *A Financial Information System for Community Banks, Part 5: Budgeting* (Park Ridge, IL: Bank Administration Institute, 1977), 29.

EXHIBIT 17.10 A Summary Budget Variance Report (Second Quarter)

	This Quarter				Year-to-Date			
	Actual	Budget	Variance[a]	Prior-Year Actual	Actual	Budget	Variance[a]	Prior-Year Actual
Interest and fees on loans	$ 936,525	948,900	(12,375)	921,100	$1,861,065	1,872,560	(11,495)	1,795,000
Interest income on investment securities[b]	718,015	718,395	(380)	709,000	1,426,370	1,434,720	(8,350)	1,415,000
Income on federal funds sold and securities purchased under agreements to resell	35,740	34,410	1,330	35,000	66,645	63,910	2,735	70,000
Interest income on balances with banks								
Total interest income	1,690,280	1,701,705	(11,425)	1,665,100	3,354,080	3,371,190	(17,110)	3,280,000
Interest expense on deposits	743,250	733,280	(9,970)	675,000	1,457,775	1,444,905	(12,870)	1,335,000
Interest expense on federal funds purchased and securities sold under agreements to repurchase	—	—	—	—	—	—	—	—
Interest expense on liabilities for borrowed money	10,400	10,400	—	19,000	22,100	22,100	—	35,000
Total interest expense	753,650	743,680	(9,970)	694,000	1,479,875	1,467,005	(12,870)	1,370,000
Net interest income	936,630	958,025	(21,395)	971,100	1,874,205	1,904,185	(29,980)	1,910,000
Provision for loan losses	15,000	20,000	5,000	20,000	31,000	38,000	7,000	38,000
Adjusted net interest income	921,630	938,025	(16,395)	951,100	1,843,205	1,866,185	(22,980)	1,872,000
Noninterest income	109,200	103,000	6,200	102,900	218,400	213,500	4,900	190,000
Subtotal	1,030,830	1,041,025	(10,195)	1,054,000	2,061,605	2,079,685	(18,080)	2,062,000
Noninterest expense	513,300	515,345	2,045	454,410	1,010,325	1,012,605	2,280	889,500
Income before income taxes and securities gains (losses)	517,530	525,680	(8,150)	599,590	1,051,280	1,067,080	(15,800)	1,172,500
Provision for federal income taxes	235,105	238,860	3,755	270,290	477,680	484,960	7,280	533,540
Provision for state income taxes	20,700	21,025	325	23,985	42,050	42,680	630	46,900
Net income before securities gains (losses) net of income taxes	261,725	265,795	(4,070)	305,315	531,550	539,440	(7,890)	592,060
Securities gains (losses)—net	15,000	10,000	5,000	(5,000)	22,000	20,000	2,000	15,000
Net income	$ 276,725	275,795	930	300,315	$ 553,550	559,440	(5,890)	607,060

[a]Parentheses denote unfavorable variance (income under budget, expense over budget).
[b]Interest income on investment securities is stated on a fully taxable equivalent basis.

Source Bank Administration Institute, *A Financial Information System for Community Banks. Part 5 Budgeting* (Park Ridge, IL Bank Administration Institute, 1977), 32.

SUMMARY

Cost accounting provides management with important data for cost control and measuring profit contribution by function. Cost accounting data assists in preparing flexible budgets where volume changes produce expense levels significantly different from those in a fixed budget. The determination of customer profitability requires accurate cost data. Unit cost data are also important in setting prices for services. The appropriate profitability techniques and philosophies for analyzing customer profitability and establishing pricing policies are discussed in Chapter 18.

Questions and Problems

1. What developments have led to a need for cost data?

2. How does responsibility accounting differ from functional cost accounting?

3. How do costing results differ between full absorption and the contribution approach?

4. Describe three possible methods used to allocate functional costs.

5. Describe the steps in a functional cost analysis.

6. Discuss alternative funds-costing methods.

7. How does a fixed budget differ from a variable budget?

8. What should be accomplished by the budgeting process?

References

Anderson, P. S. "Costs and Profitability of Bank Functions." In *Bank Management: Concepts and Issues*, ed. J. R. Brick, 431–454. Richmond, VA: Robert F. Dame, 1981.

Bank Administration Institute. *A Financial Information System for Community Banks, Part 4: Cost Accounting* and *Part 5: Budgeting*. Park Ridge, IL: Bank Administration Institute, 1977.

Johnson, F. P. *Systems and Techniques for Analyzing Bank Costs and the Pricing of Bank Services.* New York: American Institute of Certified Public Accountants, to be published in 1985, 5.

Johnson, F. P., and C. F. Muenzberg. "Can Cost Analysis Improve Your Mortgage Loan Function?" *Management Accounting*, February 1980: 22–25.

Lucien, K. "Transfer Pricing for the Cost of Funds in a Commercial Bank. *Management Accounting*, January 1979: 23–24, 36.

Tewes, J. A. "Valuing Bank Funds for Allocation and Pricing Decisions." *Management Accounting*, November 1976: 27–33.

Watson, R. D. "Estimating the Cost of Your Banking Funds." In *Bank Management: Concepts and Issues*, ed. J. R. Brick, 421–430. Richmond, VA: Robert F. Dame, 1981.

CHAPTER 18

The Costs and Pricing of Bank Services: Part 2

In Chapter 17 we developed a cost accounting framework for preparing average cost data and budgets. Deregulation of deposits has produced increased interest expenses. To compensate for these increased expenses, banks must give significant attention to pricing loans and other bank services.

The customer profitability analysis is important in recognizing the services used and deposits provided by corporate customers. The overall customer relationship and the matching of income and expense associated with the relationship provide the basis for setting appropriate loan rates to carry the relationship.

Not all customers use each service. A bank should determine the cost of each service and establish appropriate prices to produce net revenues. However, certain services may not generate sufficient volume to cover their fixed costs. Therefore pricing decisions may include packaging strategies for combining various services to generate sufficient demand for certain services. The considerations for analyzing the profitability of the corporate customer and for pricing various bank services to contribute to the bank's profit margin are presented below.

CUSTOMER PROFITABILITY ANALYSIS

The corporate customer uses a variety of bank services, including loans, deposits, and data processing. Historically banks have given significant attention to the customer's deposit relationship. The deposit relationship has been viewed as an important source of funds. The collected balances have served two primary purposes—to cover processing costs and as a vehicle to loan access. Many times, however, banks have double counted the balances, i.e., ignored the balances with regard to profitability for processing while giving full credit for the balances in lending relationships.

Customer profitability analysis encompasses the total customer relationship and analyzes each customer service to determine the total profitability instead of the profitability of each specific service. The analysis assists in setting proper terms for loans that will meet the minimum profit objectives of the bank.

Deposit and loan relationships are considered balance-based services; i.e., the size of collective deposit balances affects loan terms if the customer is assumed to be a net provider of funds. Not all customers, however, provide sufficient funds to support their own loan requirements. Those who do not are termed net borrowers. Loan terms should be sufficient to cover deposit deficiencies, cover the cost of funds, and provide profit contribution from the loan.

Fee-based services include data processing, lockbox, and other services the bank provides for a fee. Not all corporate customers use such services. As corporate treasurers have become more aware of the earning potential of idle balances, it has become necessary to consider each service independently with respect to pricing. Corporate treasurers have become selective in seeking out specific services rather than maintaining a single banking relationship. Therefore banks must price each service on the assumption that deposit balances will not be sufficient to carry the total relationship. The unbundling of services has placed many banks in a better profit position because they know to what extent price covers cost. When a corporate customer requests price estimates for specific services, the bank can respond with a high degree of accuracy.

Customer Profitability Analysis Record

There are many variations of customer profitability analysis employed by banks. Our purpose in presenting only one such analysis is to illustrate the concepts of the deposit and loan relationship (balance-based services and fee-based services). It is not our intent to suggest that this format is superior to others. Each different format serves special purposes and should be considered according to bank requirements for profitability data.

Exhibit 18.1 is a sample profitability analysis. The important attributes of this analysis include the determination of the customer's status as a net borrower or net provider of funds, the income generated from loans, the cost of funds, and loan administration costs. This example uses a funds-transfer rate, which may be the bank's pooled cost of funds or, alternatively, the marginal cost. The analysis determines the size of balances required to maintain a break-even deposit relationship and separately determines the amount and cost of funds necessary to carry the lending relationship.

The unit cost of each service multiplied by the activity level for each specific service compared with the income results in the profit or loss for balance-based or fee-based services. The importance of this analysis is that it is tailored to the customer relationship. If total services are unprofitable, the analysis indicates those services that are profitable or unprofitable. The customer contact officer can restructure the fees or require additional deposit balances in concert with the customer's ability to absorb additional fees or to provide balances.

EXHIBIT 18.1 Customer Profitability Analysis Record

Customer name: Smith Inc.
Customer ref. number: 135 460 73

Period covered: 1/1/7—12/31/74
Contact officer: W. L. Barney

Balanced Based Services
Funds provided by customer:
Commercial checking account 123 345 12

Total average gross balance		$479,580
Less: Uncollected funds		65,800
Reserve requirements		53,780
Net available balance		$360,000

Service fee income from funds providing services $ 3,168

Less expenses:

Checks processed	243,794 @	.04108	10,015
Other debits	11,572 @	.06149	712
Transit items processed	332,096 @	.05638	18,724
Money transfers	755 @	1.00603	760

Net profit (cost) funds provided $ (27,043)

Balance required to cover costs @ transfer pool rate 10.05% ($27,043 ÷ 10.05%) = → (269,084)

Net funds available for loans and investments $ 90,916

Funds used by customer:
Average loan balances outstanding

Demand loans, accounts: 832 157	$ 60,000
Commercial long-term loans, accounts: 171 641	182,000
Commercial short-term loans, accounts: 127 351	100,000
Commercial mortgages accounts: 761 388	205,000
Other funds advanced accounts: 355 391	15,000

Total funds used by customer (562,000)

Net funds provided by customer (by bank) $(471,084)

Profit or (cost) @ transfer pool rate 10.05% ($471,084 × 10.05%) ⟶ $ (47,344)

Net income provided by commercial loans

Interest income @ 12.3% average ($562,000)		$ 69,126
Commitment, credit & other fees		4,083
Total		73,209
Less expenses:		
Make credit check	10 @ .10573	$ 0
Send interest bills	10 @ .09130	1
Receive & process pymts.	2 @ 27.60134	1
Maintain collateral	2 @ 36.01491	55
Maintain account	0	72
Other expenses		43
Total expenses		(172)
Net profit (loss) balanced based services		$ 25,693

Fee Based Services

Commercial letters of credit: Letters 15 731: 15 919

Income:		
Discount earned on customer acceptances purch.	0	0
Issuance & other fees		1,095
Total income		$ 1,095
Expenses:		
Credit check	0	$ 0
Letters issued	2 @ 32.21303	64
Process inquiries	4 @ 1.90106	8
Purchase acceptance	0	0
Terminate letter of credit	1 @ 22.89139	25
Other expenses	0	0

EXHIBIT 18.1 *(continued)*

Total expenses			95
Profit (loss) commercial letters of credit			$ 1,000
Data processing—payroll processing, accounts: 817 336			
Income:			
Fees earned		$ 3,073	
Total income			$ 3,073
Expenses:			
Record processing	4,895 @ 2.79351	$ 13,674	
File maintenance	896 @ 3.79350	3,399	
Total expense			17,073
Profit (loss) data processing—payroll processing			($ 14,000)
Net profit (loss) fee based services ($14,000 − $1,000) = ⟶			$ (13,000)
Total profit (loss) all services			$ 12,693

Source: Pagano, T. G., "Measuring Customer Profitability in a Commercial Bank," *Management Accounting*, May 1975, p. 47.

Alternative Concepts and Issues

Specific methods of analyzing customer profitability vary among banks. Primary differences in these methods may be attributed to the relationships being considered (all services or the primary loan/deposit relationship), the measures of profitability to be determined, and the calculation methods used for costing funds, collected balances, and profit margins.

The description of the customer relationship may pose definitional problems. Some banks include those services that directly relate to the primary loan/deposit relationship. For example, some banks exclude repurchase agreements or large certificates of deposits, since the customer's option is to remove nonearning balances and to seek higher-earning investments from bank competitors. The bank's action to retain funds can be considered separate from the normal customer relationship and therefore excluded in computing profitability.

In addition to the basic profitability statement, many banks relate profits to capital or net funds used. The allocation of capital as a source of funds involves the appropriate amount of capital to be allocated to the relationship and target rates of return. Additional computational problems exist in the determination of the appropriate rate to be used in costing funds and the inclusion of unallocated general overhead in cost data. Alternatives are numerous and are extensively discussed by Robert E. Knight.[1]

PRICING POLICIES

As deregulation continues and banks enter more of the traditional non-banking markets, the need for pricing decisions will increase in importance. Corporate deposits have been declining. Corporate borrowers are becoming increasingly reluctant to maintain compensating balances and have shown a willingness to pay for bank services on a fee basis. The competition for the retail deposit has increased, as has the cost. As banks develop more fee-based services, greater attention must be paid to pricing because banks lack experience in offering such services.

Pricing Approaches

Historically banks have taken one of three approaches to pricing—cost-plus pricing, volume pricing, and follow-the-leader pricing. Cost-plus pricing requires that unit costs be known and target profit margins be

---

[1]See R. E. Knight, "Bank Customer Profitability: An Analysis of Alternative Approaches," *The Magazine of Bank Administration*, May 1977, 12–24.

added to determine the final prices. Addition of the profit margin ensures that each service contributes something to bank profits.

In volume pricing prices are kept low to attract large volumes of customers. It is assumed that bank costs do not vary extensively with higher volumes. As additional volume is added, additions to profits occur because of economies of scale. Follow-the-leader pricing has been a predominant approach in banks because of the historical regulatory constraints on deposit pricing. Examples of follow-the-leader pricing are free checking accounts and premium wars.

None of these approaches will work in every situation. Guiltinan describes the pitfalls one should be aware of before using these approaches:

1. The search for economies of scale is limited. Increasing volume does not always yield lower average costs, because not all costs are fixed. Furthermore, there are practical limits to the number of transactions a bank can process without reducing the quality of service—especially on demand deposit services. Finally, not all customers are equally profitable. Frequently, customers drawn to a bank by low prices will have lower balances yet be just as costly to serve as those with higher balances.

2. Customer sensitivity to price may vary across services and across groups of customers. Consequently, neither simple cost-plus nor volume-building approaches will be appropriate for all services or all markets.

3. All competitors are not alike. They may offer similar prices but differ in terms of other strategies that can influence customers. Furthermore, their cost structures may vary, especially on fee services. A price that is profitable to a competitor may not be profitable to your bank.

4. Measuring profit margins is difficult because of joint costs and interrelated demand. That is, many costs are shared among several services, and demand for one service often influences demand for a second service—either because the potential services are substitutes or because they complement one another. Thus, cost-plus pricing policies must be adjusted to reflect these realities, especially as new services are added.

5. Cost-plus pricing may ignore profit opportunities that exist in markets where pricing at small margins can yield very large volumes.

6. Price is not independent of the rest of marketing strategy. Although the price sensitivity of buyers will be influenced in part by other marketing policies and the quality of service provided, a strategy that is based on very low prices will

ultimately condition the buyer to expect low prices or to undervalue the services.[2]

Costing Approaches in Bank Pricing Decisions

Three basic costing approaches are useful in bank pricing decisions. Average costing, derived from functional cost data, reflects the average cost of each service at the current level of volume. Pricing at average cost ensures that the bank covers all costs. Total cost comprises direct and indirect costs. Cost-plus pricing easily incorporates average cost data for price determination.

Cost/volume/profit analysis is an appropriate cost approach when volume changes are expected or desired. With a change in volume, some costs will change as the number of transactions changes. Principally it is assumed that fixed costs will remain relatively unchanged and variable costs will be small in proportion to total cost because of economies of scale. Total cost includes direct and indirect costs. Volume pricing incorporates the cost/volume/profit analysis in price determination for existing services.

Incremental costing is adaptable to situations not only where new services are to be added or old services are to be deleted but also where existing services are to be expanded or contracted. Incremental costing is a direct costing method wherein only variable costs are considered relevant to the analysis. Incremental costing derives the cost difference that would result if a new service were added, an old service were deleted, or if volume increased because of a lowering of prices.

Cost/Volume/Profit Applications.   Cost/volume/profit analysis is an appropriate method for analyzing services whose average cost declines as additional volume occurs. Certain bank services, such as cash management or data-processing services, follow a basic cost/volume/profit formulation:

$$\text{Profit} = (\text{Price} - \text{Variable cost per transaction}) \times \text{Volume} - \text{Fixed cost}$$

For an existing service where volume is expected to increase, we should examine current profitability vs. profitability after the expected or desired volume change. For any contemplated change we want to ensure

---

[2]Guiltinan, J. P., *Pricing Bank Services: A Planning Approach*, American Bankers Association, 1980, 3–4.

that at least the current profit level is maintained. For example, assume the following conditions:

Current profit = $23,000   Expected profit = $?
Price = $0.50   Price = $0.40
Variable cost = $0.15   Variable cost = $0.15
Volume = 100,000   Expected volume = 150,000
Fixed cost = $12,000   Fixed cost = $12,000

Solving for expected profit, a price reduction of $0.10 per transaction and an increase in expected volume of 50,000 transactions results in profits of $25,500, or an increase of $2,500. Alternatively, given a price decrease to $0.40 per transaction and maintaining profits at $23,000, we can determine the volume level to break even at the new price, where

$$\text{Required volume} = \frac{\text{Fixed cost} + \text{Profit}}{\text{New price} - \text{Variable cost}}$$
$$= \frac{\$12,000 + \$23,000}{\$0.40 - \$0.15}$$
$$= 140,000 \text{ transactions}$$

If this volume can be achieved with the current cost structure unaffected, then the current profit can be maintained. Factors that influence achievement of a given volume level are customer reaction and the competitive environment. Additional volume may increase customer waiting time and result in customer dissatisfaction, which may in turn result in decreased demand and volume.

In our example we know that the expected volume from a price change is 150,000 transactions and that the volume required to maintain profits of $23,000 is 140,000 transactions. If the increased volume results in customer dissatisfaction and volume increases to only 130,000 transactions, the taraget profit level will not be attained. Therefore, when predicting attainable volumes, a bank must be responsive to customer attitudes at certain volume levels.

The pricing of deposit accounts is more difficult to analyze. The reason is that many different assumptions may be employed regarding the construction of revenue and cost statements. The general equation that describes a deposit relationship is

$$\text{Profit} = \begin{array}{c}\text{Earnings}\\\text{on deposit}\\\text{balances}\end{array} - \text{Transaction costs} - \begin{array}{c}\text{Fixed}\\\text{maintenance}\\\text{costs}\end{array}$$

where

$$\text{Earnings on deposit balances} = \text{Rate} \times \text{Average balance}$$
$$\text{Transaction costs} = \text{Variable cost} \times \text{Volume}$$

Banks can recover costs through the money they earn from using deposits in funding earning assets or from charging service fees. The general equation above ignores cost recovery from service fees.

Several alternatives are available for determining the earnings rate on deposits:

- *Money market rates.* Since the net yield on earning assets exceeds money market rates, the value of deposit funds will tend to be understated. These rates are also highly volatile.
- *Cost-of-funds rates.* This rate reflects what the bank would pay for alternative sources of funds if deposits were not available. In periods of rising rates the value of deposits would be understated, and they would be overstated in periods of declining rates.
- *Return on bank portfolio.* This rate is the net current earnings after tax divided by the average earnings assets. This rate reflects the past value of sources of funds, not the current value.
- *Weighted average of rates on expected portfolio mix.* This rate is based on estimates and is subject to frequent changes if portfolio rates are volatile.

The choice of an appropriate earnings rate is difficult. It should be based on the conditions that best reflect the bank's portfolio conditions over the period in which the earnings rate will be in effect.

Assuming the following conditions, we can prepare a chart (see Exhibit 18.2) that identifies the annual profitability of checking accounts:

Net earnings rate on all deposits = 10%
Transaction cost = $0.15
Maintenance cost = $36

By scaling average deposit balances from $100 to $1000 and transactions from 100 to 300 per year, we note that an average balance must exceed $500 before an account with 100 transactions breaks even. We can compute the break-even balance for the level of transactions that can serve as the "floor" for determining further price adjustments:

$$\text{Profit} = (\text{Rate} \times \text{Average balance}) - (\text{Volume} \times \text{Variable cost}) - \text{Maintenance cost}$$

Solving for the average balance with 100 transactions:

EXHIBIT 18.2   Pricing Using Cost/Volume/Profit Analysis

Average Account Balance ($)	Checking Accounts per Year				
	Net Earnings ($)	Maintenance Cost ($)	Number of Transactions	Transaction Cost ($)	Profit ($)
100	10	36	100	15	−41
			200	30	−56
			300	45	−71
300	30	36	100	15	−21
			200	30	−36
			300	45	−51
500	50	36	100	15	− 1
			200	30	−16
			300	45	−31
600	60	36	100	15	9
			200	30	− 6
			300	45	−21
800	80	36	100	15	29
			200	30	14
			300	45	− 1
1000	100	36	100	15	49
			200	30	34
			300	45	19

$$\text{Average Balance} = \frac{\text{Profit} + (\text{Volume} \times \text{Variable cost}) + \text{Maintenance cost}}{\text{Rate}}$$

$$= \frac{0 + 100(0.15) + 36}{0.10}$$

$$= \frac{15 + 36}{0.10} \text{ or } \frac{51}{0.10}$$

$$= \$510 \text{ average balance}$$

For 200 transactions, average balance = $660
For 300 transactions, average balance = $810

With the knowledge of our break-even balances, we may wish to recover part or all of our costs through service charges. For example, if we expand our revenue statement to recover a $30 maintenance fee, the average balance required for break-even becomes

For 100 transactions, average balance = $150
For 200 transactions, average balance = $300
For 300 transactions, average balance = $450

In judging customer acceptance, we need to know what the competition is charging and what our customer's average balance and number of transactions are normally. For example, if the average number of transactions is 300, we know we can offer service charge free checking if the average balance is approximately $800, or with a service charge of $3 per month and an average balance of approximately $450 no other charges (transaction charges) need be assessed.

One further adaptation of this analysis is used for NOW account pricing. The cost statement must be expanded to include interest paid on the average balance. One key to pricing NOW accounts is the selection of an average balance that sets the floor, or minimum balance, that will cover all costs, assuming a given level of checks that will be processed.

Incremental Cost Application.   An assumption involved in incremental costing is that the service to be added, deleted, or changed for volume typically shares costs with other services. Therefore, because the service in question shares fixed costs with other services, a change contemplated in that service will not affect a bank's fixed-cost structure unless the bank is operating at full capacity.

For simplicity, let us assume that an analysis of our demand deposit customers by average balance indicates that an equal number of customers are in each of the following groups:

Average Balance ($)	Annual Transactions per Account	Cost per Transaction ($)	Incremental Cost per Account ($)
0–100	300	0.15	45.00
101–300	300	0.15	45.00
301–500	250	0.15	37.50
501–800	250	0.15	37.50

If the earnings rate (10 percent) and maintenance cost ($36) remain constant, the account profitability would be as follows:

Account Range ($)	Average Balance for Range	Earnings ($)	Maintenance Cost ($)	Incremental Cost ($)	Profit ($)
0–100	50	5	36.00	45.00	−76.00
101–300	200	20	36.00	45.00	−61.00
301–500	400	40	36.00	37.50	−33.50
501–800	650	65	36.00	37.50	− 8.50

Rather than set service charges to cover all costs and thereby possibly lose customers, we may choose to set service charges for all accounts under $500 at a rate of $4 per month and for all accounts from $500 to $800 at a rate of $3 per month. The following would result:

Account Range ($)	Profit before Service Charge ($)	Service Charge ($)	Profit after Service Charge ($)	
0–100	−76.00	48.00	−28.00	} −41.00
101–300	−61.00	48.00	−13.00	
301–500	−33.50	48.00	14.50	} 42.00
501–800	− 8.50	36.00	27.50	

In this example, with an equal number of customers in each group, the loss on accounts ranging from $0 to $300 would be fully recovered by profits on accounts ranging $301 to $800. The possibilities for pricing become infinite. However, the constraining factors are customer acceptance and competitive pricing.

Cost/Volume/Profit Analysis vs. Incremental Costing. When volume changes are desired or expected, cost/volume/profit analysis or incremental costing may be used for making decisions. The question is: Which is appropriate and under what decision-making circumstances should each be used? Cost/volume/profit uses fully allocated costs, which include incremental cost and the specific service's allocated share of fixed and indirect costs. Incremental cost ignores fixed and indirect costs.

Proponents of the use of fully allocated costs state that price should cover all costs and provide a satisfactory return. If the costing system has a clearly defined allocation system for indirect costs and if management is satisfied with the "results" for decision making, then cost/volume/profit analysis can be the appropriate method. Since there are many ways to allocate indirect costs, results may be skewed. Therefore, management must be satisfied with the system to accept the results from a cost/volume/profit analysis. Finally, pricing that will recover part or all of fixed and indirect costs should be based on cost/volume/profit analysis.

For decisions to be based on recovery of variable costs only, incremental costing produces consistent results. This is because cost allocation systems for fixed and indirect costs will not influence the decision. Whereas fully absorbed cost is based on past costs, incremental costing deals with future costs. Proponents of incremental costing argue that changes in total revenue and total cost reflect the future; therefore incremental costing is more appropriate as an analytical tool. A major problem with incremental costing is that all costs may not be recognized. For example, a proposed reduction in transaction processing may affect the total services provided by a data-processing operation. Thus we must look not only at the proposed service changes but also at their effect on other services as well.

As a rule, incremental costing is preferable when new services are to be added. Cost/volume/profit analysis is preferable when basic services that are not expected to be eliminated and services where volume changes are easily predictable are under consideration. Combinations of pricing may also be used where a target profit and a price floor are established. Average costing plus a profit margin or cost/volume/profit would be used to identify target price, while incremental costing would be used to identify the price floor.[3]

Pricing Strategies

Bank services may be neutral services, substitute services, or complementary services. If the introduction of a new service will be purchased by customers who are not existing customers, the service is a neutral service. If the customers for the new service are existing customers who switch from existing services, the new service is a substitute service. If the introduction of a new service brings in new customers who are also expected to use other bank services, the new service is a complementary service. Banks often offer bundles of services such that an increased demand for one service leads to increased demand for other services.

A major concern in pricing substitutes is pricing each service to enhance total profitability. For example, a NOW account is a substitute

[3]See Guiltinan, ibid., for discussion of determining price floors. This publication also provides excellent discussion and worksheets for pricing services.

NOW Account Pricing Strategies

Pricing for NOW accounts, which are substitutes for checking accounts, is relatively complex. Competitive pricing schedules among institutions vary in such components as minimum balance, monthly charge, per-check charge, and possibly other elements as well. The minimum balance required may range from zero to $1500 or more. The lower minimum balance appeals to the low-balance customer. The higher minimum balance requirement tends to retain profitable high-balance customers while eliminating unprofitable low-balance customers.

Low minimum balances are usually accompanied by higher monthly charges and per-check charges. The opposite is true for higher minimum balances. The following schedule outlines the variety in NOW account pricing found in the Massachusetts banking markets:

	Number of Institutions	Minimum Required Balance		Monthly Charge	
		Low	High	Low	High
North Adams	3	$300	$1000	0	$4.00
Pittsfield	7	250	1000	$2.50	5.00
Greenfield	6	200	1000	0	1.50
Northampton	11	200	1000	0	5.00
Springfield	19	200	1000	0	5.00
Athol	4	200	500	0	3.00
Worcester	13	200	1000	0	4.00
Fitchburg	5	500	1000	0	4.00
Boston	15	0	1500	0	5.00
Fall River	6	25	1500	0	4.50
Taunton	5	300	700	1.50	4.50
New Bedford	7	300	600	0	4.00
Cape Cod	8	25	1000	0	4.00

Note: For market boundary definitions, see Steve Yokas and Joe Gagnon, *1981 Bank Structure in New England*, Research Report No. 67, Federal Reserve Bank of Boston, October 1982.

Source: Federal Reserve Bank of Boston, 1982 NOW account price survey.

Several trends are occurring for NOW account pricing:

- Most NOW accounts are priced according to one of three pricing schedules: (1) flat-rate pricing incorporates monthly and per-check charges; (2) free monthly and per-check charges are waived; (3) conditionally there is no charge: if minimum balances are held, no charges are incurred.
- Conditionally free pricing has become predominant.
- Minimum balance levels, monthly charges, and per-check charges are increasing principally because of increased costs imposed by the Depository Institutions Deregulation and Monetary Control Act and by explicit pricing of Federal Reserve Bank services.
- Customers have many alternative price schedules from which to select. The schedules may vary significantly but one may be no more expensive than another.
- The wide variety of pricing suggests a highly competitive market among institutions that offer NOW accounts.

Per-Check Charge		Notice of Insufficient Funds		Stop-Payment Order	
Low	High	Low	High	Low	High
0	$.15	$5.00	$12.00	$5.00	$6.00
0	.15	5.00	12.00	2.00	10.00
$.15	.25	3.00	8.50	2.00	6.00
0	.20	5.00	10.00	2.00	7.50
0	.20	4.00	8.00	3.00	7.50
0	.15	4.00	10.00	3.00	7.50
0	.15	3.00	10.00	1.00	10.00
0	.25	5.00	10.00	3.00	10.00
0	.55	3.00	15.00	1.00	15.00
0	.25	5.00	10.00	4.00	10.00
0	.25	5.00	10.00	3.00	10.00
0	.20	5.00	10.00	2.00	10.00
0	.25	4.00	10.00	2.00	7.50

for a checking account. Pricing should be developed to meet customer demand for each distinct account type and to increase total profitability. This strategy may include increasing the prices for some services and decreasing the prices for others. Pricing for new substitutes may achieve one or more of the following objectives:

1. Appeal to certain segments that might be made profitable (for example, by pricing VISA or Master Charge cards to replace small personal loans).

2. Reach new users who would not otherwise buy any of the substitutes. (Treasury bill-tied CDs and retail repurchase agreements often appeal to those who do not use passbook savings accounts.)

3. Encourage a shift to services that have a lower operating cost. (For example, Louisiana National Bank's ATM, debit card, and bill-paying-by-phone services were all implemented not only to generate fee income but also to reduce personnel costs by reducing check writing.)

4. Retain customers who would otherwise switch banks. (Incremental revenue can be negative if the failure to offer a new service at a reasonably competitive price leads to lost accounts. A bank's best customers should be retained. Rockingham National Bank in Virginia initiated Automatic Transfer Accounts (ATS) primarily to avoid inroads by the state's large holding-company banks. That is, the purpose of ATS was to encourage consolidation of savings and checking by setting a $4,000 minimum balance for no-transaction fees and a $5,000 minimum for free checking.)[4]

Complementary services may be priced to increase profitability or to increase volume. If we offer a new service that will lead to increased value of existing services, then the opportunity to receive a high price on the new service exists. If we expect certain services to lead to cross-selling other services, a price strategy may be to lower the price on the "leader." Complementary services are often bundled at a single price. Many times this bundling leads to greater profitability of all services, since certain services would not be used as much if they were marketed separately.

In setting initial prices for neutral products, there are at least two alternatives. One is skimming and the second is penetration pricing. In

---

[4]Ibid., 60.

the skimming approach the initial price is set high to take advantage of the novelty of the product. Since prices are set at high levels, competition will seek to compete on price. As the market becomes saturated at the price level, prices are decreased to successively lower levels to absorb market demand. By setting high prices a bank protects itself from uncertainties related to demand and cost factors. Significantly, prices are easy to lower but more difficult to raise.

Penetration pricing is the opposite of skimming. Prices are set as low as possible to capture the greatest share of the market. The higher volume lowers the unit costs of production and keeps competition out of the market. After the market is secured, prices may be increased.

A bank cannot ignore competition when setting prices. The pricing decision becomes more difficult, when analyzing profitability among substitutes, where existing customers may shift between bank services or to another bank. Two strategies are possible in competing directly with other banks. The first is head-on pricing, which implies direct or cutthroat pricing. Generally, this type of price competition exists where volume increase is desired and services among banks are undifferentiated.

The second strategy is differentiated pricing. This strategy emphasizes differences between the bank's service and its superiority to competitors' products. To implement a differentiated strategy, the bank must know where the competitive advantage lies and what price and benefit combinations will appeal to the target customers.

SUMMARY

The development of bank cost data provides bases for analyzing bank systems and for controlling bank costs. A formal budgeting process is an effective way to obtain management participation in setting bank goals and objectives and to establish accountability for managerial action. Customer profitability analyses are particularly important for considering total customer relationships and their profitability. The source of information for determining costs is the cost-accounting system.

Pricing strategy is important in recovering costs and meeting profit objectives. Each service has distinct characteristics and market demand. Therefore prices must be designed to meet bank objectives, which may include the introduction, expansion, or contraction of services. A bank cannot ignore the benefits of cost accounting. In periods of significant variation in cost structures, a bank must be ready to alter its pricing structures in order to maintain or improve profit margins. Cost accounting, budgeting, and customer profitability analyses are important components of an effective cost control and pricing system.

Questions and Problems

1. What is a customer profitability analysis?

2. What is a balance-based service?

3. What problems arise in defining the customer relationship?

4. Define: *cost-plus pricing, volume pricing,* and *follow-the-leader pricing.*

5. Compare average costing, cost/profit/volume analysis, and incremental costing.

6. Describe the alternatives for pricing neutral services.

Suggested Case

Case 7, Customer Profitability Analysis: Computer Software, Inc.

References

Bunkam, C. "Unraveling the Complexity of NOW Account Pricing." *New England Economic Review, Federal Reserve Bank of Boston,* May-June 1983: 30–45.

Guiltinan, J. P. *Pricing Bank Services: A Planning Approach.* Washington, DC: American Bankers Association, 1980.

Knight, R. E. "Bank Customer Profitability: An Analysis of Alternative Approaches." *The Magazine of Bank Administration,* May 1977: 12–24.

Kohn, S. T., and C. W. Scott. "Effective Pricing of EFTS." *Bankers Magazine,* March–April 1981: 40–42.

Levine, J. B. "How a Bank Performs a Customer Profitability Analysis." *Management Accounting,* June 1978: 10–14.

Pagano, T. G. "Measuring Customer Profitability in a Commercial Bank." *Management Accounting,* May 1975: 43–47, 50.

Ulrich, T. A. "The Financial Planning Implications of Bank Loan Pricing." *Management Accounting,* September 1980: 64–72.

Zimmerman, J., and H. B. McDonald. "Profitability Analysis, Cost Systems and Pricing Policies." In *The Bankers' Handbook,* 2d ed., ed. W. H. Baughn and C. E. Walker, 295–312. Homewood, IL: Dow Jones-Irwin, 1978.

CHAPTER 19

Strategic and Tactical Planning

Given the events of recent years with regard to expansion of bank services and relatively high rates of inflation and interest, strategic or long-range planning is becoming increasingly important. Formal strategic planning is a management technique for determining where the organization is going and how it will get there through regular, consistent, rational, comprehensive, and coordinated decision making that commits resources to action.[1] Strategic planning is concerned with the process of how the bank makes its money, what its strengths and weaknesses are, and from the analysis of those strengths and weaknesses what its advantages and constraints are expected to be in exploiting opportunities for growth. Tactical planning involves the short- or medium-range plans that contribute to the overall strategic objectives. These plans are represented in short-term annual operating plans and include the particular procedural and mechanical aspects of achieving the goals established within the framework of the long-range plan.

Planning is not forecasting, budgeting, or capital rationing; nor is it a panacea. Forecasting environmental changes is an important component of planning. The development of plans is an active response to forecasts. Budgeting is another component of planning and is a translation of the purpose, objectives, and strategies of the long-range plan into quantifiable targets. These targets can be used to measure the success or progress in completing elements of a plan. The allocation of capital is an element of planning and establishes priorities among various projects. The plan establishes the priorities and the allocation process follows. Planning is a tool that is used to improve performance. The purpose of planning is ultimately to improve the decisions that determine performance.

Planning provides a structure for decision making. Decisions become more regular and consistent as the plan is carried out. A planning framework leads to decision making that is rational, impersonal, and less political. Established standards and guidelines that are recognized throughout the organization reduce conflicts among personnel and project priorities.

---

[1] T. W. Thompson, L. L. Berry, and P. H. Davidson, *Banking Tomorrow* (New York: Van Nostrand Reinhold, 1978), 34.

A comprehensive and coordinated plan allows decisions to be made without the need to understand the impact of those decisions on other operating functions. Decisions follow existing goals, guidelines, and strategies incorporated in an integrated plan and result in reduction of conflict, complication, and duplication of effort. Planning forces decisions because it outlines what is to be accomplished. Therefore avoidance of a decision will result in disruption of progress toward objectives and can thus be pinpointed. The manager realizes that a decision must be made because the result of not making a decision may impact other functions, projects, objectives, or goals.

A plan should be flexible to adjust to changing conditions, but it should not be so flexible as to cause abandonment of the plan. Integrating changing conditions into a plan modifies certain elements but retains the basic plan's framework.

The assignment of responsibilities and the tracking of performance determine whether specific tasks are being executed. Budgeting partly answers whether goals are being met, but qualitative judgments must also be considered.

Finally, planning enhances management's ability to cope with risk. The plan identifies the risks involved in different courses of action. If problems arise, managers will be better prepared to address them since various risk scenarios will have been discussed in the process of establishing the plan.

THE PLANNING PROCESS

The corporate planning process incorporates an extensive examination process including both the external environment and the bank's internal environment. Examination of the internal environment consists of evaluation of past strategies, performance, strengths, and weaknesses. Additionally, the components of the bank or holding company are subjected to critical analysis. Examination of the external environment and the internal environment in terms of corporate-level functions is usually performed by staff-level personnel. The characterization and nature of the business are inputs received from functional and line managers.

Exhibit 19.1 presents a conceptual view of the planning process. The external environment analysis leads to a range of possible alternative assumptions regarding competition, regulation, and economic growth. The strategic plan is concerned with longer-range possibilities, whereas the tactical plan includes prediction of interest rates and structural changes in the short run. Each of the inputs, including statements from functional and line personnel, presents a body of data and information from which possible sets of strategies and levels of performance can be selected. The internal data is compared with the external data, and objectives, goals, and strategies are selected for the long and short

EXHIBIT 19.1 The Planning Process

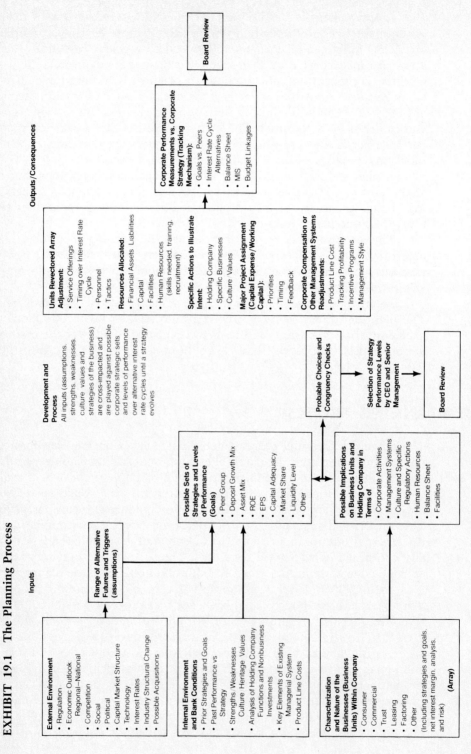

Reprinted by permission of the publisher, from B. Cox et al., *The Bank Director's Handbook* (Boston: Auburn House Publishing Company, 1981).

runs. Finally, the plan is disseminated for the development of action plans.

A control phase is important in that it provides a measurement of progress toward corporate goals and objectives. The controls are both quantitative (accounting and operations-level statistics) and qualitative (project or product development and completion results).

External Analysis

The purpose of an analysis of external factors is to clearly establish the sensitivity of bank policies to possible changes in the external environment. Importantly, favorable changes in legislation and regulations create opportunities if the timing and extent of the changes are correctly anticipated. If these factors are not considered, the bank operates in a vacuum and opportunities are lost. Unfavorable legislation and regulation may have significant impact upon plans and operating systems. For example, the change from lagged reserve accounting to contemporaneous reserve accounting imposed costs and disruptions of computer and accounting systems. If external factors are ignored, the bank is completely unprepared. Proper planning considers all external factors to derive possible scenarios on how the bank might react if these factors are correctly assessed.

Factors that should be considered are:

- Regulation
- Economic outlook: regional, national, international
- Competition
- Political and social changes
- Capital market structure
- Technology
- Interest rates
- Industry structural change
- Legislation: banking, tax, federal and state budgets

Internal Analysis

The internal analysis includes examination of the bank's past performance related to its past strategies, key financial factors, operating systems and facilities, and personnel capabilities. The analysis is self-critical and should include both the strengths and weaknesses of the organization.

Certain key data should be gathered and analyzed, including but not limited to the following:

Financial and operational
- Deposit size and mix
- Loan portfolio (size, functional distribution, and yield)

- Capital structure
- Income from trust fees, EDP services, and other service charges
- Annual growth objectives
- Level of operating expenses
- Income tax management
- Capacity constraints
- Operating efficiency
- Liquidity

Organization and manpower
- Planning and manpower requirements to meet growth objectives
- Future organizational structure
- Management development and training programs
- Salary structure, employee benefits, and personnel policies

EDP systems and control
- Effects of computer technology and the role of automated systems
- Revision and creation of internal accounting systems to meet the increasing demand for more complete, more accurate, and more timely management information
- Projected cost savings that would accrue to the bank through implementation of proposed long-range systems projects
- Projected costs of computer equipment

Facilities and equipment
- Space requirements
- New branch sites (in states where branching is permitted)

Expansion of activities
- Foreign operations
- Holding company

Marketing
- New corporate and personal services
- Share of market objectives and strategies to meet the competition from banks and other financial institutions
- Degree and type of advertising desired
- Desirability of campaigns and other promotional programs and the cost of such projects[2]

---

[2]J. W. Ernest and G. E. Patera, "Planning and Control Systems for Commercial Banks," in *The Changing World of Banking*, ed. H. V. Prochnow and H. V. Prochnow, Jr. (New York: Harper & Row, 1974), 263–264.

Each major function and subsidiary should provide proposed operating objectives and goals for the planning period. The data should include strategies and goals, financial performance including interest margin analysis, and determination of the risk factors confronting the unit.

The financial analysis should address the questions of capital adequacy, profitability and productivity, maximization of assets, and gap management. Metzger and Rau suggest that the minimum data that should be gathered to answer these questions are:

- The bank's most current balance sheet and P&L
- The bank's balance sheet and P&L data in the form of sixty key ratios
- A five-year balance sheet and P&L history
- A two-year trend projection of the balance sheet and P&L based on the historical data, with regard to the most crucial performance ratios
- A comparative analysis of the bank's performance data with six peer institutions
- A rate and maturity schedule and portfolio analysis utilizing an asset/liability model[3]

Certain market data will identify the key segments of a bank's present customer base and suggest trends in customer relationships in the future. According to Metzger and Rau, the market analysis should include:

- Market share overall
- Market share by loans and deposits
  —by category
  —by branch
- Market share comparisons to peer institutions including S&Ls and credit unions (any peer so long as it is an FDIC or FSLIC member)
- Demographic data with respect to census, SMSA [standard metropolitan statistical area], age, income, sex, etc.
- Key demographic trends of those profiles projected out in its market area, if the bank can provide the model with its own customer demographic profiles[4]

Exhibit 19.2 lists possible strengths and weaknesses that may be identified as a result of an internal analysis.

---

[3]R. O. Metzger and S. E. Rau, "Strategic Planning for Future Bank Growth," *Bankers Magazine,* July-August 1982: 59.

[4]Ibid.

EXHIBIT 19.2   Possible Strengths and Weaknesses

Financial

Strengths	Weaknesses
Historically high profitability	Poor retention of capital and erosion forecast to continue
Good financial information systems	
Adequate capital for expansion or reinvestment in new facilities	Little financial data available
	Poor yields on securities investments
Strong capital-to-assets ratios	Imbalance of loan portfolio with respect to long-term fixed-rate loans
Rich dividend policy	
	Cost of delivering products and services not identified
	Poor public image leading to depressed price of stock below book value
	Failure to develop sources of noninterest revenue
	Failure to develop trust income

Human Resources

Strengths	Weaknesses
Well-developed, competitive salary administration program	Lack of salary administration program
Salary increases tied exclusively to well-understood criteria for performance and productivity	Salary administration program that has not kept pace with the Consumer Price Index or any other index over the last five years
Bonus programs for all officers and supervisors based on overall bank performance	Salary increases decided on basis other than merit
Well-established communication between employees and the top of the organization	Salary increases decided secretly by other than direct supervisors or department heads
Multiple training programs, especially to develop supervisory, managerial, and communications skills	Lack of formal performance appraisal and feedback system
	No bonus program, a bonus program only for senior officers, or a bonus program not based on performance
Employees reimbursed for continuing education programs	
Effective appraisals of performance and feedback programs	Employees' perceptions that management does not care and will not listen to ideas or suggestions
Employees' perception that management does care and will listen	Employees' perceptions that women and/or minorities do not have equal opportunities for promotion
High morale and team spirit	
A full-time marketing staff of professional marketing personnel	No formal training programs or few training programs for supervisors and managers
Ongoing market research programs to test customers' profiles, attitudes, and needs and the marketplace	Bank goals and objectives not shared throughout the organization
	No professional marketing staff and no marketing performed other than local advertising

EXHIBIT 19.2 *(continued)*

Marketing

Strengths	Weaknesses
Branch sales training programs supporting a branch management and staff held accountable for acquisition and retention of deposits	No market research data on the bank's market or customer profiles
A central information file that allows evaluation and profit analysis of a customer's total relationship, usually accessible by a terminal	No information on costs and benefits of products and services
Positive customer awareness of the bank's image as a progressive, innovative institution	No product development and a follow-the-leader mentality with respect to new services
Formal marketing planning and budgeting with all products and services costed and priced profitably	No central information file to evaluate customer relationships or profitability of accounts
Additional funds available for promotions based on "ex" new accounts per $1000 expended	No formal business development responsibility assigned to branch managers for acquisition and retention of deposits
	No formal sales training program for branch managers or staff
	No formal marketing budget or a budget that is perceived to be purely an expense item to be cut at the first sign of declining earnings

Operations

Strengths	Weaknesses
Support from a service bureau willing to work with and develop new services for bank customers	Support from a service bureau that will develop new services only if the majority of users demand them
A data processing priorities committee that directs data processing and operations hardware and software development in support of line and branch needs and in parallel with the bank's long-range plans and objectives	In-house support from a data center that sets priorities for the bank rather than vice versa
Proof and data processing capacity to absorb a great deal of growth and even to provide services and time to other users for a fee	Operations center that has a high turnover of employees and programmers
High cost/budgeting orientation and accountability by operations/data processing management	No product line operational support
	Old, obsolete proof equipment
	Proof operator staff working in fits and starts in reaction to poorly planned work flow
	Item-processing growth projected to exceed processing volume within twelve months
	No operational planning in support of the bank's plans or objectives
	No operations budgeting or accountability for expense control
	No overall data processing priorities committee at the highest levels of management
	Operations procedures established without coordination with branch management

CONSOLIDATION OF INPUTS

The consolidation of data requires an interchange of information among key functional personnel. The purpose of this interchange is to judge the relevance of the data and to provide a forum for discussion of possible alternative objectives, goals, and strategies. Many times trade-offs will be negotiated among various unit leaders to formulate a plan that can be attained.

The proposed set of objectives, goals, and strategies will require a second analysis by the financial support staff. This analysis should identify any financial implications that may pose problems for the financing of the bank. If reasonable financing cannot be expected to be available, certain parts of the plan may be eliminated or reduced in scope.

Strategic Alternatives

The consolidation of inputs sets the stage for consideration of a bank's long-range objectives. A number of alternatives are possible:

1. Preservation of status quo
2. Slow growth
3. Rapid growth
4. Seek to be acquired
5. Transition to a different industry, such as a financial services conglomerate

The status quo position assumes that the bank will not materially change its structure of existing services and that it will continue its same profitability levels. In an environment of significant changes in specific services, the bank may be faced with making modifications over time, but for the present it maintains a wait-and-see posture. For a small bank this may be a reasonable alternative in the short run, but over the long run the position probably cannot be maintained and will be modified. Larger banks in today's environment simply cannot wait and see. They must commit to meeting existing competition or anticipating that certain structural changes must occur within the bank.

The slow-growth alternative assumes that the bank will examine its structure such that it may form a bank-holding company and begin to examine the possibilities for engaging in other operations related to banking or begin to change its conceptual focus from a bank to the broader financial services industry. The bank may select the slow-growth alternative to have the opportunity to gain hands-on experience with a single bank in manipulating services into subsidiaries. Engaging in this strategy to restructure for a short period of time provides the opportunity to develop scenarios for new services or operating units.

A rapid-growth scenario typically appeals to banks that are entrepreneurs or are looking to expand through formation of a multibank holding company and/or through the development of different financial services that do not exist in the current framework. Several implications of this choice are that management's responsibilities will evolve away from day-to-day management to direction and coordination of a group of activities in different markets with different needs and examination of possible new business ventures.

The changeover in a rapid-growth period, wherein senior management is more concerned with the longer range, requires the development of a new management team within the core banking structure at an even greater pace than in the past. Additional expertise may be required to complement senior management as the banking group enters new activities and markets. The development of the bank's own personnel in a short run is not usually feasible. The more reasonable course is to hire the expertise to formulate strategies and to conduct the day-to-day operations of new activities. Within the total structure of a rapid-growth scenario, the personnel structure will also begin to change. Therefore the compensation structure of the bank should be examined to produce incentives for personnel to be high performers.

The seek-to-be-acquired alternative is more likely for the small- to medium-sized organization. However, in today's environment with tender offers being made for large banking organizations by other large banking organizations, it is likely that a defensive posture, in the sense of working the banking organization to a position where it is desirable to be acquired, may be a focal point for a bank. The implications of such a decision may be as follows:

- Very little may be done to resolve the weaknesses found in the organization as the costs involved may be too significant to resolve in the short term.
- Effort should be made to reduce operating expenses and to preserve and improve the operating earnings to make it appear more attractive to potential purchasers.
- This is the most risky alternative, since the attractiveness of the bank may not be noticed by other organizations, nor may legislation produce the required effects that would make the bank attractive as a branch site, for example.[5]

There are no guarantees that the bank will actually be acquired. Given a longer-term scenario, if the bank has not been sold, management and shareholders may find themselves with a bank that has fallen behind its competitors and simply has not kept up with the changes in the marketplace.

---

[5]Ibid., 63.

The transition scenario is one in which the bank changes the over-all structure of its organization and concentrates on new services, which may include the following:

- Real estate brokerage
- Mortgage banking
- Construction financing
- Property management
- Real estate development
- Building supply
- Leasing companies
- Factoring services
- Agrimanagement companies
- Consumer finance
- Investment advisory services
- Mutual fund management
- Money market fund management
- Insurance companies
- Insurance agencies
- Travel agencies
- Pension plan advisory services
- Other related business[6]

Several consequences occur during a transition. Although the bank is aware that it will still be in the business of banking and managing money, it must also avail itself of a much broader use of funds by incorporating different techniques to acquire and utilize funds that will change the overall operational systems of the bank. Additionally, the scope of the bank's markets could change from local to regional or national. Finally, because a nonfinancial service organization will experience greater access to equity and debt markets, it will have the opportunity to expand services at a much faster rate than might be possible under a simple banking structure.

There are additional consequences that are not so positive. Senior management, in attempting a transition, must shift its management personnel from banking into diversified financial areas that may be totally unfamiliar to them. In addition, management must develop the skills required to direct these enterprises and hire the appropriate operating managers, many of whom are expensive. Importantly, the change in style of management that is required is to let the managers manage, deal with policy, and maintain a hands-off approach to the day-to-day operations. Senior management's role, again, is to develop the overall strategies with respect to business lines, market areas, and the allocation of resources among the various entities.

It is essential that communication be very evident within the organization, including a reliance on financial reports and meetings with the subsidiary chief operating officers. It is also important to establish extensive training programs, which may be developed through various seminars with the operating personnel at various levels in the operation. Effective communication alerts management personnel to deficiencies in their operation and to opportunities to enhance the overall organization.

---

[6]Ibid., 39.

In hiring new personnel, a full system of compensation and a reward system that works with a particular activity should be developed. This means that there may be several types of compensation systems existing within the entire organization, each of which must be managed with care. The marketing success of the overall plan is heavily dependent on continuing sophisticated research. This research may be obtained within the organization or professional consultants may be hired.

The Written Plan

Commitment to planning requires a formal written plan. The written plan provides a document that incorporates the plan's significant elements—purpose or mission statement, objectives, goals, policies and guidelines, and action strategies. All but the action strategies are determined at the corporate level. The purpose or mission statement identifies the business the bank is in. Objectives state where the bank is going. Goals specify quantitative statements and time dimensions. Policies and guidelines establish the parameters within which activities will occur. Action strategies, which are developed at lower levels in the organization, identify customers, products and services, people resources, and delivery systems. Exhibit 19.3 presents sample statements to be incorporated in a formal written plan.

EXHIBIT 19.3   Sample Statements for the Written Plan

Sample Statement of Mission

The bank's mission is to earn substantial profits for its stockholders. This aim is entirely compatible with and indeed can be achieved only by satisfaction, to the extent possible, of the needs of customers, employees, and the public. Those needs can be satisfied only if the bank aggressively markets a broad array of financial services in selected state, regional, national, and world markets.

Sample Objectives

Fastest profitable growth in selected geographic/product markets

Profitability superior to that of major competitors

Highest possible rating for debt securities

Equal opportunity through affirmative action

A reputation as a first-class wholesale banking organization

Sample Goals

Annual percentage growth rates for earnings, total assets, various categories of assets and deposits

Ratios of fixed expenses to total assets

Explanations for why these specific goals were chosen

EXHIBIT 19.3 *(continued)*

Sample Policies and Guidelines
Loans
Customers
Emphasize relationships for which this is a primary or secondary bank
Make loans of strong to moderate quality
Products/services
Diversify loans to avoid concentration in portfolios
People resources
Encourage opportunities for education and training
Delivery systems
Emphasize specific lending activities at certain locations
Develop prospects for new customers and expand services to existing
  customers through these programs

Sample Strategies for Action
Commercial or Wholesale Banking
Customers
Establish only total relationships, customers with whom the bank can
  reasonably expect to become the primary or secondary bank
Emphasize medium to large businesses of strong to moderate credit quality
Products/services
Offer a broad array of credit arrangements and financial services
Promote revolving credits and intermediate-term loans
People resources
Know the types of individuals and the number of each
Develop an organization chart
Include courses in education and training
Delivery systems
Emphasize commercial lending in certain locations
Develop prospects and existing customers through a systematic call program

Source: T. W. Thompson, L. L. Berry, and P. H. Davidson, *Banking Tomorrow* (New York: Van
Nostrand Reinhold, 1978), chaps, 2, 3, 4, 11.

Short-Term Planning

The annual operating plan is a specific segment of the overall long-range plan. Strategic planning is usually formalized in a written document. Underlying the concept of the strategic plan is the importance of formally integrating the individual one-year plans within the total plan. Annually each division or major group of a division and each profit center should prepare a plan reflecting an organized, documented, written communication that does the following:

- Defines the divisional and/or profit center situation—past, present, and future.
- Defines the opportunities and problems facing the division or profit center.
- Establishes specific and realistic objectives.
- Defines management strategy and programs required to accomplish the objectives.
- Pinpoints responsibility for execution of programs.
- Translates goals and programs into dollars and manpower—that is, planned deposits, loans, and income—and expense budgets to implement plans and meet objective goals.
- Provides a basis for planning for other departments of the bank.[7]

The process of designing the annual plan should incorporate specific directions from senior management with regard to any changes in the long-range plan. The annual operating plan provides the lower-level managers with the framework within which to define the plan's objectives. In Chapter 17 we discussed the importance of budgeting on an annualized basis. We stressed the strategy of organizing for budgets on either a top-down or a bottom-up basis. The same concept holds true for the development of the annual operating plan. The annual plan states how each activity will be expected to occur, who will be responsible for each activity, and to what extent that person or persons have the authority to execute the particular program.

There are many formats for an annual operating plan in banking. A typical plan would include the following:

Market and situation analysis. This section of the plan should include a written assessment of the factors affecting the operation and performance of each division/profit center. Following are some recommended topics for analysis purposes:

- Prior year's performance
- External factors
- Internal factors
- Opportunities and problems

Objectives. This section of the plan should contain written quantitative and qualitative goals and objectives that will be pursued during the

---

[7]Ernest and Patera, op. cit., 267.

budget year. These goals and objectives should reflect any significant problems or opportunities that were highlighted in the market and situation analysis. The development of these goals should include a correlation of the corporate goals. Following are some recommended areas for establishing goals:

- Loan and deposit levels
- Yields
- Manpower and expense levels
- Production efficiency
- Share of market
- Customer account profitability

Plans and programs. This section of the plan should contain the specific programs which will be implemented to achieve the objectives.

Expense budgets. Expense budgets are prepared to determine the "cost" of the plan. The budgeting phase of the annual operating plan is extremely critical to an effective cost-control program. [This topic was discussed in Chapter 17.]

Profit contribution. Each profit center, in addition to planning expense budget items, should determine profit contribution anticipated for the subsequent year.[8]

SUMMARY

Important to the overall planning process is the development of strategies and policies that will bring about the desired objectives. In this regard it is important to communicate and to document the entire process as well as the progress toward meeting these goals. The review process takes on a significance in that periodic consultation with unit managers is extremely important. Such consultation avoids a push-pull situation wherein certain activities are moving forward at a rate faster than other activities. It is important to coordinate the activities so that the goals are realized at approximately the times outlined in the overall plan.

In the planning process there are three potential pitfalls that must be avoided:

1. The bank talks a lot about it but never begins the process.
2. The bank attempts to go through the process without bothering to obtain the hard data required and, instead, works off emotional assumptions.

---

[8]Ibid., 268–269.

3. While the bank starts the process and works off hard data, there is little or no follow-through with the rest of the organization and, obviously, no document or plan is ever developed.[9]

There are also several points of caution with respect to the entire success of the planning process:

- The process cannot succeed if senior management is not totally candid in its self-analysis and works hard to maintain objectivity.
- It cannot succeed if the senior management team is not experienced at group-consensus decision making.
- The process cannot succeed unless there is a commitment to specific action steps to be taken.[10]

Questions and Problems

1. What is the difference between strategic and tactical planning?
2. Describe a typical planning process.
3. Describe how external environmental factors should be employed in the planning process.
4. Since banking regulations and banking structure are rapidly changing, should long-range planning be ignored? Why or why not?

References

Ernest, J. W., and G. E. Patera. "Planning and Control Systems for Commercial Banks." In *The Changing World of Banking,* ed. H. V. Prochnow and H. V. Prochnow, Jr., 244–277. New York: Harper & Row, 1974.

Johnson, H. E. "Comprehensive Corporate Planning for Banks." In *The Bankers' Handbook,* 2d ed., ed. W. H. Baughn and C. E. Walker, 273–287. Homewood, IL: Dow Jones-Irwin, 1978.

Jones, C. L. "Know Thy Niche." *Bankers Magazine,* July-August 1982: 32–35.

Kohn, S. J. "Management Strategies for the '80s." *The Southern Banker,* June 1982.

Metzger, R. O., and S. E. Rau. "Strategic Planning for Future Bank Growth." *Bankers Magazine,* July-August 1982: 57–65.

Nelson, R. R. "Strategic Marketing." *Bankers Magazine,* July-August 1982: 43–46.

Rockwell, G. B. "Strategy Development." In *The Bank Director's Handbook,* ed. B. Cox et al., 153–170. Boston: Auburn House, 1981.

Thompson, T. W., L. L. Berry, and P. H. Davidson. *Banking Tomorrow,* chap. 2, 3, 4, 11. New York: Van Nostrand Reinhold, 1978.

Yalif, A. "Strategic Planning Techniques." *The Magazine of Bank Administration,* April 1982: 22–26.

---

[9]Metzger and Rau, op. cit., 65.
[10]Ibid.

PART FOUR

◆

Bank Expansion and the Future of Banking

CHAPTER 20

Expansion of Commercial Banking

To maintain market position and to grow, banks have developed means to expand. As population increases or shifts within communities, the bank's customer base changes. As businesses form, expand, contract, or go out of existence, their banking needs also change. As customers move from primary banking areas to the suburbs or change their housing patterns, banks find a need to expand their market areas to include their customers or risk losing them to competing institutions.

Markets and permissible banking activities also change. When banks find they must diversify their assets, they may change their legal organizational form from a bank to a bank holding company with subsidiaries to extend the banking organization's market. In this chapter we shall review the basic regulations involving branching and holding company formation that have an impact on the ability of commercial banks to expand their operations. We shall also discuss the factors that banks must consider in making their expansion decisions.

BRANCH BANKING

Expansion through branching is governed by the McFadden Act of 1927. The original intent of this act was to give national banks the same opportunity to branch in those states that allowed state banks to operate branches. Since the passing of the act, branching has become a hotly debated issue. Recent events have created an environment in which banking organizations are expanding in spite of prohibitive state policies regarding branching. Much of the expansion is also across state boundaries. The primary vehicle to circumvent branching laws has been the bank holding company. Before we discuss the aspects of expansion through bank holding companies, let us examine the expansion potential of branching.

Branch banking is a means by which a bank can extend its market through establishing physical facilities to meet the banking needs of its customers. The limits on branching differ among states. Some states permit a bank to operate full-service facilities on a statewide basis. Certain states permit limited-service facilities in which customers can make deposits and withdrawals but cannot open accounts or make loan applications.

Geographic limitations on banks vary. State laws may permit statewide, limited, or unit banking (no branching). In those states that permit limited-service facilities, the facilities are limited as to number, types of services, and distance from the main office. Limited branching may restrict branching to areas such as a specific city, county, county plus adjacent counties, or other regional variations. Exhibit 20.1 outlines the states in which particular types of branching are permissible.

Physical facilities for branch banks vary. In large cities branches may be restricted to pedestrian traffic, although drive-in facilities are also found. As technology improves, many banks are replacing typical brick-and-mortar facilities with automated teller machines (ATMs). These machines permit customer access through bank debit or credit cards. The functions of the ATM are limited to consumer transactions, including checking and credit card transactions. The use of ATMs has allowed banks to restrict their banking week to Monday through Friday for primary services in brick-and-mortar facilities such as branches and drive-in facilities and to rely on ATMs to provide customer access on weekends. For banks that offered Saturday banking, the substitution of ATMs has reduced personnel costs substantially. Most states have de-

---

EXHIBIT 20.1 The Crazy Quilt of State Laws on Bank Branching

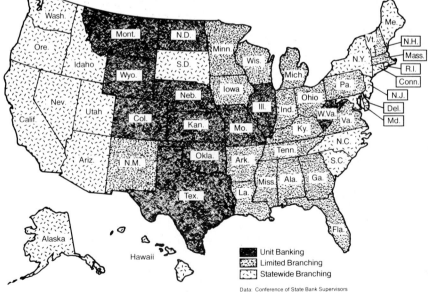

Data: Conference of State Bank Supervisors

Source: Reprinted from the November 17, 1982 issue of *Business Week* by special permission, copyright 1980 by McGraw-Hill, Inc.

termined that ATMs do not constitute branching, although certain states have imposed operational and geographic constraints on their use.

Procedural Requirements to Open a Branch

An application to establish a national bank branch requires the following information:

1. Resolution by the board of directors.
2. Summary financial condition of the bank.
3. Location of each current and pending branch.
4. Planned premises for the proposed branch.
5. Three-year deposit and earnings projections for the proposed branch.
6. Proposed officers of the proposed branch.
7. Economic and demographic data that demonstrate how the proposed branch would meet community convenience and needs.

Requirements for state bank charters vary considerably in content. Exhibit 20.2 outlines various state application requirements.

Branch Expansion Strategies

Strategy to expand through branch offices may include a plan defining the geographic and customer markets to be served. Definition of a total system and objectives for expansion minimize expansion errors. Incorporated in the plan will be the potential locations and the type of facility, which may be manned or unmanned. Since branches may be established *de novo* or through acquisition and merger with another bank, evaluation of the method of expansion should include both alternatives. Some states require expansion beyond geographic limits through merger rather than *de novo*.

The selection of branch sites includes certain basic strategies. Defensive branching is a strategy wherein a bank solidifies its current deposit base by adding convenient branches near its current locations. A bank's seeking to broaden its branch network in areas where it has no or only a few branches is known as market representation branching. A third strategy is preemptive branching, in which a bank seeks prime locations in advance of its competition. A bank may include one or more of these strategies in its plan.

A profitable expansion policy should include proper evaluation of the potential expansion and diversification of loans and deposits, possible operating economies, and the flow of funds within the branch system. Branches may be deposit generators wherein deposits exceed loans or they may be loan generators wherein loans exceed deposits. Respon-

EXHIBIT 20.2 Bank Branching Requirements by State

State	Limitations on Branching	Application Form	Verification of Minimum Capital Requirement	Resolution	Demographics	Definition of Primary Service Area	Definition of Secondary Service Area	Data on Competition Within Service Area	Map Showing Market/Traffic	Economic Development of Area	Agricultural	Residential	Commercial	Industrial	Resort/Recreational	Evidence of Need	Management Profiles/Skills	Financial Trends of Bank Three Past Years	Income/Expenditures of New Branch-3-Year Projections	Anticipated Interest Rates	Planned Investment in Building, Fixtures, Equipment	Feasibility Survey
Alabama	County	x	x	x	Rough	—		x										2 yr.	2 yr.		x	
Alaska	State	x	x	x	—	—	—	—	x	x	x	x	x	—	x	x	x		x		x	x
Arizona	State	x	x	x	Rough	General		x	x	—	—	x	x	x	x	—	x	x	x		x	—
Arkansas	County	x	—	x	Rough	General		x		x	x	x	x	x	—	x	x	x		x		x	x
California	State	x	x	x	Detail	x	x	x	x	x	x	x	—	x	x		—	Part	—	x	—	
Colorado	Unit																					
Connecticut	State	x	—	x	Rough	—		x		x		x	x	x	—	x		x		x		
Delaware	State	FDIC	x	x	Detail	x	—	x	x	x	x	x	x	x	x	x		x	x	x		
Florida	Unit																					
Idaho	State	x	x	x	x	General		x		x		x	x	x	—	x	x	x		x		x
Georgia	County	x	—	x	Rough	—	—	x					x	x	—	x		x		x		
Hawaii	Zones	FDIC	x	x	Detail	x	—	x	x	x	x	x	—	x	x	x		x		x		
Illinois	Unit																					
Iowa	County	x	x	x	Rough	—		x		x		x		x	x	x		x		x		
Indiana	County	x	x	x	x	General		x		x	x	x	x	x	—	x	x	2 yr.	x		x	
Kansas	City	FDIC	x	x	Detail	x	—	x		x	x	x	x	x	—	x	x	x		x		
Kentucky	County	x	x	x	x	General		x		x		x	x	x	—	x	x	x		x		
Louisiana	Parish	FDIC x	x	x	Detail	x	—	x		x	x	x	x	x	—	x	x	x		x		
Maine	State	FDIC	x	x	Detail	x	—	x		x		x	x	x	—	x		x		x		
Maryland	State	x	x	x	Rough	General		x	x	x	—	—	—	x	x		—	Part	—	x		
Massachusetts	County			x			—																
Michigan	County	x	x	x	x	x	—	x	x	x	x	x	x	x	x			x		x		
Minnesota	Unit																					
Mississippi	City/County	x	x	x	Rough	General		x								x				Part		x	
Missouri	Unit																					
Montana	Unit																					
Nebraska	Unit																					
Nevada	State	x	—	x	Rough	General		x	x	x	x	x	x	—	x	—	—	Part	x	x	x	
New Jersey	State	x	x	x	Detail	x	x	x	x	—	x	x	x	—	x	—	1 yr.	x		x		
New Hampshire	Town	x	x	x	Rough	General		—	—	—	—	—	—	—	—	x		x		x		
New Mexico	County	FDIC	x	x	Detail	x	—	x		x	x	x	x	x	x	x		x		x		
New York	County	x	x	x	x	x	x	x	x	x	x	x	x	x	x		x	x	x		x	
North Carolina	State	FDIC	x	x	Detail	x	—	x		x	x	x	x	x	—	x	x	x		x		
North Dakota	Unit																					
Ohio	County	x	x		x	—	—	x	x	x	x	x	x	—	x			x		x		
Oklahoma	Unit																					
Oregon	State	x	—	x	Rough	x		—		x	x	x	x	x	—	x		x		x		x
Pennsylvania	County	x	x	x	x	x	x	x	x	x	x	x	x	x	x	x		x		x	x	x
Rhode Island	State	—	—	—	—	—		x		—		—	—	—		—		x		x		
South Carolina	State	x	x	x	Rough	x		—		x	x	x	x	x	x	x	1 yr.	x		x		
South Dakota	State	x	x	x	Rough	—		x		x	x	x	x	x	—	x		x		x		
Tennessee	County	x	x	x	Rough	—	—	x		—	x	x		x	x		x	Part	—	x		
Texas	Unit																					
Vermont	State	FDIC	x	x	Detail	x	—	x		x	x	x	x	x	—	x		x		x		
Virginia	City/County	x	—	x	—	—		x	x	—	—	—	—	x	x	1 yr.	Part	x	x			
Utah	City/County	x	x	x	Rough	—		x		—		x	x	x	—	x		x		—		
Washington	State	FDIC	x	x	Detail	x	—	x		x	x	x	x	x	—	x	x	x		x		
West Virginia	Unit																					
Wisconsin	Unit																					
Wyoming	Unit																					
FDIC	See States	x	x	x		x	—	x		—	x	x	x	x	—	x	x	x		x		x
Comp/Currency	See States	x	x	x		x	—	x		—	x	x	x	—	x	x	x		x		x		—

Source: Meyer, C. S., "How to Branch Yourself Out of Profits." Reprinted by permission from *The Bankers Magazine*, Volume 159, No. 1, Winter 1976, p. 108. Copyright 1976, Warren, Gorham & Lamont Inc., 210 South Street, Boston, Mass. All Rights Reserved.

sibility for cash, reserve requirements, investments, and capital is centralized in the main office. Expansion through branches may create imbalances in the loan and deposit relationships among branches and may bring pressure upon the main office to resolve operating problems. At the same time branching allows deposits to be attracted from areas with lower loan demand and funds to be transferred to areas in which loan demand exceeds funds availability. Proper consideration of the timing of expansion can mitigate imbalances, particularly if the market attributes have been properly evaluated.

Restructuring and Closing Branches

A branch should not be considered a permanent fixture. As profit margins narrow, each branch should be examined to determine if it is and will continue to be profitable. Additionally, the market attributes should be reevaluated to ascertain if the original market objectives are continuing to be met. If they are not, it should be determined if the existing attributes are consistent with the bank's existing or future market objectives. If they are not, then relocating or closing the branch may be considered. Alternatively, management may alter the services offered at a particular branch by, for example, eliminating loan services.

Relocation may be required when the physical facilities need expanding and the bank cannot secure additional property to provide for the expansion. Changing traffic patterns and declining neighborhoods also contribute to relocation decisions. Certain bank organizations such as Bankers Trust and Security Pacific have recently abandoned consumer branches. Bankers Trust based its decision to sell its retail branches upon a desire to concentrate on wholesale banking. Bank-America closed 120 branches in 1984 because of its decreasing deposit opportunities and profit reductions. It plans to expand its automated teller network to 1200 machines. Wells Fargo Bank planned to close 29 of its 390 branches in 1984 as a cost-cutting measure.

Brick-and-mortar branches represent significant investment in physical assets. As technology is developed, it is highly likely that brick-and-mortar facilities will be reduced in number and size. Innovations such as ATMs and home banking through computer terminals will reduce the need for permanent facilities, and old-line products may be delivered without the customer's interaction with bank personnel.

Movement toward Removal of Branching Restrictions

Branching powers were given to the states by federal legislation. Some states have granted reciprocity to other states to encourage branching beyond state lines. It appears that federal legislation may be required to provide an organized framework for interstate banking.

States that do not permit branching do not appear to favor branching, much less interstate branching. In 1980 a referendum proposing branching was promoted by two of the largest banking organizations in Colorado. The referendum was soundly defeated. Observers indicated that the issues were not clear and the opposition from independent bankers was very strong.

The primary benefits of branching posed by proponents of branching include:

1. Larger banks have the resources and systems to deliver low-cost, broad-based services.
2. A large banking organization can diversify its sources and uses of funds among various users. It can direct funds into a market requiring financing. A larger organization can efficiently use its larger capital base to meet customer needs.
3. A large bank system is generally safer. Fewer bank failures have occurred among large banks.
4. A greater variety of services such as trust and specialized lending programs become available to a broader banking public.
5. Branching is competitive and offers opportunities for shopping rates, prices, and terms.

Opponents suggest that:

1. The correspondent bank system offers the independent bank specialized services that it could not economically provide itself. Therefore there is no detriment to the local customer.
2. A local bank can diversify through loan participations and through the purchase and sale of federal funds from and to correspondents.
3. A branching organization is likely to transfer funds from local communities to its major office and give preferential service to large corporate customers. A local bank will concentrate on local needs.
4. Branching promotes concentration of banking in a few large organizations. Branching erodes the smaller bank's ability to provide significant competition.

Economic studies have clearly proved neither the merits of branching nor the opposition's view of branching. In our view, interstate branching is inevitable—the only question is when. A flurry of activity among large banks and bank holding companies has resulted in their positioning themselves in certain banking markets. This positioning includes mergers and the introduction of new services through subsidiaries. These events have occurred in anticipation of federal branching legislation and as a result of the deregulation movement among banks and thrift institutions.

BANK MERGERS

Bank mergers fall under the Bank Merger Act of 1960 and the amendments of 1966, which address issues of concentration in banking. Concentration is the amount of deposits that are controlled by a few banking organizations in a given relevant market. If a merger involves a successor bank that is a national bank, the merger will be approved/disapproved by the Comptroller of the Currency. A successor bank that is a state member of the Federal Reserve System or a state nonmember insured bank comes under the jurisdiction of the Board of Governors of the Federal Reserve or the FDIC, respectively.

The Bank Merger Act specifies the following factors to be considered in approving or disapproving a merger:

1. The financial history and condition of each bank involved.
2. The adequacy of each bank's capital structure.
3. The merged banks' earning prospects.
4. The general character of the merged banks' management.
5. The convenience and needs of the community to be served.
6. The consistency of the merged banks' corporate powers with the purposes of the FDIC.
7. The effect of the merger on competition.

Since the wording of the act was unclear, a great deal of flexibility was found in applying the act. Consequently, the Justice Department began to examine bank mergers closely. The most significant challenge was made in the Philadelphia National Bank case, which reached the Supreme Court. In determining the measurement of concentration, the Court ruled that banking was a distinct line of commerce. Therefore the measurement of concentration was the amount of deposits and services offered by the resulting bank compared to the competing banks in the relevant market area. Even though banks compete for deposits with thrift institutions and compete for consumer and mortgage loans with consumer finance companies and thrift institutions, concentration would be determined only among commercial banks. This ruling has been applied even though thrift institutions are direct competitors for time deposits.

The amendments of 1966 strengthened the original act and accorded specific responsibilities in examining proposed bank mergers under the Clayton Act, one of the major antitrust acts. The 1966 amendments provided: "The responsible agency shall not approve . . . any proposed merger transaction which would result in a monopoly, or

would be in furtherance of any combination or conspiracy to monopolize or attempt to monopolize the business of banking in any part of the
United States."[1]

In the Philadelphia National Bank case it was determined that the
amount of deposits held by the resulting bank would result in 36 percent of all deposits in a four-county area and therefore was anticompetitive. In a 1967 case involving Crocker Citizens Bank, San Francisco,
the merger was approved because the largest banking organization held
approximately 40 percent of all deposits among banks in California and
had no significant competitors that could offer effective competition.
Even though the merger resulted in greater statewide concentration, the
Court was concerned with rivalry among competing banks that would
result in a more competitive atmosphere.

Regulatory economists are concerned with preserving a competitive market. In assessing competition economists provide two distinct
theories of competition: the theory of existing competition and the theory of probable future competition. The theory of existing competition
is based on a proposed merger of two firms that compete in the same
market. The courts have accepted this theory and examine the concentration of the market in which firms compete and the market shares of
the combining firms. A merger that produces an unduly large percentage
share of the market would be prohibited in most cases because it would
eliminate substantial existing competition.

The theory of probable future competition is a relatively new theory and applies to market extension mergers. These mergers involve
firms in different markets. The theory applies to the merger of two
firms, one of which competes in an oligopolistic market. An oligopolistic market is one in which a small number of firms possess the power
to determine price. The theory assumes that a merger of two firms in
such a market will continue oligopolistic pricing policies. Therefore it
is assumed that a potential entrant may have the financial ability to
enter the market and that the market will support a *de novo* entrant.

If evidence shows a history of a merger candidate entering markets
on a *de novo* basis after denial, then a high likelihood that the merger
is anticompetitive can be presumed and the merger will be denied. If no
such evidence exists, then the issues are more clouded. The courts have
discussed the theory but have not accepted it in a definitive manner.
(See the discussion below regarding mergers among bank holding
companies.)

With regard to *de novo* entry, the courts also examine the regulatory view toward approval of new entrants in the market. Barriers to
entry exist in the need for regulatory approval and in the high cost of
capital. As indicated earlier, management experience and expertise are

[1]Bank Merger Act of 1966, 80 Stat. 7: Public Law 356, 89th Cong., 2d sess., 1966

considered important to any merger proposal. This concern is also present in the formation of new banks. The result is the existence of a small number of banks in small markets and a few banking organizations controlling large banks in large markets.

Concern with competition is based upon the assumption that the few firms may influence prices of services to the detriment of the banking public. Many economic studies have investigated the interrelationships of size, concentration, and prices of services. No definitive conclusions have resulted that substantiate the primary hypothesis that few firms in a highly concentrated market price services higher than "normal" banking practice.

Assuming that interstate banking will be allowed and deregulation will continue, thereby producing fewer differences between banks and thrifts, mergers will continue to be proposed. Whether the courts can continue to hold banking to a distinct line of commerce is doubtful. For example, Merrill Lynch's CMA account is clearly offering services that compete with services offered by commercial banks. One should expect that broader views of competition will result as banking and thrifts expand into the financial services industry.

BANK HOLDING COMPANIES

A holding company is a corporation formed to hold the stocks of other corporations as an investment. In banking, the holding company has taken on greater importance because of the impediments created by various state laws in allowing bank expansion. A one-bank holding company owns a single bank. A multibank holding company owns two or more banks. Importantly, however, a bank holding company may form subsidiaries to conduct banking or activities related to banking without consideration of the impediments imposed by restrictive branching laws.

A bank holding company cannot expand its activities without prior approval of the Federal Reserve Board. Bank holding companies are subject to laws and regulations, including the Bank Merger Act and its amendments, antitrust laws, and the Bank Holding Company Acts.

Banking Acts

The Banking Act of 1933 started the process of regulating bank holding companies. That act defined a holding company as:

> Any corporation, business trust, association or similar organization . . . (1) which owns or controls, directly or indirectly, either a majority of the shares of capital stock of a member bank or more than 50 per *centum* of the number of shares voted for the election of directors of any one bank at the preceding election, or

controls in any manner the election of the majority of directors of any one bank; or (2) for the benefit of whose shareholders or members of all or substantially all the capital of a member bank is held by trustees.[2]

The act was broad and caused definitional problems. Majority ownership was the basic standard of control. It covered one-bank holding companies; however, the Banking Act of 1935 exempted one-bank holding companies since they were technically engaged in group banking.

An important consideration included in the 1933 act was that banks and bank holding companies were to separate themselves from securities companies within five years. This provision has been commonly referred to as the Glass-Steagall Act. Another important provision (Section 23A) stated that a bank could not lend more than 10 percent of its capital and surplus to any one affiliate and no more than 20 percent of its capital and surplus to all affiliates.

Although the 1933 act restricted bank holding companies from engaging in the underwriting and distribution of securities, they could engage in any line of commerce. Because further interstate operations were not anticipated at the time, the act did not limit bank acquisitions.

Bank Holding Company Act of 1956

During the period from 1935 to the mid-1950s bank holding company expansion through acquisition of banks accelerated. This expansion induced legislative concern about reduction of competition in local markets. In the Transamerica case, which reached the Supreme Court in 1953, the Court failed to uphold the Federal Reserve Board's charges that Transamerica had violated Section 7 of the Clayton Act by its purchase of banks in five Western states. The Board based its charges on statewide concentration data, but the Court narrowed the relevant market to local communities. Motivated by the concern about Transamerica's expansion, significant political pressure was put on Congress to limit such holding company action. In response, Congress enacted the Bank Holding Company Act of 1956.

The 1956 act defined a bank holding company as an organization owning 25 percent or more of the stock of two or more banks. The act established standards for forming bank holding companies and for acquisition of a bank by a bank holding company. Expansion across state lines was prohibited unless specifically authorized by statutes of the state in which the bank was located, and states were given the authority to restrict bank holding companies altogether. Certain bank holding companies such as First Interstate Corporation and Norwest Corporation were allowed to retain pre-act interstate acquisitions under "grand-

---

[2]48 Stat. 162 (1933).

father" clauses of the act. The act also delineated nonbanking activities that could be engaged in by bank holding companies. The Federal Reserve Board was permitted to allow other nonbanking activities that were "of a financial, fiduciary, or insurance nature" if they could pass the test of being "so closely related to the business of banking or managing or controlling banks as to be proper incident thereto."[3]

1966 Amendments

The 1966 Amendments to the Bank Holding Company Act of 1956 expanded the number of organizations covered by the legislation. The act applied Section 23A of the Federal Reserve Act to transactions between a subsidiary bank and its parent holding company and sister subsidiaries. Principally, deposit relationships that had previously been permitted became prohibited, and purchase of loans on a nonrecourse basis also became subject to the competitive tests applied by the Sherman Act and the Clayton Act.

1970 Amendments

The principal provisions of the 1970 amendments to the Bank Holding Company Act of 1956 included the extension of previous bank holding company acts to one-bank holding companies. The act left the determination of permitted activities to the Board of Governors under two conditions: (1) activities must be "so closely related to banking or managing or controlling banks as to be proper incident thereto"; and (2) the performance of any activity by a holding company subsidiary must "reasonably be expected to produce benefits to the public, such as greater convenience, increased competition, or gains in efficiency, that outweigh possible adverse effects, such as undue concentration of resources, decreased or unfair competition, conflicts of interest, or unsound banking practices."[4]

Permissible Activities

Activities that are permitted by the Federal Reserve Board for bank holding companies under Section 4(c)(8) include:

1. Management consulting for nonaffiliated banks and nonbank depository institutions under certain conditions.

2. Full-payout leasing of personal and certain real property.

---

[3]D. T. Savage, "A History of the Bank Holding Company Movement, 1900–78," in *The Bank Holding Company Movement to 1978: A Compendium*, ed. staff of the Board of Governors of the Federal Reserve System, September 1978: 46.

[4]Savage, op. cit., 60.

3. Mortgage banking and servicing loans.

4. Consumer credit, industrial bank operation.

5. Commercial finance and factoring.

6. Providing trust services/company (fiduciary).

7. Investment advisory service.

8. Investing in community welfare projects.

9. Data-processing and bookkeeping services.

10. Acting as insurance agent or broker where insurance is connected with the extension of credit in a community of less than 5000 people.

11. Underwriting credit life insurance (reinsurance).

12. Armored car and courier services on explicit fee basis.

13. Operating credit card company.

14. Economic information and advisory service.

15. Selling traveler's checks, U.S. savings bonds, and money orders.

16. Check verification service on a case-by-case basis.

17. Real estate appraisal.

In Chapter 21 we shall examine certain of the above activities in depth. Activities that have been denied by the Board include:

1. Equity funding (combined sales of mutual funds and insurance).

2. Underwriting general life insurance.

3. Real estate brokerage.

4. Land development.

5. Real estate syndication.

6. General management consulting.

7. Property management.

8. Non-full-payout leasing.

9. Commodity trading.

10. Issuance and sale of short-term debt obligations (thrift notes).

11. Travel agency.

12. Savings and loan association.

Bank Holding Company Acquisitions

The Bank Merger Act and the Bank Holding Company Act and their amendments require the Federal Reserve Board to consider the impact of proposed bank holding company mergers and acquisitions on competition. Since the deregulation movement began and the competition from nondepository firms has increased, many bank holding companies have positioned themselves in larger geographic markets through mergers. We earlier discussed the application of the theory of actual competition in weighing bank mergers. With regard to bank holding company expansion, the Board has attempted to apply the theory of probable future competition.

Two bank holding company mergers were denied by the Board on the ground that the mergers would lessen competition under the theory of probable future competition. Mercantile Texas Corporation, Dallas, proposed to acquire Pan National Group, Inc. of El Paso, and Republic of Texas Corporation, Dallas, proposed to acquire Citizens National Bank of Waco. Each case was appealed and the court vacated the denials and declared that the Board had failed to prove its case based upon the following four findings:

1. The market of the firm to be acquired was concentrated.
2. Whether the pool of potential entrants into the market was so large as to "vitiate" the importance of the acquiring firm as a potential competitor.
3. Upon denial that an institution would prefer the opportunity to enter the market independently—either *de novo* or through a toehold acquisition—to some other investment.
4. Independent entry will be substantially likely to bring about deconcentration of the market or other significant procompetitive effects. Supposition that entry in the remote future as a possible means to promote competition could not be used by the Board to deny an application.[5]

The Board responded with guidelines that would subject merger applications to intensive examination. The Board indicated the guidelines were not rigid and therefore certain applications outside the guidelines might also be examined. The guidelines are based on the following four criteria:

1. A highly concentrated area was defined as one for which the three-firm concentration ratio was at least 75 percent. The

---

[5]A. S. Winer, "Applying the Theory of Probable Future Competition," *Federal Reserve Bulletin*, September 1982: 527–532.

Board would also take into account effects of competition from thrifts and near-banks on market concentration.

2. The number of probable entrants was set at six excluding the applicant to determine if the pool was large enough. Also a future probable entrant was defined as any commercial banking organization not already in the market that was either of the state's four largest or was a lower-ranking organization with assets of $1 billion or more (or $500 million or more if the state had no lower-ranking organization with at least $1 billion in assets).

3. The firm to be acquired must be in a standard SMSA (standard metropolitan statistical area) and be in a market that had more than $250 million in deposits and had a rate of growth of deposits in the two most recent years at least matching that for its state or the country as a whole.

4. The firm to be acquired must be a "market leader." This was defined as any firm that ranks among the top three firms in a market, in terms of deposit holdings, and accounts for 10 percent or more of the market's deposits.[6]

The Department of Justice also established guidelines similar to the Board's guidelines. Although its guidelines differ in the degree of preciseness of certain competitive factors, they should also be considered in any proposed merger or acquisition.[7]

In addition to acquisitions that obtain control, the Board requires the filing of an application if a proposed stock purchase is 5 percent or more of the outstanding shares of a firm. Many bank holding companies have acquired 4.9 percent of the shares of other banking organizations beyond state lines to gain toehold positions in anticipation of interstate banking.

The Federal Reserve Board has required divestiture of some branches and subsidiaries before consummating certain mergers. This is a likely occurrence if branches of the two firms compete in the same market and the merger would consequently lessen competition in that market. Therefore firms either sell or close branches in order to consummate the proposed merger or acquisition.

The changes in banking structure and state banking laws are occurring rapidly. Exhibit 20.3 summarizes some of the changes to illustrate their extent. It should be noted that these events represent only a small portion of the total merger/acquisition and market extension activity.

---

[6]Ibid.

[7]Ibid.

EXHIBIT 20.3   Expansion of Banking Legislation and Activity

Activity	Action	Impact
State Laws		
Iowa	State allows acquisition of banks by out-of-state holding companies.	Banks may be acquired subject to 8% limitation of the state's deposits. Norwest Corporation (Minnesota) is an aggressive acquirer.
Maine	State allows acquisition only if there is reciprocity from other states.	
Massachusetts Rhode Island Connecticut	States allow acquisition of banks by holding companies based in other New England states on a reciprocal basis.	Rhode Island extends reciprocity beyond New England effective July 1986. Citicorp has sued in Massachusetts to remove reciprocal restrictions among New England states.
New York	State allows acquisition on a reciprocal basis.	
South Dakota	State permits out-of-state activity subject to certain restrictions. Holding companies may acquire a *de novo* bank and/or a service affiliate if customers are not drawn from existing banks.	Citicorp has moved its credit card operations to South Dakota to avoid New York State usury laws and limits on annual fees. Certain California bank holding companies have received state approval for bank charters including insurance activities. The Federal Reserve Board has disapproved the acquisition of these banks with insurance operations.
Alaska	State allows bank holding companies to acquire and to operate full-service banks without requiring reciprocity.	Law became effective July 1, 1982.
Acquisition of Banks	Bank holding companies continue to be active in bank acquisitions. Noteworthy areas are Colorado, Texas, and Florida.	Colorado and Texas are unit-banking states. No legislation permitting branching appears likely. Florida, a branching state, permits out-of-state acquisitions if a holding company owned a bank prior to enactment of the 1956 act.
Illinois	Laws prohibiting multibank holding companies have been repealed.	Multibank holding companies are rapidly being formed and bank acquisitions are actively being pursued.
Pennsylvania	Laws prohibiting multibank holding companies have been repealed. Branch banking laws have been expanded.	(see Bank Holding Company Mergers below).

EXHIBIT 20.3 *(continued)*

Activity	Action	Impact
De novo Banks Delaware	Delaware permits the establishment of *de novo* banks by out-of-state bank holding companies. Each bank must be capitalized initially at $10 million and is expected to employ at least 100 people. At the end of the first year, capital must be at least $25 million. The activities must not attract customers from the general public to the detriment of existing banking institutions.	Citicorp, J. P. Morgan, Chase Manhattan, Chemical Bank, Provident National Corporation, and Philadelphia National Bank have established *de novo* banks principally to conduct commercial lending and international banking.
Bank Holding Company Mergers	Mellon National Corporation (Pittsburgh) agreed to merge with Girard Company (Philadelphia).	Merger approved.
	Pittsburgh National Corporation agreed to merge with Philadelphia's Provident National Corporation.	Merger approved.
	Bank One Corporation (Columbus, Ohio) agreed to acquire Winters National Corporation (Dayton, Ohio).	Merger would create an organization located in every major Ohio city except Toledo.
Purchase of 4.9% Stock in Certain Bank Holding Companies	Texas Commerce Corporation acquired 4.9% interest in First Wyoming Bancorporation.	Texas Commerce Corporation serves as a major correspondent for energy-related loans. Texas Commerce Corporation has also provided long-term debt financing to First Wyoming Bancorporation.
Agreements to Purchase if Interstate Banking is Approved	Chase Manhattan plans to purchase nonvoting stock and an option to purchase all of the stock of Equimark Corporation, Pittsburgh.	Plan represents major agreement to expand large banking markets across state lines.

Note: These examples are illustrative of recent transactions or events. They represent only a small portion of the total expansionary activity.

Bank Holding Company Formation

Formation of a bank holding company requires an application to be filed with the Board of Governors. The applicant must provide information and data regarding the financial and managerial resources and future prospects of the proposed bank holding company and its proposed affiliation. The application requires demonstration of the convenience and need factors and the benefits that the holding company will produce in the formation of the bank holding company and acquisition of the affiliate. The Board will review the anticompetitive effects of the proposed transaction.

A bank holding company that wants to acquire a bank or other subsidiary prepares a detailed application that includes description of the applicant and the proposed transaction, financial and managerial information, a statement regarding convenience and needs, and a description of the competitive environment including nonbanking activities. The application is submitted to the district Federal Reserve Bank, which reviews it and makes a recommendation to the Board. If the application is approved, the applicant proceeds to consummate the transaction. The transaction may be approved subject to certain conditions. Once the conditions are met, the transaction may then be completed. If the application is not approved, the Board order may be appealed through the federal courts.

Tax Benefits of Bank Holding Company Formation

A principal tax benefit of holding company formation derives from financing the corporation through debt.[8] Briefly, if a holding company owns at least 80 percent of the outstanding stock of a subsidiary, dividends received by the holding company will be untaxed with the filing of a consolidated tax return. For the closely held holding company, debt acquired to finance acquisition of a subsidiary may be serviced without reduction for income tax. The following example illustrates the advantage of a bank purchase through holding company ownership over direct purchase.

Assume that an individual desires to purchase a bank and must finance the acquisition with debt. If the bank is purchased directly, bank dividends, diminished by income taxes, must be relied on to service the debt burden. Through the formation of a bank holding company to acquire bank stock with debt in the holding company, dividends received

---

[8]R. D. Rutz, "The Tax Benefits of Forming One-Bank Holding Companies Under the Fed's New Guidelines," *Banking Law Journal*, January 1981: 24–25.

by the holding company from the bank are not taxed and may be used to reduce acquisition debt more quickly. The following table illustrates this advantage:

Dividends in Direct Purchase		Dividends in Holding Company Purchase
Received	$100	$100
Tax 50%	50	0
Available for debt reduction	$ 50	$100

The Federal Reserve Board has established guidelines for the amount of debt that can be used for acquisition by a bank holding company. The holding company debt must be reduced to no more than a debt-to-equity ratio of 30 percent within 12 years. A holding company must demonstrate that its income projections are reasonable and that it will reduce debt on schedule. If it does not, the application may be denied. The Depository Institutions Deregulation and Monetary Control Act of 1980 contains a provision that prohibits the Board from denying applications to form one-bank holding companies in cases involving acquisition debt with a maturity of not more than 25 years. It is expected that the Board's policy will be modified to conform with the legislative change.

The tax benefits described above are not limited to small and/or one-bank holding companies. Any bank holding company with at least 80 percent ownership of a subsidiary and filing a consolidated tax return receives the same benefits.

Bank Holding Company Operations

A bank holding company serves as a vehicle for expansion into additional geographic and product markets with banks and/or other subsidiaries. Several benefits are normally expected to result from the formation of a holding company. The holding company organization is expected to provide support to the banking and nonbanking subsidiaries. This is generally accomplished by centralizing or concentrating expertise in certain functional support areas. This centralization or concentration may include some or all of the following functions:

Function	Objective
1. General administration	Establish corporate goals and objectives. Define operating plans and direct and control progress toward corporate objectives.
2. Accounting and taxation	Provide technical support to subsidiaries. Define internal accounting systems and reporting. Advise corporation and subsidiaries on tax consequences of transactions. Establish budgets and review. Prepare external reports to shareholders and regulatory agencies.
3. Data processing	Coordinate and/or provide data-processing services to the internal organization. Direct and control data systems.
4. Investments	Advise subsidiaries on investment securities. Possibly perform execution functions and consolidate purchases and sales to obtain better prices.
5. Auditing	Perform directors' and other examinations.
6. Insurance	Obtain and manage blanket bond and casualty insurance for all units.
7. Personnel	Administer corporate compensation and benefit plans. Assist subsidiaries in identifying key personnel for selection.
8. Marketing	Establish corporate identity programs. Direct and coordinate corporate-level marketing activities.
9. Loan administration	Administer loan review function. Coordinate placement of loan participations internal and external to organization.
10. Federal funds	Consolidate daily federal funds purchases and sales.
11. Finance	Provide sources of financing to subsidiaries. Obtain access to capital markets that individual units could not access on their own.

Management of the Bank Holding Company.   In addition to defining the functions to be performed by the holding company, the board of directors, with recommendations from management, should determine how the holding company should direct the policies and activities of subsidiaries. Three basic alternatives are possible.

The first, a "hands-off" policy, is a passive policy wherein the subsidiary is free to determine its own goals, objectives, and operating plans. This strategy is possible, for instance, when the officers of the holding company are also officers of the lead bank and the holding company is a legal structure formed primarily to gain leveraging and tax benefits. Also, some acquired banks or subsidiaries retain prior management and are given limited direction by the holding company. The holding company activities may be solely related to corporate accounting, finance, and audit functions.

The second alternative, a "hands-on" operation, usually includes direct intervention into a subsidiary's activities. This may include running each subsidiary with the same operating, accounting, and data-processing systems, similar definitions of products and markets, common personnel policies regarding salary and benefit structure, hiring, and promotion, and the same method of approval of operating and capital expenditure budgets.

The third alternative is a "middle-of-the-road" combination of the two extremes described above. Because no bank holding company should be expected to operate in a total "hands-on" or "hands-off" manner, a middle-of-the-road approach assigns those functional responsibilities to the holding company that can best be centralized. It gives to each subsidiary the responsibility for charting its own course in terms of how to meet the objectives established by the holding company and lets managers manage.

Operations with Lead Bank.   Some holding company organizations have emanated from a large-city or money-center bank. The holding company group may be located adjacent to or within the "lead bank." Certain operations such as investments, purchases and sales of federal funds, and loan participations and review may be conducted by the lead bank. Other administrative activities may be concentrated at the holding company level. The lead bank also usually has a significant correspondent bank activity.

Affiliated Bankshares of Colorado presents an interesting case study. This group at one point in its history was a company with banks located in several large communities but without any banks in the Denver metropolitan area. In the 1960s ABC merged with another holding company that had four banks in metropolitan Denver, including one bank in downtown Denver. Subsequent to the merger the acquired Denver banks operated as a division of ABC. All of the banks were approximately the same size. Denver National Bank, the downtown bank, had experienced serious operational problems. New management was brought in to "clean up" the bank. This management also established a correspondent bank division.

Yet it was not until the mid-1970s that the holding company banks could agree to use Denver National as its principal correspondent and to create a bank to take on the role of lead bank. Denver National has grown larger than the other banks principally through the transfer of holding company correspondent deposit balances to Denver National. Even today ABC operates with a divisional organization that preserves local-area autonomy for the former owners, now the managers, of the group's banks.

Some holding companies operate with a lead bank, much as branching organizations do. Other holding companies, particularly small holding companies in sparsely populated states, operate without a lead bank. In a nonbranching environment the lead bank can serve as a highly visible competitor in highly competitive markets. When interstate banking finally occurs, a banking organization having a lead bank with correspondent bank services can attract independent banks to be acquired. Holding company banks without a lead bank are likely to be acquisition candidates of larger organizations.

Acquisition Strategy.   One of the following three strategies may be selected by an acquisition-minded holding company:

- *Top-down No. 1:* Large bank acquires a string of smaller banks. It combines the resources and expertise of a lead bank with an attractive target bank in an attractive market. Offensive strategy.
- *Top-down No. 2:* Large bank acquires a small bank for its location. It does not try to buy management-established customer relationships or other business assets. It plans to expand its services through the acquired bank and to operate the location much as a branch. Offensive strategy.
- *Bottom-up:* A group of banks combine to avoid being acquired by a large bank holding company. Banks usually continue as autonomous units. Defensive strategy.

A bank acquisition program should set goals that are consistent with overall corporate objectives. Two steps can contribute to a successful acquisition program:

- Determine internal growth projections for the existing organization.
- Determine acquisition goals, including trade-off parameters that will be acceptable in acquisition negotiations.

The trade-offs may include form of payment and amount to be paid to acquire the stock, retention of existing management and staff, and, if securities are to be exchanged, a determination of the amount of dilution that will be acceptable.

The valuation of a bank stock is influenced by several factors. The holding company should (but does not always) consider all factors in determining an appropriate acquisition candidate. Sometimes a decision may be based solely upon seeking a target bank in a market that is open to acquisition-minded holding companies and selecting the most likely candidate from among those willing to sell or merge. Such a decision may also include the assumption that the acquisition of a bank of a certain size has a better chance of obtaining Federal Reserve Board approval. In a small-bank environment this "seat of the pants" strategy may succeed or fail without significant impact on the overall holding company. However, an unsatisfactory acquisition may haunt holding company management for a significant period of time.

Proper selection and valuation are more likely to result in minimum dilution of earnings per share and faster integration of an acquired bank into the holding group operations. To assess value and select an appropriate acquisition method, the bank holding company should:

- Evaluate the economic growth potential of the market.
- Evaluate the existing management. This may result in an early decision to replace the existing management to accomplish corporate objectives and will be a negotiating point in the acquisition.
- Evaluate the bank's assets and liabilities composition. This will determine the existing earnings' capability and also whether the assets pose any problems due to concentration among certain customers or industries. Deposit assessment is important, particularly if the deposits are concentrated among certain customers or industries that may or may not be retained after acquisition. If the deposit base is lost after acquisition, replacement and potential growth may be stifled for a significant time. Additionally, consideration should be given to how, if the acquisition is consummated, asset and liability changes can be made to increase bank earnings.

A number of valuation techniques may be used to determine a bank's worth. These include earnings comparisons before and after acquisition, market value comparisons, price/earnings comparisons, market/book value comparisons, and book/book value comparisons.[9]

Considerations following Acquisition. Integrating an acquired bank into a holding company may require significant effort in a "hands-on" operation. Usually the accounting, data-processing, and data base systems will require conversion to common systems. Integration of personnel policies may be more difficult because resistance from personnel may impede progress. Additionally, benefit plans will require legal and administrative attention.

Management continuity of the bank may be important in the short run. However, it may be desirable to replace management in order to integrate the bank more quickly into the holding company operating philosophy. Acquisition negotiations should give significant attention to the desirability of retaining former owners as managers. Former owners accustomed to having complete autonomy over bank operations may resist change.

---

[9]For a more detailed discussion, see R. Terry and M. C. Sexton, "Valuation of Banks in Acquisitions," *Bankers Magazine*, November-December 1981: 86–89.

Another consideration is the retention of local directors on the bank's board. Local directors continue to be particularly important to a local bank in order to represent the local community's needs for banking services. Representation on the bank board by holding company personnel may provide an important integration of holding company goals and objectives with local needs.

A former owner may seek to become a director of the holding company. A holding company board composed of former owners may create an environment of conflict of personal interests with corporate objectives. Some holding companies have adopted policies of denying directorship to subsidiary bank management. Instead, a management council composed of bank presidents and holding company management can resolve issues and cooperatively carry out policies and objectives adopted by a board that does not represent individual bank interests.

Income to support holding company operations is important. Dividend policies vary with regard to subsidiary banks. Some holding companies support holding company operations and holding company dividends to shareholders solely through bank dividends. Others charge management fees for specific specialized services performed centrally by the holding company to cover those operating costs and rely upon dividends for other cash requirements.

Integration will proceed more rapidly with frequent communication between bank and holding company personnel. If objectives are effectively communicated and bank personnel feel they are participants in the process rather than recipients, integration will proceed on an orderly basis.

SUMMARY

Expansion of bank activity requires careful consideration of banking and bank holding company laws and regulations. Bank acquisition requires painstaking analysis and planning in negotiations and implementation. A large number of alternatives and opportunities exist in managing an expanding organization. Future changes in banking laws may bring about interstate banking, which will require even greater attention to expansion. This activity will require reexamination of operational policies and structural organization. Flexibility and adaptability to change will be very important.

Questions and Problems

1. Describe possible branch-bank expansion strategies.

2. Why might a branch bank be closed?

3. Contrast the issues regarding permitting branch banking.

4. What is a bank holding company and how is it defined by law?

5. Briefly describe the types of legislative and regulatory changes that are affecting bank holding companies.

6. What functions may be centralized by bank holding companies and how do they operate?

7. What tax benefits accrue to shareholders when a bank holding company uses debt to acquire a bank?

8. Contrast the operating management styles that may be adopted by a holding company.

9. Contrast the three possible acquisition strategies.

References

Bradley, G. M. "Financial Issues and Considerations." Paper presented at seminar, *Bank Acquisitions and Mergers.* Washington, DC: Bank Administration Institute, Oct. 19–20, 1981.

Ginsburg, D. H. "Bank Holding Company Expansion Strategies: The Illinois Bank Holding Act." *Banking Law Journal*, August 1982: 598–605.

Haugh, J. W. "Bank Acquisitions in a High Rate Environment." Paper presented at seminar, *Bank Acquisitions and Mergers.* Washington, DC: Bank Administration Institute, Oct. 19–20, 1981.

Jesser, E. A., Jr., and K. H. Fisher. "Guidelines for Bank Holding Company Management." *Bankers Magazine*, November-December 1981: 13–20.

McCall, A. S. "The Impact of Bank Structure on Bank Service to Local Communities." *Journal of Bank Research*, Summer 1980: 101–109.

McCall, A. S., and D. T. Savage. "Branching Policy: The Options." *Journal of Bank Research*, Summer 1980: 122–126.

"Mellon National Agrees to Acquire Girard for Stock." *The Wall Street Journal*, Aug. 3, 1982, 4.

Meyer, C. S. "How to Branch Yourself Out of Profits." *Bankers Magazine*, Winter 1976: 108.

Nathan, H. C. "Nonbank Organizations and the McFadden Act." *Journal of Bank Research*, Summer 1980: 80–86.

"The Perennial Issue: Branch Banking." *Business Conditions, Federal Reserve Bank of Chicago*, February 1974: 3–23.

Rhoades, S. A. "A Clarification of the Potential Competition Doctrine in Bank Merger Analysis." *Journal of Bank Research*, Spring 1975: 35–42.

Rutz, R. D. "The Tax Benefits of Forming One-Bank Holding Companies Under the Fed's New Guidelines." *Banking Law Journal*, January 1981: 24–25.

Savage, D. T. "A History of the Bank Holding Company Movement, 1900–78." In *The Bank Holding Company Movement to 1978: A Compendium*, ed. staff of the Board of Governors of the Federal Reserve System, September 1978: 21–68.

Savage, D. T., and E. H. Solomon. "Branch Banking: The Competitive Issues." *Journal of Bank Research*, Summer 1980: 110–121.

Terry, R., and M. C. Sexton. "Valuation of Banks in Acquisitions." *Bankers Magazine*, November-December 1981: 86–89.

Watkins, T. G., and R. C. West. "Bank Holding Companies: Development and Regulation." *Economic Review, Federal Reserve Bank of Kansas City*, June 1982: 3–13.

Winer, A. S. "Applying the Theory of Probable Future Competition." *Federal Reserve Bulletin*, September 1982: 527–532.

CHAPTER 21

Expansion into Activities Related to Banking

As deregulation is implemented, several implications become very clear. Survival of individual banks will depend on their ability to find a proper niche for their services. Certain large banking firms are already engaged in expanding their product lines geographically (nationally and internationally) and in different customer markets (banking and nonbanking).

Donald C. Waite has provided an excellent analysis of the dimensions of deregulation and its possible effects on the banking industry.[1] Exhibit 21.1 illustrates the primary dimensions of deregulation in certain industries that are important to banking. In Chapter 20 we covered the various laws governing banking and nonbanking expansion. The range of regulation covers geographic location, price of input or output, range of products and services, and entry. As barriers to geographic, product, and service expansion fall through deregulation, the structure of the banking industry will change in regard to price of input or output and entry. Banking firms must be prepared to adjust to this new environment.

Waite has identified events that are expected to occur in the first phase of deregulation (two to four years).

- Performance variability among firms within the industry occurs. The weak become weaker and look for a merger partner. This is a result of loss of "trade territory" and local market access to a broader range of products and services from large, stronger firms.
- The previously most profitable products come under the most severe price pressure. Competition from investment firms and other specialized industries to provide banklike services will intensify.
- Products become unbundled with a proliferation of new, complex product/service trade-offs. Competition in broad service ranges will increase among firms, with customers

---

[1]D. C. Waite III, "Deregulation and the Banking Industry," *Bankers Magazine,* January-February, 1982: 26–36.

EXHIBIT 21.1   Primary Dimensions of Deregulation

| | Dimensions | | | |
Industry	Geography	Price of Input or Output	Range of Products and Services	Entry
Brokerage		●		
Business Terminal Equipment (BTE)		●	●	●
Banking	●	●	●	●
Current Banking Regulations	McFadden Act Douglas Amendment to Bank Holding Company Act	Regulation Q Usury Laws	Glass-Steagall Act Bank Holding Company Act	Federal Reserve Act Banking Act of 1933

Source: Extracted from D. C. Waite III, "Deregulation and the Banking Industry." Reprinted by permission from *The Bankers Magazine*, Volume 165, No. 1, January–February, 1982, p. 27. Copyright 1982, Warren, Gorham & Lamont Inc., 210 South Street, Boston, Mass. All Rights Reserved.

selecting from low-price/low-service to high-price/high-service options.

♦ An industry profit squeeze forces rapid cost cutting, particularly in the form of staff reductions. Service delivery will use greater degrees of technological advances with a commensurate reduction in personnel costs.

♦ Capital requirements increase; at the same time, access to capital markets is reduced. Uncertainty and risk related to industry adjustments to a changing environment will make investors uneasy about equity investments in these "new" firms.[2]

Successful firms under deregulation will be of three types, according to Waite. Well-established firms (Type 1) will continue to market broad-based products and services to expanded geographic areas. Type 2, low-cost producers, many of whom may not have existed before deregulation, will expand services in which they enjoy a competitive advantage because of well-developed, low-cost technology. Type 3 firms, specialty firms, will concentrate on specialized products or services in

---

[2]Ibid., 28.

EXHIBIT 21.2 Key Characteristics of Successful Firms

National Distribution Companies (Type 1)

Type 1 characteristics before deregulation:

Heavy capitalization with relatively low debt-to-equity ratios.

Well-developed information on costs of individual products and customers.

Expertise in managing a broad distribution network with integrated operational capability.

Product development and marketing expertise with capability to maintain a flow of innovative products.

Clear sense of corporate direction, with effective planning capability.

Type 1 early actions following deregulation:

Make major and rapid price adjustments to bring prices in line with costs.

Emphasize cost control and cost reduction.

Increase marketing awareness.

Raise advertising and promotional expenditures, especially those related to products and image.

Undertake selective acquisitions, usually of weaker firms, to broaden expertise or sales coverage.

Low-Cost Producers (Type 2)

Type 2 characteristics before deregulation:

Narrow, simple product lines requiring minimal service.

Line (rather than staff) emphasis, with low structural personnel costs.

Minimal internal systems, except those monitoring costs.

Type 2 early actions following deregulation:

Aggressively discount price relative to conventional producers.

Eliminate or dramatically modify a substantial element of the distribution system.

Vigorously hire key personnel from existing companies.

Expand through reproduction of low-cost system.

Emphasize low price in advertising.

Speciality Firms (Type 3)

Type 3 characteristics before deregulation:

Product or customer segments rather than geographic niches.

Expertise in products or markets that cannot be unbundled easily or are not highly price-sensitive.

Type 3 early actions following deregulation:

Deemphasize remaining price-sensitive products and increase emphasis on fees for service.

Delineate a well-defined market segment, often one recently vacated as existing broad-line competitors retrench.

Selectively acquire competitors to deepen rather than broaden expertise.

Emphasize information advertising, as opposed to image or price advertising.

Source: D. C. Waite III, "Deregulation and the Banking Industry." Reprinted by permission from *The Bankers Magazine*, Volume 165, No. 1, January–February 1982, pp. 31–33. Copyright 1982, Warren, Gorham & Lamont Inc., 210 South Street, Boston, Mass. All Rights Reserved.

**EXHIBIT 21.3   Primary Strategic Options for Financial
Institutions Emerging from Deregulation**

	Strategy Option			
Institution	Type 1	Type 2	Type 3	Types 1 and 3[a] Combined
Major Money Center Banks (top 7 to 10 banks)	●		●	●
Second-tier Banks (Nos. 11 through 100)			●	●
Major Nonbank Financial Institutions (Merrill Lynch, American Express, etc.)	●	●		
Second-tier Nonbank Financial Institutions (major savings and loans, finance companies, etc.)			●	
Local Institutions (small banks, savings and loans, etc.)			●	
New Entrants		●		

[a]Type 1 firm along one or several key banking dimensions; Type 3 along other banking dimensions.

Source: D. C. Waite III, "Deregulation and the Banking Industry." *The Bankers Magazine,* Volume 165, No. 1, January–February, 1982, p. 34. Copyright 1982, Warren, Gorham & Lamont Inc., 210 South Street, Boston, Mass. All Rights Reserved.

---

local/regional markets in which they have established reputations. Exhibit 21.2 outlines the characteristics of successful firms that will survive deregulation.

Exhibit 21.3 suggests the primary strategic options for each of these types of firms and possible combinations. The large banking firms such as Citicorp will be expected to expand their banking services nationwide and to concentrate on specialized markets. Nonbank competitors seeking to attract certain banking customers will continue to develop and market products and services with which they can effectively compete in a price-competitive environment. Non-money-center banks and nonbank financial institutions will adjust to specialized services in order to survive.

In summary, firms will develop certain organizations consistent with Type 1, 2, or 3 characteristics, as summarized in Exhibit 21.4.

EXHIBIT 21.4   Organizational Implications of Type 1, 2, and 3 Firms

Organizational Element	Organizational Characteristics		
	Type 1	Type 2	Type 3
Style	Established, but alert and responsive	Entrepreneurial; aggressive; lean	Creative and flexible
Structure	Strong functional support for decentralized network	Centralized with few functional departments; line-driven	Usually centralized with targeted functional departments
Systems	Emphasis on marketing, planning, and cost systems	Minimal systems orientation; emphasis on cost control	Light systems orientation; emphasis on creative planning and marketing approaches
Skills/staff	Broad spectrum of management skills required	Operating capability is primary attribute	Service orientation and tailored training important

Source: D. C. Waite III, "Deregulation and the Banking Industry." Reprinted by permission from *The Bankers Magazine*, Volume 165, No. 1, January–February, 1982, p. 35. Copyright 1982, Warren, Gorham & Lamont Inc., 210 South Street, Boston, Mass. All Rights Reserved.

PRIMARY APPROVED ACTIVITIES RELATED TO BANKING

A number of activities related to banking that have been approved by the Federal Reserve Board and specialized services are discussed below. The specialized services require particular expertise. Many services are attractive because they provide fee income without the problems associated with managing bank sources and uses of money. Certain activities, such as consumer, mortgage, and commercial finance, allow expansion into geographic markets beyond the home state of the parent banking organization. In some cases this expansion provides toehold entry into markets that could be served by branches, assuming removal of interstate banking prohibitions.

Certain services require significant capitalization and investment in facilities and equipment. Some incur significant start-up costs before profits can be realized. Some require specialized expertise in managing the activity to minimize and limit exposure to losses. In some circumstances activities are operated through the bank rather than through the operating subsidiaries.

Citicorp has established an aggressive plan to expand its services nationwide. It has taken advantage of its holding company structure to acquire consumer finance subsidiaries, to establish *de novo* credit card operations, to acquire ailing financial institutions, to plan bank acquisitions in states that allow reciprocity, and to attack state laws that grant reciprocity to certain regional states but exclude New York State. The map below indicates the extent of Citicorp's emergence as a financial services leader on an interstate basis.

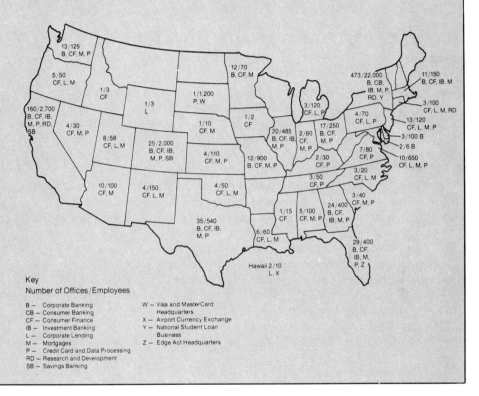

Key
Number of Offices/Employees

B — Corporate Banking	W — Visa and MasterCard
CB — Consumer Banking	Headquarters
CF — Consumer Finance	X — Airport Currency Exchange
IB — Investment Banking	Y — National Student Loan
L — Corporate Lending	Business
M — Mortgages	Z — Edge Act Headquarters
P — Credit Card and Data Processing	
RD — Research and Development	
SB — Savings Banking	

Consumer Finance

Consumer finance activities include small loans for household purposes, sales finance (direct and indirect loans), and home equity lending. Major consumer finance firms have been acquired by major bank holding companies, including Nationwide (by Citicorp) and Dial Corporation (by Norwest Corporation). Major bank holding companies with consumer finance subsidiaries include, but are not limited to, Security Pacific Corporation, Bank of America, and Manufacturers Hanover.

Consumer finance organization activities have broadened. Dial engages in leasing of industrial and agricultural equipment; commercial financing, including accounts receivable financing; offering thrift certificates and accepting passbook savings; and acting as agent for the sale of credit-related insurance and underwriting as reinsurer credit-related insurance. It operates in 37 states, with 489 offices.[3]

Norwest Corporation intends to offer new services through Dial Corporation offices, benefiting individual customers, small- to medium-sized businesses, and agricultural customers. These services will include additional credit to finance agriculture, small- to medium-sized businesses, education, and home improvements. Dial will also extend SBA-guaranteed and fixed-rate loans for commercial and agricultural purposes.

The acquisition provides geographic expansion principally through lending. Before the acquisition Norwest operated in a seven-state area, and its subsidiaries presently engage in banking, basic financing, mortgage banking, agricultural financing, secured commercial lending, data processing, credit-related insurance sales and reinsurance, municipal bond underwriting, corporate trust services, and securities-clearing services. The acquisition expands geographic and bank product markets. In the event of interstate banking, this acquisition produces toehold entry for further expansion into banking directly.

The consumer finance organization requires external financing for the most part, since it is not a depository institution. This financing varies but includes reliance on bank lines of credit, commercial paper, and other debt financing. Its operations are very similar to those of branch banking. Loans are typically small and standardized. Its operating costs are usually low for personnel and facilities but high for financing.

Mortgage Banking

Mortgage banking is an activity in which a corporation originates, packages, and sells loans to investors and retains servicing rights for a fee. Interim financing is required to support originated loans until the package is completed for sale. "Warehouse" financing is normally required. A warehouse arrangement is one in which a bank provides a secured or unsecured line of credit to the mortgage company to acquire or originate loans for sale to investors. Investors include mutual savings banks and other thrift institutions, insurance companies, trust organizations, and pension funds.

Although certain bank holding companies have established *de novo* mortgage banking operations, there has also been recent activity

---

[3]"Legal Developments, Northwest Bancorporation, Minneapolis, Minnesota," *Federal Reserve Bulletin*, August 1982: 519–520.

in acquisitions. Chase Manhattan acquired Suburban Coastal Corporation, Wayne, New Jersey, and Seafirst Corporation acquired Arden Mortgage, Walnut Creek, California.[4]

Arden engages in mortgage lending and servicing and construction lending activities. Seafirst plans to expand Arden's services to include extension of single-family home construction loans, acquisition and development loans, apartment house loans, multifamily project loans, and commercial and industrial financing. Seafirst operated mortgage banking and construction finance firms in Washington and Arizona, and the Arden acquisition provides entry to the California market.

Financing requirements include capital for operations and for meeting the capitalization requirements of such secondary market organizations as GNMA and FNMA. Debt financing through warehousing arrangements provides seasonal and working capital funds. Mortgage financing requires specialized skills, including expertise in origination, sales and servicing, and loan brokerage to investors.

Commercial Finance

Banks have extended their commercial loan and leasing activities through two principal vehicles. The loan production office is an extension of the main office, much like a branch office except that it originates and services loan from offices that do not accept deposits. These offices frequently are located in many major cities without regard for state boundaries. When energy development in the Mountain states accelerated, a number of major banks located loan production offices in Denver to expand their market in large-scale, profitable lending.

The second alternative is the establishment of commercial finance subsidiaries or the acquisition of existing companies. For example, Security Pacific Corporation acquired A. J. Armstrong Company, New York City.[5] Armstrong engages in activities of commercial finance and factoring, arranging letters of credit for use in international trade, and holding full-pay-out leases. The acquisition represented movement into the New York area for commercial loan services and toehold entry for future expansion.

Financing for the commercial finance organization includes bank financing, commercial paper, debt, and equity financing. Much of commercial finance activity is funding asset-based loans. This specialized activity allows standardized collection and monitoring. It has become

---

4"Legal Developments, Chase Manhattan, New York, New York," *Federal Reserve Bulletin,* June 1982: 383–384; and "Legal Developments—Seafirst Corporation, Seattle, Washington," *Federal Reserve Bulletin,* January 1981: 68.

5"Legal Developments, Security Pacific Corporation, Los Angeles, California," *Federal Reserve Bulletin,* August 1981: 637–638.

particularly attractive to those banks with loss of large business customers to the commercial paper market. Asset-based lending has become a very competitive market, with interest rates about two points over prime. Additionally, competition has undermined loan standards. Lenders used to advance 35 percent to 40 percent of an inventory value, but recently they have extended credit at 60 percent to 70 percent of inventory value. The market has been especially attractive to regional banks because of their traditional banking relationships with small- to medium-sized borrowers.

About 70 banks have entered venture capital financing to attempt to reap large rewards that cannot be achieved through normal bank lending. Whereas bank lending typically is against assets, venture capital financing invests against future profits. It provides early financing to young or start-up companies that have potential for rapid growth. Banks are allowed to invest up to 5 percent of their capital in venture capital firms.

In 1980 BankAmerica's venture capital subsidiary invested $1 million in Quantum Corporation, a manufacturer of disk drives. Its investment was valued at about $20 million when Quantum sold stock publicly. Continental Illinois invested $500,000 in Apple Computer in 1978 and expects to net more than $40 million in profits.

Data Processing

Until recently data-processing services included bookkeeping or data-processing services to the internal operations of a bank holding company and its subsidiaries, as well as storing and processing other banking, financial, and related data such as performing payroll, accounts-receivable, accounts-payable, and billing services for correspondent banks and bank customers. These activities were permissible under Regulation Y of the Federal Reserve Board. Most activities were engaged in on a local or regional basis.

Citicorp applied for approval to engage in data-processing activities that would significantly expand the data-processing limitations outlined above. On July 1, 1982 Citicorp received approval to engage in the following activities through its subsidiary Citishare Corporation:

- Processing and transmitting banking, financial, and economic data for others through time-sharing.
- Electronic funds transfer.
- Home banking.
- Authentication.
- Provision of packaged financial systems to depository or other institutions to perform traditional banking functions.
- Selling excess capacity on data-processing and -transmission facilities.

* Providing data processing and data services for internal
  operations of Citicorp and its subsidiaries.[6]

The geographic area approved encompassed the entire United States.

The Federal Reserve Board, however, placed certain restrictions on
the proposed services. Citicorp intended to provide hardware to potential users. The Board determined that Citicorp may provide general-pur-
pose hardware in connection with its data-processing services if the cost
to Citicorp of such hardware does not exceed 30 percent of the total cost
of the services provided. This criterion was used to establish the activity
as incidental to banking activity. Consistently exceeding the limitation
would indicate that Citicorp is engaging in a primary activity.

This activity represents a major step in engaging in electronic
banking on a national scale. The investment in data-processing and
data-transmission capability is a specialized and high-cost investment
that could be attempted only by a large, well-capitalized firm.

Electronic banking through automated teller machines (ATMs) has
expanded rapidly. Several large banking organizations have agreed to
link ATMs to provide customers access to their bank accounts regardless of location of the ATMs.[7] The group includes Manufacturers Hanover, First Interstate Corporation, Mellon National Corporation, Norwest Corporation, National Bank of Detroit, and five other banking
organizations. The network will represent about 3500 machines and 10
million customers in 35 states. One can only guess that other banking
services may be linked or offered on a consortium basis if interstate
banking is approved.

Several banking organizations have entered the home banking market. Chemical New York was one of the first to experiment with home
banking. It has spent $20 million on its Pronto System, which is com-
patible with Atari, Apple, and IBM personal computers. It has also fran-
chised its system to nine other banks including Crocker National.
Chemical New York plans to add discount brokerage and other financial
services. Other organizations testing the market for home banking services include Citicorp, BankAmerica, and four regional banks in
Florida.

Bank One Corporation, in Columbus, Ohio, has determined that
the processing of credit card transactions and transactions for firms offering money market funds is within its expertise. Consequently the
bank has devoted significant resources to establishing itself as a primary
processor and Visa card issuer for these services.

State Street Bank and Trust Company of Boston has targeted processing for mutual funds. The Bank of New York is also engaging in

[6]"Legal Developments, Citicorp, New York, New York," *Federal Reserve Bulletin,* August 1982: 504–514.

[7]"Bank Teller Network Is Seen by Year's End," *The Wall Street Journal,* June 15, 1982, 37.

similar activity. Mellon National Corporation provides data-processing services for 200 institutions in 11 states. Mellon's fees for data-processing services amounted to approximately 18 percent of its 1981 operating revenues.

Stock Brokerage

Recently large banking organizations have applied to the Federal Reserve Board for approval to establish or acquire stock brokerage operations as an adjunct service in banks. The brokering of stocks is distinguished from typical investment-banking operations in that brokering involves matching unsolicited orders for purchase and sale of securities, whereas investment banking includes underwriting, syndication, and market-making activities as well as brokerage. The brokerage activity represents fee-generation opportunities without investment in securities.[8]

BankAmerica has purchased Charles Schwab and Company, a discount broker. Security Pacific Corporation has arranged with Fidelity Brokerage Services, Boston, to execute securities transactions for those customers who can use any of the bank's 640 branches in California for such transactions. One view toward engaging in securities transactions is that existing customers of the bank can access the securities markets, and securities customers can access the bank and become its customers.

Special Niches and Opportunities

Opportunities for expansion are numerous. Many opportunities arise from financial crises. For example, the financial condition of thrifts and liberal policies toward large-bank and bank holding company bailouts of thrifts may create merger opportunities that would not exist except for crisis. Recently Citicorp was allowed to acquire Fidelity Savings and Loan Association of San Francisco, First Federal Savings and Loan Association of Chicago, and New Biscayne Federal Savings and Loan Association of Miami. The acquisitions are restricted but may well set the stage for additional acquisitions and speed up interstate banking.

Pending legislation is considering expansion of commercial loan powers for thrifts. Differences between thrifts and banks are becoming less apparent. We speculate that more mergers will occur among banks and thrifts under stress conditions but that banks and thrifts will be allowed to merge under favorable conditions in a short- to medium-term horizon.

Regulatory approval on two fronts also allows banks to compete head-on with the securities industry. These approvals allow the creation

---

[8]See "The Search for Special Niches," *Business Week,* Apr. 12, 1982, 70 ff.

of money-market-like accounts and the sale of commercial paper. Bankers Trust Company, New York, has engaged in the activity since 1978, and the regulatory approval was challenged in the courts. The federal appeals court upheld Bankers Trust, and other banks are expected to enter the market. The approval of the money-market-like account is now under challenge in the courts by the securities industry.

Recently Citicorp received approval to engage *de novo* in the activities of soliciting, underwriting, dealing in, purchasing, and selling obligations of the United States, general obligations of various state and political subdivisions, and other obligations, including money market instruments such as bankers' acceptances and certificates of deposit. The activities will be conducted from New York City and will encompass the entire United States. The activities had not been previously included in the Federal Reserve Board's list of permissible activities.

Small and large banking organizations have taken actions to establish special market niches. These niches include nationwide check processing services (First Tennessee National Corporation), farm management for absentee owners (Hawkeye Bancorporation, Des Moines), investment advisory services to mutual funds (Provident National Corporation), cash-flow and strategic planning to middle-market companies (Mark Twain Bankshares, Missouri), franchising name and services (First Interstate Corporation), wholesale banking (Texas Commerce Bankshares, Houston), retail banking (First City Bancorporation of Texas, Houston), and lending to machine tool companies (Ameritrust Corporation, Cleveland).[9]

COMPETITION TO BANKING ORGANIZATIONS

Foreign Banks

Foreign banks have been engaged in banking activities in the United States. Before the International Banking Act of 1978 (IBA), foreign banks were permitted to operate and accept deposits in more than one state and did not have to meet reserve requirements. The purpose of the act was to place foreign banks on relatively the same competitive level as domestic banks. However, foreign banks enjoy a competitive edge in lending that is less restricted. Most foreign banks have concentrated their operations in New York City and California.

Foreign banks are also subject to the Bank Holding Company Act and the Federal Reserve Board's permissible activities. The one notable exception is the securities activity conducted by these banks, which was grandfathered by new activity related to government securities of the banking organization's home country.

---

[9]Ibid.

Probably one major event that suggests more direct domestic banking activity is the London-based Midland Bank, Limited's formation of a bank-holding company and the acquisition of a 51 percent interest of Crocker National Corporation, San Francisco, and its subsidiaries. In its approval the Federal Reserve Board considered the public benefits, concluding that elimination of probable future competition was not significant and that Midland would inject additional capital into Crocker. The resulting acquisition places Midland as the tenth largest banking organization in the world. Midland owned approximately 20 percent of European American Bank of New York at the date of acquisition and is under Federal Reserve Board orders to reduce its interest to 5 percent or less within three years. The acquisition of Crocker places Midland as a substantial worldwide competitor of major U.S. banking organizations.

With regard to acquisitions of domestic banks, foreign banks enjoy a competitive advantage over out-of-state domestic banks because of interstate banking limitations. Domestic banks were prohibited from acquiring BanCal Tri-State, acquired by Mitsubishi Bank, and Harris Trust, acquired by Bank of Montreal.

Nonbank Banks

Several industrial, commercial, and investment and insurance firms have formed *de novo* banks or acquired banks but have divested the commercial lending activities to avoid classification as bank holding companies. In 1983 Chairman Volcker of the Federal Reserve Board announced a moratorium on nonfinancial institution acquisition or formation of nonbanks. According to the Fed, there are about 60 to 70 nonbanks. In December 1983 the Fed broadened the definition of commercial lending to include purchase of commercial paper, certificates of deposit, and bankers' acceptances.

Major corporations owning nonbanks are Prudential Insurance Company of America, Beneficial Corporation, Gulf & Western Industries, and J. C. Penney. The principal use of the nonbank format is entrance to the retail banking markets. Under the new rules these companies will be required to register as bank holding companies within six months or divest bank or nonbanking operations within two years. Any company that offered banking services before December 10, 1982 would be exempt under grandfather clauses.

In January 1983 Merrill Lynch received approval from the New Jersey banking commissioner to form a state bank. This form of nonbank differs from previous formations principally in that the bank will not accept demand deposits. Although the bank is expected to make commercial loans, under present rules Merrill Lynch does not expect to be classed as a bank holding company because the bank will not accept demand deposits.

Securities Industry

Earlier we discussed money market fund competition for depositor balances. As banks move toward entering certain segments of activities previously the sole territory of investment firms, securities firms are similarly taking steps to engage in banking or bank-related activities.

Consider the following:

+ Dreyfus Corporation, a New York-based mutual fund company, obtained approval to establish a national bank. The purpose of the bank is to provide a full-service package to small- and medium-sized corporate pension and individual retirement plans. The bank will provide trust, investment management, and administrative services. It will eventually offer deposit accounts to its customers and the public but will not make commercial loans.[10]
+ E. F. Hutton set up a trust company to manage certain pension and retirement accounts. Shearson/American Express and other investment companies own trust companies. The principal advantage is the pooling of funds under trust agreement that is exempt from registration under the Investment Company Act.
+ Merrill Lynch has begun selling certificates of deposit and brokering CDs to banks and thrifts.[11]
+ Merrill Lynch has created Capital Resources to offer loans to middle-market firms.

Savings and Loan Associations

Savings and loan associations have received expanded powers that allow these organizations to become more like banks. In October 1982 Congress authorized savings and loan associations to place as much as 10 percent of their assets into commercial loans. It increased the limit on commercial real estate loans from 20 percent to 40 percent of assets and on consumer loans from 20 percent to 30 percent of assets. Additionally, savings and loan associations may offer checking services to business customers and may offer interest-bearing checking accounts to government agencies. As of January 1, 1984, interest rate differentials on deposits between banks and thrifts have disappeared.

The Federal Reserve Board continues to treat savings and loan associations as separate from the business of banking. Except for troubled savings and loan associations, it can be expected that mergers with or

---

[10]C. Conte, "Dreyfus Seeks Clearance to Start a Bank," *The Wall Street Journal*, Oct. 20, 1982, 2.

[11]"Merrill Lynch Plays Bank—Again," *Business Week*, June 28, 1982, 92.

acquisitions of savings and loans by banks or bank holding companies will be denied in the short run. However, if savings and loan association powers are expanded further and banking powers are continued, we may see legislation that combines the banking and thrift industries into a single line of commerce. If this occurs, merger and acquisition activity may accelerate. The increase in competition may create additional erosion in the community banks' ability to compete with larger and expanded banking organizations.

SUMMARY

Applications for new banking-related activities are occurring with increasing rapidity. Similarly, investment bankers are seeking to expand their activities into areas previously relegated to banking. Banking organizations must plan to overcome their biases toward traditional services to survive and maintain their profitability.

For bankers to emerge as winners in the battle for consumer and corporate dollars, they must:

- Create innovative products to set each bank apart from the competition.
- Focus on fewer lending and nonlending areas, thereby rejecting some customer groups.
- Project an image that clearly registers with corporate treasurers and consumers alike.
- Develop much more sophisticated marketing and operational skills.
- Anticipate and react to change by consorting with such enemies as money market funds, brokerage firms, and insurance companies and by emphasizing fee-generating services to offset narrowed lending margins.[12]

Questions and Problems

1. Describe the types of firms identified by Waite that are likely to succeed during the deregulation movement and the possible strategies that will promote success.

2. Analyze the expansion of banking organizations into related activities and determine the extent to which interstate banking exists in fact rather than by law.

3. What are the trends that are occurring among regional and small banks as they seek to service "special niches"?

---

[12]"The Search for Special Niches," op. cit., 70.

4. Analyze the extent to which securities firms have entered banking.

5. Discuss the foreign-bank ownership of U.S. banks and bank holding companies.

6. In what ways have nonbanking firms structured nonbanks to avoid becoming bank holding companies?

7. Discuss the expansion of electronic banking to consumers.

References

"Alaska Makes Its Bid for Interstate Banking." *Business Week,* May 24, 1982, 47.

"An End Run That Spurs Interstate Banking." *Business Week,* Apr. 5, 1982, 29–30.

Andrew, J. "National Steel's First Nationwide S&L Striving to Profit in Interstate Banking." *The Wall Street Journal,* Oct. 27, 1982, 2.

———. "S&Ls Wary about Flexing New Muscles in the Riskier Commercial-Loan Arena." *The Wall Street Journal,* Oct. 5, 1982, 12.

"BankAmerica Plans to Acquire Charles Schwab." *The Wall Street Journal,* Nov. 25, 1981, 4.

"Bank Teller Network Is Seen by Year's End." *The Wall Street Journal,* June 15, 1982, 37.

"Banks Blend with the Funds." *Business Week,* May 24, 1982, 143.

Bell, J. F., and A. E. Wilmarth, Jr. "The Interstate Banking Controversy: President Carter's McFadden Act Report." *Banking Law Journal,* September 1982: 722–744.

Carrington, T. "Fed to Broaden Rule on Offering Bank Services." *The Wall Street Journal,* Dec. 15, 1983, 2.

Carrington, T., and E. C. Gottschalk, Jr. "Bank Sorties into Discount Brokerage Create Wall Street Fears of an Invasion." *The Wall Street Journal,* Sept. 2, 1982, 4.

"Chemical Bank Plans to Offer New Services as a Discount Broker." *The Wall Street Journal,* July 22, 1982, 29.

Conte, C. "Citicorp Buys an Oakland S&L after Fed's Nod." *The Wall Street Journal,* Sept. 30, 1982, 3, 25.

———. "Dreyfus Seeks U.S. Clearance to Start a Bank." *The Wall Street Journal,* Oct. 20, 1982, 2.

———. "Money Funds Sue Regulators over Law Letting Banks Offer Competitive Accounts." *The Wall Street Journal,* Oct. 26, 1982, 12.

"Electronic Banking." *Business Week,* Jan. 18, 1982, 70–80.

Frodin, J. H. "Electronics: The Key to Breaking the Interstate Barrier." *Business Review, Federal Reserve Bank of Philadelphia,* September-October 1982: 3–11.

Helyar, J. "Banks' Rising Interest in Commercial Finance Reshapes the Industry." *The Wall Street Journal,* Dec. 22, 1983, 1, 12.

———. "Regional Banks Search for a Niche in Face of New Rules, Competition." *The Wall Street Journal,* Feb. 4, 1983, 25.

Hertzberg, D. "Interstate Banking Spreads Rapidly Despite Laws Restructuring Practice." *The Wall Street Journal,* Dec. 19, 1983, 21.

Hertzberg, D., and T. Carrington. "Controversy Engulfs Banking Industry in Wake of Fed's Latest Nonbank Ruling." *The Wall Street Journal,* Dec. 16, 1983, 50.

"How a Crisis Is Speeding Deregulation." *Business Week,* May 31, 1982, 68.

Janssen, R. F. "Bankers Are Rediscovering America." *Business Week,* June 14, 1982, 31.

"Legal Developments." *Federal Reserve Bulletin:* "Chase Manhattan, New York, New York" (mortgage finance), June 1982: 383–384; "Citicorp, New York, New York" (electronic banking), August 1982: 504–514; "Midland Bank, Limited, London, England" (bank acquisition), September 1981: 729–734; "Northwest Bancorporation, Minneapolis, Minnesota" (consumer finance), August 1982: 519–520; "Provident National Corporation, Philadelphia, Pennsylvania" (bank acquisition), March 1982: 194; "Seafirst Corporation, Seattle, Washington" (mortgage finance), January 1981: 68; "Security Pacific Corporation, Los Angeles, California" (commercial finance), August 1981: 637–638.

Lynch, M. C. "Fidelity Group Unit Speeds Banks' Entry into Discount Stock Brokerage Business." *The Wall Street Journal,* June 18, 1982, 10.

McMurry, S. "Merrill Lynch Cleared to Form New Jersey Bank." *The Wall Street Journal,* Jan. 4, 1984, 4.

"Merrill Lynch Plays Bank—Again." *Business Week,* June 28, 1982, 92.

Oglivie, N. R. "Foreign Banks in the U.S. and Geographic Restrictions on Banking." *Journal of Bank Research,* Summer 1980: 72–79.

"S&Ls Receive Expanded Lending Powers as Bank Board Carries Out Aid Package." *The Wall Street Journal,* Nov. 5, 1982, 4.

Salamon, J. "Citibank Prepares to Duel Merrill Lynch by Testing a Cash Management Service." *The Wall Street Journal,* June 14, 1982, 8.

"SP Takes Lead Among Banks in Race to Launch Discount Broker Units." *The Wall Street Journal,* Aug. 27, 1982, 4.

"The Search for Special Niches." *Business Week,* Apr. 12, 1982, 70 ff.

"Striking Back, a Bank Joins the Revolution." *Time,* May 3, 1982, 48.

Trebing, M. E. "The New Bank-Thrift Competition: Will It Affect Bank Acquisition and Merger Analysis?" *Review, Federal Reserve Bank of St. Louis,* February 1981: 3–11.

"Visa's Bid to Keep Banks on Board." *Business Week,* Apr. 26, 1982, 101–102.

Waite, D. C., III. "Deregulation and the Banking Industry." *Bankers Magazine,* January-February 1982: 26–36.

Zonaka, V. F. "Brokers Being Added at Bank of America." *The Wall Street Journal,* Oct. 21, 1981, 1.

CHAPTER 22

Trust

The trust function of a bank involves management of customers' assets in a fiduciary capacity. The employees of a trust department act as managers for the bank and provide asset management services for a fee. This service function differs from the management of a commercial bank's assets. Customers' assets are separated and not commingled with the bank's assets.

The area of trust management is undergoing significant modification in today's changing regulatory and competitive environment. The trust department of a bank is a separate service department that offers specialized services for individuals and corporations. By regulation the trust department was, and for the most part still is, a separate unit whose operation is not integrated with other commercial bank functions. In recent years a few banks have integrated traditional trust services and other bank services. This change has come about because of a changed economic and competitive environment and because of greater emphasis on profitability of the function.

Our discussion of trust begins with a description of the basic services offered by a trust department. We shall then examine the basic elements involved in the regulation of trust. In the final section of the chapter we shall discuss the elements involved in the management of trust, including organizational and policy concepts and profitability of the function.

SERVICES OF TRUST DEPARTMENTS

Before describing the services offered by trust departments, we need to define and briefly discuss a few key terms. Bank trust departments enter into a fiduciary relationship with their clients or customers. The essence of the fiduciary relationship is that the employees of the trust department must act in the best interest of the customer. The bank itself is the fiduciary and employees of the department are acting as representatives of the bank. The basic service offered is management of others' assets in a fiduciary capacity.

There are two major types of accounts or vehicles through which the bank delivers these management services—trust and agency accounts. In a trust arrangement the trustor legally transfers title of a property to the trustee, who manages the property for the beneficiaries.

In an agency arrangement the customer engages the agent (the bank) to perform specific services.

Key differences between trust and agency accounts include the transfer of title to the property and dissolution of the agreement. With a trust arrangement title to the property is legally transferred to the trustee, whereas under an agency agreement the title to the property does not pass to the agent. An agency agreement can be terminated by either party but this is not the case with a trust agreement.[1]

Bank trust departments provide a variety of asset management services to both individuals and corporations under trust and agency agreements. Asset management services vary from complete discretionary management of assets to such limited services as safekeeping and accounting.

The types of accounts and services offered by a trust department can be classified into personal and corporate areas. In the personal account area, trust departments offer the following services:

- *Estate settlements.* The trust department settles the estate of an individual according to the instructions of the individual's will. The services provided include securing property for the estate, handling all income, paying estate and inheritance taxes, providing a final accounting of the estate, and distributing the assets to the beneficiaries. The trust department may also provide additional management services to the beneficiaries upon settlement.
- *Personal trusteeships.* Personal trusteeships can be classified as living trusts or testamentary trusts. A living trust is a contract between a living individual and the trust department. Motivation for a living trust can include avoidance of taxes, obtaining specialized management of real or personal property, alleviating concern an individual may have over potential incapacity, and eliminating the necessity of probate. A testamentary trust arises from a customer's will. A person writing a will may decide to leave property to beneficiaries in the form of a trust.
- *Guardianships.* A trust department may serve as guardian of property for minors or those mentally incompetent. The duties involved are similar to those of personal trusteeships. The guardian gathers assets and manages the property in the best interest of the protected person.
- *Personal agencies.* Services provided in a personal-agency account vary from safekeeping services to management of

---

[1]R. L. Blevens et al., *The Trust Business* (Washington, DC: American Bankers Associations, 1982). The authors discuss basic concepts and types of accounts in Chapter 1.

assets. In this type of account the trust department is acting as an agent in some capacity of asset management. A typical personal-agency account is a custodial agency. The duties of the trust department include receiving dividends and interest from the property and dispersing or reinvesting them according to the customer's instructions, notifying the customer of rights, offerings, and defaults, buying and selling securities according to the customer's instructions, and providing record-keeping services. In a management agency the trust department has some discretion in managing the customer's assets.

The following are typical services offered in the corporate area:

- *Corporate trusteeships.* Banks, through the trust departments, act as trustees for issues of corporate bonds. In this capacity the bank acts as watchdog for the bond holders, making sure that all provisions of the indentures are met.

- *Corporate agencies.* Two major types of corporate agencies are transfer agencies and registrar agencies. In these capacities the trust department acts as agent in transferring and registering financial securities, both debt and equity. In addition to the record-keeping and verification services provided by transfer and registrar agencies, the trust department also provides paying-agency services. In this capacity the trust department disburses dividend and debt payments on corporate securities.

- *Employee benefit trusts.* An employee benefit trust encompasses all forms of services to business firms in the management of pensions, profit-sharing plans, and other benefit plans offered to employees. Services provided in these trust accounts vary from full discretionary management of funds in the form of a trust to partial discretionary management of funds in an agency relationship. In addition to management, other services include record-keeping, preparation of periodic reports, paying of benefits, and assuring compliance with regulations concerning pension funds.

- *Charitable trusts and agencies.* A charitable trust or agency account is created for a legal charity. A variety of trusts exist, such as community trusts and public or private foundation trusts. The services provided are similar to those provided to other types of trust and agency accounts; the only significant difference is the ownership of the account.

REGULATION

The first comprehensive government supervision of trust activities of national banks was put into effect by the Federal Reserve Board in 1934.[2] The Federal Reserve Board remained the primary regulator of national banks until 1963, when regulatory responsibility was transferred to the Comptroller of the Currency. Since most trust activity by banks is concentrated in larger banks, the Comptroller has regulatory responsibility for the majority of trust activity in the United States.

Primary regulatory responsibility for trust activity is divided among the three federal regulatory agencies in the same manner as for other banking operations. The Comptroller examines national banks. State-chartered member banks are examined by the Federal Reserve Board. The FDIC has primary regulatory responsibility for state-chartered insured banks that are not members of the Federal Reserve System. Given the dominance of national banks, we shall describe the major trust regulations for national banks that are contained in Regulation 9.

The major provisions of Regulation 9 include sections that:

- define the various types of accounts and the responsibilities of the bank's board regarding the bank's exercise of fiduciary powers.
- regulate the investment and disbursement of idle funds of trust and agency accounts. This regulation is designed to prevent a conflict of interest between the trust department and the commercial bank.
- prohibit self-dealing and set forth provisions that must be followed in protecting the trust customer from the bank's self-dealing. Self-dealing would involve the trust department's breaching its fiduciary responsibility by making investment decisions that benefit the bank and not the trust customer.
- prohibit the commingling of trust department assets with the assets of the bank.
- set forth provisions for managing collective investment funds and employee benefit funds.[3]

The basic purpose of these regulations is to assure that the bank does not breach its fiduciary responsibilities in its trust operations. The regulations require, from a practical standpoint, that trust operations be separate. The so-called "Chinese wall" that separates trust and other commercial bank operations is designed to protect the trust customer.

---

[2]Ibid., chap. 1.

[3]For a detailed summary of Regulation 9, see Bank Administration Institute, *Bank Administration Manual*, vol. 2 (Park Ridge, IL: Bank Administration Institute, 1974), 856–857.

The regulatory provision of separation has negative influences on trust operations. Historically the trust department has been viewed as a separate service function and not as a critical element in a bank's overall planning. The separation has contributed to lack of profitability and lack of coordination between banks and their trust departments.

Trust department operations are also influenced by regulations that apply to the entire bank. The Glass-Steagall Act, which required banks to eliminate most investment-banking activity, has a limiting effect on activities that could be undertaken by the trust function. In delivering financial services, the trust department of a commercial bank has greater restrictions on its activity than a brokerage firm. In the current environment many of the provisions of the Glass-Steagall Act appear to be crumbling.[4] Depending on the eventual outcome concerning relaxation of the Glass-Steagall Act, the trust department may be able to offer extended services in the future.

The trust function has also been limited by regulations prohibiting interstate banking. The limitation on establishing physical locations outside of a bank's service area has limited the expansion of trust operations. The investment industry is not subject to the same limiting regulations.

Trust operations and services have also been influenced by the relaxation of controls relating to the characteristics of deposit services offered by banks. Exhibit 22.1 presents a summary of the major regulatory changes in this area. The effect of elimination of interest rate restrictions on deposit services has been a gradual change that allows banks to offer deposit services that have more investment characteristics than previously. This in turn has resulted in a potential loss in trust business and duplication of effort of the trust and commercial banking functions. We shall address this issue in greater detail in a later section of this chapter.

The regulations discussed to this point have a direct influence on trust services. The economic and competitive environment in which trusts operate has been influenced by regulatory changes of a broader nature. Although it would be impossible to discuss in a thorough manner all of the elements that have had an impact on the trust department's operational environment, a few major changes that will influence it (in some cases have already influenced it) need to be discussed. These changes affect the market served by trust departments and the products offered by trust departments. Three areas of change that have an impact on trust services are (1) changes in the structure of secondary securities markets and in commission structures, (2) pension fund reforms, and (3) changes in tax regulations.

---

[4]"Bankers as Brokers," *Business Week*, Apr. 11, 1983, 70–74.

EXHIBIT 22.1 Summary of Regulatory Changes on Deposit Services

Date	Change	Date	Change
June 1970	Regulation Q ceilings on time deposits of $100,000 or more with maturities of 30–89 days suspended.	November 1975	Commercial banks authorized to offer savings accounts to businesses.
September 1970	Federally chartered savings and loan associations permitted to make preauthorized nonnegotiable transfers from savings accounts for household-related expenditures.	February 1976	Congress extended NOW accounts to all New England states.
		May 1976	New York permitted checking accounts at state-chartered mutual savings banks and savings and loans.
June 1972	State-chartered mutual savings banks in Massachusetts began offering NOW accounts.	June 1978	Six-month money market certificates (MMCs) introduced at banks and thrifts.
May 1973	Regulation Q ceilings on time deposits of $100,000 or more with maturities exceeding 90 days suspended.	October 1978	Congress extended NOW account authority to New York State.
January 1974	All depository institutions in Massachusetts and New Hampshire authorized by Congress to offer NOW accounts.	November 1978	Commercial banks and mutual savings banks authorized to offer automatic transfer (ATS) from a savings account to a checking account or other type of transactions account.
August 1974	Selected federal credit unions permitted to issue credit union share drafts, check-like instruments payable through a commercial bank.	July 1979	A floating ceiling for time deposits at banks and thrifts with a maturity of 4 years or more established.
November 1974	Commercial banks authorized to offer savings accounts to state and local government units.	January 1980	The floating ceiling extended to time deposits with a maturity of 2½ years or more.
April 1975	Member banks authorized by the Federal Reserve to make transfers from a customer's savings account to a demand deposit account upon telephone order from the customer.	March 1980	The Depository Institutions Deregulation and Monetary Control Act of 1980 enacted.

Source: *Synergy in Banking in the 1980's*, American Bankers Association, 1982, 24–25.

In the late 1960s the movement away from the fixed-commission structure of the New York Stock Exchange began. The movement culminated in May 1975 with the elimination of fixed commissions. Related to the changes in the price of transaction services are changes in the structure of the investment industry and movement toward a national market system.[5]

Under fixed commissions, the charges to institutional investors for transaction services exceeded the cost of providing those services. The brokerage industry charged the fixed commission rate but also offered investment advisory services to institutional investors to partly compensate them for the excess charges. Since May of 1975, when fixed commissions were eliminated, transaction services and other related services have been "unbundled" without the tie-in pricing arrangement. Since institutional investors now must pay directly for advisory services, trust departments offering advisory services are on a more favorable competitive basis than they were under fixed commissions.[6]

With the enactment of the Employee Retirement Income Security Act (ERISA) in 1974, the area of pension fund management experienced significant changes. Among the major provisions of the 1974 act were increased funding requirements and controls on pension fund management. The prudent-man provision of ERISA extended the fiduciary responsibilities of pension fund managers beyond the preservation of principal to earning a rate of return through prudent investments sufficient to pay retirement benefits when due. The prudent-man provision placed greater responsibility on the manager of pension funds. A companion to ERISA, the Public Employee Retirement Income Security Act, extended similar provisions to public-employee pension plans.

Several potential effects of these pension reforms may influence the trust department's service market. First, in a direct sense, trust departments that manage employee benefit plans are subject to the prudent-man rule and its greater fiduciary responsibility. Second, the long-run effects of the reforms may increase the assets available to be managed. To the extent that pension funds were undercapitalized, larger commitments of funds may be expected. Third, the increased fiduciary responsibilities and the associated liability are likely to lead to extended use of third-party managers of employee benefit funds.

Major tax reforms have influenced the market for trust services. Tax reforms have had both a direct and an indirect influence. On a direct basis, changes in tax laws require that previous trust plans for individuals be updated to accommodate the changes in regulations. On an

---

[5]Some of the structural changes are discussed in J. J. Mulhern, "The National Market Taking Shape," *Business Review, Federal Reserve Bank of Philadelphia.* September–October 1980: 3–11.

[6]On a direct basis, the removal of fixed commissions has potentially reduced the cost to the trust department of securing transaction services.

indirect basis, changes in tax regulations may increase or decrease the potential need for trust services.

As an example, the Economic Recovery Act of 1981 has both a direct and an indirect influence. On a direct basis, plans formulated under previous regulations must be revised. The 1981 act increases the exemptions on estates and requires the replanning of many personal trusts. On an indirect basis, when all changes of the act are incorporated, the larger exemptions from estate taxes will potentially reduce the market for trust services. The exemption from estate taxes is scheduled to shift to a potential $1.2 million by 1986, leading one author to conclude that estates subject to tax may be reduced by 90 percent.[7]

MARKET STRUCTURE

Trust is a specialized service that requires specialized personnel and systems. A bank must have a potential market for its trust services that is large enough to overcome the fixed administrative costs associated with offering the services. For this reason most banks do not offer trust services.

In 1981 less than one third of insured banks offered trust services. *Trust Assets of Banks and Trust Companies—1981* indicated the 4965 banks had approved trust powers and 4005 of these banks actually offered the services.[8]

Market structure analysis indicates that a positive relationship exists between the size of a trust department and the average size of its managed accounts. Exhibit 22.2 displays a breakdown of trust department average account size by the size of the trust department. The table demonstrates the differences in average account size for large and small trust departments. The average account size for trust departments with assets of less than $10 million is $62,000, whereas the average account size for trust departments whose assets exceed $1 billion is $831,700.

All of the different accounts vary with the size of the trust department, but the largest disparity is in the employee benefit trust and agency accounts. Larger trust departments offer employee benefit services to much larger customers.

Exhibit 22.3 displays the trust and agency accounts of the ten largest trust departments in 1981. Morgan Guaranty Trust is by far the largest trust organization, with managed assets in excess of $35 billion. The

---

[7]E. J. Gamble, "New Tax Law May Reduce Estates Subject to Tax by 90%," *Trust and Estates,* October 1981: 39–47.

[8]*Trust Assets of Banks and Trust Companies—1981"* (Washington, DC: Federal Financial Institutions Examination Council, 1982), 11.

EXHIBIT 22.2   Average Account Size for Trust Departments of Varying Assets Size

| | Trusts and Estates | | | | Agencies | | |
| | Employee Benefit | Personal Trusts | Estates | Subtotal | Employee Benefit | All Others | Total |
Assets							
Less than 10 Million	$ 50.5[a]	$ 63.5	$ 83.5	$ 62.8	$ 33.8	$ 63.4	$ 62.0
10–25 Million	79.0	95.3	100.1	91.9	173.7	121.5	96.2
25–100 Million	126.2	135.9	127.3	132.7	268.8	187.1	141.6
100–500 Million	204.6	188.5	152.7	189.7	697.7	399.6	215.4
500 Million–1 Billion	127.7	222.6	199.5	181.6	2,030.0	535.9	215.4
Greater than 1 Billion	1,972.4	360.7	301.9	611.1	14,202.5	1,788.7	831.7
All Trust Departments	583.7	243.7	184.5	320.5	3,587.0	866.4	412.6

[a]All figures are in thousands of dollars.

Source: *Trust Assets of Banks and Trust Companies—1981* (Washington, DC: Federal Financial Institutions Examination Council, 1982), 14.

EXHIBIT 22.3 Ten Largest Trust Departments by Size of Assets Managed in 1981

| Bank | Trusts and Estates | | | | Agencies | | Total |
	Employee Benefit	Personal Trusts	Estates	Subtotal	Employee Benefit	All Others	
1. Morgan Guaranty Trust Company New York City, New York	$ 8,835,549[a]	$3,951,173	$132,577	$12,919,299	$14,264,533	$ 8,016,442	$35,200,274
2. Citibank New York City, New York	7,716,293	2,571,915	57,953	10,346,161	1,490,103	7,979,068	19,815,332
3. Bankers Trust Company New York City, New York	11,690,490	1,971,776	120,293	13,782,559	3,148,116	2,556,367	19,487,042
4. Provident National Bank Bryn Mawr, Pennsylvania	211,530	2,234,661	90,053	2,536,244	660,687	12,720,963	15,917,894
5. Continental Illinois National Bank Chicago, Illinois	3,062,316	2,567,129	142,429	5,771,874	1,179,297	6,271,872	13,223,043
6. Mellon Bank Pittsburgh, Pennsylvania	2,983,029	3,077,835	124,159	6,185,023	5,437,694	746,318	12,369,035
7. Harris Trust and Savings Bank Chicago, Illinois	4,994,755	2,827,851	242,722	8,065,328	1,011,402	2,306,406	11,383,136
8. Manufacturers Hanover Trust Company New York City, New York	4,509,146	2,569,259	240,275	7,318,680	2,030,004	1,872,150	11,220,834
9. The Northern Trust Company Chicago, Illinois	4,393,002	3,836,475	177,051	8,406,528	370,831	1,989,841	10,767,200
10. Bank of America National Trust and Savings San Francisco, California	4,848,276	3,674,148	365,483	8,887,907	224,424	954,515	10,066,846

[a]All figures are in thousands of dollars.

Source: *Trust Assets of Banks and Trust Companies—1981* (Washington, DC: Federal Financial Institutions Examination Council, 1982), 78.

next largest trust department, Citibank, has less than $20 billion in assets. The list is dominated by large money-center banks as expected, but the ranking is not the same as ranking by bank assets or deposits. Some institutions, particularly Morgan Guaranty Trust, place greater relative emphasis on trust. The data in Exhibit 22.3 indicate different product emphasis as well.

Exhibit 22.4 displays a breakdown of trust institutions by size. In 1981, 103 trust institutions managed assets in excess of $1 billion. This comprised 3 percent of banks offering trust services. In contrast, 88 percent of institutions that offered trust services managed assets of less than $100 million. These figures have important implications for profitability, which is analyzed later in this chapter. It is difficult for a department with less than $100 million in assets to be profitable; yet 88 percent of all trust institutions manage assets of less than $100 million.

Some trust departments do not offer as many services as others. One important service, collective investment, is typically offered by larger trust departments. Collective investment funds, also known as common trust funds, are pooled investment funds that are managed by trust institutions. They are similar to mutual funds with the exception that such funds can be offered only to trust department customers.

In 1981, of the 4005 trust departments of banks insured by the FDIC, 995 offered collective investment funds. There must be sufficient volume of assets to warrant the offering of common trust funds. Only larger departments have such volume.

Similar to mutual funds, collective investment funds can offer specialized investment by type of security, such as common stocks, bonds, municipal bonds, and short-term money market instruments. Specialized investments such as real estate equity and foreign equity are also offered by trust institutions.

EXHIBIT 22.4   Number and Percentage of Trust Institutions by Size of Assets Managed

Size	Number of Banks	Percent
Greater than 1 Billion	103	3
500 Million to 1 Billion	56	1
100 Million to 500 Million	334	8
Less than 100 Million	3605	88
Total Trust Institutions	4098	100

Source: Based on figures of all trust institutions. *Trust Assets of Banks and Trust Companies—1981* (Washington, DC: Federal Financial Institutions Examination Council, 1982).

The funds can be actively or passively managed. With an actively managed fund, the management of the trust institution attempts to secure superior performance through selection or timing of purchases or sales of securities in the fund. With a passively managed fund, no attempt is made to secure abnormal profits. The funds are invested in an index such as the Standard and Poor's 500 and the fund's goal is to match performance of the index. Index funds became popular in the 1970s as evidence of market efficiency and as the difficulty in securing abnormal profits began to mount. The vast majority of funds are actively managed but indexed funds are available.

Exhibit 22.5 presents a breakdown of collective investment funds by type of fund. In terms of assets the largest type of fund is in the short-term money market area. This type of account competes directly with the money market funds. Traditional equity, income, and balanced funds are also large components of total offerings.

Collective investment activity is dominated by the larger trust institutions. Exhibit 22.6 displays collective investment fund operations by banks. Morgan Guaranty Trust operates 27 different funds with a total of $13.8 billion in assets. This composes over one third of its total managed assets. The pooled funds are a very important component of the large trust departments.

EXHIBIT 22.5 Collective Investment Funds by Type of Fund

Type of Fund	No. of Funds	No. of Banks	Total Assets ($ Thousand)	Total Number of Accounts
01—Equity	1,831	852	$ 25,803,944	267,062
02—Diversified Balanced	340	252	4,038,860	71,023
03—Fixed Income	1,743	863	20,891,857	312,719
04—Municipal Bond	342	315	4,550,634	70,109
05—Real Estate Equity	38	33	1,884,182	3,431
06—Short-Term Investment	333	181	46,174,799	305,520
07—Mortgage	71	33	1,208,665	4,504
08—Foreign Equity	29	18	1,017,936	1,407
09—Foreign Fixed Income	9	6	456,771	920
10—Index Equity	38	18	7,538,660	1,348
11—Index Fixed Income	2	2	12,767	538
12—Other	38	30	1,890,521	13,472
Total	4,814	2,603	115,469,596	1,052,053

Source: *Trust Assets of Banks and Trust Companies—1981* (Washington, DC: Federal Financial Institutions Examination Council, 1982), 112.

EXHIBIT 22.6   Collective Investment Fund Operations by Banks: 15 Largest Banks

Bank	Number of Funds	Total Assets ($ Thousand)	Total Number of Accounts
Morgan Guaranty Trust Company New York City, New York	27	$13,806,000	14,605
Citibank New York City, New York	33	6,203,397	17,680
Wells Fargo Bank San Francisco, California	32	5,618,028	16,788
The Chase Manhattan Bank New York City, New York	22	4,405,375	8,839
The Northern Trust Company Chicago, Illinois	19	4,281,675	17,873
Bank of America National Trust and Savings San Francisco, California	19	3,826,540	36,212
Harris Trust and Savings Bank Chicago, Illinois	19	3,351,087	11,555
Manufacturers Hanover Trust Company New York City, New York	25	3,018,143	6,644
Bankers Trust Company New York City, New York	47	2,873,648	6,988
The First National Bank of Chicago Chicago, Illinois	21	2,436,719	12,272
Chemical Bank New York City, New York	15	2,389,617	5,149
Mellon Bank Pittsburgh, Pennsylvania	19	2,241,599	12,416
American National Bank and Trust Company Chicago, Illinois	14	2,198,382	2,725
State Street Bank and Trust Company Boston, Massachusetts	19	2,089,460	7,662
National Bank of Detroit Detroit, Michigan	15	1,959,326	9,474

Source: *Trust Assets of Banks and Trust Companies—1981* (Washington, DC: Federal Financial Institutions Examination Council, 1982), 118.

MANAGEMENT OF THE TRUST FUNCTION

Traditionally the trust department has operated as a unit separate from other bank functions. Also, banks have viewed trust as more of a complementary service than a potential profit center. The typical notion of a trust customer was that of a very wealthy individual who relied on the trust department to help manage his vast holdings of assets.

Within the last two decades the traditional view of trust has been undergoing change. This change has been in the areas of product structure, services, and concern for profitability. The managements of banks and trust departments have begun to view the trust department in terms of a profit center. Banks are looking at possible methods of expansion of trust services to new markets.

The general trends in the competitive, economic, and regulatory markets have led managements to assess the profitability of trust operations. As margins have been squeezed, cost reduction programs have become popular. The structural organization of trust departments is being reviewed to determine if services can be offered in a more efficient fashion. We shall address in the last section of this chapter some of the more radical changes that are being observed. In this section we shall discuss the traditional trust department organization and the profitability of trust departments.

Organizational Structures

The traditional organization of the trust department is based on functions. A sample organizational chart based on functions is displayed in Exhibit 22.7. The main functional areas are business development, administration, investment, and support services. Both personal and corporate accounts are serviced through the main functional areas.

Exhibit 22.8 displays an alternative organizational breakdown by customer markets. In recent years many banks have reorganized their commercial services by customer markets, and this alternative is also feasible for the trust department. The product-line structure organizes the trust department under personal and institutional areas with all functional elements provided separately for personal and institutional accounts. The advantage of this form is that because the product markets are different, the bank can offer the specialized services more efficiently.

The final possibility is a structure that combines both the functional and the product-line concepts. A sample of a combined structure is displayed in Exhibit 22.9. This structure features personal and institutional product areas and the functional areas of investment and support services. Some form of combined structure is the most common since such a form results in greater efficiency. The major product lines are separate but there is not the duplication of departments that is present with a strict product-line organization. For example, it is likely to be more efficient to have a single research department rather than duplicate the function for both personal and institutional services.

The organization of the trust department is very important to overall profitability. The key to operating the trust function profitably is to deliver the service while minimizing overhead and operational costs. Unnecessary duplication of services will result in increased salary and overhead expenses. Efficient organization will enhance profitability.

EXHIBIT 22.7 Organizational Structure—Functions

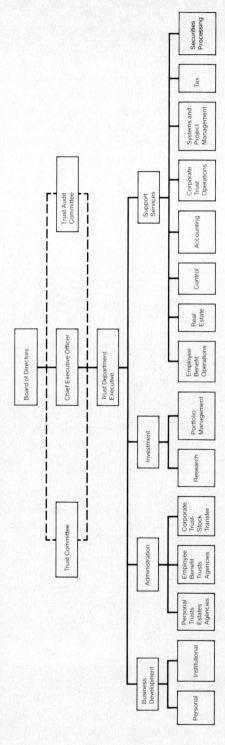

Source: Ronald L. Blevens et al., *The Trust Business* (Washington, DC: American Bankers Association, 1982), 188.

EXHIBIT 22.8   Organizational Structure—Product Lines

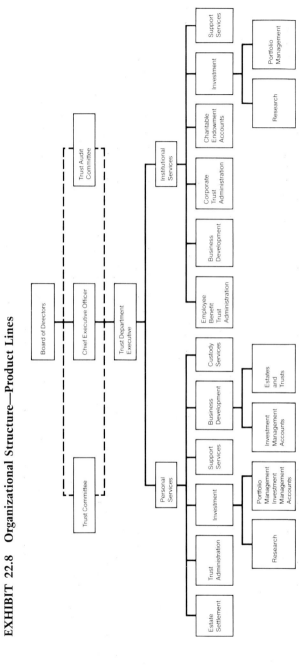

Source: Ronald L. Blevins et al., *The Trust Business* (Washington, DC: American Bankers Association, 1972), 189.

EXHIBIT 22.9 Organizational Structure—Functions and Product Lines Combined

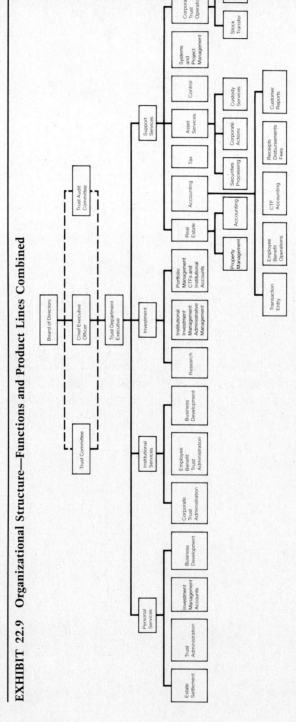

Source: Ronald L. Blevens et al., *The Trust Business* (Washington, DC: American Bankers Association, 1982), 190.

Profitability of Trust Operations

Measuring trust profitability is a very difficult task. In some sense the profitability of a trust department or function is dependent on the allocation of costs and revenues. Key elements involved with the allocation problem include the corporate overhead and credit on balances related to trust services.

The profitability of a trust department depends on the cost allocation system. If an unreasonable proportion of total overhead is allocated to trust, the function will appear less profitable. Operation of a trust department also creates deposit balances that the bank is able to invest in earning assets. The measured profitability of the trust department depends in part on the extent to which the trust department receives credit for the earnings generated from such balances.

The issue of whether the earnings credit on trust department balances should be counted in trust profitability has been widely discussed and debated.[9] Most studies of profitability show that trust departments are not profitable without the earnings credit. For example, the 1981 *Functional Cost Analysis* shows that both large and small trust departments are not profitable without consideration of earnings balances.[10]

The balances income issue was discussed in a recent *Trust Management Update*.[11] The article points out that there is a difference between fiduciary and nonfiduciary balances. Balances on fiduciary accounts such as estate settlements are not or should not be considered as a component of operating income. The bank has a fiduciary responsibility to keep idle cash balances at a minimum. Balances on nonfiduciary accounts bear characteristics of operating income and therefore earnings on such balances should be considered in trust department profitability. For many services compensating balances are an integral component of pricing.

For large trust departments with assets in excess of $5 billion, pretax operating profit margin with nonfiduciary-balances earnings credit included was 23 percent, whereas the margin without the credit was 7 percent.[12] The earnings credit effect is more significant for larger trust departments, but the credit has some impact for trust operations of all sizes.

---

[9]J. Asher, "To Build Profits: Which Way Trust?" *ABA Banking Journal*, February 1977: 37–62; and "Can Trust Officers Solve the Cost Accounting Puzzle?" *Banking*, March 1978: 54–57.

[10]Board of Governors of the Federal Reserve System, *Functional Cost Analysis, 1981 Average Banks* (Washington, DC, 1982).

[11]Cates Consulting Analysts, "Trust Profit: The Balances Income Issue," *Trust Management Update* (New York: Cates Consulting Analysts, March 1983 reprint).

[12]Ibid. The article makes a distinction between trust profitability and the contribution that the trust department makes to overall bank or bank holding company profit. The authors argue that when measuring the contribution to the holding company, fiduciary-balances credits should be considered.

Another issue involved in measuring profitability concerns the measurement of overall customer profitability. It may well be that one component of the overall customer relationship does not appear profitable but the overall customer relationship is profitable. This issue may be critical for large corporate customers that may use commercial loan and deposit services as well as trust services. Measurement of one element of the package of services may be very misleading.

In 1980 a new profitability measurement service, called Trustcompare, began operation. The service is offered through Cates Consulting Analysts, Inc., with sponsorship by the Trust Division of the American Bankers Association. The goal of the program is to analyze revenues, expenses, and profitability of trust departments and to compare performance of banks of similar size. The program uses standardized accounting procedure and presents greater detailed analysis than is available with the *Functional Cost Analysis* program. It is a tiered approach that presents different profile levels depending on the degree of sophistication of the trust operation.

Exhibit 22.10 summarizes some key revenue expense and profitability measures for participating banks in 1982. The profit margins and income sections show that trust departments with managed assets in excess of $100 million are more profitable than those with assets of less than $100 million. The 1982 figures are consistent with previous studies that tend to show that larger operations are more profitable.[13] The earnings components also show that trust operations significantly contribute to overall returns. For banks with trust assets in excess of $5 billion, 10.2 percent of total bank earnings were contributed from trust in 1982. The percentages of trust income and earnings, with larger departments making larger contributions, also highlight trust contributions.

The expense and product-mix sections of the report point out some key elements and indicate certain differences between large and small banks. In terms of product mix, estate services are more important for small trust operations, and corporate services and employee benefit management are more important for large trust operations. Personal trust accounts represent over 35 percent of operating income for all but the very largest trust operations. The largest expense element is personnel expenses, which range from 53 percent of operating income for small departments to 44 percent for the largest departments. Contract services are larger for small operations, indicating that they purchase more outside services than larger trust departments. Returns to scale appear to be most predominant in the personnel area.

The figures in Exhibit 22.10 are based on averages for a rather small component of total trust departments. Two points concerning this

---

[13]K. V. Smith and M. B. Goudzwaard, "The Profitability of Commercial Bank Trust Management," *Journal of Bank Research,* Autumn 1972: 166–177.

EXHIBIT 22.10 Selected Trustcompare Results for Five Asset-Size Categories, 1982

	Managed Assets				
	$40–100 Mil.	$100–500 Mil.	$500 Mil. 1 Bil.	$1–5 Bil.	Over $5 Bil.
Profitability					
Pretax operating profit margin					
1982	14.8%	25.2%	22.2%	27.4%	22.4%
1981	13.4	26.3	27.1	28.0	25.7
Profit margin ex nonfiduciary balances credit, 1982	6.9	15.4	16.9	20.0	5.8
Product Mix					
As % of total operating income					
Estates	8.4%	8.6%	8.8%	7.4%	3.7%
Personal trust	35.2	36.1	37.6	36.0	27.3
Investment advisory	3.8	3.9	5.8	7.3	6.0
Managed EB	12.7	13.1	11.5	13.1	9.7
Nonmanaged EB	1.3	2.1	3.5	3.1	3.4
Custody	4.3	2.9	4.5	4.7	5.7
Corporate services	5.4	5.1	5.8	8.8	9.9
Other	1.0	1.8	1.2	2.5	4.9
Nonfiduciary bal. credit	4.6	9.7	6.6	8.8	12.3
Expense Control					
As % of total operating income					
Personnel	53.4%	45.9%	48.1%	44.1%	44.0%
Contract services	11.7	10.0	11.5	5.5	3.4
Other direct	12.5	11.4	11.9	12.2	13.8
Indirect	9.4	8.0	9.9	9.8	16.0
(Computer)	9.4	6.3	5.9	6.3	9.9
Corporate overhead as % of total operating income	5.3%	6.5%	5.7%	7.2%	8.5%
Contribution to Bank					
Bank return on assets	1.03%	0.85%	0.82%	0.76%	0.58%
Trust contribution to bank ROA	0.02	0.04	0.04	0.05	0.08
Trust as % of bank					
Income	5.5%	6.0%	6.6%	8.1%	8.1%
Earnings	1.5	4.8	4.0	6.1	10.2
No. of Trust Banks	*17*	*71*	*33*	*53*	*19*

Source: Cates Consulting Analysts, Inc. (New York, New York).

summary seem important. First, trust departments that manage assets in excess of $100 million tend to be more profitable than smaller departments. Second, these are average figures. Size per se does not assure profitability. The Trustcompare results show some decline in profitability between departments with assets of $1–5 billion and those with assets of over $5 billion.

TRUST—FUTURE DIRECTIONS

Throughout this text we have attempted to describe those areas of banking in which we expect to see changes. The trust area may be the area in which we shall see the greatest change. It is in the trust area that banks may offer personal financial-planning services that will compete directly with brokerage and investment institutions. Banks with trust departments in place have personnel with investment backgrounds, and many banks have business-development personnel in place. Many trust operations are beginning to offer innovative services to compete with investment institutions, and many are repackaging services to attract additional customers.

The environment of change is reflected in the structural changes that integrate trust and other commercial bank services, and in the cooperative trust efforts that allow smaller institutions to offer trust in an efficient fashion. These developments indicate an emphasis on collective-investment-funds products. The structure and products that eventually emerge will depend on regulatory changes and the view of regulators concerning separation of trust powers.

The movement to broaden the operations of trust and to integrate trust and other commercial bank operations has been spurred by the brokerage firms' invasion into banking services and by changes in regulation that allow banks to offer deposit services that are more investment-like in character. The results of a major study commissioned by the American Bankers Association Trust Division, entitled *Synergy in Banking in the 1980s: A Strategic Assessment of Trust Banking Opportunities in the Financial Services Industry*, were published in 1982.[14] The study evaluates technological, competitive, economic, and regulatory changes as they apply to the financial services industry in general and to trust operations specifically. The major conclusion of the study is that changes in a bank's operating environment call for a complete reevaluation and reorganization of the products it offers.

---

[14]A summary of the ABA publication was presented in "ABA Study Looks at Future Services and Changes for the Banking Industry," *Trust and Estates*, February 1982: 26–30.

The report calls for greater market segmentation in the personal financial services area, with different levels of product services ranging from those that can be marketed on a general basis to the broad market to those that require detailed knowledge of a customer's specific circumstances. A summary of the suggested market-segmented accounts appears in Exhibit 22.11.

Examination of Exhibit 22.11 reveals the movement toward integration of trust and traditional bank services. In Level III services include tax planning, investment, lending, and transaction services. It is through this integration that banks will be able to compete with the investment industry.

Our discussion to this point has been forward-looking, but some evidence exists to point out that the industry is moving in the direction of offering financial-planning services that combine investment management and lending services. Several banking organizations have moved toward integrating trust and commercial operations. Included are majors such as Norwest Corporation, Crocker National Bank, and Citicorp. There is also evidence of innovation in smaller organizations such as F&M Marquette National Bank of Minneapolis and Fleet National Bank of Providence, RI.[15]

Several areas of product innovation are beginning to be developed in the current environment. Trust departments are evaluating packages of services and rebundling services to meet the demands of the marketplace.[16] While some departments are bundling new packages, others are experimenting with unbundling to attract additional customers.[17] Banks are offering customers the choice of selecting elements of packages of services.

The trust function can achieve potential gains from automation. As our investigation of profitability indicated, personnel costs are the largest component of operating costs for trust. Many of the services that previously required officers' time can be automated.[18] The end result will be delivery of services at lower cost.

---

[15]T. Bisky, "The Challenges of Trust Fascinate Steve Farley," *ABA Banking Journal*, January 1983: 42–44; and J. Asher, "To Build Profits: Which Way Trust?" *Banking*, February 1977: 37–62.

[16]D. C. Cates, "Trust/Bank Cooperation: An Interview Series," *Trust Management Update, American Bankers Association*, January 1983: 11–15; C. Gozarek, "Developing Trust Business Through Branch Banks," *Trust and Estates*, November 1981: 20–22; J. K. Milne and S. X. Doyle, "Rx for Ailing Bank Trust Departments," *Bankers Magazine*, January-February 1980: 54–58; and W. W. Peters, "Realizing the Trust Potential in Cash Management Services," *Bankers Magazine*, September-October 1982: 46–48.

[17]R. W. Prensner, "Unbundling Trust Services," *Trust and Estates*, November 1980: 10–16.

[18]J. M. Dillion, " Invading the Cash Management Services Market," *Trust and Estates*, August 1982: 25–27; R. J. Sywolski, "Is Automated Cost Accounting the Key to Trust Profits?" *Trust and Estates*, February 1980: 38–39; R. J. VanArt, Jr., "Outlook for Trust Automation in the 1980s," *Trust and Estates*, March 1981: 32–35.

EXHIBIT 22.11 Market-Segmented Personal Service Products

Level and Description	Products and Services	Marketing Implications
Level IV: Products and services which require detailed knowledge of the customer's family or personal situation, sound judgment, and good technical knowledge.	**Complex estate planning** **Complex financial planning** **Complex tax-planning consulting** **Fiduciary services**	Customer contact staff adds value through detailed knowledge of the customer, sound judgment, and good technical knowledge.
Level III: Products and services which require detailed technical knowledge or access to superior judgmental advice.	**Full-service broker dealer services (equities, bonds, options, government/government agencies, commodities, financial futures, currency futures, tangibles)** **Commingled asset management** **Simple financial planning** **Simple personalized insurance planning** **Simple tax planning** **Packaged tax shelters** **Other limited partnership investments** **Lending as part of a financial plan** **Complex tax return preparation** **Real estate brokerage** **Real estate management** **Personal services (bill payment, completion of medicare forms, arrangement of health care services, etc.)**	Customer contact staff adds value through personal contact and input of judgment into decisions. Comprehensive customer information to support customer contact staff and free them up for personal contact and for decision making.

Level II: Products and services which require a low level of judgment or which can be delivered on an impersonal packaged basis.

Money market funds
Other mutual funds
Directed insurance products
Annuity products
Discount brokerage services
Variable-rate mortgages
Standard tax return preparation
Comparative shopping services

Opportunity to combine individual products and services into integrated, modularized packages to establish a systems-based customer relationship. Services can be delivered electronically and comprehensive statements can be prepared.

Level I: Commodity products and services which can be understood and evaluated on an unaided basis by most consumers.

Checking/NOW accounts
Savings accounts
Auto and home insurance
Term life insurance
Auto loans
Fixed-rate mortgages
Credit/debit cards
Revolving-credit facilities
Second mortgages

Source: American Bankers Association, *Synergy in Banking in the 1980s: A Strategic Assessment of Trust Banking Opportunities in the Financial Services Industry* (Washington DC: American Bankers Association, 1982), 106–107.

The evidence on profitability indicates returns to scale for trust operations. This combined with the market movement toward personal financial-planning services will place new competitive pressures on small regional banks. To offer services that will be competitive with the integrated services of larger institutions will require innovation. Possibilities include cooperative efforts with and purchasing of services from larger organizations. An example of a cooperative effort is the Trust Company of Oklahoma, which was formed in 1980 and is owned by 40 community banks that could not efficiently offer trust services independently.[19] The combined assets of the cooperative are approximately $200 million.

The collective funds area also represents an area in which trust departments could extend market potential. Under current regulation banks can market collective funds services only to trust customers. Through product redesign banks could effectively compete with mutual funds by offering investment management and diversification services to a broader market. The collective funds management systems are in place for many organizations, and services could be expanded if packages combining financial-planning services and collective funds services were available.

SUMMARY

The traditional services offered through the trust department include personal and corporate agency and trust accounts. Personal services include estate planning and settlement, personal agency, and trusteeship and guardianship. Corporate services include employee benefit administration, transfer and registrar agencies, and charitable trusts.

Regulation of trust operations has resulted in trust operations being separated from other banking operations. Trust services are significantly affected by regulation in both a direct and an indirect way. In a direct way, regulations such as the Glass-Steagall Act limit the investment activity that a bank may undertake. In an indirect way, regulations such as ERISA and the Economic Recovery Act of 1981 influence the market for trust services.

Profitability of the trust function is related to size. Generally, larger departments are more profitable. The key factor in the profitability of larger banks appears to be lower personnel costs. The services offered by large and small trust departments also vary. Larger trust de-

---

[19]P. Mindeman, "Trust Services—A Cooperative Approach," *Trust Management Update, American Bankers Association,* January 1983: 18–20.

partments offer expanded corporate services, and a larger percentage of their income is derived from employee benefit account management. Smaller departments secure a larger percentage of their operating income from estate settlements.

The services offered by trust departments and the organizational structure of trust operations are undergoing significant changes in the current environment. As we move toward a market in which personal financial planning is emphasized, we can expect to see greater integration of trust and other commercial bank services.

Questions and Problems

1. Briefly describe the types of accounts and services offered by trust departments of commercial banks.

2. Describe the relationship between the size of a trust department and the average size of the accounts managed by that trust department.

3. Define the term *collective investment fund* and describe the various types of funds offered by commercial bank trust departments.

4. What are the alternative forms of organizational structures that may be employed in the delivery of trust services?

5. In the consideration of measurement of trust profitability, the issue of earnings credit on deposit balances generated by a trust department was discussed. **a.** Describe the findings with respect to profitability and earnings credit. **b.** Discuss the issue of considering earnings credit on fiduciary and nonfiduciary balances.

6. Compare the profitability of small trust departments with the profitability of large trust departments. For your discussion consider small trust departments to be those that manage assets of less than $100 million.

References

American Bankers Association. "ABA Study Looks at Future Services and Changes for the Banking Industry." *Trust and Estates*, February 1982: 26–30.

Asher, J. "Can Trust Officers Solve the Cost Accounting Puzzle?" *Banking*, March 1978: 54–57.

Asher, J. "To Build Profits: Which Way Trust?" *ABA Banking Journal*, February 1977: 37–62.

Blevins, R. L., et al. *The Trust Business*. Washington, DC: American Bankers Association, 1972.

Bexley, J. B. "Establishing a Trust Department in a Small Bank." *The Magazine of Bank Administration*, August 1973: 34–36.

Bisky, T. "The Challenges of Trust Fascinate Steve Farley." *ABA Banking Journal*, January 1983: 42–44.

Board of Governors of the Federal Reserve System. *Functional Cost Analysis, 1981 Average Banks* (Washington, DC, 1982).

Booker, I. "How and Why to Value a Trust Business." *Trust and Estates*, October 1982: 30–31.

Cates Consulting Analysts. "Trust Profit: The Balances Income Issue." *Trust Management Update* (New York: Cates Consulting Analysts, March 1983 reprint).

Cates, D. C. "Trust/Bank Cooperation: An Interview Series." *Trust Management Update, American Bankers Association*, January 1983: 11–15.

Clarke, J. M. "Why Talk Trust When Clients Really Respond to Problem Solving?" *ABA Banking Journal*, January 1983: 38–39.

Dillion, J. M. "Invading the Cash Management Services Market." *Trust and Estates*, August 1982: 25–27.

Ellison, D. E. "Fiduciary Services by Business Line." In *The Bankers' Handbook*, 2d ed., ed. W. H. Baughn and C. E. Walker, 929–935. Homewood, IL: Dow Jones-Irwin, 1978.

Ellison, D. E. "The Function and Organization of Fiduciary Services." In *The Bankers' Handbook*, 2d ed., ed. W. H. Baughn and C. E. Walker, 923–928. Homewood, IL: Dow Jones-Irwin, 1978.

Ellison, D. E. "Investment Management of Securities as Fiduciary Assets." In *The Bankers' Handbook*, 2d ed., ed. W. H. Baughn, and C. E. Walker, 936–946. Homewood, IL: Dow Jones-Irwin, 1978.

Evans, R. B. "Starting a Trust Department in a Community Bank." *The Magazine of Bank Administration*, June 1976: 28–31.

Gamble, E. J. "New Tax Law May Reduce Estates Subject to Tax by 90%." *Trust and Estates*, October 1981: 39–47.

Gozarek, C. "Developing Trust Business Through Branch Banks." *Trust and Estates*, November 1981: 20–22.

Heirs, R. W. "Michigan's Trust Branching System." *Trust and Estates*, November 1981: 25–26.

Kennedy, J. C., and R. I. Landau. *Corporate Trust Administration and Management*, 2d ed. New York: New York University Press, 1975.

Martell, T. F., and R. L. Fitts. "Determinants of Bank Trust Department Usage." *Journal of Bank Research*, Spring 1978: 8–14.

Milne, J. K., and S. X. Doyle. "Rxfor Ailing Bank Trust Departments." *Bankers Magazine*, January-February 1980: 54–58.

Mindeman, P. "Trust Services—A Cooperative Approach." *Trust Management Update, American Bankers Association*, January 1983: 18–20.

Mulhern, J. J. "The National Market Taking Shape." *Business Review, Federal Reserve Bank of Philadelphia*, September-October 1980: 3–11.

Person, R. J. "Here Come the S&L's." *Trust and Estates*, July 1979: 8–12.

Peters, W. W. "Realizing the Trust Potential in Cash Management Services." *Bankers Magazine*, September-October 1982: 46–48.

Prensner, R. W. "Unbundling Trust Services." *Trust and Estates*, November 1980: 10–16.

Seidel, R. B. "Writing Trust Policy, Parts 1, 2, and 3." *The Magazine of Bank Administration*, January-March 1983: 33–35, 40–43, 46–48.

Smith, K. V., and M. B. Goudzwaard. "The Profitability of Commercial Bank Trust Management." *Journal of Bank Research*, Autumn 1972: 166–177.

Sywolski, R. J. "Is Automated Cost Accounting the Key to Trust Profits?" *Trust and Estates*, February 1980: 38–39.

Trust Assets of Banks and Trust Companies—1981. Washington, DC: Federal Financial Institutions Examination Council, 1982.

VanArt, R. J., Jr. "Outlook for Trust Automation in the 1980s." *Trust and Estates*, March 1981: 32–35.

CHAPTER 23

International Banking

Domestic banks were not authorized to establish international offices until the passage of the Federal Reserve Act of 1913. The first bank to establish a foreign branch was Citibank, which opened a branch in South America in 1914. With a few exceptions, domestic banks were not active in international banking until the 1960s.

In today's market international banking is an integral part of many large bank operations. Large money-center banks expanded international operations very aggressively in the 1960s, and expansion continued in the 1970s. The 1970s also saw foreign banks expand their operations in the United States. The banking system has become progressively more interconnected as international banking becomes more important to the global banking system.

International banking is more complex than domestic banking for a variety of reasons. First, regulations are more complicated in that two sets of regulations must be adhered to—domestic regulations and regulations of the country in which operations are undertaken. Second, additional risks are present with international banking. Financial reporting standards are not so rigorous in foreign countries, which makes it more difficult to evaluate credit risk. In some countries political instability increases risk of operations. Third, a bank has many options in the form of organization it uses to deliver international services. The process of evaluating how to deliver services is more complicated.

The activity in international banking by domestic banks has been increasing in the last two decades. While overall activity has been increasing, most of the international banking activity has been undertaken by large money-center banks. For many money-center banks international business comprises a very large part of overall business. In 1982, for example, 60 percent of Citibank's net income and 67 percent of its total deposits were generated from international operations.[1]

The relatively recent increase in international banking activity on the part of American banks can be traced to a variety of factors. In the 1960s banks expanded international operations to skirt regulations. Much of the initial activity in the Eurodollar market can be traced to banks' raising funds at market rates that could not be raised domestically because of Regulation Q. Limitations on foreign lending by

---

[1]"Citibank's Pervasive Influence on International Lending," *Business Week*, May 16, 1983, 124.

domestic banks led to the formation of foreign branches and foreign subsidiaries. In the 1960s nonfinancial domestic corporations took on multinational characteristics. Domestic banks extended their international operations to service their customers' needs.[2]

In the 1970s much of the expansion of international activity could be traced to the recycling of "petro dollars." With the large increases in oil prices, oil-exporting countries experienced large inflows of funds, which were deposited in banks. The banks securing these deposit funds expanded their international loans to employ these funds.

In recent years banks have also used international operations to expand deposits and loans. Some bank activity in international operations can be traced to defensive strategies to protect market share. Foreign banks have become very active in competing for the international business of domestic corporations. In addition, some banks are using international banking locations to position for interstate banking.

In this chapter we shall consider three major aspects of management of international banking: (1) the various organizational forms available to deliver international services and the basic structure and regulations, (2) the Eurodollar market, and (3) the basic concepts of international lending.

DELIVERY OF SERVICES

A bank that decides to become involved in international banking may select from a variety of organizational forms for the delivery of services. The choice of form depends on what services the bank wants to offer, the expected volume, the size of the bank, the capital commitment necessary to establish the organizational form, personnel requirements, and regulations. Large money-center banks provide extensive services through a number of organizational forms, including representative offices, full-service branches, subsidiaries, and specialized-service offices. A large bank may have to use all of the available organizational forms to provide services to different areas. A smaller regional bank may provide limited international services through one organizational form.

A bank can provide limited international services to its customers through correspondent banks. A bank using this method of delivering service would not aggressively expand its international services but would simply service the needs of its domestic customers. The types of services that can be offered through correspondents include foreign exchange, honoring letters of credit, and furnishing credit information.[3]

---

[2]B. B. White, "Foreign Banking in the United States: A Regulatory and Supervisory Perspective," *Quarterly Review, Federal Reserve Bank of New York,* Summer 1982: 48–58.

[3]D. K. Eitman and A. I. Stonehill, *Multinational Business Finance,* 3rd ed. (Reading, MA: Addison-Wesley, 1982), 494–495.

The advantage to a bank in using correspondents is that the bank employs no personnel to provide the service. The bank provides the service in exchange for providing similar services for the foreign bank. In this way the bank can provide limited services to accommodate some of the needs of its customers; but using correspondents does not generate business for the bank's own account. Even if a bank provides full-service international banking in some geographic locations, correspondent relationships will be maintained to provide services in other areas.

Basic Organizational Forms

Exhibit 23.1 displays the basic organizational forms a bank can employ to deliver international services. Examination of Exhibit 23.1 reveals a wide variety of forms, ranging from a representative office, which has a very limited staff and scope, to a subsidiary bank, which has full-banking services offered by a subsidiary of the holding company. The exhibit also provides an overview of services that may be offered and advantages and disadvantages of the various forms.

Representative Office. The primary use of a representative office is as a business development office. In a representative office a bank has one or more representatives located in a foreign city who develop business for the home office of the bank. This form of organization is often used in advance of opening a branch. A bank cannot actually make loans or accept deposits directly in the representative office under this organizational form.

Shell Branch. Shell branches are used as booking offices to gain access to the Eurocurrency market. Shell branches are characterized by the absence of an effective operational staff; the main office of the bank performs the work. It is common for shell branches to be located in tax-advantage countries. The two most popular locations are the Bahamas and the Cayman islands.

Full-Service Branch. Full-service branches probably represent the most flexible organizational form to deliver services. Through a branch a bank can provide any or all of the services permissible under joint regulations of the United States and the host country. Personnel requirements are more extensive than with a shell or representative office, since a full staff must be maintained. Branches are not a viable option in all countries, however, since some countries—Mexico and Canada, for example—prohibit branching by foreign banks.[4]

---

[4]R. K. Abrams, "Regional Banks and International Banking," *Economic Review, Federal Reserve Bank of Kansas City*, November 1980: 11.

EXHIBIT 23.1 Basic Organizational Forms

Form	Services Provided	Advantages	Disadvantages
Representative Office	Limited personnel who serve in an advisory capacity to customers of the parent bank in the particular location.	Personnel can establish contact in the local banking community, enabling the parent bank to better service its customers. Lower personnel and administrative costs.	Limited service—the bank cannot provide general banking activities, which limits the services that can be provided.
Shell Branch	Used as a booking office to gain access to the Eurocurrency markets. Actual banking activities take place at the organization's main office.	Access to Eurocurrency market for domestic funding. Reserve-free location from which to issue foreign loans.	Does not provide full-service operations. Limited personnel results in limited service.
Full-Service Foreign Branch	Develops foreign business. Gathers foreign credit information. Provides full service to the bank's foreign customers.	Branch is a legal extension of the parent bank and does not require separate capitalization. Branch has the same status as the parent bank in the international market. Organizational form is flexible, and services can be integrated with the parent bank.	Expense of establishing and maintaining a full-service branch. Income of foreign branch may be heavily taxed. Branch is prohibited from undertaking activities prohibited for its parent.
Subsidiary Bank or Affiliate Bank	Provides full-service banking activities in a foreign location. Can provide all services allowed by local banking regulations; may provide more services than a branch.	Potential for offering services not allowed by U.S. banking regulations. Viewed as a separate bank; it may be easier to develop more extensive services in the local market. May have more favorable tax treatment.	Requires separate capitalization. Operational aspects may be less flexible than a branch. Separate capital, deposits, and loans cannot be transferred easily. Greater organizational development costs and personnel costs.

EXHIBIT 23.1 *(continued)*

Form	Services Provided	Advantages	Disadvantages
			If the parent bank is a minority owner, control is a potential area of difficulty.
Consortium Bank	Full-service banking. Related investment and underwriting services. Consulting services for banking entities.	Allows large banks to pool operations in a separately owned banking operation. Pooling of loan risks. Pooling of different expertise. Establishment of wide network of facilities.	Effectively available only to the largest international banking organizations. The domestic bank has less control than it would have over a subsidiary.
Edge Act or Agreement Corporation	Banking services related to international banking. Investment services, including equity positions in corporations.	Can establish international banking offices with limited capital commitment in the United States. Allows domestic banks to set up interstate locations, even though activities are limited to international business. Flexible in terms of scope; both banking and investment services can be offered.	Lending limits of 15% of capital apply to loans to any single customer. Limited to deposits related to foreign transactions; some limits on types of deposits that can be accepted.
International Banking Facility	Deposit and lending service to foreign residents and banks. Business limited to a wholesale nature.	Allows a bank to use a domestic office to book Eurocurrency transactions without employing a shell branch. No formal application is necessary to form a facility. Extremely flexible.	Activity is limited to foreign residents. Activity is limited to large accounts.

Subsidiary or Affiliate Bank. A subsidiary or an affiliate bank is a separate organization of the holding company that is an entirely separate banking organization and is chartered through the host country. A *subsidiary* bank in which the parent bank owns a minority interest is referred to as an *affiliate.*

A subsidiary or affiliate bank requires separate capitalization and charter approval by the host country. Some advantages of this form of organization over branches include a wider range of banking activities, less restrictive regulation, and a separate identity. It may be possible for the bank to become more widely accepted in the local market because of the separate organization. As a separate banking organization offering services similar to those of local banks, the bank may be able to compete more effectively with local organizations.

The separate identity can also be a limiting factor, since the full backing of the parent bank does not apply. The financial strength of the subsidiary bank is evaluated separately from that of the parent bank. Also, commitment of funds in the form of capital is substantially more than that required for a branch.

Consortium Bank. A consortium bank is a separate banking organization that is a joint venture of several parent banks. The parent banks are typically from different nations. Consortium banking is generally limited to large multinational banks. An example of a consortium bank is the Société Financère Européene, which is owned by nine large multinational banks (including BankAmerica) of different nationalities. This consortium bank has a complex structure of three separate organizations and engages in a broad range of financial services.[5]

This range of activities is available only to the large multinational banks. It presents options that may be unavailable to subsidiary banks because of personnel limitations and capital requirements. Activities of consortia include complex loan syndications and investment banking.

Edge Act or Agreement Corporation. Domestic banks can also service the international market through Edge Act corporations (typically referred to as "Edges") and agreement corporations. Agreement corporations were authorized for formation with amendments to the Federal Reserve Act in 1913 and 1916. Edge Act corporations were authorized with a similar amendment in 1919.

One essential difference between an agreement corporation and an Edge corporation is the charter. Agreement corporations are chartered by the state, whereas Edges are federally chartered. Another key difference is a minimum capital requirement of $2 million for an Edge, whereas no minimum capital requirement applies to agreement corpo-

---

[5]Eitman and Stonehill, op. cit., 501–502.

rations.[6] The 1916 amendment allowed national banks with capital of $1 million or more to commit up to 10 percent of their capital in institutions for conducting international banking business. In 1919 the Federal Reserve Act was amended to allow the Federal Reserve Board to charter corporations that engage in international banking.

Edge Act and agreement corporations can engage in both banking and investment activities. Originally the investing capability of Edges and agreement corporations was the only means by which banking organizations could make equity investments in foreign corporations, but later amendments to the Federal Reserve Act in 1966 and the Bank Holding Act in 1970 allowed banking organizations to make direct equity investments in foreign corporations.[7]

An Edge that is engaged in banking activity can accept demand and time deposits as long as they are identifiable as international transactions. It can offer a variety of services, including foreign exchange, acceptance transactions, and lending. Lending limits of 15 percent of capital apply to loans to a single customer.

Investment Edges can make long-term loans and equity investments with much less stringent requirements on limits. For example, an investment Edge can lend as much as 50 percent of its capital to a single customer. Investment Edges are commonly used as holding companies for a bank's foreign subsidiaries and affiliated companies.

International Banking Facility.   In December 1981 the Federal Reserve Board permitted an additional form of delivering international banking services, called International Banking Facilities (IBFs). IBFs are allowed to conduct deposit and loan business with foreign residents and foreign banks without being subject to reserve requirements, interest rate ceilings, and FDIC insurance requirements.[8] IBFs effectively allow a bank to conduct business in a Eurocurrency environment without establishing an offshore facility.

An IBF is a separate set of asset and liability accounts, segregated on the books of an establishing institution, rather than a separate institution. An IBF can be established by a U.S.-chartered depository institution, a U.S. branch or agency of a foreign bank, or a U.S. office of an Edge or agreement corporation.[9]

Regulations that apply to IBFs are designed to control activities so that business activity is restricted to foreign customers and not used by

---

[6]For a complete discussion of Edge Act and agreement corporations, see N. Pinsky, "Edge Act and Agreement Corporations: Mediums for International Banking," *Economic Perspectives, Federal Reserve Bank of Chicago,* September–October 1978: 25–31.

[7]Ibid., 28.

[8]S. J. Key, "International Banking Facilities," *Federal Reserve Bulletin,* October 1982: 565.

[9]Ibid., 566.

banking institutions to skirt regulations that apply to the domestic market. No deposit or lending activity can be done with any U.S. resident. Deposits cannot be negotiable and must have a maturity of at least two business days. Loans made to foreign customers are restricted to the financing of their operations outside the United States.[10] There is very little history on IBFs, since they were approved only in December 1981. By early September 1982 nearly 400 banking institutions had established IBFs, and total assets amounted to more than $150 billion.[11]

Structure of International Banking Activity

As our discussion to this point has indicated, a variety of organizational forms are possible for delivering international banking services. Most of the activity by U.S. banks in establishing international banking organizations has been undertaken by money-center and large regional banks. Small regional banks may provide limited service through correspondent banks or representative offices, but delivery of service through actual banking facilities has been dominated by the largest domestic banks.

Domestic banks have had the authority to organize international banking operations since the early 1900s, but, with a few exceptions, no banks were active in this area until the 1960s and 1970s. As recently as 1959 there were only six Edge Act corporations in existence, whereas by 1983, 143 Edge Act corporations were in existence.[12] In 1960 international banking was undertaken solely by the largest money-center banks. In the late 1960s and 1970s activity was expanded by money-center and large regional banks. The majority of international banking activity is still undertaken only by banks whose domestic assets exceed $1 billion.

Exhibit 23.2 presents a summary of banking activity by bank size as of December 31, 1979. The activity of most banks with assets of $1 billion or less is limited to shell branches. The number of banks in this category with Edge Act corporations is less than 1 percent, whereas 100 percent of banks with assets in excess of $10 billion operate Edge Act corporations. The dominance of very large money-center banks is most apparent in foreign-branching activity. Banks with assets in excess of $10 billion operate 501 branches, with almost all branching activity undertaken by banks whose assets exceed $3 billion.

---

[10]For a complete discussion of the requirements and permissible activities of IBFs, see Key, op. cit.

[11]Key, op. cit., 565.

[12]C. M. Korth, "The Evolving Role of U.S. Banks in International Finance," *Bankers Magazine,* July–August 1980: 69; and D. D. Whitehead, "Interstate Banking: Taking Inventory," *Economic Review, Federal Reserve Bank of Atlanta,* May 1983: 15.

EXHIBIT 23.2   International Banking Activity by Bank Size as of December 31, 1979

Domestic Assets ($ Billion)	Number of Banks with Edge Act Corporations	Number of Banks with Shell Branches	Number of Banks with Foreign Branches[a]	Number of Foreign Branches
Under 1.0	3	29	—	—
1.0–1.999	5	49	4	4
2.0–2.999	25	25	5	5
3.0–9.999	24	38	23	85
10.0 and over	14	12	14	501

[a]Does not include shell branches.

Source: Adapted from Richard K. Abrams, "Regional Banks and International Banking," *Economic Review, Federal Reserve Bank of Kansas City,* November 1980.

For the largest domestic banks international earnings have grown to become a very significant component of total earnings. For the 10 largest U.S. banks international earnings comprised nearly 50 percent of total earnings in 1977.[13] This has grown from a comparable figure of less than 20 percent in 1970.

Regional banks have entered the international market, but the majority of these banks have entered the market on a very limited basis. Although some regionals have opened shell branches, the majority of their activity has been limited to operation of an international department. Many regionals offer only basic services such as foreign exchange and letters of credit.[14]

International Banking Services

Banks provide a variety of services in the international area, ranging from payment transfers to Eurocurrency borrowing and lending. The degree of complexity of services is highly variable. Bank size is an important determinant of services offered. Some of the services discussed below can be provided by small banks through correspondents, whereas others require the investment capital and expertise of a money-center bank.

Money Transfers.   A basic international service provided by banks is money transfer. Money transfer can be requested by both retail and wholesale customers. An individual might want to transfer funds from

---

[13]Korth, op. cit., 71.

[14]For a summary of the activity of regional banks, see Abrams, op. cit.

the United States to an individual in a foreign country. Wholesale customers such as importers may want to transfer funds from the United States to a foreign country for payment to an exporter. In addition, the need to transfer funds on an interbank basis arises from traveler's check transactions. A foreign bank needs to collect funds from a U.S. bank when dollar-denominated traveler's checks are cashed at the foreign bank.

Funds transfer services are usually provided for a fee and can be accomplished by several methods, including airmail remittances, cable remittances, foreign drafts, and cash letters. As the name implies, airmail remittances are instructions between banks to transfer funds by airmail. Cable remittances refer to transfers via wire or electronic means. Foreign drafts are used when a client wants a negotiable instrument to replace an instructional type of transfer. Cash letters are employed for interbank transfers.

Foreign Trade Transactions.   Much of the activity in international banking entails the financing of foreign trade. Major services provided include collection services associated with drafts, issuing letters of credit, and bankers' acceptance activity. The most important activity entails issuing letters of credit.

To facilitate international trade, importers and exporters need to coordinate payment transfer and transfer of title of the goods while controlling risk. If the exporter wishes the importer to pay for the goods immediately, a sight draft is issued when the goods are shipped. This requires the importer to pay for the goods when the draft arrives (is sighted).[15]

A more common method in financing international trade is the use of letters of credit. In essence, a letter of credit is an agreement by an importer's bank to pay a specified sum on a specified date, providing the terms of the sale are met by the seller (exporter) of the goods. The promise to pay is made by the bank providing the letter of credit. Most letters of credit are irrevocable; so once the terms of the sale are met, the exporter has the bank's promise to pay. This is different from the collection of a draft discussed above. With a sight draft the promise to pay is that of the importer.

Letters of credit can be arranged as drafts payable on sight, in which the funds are to be paid once the draft is received. Time or usance letters of credit are also commonly used in international trade financing. With a time or usance letter of credit, the bank promises to disburse funds not on sight of the draft but at some specified future date. A

---

[15]In some countries regulations allow the importer to wait until the vessel in which the goods were shipped arrives. See P. K. Oppenheim, *International Banking.* 4th ed. (Washington, DC: American Bankers Assoication, 1983), 126.

common arrangement is *x* days after sight. The use of a time draft may give the importer enough additional time to take possession of the goods and sell them before the bank is required to pay the exporter. If the goods are sold within the alotted time, funds will be available for the importer to deposit in the bank before the bank disburses on the letter of credit. In the case described above, the bank would not disburse funds, although the liability to disburse exists.

A time draft is the basis for a bankers' acceptance, which is a negotiable instrument. The exporter is able to secure funds in advance of the maturity of the draft by discounting the draft through his bank. The term *acceptance* arises from the process of the importer's bank's accepting the draft and having the primary responsibility for providing payment at maturity.[16]

Exhibit 23.3 details the process of a line of credit becoming a bankers' acceptance and traces the process of creation to final payment of the draft. Steps 1–7 detail the process of the line-of-credit creation preceding the actual creation of the bankers' acceptance. Steps 8–15 detail the process following creation of the acceptance. With a straight line of credit, face-value funds would be distributed to the exporter's bank at maturity. With an acceptance, discounted funds are disbursed when the draft and shipping documents are received. The issuing bank then sells the bankers' acceptance (its obligation) to a third party in the money market and receives payment for its promise to pay at a later date. In this fashion the bank has not tied up its funds. Steps 13–15 detail final payment of funds for acceptance.

To be an effective competitor in the bankers' acceptance market, a bank must have a specialized staff and an established name. Most of the activity in this area is done by money-center banks with assets in excess of $5 billion.[17] Small regional banks have limited activity, although it does exist. It is more costly for a small bank to sell its acceptances in the secondary market since large discounts are necessary to sell the paper.

Foreign Exchange Services.   Foreign exchange services are important for international banking transactions since such transactions often entail foreign currency. A U.S. importer may be required to pay for goods in a foreign currency. A U.S. exporter may receive payment in foreign currency for goods sold to a foreign importer. Both of these cases require an exchange of currency, and banks provide exchange services for their customers.

---

[16]For a complete discussion of bankers' acceptances, see J. M. Duffield and B. J. Summers, "Bankers' Acceptances," in *Instruments of the Money Market*, 5th ed., ed. T. Q. Cook and B. J. Summers (Richmond, VA: Federal Reserve Bank of Richmond, 1981), 114–122.

[17]Ibid., 121.

EXHIBIT 23.3 Creation of a Bankers' Acceptance

Example of Bankers' Acceptance Financing of U.S. Imports:
A Banker's Acceptance is Created, Discounted,
Sold, and Paid at Maturity

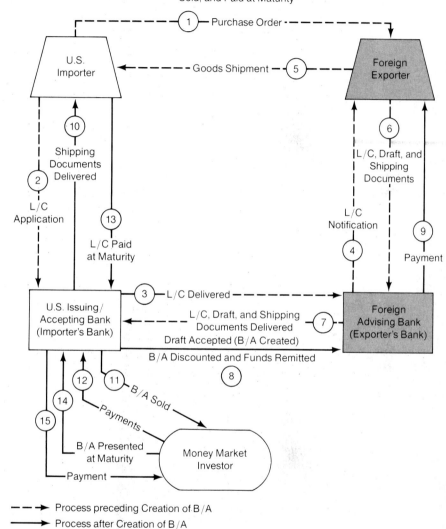

Source: J. G. Duffield and B. J. Summers, "Bankers' Acceptances," in *Instruments of the Money Market*, 5th ed., ed. T. Q. Cook and B. J. Summers (Richmond, VA: Federal Reserve Bank of Richmond, 1981), 116.

Two major types of foreign exchange services can be provided by banks: current exchange services and forward-commitment exchange services. With a current exchange the bank is exchanging one currency for another immediately. For example, an exporter could request an immediate exchange of pesos received for payment for dollars. The bank can provide for the exchange in several ways. If the bank holds an inventory of pesos, the exchange can be made at the current rate and delivery can be accomplished through an inventory adjustment. Alternatively, the bank could agree to the exchange at the current rate and then cover its position after the agreement. In this case the bank is at risk in relative value of the currencies until its open position is covered. The bank could also not commit to the exchange rate until the offsetting transaction is arranged.

Large banks that are active in foreign exchange services will maintain working balances in currencies to accommodate exchanges. In addition, these banks will have traders active in the currency markets, making it easier for the banks to adjust inventory positions to accommodate immediate exchanges. A small regional bank without working balances in currencies or an active trading department is likely to incur greater risk when it has an open position.

A bank providing forward-commitment exchange services agrees to exchange currency at a later date for a specified exchange rate today. Forward delivery dates from one month to a year are common, with some contracts in actively traded currencies extending to several years.[18] From the customer's perspective, the advantage of arranging forward-commitment exchange is that risk can be avoided. A bank that arranges forward commitments for its customers must be certain that its customers will deliver their portions of the transactions; otherwise the bank could experience losses.

Bank activity in foreign exchange services varies with size and expertise of specialized staff. Money-center banks with large volumes of transactions are able to maintain large trading staffs and are better able to evaluate risk. Regional bank activity is limited by specialized trading staff necessary to accommodate trading. Some regional banks maintain active foreign exchange services, whereas others offer limited services.[19]

Two additional services of banks in the international banking area are Eurodollar market participation and making foreign loans. These areas, both of which are very important to large money-center banks, are discussed in the following sections.

---

[18]Oppenheim, op. cit., 220.

[19]Abrams, op. cit., 5.

Regulation and Regulatory Issues

Probably no area of international banking is more complex than regulation. Regulatory issues are complicated by the fact that different countries impose different types and different degrees of regulation on banking institutions. The particular regulations a bank must adhere to in its international banking operations depend on the form through which it is delivering its service and the country or countries in which it is operating. For example, most foreign countries do not place the constraints that U.S. banking regulators impose on investment banking. Therefore, if a domestic bank delivers services through a subsidiary in a host country that allows investment banking, these services can be provided. If international services are offered via a branch, the bank must adhere to U.S. regulations, which do not allow investment banking. Thus a domestic bank servicing a particular market through different organizational forms may be subject to vastly different sets of regulations.

The regulation of domestic and foreign banks presents problems for regulators of a given country. If the banking regulations of one country are more restrictive than those of other countries, the regulations, if imposed on foreign banks in the host country, may make the market unattractive for foreign entry. The restrictive regulations may discourage foreign entry, making the market less competitive. Furthermore, the restrictions may make it more difficult for the host country's banks to enter foreign markets. If foreign regulators adopt a "reciprocity" principle, allowing foreign banks opportunities similar to those offered the country's banks in foreign operations, the regulatory constraints may impose hardship on the host country's banks.[20]

If regulators allow foreign banks greater freedom in operations than its domestic banks, an obvious problem exists. The foreign banks will have a competitive advantage over domestic banks. The only possible benefit to such a regulatory policy would be that it may give the country's banks greater freedom in the international market (assuming that other countries reciprocate).

A problem of this sort was addressed in the International Banking Act of 1978. Foreign banks had a competitive advantage over U.S. banks in establishing interstate banking offices. The primary goal of the 1978 act was to place domestic and foreign banks on equal footing. In passing this act, the United States has adopted the principle of national treatment based on the principle of nondiscrimination.[21]

---

[20]For a discussion of the philosophies of regulation, see J. P. Segala, "A Summary of the International Banking Act of 1978," *Economic Review, Federal Reserve Bank of Richmond.* January–February 1979: 16–21; and White, op. cit.

[21]Segala, op. cit.

The banking system has become more interdependent and interconnected, with international banking emphasized by most major banks. This expansion into international banking would present only minor regulatory problems if all countries had similar regulations and control procedures. The banking regulations are highly variable, however, and the principle of national autonomy is the rule in banking regulations. This leads to wide variation in banking regulation.[22]

World banking leaders have begun to recognize the problems in international regulations. Following some large bank failures in the mid-1970s, the Bank for International Settlements formed a committee on banking regulations and supervisory practices.[23] The committee, which is made up of 11 members from major countries, has made very limited progress in improving the coordination of international regulations. At least the attempt is being made to coordinate regulations.[24]

The importance of international banking regulation has again reached center stage with the current problems arising from large losses and potential losses on international loans. Many of the world's major banks could potentially experience devastating loan losses, which could lead to failures. The issues involved in coordinating regulation are extremely complex and not easily resolved.

Eurodollar and Eurocurrency Market Operations

The market through which most money-center banks conduct the majority of their international banking operations is the Eurodollar market. The Eurodollar market is largely an unregulated market that is wholesale in nature. The growth of the Eurodollar market is related to many factors that range from attempts to avoid national banking regulation to fear of deposits of one country being seized by another country.[25]

A Eurodollar deposit is defined as a deposit liability, denominated in U.S. dollars, of banks located outside the United States.[26] Dollar-denominated deposits with a branch, affiliate, or subsidiary of a U.S. bank and more recently with an international banking facility of a U.S. bank are classified as Eurodollar deposits even though the affiliation is with a bank whose head office is in the United States. Dollar-denomi-

---

[22]For an excellent discussion of the variability in banking regulations, see R. Dale, "Safeguarding the International Banking System," *The Banker*, August 1982: 49–82.

[23]In June 1974 the Eurodollar market was shocked by the collapse of the Herstatt Bank and the near collapse of Franklin National Bank. See L. L. Kreicher, "Eurodollar Arbitrage," *Quarterly Review*, *Federal Reserve Bank of New York*, Summer 1982: 10–21.

[24]For a discussion of the problems faced by the committee, see Dale, op. cit.

[25]For a complete discussion of the factors contributing to the development of the Eurodollar market, see M. Goodfriend, "Eurodollars," in *Instruments of the Money Market*, 5th ed., ed. T. Q. Cook and B. J. Summers (Richmond, VA: Federal Reserve Bank of Richmond, 1981), 123–133; and Oppenheim, op. cit., chap. 16.

[26]Goodfriend, op. cit., 123.

nated deposits with foreign banks are also classified as Eurodollar deposits. Virtually all Eurodollar deposits are interest-bearing time deposits even though such deposits may have a maturity of only one or two days.

The term *Eurocurrency* is broader in scope and includes deposits denominated in other currencies that are held by banks outside of the home office country. A deposit liability denominated in Swiss francs held by a London bank would be referred to as a *Eurofranc* deposit. Dollar-denominated deposits are by far the most important component of the Eurocurrency market, making up over 70 percent of total deposits.[27] But the market is broader than just Eurodollars.

The term *Eurodollars* is misleading since a deposit located in any bank outside the United States is referred to in a broad sense as a Eurodollar. The majority of trading activity is still centered in Europe, but significant activity also takes place in the Caribbean and Asian markets. Some authors refer to a dollar-denominated deposit in Singapore as an Asian dollar deposit. Here we are referencing all offshore deposits as Eurodollars.

A few significant differences exist between Eurodollar and domestic dollar deposits. First, all Eurodollar deposits are time deposits even if the maturity is only one day. Second, all Eurodollar deposits are interest-bearing. Third, Eurodollar deposits are not subject to reserve requirements or deposit insurance assessments.[28] Except for these differences Eurodollar deposits and domestic deposits are indistinguishable.

TYPES OF DEPOSITS

All deposits in the Eurodollar market are time deposits. Maturities can range from one day to several years, but most activity is in the maturity range of one week to six months.[29]

Other forms of deposits include fixed-rate CDs, floating-rate CDs, and floating-rate notes. Fixed-rate Eurodollar CDs are similar to domestic CDs. They offer the holder the ability to sell the deposit in the secondary market, and an active secondary market exists. The high and unpredictable rates of inflation of the late 1970s and early 1980s spawned floating-rate CDs and notes. Floating-rate CDs have been issued with maturities that range from one and one-half to five years. Floating rate notes have been issued with maturities that range between four and twenty years. Secondary markets for both floating-rate CDs and

---

[27]Ibid., 125.

[28]Eurodollar deposits borrowed by a U.S. bank head office for domestic use are subject to reserve requirements. Reserves are required regardless of the fact that the deposits were raised from a foreign branch or subsidiary.

[29]Goodfriend, op. cit., 126.

notes exist, but the markets are not as active as the market for fixed-rate CDs. Floating-rate liabilities of this type have been aggressively pursued by some banking organizations as a source of permanent funding.[30]

Eurodollar deposits are provided by a bank's customers and by other banks through the interbank market. The interbank market comprises the majority of trading in Eurodollar deposits, and the market is very active.

The interbank market developed because banks seldom have exact matches in Eurodollar deposits and demand for loans. The active interbank market allows a bank to employ surplus deposit funds or secure additional funds needed to support additional loans. Major banking institutions can obtain or employ Eurodollar deposits at the London Interbank Offer Rate (LIBOR). Banks secure or employ Eurodollar deposits both on a direct basis and through brokers who bring buyers and sellers together.[31]

RATES ON DEPOSITS

Rates on Eurodollar deposits are closely related to rates on domestic deposits. As we have indicated, there are differences between Eurodollar deposits and domestic deposits in reserve requirements and deposit insurance assessment, but with these exceptions the two types of deposits are close alternatives.

Exhibits 23.4 and 23.5 display rates on Eurodollar deposits and similar-maturity domestic deposits. The rates on overnight Eurodollar deposits and federal funds are very similar. The rates on domestic and Eurodollar CDs are also very similar, although they have a little more variability in spread than the overnight rates.

The process that keeps the rates on domestic and Eurodollar deposits very close is arbitrage. Since the two sources of funds are close substitutes, if the spread between the rates gets too large, then opportunities for profits arise that banks will take advantage of, causing the spread to decrease.

A simple example of an arbitrage transaction can be constructed assuming the Eurodollar CD rate exceeds the domestic CD rate for similar maturities. Banks could sell domestic CDs and employ the funds in Eurodollar CDs. This would be a matched transaction with very little

---

[30]D. S. Howard, "Dynamics of Interest Differential Earnings," in *Funds Management Under Deregulation*, ed. G. Hempel (Washington, DC: American Bankers Association, 1981), 554–561.

[31]Oppenheim, op. cit., 299.

EXHIBIT 23.4   Rates on Federal Funds and Overnight Eurodollar Deposits

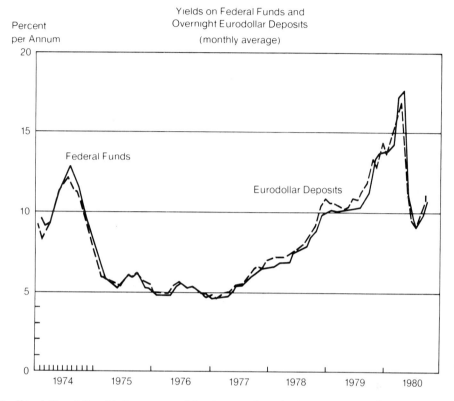

Source: M. Goodfriend, "Eurodollars," in *Instruments of the Money Market,* 5th ed., ed. T. Q. Cook and B. J. Summers (Richmond, VA: Federal Reserve Bank of Richmond, 1981), 129.

risk, and if the spread between the CDs was large enough banks would move to arbitrage the opportunity for profits.

The above example is simplified to demonstrate the motivation behind the trade. The process involved in an actual arbitrage transaction is complicated by additional cost and constraint factors.[32] Effective cost factors for the alternative deposits must include the reserve requirements and FDIC insurance assessment on the domestic deposits and a risk premium on the Eurodollar deposits. Constraint factors include cap-

---

[32]For a thorough discussion of arbitrage opportunities in the Eurodollar market, see L. L. Kreicher, "Eurodollar Arbitrage" *Quarterly Review,* Federal Reserve Bank of New York (Summer 1982): 10–21. The author develops an arbitrage tunnel based on effective costs of domestic and Eurodollar deposits.

EXHIBIT 23.5 Rates on Three-Month Domestic and Eurodollar CDs.

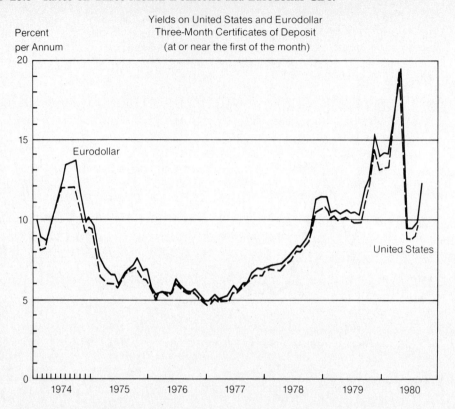

Source: M. Goodfriend, "Eurodollars," in *Instruments of the Money Market*, 5th ed., ed. T. Q. Cook and B. J. Summers (Richmond, VA: Federal Reserve Bank of Richmond, 1981), 130.

ital controls and internal balance-sheet constraints.[33] For example, our illustrative arbitrage transaction expands the bank's balance sheet, which places additional constraint on capital. If a bank is at its perceived capital limit, even though the transaction presents a profitable opportunity, the transaction may not be undertaken since it would reduce the capital adequacy ratio.

Rates on Eurodollar CDs and floating-rate instruments are closely related to the LIBOR. The rate on three-month Eurodollar CDs has averaged 30 basis points less than the three-month LIBOR. Rates on floating-rate instruments are usually tied to the LIBOR and have aver-

[33]Ibid.

aged 12.5 to 25 basis points over the six-month LIBOR.[34] The rates on floating-rate instruments are typically adjusted every three or six months.

INTERNATIONAL LOANS

For banks with extensive international operations, loans generate the largest component of earnings from international operations. Loans made to foreign enterprises and governments are complex credits that possess all the elements of risk involved with a domestic loan plus additional unique elements of risk. When a bank makes international loans, additional investigation of economic performance is necessary to evaluate credit risk. The stability of the government must also be assessed to evaluate probable performance of the credit.

In this section we shall overview the major types of loans made to foreign borrowers, describe the types of borrowers and relate the elements of risk to the particular borrowers, and describe the current environment in international lending. We shall limit our discussion to the unique elements involved in international lending. All of the elements involved in the administration of loans discussed in Chapters 7–9 apply to international loans, but additional elements must be incorporated into the administrative process of international lending.

Loan Types and Customers

International loan types are similar to domestic loan types. Loans can be short term or long term and can be secured or unsecured. The loans can be granted for a fixed amount or can be made on a credit line basis. Similar to participation loans, international loans can be made on a syndicate basis. In a syndicate loan a bank will enter into an agreement with other banks to fund a large international credit.

Certain specialized types of loans are more common in the international sphere than in domestic operations. Complex asset-based financing arrangements are common in the international area. We recall from Chapter 8 that with an asset-based loan the assets backing the loan become the basis for repayment of the loan. The qualification process involves evaluation of the conversion of the assets into funds to repay the credit. Asset-based project loans involving joint-venture operation and ownership are often encountered in the international area. These types of loans require a specialized analysis of the worth of the assets and often require complex loan agreements.

---

[34]Goodfriend, op. cit., 127–128.

An example of this type of loan is a production-payment loan that is based on mineral production. For example, a number of companies may be involved in a joint venture to extract minerals from a Third World country. The companies agree to produce a certain quantity of minerals each year and the bank looks to production of the minerals to repay the loan. The production agreement becomes the basis of the loan rather than the cash flow of the companies involved in the joint venture.[35]

Customers for international loans include individuals, business enterprises, correspondent banks, and foreign governments or their subsidiaries. Of these, individuals are the least important for most banks. The emphasis is on commercial loans or loans to foreign governments.

U.S. banks make a variety of loans to correspondent banks, with most being short term. Loans involve letters-of-credit financing, bankers' acceptance financing, and advances against collections. Some loans to correspondent banks are made on a seasonal basis to assist correspondent banks in the financing of agricultural production.[36]

Loans made to business enterprises range from trade financing for smaller businesses to working-capital and term loans for larger enterprises. In addition, project-financing arrangements for joint ventures, as described above, are common.

A large component of international lending involves direct loans to foreign governments, central banks of foreign governments, and corporations under the control of foreign governments. Loans made to foreign governments may include loans to cover balance-of-payments deficits and loans for specific projects similar to those made to private enterprises.

In a sense, loans made to a foreign government or foreign government bank are the safest loans that can be made in a country. The government is likely to be the safest risk in a given country. The government cannot go bankrupt (although the current government can fail), but at the same time a bank making a loan to a foreign government has little leverage.[37] The government may force banks to reschedule debts and extend maturities, as we are currently witnessing. Balance-of-payments deficits are causing many foreign governments to reschedule, and banks have little leverage over these reschedulings.

Evaluation of the creditworthiness of loans made to foreign governments often involves prediction of world economic performance. Events such as OPEC's raising of oil prices in the 1970s can have a drastic impact on the ability of a government to repay its debt. So while the

---

[35]For a complete discussion, see Oppenheim, op. cit., 280–284.
[36]Ibid., 277–280.
[37]Ibid., 282–284.

loans are safe in the sense that the countries may not go bankrupt, they can also be very risky.

Risks in International Lending

In addition to the elements of risk present in domestic lending, several unique elements of risk are encountered in international lending. In attempting to predict possible default on an international loan, a banker must address issues concerning the stability of the government that is involved directly or indirectly with the loan, foreign exchange implications, and the impact of world economic performance on the ability of the borrower to repay the loan.

The major elements of risk involved in international lending are:

- *Foreign Exchange Risk:* The bank may face foreign exchange risk if the loan is not denominated in dollars unless the open currency position is hedged. This is typically a smaller problem for U.S. banks than foreign banks, given the dominance of the dollar, but foreign exchange risk may be a factor in some loans. From a broader perspective, foreign exchange risk may be an important consideration in evaluating the ability of a foreign borrower to pay. If the exchange rate between the borrower's home currency and the dollar change dramatically over the life of a loan, the borrower's ability to produce the cash flow to repay could be drastically affected.
- *Sovereign Risk:* Refers to the possibility of political measures preventing or delaying the payment of external obligations. The significance of sovereign risk depends on the borrower, but all international loans are subject to sovereign risk to some extent. In evaluating sovereign risk, the bank must assess the stability of the political system and the impact that any instability could have on repayment of the loan.
- *Transfer Risk:* Refers to the ability of a borrower to obtain foreign exchange in order to make payments in the currency agreed upon in the loan agreement. The possibility exists that the country may block convertibility of currency, which may affect the customer's ability to repay the loan. At the time of the loan, currency could be freely exchangeable, but the government could enforce a change restricting foreign exchange following the initiation of the loan.
- *Fund Availability Risk:* Refers to longer-term loans that are funded by shorter-term Eurodollar deposits. If a bank makes a long-term loan and funds that loan with shorter-term Eurocurrency deposits, disruptions in the Eurodollar market could cause liquidity problems for the lending bank.

♦ *Regulatory Risk:* Refers to the possibility that regulations in the bank's country of operation could be changed following the loan transaction. Imposition of reserve requirements is an example of the type of regulatory change that could occur. The profitability of the loan could be affected unless the agreement is structured in a fashion that allows the bank to adjust the interest rate on the loan in order to pass through the additional costs associated with regulation.[38]

In evaluating the risk involved with an international loan, the bank's management must assess how these additional elements of risk will affect eventual repayment of the credit. The importance of each of the elements of risk depends on the type of loan, the borrower, and the maturity of the loan. It is possible to structure the loan agreement to minimize the impact of some of these elements, but some elements are unavoidable and can be controlled only through diversification and restriction of the amount of funds committed to specific countries.

National and International Lending Agencies

International lending may involve government agencies as well as private banks. Several national and international agencies are involved in foreign lending. Agency involvement ranges from direct lending to insuring loans made by private institutions.

The major domestic agencies include the Export-Import Bank (Eximbank), the Foreign Credit Insurance Association (FCIA), and the Overseas Private Investment Corporation (OPIC).[39] All of these national government agencies provide some assistance in the international trade area. The Eximbank, which is the most important national agency, makes direct loans to exporters of U.S. goods as well as providing assistance for private financing. The FCIA is a voluntary association of private insurers that provides insurance on trade credits of U.S. exporters against losses from commercial and political hazards. The OPIC offers insurance against political hazard for U.S. equity investments in foreign countries.

The major international organizations involved in international lending are the International Monetary Fund and the World Bank. These organizations were created at the conclusion of World War II and are jointly owned by member countries. The World Bank raises funds for

---

[38]This section draws heavily on discussions of risk in L. S. Goodman, "Bank Lending to Non-OPEC LDCs: Are Risks Diversifiable?" *Quarterly Review, Federal Reserve Bank of New York*, Summer 1981: 10–20; and H. S. Bloch, "Foreign Risk Judgement for Commercial Banks," *Bankers Magazine*, Autumn 1977: 90–96.

[39]For a complete discussion of national and international agencies, see Oppenheim, op. cit., chap. 17.

international lending through capital contributions of its members and by borrowing in the capital markets. The World Bank provides direct financing and also assists in cofinancing projects that involve both World Bank and private bank funds. The International Monetary Fund (IMF) was founded to assist developing countries in balance-of-payments problems. Similar to the World Bank, the IMF is funded through capital contributions of its members. As of 1982 the World Bank had 143 members and the IMF had 146 members.[40] In addition to financing, the World Bank and the IMF provide technical assistance to developing countries.

In addition to international agencies, regional-development banks have also been formed to provide assistance in regional international finance. Examples of banks in which the United States is a member are the Inter-American Development Bank and the Asian Development Bank.[41]

THE CURRENT INTERNATIONAL LOAN SITUATION

The complex set of events triggered by OPEC's dramatic increase in oil prices in the 1970s has brought about significant problems in international finance. The dramatic increases in oil prices in the early and late 1970s caused balance-of-payments deficits for importing countries and at the same time created huge surpluses for exporting countries. U.S. banks were involved in the recycling of the surpluses, known as "petrodollars."[42] The surpluses were deposited in the Eurodollar market, and U.S. banks employed much of the funds by making loans to non-OPEC lesser-developed countries (LDCs).

Although loan limits apply to nongovernment borrowers, no similar limits apply to bank loans to government borrowers. Loans to non-OPEC LDCs comprise over 200 percent of the equity capital for the nine largest U.S. banks.[43]

As the world recession grew worse and balance-of-payments deficits widened, significant problems developed. Some oil-producing LDCs such as Mexico enjoyed increases in revenue as oil prices rose. Mexico expanded its development programs, using increased revenues from oil and extended borrowing to finance a portion of its projects. When oil prices declined, Mexico saw its oil income dramatically decrease and

---

[40]Ibid., 318, 320.

[41]For further discussion see Eitman and Stonehill, op. cit., 425–430.

[42]For complete discussions on the problems associated with international finance, see A. Burns, "The Need for Order in International Finance," *Economic Review, Federal Reserve Bank of Richmond*, July-August 1979: 13–18; A. Smith, *Paper Money* (New York: Summit Books, 1981); P. Erdman, "Living on the Default Line," *Playboy*, January 1983: 94–253.

[43]B. Steinberg, "How the Debt Bomb Might Be Defused," *Fortune*, May 2, 1983, 130.

found itself needing to refinance $29.2 billion, which it was unable to pay when it came due in 1982.[44] Mexico, though it was the largest, was not the only LDC to expand its development programs. Others included Venezuela, Indonesia, the Philippines, and Nigeria.

The problems in international lending are traced to shorter maturities. The recycling process with OPEC surpluses led banks to shorten maturities on loans. Shortened maturities on loans are more closely associated with the funding obtained in the Eurodollar market, but shorter maturities present default problems if the borrowers are unable to pay at maturity. Larger and larger percentages of LDCs' debt are coming due. The shorter maturities, coupled with high rates of inflation and short-term interest rates, lead to rapid deterioration of the debt service ratios. A recent *Fortune* article reports that debt service as a percentage of export earnings has risen from approximately 35 percent in 1975 to nearly 80 percent in 1983 for 21 major borrowing countries.[45]

The near-term prospects for loans to foreign governments are not glowing. The ability of the LDCs to repay their debts will depend on global economic performance. We have witnessed some massive debt restructurings (Mexico, $20 billion in 1983) and it seems probable that many more countries will also have to restructure their debt.[46] Some analysts are predicting that maturities on some LDC debt will be lengthened to as much as 25 or 30 years to remedy the current problem. Furthermore, banks are likely to see changes in legislation that will place limits on lending to foreign countries. Possible changes include loan limits to specific countries, required diversification for international loans, and stronger and more timely disclosure of exposure.[47] One change that has been enacted requires banks to establish special reserves.

The International Lending Supervision Act of 1983 requires banking institutions to establish special reserves against certain international assets (loans). The reserves are termed *allocated transfer risk reserves* (ATRR). Transfer risk means the possibility that an asset cannot be serviced in the currency of payment because of a lack of, or restraints on the availability of, foreign exchange in the country of the obligor.

The federal banking agencies are required to apply the following criteria to determine if an ATRR is required:

a. Whether the quality of a banking institution's assets has been impaired by a protracted inability of public or private obligors in a

---

[44]Erdman, op. cit., 134.

[45]Steinberg, op. cit., 134.

[46]"Third World Debt: It's the Feds vs. the Bankers," *Business Week,* Jan. 9, 1984, 47. Federal Reserve Board Chairman Paul Volcker puts pressure on banks to lower interest rates on loans to third-world countries to avoid "a wave of massive defaults."

[47]Steinberg, op. cit., 134; and Goodman, op. cit., 20.

foreign country to make payments on their external indebtedness as indicated by such factors, among others, as whether:
—such obligors have failed to make full interest payments on external indebtedness;
—such obligors have failed to comply with the terms of any restructured indebtedness; or
—a foreign country has failed to comply with any International Monetary Fund or other suitable adjustment program; or

b. whether no definite prospects exist for the orderly restoration of debt service.[48]

The amount of the ATRR that normally is kept separate from general loan loss reserves should be determined by the length of time the quality of the asset has been impaired, recent actions taken to restore debt service capability, the prospects for restored asset quality, and other relevant factors. The initial-year provision is established at 10 percent of the amount of each international asset. In subsequent years the provision increases to 15 percent of the principal amount. At the end of seven years, the asset would be completely reserved if conditions in the respective country had not improved.

SUMMARY

International banking has become a more significant and integral component of banking in the United States. The last two decades have witnessed rapid expansion of international banking activities. The majority of international banking activities are still undertaken by money-center banks, although some regional banks have increased their international banking activities.

A bank has a great amount of flexibility in the manner in which its international banking services can be delivered. Options range from representative offices to full-service subsidiary banks. In addition, specialized forms, such as Edge Act corporations and international banking facilities, can be established interstate to deliver international services.

The types of international services offered by banks include money transfers and draft collection, foreign exchange activities, international trade financing, Eurodollar market activity, and full-service lending. Revenue from international loans is the largest component of income on international services, but additional components of risk are associated with lending. Key elements include foreign exchange risk, sovereign risk, and transfer risk.

---

[48]"Subpart D—International Lending Supervision," Regulation K, Federal Reserve System, February 1984, 4.

Questions and Problems

1. Identify several factors that have led U.S. banks to increase their activity in international banking.

2. Identify and briefly describe the various organizational forms that banks may employ to deliver international banking services.

3. Describe the following international banking services: *money transfer, foreign trade transactions,* and *foreign exchange services.*

4. Discuss the difficulties encountered in attempting to regulate international banking activity.

5. Define the term *Eurodollar market* and discuss how banks use the Eurodollar market.

6. What are the major elements of risk involved in making international loans?

7. Discuss the relationship of the current international loan situation and the oil crisis and world recession problems of the late 1970s and early 1980s.

References

Abrams, R. K. "Regional Banks and International Banking." *Economic Review, Federal Reserve Bank of Kansas City,* November 1980: 3–14.

Bloch, H. S. "Foreign Risk Judgement for Commercial Banks." *Bankers Magazine,* Autumn 1977: 90–96.

Burns, A. F. "The Need for Order in International Finance." *Economic Review, Federal Reserve Bank of Richmond,* July–August 1977: 13–18.

"Citibank's Pervasive Influence on International Lending." *Business Week,* May 16, 1983, 124–126.

Dale, R. "Safeguarding the International Banking System." *The Banker,* August 1982: 49–82.

Dod, D. P. "Bank Lending to Developing Countries: Recent Developments in Historical Perspective." *Federal Reserve Bulletin,* September 1981: 647–656.

Duffield, J. G., and B. J. Summers. "Bankers' Acceptances." In *Instruments of the Money Market,* 5th ed., ed. T. Q. Cook and B. J. Summers, 114–122. Richmond, VA: Federal Reserve Bank of Richmond, 1981.

Eitman, D. K., and A. I. Stonehill. *Multinational Business Finance,* 3rd ed. Reading, MA: Addison-Wesley, 1982.

Erdman, P. "Living on the Default Line." *Playboy,* January 1983, 94–253.

Frydl, E. J. "The Eurodollar Conundrum." *Quarterly Review, Federal Reserve Bank of New York,* Spring 1982: 11–19.

Goodfriend, M. "Eurodollars." In *Instruments of the Money Market,* 5th ed., ed. T. Q. Cook and B. J. Summers, 123–133. Richmond, VA: Federal Reserve Bank of Richmond, 1981.

Goodman, L. S. "Bank Lending to Non-OPEC LDC's: Are Risks Diversifiable?" *Quarterly Review, Federal Reserve Bank of New York*, Summer 1981: 10–20.

Howard, D. S. "Dynamics of Interest Differential Earnings." In *Funds Management Under Deregulation.*, ed. G. H. Hempel, 554–561. Washington, DC: American Bankers Association, 1981.

Key, S. J. "International Banking Facilities." *Federal Reserve Bulletin,* October 1982: 565–576.

Korth, C. M. "Developing a Country-Risk Analysis." In *Classics in Commercial Bank Lending,* ed. W. W. Sihler, 68–73. Philadelphia, PA: Robert Morris Associates, 1981.

———. "The Evolving Role of U.S. Banks in International Finance." *Bankers Magazine,* July–August 1980: 68–73.

Kreicher, L. L. "Eurodollar Arbitrage." *Quarterly Review, Federal Reserve Bank of New York*, Summer 1982: 10–21.

Oppenheim, P. K. *International Banking,* 4th ed. Washington, DC: American Bankers Association, 1983.

Pinsky, N. "Edge Act and Agreement Corporations: Mediums for International Banking." *Economic Perspectives, Federal Reserve Bank of Chicago,* September–October 1978: 25–31.

Seawahl, N. "Getting Started in International Lending: A Guide to Sources of Printed Information." In *Classics in Commercial Bank Lending,* ed. W. W. Sihler, 496–515. Philadelphia, PA: Robert Morris Associates, 1981.

Segala, J. P. "A Summary of the International Banking Act of 1978." *Economic Review, Federal Reserve Bank of Richmond,* January-February 1979: 16–21.

Smith, A. *Paper Money.* New York: Summit Books, 1981.

Steinberg, B. "How the Debt Bomb Might Be Defused." *Fortune,* May 2, 1983, 128–146.

"Subpart D—International Lending Supervision," Regulation K, Federal Reserve System, February 1984: 1–11.

"Third World Debt: It's The Feds vs. The Bankers." *Business Week,* Jan. 9, 1984, 47.

White, B. B. "Foreign Banking in the United States: A Regulatory and Supervisory Perspective." *Quarterly Review, Federal Reserve Bank of New York*, Summer 1982: 48–58.

Whitehead, D. D. "Interstate Banking: Taking Inventory." *Economic Review, Federal Reserve Bank of Atlanta*, May 1983: 1–50.

"Worry at the World's Banks." *Business Week,* Sept. 16, 1982, 80–86.

CHAPTER 24

The Future of Banks in the Financial Services Industry

ISSUES IN THE FINANCIAL SERVICES INDUSTRY

The financial services industry is an evolving industry. The industry includes diverse primary activities such as securities, banking, insurance, leasing and real estate, and support activities such as data processing and management consulting. The participants in the industry are commercial banks, thrifts, money market funds, finance companies, investment bankers, securities brokers, insurance companies, and nonfinancial firms such as manufacturers and retailers.

In a recent study Rosenblum and Siegel compared 34 major companies, including manufacturers, insurers, retailers, and diversified financial companies, with 15 of the largest bank holding companies and the commercial banking system. Their findings are as follows:

- Nonfinancial companies have continued to enter the product lines of commercial banks.
- The pace of this entry has accelerated in both lending and deposit-taking activities.
- Market shares in consumer and installment lending have been very fluid. In auto loans, for example, the captive finance companies of the auto manufacturers have gained market shares largely at the expense of commercial banks.
- Banks have been very successful in the credit card business, with both VISA and MasterCard having passed Sears (which was the number one credit card in 1972) by most conventionally used measures.
- Banks remain dominant in short-term commercial and industrial loans, but their dominance may be on the wane.
- In longer-term lending to businesses, commercial banks are not the leading institutional lenders. Commercial mortgage lending is dominated by insurance companies, and leasing is dominated by manufacturers and leasing companies.

+ The money market funds sponsored by several of the companies in this study have made significant inroads into the deposit base of the nation's commercial banks.[1]

The conclusion from the study is that two policy issues have become predominant:

+ The markets for most credit services are rapidly becoming national in scope; the geographic market of retail deposits has recently become national. The market for wholesale deposits had, of course, been national for about two decades and international for about one decade.
+ Banking is no longer a distinct line of commerce. That is, in spite of the opposition held by the courts in the two decades since the U.S. Supreme Court ruled in the *Philadelphia National Bank*, commercial banks do face significant competition from finance companies, manufacturers, retailers, S&L's, mutual savings banks, and other depository institutions.[2]

Importantly, what is not clear is whether the "players" in the market will compete according to the same set of rules and whether legislative and regulatory changes will be made to allow parity to exist. Often raised is the question: "What is the future of banks?" It is clear that the distinct line of commerce for banking is now blurred. The issue of nonbanks with bank charters has brought about the separability of the demand deposit function and the commercial lending function. As we stated in the first chapter, the two characteristics that identify banking are these two functions. In fact, the product line competition is independently occurring for deposits by different categories, for loans by different categories, and for other traditional banking activities as well. Therefore the basic question should be: "How will banks perform and will they be able to compete successfully in the financial services industry?"

With new regulations supporting increased lending and deposit activities of thrift institutions and the movement of investment bankers and nonfinancial companies into the traditional realm of banking, the distinction between these entities will become increasingly blurred and, in fact, may lead to specialization among firms in specific product markets. We believe the survival of banks in this structure is dependent on the ability to compete in distinct markets, whether they be deposit-taking

---

[1]H. Rosenblum and D. Siegel, *Competition in Financial Services: The Impact of Nonbank Entry* (Chicago: Federal Reserve Bank of Chicago, 1983), i–ii.

[2]Ibid., ii.

or credit-granting functions. We also believe that banks will expand into noncredit services to diversify their income base and to derive greater proportions of their income from noncredit sources.

In Chapter 1 we identified several functions that banking serves today. In considering their importance through the 1980s and beyond, we expect certain trends to evolve as follows:

1. *Originating credit contracts*
   - Greater emphasis will be put on origination of credit contracts for placement with other banks who can inventory these contracts better than the originating banks.
   - Greater market awareness of pricing must be performed by banks of varied sizes to properly make such contractual sales and purchases.
   - Expertise in originations and specialization in certain types of credits will increase within the banking industry.
2. *Investigating investment contracts*
   - The cost of financing inventory is expressed as the cost of debt and equity to the banking firm. Whereas competitors such as pension funds, the commercial paper market, mutual funds, money market funds, and foreign banks have lower equity requirements, the shift to origination will occur simply because the cost of inventorying credit contracts will become too great for banks.
3. *Financing the bank*
   - Deregulation of deposits with regard to rates and minimum balances is almost complete. The result will be higher costs of deposits to banking institutions.
   - Larger banks will continue to have greater access to the capital markets. Smaller banks will continue to rely on primarily local funds to support their activities. Although brokers are packaging deposit funds for larger banks and selling them to smaller banks, it is clear that the cost of financing the bank will increase.
4. *Originating noncredit transactions*
   - Banks are finding competitors for funds-transfer mechanisms, including S&Ls and money market funds.
   - Banks will have to aggressively market deposit services because customers will no longer have to go to a bank to establish checking accounts.
   - Competition in telecommunications and information processing already includes such firms as AT&T, IBM, ITT, RCA, GE, TRW, and Dunn & Bradstreet. Therefore funds-transfer technology is not likely to be controlled by banks in the future.

- With the increase in computer technology available to small businesses and homes, expansion of home and office banking can be expected to continue on two fronts: banking services and brokerage services.
5. *Selling financial and management services*
- Corporate finance, merchant banking, and investment and financial counseling will be activities in which larger banks will expand their services. This expansion will require increased expertise, and experienced personnel will be sought within and outside the existing banking framework. The cost of doing business will thus be increased, with the expectation, however, that the additional expertise will produce higher returns on these nontraditional banking services.

We believe that the restrictions on branch banking and expansion of bank holding companies will be lifted. These limitations will most probably be lifted on a regional basis, and a full interstate banking system is likely to come into existence in the next five to ten years. Federal legislation will be required to overcome the resistance to interstate banking in those states that continue to have unit or limited branch banking.

We also believe that the Federal Reserve Board's list of permissible activities for banks will be expanded to include, on a phased-in basis, increased activity in full-line insurance (both life and casualty), investment banking, money market funds, and real estate joint ventures. Presently credit contracts are being written that, in effect, grant banks equity interest through participation in profits from commercial real estate ventures. Resistance from insurance companies, investment bankers, and brokerage houses will be expected to continue.

One issue that will probably take a considerable amount of time to resolve is the entry of nonfinancial companies into the business of banking, although the Federal Reserve Board has taken steps to restrict nonbanking activity. A recent example of potential problems associated with operating full-line insurance services is the Baldwin-United reorganization. Baldwin-United began as a manufacturer of musical instruments and expanded into banking, S&Ls, and insurance. As a result it took on significant debt in acquiring large corporations. The consequence was that Baldwin-United failed to make certain interest payments and has since gone into reorganization. This experience may be used by bankers as an argument for preventing the expansion of nonfinancial companies into the business of banking. However, we believe that in the longer run, unless all participants in the financial services industry are regulated on the same basis, nonfinancial firms will continue to be allowed to make inroads into the financial services industry.

Several problem areas become apparent. These include the increased risks that banks will be forced to take to compete for funds. The higher costs of funds will have to be offset by higher rates of return on invested funds in order to maintain interest spreads. We believe that there will be a shakeout of the banking industry as this occurs and that all banking institutions will experience some problems in survival during the 1980s. If we draw upon the experience of the deregulation of the airline industry, we may well see more bank failures and more mergers resulting simply from the need to absorb the banks that are unsuccessful competitors. The protection provided by banking regulation has allowed noncompetitive banks to exist. With full deregulation and the inroads made by other institutions and financial organizations, these noncompetitive institutions may find themselves in insolvent positions and unable to cope with the changing structure of the industry. The policy implications on a national basis will place severe pressure on the regulatory agencies to prevent the occurrence of these problems.

To accommodate the changes that we have outlined, several regulatory issues must be resolved, including granting the right to banks to expand into traditional nonbanking financial services. A second issue is whether nonfinancial firms and foreign banks should conform substantially to the same regulations to which banks must adhere. The final issue is to what extent all participants in the financial services industry should be regulated and to what extent depositors should be protected.

ISSUES IN REGULATORY CHANGE

Several issues have been raised concerning regulatory change. These issues fall into four separate categories as follows:

1. *Depositor protection and monetary stability*

• New types of transactions for debiting and crediting customer accounts are creating quasi-deposit accounts. These may involve tapping the holdings of liquid investments or securities held by a bank or other financial institution, making these accounts, in effect, checking accounts. A regulatory question is whether these new types of accounts should be regulated in whole or in part and whether they should be given deposit protection.

• With regard to risk measurement, there will probably be required (1) the assessment of deposit insurance premiums according to portfolio risk and (2) audits by certified public accounting firms using extended procedures to comply with regulatory requirements. Within the next three to five years all banks that are federally insured or chartered are likely to be required to have audits performed by certified public accounting firms. During the same period, for deposit insurance purposes, banks are likely to be assessed on the basis of the relative risks, including default risk and interest rate risk, that are present in their asset portfolios.

+ Both Congress and the regulatory agencies need to address competitive standards, equality in reserve requirements, and control of the monetary system as new types of payment accounts are created that may bypass today's payment system.

2. *Efficient and competitive banking system*

+ As discussed in earlier chapters, interstate banking will probably occur. The question of whether states should be allowed to remove barriers to interstate banking on a gradual basis or whether federal legislation will be required to remove branching and bank holding company restrictions will become a primary issue. We believe that federal legislation will be required to bring about a gradual conversion to interstate banking and that it will first occur regionally and then nationwide.

+ With regard to electronic funds transfer systems (EFTS), the distinction between bank branches and EFTS facilities depends on state law. Any expansion to interstate banking should be subjected to expansion of EFTS on a national basis. Expansion of EFTS services is presently governed by state law, and access to these services is generally shared among the participants. What is required on a regional and national basis is a consistency in the policies and regulations for employing EFTS services.

+ With regard to expanded services, the expansion into full-line insurance and securities activities is a distinct possibility in a shorter run. There are likely to be more joint-venture activities between deposit and nondeposit institutions as well as more financial institution participation in profits and projects with customers. Existing laws and regulations are inadequate to either control or allow expansion in these activities. Therefore some phased-in approach to addressing the longer-run concerns of participants conducting expanded activities on a joint-venture basis must be considered.

+ With regard to the structure of the banking industry, mergers and acquisitions will increase. Among these mergers and acquisitions we believe there will be a melding of present financial institutions, both banking and thrift, with other financial industry participants and that a framework for the industry must be developed to allow these activities to occur on a systematic basis. Also, branching facilities as we presently know them will diminish, and there will be an increased emphasis on electronic technology to provide banking services.

The technology for credit cards is significantly advanced and is presently serving as a model for the expansion of other banking and securities activities.

• With regard to reserves on transaction accounts, the regulatory issues are (1) whether reserves should be required on transaction accounts for all institutions and (2) whether reserve requirements should apply to other firms engaged in the financial services industry and, if so, whether the Federal Reserve should pay interest on such accounts held as reserves or the required reserves should be significantly reduced.

3. *Consumer protection*

• Several issues are unresolved: (1) increasing consumer protection in the areas of both banking and investment activities, (2) consumer privacy in the EFTS environment, and (3) operating standards on EFTS transactions to provide for error resolution and authorized use of EFTS facilities.

4. *Structure of regulatory authorities*

• In all likelihood, with interstate banking the dual banking system will be under threat simply because of the problems posed by examining banks which are domiciled in other states. This would pose significant problems for state examiners for locally domiciled banks and those which expand into other geographic jurisdictions not under their control. As more institutions become alike, consolidation among the participants becomes more likely, therefore posing problems of dealing with industries in which examiners are unfamiliar.

STRATEGIES FOR A BANK'S SUCCESS IN THE FINANCIAL SERVICES INDUSTRY

For banks to perform well and survive in the new financial services industry, we believe the well-capitalized and better-performing firms have more of a chance to survive and succeed. The better-performing companies must attract competent people, for the public continues to identify a good bank as one that translates to competent people. One strategy for the changing banking environment requires that banks attract competent people and then recruit, hire, and place them in the right jobs. Banks need to recruit and hire many different kinds of people—salespersons, analysts, programmers, teleprocessing experts, financial staff members, systems specialists, and loan originators. To retain such personnel, adequate compensation, incentive, and individualized training programs must be developed. Solid employee relations are essential if a bank is to meet the increased demands of the new banking environment.

To survive and succeed, a bank must develop a sound business plan based on a thorough understanding of market demands, costs, trends, and integration of domestic and foreign activities. It must take into account its competitors' strengths and weaknesses and must build upon its own inherent advantages. The bank must position itself so that it is stronger and smarter than its competitors or offers services superior to those of any competitor in its line of business. Good performance through good planning can be implemented only through a good personnel and organizational climate.

The path to the top in the new banking environment is not so clear as it has been in the past. Bankers with credit experience formerly found easy access to the senior management levels. With the current demands for increased operational and financial expertise, doors are opening more often to noncredit personnel to succeed at the senior levels of the organization. What is clear is that the emerging industry will be dominated not by banks but by financial services institutions that have more generalized expertise and an understanding of the complexities of operating a business in a competitive environment.

References

"Bills on Combining Banks, Non-Banks to Be Taken Up in July by Senate Panel." *The Wall Street Journal*, June 28, 1983, 6.

Bowden, E. V. *Revolution in Banking*. Richmond, VA: Robert F. Dame, 1980, 185–203.

Conte, C. "Financial Morass, Deregulation of Banks Stirs Confusion, Splits Fed and White House." *The Wall Street Journal*, July 1, 1983, 1, 7.

Helyar, J. "Medium-Sized Banks Leading Merger Rush." *The Wall Street Journal*, Aug. 11, 1983, 23, 27.

Hertzberg, D. "Insurers Fighting Bank's Attempts to Gain Broad Underwriting Power." *The Wall Street Journal*, Aug. 8, 1983, 17.

Kaufman, G., L. R. Mote, and H. Rosenblum. *The Future of Commercial Banks in the Financial Services Industry*. Chicago: Federal Reserve Bank of Chicago, 1983.

Rosenblum, H., and D. Siegel. *Competition in Financial Services: The Impact of Nonbank Entry*. Chicago: Federal Reserve Bank of Chicago, 1983.

Spong, K. *Banking Regulation, Its Purposes, Implementation and Efforts*. Kansas City: Federal Reserve Bank of Kansas City, 1983, 133–147.

PART FIVE

◆

Cases

CASE 1

Increase in Revolving Line of Credit: Johnco Manufacturing Company

As of November 21, 1983 Johnco Manufacturing Company has requested an increase in its revolving line of credit. The primary bank of account, First Intermountain Bank—Buffalo, Wyoming (FIBB), has transmitted the request to its primary correspondent bank, First Intermountain Bank—Salt Lake City (FIBSL).

FIBB indicates that Johnco requests a $200,000 increase to the line of credit that was approved for renewal in September 1983. Johnco requests increased financing to support higher levels of accounts receivable and inventory associated with the current volume of production and sales. In addition, Johnco requests that the advance ratio of 50 percent on accounts less than 60 days past due be increased to 75 percent.

For the three months ended September 30, 1983, actual sales ranged between $500,000 and $700,000 per month. The company's new product line in personal computer furniture, which has proved to be successful, is very important to the firm. Although the company currently generates 70 percent of its sales from sewing cabinets and 30 percent from personal computer furniture, it expects to achieve equivalent sales from each product line in the future.

Using a Loan Relationship ROA Computation for analyzing loan profitability, FIBSL estimates that the total line of credit for Johnco will be approximately $1,100,000. FIBSL requires a hurdle rate of 2.5 percent. Interest income is estimated at 13.5 percent and funds cost at 8.75 percent. FIBSL assesses a loan expense charge of $10,000 and estimates the loan loss provision on this type of loan to be .58 percent.

Johnco has supplied current financial statements which have been added to the loan analysis computer spread sheet. However, FIBSL has not updated the spread sheet for the bad debt reserve of $59,000, which is reflected in the following information:

| | Percent of Total Accounts Receivable | | | | | |
	Current	30 Days	60 Days	90 Days	120 + Days	Total A/R
July	55	28	6	8	3	$ 919,800
August	58	22	12	1	7	826,800
September	66	21	3	6	4	1,062,000

	Total Inventory	Eligible Inventory
July	$799,200	$757,000
August	801,000	754,200
September	798,700	755,900

Credit history for the September 1983 renewal is provided.

Requirements

1. Analyze the loan request, giving consideration to the accounts receivable margin of 50 percent and requested margin of 75 percent. Assess the risk associated with the increase.

2. Prepare a Loan Relationship ROA Computation.

3. Determine whether the loan request should be granted and under what conditions.

LOAN RELATIONSHIP ROA COMPUTATION

Customer:

Type of loan:

Funds Statement

1. Total line of credit _____
2. Unused portion of line _____
3. Average collected demand balance _____
4. Average time balance _____
5. Total deposits _____
6. Less: Required reserves _____
7. Total sources _____
8. Net funds used _____

(continued)

Profit Contribution

9. Interest income on loans average rate _____%   _____
10. Loan fees   _____
11. Miscellaneous income   _____
12. Total income   _____
13. Funds cost _____ % × Line 1   _____
14. Less: Funds credit _____ % × Line 7   _____
15. Net funds cost (Line 13 − Line 14)   _____
16. Loan expense   _____
17. Loan loss provision _____ % × Line 1   _____
18. Total charges
19. Profit contribution (loss)   _____

Profitability Objective

20. Return on assets (Line 19 ÷ Line 1)   _____
21. Hurdle rate   _____
22. Profitability index (Line 20 ÷ Line 21)   _____

MEMORANDUM FOR THE CREDIT FILE

Name: Johnco Manufacturing Co. Ltd
           c/o First Intermountain Bank (FIBB)
           Buffalo, Wyoming

Business: Office and Institutional Furniture Mfg.

Date: September 27, 1983

I. Summary of Credit Request
Renewal

Amount/Structure   A. $450,000 all

$450,000 First Intermountain Bank, Salt Lake City (FIBSL); revolving operating line.

Rate: 2½% over prime, floating and adjusting first of month; 13½% floor, 21½% ceiling; interest payable monthly.

B. $350,000 all

$300,000 FIBSL; term operating line.

Rate: 2½% over prime, floating and adjusted first of month; 13½% floor, 21½% ceiling; interest payable monthly; principal reduction of $12,000 monthly, less FSB interest.

C. $303,056 all

$303,056 FIBSL; amortizing term loan.

Rate: 2½% over prime, floating and adjusted first of month; interest payable monthly; principal reduction of $7,500 monthly, less FIBB interest.

(continued)

Collateral	A & B.	Borrowing base includes 50% of accounts receivable to 60 days; 50% of inventory at cost.
	C.	First mortgage on Buffalo plant property, appraised value 11/16/81 $425,000.
		Furniture and fixtures are taken in an abundance of caution.
Maturity:		All three commitments expire September 15, 1984. All obligations are on a demand basis.

II. Borrower History

A. *General:* Johnco Manufacturing was started by Ken Johnson 25 years ago. The company, with manufacturing facilities in Buffalo, Wyoming and Madison, Wisconsin manufactures a full line of sewing machine cabinets and office furniture. The furniture line is moderately priced and competes on a national basis with other office furniture companies such as Samsonite, Hon Desk Company, and Modar Company. Johnco has no competition in the sewing cabinet market due to its early emergence as the leading manufacturer and its dominance of the market. The company's Buffalo facility is a modern light-manufacturing facility of 28,000 square feet, and the Wisconsin plant has approximately 43,200 square feet.

B. *Product Line:* The company's main product line is sewing machine tables and cabinets. This product line accounts for 60 to 65 percent of its current sales volume. Major customers for the sewing cabinet line include all operating equipment manufacturers (OEM) (Singer, Pfaff, Viking, Bernina) as well as some of the nation's major retailers (Montgomery Ward and J. C. Penney). Sales to Montgomery Ward and Penney accounted for approximately 33 percent of Johnco's total sales during FY 1982 (Penney did $1.5 million in sewing cabinet volume in FY 1981). Sales are solicited by company reps and are generated through catalogs, retail stores, and OEM retail outlets.

Johnco diversified into office and personal computer furniture because of a continued softness in the sewing machine market. Products are sold to major wholesalers of office furniture (Quill, Fidelity House, Boise Cascade), retail outlets, and catalog distributors. Customers are solicited nationwide by commissioned reps working under the direction of Gary Smith. In FY 1981 office furniture sales represented 35 to 40 percent of the company's annual volume. The company's goal is to balance the product mix to the point where each represents 50 percent of annual sales.

C. *Management:*

Ken Johnson

President—100 percent ownership

Because of the success of the company and Ken's desire to have more leisure time, he has gathered a management team of young but experienced men to run the company on a daily basis. Ken continues to take an active role in critical sales (Sears, Montgomery Ward, Penney, etc.) as well as overseeing the company's sales program.

(continued)

Bob Jones
Vice-President, Finance

Bob is the number 2 man in the company, reporting to Ken for its overall operation. Bob is a CPA and helped design the computerized management information system utilized by Johnco.

Gary Smith
Sales, Office Furniture

Phillip James and Brian Johnson (Ken's son)
Sales, Sewing Machine Cabinets

Ralph Roberts
Plant Manager, Madison, Wisconsin

All of these men are in their 30s and early 40s and have been with the company a number of years. Ken believes that these men can run the company without his intervention, and this is a major part of his overall plan. Ken also believes that to attract and retain quality management personnel he must pay attractive salaries. The following salaries and bonuses are paid to the key staff:

Name	Position	Salary	Bonus
Bob Jones	Vice-President	$ 34,000	$ 7,500
Gary Smith	Sales, Office Furniture	31,500	5,000
Phillip James	Sales, Sewing Machine Cabinets	31,500	5,000
Ralph Roberts	Plant Manager, Madison	42,500	6,000
Jerry Roberts	Production Manager, Madison	26,000	5,000
Bud Wallock	Production Manager, Buffalo	26,000	5,000
		191,500	33,500
Ken Johnson		100,000	6,500
		$291,500	$40,000

C. Ken is aware of the salary and bonus impact on current earnings. As the owner of the company, he believes that as long as the company is generating enough to meet its debt requirements, earnings alone are not the key indicator.

III. Financial Analysis

FYE statements for 6/30/79 through 6/30/82 were audited by Higgins and Co. Unqualified opinions were received in 1979 and 1982. Qualified opinions were received in 1980 and 1981. The company changed its accounting method of treating miscellaneous hardware items from expensing when purchased to expensing when used in the manufacturing process.

A. *Operations:*

	1980	%	1981	%	1982	%	1983	%
Sales	$4,233,951	100.0	$4,429,348	100.0	$4,531,872	100.0	$5,561,863	100.0
Gross Profit	1,405,977	33.0	1,586,787	35.0	1,063,602	24.0	1,600,439	29.0
Operating Expense	1,419,052	33.0	1,549,868	35.0	1,128,451	25.0	1,377,768	25.0
Operating Profit	(13,075)	(.3)	36,919	.8	(64,849)	(1.4)	222,671	4.0
Net Income	19,966	.5	39,697	.9	(23,572)	(.5)	138,513	2.5

In response to a continued softness in the sewing machine market, Johnco modified its product mix during FY 1981 by expanding into office and computer furniture. Hoping to boost what otherwise had been a slow 1982 FY (sales rose by only 2 percent), Johnco negotiated in early 1982 to feature its furniture line in Boise Cascade's catalog and showrooms.

The effect of the change in product mix became apparent during fiscal 1983, when net sales increased by 23 percent.

Increased overhead expenses, occasioned by the new Wyoming plant and equipment, caused a 14 percent increase in cost of goods sold. However, due to increased purchasing economies and reduced lumber costs, Johnco's COGS margin decreased 5 percent during FY 1983.

Operating expenses increased 35 percent during the period, influenced primarily by a 45 percent increase in salaries and benefits. These increases are in keeping with Johnson's policy of retaining quality management and labor through ample compensation.

In summary, the combination of product diversification and an improving general economy has allowed Johnco to rebound from a FY 1982 net loss to a year of record sales and profits.

B. *Balance Sheet:* For FY 1983 Johnco recorded total footings of $2,642,000, representing a 12 percent increase over the previous year. Total receivables increased 28 percent in actual dollars and increased from 26.5 percent to 30.3 percent of footings. Inventories increased 18 percent, going from 30 percent to 32 percent of footings, and net fixed assets showed a nominal 1.5 percent increase.

Johnco's liquidity declined slightly during FY 1983, the current ratio going from 1.88 to 1.70. Increases in receivables and inventory were the primary causes of the decline.

The firm's leverage position did decrease somewhat during fiscal 1983, going from a debt to worth of 3.72 to 3.09. The improvement is the result of increased retained earnings during the year.

IV. Cash Flow

The actual cash position of Johnco remained healthy at FYE 1983. Cash generated from operations was adequate to cover cash operating expenses, financing costs, and debt amortization. The company recorded gross cash margins of $1,329,000 in 1981, $1,751,000 in 1982, and $1,212,000 in 1983, indicating an excess of direct revenues over direct costs.

V. Loan Structure

A. *Revolving Line and Term Operating Line:* Secured by a first lien on accounts receivable and inventory and cross-collateralized with security of term loan. Interest payable monthly. Principal due at maturity 9/15/83.

   The borrowing base is computed at 50 percent of accounts receivable less than 60 days plus 50 percent of inventory, reporting monthly. First Intermountain Bank collects Johnco receivables, depositing them daily in a central account. This account is charged on a collected-funds basis and applied to the line.

   Based on company-provided information as of 6/30/83, the borrowing base would approximate the following:

Raw materials	$555,100	
Finished goods	242,435	
Total eligible inventory	$797,554	
Advance base of 50 percent of eligible inventory		$398,777
Total eligible accounts receivable (pending 60 days)	$799,785	
Advance base of 50 percent of eligible receivables		$399,893
Maximum borrowing available under formula		$798,670

B. *Term Loan:* In addition to the revolving line and term operating loans, the banks have a real estate loan secured by a first mortgage on the Buffalo plant. Cross-collateral includes accounts receivable, inventory, furniture, fixtures, and equipment in both Buffalo and Madison, and a second mortgage on the property in Madison. The original amount of this loan was $350,000, and has a current balance of $303,000.

   The Buffalo plant sits on ground leased from Burlington Northern, which has subordinated its lease position. First Intermountain Bank has taken an assignment of the lessee's interest.

MAI appraisal dated 11/16/81 on the Buffalo plant reflects a first-deed-of-trust collateralized value of:		$425,000
MAI appraisal dated 1979 on the Madison plant reflects a second-deed-of-trust collateralized value of:		
Total value	$697,609	
First deed of trust	473,633	
Second deed of trust		$223,976
Total collateral value		$648,976
Term loan (current balance)		$303,000
Loan to value		47%

The loans/commitments to Johnco are subject to a loan agreement that requires monthly financial statements, an annual audited statement, and monthly borrowing base plus accounts receivable aging. An annual inspection will be conducted in conjunction with First Intermountain—Salt Lake City.

First Intermountain Bank—Buffalo utilizes a Bank Control Account (Pledge Account) in conjunction with a lockbox. All receipts are applied to the revolving operating line.

VI. Documentation

Documentation required and received by FIBSL under this commitment includes:

1. Security agreements covering accounts receivable and inventory (blanket agreement).
2. Financing statement and search covering accounts receivable and inventory (blanket agreement). Filed in Wyoming and Wisconsin.
3. Appraisal on Buffalo plant.
4. First deed of trust on Buffalo plant.
5. Second deed of trust on Madison plant (abundance of caution). FIBSL has a subordination agreement on accounts receivable and inventory from Bank of Madison.
6. Mr. Johnson's guarantee.
7. Loan agreement.
8. Hazard insurance.
9. Title commitment on Buffalo plant.
10. Flood hazard certificate.

CONFIDENTIAL
PERSONAL FINANCIAL STATEMENT JULY 15, 1983

Kenneth A. and Lois E. Johnson
1 Old Oregon Trail
Buffalo, WY

President and Chairman, Johnco Manufacturing Company
　　Plant and main office—Buffalo
　　Plant—Madison, WI

Personal bank account: First Intermountain Bank, Buffalo

Assets		Liabilities	
Cash	$ 9,200	Johnco Manufacturing	$ 91,000
Receivables	13,500	Mortgages	170,000
Real estate	285,000	Accounts and bills due	4,300
Personal property	92,000		
Automobiles	12,000	*Total liabilities*	265,300
Insurance cash values	18,000	*Net worth*	1,099,920
Stocks	910,520		
Partnerships and interests	25,000	*Total liabilities and net worth*	$1,365,220
Total assets	$1,365,220		

(continued)

Source of Annual Income

Salary	$100,000
Bonus	50,000
Other income	4,000

	Value
Stocks	
Johnco Manufacturing Company 14,008 Shares @ $57.32 (book value)	$802,938
Partnerships & Interests	
Independent Leasing & Sales Company (at cost)	25,000
Real Estate	
Homestead—1 Old Oregon Trail, Buffalo, WY (mortgage $49,740)	110,000
Second home—1/2 acres, Jackson, WY	175,000
Contracts Owned—Receivables	
Notes due	13,500

Schedule of Life Insurance Carried

Northwestern National Life—3 policies	$ 67,000	estate
Occidental—2 policies	11,800	estate
Company groups	60,000	estate
Travel accident	200,000	estate
Northwestern National Life	400,000	Johnco

Signature

Balance Sheet Inputs: Assets (MSB, November 21, 1983)

	Unqual. June 30 1980		Unqual. June 30, 1981		Unqual. June 30, 1982		Unqual. June 30, 1983		Unaudit. Sept. 30, 1983	
	$000	% Tot.	$000	% Tot.	$000	% Tot.	$000	% Tot.	$000	% Tot.
Cash	19	1.00	27	1.28	26	1.10	21	0.79	0	0.00
Accounts receivable—trade	462	24.20	621	29.40	641	27.24	850	32.17	1,019	37.01
(bad debt reserve) (−)	(13)	(0.68)	(14)	(0.66)	(17)	(0.72)	(50)	(1.89)	0	0.00
Total accounts receivable—net	449	23.52	607	28.74	624	26.52	800	30.28	1,019	37.01
Notes receivable—current	0	0.00	0	0.00	0	0.00	0	0.00	80	2.91
Federal income tax receivable	24	1.26	0	0.00	28	1.19	0	0.00	0	0.00
Raw materials	473	24.78	568	26.89	473	20.10	555	21.01	0	0.00
Work in progress	35	1.83	14	0.66	36	1.53	45	1.70	0	0.00
Finished goods	156	8.17	223	10.56	204	8.67	242	9.16	0	0.00
Total inventory (FIFO)	664	34.78	805	38.12	713	30.30	842	31.87	799	29.02
Prepaid expenses	33	1.73	6	0.28	2	0.08	11	0.42	12	0.44
Total Current Assets	1,189	62.28	1,445	68.42	1,393	59.20	1,674	63.36	1,910	69.38
Due from officers/stockholders	98	5.13	102	4.83	105	4.46	100	3.79	0	0.00
Due from employees	16	0.84	15	0.71	11	0.47	6	0.23	0	0.00
Land	7	0.37	7	0.33	7	0.30	7	0.26	7	0.25
Buildings & improvements	348	18.23	349	16.52	707	30.05	707	26.76	714	25.94
Furniture & fixtures	74	3.88	75	3.55	105	4.46	114	4.31	114	4.14
Machinery & equipment	176	9.22	189	8.95	198	8.41	232	8.78	239	8.68
Transportation equipment	103	5.40	115	5.45	43	1.83	91	3.44	113	4.10
Capital leases	53	2.78	38	1.80	16	0.68	0	0.00	0	0.00
Gross fixed assets	761	39.86	773	36.60	1,076	45.73	1,151	43.57	1,187	43.12
(Accumulated depreciation) (−)	(206)	(10.79)	(268)	(12.69)	(270)	(11.47)	(333)	(12.60)	(345)	(12.53)
Total fixed assets—net	555	29.07	505	23.91	806	34.25	818	30.96	842	30.58
Cash value—life insurance	0	0.00	10	0.47	19	0.81	29	1.10	0	0.00
Deposits	14	0.73	14	0.66	7	0.30	14	0.53	0	0.00
Operating authority—net	4	0.21	0	0.00	0	0.00	0	0.00	0	0.00
Patents, trademarks, etc.—net	31	1.62	19	0.90	10	0.42	0	0.00	0	0.00
Other—net	2	0.10	2	0.09	2	0.08	1	0.04	1	0.04
Total intangible assets	37	1.94	21	0.99	12	0.51	1	0.04	1	0.04
Total Assets	1,909	100.00	2,112	100.00	2,353	100.00	2,642	100.00	2,753	100.00

Balance Sheet Inputs: Liabilities and Net Worth
(MSB, November 21, 1983)

	Unqual. June 30, 1980		Unqual. June 30, 1981		Unqual. June 30, 1982		Unqual. June 30, 1983		Unaudit. Sept. 30, 1983	
	$000	% Tot.	$000	% Tot.	$000	% Tot.	$000	% Tot.	$000	% Tot.
Overdraft	41	2.15	0	0.00	0	0.00	0	0.00	2	0.07
Notes payable S/T—bank	108	5.66	350	16.57	215	9.14	266	10.07	362	13.15
Current maturities—LTD	96	5.03	105	4.97	101	4.29	160	6.06	0*	0.00
Current capital lease obligations	14	0.73	10	0.47	2	0.08	0	0.00	0	0.00
Accounts payable—trade	182	9.53	222	10.51	354	15.04	270	10.22	258	9.37
Wages/salaries payable	28	1.47	44	2.08	49	2.08	75	2.84	0	0.00
Interest payable	5	0.26	7	0.33	4	0.17	3	0.11	0	0.00
Tax accruals	12	0.63	12	0.57	11	0.47	8	0.30	0	0.00
P/S plan contribution	0	0.00	9	0.43	0	0.00	50	1.89	0	0.00
Bonuses payable	30	1.57	40	1.89	5	0.21	92	3.48	0	0.00
Other accrual (settlement)	41	2.15	0	0.00	0	0.00	0	0.00	0	0.00
Total accrued liabilities	116	6.08	112	5.30	69	2.93	228	8.63	155	5.63
Income taxes payable	1	0.05	8	0.38	0	0.00	58	2.20	88	3.20
Total Current Liabilities	558	29.23	807	38.21	741	31.49	982	37.17	865	31.42
Long-term debt	757	39.65	702	33.24	1,054	44.79	945	35.77	735*	26.70
Capital lease obligations	41	2.15	30	1.42	15	0.64	0	0.00	0	0.00
Time pay n/p	0	0.00	0	0.00	0	0.00	0	0.00	354*	12.86
Deferred income taxes	25	1.31	30	1.42	35	1.49	68	2.57	68	2.47
Total Liabilities	1,381	72.34	1,569	74.29	1,845	78.41	1,995	75.51	2,022	73.45
Common stock	16	0.84	16	0.76	16	0.68	16	0.61	16	0.58
Paid-in capital	122	6.39	122	5.78	122	5.18	122	4.62	122	4.43
Retained earnings	390	20.43	430	20.36	398	16.91	537	20.33	620	22.52
(Treasury stock) (−)	0	0.00	(25)	(1.18)	(28)	(1.19)	(28)	(1.06)	(27)	(0.98)
Total Net Worth	528	27.66	543	25.71	508	21.59	647	24.49	731	26.55
Total Liabilities & Net Worth	1,909	100.00	2,112	100.00	2,353	100.00	2,642	100.00	2,753	100.00
Tangible net worth	491	25.72	522	24.72	496	21.08	646	24.45	730	26.52
Working capital	631	33.05	638	30.21	652	27.71	692	26.19	1,045	37.96

*Amounts reclassified from prior period into amount of term operating line.

Income Statement Inputs
(MSB, November 21, 1983)

	Unqual. June 30, 1980 (12 mos.)		Unqual. June 30, 1981 (12 mos.)		Unqual. June 30, 1982 (12 mos.)		Unqual. June 30, 1983 (12 mos.)		Unaudit. Sept. 30, 1983 (3 mos.)	
	$000	% Rev.	$000	% Rev.	$000	% Rev.	$000	% Rev.	$000	% Rev.
Sales	4,234	100.00	4,429	100.00	4,532	100.00	5,562	100.00	1,697	100.00
Net revenues	4,234	100.00	4,429	100.00	4,532	100.00	5,562	100.00	1,697	100.00
Cost of goods sold	2,828	66.79	2,843	64.19	2,987	65.91	3,412	61.34	1,195	70.42
Other costs of business (overhead)	446	10.53	456	10.30	481	10.61	549	9.87	108	6.36
Gross Profit	960	22.67	1,130	25.51	1,064	23.48	1,601	28.78	394	23.22
General & administrative expense	536	12.66	560	12.64	508	11.21	692	12.44	172	10.14
Selling expense	125	2.95	203	4.58	244	5.38	332	5.97	43	2.53
Lease/rent expense	40	0.94	40	0.90	24	0.53	4	0.07	0	0.00
Depreciation	64	1.51	59	1.33	66	1.46	73	1.31	0	0.00
Amortization	11	0.26	10	0.23	10	0.22	10	0.18	0	0.00
Bad debt expense	11	0.26	13	0.29	11	0.24	51	0.92	0	0.00
Operating Profit	173	4.09	245	5.53	201	4.44	439	7.89	179	10.55
(Interest expense)　(−)	(186)	(4.39)	(208)	(4.70)	(265)	(5.85)	(215)	(3.87)	(48)	(2.83)
Gain on sale of assets	0	0.00	0	0.00	21	0.46	5	0.09	0	0.00
Other income	14	0.33	9	0.20	3	0.07	3	0.05	8	0.47
(Other expense/settlement)　(−)	(11)	(0.26)	0	0.00	0	0.00	0	0.00	0	0.00
Income from subsidiary	1	0.02	4	0.09	0	0.00	0	0.00	0	0.00
Profit before Taxes	(9)	(0.21)	50	1.13	(40)	(0.88)	232	4.17	139	8.19
Current taxes payable (refundable)	(12)	(0.28)	6	0.14	(22)	(0.49)	60	1.08	56	3.30
Deferred taxes	3	0.07	4	0.09	6	0.13	33	0.59	0	0.00
Profit before Extraordinary Items	0	0.00	40	0.90	(24)	(0.53)	139	2.50	83	4.89
Accounting change	20	0.47	0	0.00	0.	0.00	0	0.00	0	0.00
Net Profit	20	0.47	40	0.90	(24)	(0.53)	139	2.50	83	4.89
Prior period adjustment to retained earnings	0	0.00	0	0.00	(8)	(0.18)	0	0.00	0	0.00
Treasury stock purchase (retirement)	0	0.00	(25)	(0.56)	(3)	(0.07)	0	0.00	1	0.06
Change in Net Worth	20	0.47	15	0.34	(35)	(0.77)	139	2.50	84	4.95

Financial Ratios
(MSB, November 21, 1983)

	Unqual. June 30, 1980	Unqual. June 30, 1981	Unqual. June 30, 1982	Unqual. June 30, 1983	Unaudit. Sept. 30, 1983
Profitability and Growth					
Gross margin	22.67%	25.51%	23.48%	28.78%	23.22%
Net margin	0.47	0.90	(0.53)	2.50	4.89
Return on assets	1.05	1.89	(1.02)	5.26	12.06
Return on net worth	4.07	7.66	(4.84)	21.52	45.48
Net sales growth		4.61	2.33	22.73	22.04
Net income growth		100.00	(160.00)	679.17	138.85
Total assets growth		10.63	11.41	12.28	4.20
Total liabilities growth		13.61	17.59	8.13	1.35
Net worth growth		2.84	(6.45)	27.36	12.98
Turnover and Efficiency					
Total assets/net sales	45.09%	47.69%	51.92%	47.50%	40.56%
Gross plant/net sales	17.97	17.45	23.74	20.69	17.49
SG&A expense/net sales	16.82	18.42	17.37	19.40	12.67
Receivables in days	41 days	50 days	53 days	52 days	59 days
Inventory in days	74	89	75	78	56
Payables in days	20	25	37	25	18
Financial Condition					
Current ratio	2.13%	1.79%	1.88%	1.70%	2.21%
Quick ratio	0.88	0.79	0.91	0.84	1.27
Working capital ($000)	$631	$638	$652	$692	$1,045
Debt/tangible net worth	2.81%	3.01%	3.72%	3.09%	2.77%
Senior liab./tang. net worth + sub. debt	2.81	3.01	3.72	3.09	2.77

Cash Flow
(MSB, November 21, 1983)

	Unqual. June 30, 1981	Unqual. June 30, 1982	Unqual. June 30, 1983	Unaudit. Sept. 30, 1983
Sales, net	4429	4532	5562	1697
Change in receivables	(158)	(17)	(176)	(299)
Cash from Sales	4271	4515	5386	1398
Cost of goods sold	(3299)	(3468)	(3961)	(1303)
Change in inventories	(141)	92	(129)	43
Change in payables	40	132	(84)	(12)
Cash Production Costs	(3400)	(3244)	(4174)	(1272)
Gross Cash Margins	871	1271	1212	126
SG&A expense	(816)	(787)	(1079)	(215)
Change in prepaids	27	4	(9)	(1)
Change in accruals	(4)	(43)	159	(73)
Cash Operating Expense	(793)	(826)	(929)	(289)
Cash after Operations	78	445	283	(163)
Miscellaneous cash income	16	32	12	157
Income taxes paid	26	(15)	26	(26)
Net Cash after Operations	120	462	321	(32)
Interest expense	(208)	(265)	(215)	(48)
Dividends paid	0	0	0	0
Financing Costs	(208)	(265)	(215)	(48)
Net Cash Income	(88)	197	106	(80)
Current portion long-term debt	(110)	(115)	(103)	(160)
Cash after Debt Amortization	(198)	82	3	(240)
Capital expenditures	(19)	(377)	(95)	(24)
Long-term investments	0	0	0	0
Financing Surplus/(Requirements)	(217)	(295)	(92)	(264)
Change in short-term debt	201	(135)	51	98
Change in long-term debt	49	440	36	144
Change in equity	(25)	(11)	0	1
Total External Financing	225	294	87	243
Cash after financing	8	(1)	(5)	(21)
Actual Change in Cash	8	(1)	(5)	(21)

ASSUMPTIONS USED IN PREPARATION OF BUDGET AND CASH FLOW PROJECTIONS

1. Gross sales are considered to be net of returns.

2. Commissions will be 5 percent of gross sales.

3. The amount of material used will be 50 percent of net sales.

4. Production labor will be 15 percent of net sales.

5. Overhead will be computed at 75 percent of production labor.

6. Accounts receivable will turn every 60 days.

7. An attempt will be made to maintain an inventory level equal to a 90-day supply. Payments for inventory will be made the month following the sale.

8. SG&A expenses, excluding interest, will remain constant over the term of the budget regardless of the sales volume.

9. The effective income tax rate is 40 percent (32 percent federal, 4 percent Wyoming, and 4 percent Wisconsin).

10. All net profit after tax is used for operating cash. No capital expenditures are included in the budget. No sales of assets are planned.

11. Depreciation will remain constant throughout the period. Depreciation expense per month is distributed as follows: overhead, $5200, SG&A, $2150, for a total of $7,350.

GENERAL AND ADMINISTRATIVE BUDGET JULY 1983 TO JUNE 1984

Automotive	$ 1,350
Credit expense	1,500
Advertising expense	5,000
Insurance expense	4,500
Payroll expense	2,200
Administrative payroll	21,500
Office expense	7,100
Data processing expense	6,100
Miscellaneous general and administrative expense	2,300
Licenses and taxes expense	350
Marketing expense	1,200
Professional services expense	2,400
Telephone expense	2,500
Travel and entertainment expense	5,500
	$63,500

JOHNCO MANUFACTURING PRO FORMA INCOME STATEMENT, JULY 1983 THROUGH JUNE 1984

	7/83	8/83	9/83	10/83	11/83	12/83	1/84	2/84	3/84	4/84	5/84	6/84
Gross sales	$360,000	$435,000	$540,000	$590,000	$570,000	$630,000	$540,000	$465,000	$585,000	$410,000	$435,000	$440,000
Commissions	18,000	21,750	27,000	29,500	28,500	31,500	27,000	23,250	29,250	20,500	21,750	22,000
Net sales	342,000	413,250	513,000	560,500	541,500	598,500	513,000	441,750	555,750	389,500	413,250	418,000
Cost of sales												
Materials	171,000	206,625	256,500	280,250	270,750	299,250	256,500	220,875	277,875	194,750	206,625	209,000
Labor	51,300	62,000	77,000	84,000	81,250	89,750	77,000	66,250	83,350	58,425	62,000	62,700
Overhead	38,500	46,500	57,750	63,000	61,000	67,300	57,750	49,700	62,500	43,800	46,500	47,000
Total	260,800	315,125	391,250	427,250	413,000	456,300	391,250	336,825	423,725	296,975	315,125	318,700
Gross profit	81,200	98,125	121,750	133,250	128,500	142,200	121,750	104,925	132,025	92,525	98,125	99,300
SG&A expense	63,500	63,500	63,500	63,500	63,500	63,500	63,500	63,500	63,500	63,500	63,500	63,500
Income from operations	17,700	34,625	58,250	69,750	65,000	78,700	58,250	41,425	68,525	29,025	34,625	35,800
Interest expense												
Long-term	11,633	11,480	10,962	11,164	10,652	10,844	10,681	9,853	10,374	9,894	10,065	9,589
Short-term	2,369	2,378	3,751	4,696	4,640	5,745	5,632	4,567	4,559	4,175	3,726	3,488
Total	14,002	13,858	14,713	15,860	15,292	16,589	16,313	14,420	14,933	14,069	13,791	13,077
Profit (loss) before tax	3,698	20,767	43,537	53,890	49,708	62,111	41,937	27,005	53,592	14,956	20,834	22,723
Provision for income tax (40%)	1,479	8,307	17,415	21,556	19,883	24,844	16,775	10,802	21,437	5,982	8,334	9,089
Net income	$2,219	$12,460	$26,122	$32,334	$29,825	$37,267	$25,162	$16,203	$32,155	$8,974	$12,500	$13,634
Year-to-date income	$2,219	$14,679	$40,801	$73,135	$102,960	$140,227	$165,389	$181,592	$213,747	$222,721	$235,221	$248,855

JOHNCO MANUFACTURING CASH FLOW BUDGET AND BORROWING BALANCES, FISCAL YEAR ENDING JUNE 30, 1984

	7/83	8/83	9/83	10/83	11/83	12/83	1/84	2/84	3/84	4/84	5/84	6/84
Beginning cash	0	0	0	0	0	0	0	0	0	0	0	0
Cash receipts												
Accounts receivable collections	$431,250	$380,000	$317,500	$468,750	$538,750	$567,500	$605,000	$570,000	$525,000	$543,750	$467,500	$466,250
Cash disbursements												
Inventory purchases	190,000	171,000	206,625	256,500	280,250	270,750	299,250	256,500	220,875	277,875	194,750	206,625
Production labor	51,300	62,000	77,000	84,000	81,250	89,750	77,000	66,250	83,350	58,425	62,000	62,700
Clerical salaries	6,700	6,700	6,700	6,700	6,700	6,700	6,700	6,700	6,700	6,700	6,700	6,700
Management salaries	21,500	21,500	61,500	21,500	21,500	21,500	21,500	21,500	21,500	21,500	21,500	21,500
Plant mgrs. & plant secs.	7,200	7,200	7,200	7,200	7,200	7,200	7,200	7,200	7,200	7,200	7,200	7,200
Payments within 30 days												
Commissions	20,000	18,000	21,750	27,000	29,500	28,500	31,500	27,000	23,250	29,250	20,500	21,750
SG&A	33,150	33,150	33,150	33,150	33,150	33,150	33,150	33,150	33,150	33,150	33,150	33,150
Overhead	37,550	33,300	41,300	52,550	57,800	55,800	62,100	52,550	44,500	57,300	38,600	41,300
Debt payments [P&I]	25,619	25,619	25,619	25,619	25,619	25,619	25,619	25,619	25,619	25,619	25,619	25,619
Taxes			60,000	25,000		60,000	25,000		25,000			25,000
Profit sharing						50,000						
Working capital interest	2,760	2,369	2,378	3,751	4,696	4,640	5,745	5,632	4,567	4,559	4,175	3,726
Total cash out	395,779	380,838	543,222	542,970	547,665	653,609	594,764	502,101	495,711	521,578	414,194	455,270
Ending cash	35,471	(838)	(225,722)	(74,220)	(8,915)	(86,109)	10,236	67,899	29,289	22,172	53,306	10,980
Cash advanced		838	225,722	74,220	8,915	86,109						
Note payments	(35,471)						(10,236)	(67,899)	(29,289)	(22,172)	(53,306)	(10,980)
Cash forward	0	0	0	0	0	0	0	0	0	0	0	0
Borrowing balance, working capital												
Beginning balance	$250,000	$214,529	$215,367	$351,089	$425,309	$434,224	$520,333	$510,097	$442,198	$412,909	$390,737	$337,431
Advances	35,471	838	225,722	74,220	8,915	86,109						
			90,000*									
Payments							10,236	67,899	29,289	22,172	53,306	10,980
Ending balance	214,529	215,367	351,089	425,309	434,224	520,333	510,097	442,198	412,909	390,737	337,431	326,451
Interest on ending balance at 13%	$ 2,369	$ 2,378	$ 3,751	$ 4,696	$ 4,640	$ 5,745	$ 5,632	$ 4,567	$ 4,559	$ 4,175	$ 3,726	$ 2,488

*During September approximately $90,000 will be transferred into the intermediate-term loan to reestablish the balance at $350,000.

JOHNCO MANUFACTURING
ACCOUNTS RECEIVABLE COLLECTIONS
(AVERAGE 60-DAY TURN)

Month	Sales	Sales Collection at			Total Cash Received
		30 Days 50%	60 Days 25%	90 Days 25%	
April 1983	$525,000				
May	400,000	$265,500			
June	400,000	200,000	$131,250		
July	360,000	200,000	100,000	$131,250	$431,250
August	435,000	180,000	100,000	100,000	380,000
September	540,000	217,500	90,000	100,000	317,500
October	590,000	270,000	108,750	90,000	468,750
November	570,000	295,000	135,000	108,750	538,750
December	630,000	285,000	147,500	135,000	567,500
January 1984	540,000	315,000	142,500	147,500	605,000
February	465,000	270,000	157,500	142,500	570,000
March	585,000	232,500	135,000	157,500	525,000
April	410,000	292,500	116,250	135,000	543,750
May	435,000	205,000	146,250	116,250	467,500
June	440,000	217,500	102,500	146,250	466,250

CASE 2

Problem Loan: Ramco Inc.

Ski Country Bank (SCB), located in Summit County, Colorado, is a $500 million deposit bank. The bank has experienced turnover in lending personnel due to promotions, reorganization, and terminations.

Bank loan officers grade loans as does the loan review department, which reports to the head of commercial loans. If the loan officer's grade is higher than the loan review officer's grade, each officer is required to submit an analysis of the grading to the head of commercial loans for review and assignment of the appropriate grade.

The following personnel have been involved in the administration of a line of credit to Ramco:

- Bob Westberg—hired on April 15, 1984 to take over the commercial loan division.
- Steve Vaughn—loan review officer.
- Al Long—loan officer in the Enterprise Market lending group. Ramco was initially approved in this group but subsequently transferred to the Ski Industry lending group.
- Bill Davis—loan officer in Ski Industry lending group.
- Ken Jones—took over the Ramco loan after Bill Davis was promoted to head of the Ski Industry lending group.
- Don Harris—former head of the commercial loan division.
- Chuck Parker—loan officer in the Ski Industry lending group who took over Ken Jones's duties while Jones was on vacation at the Winter Olympics.

The loan committee includes the head of commercial loans and the heads of the lending groups, including the Enterprise Market and Ski Industry groups. The group approves/disapproves all loans over $500,000 and those that are graded C− and below or that exceed the loan officer's lending limit.

Due to increased loan volume, the bank periodically moves credit analysts into direct lending positions. Existing loans are reassigned to these new loan officers from the loan portfolios of other officers within the lending group. Normally assignments are made based on the dollar amount of loans to relate to the lower lending limits of these new officers. At the time of transfer of the Ramco loan responsibility among the various officers, the lending limits were: Al Long, $200,000; Bill Davis, $400,000; and Ken Jones, $500,000.

Upon assuming his new position as head of the commercial loan division, Bob Westberg asked for memorandums from the loan review department on all C− and below loans.

Requirements

1. Determine the possible resolutions to the Ramco situation.

2. Identify the early warning signs that have been ignored over the life of the loan.

3. Identify the weaknesses in the lending process associated with the Ramco loan and determine how the loan should have been handled at each stage.

4. Identify the control aspects from analysis to approval to ongoing administration that are important in ensuring loan performance and that would improve Ski Country Bank's lending process.

SKI COUNTRY BANK: LOAN GRADES

Class A: Prime loans based on liquid collateral with adequate margin or supported by a strong financial statement of recent date. Character and ability of individuals or company principals are excellent and unquestioned. Position of company in its industry and in its community is excellent. High liquidity, minimum risk, good ratios, low handling cost.

Class B: Desirable loans of somewhat less stature than Class A but with strong financial statements or secured by other marketable securities (where there is no significant concentration or impairment to liquidation). Probability of serious financial deterioration is unlikely. Possesses a sound source of repayments (and backup) that definitely will allow repayment in a reasonable period of time. Individual loans backed by sound assets and personal integrity. (Some potential Class A borrowers who do not provide a valuable relationship for the bank might fall here.)

Class C: Satisfactory loans of average or mediocre strength having some deficiency or some vulnerability to changing economic or industry conditions, but currently collectible. Secured loans lacking in margin or liquidity. Loans to individuals perhaps supported in dollars of net worth but with supporting assets that are not liquid. Sometimes a temporary classification for untested borrowers or where information is not entirely complete or acceptable.

Class C−: First classification that is related to a bank examiner class—i.e., Other Assets Especially Mentioned. A warning classification that portrays one or more deficiencies that cannot be tolerated, even in the short run. Pertinent ratios have deteriorated, deserving immediate attention and correction. Sometimes represents an interim or temporary classification of credits, new or on probation, moving to Class C or D.

Class D: Substandard because of deficiencies; related to bank examiner grade Substandard. Company or individual loans with no evident future that are unfavorably affecting the loan-to-deposit ratio or cost of funds. Heavy leverage accounts, with no immediate relief in sight or compensating features. Accounts requiring excessive attention of the loan officer because of borrower's lack of cooperation. Credits unable to adjust to unfavorable industry or general economic conditions. Individual loans where character or ability has become suspect. Credits on the brink of potential charge-off, particularly for operating at a loss.

Class E: Loans related to bank examiner grades Doubtful and Loss where an element of probable loss exists; at least a portion would be charged off if liquidated at present. Critical credits requiring immediate and drastic action. Secured loans with insufficient collateral or other sources to see the bank fully paid. Nonperforming assets where day-to-day circumstances leave the loans in question. Loans believed not to be tolerated as live assets by the examiners at their next visit or review.

MEMORANDUM FOR THE CREDIT FILE

To: Bob Westberg

From: Steve Vaughn

Date: April 21, 1984

Subject: Ramco, Inc.

The company is a wholesaler of ski and tennis apparel manufactured through contract labor shops and its own facility. The credit originated in the Enterprise Market lending group with Al Long in 1980 as an $80,000 line of credit, secured by inventory, accounts receivable, and securities.

The credit was reviewed by Loan Review November 1, 1980 and was graded C. It was adequately secured with a 32 percent collateral margin, and management was considered capable. The guarantor and founder, Theodore Walters, provided additional support with a personal net worth of $151,000. The financial statement dated September 3, 1980 reflected working capital of $20,000, current ratio of 1.4 to 1, and a debt to worth of 1.9 to .1. Although this reflects a strained liquidity and leveraged position, it was a new corporation, which could justify the ratios. Also, a net income of $17,000 by January 31, 1981 had been projected.

Loan Review again reviewed the credit on August 20, 1981. It was then a $100,000 line of credit with $87,000 outstanding. There was also a commitment for $40,000 to cover letters of credit. These were collateralized by accounts receivable and inventory. The credit was again assigned a C grade, based on the control program of inventory and accounts receivable by Ski Country Bank (SCB), the experience of management, and profitable operations.

Noteworthy is the growth of total assets from $83,000 on August 31, 1980 to $238,000 on April 30, 1981, primarily from increases in inventory and accounts receivable. Another noteworthy fact was that the current ratio deteriorated to 1.1 to 1 and debt to worth increased to 4.5 to 1. The positive factor was that operating information showed increasing sales and income.

On October 24, 1981 the line of credit was increased to $225,000 to replace the $100,000 line and a $75,000 overline. At that time $33,000 was outstanding on the letter of credit commitment. The total amount outstanding was $207,000, with total collateral valued at $343,000 (40 percent margin).

At this point scheduling problems began to appear. The reason for the increased line was that receipt of contract work was late. This meant late shipments to retailers who required timely shipments for seasonal sales.

On February 28, 1982 the line of credit was increased to $450,000; however, on April 30, 1982 it was reduced to $350,000. Here, on the April 30, 1982 loan write-up, Bill Davis indicated that problems existed with personnel and systems, which were not keeping pace with the company's growth. Davis also indicated that production problems existed and that certain piece-goods suppliers, covered under our letters of credit, were not being paid. At that time collateral controls were strengthened, as was the letter agreement.

On July 21, 1982 Loan Review, at the request of the head of the Ski Industry lending group, graded the credit C— for the following reasons:

1. Lack of adequate accounting procedures
2. Production problems
3. High administrative expenses
4. Increased reliance on bank funding to support working capital
5. Negative net worth
6. Out-of-margin condition

The credit was presented to the Loan Administration Committee September 7, 1982. It was informed that the company was in need of a $50,000 to $100,000 equity injection and was out of margin by $40,000. In his presentation Bill Davis said that the company continued to experience trade-payables pressure; however, the company had returned to profitability, had rescheduled its trade payments, and expected a capital injection of $25,000 during the month. Also, additional collateral in the form of second-trust deeds was taken to protect the overline. Additionally, new management staff had been engaged in the area of accounting, production, and scheduling.

On January 3, 1983 the credit was again presented to the Loan Administration Committee by Bill Davis. The Committee was informed that Ramco had purchased Resource Services Company, a company that did contract work for them. Ramco had also paid a tax liability, resulting in a cash drain of $30,000. These funds should have been used to retire past-due trade debt. Also, ski order cancellations and $36,000 in returns, due primarily to poor ski conditions, had forced SCB to advance against real estate equities, and the bank had overadvanced an additional $27,000. However, positive operating results and a reduction in ski inventory, which had been replaced by more seasonal tennis inventory, caused the situation to remain "virtually unchanged." The loan was classified D.

Efforts to attract $250,000 in equity capital or the company's movement to another institution were desired. These possibilities were given as the reason to approve a $35,000 overline for 90 days. SCB was also to perfect a second mortgage on the company's office building.

At the May 27, 1983 Loan Administration Committee presentation, recognition of a $56,000 collateral shortfall was made. The outstanding balance of $883,000 on a $950,000 line was collateralized by $777,000. The business continued to deteriorate for the following reasons:

1. A poor skiing season

2. Ineffective pricing

3. Weak management

4. Expansion through acquisition

5. Returned merchandise

6. Missed delivery dates

7. Slowed collection of accounts receivable due to the poor skiing season

The course of action taken by Commercial Lending was to:

1. Place Ramco's accounts receivable on direct notification

2. Audit the inventory

3. Position SCB personnel in the company to administer disbursements

4. Place payables, in the amount of $190,000 on an 18-month payout

The company during this time was to continue to pursue outside capital sources. It was also to find a full-time controller and a general manager. Also, the $56,000 shortfall in collateral was not to be allowed to increase but was to amortize over a 10-month period.

At the August 3, 1983 Loan Administration Committee presentation, Ken Jones presented a report that was essentially a repetition of the May 27, 1983 presentation. Amounts and figures were changed to represent the current situation, but basically the same problems existed—poor management and inefficient administration. Ramco had, however, obtained a full-time controller.

Jones sought and received from the Loan Administration Committee an increase in the line to $1,150,000 from $950,000. The increase was permitted with the provisions that stock in Resource Services Company be obtained, close analysis of cash flow be made, and restrictions be placed on growth without adequate additional capital. Also, the $56,000 overadvance was to be reduced to $25,000 by maturity.

A February 6, 1984 memo to Don Harris from Chuck Parker requested a 30-day extension on the line. This request was based on an outside consultant's determination that the company was viable and could operate profitably. It was also noted that the company would reflect a $50,000 profit from the prior year and that a Japanese firm, Moonbeam, had made a tentative proposal for a $200,000 capital injection. The extension was granted.

On March 8, 1984 Jones presented to the Loan Administration Committee a request for an increase in the line to $1,700,000 from $1,150,000. Everything appeared to have remained the same except that an infusion of funds was received from the Japanese firm. In exchange for a long-term loan of $220,000, Ramco would design, manufacture, and distribute golf wear for Moonbeam. In any event, approval was not granted, pending clarification of the operation, the cash flow, the collateral position, and the transaction negotiated with Moonbeam.

On April 12, 1984 the Loan Administration Committee approved a $1,300,000 line commitment running to June 30, 1984. Action would then be taken on progress in receivables collection. Guarantor Walters's personal loan of $13,000 was to be paid through liquidation of securities held as collateral. Presently an overadvanced position is anticipated through the summer, with a corrected position considered possible in the fall.

This summary reflects the present situation of Ramco, Inc. as of April 20, 1984, based on information found in the Commercial Lending and Loan Review files.

CASE 3

Consumer Credit: Credit-Scoring Charge Card Applications, Rocky Ford National Bank

Bruce Smith was hired by Rocky Ford National Bank (RFNB) in the management training program. He has spent the last three weeks in the training program studying operations in the consumer loan department. Bruce has observed the installment loan officers servicing direct loan requests.

As part of his training in the consumer loan area, Bruce is now going to observe the operation of Rocky Ford's charge card operations. RFNB uses a credit-scoring model in approving requests for check guarantee cards, the bank's overdraft credit line that is called "Balance Plus," and for MasterCard and Visa credit cards.

In a meeting with Susan Jensen, who is the vice president in charge of charge card operations, the credit-scoring model was described. The model was developed from the extensive data base of RFNB by means of multiple discriminant analysis. The model is shown in Exhibits C3.1 and C3.2. Susan explained that the bank uses the model to identify applicants who are clearly acceptable, those who clearly do not meet the bank's standards, and those for whom further credit analysis should be done.

Susan explained the procedure that is followed in processing a credit application. The first step in the procedure involves scoring the application using the model in Exhibits C3.1 and C3.2. If a score of 120 or less results, the request for the cards is denied and the applicant is notified by mail. If a score of 160 or greater results, the application is approved and is then forwarded to a loan officer to determine the credit limit(s). The loan officer assesses the credit limit through the use of traditional methods of analysis. If the credit line requested by the customer is acceptable, the customer is notified of the approval and the card(s) are ordered. If the credit line requested by the applicant exceeds the amount that the loan officer judges to be appropriate, the customer is contacted by phone and notified of the approval for the lesser amount. If the customer accepts the counteroffer, the card(s) are ordered.

On applications for which the score is between 121 and 159, the application is referred to the loan officer for analysis. For these applications the loan officer, using traditional analysis, approves or declines the

EXHIBIT C3.1 Sample Credit Scoring: Application Information

Category	Below .5	.5–1.49	1.5–3	3.1–6	6.1–10	10.1–20	Over 20/Ret.
Years on Job	5	15	18	20	22	27	35
Previous Job	Below 2 0	2.1–5 10	Over 5 20				
Years at Address	Below .5 0	.5–1.49 8	1.5–5 15	5.1–10 20	Over 10 25		
Home/Real Estate Status	Own 25	Rent 0					
Home Phone	Yes 20	No 0					
Credit Cards	None 0	Dept. Store 10	Dept. Store & Oil 12	Visa or Mastercard 30			
Source	New Customer 0	Present Customer, Checking 8	Present Customer, Checking/ Savings 16	Previous Customer 18			

EXHIBIT C3.2   Sample Credit Scoring: Credit Bureau Information

Derogatory Information	One Derog. Citation	Two Derog. Citation	More Than Two Cita.	No Report	No Derog.
	−10	−20	−35	−5	0
Satisfactory Information	One Satis.	Two Satis.	More Than Two Satis.		
	10	15	25		

request and sets the dollar amount of credit. The loan officer considers character, capacity, capital, and conditions as they apply to the specific request.

Susan discussed with Bruce the advantages of using the credit-scoring model. She indicated that response time has been greatly improved since the scoring procedure was implemented. She also indicated that the efficiency of the charge card department has improved. A larger number of applications can be processed with the same personnel and, even when the costs of development and implementation of the scoring model are considered, operating costs are lower.

After further discussion of the model, Bruce feels confident that he understands the basic operation of the scoring model. As his first assignment in the department, Susan gives Bruce two applications and corresponding credit bureau reports to score and process (see Exhibits C3.4 through C3.7). Bruce is required to process the credit applications and follow the bank's policy with respect to scoring (see Exhibit C3.3). If the score falls between the automatic accept or reject scores, Bruce is required to perform traditional analysis and recommend approval or rejection. If he recommends approval, he must specify a dollar amount of credit.

EXHIBIT C3.3   Scoring Form

Applicant: _____

Category—Application	Points
Years on Job	_____
Previous Job	_____
Years at Address	_____
Home/Real Estate Status	_____
Home Phone	_____
Credit Cards	_____
Source	_____
Subtotal	_____

Category—Credit Bureau	
Derogatory Information	_____
Satisfactory Information	_____
Subtotal	_____
Total Points	_____

Additional Requirements

1. In addition to the advantages of implementing the scoring system that were described by Susan, describe any additional advantages there might be in using the credit-scoring model.

2. With respect to the particular credit applications, discuss the potential bias for the credit-scoring model.

3. List factors that could be important determinants in the acceptability of the credit applications that are not included explicitly in the credit-scoring model.

4. As the model is currently used, credit bureau reports are ordered on all applications. Describe an alternative procedure that could be implemented for even more efficiency.

EXHIBIT C3.4   Credit Application, Rocky Ford National Bank: Applicant No. 1

Rocky Ford
National Bank

Personal Information

your name *Margaret Courtney*
street address *1213 Oline St.*
city, state, zip *Boulder, CO   80372*
home phone *297-6300*   years there *1 yr 1 mon*
social security number (optional) *123-45-5797*   age *23*

are you a United States citizen? ☒ yes   ☐ no

number of dependents (including self) *1*
name of mortgage holder or landlord *Home Savings of Boulder*
amount of rent or mortgage payments *472.29*   ☒ own ☐ rent
market value *$66,000* amount owing *$30,000*
former street address *401 N. Main #12* years there *3 yrs*
city, state, zip *Boulder, CO   80372*
other real estate owned

Co-Applicant You need only complete this section if this is a joint account, if another person is an authorized user, or if you are relying on the income of a spouse or another person as a basis for the credit requested.

name *Chuck Courtney*
address *1213 Oline St.*
relationship to applicant *husband*   age *27*
social security number (optional) *123-89-2168*
employer *Ralph Knudsen*
work phone *Contract labor*
years there *2 yrs* gross monthly earnings *1200.00*

Your Income Only that income you wish to be considered in evaluating this credit request need be disclosed, including alimony, child support or separate maintenance. If you are Self-Employed, Attach Current Financial Statement and/or Latest Income Tax Return.

your present employer *Softwave Beauty Salon*
street address *1335 S. Shore*
city, state, zip *Boulder, CO   80371*
work phone *492-7701*
kind of business *Cosmotology*
gross monthly earnings *1100.00*
your occupation or position *Cosmotologist* years there *4½ yrs*
last employer *Mary Jo's Skin Care*
street address *402 Parker*
city, state, zip *Boulder, CO 80371* years there *3 yrs*
other sources of income
other monthly income (before taxes) $

Personal reference

nearest relative not living with you *Chris Smith*
street address *400 Mellow Way*
city, state, zip *Boulder CO   80377*
phone *271-6065* relationship *Sister*

Previous bank information

previous bank name *First Bank*
city, state, zip *Boulder, CO*
branch, if applicable
checking acct. # *Unknown* savings account ☒ yes ☐ no
date closed *2/81*

FOR BANK USE ONLY

Please mark services desired:

☐ Visa Banking Card with Balance Plus $_____
☐ Check Guarantee Card
☐ Bancard
☐ Balance Plus $_____
☒ Visa Credit $_____
☒ Master Card $_____
☐ PLEASE MAIL ME A PERSONAL IDENTIFICATION NUMBER (PIN) TO BE USED IN THE AUTOMATED TELLER MACHINES.

checking account number *1076640*
savings account number *6112175*

Master Card number
Visa Credit Card Number
Other credit cards *J.C. Penney # 617-729-31111*
#

Your present debts and past credit references (Be sure to list all your debts. Use additional sheet if necessary)

1. car financed by *Vehicles are paid for*
   address
   balance still due or date paid off $ _____ monthly payment $ _____
   account #

2. creditor
   address
   balance still due or date paid off $ _____ monthly payment $ _____
   account #

3. creditor
   address
   balance still due or date paid off $ _____ monthly payment $ _____
   account #

4. creditor
   address
   balance still due or date paid off $ _____ monthly payment $ _____
   account #

Are you obligated to pay alimony, child support or separate maintenance?
Yes ____ No *X* Amount _____

Student information (if applicable)

school name _____ year in school _____
major
parents' name
street address
city, state, zip

I certify that all the information I've given in this application is true, accurate, and complete. You have my permission to investigate my credit history. You can release credit information on this application to others who have a legitimate reason for asking about my credit.
Please send me the Agreement(s) pertaining to the bank services for which I qualify.

your signature x *Margaret Courtney*
co-applicant's signature x *Chuck Courtney*
(if joint account desired)   date *2/27/84*

	Approval	Date	Credit Limit	Acct. #	Expiration Date	Uses
Visa Banking Card						
Balance Plus						
Gold Card						
Red Card						
Visa Credit						
Master Card						

EXHIBIT C3.5   Credit Bureau Information: Applicant No. 1

Name: Margaret Courtney

SS #:   123-46-5797

IB report from Boulder, CO   ID #197-1617406

Current Address: 1213 Olive Street, Boulder, CO 80372   S10/83
Current Employer: Softwave Beauty Salon, Boulder, CO

Former Address: 401 N. Main #12, Boulder, CO 80372
Former Employer: Mary Jo's Skin Care, Boulder, CO

File 08/81   AC2/28/84

Firm Name Identity Code	Type Terms	Reported Method	Open Paid	High	Owes	Past Due	Payments Late Hist. 30/60/90+
Home Savings FS-136---115 Acct. #221010101	I 354	10/03/83M	08/82 09/83	22K	21K	00 ---	00/00/00
Home Savings FS-136---115 Acct. #22021797	I 170	10/03/83M	05/73 09/83	13K	10K	00 ---	00/00/00
First Bank BB-136---45 Acct. #46464949	I 131	09/02/82A	08/81 08/82	1409	00	00 ---	00000000000000-0000 000-0000

Inquirer Name	KB-BUR-GP-CODE	Inq. Date
Rocky Ford	BC-187------1282	02/28/84
Rocky Ford	BB-136------4001	02/22/84
Penney J C	DC-103----------4	10/20/83
Home Savings	FS-136--------115	10/03/83

End #136-1617406

Report 137   02/29/84   14H   12M   Term 283   Oper 220

EXHIBIT C3.6   Credit Application, Rocky Ford National Bank: Applicant No. 2

**Rocky Ford
National Bank**

Personal Information

your name Carol Holden

street address 128 King Street

city, state, zip Boulder, CO 80378

home phone (303) 298-7654   years there 1.5

social security number (optional) 123-45-6789   age 32

are you a United States citizen? ☑ yes ☐ no

number of dependents (including self) 1

name of mortgage holder or landlord Mrs. W. D. Holley

amount of rent or mortgage payments $185/month   ☐ own ☑ rent

market value $ _____ amount owing $ _____

former street address 123 S. Slowm   years there 2

city, state, zip Boulder, CO 80378

other real estate owned 2 houses & lots in Lyons, CO

Please mark services desired:

☐ Visa Banking Card with Balance Plus $ _____
☐   Check Guarantee Card
☐   Bancard
☐ Balance Plus $ _____
☑ Visa Credit $ 1,000
☐ Master Card $ _____
☐ PLEASE MAIL ME A PERSONAL IDENTIFICATION NUMBER (PIN) TO BE USED IN THE AUTOMATED TELLER MACHINES.

checking account number 71-3162-5

savings account number 6256083

Master Card number _____

Visa Credit Card Number _____

Other credit cards   Amoco   #577-43-9991
                     The Denver   #123-456-789

Your present debts and past credit references (Be sure to list all your debts. Use additional sheet if necessary).

1. car financed by paid cash
   address —
   balance still due or date paid off $ —   monthly payment $ _____
   account # —

2. creditor Roger Johnson
   address Lyons, CO 80761
   balance still due or date paid off $ 30,000.   monthly payment $ 375
   account # _____

3. creditor The Denver
   address Denver, CO
   balance still due or date paid off $ 120.   monthly payment $ 20.
   account # 123-456-789

4. creditor May D&F
   address Denver, CO
   balance still due or date paid off $ 50.   monthly payment $ 25.
   account # 987-654-321

Are you obligated to pay alimony, child support or separate maintenance?
Yes _____ No X   Amount _____

Co-Applicant You need only complete this section if this is a joint account, if another person is an authorized user, or if you are relying on the income of a spouse or another person as a basis for the credit requested.

name _____

address _____

relationship to applicant _____

social security number (optional) _____

employer _____

work phone _____

years there _____ gross monthly earnings _____

Your Income Only that income you wish to be considered in evaluating this credit request need be disclosed, including alimony, child support or separate maintenance. If you are Self-Employed, Attach Current Financial Statement and/or Latest Income Tax Return.

your present employer University of Colorado

street address _____

city, state, zip Boulder, CO 80388

work phone (303) 278-4442

kind of business University Food Service

gross monthly earnings $1,280/month

your occupation or position Supervisor   years there 5

last employer Storage Plant, Inc.

street address 123 Smith Street

city, state, zip Denver, CO   years there 3 mo.

other sources of income Rental Income from prop. in Lyons

other monthly income (before taxes) $ income = $475/mo.

Student Information (if applicable)

school name _____   year in school _____

major _____

parents' name _____

street address _____

city, state, zip _____

Personal reference

nearest relative not living with you W. C. Smith

street address Box 1273

city, state, zip White Spgs, GA 50731

phone (212) 429-7772   relationship Father

Previous bank information

previous bank name First Nat'l Bank of Boulder

city, state, zip Boulder, CO

branch, if applicable _____

checking acct. # N/A   savings account ☑ yes ☐ no

date closed approximately May 1978

I certify that all the information I've given in this application is true, accurate, and complete. You have my permission to investigate my credit history. You can release credit information on this application to others who have a legitimate reason for asking about my credit.
Please send me the Agreement(s) pertaining to the bank services for which I qualify.

your signature x Carol Holden

co-applicant's signature x _____
(if joint account desired)
date 2-1-84

FOR BANK USE ONLY

	Approval	Date	Credit Limit	Acct. #	Expiration Date	Uses
Visa Banking Card						
Balance Plus						
Gold Card						
Red Card						
Visa Credit						
Master Card						

EXHIBIT C3.7 Credit Bureau Information: Applicant No. 2

Name: Carol Holden

SS#: 123-45-6789

IB report from Boulder, CO ID #185-1238302

Current Address: 128 King Street, Boulder, CO 80378 SC1/81
Current Employer: University of Colorado-Boulder

Former Address: 123 S. Slocum Street, Boulder, CO 80378
Former Employer: Storage Plant, Inc.

File 10/79 A11/17/83

Firm Name Identity Code	Type Terms	Reported Method	Open Paid	High	Owes	Past Due	Payments Late Hist. 30/60/90+
Denver Dry Goods DC-136---77 Acct #123-456-789	R	04/29/81A	09/79 04/81	136	—	00	00000000-000 00-00000
May D F DC-136---700 Acct #987-654-321	R 18	11/28/83A	08/79 09/83	138	18	00	000000000000 00000000-000
Conoco OC-187---197 Acct #264271297	R	12/08/83A	04/79 01/83	48	00	00	00000000000-

End # 136-1237302'

Report 137 02/02/84 14H 39M Term 299 Oper 22C

CASE 4

Analysis of Bank Performance: Laramie County Bank

This exercise is designed to lead you through a basic analysis of bank operations. Certain data are purposely excluded so that you are forced to examine the limitations of the analysis and to identify the need for additional information that will explain variances in operating data or help you arrive at sound conclusions.

Laramie County Bank was founded in 1960 in Cheyenne, Wyoming, the state capital. The city has a population of approximately 55,000 people. It has seven banks, of which Laramie County Bank is the second largest. Wyoming does not allow branch banking. During the past two years three new banks have been chartered in Cheyenne. The principal economic activities of the area are federal and state government, light industry, and ranching. Over the past eight years bank deposits have approximately doubled. Growth has been attributed to increased government activity and to the expansion of light industry. Agricultural activity in Laramie County is primarily livestock and raising the related hay. Laramie County Bank operates an agricultural credit subsidiary, which initiates and discounts loans with the Federal Intermediate Credit Bank.

The Maxfield family has owned and operated the bank since its founding. Thomas Maxfield, chairman and president, has headed the bank for several years and recently considered an early retirement to devote his time to certain real estate and oil and gas interests. In 1980 he employed his grandson Dick as a management trainee. Dick has worked in all departments of the bank, and his grandfather considers him his successor at retirement. Recently Dick began making commercial loans and has progressed fairly well.

Tom Maxfield has administered the bank with little input from bank officers. Annually he compares the bank's performance to the previous year's performance and to the performance of other banks in the Tenth Federal Reserve District for Colorado, New Mexico, and Wyoming. He decides to involve Dick in the analysis of bank data to give him additional exposure to the management of a bank.

Tom calls Dick into his office and briefly outlines the analysis to be completed. Tom tells Dick that he had Harry Jones, the cashier, prepare comparative statements of condition and income for the current year and the past year. Additionally, he had Harry format the necessary worksheet columns that Dick will need for his analysis. Harry has also included a copy of the current year's operating ratios for member banks in the Tenth Federal Reserve District. Tom tells Dick he should complete the worksheets and the columns for Laramie County Bank for the comparison to other banks.

Follow the instructions for each stage of the analysis. You may want to record observations regarding the analysis as you proceed.

LARAMIE COUNTY BANK BALANCE SHEET

Assets	December 31 ($000) 19X2	19X1	Change in Amount 19X2–19X1	Percentage Change 19X1 to 19X2	19X2 Percentage Composition of Total Assets	19X1 Percentage Composition of Total Assets
Cash and due from banks	$ 9,109	$14,741	___	___	___	___
Investment securities	17,634	19,506	___	___	___	___
Federal funds sold and securities purchased under repurchase agreement	203	0	___	___	___	___
Loans and lease financing	33,905	25,233	___	___	___	___
Unearned income	(276)	(304)	___	___	___	___
Total loans	33,629	24,929	___	___	___	___
Allowance for loan losses	(234)	(334)	___	___	___	___
Net loans	33,395	24,595	___	___	___	___
Bank premises and equipment	527	520	___	___	___	___
Investment in subsidiaries	2,308	2,104	___	___	___	___
Accrued interest receivable	938	739	___	___	___	___
Real estate acquired by foreclosure	0	8	___	___	___	___
Other assets	318	380	___	___	___	___
Total Assets	$64,432	$62,593	___	___	___	___

Liabilities	December 31 ($000) 19X2	19X1	Change in Amount 19X2–19X1	Percentage Change 19X1 to 19X2	19X2 Percentage Composition of Total Assets	19X1 Percentage Composition of Total Assets
Deposits:						
Demand	$19,708	$23,664	___		___	___
Savings	7,678	4,516	___		___	___
Time	24,208	18,481	___		___	___
Total deposits	51,594	46,661				

Federal funds purchased and securities sold under repurchase agreement	6,000	10,350		
Accounts payable and accrued liabilities:				
Interest payable	585	349		
Other	255	120		
Long-term debt	420	480		
Total Liabilities	58,854	57,960		
Stockholders' equity:				
Common stock, stated value $10 per share: authorized, issued, and outstanding, $150,000 shares	1,500	1,500		
Surplus	470	470		
Retained earnings	3,608	2,663		
Total stockholders' equity	5,578	4,633		
Total Liabilities and Stockholders' Equity	$64,432	$62,593		
FTE employees	50	45		

Instructions: 1. Complete columns "Change in Amount" and "Percentage Change" on the Balance Sheet.

2. Complete columns "Percentage Composition" on the Balance Sheet.

3. When you have completed steps 1 and 2, answer the questions below.

Questions: 1. What were the major Balance Sheet changes in amount and percentage between years 19X1 and 19X2?

2. What liability change directly contributed to the reduction of cash and due from banks?

3. Describe the major changes in Balance Sheet account percentage composition. What changes in bank policy appear to be evident?

LARAMIE COUNTY BANK INCOME STATEMENT, YEAR ENDED DECEMBER 31

	19X2 ($000)	19X1	Amount of Change 19X2–19X1	Percentage Change 19X1–19X2	Percentage of Total Operating Income 19X2	Percentage of Total Operating Income 19X1
Interest Income						
Interest and fees on loans	$3,556	$2,844	—	—	—	—
Interest on investment securities:						
U.S. Treasury and other U.S. government agencies	113	122	—	—	—	—
States and political subdivisions	807	770	—	—	—	—
Other securities	13	10	—	—	—	—
Total interest on investment securities	933	902	—	—	—	—
Interest on federal funds sold	14	11	—	—	—	—
Total interest income	4,503	3,757	—	—	—	—
Interest Expense						
Interest on:						
Deposits:						
Savings	379	226				
Time	1,573	1,339	—	—	—	—
Federal funds purchased and securities sold under agreements to repurchase	127	429				
Long-term debt	38	43	—	—	—	—
Total interest expense	2,117	2,037	—	—	—	—
Net interest income	2,386	1,720	—	—	—	—
Provision for loan losses	(120)	(98)				
Net interest income after provision for loan losses	2,266	1,622	—	—	—	—

	19X2	19X1			
Noninterest income					
Income from trust services	158	145			
Service charges on deposit accounts	132	156			
Other	663	577			
Total noninterest income	953	878			
Noninterest expense					
Salaries and employee benefits	866	811			
Net occupancy expense	278	258			
Furniture and equipment expense	134	118			
Other operating expense	580	518			
Total noninterest expense	1,858	1,705			
Income before taxes on income and securities transactions	1,361	795			
Taxes on income	(254)	(12)			
Income before securities transactions	1,107	783			
Securities transactions (net of tax)	(112)	120			
Net Income	$ 995	$ 903			
Per Share	$ 6.63	$ 6.02			

Instructions:
1. Complete columns "Amount of Change" and "Percentage Change" on the Income Statement.
2. Complete columns "Percentage of Total Operating Income" on the Income Statement.
3. Answer the questions below.

Questions:
1. What were the major Income Statement changes in amount and percent between years 19X1 and 19X2?
2. Are any major changes in Income Statement account percentage composition apparent? If so, describe them.

LARAMIE COUNTY BANK
AVERAGE BALANCE DATA

	Average Balance ($000)	
	19X2	**19X1**
Cash	$11,925	$ 2,023
Investment securities		
U.S. Treasury	1,603	2,023
Municipals	18,754	18,334
Other securities	187	204
Federal funds sold and securities purchased under repurchase agreements	172	193
Loans		
Commercial	13,981	10,146
Agricultural	2,934	2,474
Installment	5,170	4,412
Real estate	10,719	9,340
	32,804	24,372
Deposits		
Demand	21,686	18,517
Savings	7,580	4,520
Time	22,439	19,866
Long-term debt	422	478
Federal funds purchased and securities sold under repurchase agreements	1,591	7,246
Average capital	5,106	4,283
Average assets	63,513	61,225
Average earning assets	53,520	45,126
Average risk assets	48,277	40,473

LARAMIE COUNTY BANK
RATIOS

	19X2	19X1
Liquidity		
$\dfrac{\text{Cash}}{\text{Demand deposits}}$	____ =	____ =
$\dfrac{\text{Cash}}{\text{Total deposits}}$	____ =	____ =
$\dfrac{\text{Cash and short-term U.S. governments}}{\text{Total deposits}}$	$\dfrac{+\ 1{,}000}{\ }$ =	$\dfrac{+\ 1{,}500}{\ }$ =

Observations:

	19X2	19X1
Investment Policy		
$\dfrac{\text{Earning assets}}{\text{Total assets}}$	____ =	____ =
$\dfrac{\text{Loans}}{\text{Deposits}}$	____ =	____ =

	19X2		19X1	
	Amount	**%**	**Amount**	**%**
Loan Mix				
Commercial	____	____	____	____
Installment	____	____	____	____
Mortgage	____	____	____	____
Agricultural	____	____	____	____
Total	____	____	____	____
Securities Mix				
U.S. government	____	____	____	____
Municipals	____	____	____	____
Other	____	____	____	____
Total	____	____	____	____
Deposit Mix				
Demand	____	____	____	____
Savings	____	____	____	____
Time	____	____	____	____
Total	____	____	____	____

(continued)

Observations:

	19X2	19X1
Leverage		
$\dfrac{\text{Average deposits}}{\text{Average capital}}$	___ =	___ =
$\dfrac{\text{Average borrowed funds}}{\text{Average capital}}$	___ =	___ =

Observations:

	19X2	19X1
Capital Adequacy Ratios		
$\dfrac{\text{Average risk assets}}{\text{Average capital}}$	___ =	___ =
$\dfrac{\text{Average total assets}}{\text{Average capital}}$	___ =	___ =

Observations:

	19X2	19X1
Efficiency		
$\dfrac{\text{Operating income}}{\text{FTE employees}}$	___ =	___ =
$\dfrac{\text{Average assets}}{\text{FTE employees}}$	___ =	___ =
$\dfrac{\text{Average deposits}}{\text{FTE employees}}$	___ =	___ =

Observations:

	19X2	19X1
Returns		
$\dfrac{\text{Income before securities transactions}}{\text{Average assets}}$	___ =	___ =
$\dfrac{\text{Net income}}{\text{Average assets}}$	___ =	___ =
$\dfrac{\text{Net income}}{\text{Average capital}}$	___ =	___ =
$\dfrac{\text{Total operating income}}{\text{Average assets}}$	___ =	___ =

Observations:

LARAMIE COUNTY BANK
YIELD ANALYSIS

	19X2			19X1		
	Average Balance	Interest Income or Expense	Average Yields or Rates	Average Balance	Interest Income or Expense	Average Yields or Rates
U.S. Treasury						
Municipals[a]						
Other						
Total						
Federal funds sold						
Loans						
Total						
Deposits						
Federal funds purchased						
Long-term debt						
Total interest-bearing liabilities						
Net interest income						
Yield spread						
Net interest income to earning assets						

[a]Tax equivalent rate = 48%.

COLORADO, NEW MEXICO, AND WYOMING MEMBER BANKS, GROUPED ACCORDING TO SIZE OF TOTAL ASSETS, 19X2

	All Banks		Group 5 $50 Million and Over		Your Figures	
	19X2	19X1	19X2	19X1	19X2	19X1
Number of banks	240	227	52	45		
Profitability						
Percentage of equity capital						
1. Income after taxes and before securities gains or losses	15.00%	12.90%	16.90%	15.00%	——— 1
2. Net income	15.00	13.20	17.00	15.30	——— 2
Percentage of net income						
3. Cash dividends paid	24.10	25.30	33.70	32.10	——— 3
Sources and Disposition of Income						
Percentage of total assets						
4. Total operating income	8.77	8.13	8.70	7.95	——— 4
5. Salaries, wages, and employee benefits	1.82	1.72	1.59	1.54	——— 5
6. Interest on deposits	3.17	3.02	3.24	2.93	——— 6
7. Interest on borrowed money and subordinated notes and debentures	0.19	0.12	0.37	0.24	——— 7
8. Net occupancy expense of bank premises and furniture and equipment expense	0.52	0.28	0.51	0.29	——— 8
9. All other operating expenses	1.57	1.73	1.43	1.56	——— 9
10. Total operating expenses	7.27	6.87	7.14	6.56	——— 10
11. Income after taxes and before securities gains or losses	1.12	0.99	1.14	1.05	——— 11
12. Net income	1.12	1.01	1.14	1.06	——— 12
Percentage of total operating income						
13. Interest on U.S. Treasury and U.S. agency securities	9.10	9.80	8.40	9.20	——— 13
14. Interest on obligations of states and political subdivisions	6.80	7.60	7.40	8.10	——— 14
15. Interest and dividends on all other securities	0.30	0.20	0.10	0.20	——— 15
16. Interest and fees on loans	70.90	70.10	72.50	70.70	——— 16
17. Income on federal funds sold	4.00	3.00	2.40	2.30	——— 17
18. All other operating income	8.90	9.30	9.20	9.50	——— 18
19. Total operating income	100.00	100.00	100.00	100.00	——— 19
20. Trust department income	1.70	1.80	2.40	2.70	——— 20
21. Salaries and employee benefits	20.70	21.00	18.20	19.30	——— 21
22. Interest on deposits	36.60	37.60	37.40	37.00	——— 22
23. Interest on borrowed money	1.80	1.20	3.80	2.50	——— 23
24. Net occupancy expense of bank premises and furniture and equipment expense	5.90	3.40	5.90	3.70	——— 24
25. Provision for loan losses	3.50	3.90	3.10	2.80	——— 25
26. All other operating expenses	14.40	17.30	13.70	17.30	——— 26
27. Total operating expenses	82.90	84.40	82.10	82.60	——— 27

28.	Interest on subordinated notes and debentures	1.00	0.90	1.00	1.00
29.	Income before taxes and securities gains or losses	17.10	15.60	17.90	17.40
30.	Income after taxes and before securities gains or losses	12.80	12.30	13.10	13.10
31.	Net securities gains (+) or losses (−) after tax effect	+0.00	+0.20	+0.00	+0.20
32.	Net income	12.80	12.50	13.20	13.30

Rates of Return on Securities and Loans

Return on securities

33.	Interest on U.S. Treasury and U.S. agency securities	7.31	6.69	7.21	6.71
34.	Interest on obligations of states and political subdivisions	5.29	5.11	5.15	5.08
35.	Interest and dividends on all other securities	6.43	6.38	6.25	6.21

Return on loans

36.	Interest and fees on loans (including valuation reserve)	10.58	9.91	10.71	9.88
37.	Net losses (−) or recoveries (+) on loans	−0.30	−0.39	−0.27	−0.25

Distribution of Total Assets

Percentage of total assets

38.	Cash assets	11.40	11.70	12.50	12.70
39.	U.S. Treasury securities	7.90	8.60	7.40	7.80
40.	Securities of U.S. government agencies and corporations	2.90	3.10	2.60	2.90
41.	Obligations of states and political subdivisions	11.10	11.80	12.50	12.80
42.	All other securities	0.30	0.20	0.20	0.20
43.	Net loans including federal funds sold	62.50	61.00	60.50	59.60
43a.	Net loans	58.40	57.20	58.30	56.30
43b.	Federal funds sold	4.00	3.70	2.30	3.30
44.	Real estate	2.20	2.00	2.50	2.30
45.	All other assets	1.70	1.60	1.80	1.70

Distribution of Loans

Percentage of gross loans and federal funds sold

46.	Real estate loans	24.30	23.10	30.00	28.90
47.	Loans to farmers	15.00	16.80	7.60	8.00
48.	Commercial and industrial loans	25.70	25.60	28.10	28.30
49.	Consumer loans to individuals	26.70	26.60	27.40	26.50
50.	Federal funds sold	6.30	6.10	3.70	5.30
51.	All other loans	2.00	1.80	3.20	3.00

Other Ratios

In percentage

52.	Total capital accounts to total assets	8.70	8.10	7.30	7.40
53.	Time and savings deposits to total deposits	60.60	61.00	60.70	61.00
54.	Interest on time and savings deposits to total time and savings deposits	5.89	5.50	6.11	5.48
55.	Interest on large CDs to large CDs outstanding	7.21	6.52	7.26	6.58
56.	Income taxes to net income plus income taxes	22.10	19.50	23.10	23.00

Questions:

1. Are any major changes in policy evident from the ratio analysis? If so, describe them.
2. What changes in net interest income, yield spread, and net interest income on earning assets have occurred between years 19X1 and 19X2?
3. For the following ratios, compare and comment on Laramie County Bank's performance related to Federal Reserve Board comparative data:

	FRB 19X2	LCB 19X2	FRB 19X1	LCB 19X1
As Percentage of Total Assets				
Total operating income	_____	_____	_____	_____
Net income	_____	_____	_____	_____
As Percentage of Total Operating Income				
Interest and fees on loans	_____	_____	_____	_____
Interest on deposits	_____	_____	_____	_____
Income after taxes and before securities gains and losses	_____	_____	_____	_____
Rates of Return				
Interest on U.S. Treasury securities	_____	_____	_____	_____
Interest and fees on loans	_____	_____	_____	_____
Distribution of Total Assets				
Net loans	_____	_____	_____	_____
Other Ratios				
Total capital accounts to total assets	_____	_____	_____	_____
Time and savings deposits to total assets	_____	_____	_____	_____

4. List additional analyses that you believe would be useful in analyzing this bank's performance.

CASE 5

Projection of Bank Performance: Laramie County Bank

Tom Maxfield was pleased with Dick's analysis (see Case 4). In planning for the coming year, Tom decided to have Dick prepare a projected statement of condition and an income statement. Tom prepared a set of planning parameters for 19X3.

Prepare a projected statement of condition and an income statement based on these assumptions. Answer the questions below after preparing the projections.

Questions:

1. Do the projections meet a target objective of 15 percent return on equity and 1.5 percent return on assets?
2. Why is the bank able to meet the equity ratio but not the return-on-assets ratio?
3. If the bank injected $1 million in capital to reduce long-term debt and other liabilities, what would be the return on equity and return on assets? Assume no change in net income.
4. Assuming regulators requested the additional capital contribution, what planning steps would you take to meet the performance objectives?

After deducting dividends from stockholders' equity, increase or decrease cash and due from banks to balance the balance sheet. Change total assets if necessary.

Using the information following, complete the balance sheet and income statement on pages 644-646.

LARAMIE COUNTY BANK
19X3 PLANNING PARAMETERS

Balance Sheet	Percent of Average Assets
Cash and due from banks	12.0 est.
Investment securities	23.0
Federal funds sold	4.0
Net loans	56.0
Bank premises and equipment	3.0
Other assets	2.0
	100.0
Deposits	83.0
Federal funds purchased	6.0
Long-term debt	0.7
Other liabilities	1.0
Stockholders' equity	9.3
	100.0

Investment Securities	Percent	Rate
U.S. Treasury and agencies	12.0	8.7%
Municipals	87.0	9.0 T.E.*
Other	1.0	7.0
	100.0	

Loans	Percent	Rate
Commercial	45.0	13.0%
Agricultural	9.0	9.0
Installment	15.0	14.0
Real estate	31.0	
	100.0	

Deposits	Percent	Rate
Demand	35.0	
Savings	15.0	5.0%
Time	50.0	8.5
	100.0	

*Tax Equivalent

(continued)

	Rate
Federal funds sold	11.0%
Federal funds purchased	11.0
Long-term debt	9.0

Income Statement	Percent of Interest Income
Provision for loan losses	5.5
Income from trust services	7.0
Service charges on deposits	6.0
Other income	25.0
Salaries and employee benefits	37.0
Net occupancy	13.0
Furniture and equipment expense	6.0
Other operating expense	24.0
Securities gains and losses	0

Other Information

Tax rate	46% *
Dividends	$60,000
Total average assets	$70,000,000

*Tax Equivalent

LARAMIE COUNTY BANK
BALANCE SHEET*

	(1) Percent of Average Assets/Acct.	(2) Balance ($000)	(3) Rate Earned/Paid	(4) Income/Expense [(2) × (3)] ($000)
Cash and due from banks				
Investment securities:				
U.S. Treasury and agencies				
Municipals				
Other securities	___	___		
Total securities				
Loans				
Commercial				
Agricultural				
Installment				
Real estate	___	___		
Total loans (net)				
Federal funds sold				
Bank premises				
Other assets	___	___		
Total Assets	100.0	$70,000		

Deposits
Demand
Savings
Time

Total deposits _____

Federal funds purchased
Long-term debt
Other liabilities

Stockholders' equity
Common stock
Additional paid-in capital
Retained earnings 12/31/X2
Plus: Income
Less: Dividends

Total stockholders' equity _____ 100.0

Total Liabilities and Stockholders' Equity $70,000

* After deducting dividends from stockholders' equity, increases or decreases cash and due from banks to balance the balance sheet, change total assets if necessary. Using the information above, complete the balance sheet and income statement.

LARAMIE COUNTY BANK
PROJECTED 19X3 INCOME STATEMENT

	Percent of Net Interest Income	Amount	Percent of Total Operating Income
Interest income			
Interest and fees on loans			
U.S. Treasuries and agencies			
Municipals			
Other securities			
Federal funds sold	____	____	____
Total interest income			
Interest expense			
Savings			
Time			
Federal funds purchased			
Long-term debt	____	____	____
Total interest income			
Net interest income	100.0		
Provision for loan losses	____	____	____
Net interest income after provision for loan losses			
Noninterest income			
Income from trust services			
Service charges on deposits			
Other	____	____	____
Total noninterest income			
Noninterest expenses			
Salaries and employee benefits			
Net occupancy expenses			
Furniture and equipment expenses			
Other operating expenses	____	____	____
Total noninterest expense			
Income before taxes on income and securities transactions			
Taxes on income	____	____	____
Net income			
Ratios			
Net income/total assets			
Loan/deposits			
Deposits/capital			
Capital/earning assets			
Earning assets/total assets			
Return on average equity			

CASE 6

Interest Margin Planning, Eighth National Bank of Denver

Chester Fields, the senior vice-president in charge of financial planning for the Eighth National Bank of Denver, has asked you, a newly hired business school graduate, to assist him in the analysis of the bank's interest margin position. Owing to changes in regulation due to take effect at the beginning of the next quarter, Mr. Fields is concerned about planning the bank's interest margin position. The changes in regulation are those being implemented according to the provisions of the Depository Institutions Deregulation and Monetary Control Act of 1980. The act will allow banks to pay money market rates on deposits in the new money market deposit accounts.

Chester made an appointment for you with Wendy Hansen, who is the vice-president in charge of marketing for the bank. You discuss the new account with her, and she indicates that the bank is going to aggressively market the new deposit account. She indicates that she feels that most other banks in the area will follow suit and she doesn't expect that Eighth National will be able to attract a large volume of new funds. Her department has conducted surveys of the bank's depositors. She is confident that as much as 75 percent of the Regulation Q savings balances would convert to money market deposit accounts almost immediately following the change in regulation. She estimates that the new deposits will offer an 8.5 percent rate initially and the rate will float thereafter.

Following your appointment with Wendy, you return to Chester's office. He discusses with you the potential problem that the switch in deposits could cause for the bank. Specifically, he is concerned about the effect that the switch could have on the bank's interest-sensitive position.

Chester shows you a planning report he currently uses to analyze changes in the bank's interest margin and gap position over time. The report, which is displayed in Exhibit C6.1, shows the bank's beginning balances and gap position. It also breaks down funds that are nonsensitive to changes in interest rates and those that are affected by changes in interest rates. The report also displays amounts of assets and liabilities that are scheduled to mature or to be repriced over the next four quarters and the balances that have maturities in excess of one year. In addition, the report contains yield figures for all of the categories. They are displayed immediately below the dollar balances.

EXHIBIT C6.1 Eight National Bank of Denver

	Beginning Balance*	Nonsensitive Funds	Floating Funds	1st Qtr.	2nd Qtr.	3rd Qtr.	4th Qtr.	Greater Than One Year
Earning Assets								
Investment securities	2,000	50 6.00%		250 14.00%	250 14.00%	250 14.00%	250 14.00%	950
Short-term investments	500		500 8.50%					0
Commercial loans, floating	2,000		2,000 12.00%					0
Commercial loans, fixed	2,000			500 13.00%	500 13.00%	500 13.00%	500 13.00%	0
Real estate, floating	500		500 14.00%					0
Real estate, fixed	1,500			50 10.00%	50 10.00%	50 10.00%	50 10.00%	1,300
Consumer loans, floating	500		500 16.00%					0
Consumer loans, fixed	1,000			50 18.00%	50 18.00%	50 18.00%	50 18.00%	800
Total earning assets	10,000	50 6.00%	3,500 12.36%	850 13.41%	850 13.41%	850 13.41%	850 13.41%	3,050

Interest-Bearing Liabilities

	Total							
Regulation Q savings	4,000	4,000 5.50%						0
Money market deposit accounts	0	0						0
CDs <100,000	2,500			500 9.25%	500 9.25%	500 9.25%	500 9.25%	500
CDs >100,000	1,000			500 9.50%	500 9.50%			0
Borrowed funds	500		500 8.00%					0
Total interest-bearing liabilities	8,000	4,000 5.50%	500 8.00%	1,000 9.38%	1,000 9.38%	500 9.25%	500 9.25%	500 9.25%
Noninterest Funding	2,000							
GAP (RSA − RSL)		−3,950 0.50%	3,000 4.36%	−150 4.04%	−150 4.04%	350 4.16%	350 4.16%	2,550
Static GAP				2,850	2,850	3,350	3,350	
Cumulative GAP				2,850	2,700	3,050	3,400	5,950

*All dollar amounts are in thousands.

The last section of the report reveals the effect on the GAP position. The change in the GAP for a particular quarter is shown along with two additional measures that display cumulative effects.

If the starting GAP is denoted as SG and each quarter as Q_1, Q_2, Q_3, and Q_4, respectively, then:

$$\text{Static GAP} = \text{SG} + Q_1, \text{ or SG} + Q_2 \text{ or SG} + Q_3 \text{ or SG} + Q_4$$
$$\text{Cumulative GAP} = \text{SG} + Q_1, + Q_2 + Q_3 + Q_4$$

Requirements

1. Construct a report similar to Exhibit C6.1 that displays the effect of the change in Eighth National's deposit structure. Assume that the change takes place immediately and consider the extent to which the change could impact the bank. Assume that the maximum conversion that Wendy predicted takes place.

2. Compare the results of your analysis with the original report. What implications does your analysis have on potential margin management problems that Chester may face over the coming year?

3. The measure of cumulative gap considers the cumulative effect of changes in gap through time. What assumption does the measure of cumulative gap make? Is this assumption appropriate for most analyses?

4. Wendy predicted no change in volume. Suppose that the bank priced the new deposit account very aggressively. Describe how an increase in volume would have to be incorporated in the analysis.

5. Develop possible strategies to compensate for the increased cost of funds.

CASE 7

Customer Profitability Analysis: Computer Software, Inc.

Computer Software, Inc. has indicated a desire to restructure its lending relationship with Anytown National Bank (the current lending relationship is summarized on page 652). Computer Software proposes the following terms:

- Interest rate: prime
- Compensating balance: none
- Decrease average collected demand balances by $25,000
- Increase time balances by $25,000

Anytown National Bank is considering Computer Software's request. Its proposal includes the following terms:

- Interest rate: prime
- Compensating balance: none
- Decrease average collected demand balances by $25,000
- Increase time balances by $25,000
- Commitment fee: 0.5 percent of approved credit line

Instructions:

1. Prepare a yield analysis worksheet for the existing relationship. Round computations to even dollars. Compute the net loan yield to the nearest tenth of a percent. Compute the interest rate required to the nearest quarter of a percent.
2. Prepare a yield analysis worksheet for the relationship proposed by Anytown National Bank. Round computations to even dollars. Compute the net loan yield to the nearest tenth of a percent. Compute the interest rate required to the nearest quarter of a percent.
3. Discuss whether the resulting computations for the restructured relationship meet either party's objectives. Consider what factors contributed to the changed relationship. What other alternatives for pricing could Anytown National suggest to meet Computer Software's objectives as well as its own?

SUMMARY OF CUSTOMER RELATIONSHIP WITH COMPUTER SOFTWARE, INC.

Approved credit line	$300,000
Average line outstanding	$240,000
Interest rate	Prime + 1%
Maturity	1 year
Collateral	Unsecured
Interest earned	$36,000
Compensating collected demand balances required	20% of approved line
Deposit balances	
Demand	
Average gross balances	$112,000
Average collected balances	$ 61,000
Time	$ 10,000
Interest paid on time	$ 1,000
Activity data	
Loans	4 promissory notes
Checking accounts	
Home debits	3,420
Deposits	526
Local items	2,632
Transit items	4,120
Account cycle periods	12
Risk	Moderate

GENERAL INFORMATION

Demand reserve requirements	12.00%
Time reserve requirements	3.00
Cost of funds	
Average rate	7.80
Marginal rate	8.25
Loan administration expense	$60 per note + .005 × average loan balance
Loan risk ratio	
Unsecured revolving credit	
Low risk	0.4%
Moderate risk	0.5
Medium risk	0.8

(continued)

Desired yield	9.5
Prime rate	14.0
Deposit activity costs	
Home debits	$ .02
Deposits	.05
Local items	.03
Transit items	.04
Account maintenance	2.50 per period

Note: Assume commercial demand accounts are exempt from deposit service charges.

Definitions for Yield Analysis Worksheet:

Service charges and other fees	Deposit service charges and commitment fees
Loan servicing costs	$60 per note
Departmental overhead expense	.005 × average loan balance
Cost of risk	Appropriate risk ratio × average loan balance

COMMERCIAL LOAN
YIELD ANALYSIS WORKSHEET

Borrower's Name _____

( ) New Loan ( ) Review Date _____

Sources of Funds Employed

1. Average loan balance $ _____
2. Demand deposit contribution [average balance × (1 − reserve requirement ____%)] $ _____
3. Time deposit contribution [average balance × (1 − reserve requirement ____%)] $ _____
4. Other deposit contribution [average balance × (1 − reserve requirement ____%)] $ _____
5. Total deposit contribution (total of Lines 2 through 4) $ _____
6. Net "pooled funds" required (Line 1 − Line 5) $ _____

(continued)

Total Gross Loan Income

7. Loan interest (Line 1 × interest
   rate charged ____%) $_____
8. Service charges and other fees $_____
9. Total gross loan income (Line 7 + Line 8) $_____

Total Loan Expense

10. Cost of funds required (Line
    6 × appropriate cost rate ____%) $_____
11. Time deposit interest expense $_____
12. Loan-servicing costs (nonrecurring)
    A. Initial costs $_____
    B. Term costs $_____   Total $_____
13. Total direct expense (subtotal
    of Lines 10 through 12) $_____
14. Departmental overhead expense $_____
15. Cost of risk (Line 1 × appropriate
    risk rate factor ____) $_____
16. Demand deposit activity costs $_____
17. Total loan expense (total of
    Lines 13 through 16) $_____

Net Loan Income and Yield

18. Net loan income (Line 9 − Line 17) $_____
19. Net loan yield (Line 18 ÷ Line 6)   _____%

Nominal Rate Calculation

20. Required net loan income (Line
    6 × desired yield on pooled funds employed)   ____% $_____
21. Required gross loan income
    (Line 20 + Line 17) $_____
22. Interest rate required (Line
    21 ÷ Line 1)   _____%

APPENDIX A

◆

Accounting and Taxation Supplement

Name of Bank: _____ **Charter Number:** _____

Balance Sheet at the close of business on _____ month _____ day _____ year

Statement of Resources and Liabilities

	Sch.	Item	Col.	Thousands	Hnds.	Cts.	
1. Cash and due from depository institutions	C	8			XXX	XX	1
2. U.S. Treasury securities	B	1	E		XXX	XX	2
3. Obligations of other U.S. government agencies and corporations	B	2	E		XXX	XX	3
4. Obligations of states and political subdivisions in the United States.	B	3	E		XXX	XX	4
5. Other bonds, notes, and debentures.	B	4	E		XXX	XX	5
6. Federal Reserve stock and corporate stock					XXX	XX	6
7. Trading account securities					XXX	XX	7
8. Federal funds sold and securities purchased under agreements to resell					XXX	XX	8
9. a. Loans, Total (excluding unearned income) [XXX XX]	A	10					9a
b. Less: Allowance for possible loan losses [XXX XX]							9b
c. Loans, Net					XXX	XX	9c
10. Lease financing receivables.					XXX	XX	10
11. Bank premises, furniture, and fixtures, and other assets representing bank premises					XXX	XX	11
12. Real estate owned other than bank premises					XXX	XX	12
13. Investments in unconsolidated subsidiaries and associated companies					XXX	XX	13
14. Customers' liability to this bank on acceptances outstanding.					XXX	XX	14
15. Other assets.	G	3			XXX	XX	15
16. **Total Assets** (sum of items 1 through 15)					XXX	XX	16
17. Demand deposits of individuals, partnerships, and corporations	F	1f	A		XXX	XX	17
18. Time and savings deposits of individuals, partnerships, and corporations	F	1f	B&C		XXX	XX	18
19. Deposits of the United States government	F	2	A&B&C		XXX	XX	19
20. Deposits of states and political subdivisions in the United States.	F	3	A&B&C		XXX	XX	20
21. Deposits of foreign governments and official institutions	F	4	A&B&C		XXX	XX	21
22. Deposits of commercial banks.	F	5&6	A&B&C		XXX	XX	22
23. Certified and officers' checks.	F	7	A		XXX	XX	23
24. a. Total deposits (sum of items 17 through 23)					XXX	XX	24a
(1) Total demand deposits [XXX XX]	F	8	A		XXX	XX	24a1
(2) Total time and savings deposits [XXX XX]	F	8	B&C		XXX	XX	24a2

25. Federal funds purchased and securities sold under agreements to repurchase . . . . . . | XXX | XX | 25
26. a. Interest-bearing demand notes (note balances) issued to the U.S. Treasury . . . | XXX | XX | 26a
    b. Other liabilities for borrowed money . . . . | XXX | XX | 26b
27. Mortgage indebtedness and liability for capitalized leases . . . . . | XXX | XX | 27
28. Bank's liability on acceptances executed and outstanding . . . . | XXX | XX | 28
29. Other liabilities   H   4 . . . . . | XXX | XX | 29
30. **Total Liabilities** (excluding subordinated notes and debentures) (sum of items 24a through 29) . . . . | XXX | XX | 30
31. Subordinated notes and debentures. . . . . . | XXX | XX | 31

32. Preferred stock   No. shares outstanding [ ] (par value) . . . | XXX | XX | 32
33. Common stock   a. No. shares authorized [ ]
                 b. No. shares outstanding [ ] (par value)

34. Surplus . . . . . . | XXX | XX | 33
35. Undivided profits . . . . . | XXX | XX | 34
36. Reserve for contingencies and other capital reserves . . . . | XXX | XX | 35
37. **Total Equity Capital** (sum of items 32 through 36) . . . . | XXX | XX | 36
38. **Total Liabilities and Equity Capital** (sum of items 30, 31, and 37) . . . . | XXX | XX | 37
    | XXX | XX | 38

Thousands of dollars

	Thousands	Hnds.	Cts.	
1. Amounts outstanding as of report date:				
a. Standby letters of credit				
(1) Standby letters of credit, total . . .	XXX	XX	XX	1a1
(2) Amount of standby letters of credit in memo item 1a(1) conveyed to others through participations . . .	XXX	XX	XX	1a2
b. Time certificates of deposit in denominations of $100,000 or more . . .	XXX	XX	XX	1b
c. Other time deposits in amounts of $100,000 or more. . .	XXX	XX	XX	1c
2. Average for 30 calendar days (or calendar month) ending with report date:				
a. Cash and due from depository institutions (corresponds to Assets, item 1). . .	XXX	XX	XX	2a
b. Federal funds sold and securities purchased under agreements to resell (corresponds to Assets, item 8) . . .	XXX	XX	XX	2b
c. Total loans (corresponds to Assets, item 9a) . . .	XXX	XX	XX	2c
d. Time certificates of deposits in denominations of $100,000 or more (corresponds to Memo item 1b above) . . .	XXX	XX	XX	2d
e. Total deposits (corresponds to Liabilities, item 24a) . . .	XXX	XX	XX	2e
f. Federal funds purchased and securities sold under agreements to repurchase (corresponds to Liabilities, item 25) . . .	XXX	XX	XX	2f
g. Other liabilities for borrowed money (corresponds to Liabilities, item 26b) . . .	XXX	XX	XX	2g
h. Total assets (corresponds to Assets, item 16). . .	XXX	XX	XX	2h

Name of Bank: _____ **Charter Number:** _____

Section A—Sources and Disposition of Income Year to Date (indicate losses in parentheses)

	Thousands of dollars		
	Thousands	Hnds.	Cts.

Operating Income:

	Thousands	Hnds.	Cts.	
a. Interest and fees on loans.		XXX	XX	1a
b. Interest on balances with depository institutions.		XXX	XX	1b
c. Income on Federal funds sold and securities purchased under agreements to resell in domestic offices of the bank and of its Edge and Agreement subsidiaries.		XXX	XX	1c
d. Interest on U.S. Treasury securities		XXX	XX	1d
e. Interest on obligations of other U.S. government agencies and corporations.		XXX	XX	1e
f. Interest on obligations of states and political subdivisions in the United States		XXX	XX	1f
g. Interest on other bonds, notes, and debentures.		XXX	XX	1g
h. Dividends on stock.		XXX	XX	1h
i. Income from lease financing.		XXX	XX	1i
j. Income from fiduciary activities		XXX	XX	1j
k. Service charges on deposit accounts in domestic offices		XXX	XX	1k
l. Other service charges, commissions, and fees		XXX	XX	1l
m. Other operating income (from Section D, item 4).		XXX	XX	1m
n. **Total Operating Income** (sum of items 1a through 1m)		XXX	XX	1n

Operating Expenses:

	Thousands	Hnds.	Cts.	
a. Salaries and employee benefits.		XXX	XX	2a
b. Interest on time certificates of deposit of $100,000 or more issued by domestic offices.		XXX	XX	2b
c. Interest on deposits in foreign offices		XXX	XX	2c
d. Interest on other deposits.		XXX	XX	2d
e. Expense of Federal funds purchased and securities sold under agreements to repurchase in domestic offices of the bank and of its Edge and Agreement subsidiaries		XXX	XX	2e
f. (1) Interest on demand notes (note balances) issued to the U.S. Treasury.		XXX	XX	2.f(1)
(2) Interest on other borrowed money		XXX	XX	2.f(2)
g. Interest on subordinated notes and debentures.		XXX	XX	2g

h. (1) Occupancy expense of bank premises, Gross	2.h(1)	XXX	XX		
(2) Less: Rental income	2.h(2)	XXX	XX		
(3) Occupancy expense of bank premises, Net	2.h(3)			XXX	XX
i. Furniture and equipment expense	2i			XXX	XX
j. Provision for possible loan losses (from Section C, item 4)	2j			XXX	XX
k. Other operating expenses (from Section E, item 3)	2k			XXX	XX
l. **Total Operating Expenses** (sum of items 2a through 2k)	2l			XXX	XX
Income Before Income Taxes and Securities Gains or Losses (item 1n minus 2l)	3			XXX	XX
Applicable Income Taxes	4			XXX	XX
Income Before Securities Gains or Losses (item 3 minus 4)	5			XXX	XX
a. **Securities Gains (Losses), Gross**	6a	XXX	XX		
b. **Applicable Income Taxes**	6b	XXX	XX		
c. **Securities Gains (Losses), Net**	6c			XXX	XX
Net Income (item 5 plus or minus 6c)	7			XXX	XX
or					
Income Before Extraordinary Items	7			XXX	XX
Extraordinary Items, Net of Tax Effect (from Section F, item 2c)	8			XXX	XX
Net Income (item 7 plus or minus 8)	9			XXX	XX

Director Reports
Balance Sheet

	Month/Day/Year					
	Prior Year		Current Year		Plan	
	Amount	Percent	Amount	Percent	Amount	Percent
Assets						
Cash and due from banks	$		$		$	
Interest-bearing balances						
U.S. Treasury securities						
Securities of other U.S. government agencies						
Obligations of states and political subdivisions						
Other securities	———		———		———	
Total investment securities						
Federal funds sold						
Real estate loans—residential						
Real estate loans—other						
Installment loans						
Commercial loans						
Other loans						
Total loans, gross	———		———		———	
Less: Unearned discount						
Allowance for loan loss	———		———		———	
Total loans, net						
Direct lease financing						
Property						
Other assets	———	———	———	———	———	———
Total assets	$____	100.0	$____	100.0	$____	100.0
Liabilities						
Demand deposits—individuals, partnerships, corporations						
Public funds—demand						
Other demand deposits	———		———		———	
Total demand deposits						
Time and savings—IPC						
Public funds—time						
Time deposits over $100,000						
Other time and savings	———		———		———	
Total domestic time and savings	———		———		———	

(continued)

Director Reports *(continued)*

Balance Sheet

	Month/Day/Year					
	Prior Year		Current Year		Plan	
	Amount	Percent	Amount	Percent	Amount	Percent
Total domestic deposits	_____		_____		_____	
Foreign deposits	_____		_____		_____	
Total deposits	_____		_____		_____	
Federal funds purchased						
Mortgage indebtedness						
Other liabilities	_____		_____		_____	
Total liabilities						
Capital notes and debentures						
Equity capital—total	_____		_____		_____	
Total liabilities— capitalization reserves	$ ____	100.0	$ ____	100.0	$ ____	100.0

Director Reports *(continued)*

Statement of Income
Year to Date
Month Ended _____

	Prior Year		Current Year		Plan		Variance
		Percent		Percent		Percent	Actual to Plan
Interest Income							
Interest and fees on loans							
Interest on investment securities							
U.S. Treasury securities							
Obligations of U.S. government agencies							
Obligations of states and political subdivisions							
Other securities and investments							
Interest on federal funds sold and securities purchased under reverse repurchase agreements							
Income on trading account securities							
Total interest income		___		___		___	___
Interest Expense							
Interest on deposits							
Savings and time deposits							
Time deposits of $100,000 or more							
Interest on short-term borrowings							
Interest on long-term debt		___		___		___	___
Total interest expense		___		___		___	___
Net Interest Income							
Less provision for loan losses							

Net Interest Income after Provision for Loan Losses

Other Income
Trust department income
Service charges on deposit accounts
Other operating income

Other Expenses
Salaries and wages
Pensions and other employee benefits
Occupancy expense of bank premises, net
Equipment and processing expense
Other expenses
  Total expenses
Income before income taxes and securities gains/(losses)
Less applicable income taxes

Income before Securities Gains/(Losses)
Net securities gains/(losses), net of related tax effect

Net Income $ \underline{\underline{\quad}}$

Director Reports (continued)

Analysis of Net Interest Income
Year to Date _____
Month Ended _____

to strip up

	Prior Year		Current Year		Plan		Variance	
	Average Balance Sheet Account	Yield/ Rate	Average Balance Sheet Account	Yield/ Rate	Average Balance Sheet Account	Yield/ Rate	Average Balance Sheet Account	Yield/ Rate
Interest Income:								
Interest and fees on loans	$	%	$	%	$	%	$	%
Interest on investment securities:								
U.S. Treasury securities								
U.S. agencies								
Obligations of states and political subdivisions								
Other securities								
Interest on federal funds sold and securities purchased under reverse repurchase agreements							+	
Income on trading account securities								
Total interest income								
Interest Expense:								
Interest on deposits								
Savings and time deposits								
Time deposits of $100,000 or more								
Interest on short-term borrowings								
Interest on long-term debt								
Total Interest Expense								
Net Interest Income								

Statement of Stockholders' Equity

	Past Years	Current Year to Date
Common Stock:		
Balance, beginning and end of year or period	———	———
Surplus:		
Balance, beginning and end of year or period	———	———
Undivided Profits		
Balance, beginning of year		
Net income		
Cash dividends declared (per share)	———	———
Balance, end of year or period	———	———
Total Stockholders' Equity, End of Year or Period	———	———

Director Reports (continued)
Statement of Changes in Financial Position

	Prior Year	Current Year
Funds Provided		
Net income		
Add noncash items included in net income		
Provision for losses on loans		
Depreciation		
Provision for deferred income taxes		
Funds provided from operations	————	————
Increase in		
Deposits		
Federal funds purchased and securities sold under repurchase agreements		
Accrued expenses and other liabilities		
Decrease in		
Cash, cash items, and demand deposits		
Investment securities	————	————
Federal funds sold	————	————
Funds Used		
Cash dividends paid		
Increase in		
Cash, cash items, and demand deposits		
Investment securities		
Federal funds sold	————	
Loans		
Bank premises and equipment		
Accrued interest receivable and other assets		

Decrease in
Accrued expenses and other liabilities
Capital notes

Investment Securities. Weighted average yields (effective yields for tax-exempt obligations are on a fully taxable basis, assuming a tax rate of 46 percent) of such securities are as follows:

	Within One Year		After One but within Five Years		Maturing After Five but within Ten Years		After Ten Years		Total	
	Amount	Yield	Amount	Yield	Amount	Yield	Amount	Yield	Amount	Yield
U.S. Treasury										
U.S. government agencies										
States and political subdivisions[a,b]										
Other										

[a]Taxable equivalent adjustment for calculation of yield.
[b]Dollar amount of taxable equivalent adjustment (annualized).

Director Reports (*continued*)

Loan Maturities and Sensitivity to Changes in Interest Rates

	Maturity				Rate Structure of Loans Due after One Year		
	One Year or Less	Over One Year through Five Years	Over Five Years	Total	With Predetermined Rate	With Floating Rate	Total
Construction and land development							
Other real estate loans (excluding one- to four-family residential properties)							
Other financial institutions							
Agricultural loans							
Commercial and industrial loans							
All other loans attributable to domestic operations	___ ___	___ ___	___ ___	___ ___	___ ___	___ ___	___ ___

Nonperformance Loans

				Period Ended X/X/XX	
	Past Due	Renegotiated Loans	Total	Interest of Original Terms	Interest Actually Recorded
Other real estate loans (excluding one- to four-family residential properties)					
Commercial and industrial loans					
Consumer loans	___ ___	___ ___		___ ___	___ ___

Director Reports *(continued)*

Summary of Loan Loss Experience.   The following table summarizes loans outstanding at the end of each period and the average during each period, changes in the allowance for losses on loans arising from loans charged off and recoveries on loans previously charged off, and additions to the allowance that have been charged to operating expense.

	19XX	19X1	19X2	19X3	19X4	Year to Date
Balance at beginning of period						
Loans charged off						
Real estate loans						
Commercial and industrial loans						
Consumer loans						
Other loans	———	———	———	———	———	———
Recoveries on loans previously charged off						
Real estate loans						
Commercial and industrial loans						
Consumer loans	———	———	———	———	———	———
Net loans charged off						
Additions to allowance charged to operating expense	———	———	———	———	———	———
Balance at end of period	═══	═══	═══	═══	═══	═══
Loans outstanding at end of period	═══	═══	═══	═══	═══	═══
Average loans outstanding during the period, net of unearned discount	═══	═══	═══	═══	═══	
Ratio of net loans charged off to average loans outstanding	═══	═══	═══	═══	═══	═══

(continued)

Director Reports *(continued)*

Average Deposits for Each Period Indicated

	Three Years					
	$	%	$	%	$	%
Demand deposits						
Savings accounts						
Time certificates of deposit of $100,000 and over						
Other time deposits						
Total average deposits						

Significant Ratios

Operating Performance as Percent or Dollar Amount of Total Assets

1. Net income
2. Interest income (fully taxable equivalent)
3. Interest expense
4. Net interest margin
5. Salaries and benefits
6. Occupancy expense
7. Earning assets
8. Equity capital
9. Employees per million dollars

Yields and Rates

10. Effective tax rate on operating income
11. Cash dividend payout ratio
12. Operating income per employee
13. Breakeven yield

Other Comparisons

14. Loans as percentage of deposits
15. Employees per million dollars of deposits
16. Growth in deposits (one year)
17. Growth in average assets (one year)
18. Growth in income before securities transactions (one year)

CHAPTER 6

Accounting for Deposits

Transaction	Entry		Effect on Financial Statement
Addition to Deposit Account	Debit:	Cash or Due from banks	Increases assets
	Credit:	Demand deposits or NOW accounts or Savings deposits or Time deposits	Increases liabilities
Check Clearing	Debit:	Cash or Federal Reserve account	Increases assets
	Credit:	Due from banks	Decreases assets
Checks Received from Other Banks for Customers' Transactions	Debit:	Demand deposits or NOW accounts	Decreases liabilities
	Credit:	Due to banks or Federal Reserve account	Increases liabilities or Decreases assets
Withdrawal of Savings or Time Deposits	Debit:	Savings deposits or Time deposits	Decreases liabilities
	Credit:	Cash or Cashier's check	Decreases cash or Increases liabilities
Clearing of Cashier's Checks	Debit:	Cashier's check or Due to banks	Decreases liabilities or Increases liabilities
Accrual of Interest Expense	Debit:	Interest expense	Increases expenses
	Credit:	Accrued interest payable	Increases liabilities
Interest Credited to Customer	Debit:	Accrued interest payable	Decreases liabilities
	Credit:	NOW accounts or Savings deposits or Time deposits	Increases liabilities
or			
Interest Paid to Customer	Credit:	Cash or Cashier's check	Decreases assets or Increases liabilities
Service Charges Deducted from Account	Debit:	Demand deposits or NOW accounts	Decreases liabilities
	Credit:	Service charge income	Increases income

CHAPTER 8

Accounting for Commercial Loans

Transaction	Entry		Effect on Financial Statement
New Loan	Debit:	Commercial loans	Increases assets
	Credit:	Cash	Decreases assets
		or	
		Demand deposit and/or	Increases deposits
		Unearned discount on commercial loans (if note is discounted in advance)	Increases asset contra account[a]
Accrual of Interest Collected	Debit:	Interest and fees receivable on loans	Increases assets
	Credit:	Loan interest income	Increases income
Accrual of Interest (on Discounted Note)	Debit:	Unearned discount on commercial loans	Decreases liabilities Increases income
	Credit:	Loan interest income	
Principal Repayment	Debit:	Cash	Increases assets
	Credit:	Commercial loans	Decreases assets
Participations Sold	Debit:	Due from banks	Increases assets
	Credit:	Participations sold— commercial loans	Increases asset contra account[b]
Receipt for Participations Sold Proceeds	Debit:	Cash	Increases assets
	Credit:	Due from banks	Decreases assets
Loan Payment Including Interest	Debit:	Cash	Increases assets
	Credit:	Interest and fees receivable on loans	Decreases assets
		Commercial loans	Decreases assets
Payoff of Participation	Debit:	Cash	Increases assets
	Credit:	Commercial loans	Decreases assets
	Debit:	Participations sold— commercial loans	Decreases contra account
	Credit:	Due to banks	Increases liabilities
Payment to Participating Bank	Debit:	Due to banks	Decreases liabilities
	Credit:	Cash	Decreases assets

[a]Asset contra account reduces commercial loan account to its principal balance.
[b]Asset contra account reduces outstanding commercial loans to net loans owned by the bank.

CHAPTER 9

Accounting for Loan Losses

Transaction	Entry		Effect on Financial Statement
Provision for Loan Losses	Debit:	Provision for possible loan losses	Increases expenses
	Credit:	Allowance for possible loan losses	Increases asset contra account (valuation)
Write-off of Bad Debts	Debit:	Allowance for possible loan losses	Decreases contra account
	Credit:	Appropriate loan account	Decreases assets
	Debit:	Interest income or Unearned discount	(1) Decreases income for income uncollected (2) Decreases contra account for uncollectible debt
	Credit:	Interest and fees receivable or Appropriate loan account	(1) Decreases assets (2) Decreases assets
Recovery of Bad Debt (Debt Previously Written Off)	Debit:	Cash	Increases assets
	Credit:	Allowance for possible loan losses	Increases contra account
Accounting for Difference between Book and Tax Provisions	Debit:	Provision for possible loan losses	Increases expenses
	Credit:	Appropriated capital	Increases capital (contingency)[a]
		Federal income taxes payable (deferred)	Increases liabilities

[a]The contingency represents the excess of the calculated provision for possible loan losses over the amount charged to income in the financial statements. The excess results in deferral of income taxes payable for the additional deduction for tax purposes. The contingency portion (excess) is accounted in effect as a reduction of undivided profits and an appropriation of capital. The contingency can be reduced only by a reversal of the relationship between the book provision and the tax provision (tax provision less than book provision).

Tax Accounting for Loan Losses (Bad Debts)

Tax accounting for bad debts can be accomplished by one of two methods: the specific charge-off method and the reserve method. The specific charge-off method allows a deduction for a bad debt when the debt becomes wholly or partially worthless. The basic problem with this method is how to determine whether a debt is worthless "in whole" or "in part." Typically, the factors to be considered are the value of the collateral securing the debt and the debtor's financial condition. The circumstances surrounding nonpayment of debt might indicate that the debt is worthless and uncollectible and that legal action would not enforce payment. Although bankruptcy may indicate that the debt is worthless, a filing for bankruptcy is not required to prove that a debt is worthless. If the debt is wholly worthless, it is charged off in the year in which it is deemed worthless. If it is partially worthless, the amount to be charged off may be written off in the current year or delayed until the loan is deemed wholly worthless. Any payments recovered in subsequent years are included in gross income in the taxable year of the recovery.

If a property owner fails to meet his obligation to a bank, the bank may foreclose the mortgage, compromise the debt, or accept the mortgage property in satisfaction of the debt. Generally, if the property securing the indebtedness is sold in a legal sale through the courts, the bank is required to bid for the property in the open market to return the property. If the bank's bid on the property is less than the basis in the loan, the bank realizes an immediate loss, which is deductible as a bad debt in the year in which the transfer of property occurs. If the property is worth less than the bid price, the bank realizes a capital loss and is entitled to an additional deduction for loss for the difference between the value of the property received and the bid price. Correspondingly, if the property value exceeds the bid price, the bank realizes a gain on the transaction when the property is sold. Generally, property taken in foreclosure normally establishes the true fair-market value of the property in the absence of clear and convincing proof to the otherwise.

Another alternative is to have the mortgagor relinquish his interest in the property in favor of the bank. The bank is then faced with selling the property to an independent third party. Any cash proceeds received from the sale that partially or totally satisfy the mortgage debt affect the determination of taxable income. Any costs incurred by the bank to protect the mortgage property before receiving the property are added to the basis of the loan. The basis of the loan is compared to the net proceeds of the sale, and if the amount received is insufficient to cover the basis of the loan, the bank can realize a deduction for bad debt.

If the amount bid for the property includes the accrued interest on the property, the interest must be included in taxable income. If the bid includes principal only, no income is recognized. If the accrued interest has been recognized in a prior taxable period, the bank is entitled to include the accrued interest as an additional deduction for bad debt.

The reserve method allows the bank to create a reasonable allowance for loan losses by providing for bad debts through the income statement. If the bank uses the reserve method, it has two alternatives for calculating a maximum allowable reserve for loan losses at the end of a taxable year: the percentage method and the experience method. In each case the method prescribes specific limits on the percentage of the loan loss allowance to the bank's outstanding loans at the end of the year. Importantly, the bank may use the percentage method in one taxable year and change to the experience method in a subsequent year without prior notification of the IRS. The reason for this is that the bank has the option of taking the larger deduction created by the use of either method in any one taxable year. It is likely that in a recessionary environment and in a period of reduced business activity actual experience will produce a higher reserve for loan losses than would be produced by the percentage method.

The initial step in using the reserve method is to define total loans. A bona fide debt arises when there is a relationship between debtor and creditor based upon a valid and enforceable obligation to pay a fixed or determinable sum of money. Loans for the purposes of deducting bad debts include customer drafts, bankers' acceptances purchased or discounted by a bank, and loan participations to the extent of the risk incurred by the bank. Loans exclude accrued interest or discounts unless they are included in income, commercial paper, and corporate and government bonds. The percentage method uses "eligible loans" for the purposes of computing the amount to increase the allowance for loan losses, whereas the experience method uses "total loans" as the base for applying the applicable experience ratio.

The percentage method allows the bank to increase its own loss reserve to a specified percentage of "eligible loans" outstanding at the end of each year. To find eligible loans, total loans are reduced by loans to banks, bank funds on deposit in a bank, federal funds sold, government-guaranteed or insured loans to the extent of the guarantee, and cash collateral. The statutory percentage for computing the allowance for loan losses is 0.6 percent for 1983 through 1987. Beginning in 1988, all banks must use the experience method.

The maximum allowable increase to the reserve depends on net charge-offs, on whether outstanding loans have increased or decreased since the base year, and on the relationship of the loan loss reserve in the base year to eligible loans at the end of the base year. For taxable years beginning after 1982, where eligible loans have increased, the maximum allowable loan loss provision is limited to the amount required to increase the current year's ending loan loss reserve to .6 percent of eligible loans at the end of the taxable year. Generally, a bank is entitled to an addition to the reserve that is at least equal to its net charge-offs for the current year. If eligible loans have decreased since the end of 1982, the current year's annual addition is limited to the amount needed to maintain the reserve at the same relationship to eligible loans as that which existed at the end of 1982. The actual computations can be very complex.

The experience method is based upon the bank's actual experience with bad debts over the six most recent years, including the current year. A newly formed financial institution with fewer than five years' operation may rely upon the experience with bad debts of comparable banks to compute its provision for bad debts, that is, all financial institutions located in the same Federal Reserve district for those years in which the new bank was not in existence.

CHAPTER 10

Accounting for Consumer Loans

Transaction	Entry		Effect on Financial Statement
New Loan	Debit:	Installment loans	Increases assets
	Credit:	Cash	Decreases assets
		Unearned discount[a]	Increases contra account
Accrual of Interest	Debit:	Unearned discount	Decreases contra account
	Credit:	Interest income on installment loans	Increases income
Loan Payment	Debit:	Cash	Increases assets
	Credit:	Installment loans	Decreases assets

[a]If credit life insurance is included in note amount, an unearned premium on credit life insurance would be credited and amortized to "other income," similar to "unearned discount" entries.

CHAPTER 11

Accounting for Mortgage Loans

Transaction	Entry		Effect on Financial Statement
New Loan	Debit:	Real estate loans	Increases assets
	Credit:	Cash	Decreases assets
Receipt of Loan Fees and Amounts for Closing Costs	Debit:	Cash	Increases assets
	Credit:	Interest and fees on real estate loans	Increases income
		Escrow account	Increases liabilities
Disbursement of Closing Costs	Debit:	Escrow account	Decreases liabilities
		Expense/cashier's checks	Increases liabilities
Receipt of Payment	Debit:	Cash	Increases assets
	Credit:	Real estate loans	Decreases assets
		Interest and fees on real estate loans	Increases income

CHAPTER 12

Accounting for Investment Securities

Transaction	Entry		Effect on Financial Statement
Bonds Purchased (Flat)	Debit:	Investment securities (appropriate account: U.S. Treasury, U.S. agencies, obligations of states and political subdivisions)	Increases assets
	Credit:	Cash	Decreases assets
Bonds Purchased with Accrued Interest	Debit:	Investment securities (appropriate account)	Increases assets
	Credit:	Cash	Decreases cash
		Purchase interest on investment securities	Increases liabilities
Bonds Purchased at Discount	Debit:	Investment securities	Increases assets
	Credit:	Discount on investment securities	Increases contra account
		Cash	Decreases assets

(continued)

CHAPTER 12 *(continued)*

Accounting for Investment Securities

Transaction	Entry		Effect on Financial Statement
Bonds Purchased at Premium	Debit:	Investment securities	Increases assets
	Credit:	Cash	Decreases assets
Interest Accrued	Debit:	Interest income receivable on investment securities	Increases assets
	Credit:	Interest income (appropriate account)	Increases income
Receipt of Interest	Debit:	Cash	Increases assets
	Credit:	Interest income receivable on investment securities[a]	Decreases assets
	Debit:	Cash	Increases assets
		Purchase interest on investment securities	Decreases liabilities
	Credit:	Interest income receivable on investment securities	Decreases assets
Amortization of Premium	Debit:	Interest income (appropriate account)	Decreases income
	Credit:	Premium on investment securities	Increases contra account (credit balance)
Amortization of Discount	Debit:	Discount on investment securities	Increases contra account (debit balance)
	Credit:	Interest income (appropriate account)	Increases income
Sale of Securities	Debit:	Cash and/or	Increases assets
		Premium on investment securities and/or	Decreases contra account
		Securities losses	Decreases income
	Credit:	Investment securities (appropriate account) and/or	Decreases assets
		Discount on investment securities and/or	Decreases contra account
		Securities gains	Increases income
Securities Pledged to Secure Municipal Deposits	Debit:	Investment securities pledged (appropriate account)	Increases assets
	Credit:	Investment securities (appropriate account)	Decreases assets

[a]For first payment after securities purchased with interest.

CHAPTER 13

Accounting for Funds Management

Transaction	Entry		Effect on Financial Statement
Transfer from Correspondent Bank to Increase Reserve Account	Debit:	Federal Reserve account	Increases assets
	Credit:	Due from banks	Decreases assets
Borrow Short-Term Funds to Increase Reserves	Debit:	Federal Reserve account	Increases assets
	Credit:	Federal funds purchased and securities sold under repurchase agreements	Increases liabilities
Funds Returned with Interest	Debit:	Federal funds purchased and securities sold under repurchase agreements	Decreases liabilities
		Interest expense	Increases expenses
	Credit:	Federal Reserve account	Decreases assets
Invest in Short-Term Funds	Debit:	Federal funds sold and securities purchased under reverse repurchase agreements	Increases assets
	Credit:	Federal Reserve account	Decreases assets
Funds Returned with Interest from Borrower	Debit:	Federal Reserve account	Increases assets
	Credit:	Federal funds sold and securities purchased under reverse repurchase agreements	Decreases assets
		Interest income	Increases income
Borrow from Discount Window	Debit:	Federal Reserve account	Increases assets
	Credit:	Borrowed funds	Increases liabilities
Repay the Fed	Debit:	Borrowed funds	Decreases liabilities
		Interest expense	Increases expenses
	Credit:	Federal Reserve account	Decreases assets

CHAPTER 14

Accounting for Capital

Transaction	Entry		Effect on Financial Statement
Initial Capitalization	Debit:	Cash	Increases assets
	Credit:	Capital stock and Surplus	Increases capital
Net Losses	Debit:	Undivided profits	Decreases capital
	Credit:	Income summary	Creates income statement
Net Income	Debit:	Income summary	Creates income statement
	Credit:	Undivided profits	Decreases capital
Declaration of Dividends	Debit:	Undivided profits	Decreases capital
	Credit:	Dividends payable	Increases liabilities
Payment of Dividends	Debit:	Dividends payable	Decreases liabilities
	Credit:	Cashier's checks	Increases liabilities
Long-Term Debt	Debit:	Cash	Increases assets
	Credit:	Subordinated debentures or Long-term debt	Increases liabilities
Accrual of Interest	Debit:	Interest expense	Increases expenses
	Credit:	Accrued interest payable	Increases liabilities
Payment of Interest	Debit:	Accrued interest payable	Increases expenses
	Credit:	Cashier's checks	Increases liabilities
Retirement of Debt	Debit:	Subordinated debentures or Long-term debt	Decreases liabilities
	Credit:	Cashier's checks	Increases liabilities

Content of an Offering Circular

Amendments to 12 CFR Part 16, *Securities Offering Disclosure Rules,* include certain instances when a bank is exempt from preparing an offering circular:

- Any transaction by a bank not involving a public offering, including a negotiated sale (private placement) to not more than 15 purchasers within any continuous 12-month period.
- Any reorganization, merger, consolidation, or acquisition of assets by a bank if the bank's shareholders are furnished a proxy statement.
- Any transaction with existing security holders involving an exercise of conversion rights.
- Any transaction involving securities offered to employees or directors pursuant to a stock purchase, stock option, or savings plan.
- The provision for an abbreviated filing if the amount of offering does not exceed $500,000 when aggregated with all other sales within the preceding 12-month period.

For those banks required to prepare it, the offering circular includes 15 basic items:

1. *Cover page:* Amounts and price of the offering and a brief statement of the plan of distribution.

2. *Plan of distribution:* Information regarding the underwriter or the bank's plan for distributing securities.

3. *Use of proceeds:* Reasons why the bank requires additional capital and *pro forma* statements indicating the improvement in capital ratios after the issuance.

4. *Capital structure:* A comparative schedule illustrating existing and proposed capital structures.

5. *Summary of earnings:* Summary of the last five fiscal years, including ratios of net income to stockholders' equity, net income to total assets, and total interest expense to gross interest income, and a discussion of the bank's earnings for the last two years.

6. *Description of business:* Primary business locations, the competition and competitive environment, the bank's business activities, properties owned, funds management practices, risks in the loan and securities portfolios, and statistical information (see the following section).

7. *Capital stock:* Description of the rights of shareholders, the bank's policy regarding dividends, and a history of dividend payments.

8. *Debt securities:* The terms and restrictions of an issue for debt securities.

9. *Other securities being offered:* The amounts and terms of exercise for rights, warrants, or convertible securities.

10. *Nature of trading market:* Names of principal market makers and high and low bid prices during last two years.

11. *Directors and officers:* Brief biographical summaries, including age, title, length of service in the capacity, and any related-party transactions with the bank.

12. *Principal security holders:* Amounts of securities held directly or indirectly by officers and directors as a group and any other individual group or corporation owning more than 5 percent of the bank's outstanding voting securities.

13. *Remuneration and other transactions with management.*

14. *Pending legal proceedings.*

15. *Financial statements:* Statements prepared in accordance with generally accepted accounting principles and in the format of a call report; may or may not be accompanied by the opinion of an independent accountant.

The amount of information required in the circular is substantial, and banks anticipating additional capital needs are well advised to seek professional legal and accounting assistance.

Compliance Reporting for Securities Issues

When a bank issues securities, it generally subjects itself to additional regulatory requirements for reporting. The annual report to the SEC on Form 10-K (not to be confused with the bank's annual report to shareholders) contains information similar to that required in a registration of securities. The purpose of the report is to update the original information included in the circular describing an offering. Many banks include certain information given in the regulatory reports in the annual report to shareholders; others simply indicate that regulatory reports are available to shareholders upon request. Management's primary concern is to supply the statistical information regarding the bank's performance. A significant portion of the information needed to comply with requirements for the regulatory annual report and proxy statements is based on performance ratios (see Chapter 15).

The statistical disclosures and management's discussion and analysis of the summary of operations emanate from the SEC's *Guide 3:*

I. **Distribution of Assets, Liabilities, and Stockholders' Equity; Interest Rates and Interest Differential**
   A. For each reported period, present average balance sheets. The format of the average balance sheets may be condensed from the detail required by the financial statements provided that the condensed average balance sheets indicate the significant categories of assets and liabilities, including all major categories of interest-earning assets and interest-bearing liabilities. Major categories of interest-earning assets should include loans, taxable investment securities, nontaxable investment securities, interest-bearing deposits in other banks, Federal funds sold and securities purchased with agreements to resell, other short-term investments, and other (specify if significant). Major categories of interest-bearing liabilities should include savings deposits, other time deposits, short-term debt, long-term debt, and other (specify if significant).
   B. For each reported period, present an analysis of net interest earnings as follows:
      1. For each major category of interest-earning asset and each major category of interest-bearing liability, the average amount outstanding during the period and the interest earned or paid on such amount.
      2. The average yield for each major category of interest-bearing asset.
      3. The average rate paid for each major category of interest-bearing liability.
      4. The average yield on all interest-earning assets and the average effective rate paid on all interest-bearing liabilities.
      5. The net yield on interest-earning assets (net interest earnings divided by total interest-earning assets, with net interest earnings equaling the difference between total interest earned and total interest paid).
      6. This analysis may, at the option of the registrant, be presented in connection with the average balance sheet required by paragraph A.
   C. For the latest two fiscal years, present (1) the dollar amount of change in interest income and (2) the dollar amount of change in interest expense. The changes should be segregated for each major category of interest-earning asset and interest-bearing liability into amounts attributable to (a) changes in volume (change in volume times old rate), (b) changes in rates (change in rate times old volume), and (c) changes in rate-volume (change in rate times the change in volume). The rate/volume

variances should be allocated on a consistent basis between rate and volume variance and the basis of allocation disclosed in a note to the table.

II. Investment Portfolio

A. As of the end of each reported period, present the book value of investments in obligations of (1) the U.S. Treasury and other U.S. government agencies and corporations; (2) states of the United States and political subdivisions; and (3) other securities including bonds, notes, debentures, and stock of business corporations, foreign governments, and political subdivisions, intergovernmental agencies, and the Federal Reserve Bank.

B. As of the end of the latest reported period, present the amount of each investment category listed above which is due (1) in one year or less, (2) after one year through five years, (3) after five years through ten years, and (4) after ten years. In addition, state the weighted average yield for each range of maturities.

C. As of the end of the latest reported period, state the name of any issuer, and the aggregate book value and aggregate market value of the securities of such issuer, when the aggregate book value of such securities exceeds 10 percent of stockholders' equity.

III. Loan Portfolio

A. *Types of Loans.* As of the end of each reported period, present separately the amount of loans in each category listed below. Also show the total amount of all loans for each reported period, which amounts should be the same as those shown on the balance sheets.

Domestic:
1. Commercial, financial and agricultural
2. Real estate—construction
3. Real estate—mortgage
4. Installment loans to individuals
5. Lease financing

Foreign:
6. Governments and official institutions
7. Banks and other financial institutions
8. Commercial and industrial
9. Other loans

B. *Maturities and Sensitivity to Changes in Interest Rates.* As of the end of the latest fiscal year reported on, present separately the amount of loans in each category listed in paragraph A (except that this information need not be presented for categories 3, 4, and 5 and categories 6 through 9 may be aggregated), which are: (1) due in one year or less, (2) due after one year through five years, and (3) due after five years. In addition, present separately the total amount of all such loans due after one year which (a) have predetermined interest rates and (b) have floating or adjustable interest rates.

C. *Risk Elements*

1. Nonaccrual, Past Due, and Restructured Loans. As of the end of each reported period, state separately the aggregate amount of loans in each of the following categories:

    a. Loans accounted for on a nonaccrual basis.

    b. Accruing loans which are contractually past due 90 days or more as to principal or interest payments.

    c. Loans not included above which are "troubled debt restructurings" as defined in Statement of Financial Accounting Standards No. 15 ("FAS 15"), "Accounting by Debtors and Creditors for Troubled Debt Restructurings."

2. Potential Problem Loans. As of the end of the most recent reported period, describe the nature and extent of any loans which are not now disclosed pursuant to Item III.C.1 above, but where known information about possible credit problems of borrowers (which are not related to transfer risk inherent in cross-border lending activities) causes management to have serious doubts as to the ability of such borrowers to comply with the present loan repayment terms and which may result in disclosure of such loans pursuant to Item III.C.1.

3. Foreign Outstandings. As of the end of each of the last three reported periods, state the name of the country and aggregate amount of cross-border outstandings to borrowers in each foreign country where such outstandings exceed 1 percent of total assets.

4. Loan Concentrations. As of the end of the most recent reported period, describe any concentration of loans exceeding 10 percent of total loans which are not otherwise disclosed as a category of loans pursuant to Item III.A of this Guide. Loan concentrations are considered to exist when there are amounts loaned to a multiple number of borrowers engaged in similar activities which would cause them to be similarly impacted by economic or other conditions.

D. Other Interest-Bearing Assets. As of the end of the most recent reported period, disclose the nature and amounts of any other interest-bearing assets that would be required to be disclosed under Item III.C.1 or 2, if such assets were loans.

IV. Summary of Loan Loss Experience

A. An analysis of loss experience shall be furnished in the following format for each reported period:

Analysis of the Allowance for Loan Losses	
	Reported Period
Balance at beginning of period	$X
Charge-offs	
Domestic:	
Commercial, financial, and agricultural	X
Real estate–construction	X
Real estate–mortgage	X
Installment loans to individuals	X
Lease financing	X
Foreign	X
Recoveries	
Domestic:	
Commercial, financial, and agricultural	X
Real estate–construction	X
Real estate–mortgage	X
Installment loans to individuals	X
Foreign	X
Net charge-offs	X
Additions charged to operations	X
Balance at end of period	$X
Ratio of net charge-offs during the period to average loans outstanding during that period	X%

B. At the end of each reported period, furnish a breakdown of the allowance for loan losses in the following format:

Allocation of the Allowance for Loan Losses

Balance at End of Period Applicable to	Reported Period	
	Amount	Percent of Loans in Each Category to Total Loans
Domestic		
Commercial, financial, and agricultural	$X	X%
Real estate–construction	X	X
Real estate–mortgage	X	X
Installment loans to individuals	X	X
Lease financing	X	X
Foreign	X	X
Unallocated	X	N/A
	$X	X%

V. Deposits

A. For each reported period, present separately the average amount of and the average rate paid on each of the following deposit categories which are in excess of 10 percent of average total deposits.

Deposits in domestic bank offices:
1. Noninterest-bearing demand deposits
2. Interest-bearing demand deposits
3. Savings deposits
4. Time deposits

Deposits in foreign banking offices:
5. Banks located in foreign countries (including foreign branches of other U.S. banks)
6. Foreign governments and official institutions
7. Other foreign demand deposits
8. Other foreign time and savings deposits

B. Categories other than those specified for deposits in domestic bank offices above may be used to present the types of domestic deposits if they more appropriately describe the nature of the deposits.

C. If material, the registrant should disclose separately the aggregate amount of deposits by foreign depositors in domestic offices. Identification of the nationality of the depositors is not required.
D. As of the end of the latest reported period, state the amount outstanding of (1) time certificates of deposit in amounts of $100,000 or more and (2) other time deposits of $100,000 or more issued by domestic offices by time remaining until maturity of 3 months or less; over 3 through 6 months; over 6 through 12 months; and over 12 months.
E. As of the end of the latest reported period, state the amount outstanding of time certificates of deposit and other time deposits in amount of $100,000 or more issued by foreign offices. If the aggregate of such certificates of deposit and time deposits in amounts exceeding $100,000 represents a majority of total foreign deposit liabilities, the disclosure need not be given, provided that there is a statement that a majority of deposits were in amounts in excess of $100,000.

VI. Return on Equity and Assets
For each reported period, present the following:
1. Return on assets (net income divided by average total assets).
2. Return on equity (net income divided by average equity).
3. Dividend payout ratio (dividends declared per share divided by net income per share).
4. Equity to assets ratio (average equity divided by average total assets).

VII. Short-Term Borrowings
For each reported period, present the following information for each category of short-term borrowings reported in the financial statements pursuant to Rule 9–04.11:
1. The amounts outstanding at the end of the reported period, the weighted average interest rate thereon, and the general terms thereof.
2. The maximum amount of borrowings in each category outstanding at any month-end during each reported period.
3. The approximate average amounts outstanding during each reported period and the approximate weighted average interest rate thereon.

INDEX